AN ANTHOLOGY OF
CANADIAN LITERATURE
IN ENGLISH

Revised & Abridged Edition

AN ANTHOLOGY OF
CANADIAN LITERATURE
IN ENGLISH

Revised & Abridged Edition

Edited by

Russell Brown

Donna Bennett

& Nathalie Cooke

Toronto
Oxford University Press

Oxford University Press
70 Wynford Drive, Don Mills, Ontario M3C 1J9

Oxford New York
Athens Auckland Bangkok Bombay
Calcutta Cape Town Dar es Salaam Delhi
Florence Hong Kong Istanbul Karachi
Kuala Lumpur Madras Madrid Melbourne
Mexico City Nairobi Paris Singapore
Taipei Tokyo Toronto
and associated companies in
Berlin Ibadan

Canadian Cataloguing In Publication Data

Main entry under title:

An Anthology of Canadian literature in English

Rev. and abr.
Includes bibliographical references.
ISBN 0-19-540785-7

1. Canadian poetry (English).*   2. Canadian
fiction (English).*   I. Brown, Russell, 1942–
II. Bennett, Donna, 1945–   .   III. Cooke, Nathalie.

PS8233.A69 1990   C811'.008   C90-094565-6
PR9194.4.A69 1990

Printed in Canada by Best Gagné Book Manufacturers

CONTENTS

ACKNOWLEDGEMENTS

MARGARET ATWOOD. 'This is a Photograph of Me' from *The Circle Game*, copyright © 1966 by Margaret Atwood (Toronto: House of Anansi Press). Reprinted by permission. 'The Resplendent Quetzal' from *Dancing Girls* is used by permission of the Canadian Publishers, McClelland & Stewart, Toronto. Reprinted by permission of Oxford University Press Canada: 'Progressive Insanities of a Pioneer', 'Further Arrivals', 'The Planters', 'The Wereman', 'Death of a Young Son by Drowning', 'Departure from the Bush', 'Dream 2: Brian the Still-Hunter', 'Thoughts from Underground', 'Tricks with Mirrors' from *Selected Poems* copyright © Margaret Atwood. 'Marrying the Hangman', 'Variation on the Word *Sleep*', 'Another Elegy' from *Selected Poems II: Poems Selected & New 1976-1986* copyright © Margaret Atwood 1986. MARGARET AVISON. 'Light I, III' from *sunblue* by Margaret Avison is reprinted by permission of Lancelot Press Limited. 'Neverness', 'The Butterfly', 'Perspective', 'Snow', 'Butterfly Bones; or Sonnet Against Sonnets', 'Tennis' from *Winter Sun/The Dumbfounding*. Used by permission of the Canadian Publishers, McClelland & Stewart, Toronto. SANDRA BIRDSELL. 'The Wednesday Circle' reprinted by permission from *Agassiz Stories* (Turnstone Press, 1987), © Sandra Birdsell. EARLE BIRNEY. 'Vancouver Lights', 'The Ebb Begins from Dream', 'Bushed', 'Can. Lit.', 'A Walk in Kyoto', 'The Bear on the Delhi Road', 'El Greco: *Espolio*' from *Ghost in the Wheels*; 'Anglosaxon Street' from *Selected Poems 1940-1966*. Used by permission of the Canadian Publishers, McClelland & Stewart, Toronto. CLARK BLAISE. 'Eyes' from *North American Education* by Clark Blaise. Copyright © 1973 Clark Blaise. Reprinted by permission of Clark Blaise. GEORGE BOWERING. From *Kerrisdale Elegies* Two and Five. Reprinted by permission of the author. DIONNE BRAND. 'At the Lisbon Plate' from *Sans Souci*. Reprinted by permission of Williams-Wallace Publishers. ROBERT BRINGHURST. 'Deuteronomy', 'Essay on Adam', 'These Poems, She Said', 'The Reader' from *The Beauty of Weapons*. Used by permission of the Canadian Publishers, McClelland & Stewart, Toronto. MORLEY CALLAGHAN. 'Watching and Waiting' from *Morley Callaghan Stories* by Morley Callaghan © 1959. Reprinted by permission of Macmillan of Canada, A Division of Canada Publishing Corporation. LEONARD COHEN. 'You Have the Lovers', 'A Kite Is a Victim', 'Suzanne Takes You Down', 'Two Went to Sleep', 'Everybody Knows' from *Selected Poems*; 'Book of Mercy 49, 50' from *Book of Mercy*. Used by permission of the Canadian Publishers, McClelland and Stewart, Toronto. LORNA CROZIER. 'Poem about Nothing', 'Forms of Innocence' from *The Garden Going On Without Us*; 'Fathers, Uncles, Old Friends of the Family', 'Afterwords' from *Angels of Flesh, Angels of Silence*. Used by permission of the Canadian Publishers, McClelland and Stewart, Toronto. MARY DI MICHELE. 'Luminous Emergency' reprinted by permission of the author. 'Snapshots' from *Immune to Gravity* used by permission of the Canadian Publishers, McClelland and Stewart, Toronto. TIMOTHY FINDLEY. 'Stones' from *Stones* by Timothy Findley. Copyright © Pebble Productions, Inc., 1988. Reprinted by permission of Penguin Books Canada Limited. MAVIS GALLANT. 'The Ice Wagon Going Down the Street' from *My Heart is Broken*. Reprinted by permission of Georges Borchardt, Inc. and the author. Copyright © 1957 by Mavis Gallant. FREDERICK PHILIP GROVE. 'Snow' from *Over Prairie Trails* is reprinted by permission of A. Leonard Grove, Toronto. JACK HODGINS. 'By the River' from *Spit Delaney's Island* by Jack Hodgins © 1976. Reprinted by permission of Macmillan of Canada, A Division of Canada Publishing Corporation. PAULETTE JILES. 'North Shore of Lake Superior: The Truth' from *Sitting in the Club Car Drinking Rum and Karma-Kola*. 'Rock Climbing', 'Horror Stories', 'Night Flight of Attiwapiskat' from *Celestial Navigation*. Used by permission of the Canadian Publishers, McClelland & Stewart, Toronto. A.M. KLEIN. 'Reb Levi Yitschok Talks to God', 'Heirloom', 'Psalm XXXVI: A Psalm Touching Genealogy', 'The Rocking Chair', 'Political Meeting', 'Portrait of the Poet as Landscape', 'Autobiographical' by A.M. Klein from *A.M. Klein: Complete Poetry*, Vol. 1 & 2, edited by Zailig Pollock, © University of Toronto Press, 1990. Reprinted by permission of University of Toronto Press. Zailig Pollock's help with the A.M. Klein selections is greatly appreciated. JOY KOGAWA. 'Obasan' reprinted by permission of the author. 'Where There's A Wall', 'Road Building by Pick Axe', and 'Minerals from Stones' from *Woman in the*

Woods Mosaic Press 1985. Reprinted by permission. ROBERT KROETSCH. 'F.P. Grove: The Finding' reprinted by permission of the author. 'Seed Catalogue' from *Complete Field Notes*. Used by permission of the Canadian Publishers, McClelland & Stewart, Toronto. PATRICK LANE. All poems reprinted by permission of the author. MARGARET LAURENCE. 'To Set Our House in Order' from *A Bird in the House*. Used by permission of the Canadian Publishers, McClelland & Stewart, Toronto. IRVING LAYTON. 'Newsboy', 'The Birth of Tragedy', 'The Cold Green Element', 'The Fertile Muck', 'Whatever Else Poetry Is Freedom', 'Keine Lazarovitch 1870-1959', 'Butterfly on Rock', 'A Tall Man Executes a Jig' from *Collected Poems*. Used by permission of the Canadian Publishers, McClelland & Stewart, Toronto. STEPHEN LEACOCK. 'The Marine Excursion of the Knights of Pythias' from *Sunshine Sketches of a Little Town*. Used by permission of the Canadian Publishers, McClelland & Stewart, Toronto. DENNIS LEE. 'Elegy 1, 2, and 9' from *Civil Elegies and Other Poems* (Toronto: House of Anansi Press, 1972). Reprinted by permission. DOROTHY LIVESAY. All poems reprinted by permission of the author. GWENDOLYN MacEWEN. 'The Death of the Lock Ness Monster', 'Polaris' from *Afterworlds*. Used by permission of the Canadian Publishers, McClelland & Stewart, Toronto. 'The Void' and 'Real Enemies' from *The T.E. Lawrence Poems* by Gwendolyn MacEwen. Published 1982, second printing 1983 by Mosaic Press. Reprinted by permission. 'Icarus', 'Manzini: Escape Artist', 'The Portage', 'Dark Pines Under Water' from *Magic Animals*. Reprinted by permission of Stoddart Publishing Co. Limited. ALISTAIR MacLEOD. 'As Birds Bring Forth the Sun' from *As Birds Bring Forth the Sun*. Used by permission of the Canadian Publishers, McClelland & Stewart, Toronto. ELI MANDEL. All poems reprinted by permission of the author. DAPHNE MARLATT. All poems reprinted by permission of the author. ROHINTON MISTRY. 'Squatter' from *Tales of Firozsha Baag* by Rohinton Mistry. Copyright © Rohinton Mistry, 1987. Reprinted by permission of Penguin Books Canada Limited. ERIN MOURÉ. 'It is Only Me' and 'Barrington' from *Wanted Alive* (Toronto: House of Anansi Press, 1983); 'Professional Amnesia' from *Domestic Fuel* (Toronto: House of Anansi Press, 1985); 'Miss Chatelaine' from *Furious* (Toronto: House of Anansi Press, 1988); Reprinted by permission. ALICE MUNRO. 'Something I've Been Meaning to Tell You'. Copyright © 1974 by Alice Munro. All rights reserved, from *Something I've Been Meaning to Tell You* published by The New American Library. Reprinted by permission of Virginia Barber Literary Agency, Inc. JOHN NEWLOVE. 'Four Small Scars', 'The Double-headed Snake', 'Samuel Hearne in Wintertime' from *The Fat Man*; 'Ride Off Any Horizon' from *Black Night Window*. Used by permission of the Canadian Publishers, McClelland & Stewart, Toronto. bp NICHOL. From *The Martyrology* Book 3, Book 5, 'Lament', 'Landscape: 1' from *Zygal*. ALDEN NOWLAN. Reprinted by permission of Stoddart Publishing Co. Limited: 'Temptation' from *Bread, Wine and Salt*; 'The First Stirring of the Beasts', 'Country Full of Christmas' from *The Mysterious Naked Man*; 'Canadian January Night' from *Between Tears and Laughter*; 'On the Barrens' from *Smoked Glass*. MICHAEL ONDAATJE. All poems reprinted by permission of the author. P.K. PAGE. All poems reprinted by permission of the author. E.J. PRATT. 'The Prize Cat', 'The Truant', 'Come Away, Death', 'From Stone to Steel', 'Toward the Last Spike' from *E.J. Pratt: Complete Poems* Parts 1 & 2, edited by Sandra Djwa and R.G. Moyles, © University of Toronto Press, 1989. Reprinted by permission of University of Toronto Press. AL PURDY. 'Wilderness Gothic', 'The Cariboo Horses', 'Trees at the Arctic Circle', 'Lament for the Dorsets', 'Roblin's Mills (2)' from *Being Alive*; 'The Country North of Belleville' from *Selected Poems*; 'The Dead Poet', 'Man Without a Country', 'For Steve McIntyre' from *Collected Poems*. Used by permission of the Canadian Publishers, McClelland & Stewart, Toronto. JAMES REANEY. Reprinted with the permission of the author, publisher, and Sybil Hutchinson, literary agent: 'Starling with a Split Tongue', 'The Alphabet', 'The Lost Child', and 'The School Globe' from *Poems* by James Reaney. Copyright Canada, 1972 by James Reaney, New Press, Toronto. DAVID ADAMS RICHARDS. 'A Rural Place' by David Adams Richards is reprinted from *Dancers at Night* by permission of Oberon Press. MORDECAI RICHLER. 'The Summer My Grandmother Was Supposed to Die' from *The Street*. Used by permission of the Canadian Publishers, McClelland & Stewart, Toronto. SIR CHARLES G.D. ROBERTS. All poems reprinted by permission of Lady Joan Roberts. 'When Twilight Falls on the Stump Lots' from *The Heart of the Ancient Wood*. Used by permission of the Canadian Publishers, McClelland & Stewart, Toronto. LEON ROOKE. 'A Bolt of White Cloth' from *A Bolt of White Cloth*. Reprinted by permission of Stoddart Publishing Co. Limited. SINCLAIR ROSS. 'A Field of

Wheat' from *The Lamp At Noon and Other Stories*. Used by permission of the Canadian Publishers, McClelland & Stewart, Toronto. DUNCAN CAMPBELL SCOTT. 'At the Cedars', 'The Onondaga Madonna', 'Night Hymns on Lake Nipigon', 'The Forsaken', 'The Height of Land' from *Selected Poems of Duncan Campbell Scott* is reproduced with the permission of John G. Aylen, Ottawa, Canada. F.R. SCOTT. 'The Canadian Authors Meet', 'Trans Canada', 'Lakeshore', 'Poetry', 'Laurentian Shield', 'All the Spikes But the Last' from *F.R. Scott: Selected Poems*. Used by permission of the Canadian Publishers, McClelland & Stewart, Toronto. A.J.M. SMITH. 'The Lonely Land', 'Far West', 'Sea Cliff', 'The Plot Against Proteus', 'The Wisdom of Old Jelly Roll' from *The Classic Shade*. Used by permission of the Canadian Publishers, McClelland & Stewart, Toronto. AUDREY THOMAS. 'The Man With Clam Eyes' from *Goodbye Harold, Good Luck* by Audrey Thomas. Copyright © Audrey Thomas, 1986. Reprinted by permission of Penguin Books Canada Limited. BRONWEN WALLACE. 'Joseph MacLeod Daffodils', 'Testimonies', 'The Watermelon Incident' from *The Stubborn Particulars of Grace*. Used by permission of the Canadian Publishers, McClelland & Stewart, Toronto. 'The Woman in this Poem' from *Signs of the Former Tenant* by Bronwen Wallace by permission of Oberon Press. PHYLLIS WEBB. All poems reprinted by permission of the author. RUDY WIEBE. 'Where Is the Voice Coming From?' from *Where Is the Voice Coming From*. Used by permission of the Canadian Publishers, McClelland & Stewart, Toronto. FRED WAH. 'I lie here and wait for life again' by Fred Wah from *Breathin' My Name with a Sigh* © 1981, Talon Books Ltd. ' Waiting for Saskatchewan', 'Relation Speaks', 'Elite 3' reprinted by permission from *Waiting for Saskatchewan* (Turnstone Press, 1985), © Fred Wah. SHEILA WATSON. 'Antigone' reprinted by permission of the author. ETHEL WILSON. 'The Window' from *Mrs Golightly and Other Stories*. Reprinted by permission of Macmillan of Canada, A Division of Canada Publishing Corporation.

INTRODUCTION

The works collected in this volume make visible four large movements in the development of Canadian literature. (1) *The first stirrings of a literary culture before Canada became a nation.* Often expressing either an immigrant's sense of loss and displacement or an explorer's excitement of discovery, pre-Confederation writers initiated the struggle to find suitable language and forms to describe new experiences in a new landscape. (2) *The emergence of a national literature.* Writers who began their careers in the era following Confederation—such as Isabella Valancy Crawford, Charles G.D. Roberts, D.C. Scott, and Archibald Lampman—drew on and transformed the Romantic and post-Romantic heritage from Britain and America to find a voice suitable to their own milieu and to create an indigenous Canadian literature. (3) *The evolution of literary modernism in Canada.* The beginnings of a modernist sensibility may be seen as early as Roberts and Sara Jeannette Duncan, but Canada did not have an identifiable modernist movement until the emergence of such writers as E.J. Pratt, A.J.M. Smith, F.R. Scott, and Morley Callaghan. These writers were generally less interested in the revolutionary aspects of modernism (with its desire to shock or astound and its tendency to break sharply with the past) than in its formal characteristics (the relation between the authorial voice and the text, the new freedom of subject matter, and innovations in language and technique). (4) *The fragmented aesthetics that has emerged in the last thirty years.* As modernism has lost its hold in recent years, we can see a number of 'movements' in Canadian writing, some of which (like the fiction-writing typified by Margaret Laurence) grow directly out of the modernist mode, while others (represented by George Bowering, bp Nichol, and Robert Kroetsch) can be grouped as postmodernist.

Superficially the Canadian literary tradition seems to be chiefly made up of 'realistic' writing, a literature that, in its tendency to focus on the events of everyday existence, has been shaped by a need for chronicling the Canadian experience and developing a sense of self-identity. A wilderness colony, a new nation based on a rural economy, an urban culture sharing the continent with a dominating, technological society, Canada has passed from infancy to maturity during a period of world-wide intellectual upheaval that has been marked by the move from an age of romantic idealism, which saw reality as part of an overall transcendent plan that the mind could perceive and understand; through one of social positivism, which sought order in a political and social reality; to one of a disillusioned scepticism, which rejected any coherent vision of reality. The question of what constitutes reality, reconceived by each of these intellectual moments, is central to the creation of a national identity and literature, because the sense of what is 'real' grounds any definition of self. Thus Canada had to come to terms not only with its own changing society, but also with the shifting intellectual climate under which it was formed. In Canada, as elsewhere, as the assumption that truth or reality was inherent in ideals seemed to disintegrate, the significance of a daily reality increased.

For Canadian writing this change was especially impressive, because writers found themselves writing for readers, first foreign and then native, who had no clear image or definition of a 'Canadian' reality. From the earliest narratives of exploration and settlement, to the Confederation period with its awareness of nationhood, to the present expressions of a more confident post-colonial self-awareness, writers have accordingly sought a reality based in or made accessible through daily experience and have therefore made their relationship to place an important element of their writing. However, while a kind of everyday realism that responds to the need for self-definition has been a prominent feature of the Canadian tradition, that has not meant a complete abandonment of idealized vision nor of a sense of literature as a social force. Within Canadian writing a number of divergent elements remain in play that speak of the romantic, positivist, sceptical inheritances, and, along with Canada's sense of place as wilderness, rural, agrarian, and urban, continue to create the complex and still emerging Canadian identity.

In their encounters with new milieus and unfamiliar landscapes, early writers such as Brooke, Hearne, Thompson, Jameson, Moodie, and Traill sought—in their chronicles of ventures into the wilderness, of stoic endurance and personal regeneration, and of the attractions of primitivism—to reconcile old realities with new, and to deal with the contradictions of a Canadian experience at odds with their models from the past. Similarly, the writers of the Confederation period created a poetry that contains fascinating tensions, work that marries—sometimes uneasily—their direct experience of the Canadian landscape to a Romantic vision, with results as various as the mythopoeic writing of Crawford or the dramatized ambivalence of the speaker in Roberts' 'Tantramar Revisited', who is unwilling to approach too closely the idealized Wordsworthian landscape he overlooks for fear of discovering 'the hands of chance and change'. While the late nineteenth-century Realist movement—so important in Europe and America—never became fully native to Canadian writing, the advent of modernism, with its sense that the notion of reality was problematic and that truth is partial, internal, and subjective, produced divergent responses in Canada. One group of Canadian writers followed the lead of modernists such as T.S. Eliot and sought the real world internally, through investigation of the psyche and the unconscious, and of the idealizing worlds that the mind can construct, such as literature and myth; a second group, more closely related to the Realist tradition, looked for a reality, unmediated by idealism, in the local and immediate world of physical experience, relegating concerns for the 'literary' to a secondary position. That first response is associated with the poets of the 'Montreal group' (such as A.J.M. Smith and F.R. Scott), and continued by the mythopoeic writing of Jay Macpherson and Margaret Atwood. The other kind of modernist writing, which had its roots in the rural realism of Raymond Knister, the imagism of W.W.E. Ross, and the early socially-conscious work of Dorothy Livesay, responded to a sense of a world dominated by random forces. This kind of modernism came to prominence in Canada in the forties in the work of those writers, such as Irving Layton, who associated themselves with John Sutherland and his little magazine *First Statement*, and it also found expression in the Saskatchewan fiction of Sinclair Ross. The influence of these writers—who sought a stripped language, a directness of expression, and an unidealized view of experience—may still be seen in the fiction and poetry of Al Purdy, Alice Munro, Margaret Laurence, Patrick Lane, and Lorna Crozier.

The general move away from modernism that begins around the middle of the twentieth century and gains impetus after the sixties is characterized by an emphasis on literary forms that are self-conscious and self-reflexive, and that express ironic doubt about the reality of both the self and the external world as objects of inquiry. As was earlier true of modernism, many Canadian writers responded to this postmodern movement because they recognized concerns that were strikingly congruent with those already existing in this country. In particular, both modernist and postmodernist anxieties about, and fascination with, language—which is seen as becoming increasingly elusive in meaning and yet as having a previously unrecognized, even dangerous, power to shape its user—and about what lies hidden under the surface of language, have significance for contemporary Canadians, since language has sometimes been identified in Canada as the most pervasive yet least visible remnant of a colonial heritage, while it is also viewed as the last place where authenticity can be created. In this context we can see how a number of writers have come to challenge existing literary forms and even language itself in order to find new means of expression. It would be misleading, however, to suggest that contemporary writing in English Canada has made a radical break with older techniques and aesthetics: a wide range of work that has been affected by these concerns nevertheless remains continuous with the literature that has come before. And, even in this recent work, the longstanding interest in mapping out the nature of the Canadian experience and the reality of the Canadian identity often remains visible.

This revised and abridged version of *An Anthology of Canadian Literature in English* is based on the earlier two-volume edition (1982, 1983). As well as shortening some previous selections and omitting some writers, the editors have updated selections and headnotes throughout, and several authors have been added, reflecting not only the emergence of new figures but the continuing reassessment of the canon.

While readers can use this anthology to discover the overall shape of the English-Canadian literary tradition, they need not feel constrained to read chronologically. Those whose interest lies first of all in contemporary writing may find it rewarding to turn back to the origins of the literary culture that produced it, while readers who particularly want to see the historical sources of Canadian culture may want not only to precede their reading of literary works with the accounts of exploration given by Hearne and Thompson and the encounters with settlement given by Jameson, Moodie, and Traill, but to supplement these pictures of the nation in its formative stages with a reading of the work of Haliburton; with *Towards the Last Spike*, Pratt's epic account of tying the nation together by rail; and with Margaret Atwood's poetic recasting of Moodie's experience in *The Journals of Susanna Moodie*.

To serve as a convenient starting point for the study of English-Canadian literature, this anthology has been arranged chronologically by the author's birth-dates, and provides introductions to the writers by locating selections from their work in relation to their larger body of writing, their personal development, their place in the Canadian literary community, and relevant contexts for further study. From among the many writers who contributed to the development of English-Canadian literature, we have chosen a representative group to give the reader an extensive sense of Canadian literature in one volume while including only complete texts. The few exceptions to this rule of not excerpting from longer works—the relatively self-contained selections from Frances Brooke's *History of Emily Montague* and from narratives of exploration and settlement—are from books that are not often read today in whole, but that remain important to students of Canadian literature. (Where omissions have been made, they are usually indicated by asterisks; those shorter than a paragraph are marked by ellipses of three spaced periods.) Obviously, therefore, the growth of the novel—a form that has become increasingly important to Canadian literature in the twentieth century—is not represented in this anthology.

The technical apparatus of this volume has been kept as simple as possible. The notes are intended to provide information rather than interpretation. They are not meant to replace a dictionary, though they do provide definitions for obscure words or words used in an unfamiliar sense. Major literary and historical figures—especially those in the English-language tradition—and easily recognizable literary allusions have usually been left unexplained. To distract the reader as little as possible, more than one item has sometimes been glossed in a single note; in such cases the superscript appears in the text appended to the first reference: the additional words glossed are repeated in the note.

Where more than one version of a text exists, we have usually chosen the author's most recent revision. We have silently corrected a few obvious typographical errors; where any doubt about texts existed, we have, whenever possible, consulted the authors. All selections are dated according to first book publication. If substantive changes were later made, we have indicated the date of the revised publication (e.g., '1962, rev. 1968'). When we thought it helpful to indicate a significantly earlier date of prior (journal) publication, two dates are provided (e.g., '1974, 1983'); if a date of composition is indicated, it has been placed in square brackets (e.g., '[1956], 1972'). In some cases writers have themselves appended dates to their poems; these have usually been retained at the end, to the right.

In annotating and correcting this edition of the anthology, we are indebted to a great many people. In addition to those whom we thanked in the earlier edition, we would particularly like to acknowledge the helpful comments of W.J. Keith, Earle Birney, Michael Darling, D.M.R. Bentley, and Zailig Pollock.

1 May 1990

RUSSELL BROWN
DONNA BENNETT
NATHALIE COOKE

Frances Brooke

1724-1789

The History of Emily Montague, published in London in 1769, is often described as the first Canadian novel (and indeed as the first North American one). Its author, Frances Brooke, was already an established writer before she came to Quebec in 1763 to join her husband, the chaplain of the garrison there. In England she had been part of a literary circle that included Samuel Richardson, usually thought of as the first English novelist. (Brooke adopted the epistolary form of her fiction from Richardson.) Before leaving England she had already published her first novel (*The History of Lady Julia Mandeville*, 1763), a book of poetry, and a play, and been editor of a weekly periodical called *The Old Maid*. A translation of a French romance gives evidence of an interest in French literature and culture that helped provide the background and disposition to respond to the milieu she encountered during her stay in Canada. Except for one visit home, Brooke seems to have lived in Quebec until 1768, when she and her husband returned to England.

In *The History of Emily Montague* Canada stands in a relationship to England that resembles the way the enchanted woods of Shakespeare's comedies stand to the everyday world. It is a place for romantic intrigues and the confusions of love, for an idyllic interlude from which all the principals will eventually emerge to return to the orderly world of their origins. The novel is composed of 228 letters, written mostly by its young English lovers. Chief among these is Ed. Rivers, a half-pay officer who plans to settle in Canada but eventually returns to England; the beautiful Emily Montague,

with whom he falls in love; and Emily's best friend, the coquettish Arabella Fermor.

Emily Montague met with a favourable reception in Europe: it was reprinted twice in its author's lifetime and was translated into French. Though her novel seems to have had little direct influence on Canadian writers, Brooke is an important figure in Canada's literary tradition because she provides some of the earliest imaginative responses to the country—responses that anticipated those of later writers. For instance, the experience of the immigrant in the New World receives one of its earliest treatments in this novel, and Brooke uses that topic to comment on, and give some freshness to, the plot of her highly conventional romance, as when Rivers says of Emily: '. . . if she loves [me] I know in my own heart, that Canada will no longer be a place of exile' (Letter 83). Even more important is the way Brooke describes not only the garrison-based society at Quebec but also the surrounding landscape and the climate, and the effect of these upon individuals; offers interesting observations about the co-existence of the French and English; examines the Indians and their culture; sees North American society as calling up new questions about the roles of women; and expresses a need for new language, metaphors, and myths to deal with the radically new experiences she encountered in Canada. At the same time, Brooke's European background is evident. It is revealed in her perception of the Indians, which seems to be founded on a reading of Rousseau, and in her reaction to landscape, which is often shaped by the eighteenth-century fascination with the sublime.

From *The History of Emily Montague*

LETTER 1

TO JOHN TEMPLE, ESQ; AT PARIS
[FROM ED. RIVERS]

Cowes, April 10, 1766

After spending two or three very agreeable days here, with a party of friends, in exploring the beauties of the Island, and dropping a tender tear at Carisbrook Castle on the memory of the unfortunate Charles the First.[1] I am just setting out for America, on a scheme I once hinted to you, of settling the lands to which I have a right as a lieutenant-colonel on half pay. On enquiry and mature deliberation, I prefer Canada to New-York for two reasons, that it is wilder, and that the women are handsomer: the first, perhaps, every body will not approve; the latter, I am sure, *you* will.

You may perhaps call my project romantic, but my active temper is ill suited to the lazy character of a reduc'd officer:[2] besides that I am too proud to narrow my circle of life, and not quite unfeeling enough to break in on the little estate which is scarce sufficient to support my mother and sister in the manner to which they have been accustom'd.

What you call a sacrifice is none at all; I love England, but am not obstinately chain'd down to any spot of earth; nature has charms every where for a man willing to be pleased: at my time of life, the very change of place is amusing; love of variety, and the natural restlessness of man, would give me a relish for this voyage, even if I did not expect, what I really do, to become lord of a principality which will put our large-acred men in England out of countenance. My subjects indeed at present will be only bears and elks, but in time I hope to see the *human face divine* multiplying around me; and, in thus cultivating what is in the rudest state of nature, I shall taste one of the greatest of all pleasures, that of creation, and see order and beauty gradually rise from chaos.

The vessel is unmoor'd; the winds are fair; a gentle breeze agitates the bosom of the deep; all nature smiles: I go with all the eager hopes of a warm imagination; yet friendship casts a lingering look behind.

Our mutual loss, my dear Temple, will be great. I shall never cease to regret you, nor will you find it easy to replace the friend of your youth. You may find friends of equal merit; you may esteem them equally; but few connexions form'd after five and twenty strike root like that early sympathy, which united us almost from infancy, and has increas'd to the very hour of our separation.

What pleasure is there in the friendships of the spring of life, before the world, the mean unfeeling selfish world, breaks in on the gay mistakes of the just-expanding heart, which sees nothing but truth, and has nothing but happiness in prospect!

I am not surpriz'd the heathens rais'd altars to friendship: 'twas natural for untaught superstition to deify the source of every good; they worship'd friend-

---

[1]Charles I was incarcerated in Carisbrook Castle on the Isle of Wight before his execution in 1649. The sentiments expressed in this passage owe much to the Gothic sensibility of Brooke's period, with its fondness for indulging in the melancholy feelings inspired by ruined castles.
[2]One discharged from active service and put on half-pay, subject to recall.

ship, which animates the moral world, on the same principle as they paid adoration to the sun, which gives life to the world of nature.

I am summon'd on board. Adieu!

Ed. Rivers

LETTER 10
TO MISS RIVERS, CLARGES STREET
[FROM ARABELLA FERMOR[1]]

Silleri, August 24

I have been a month arrived, my dear, without having seen your brother, who is at Montreal, but I am told is expected to-day. I have spent my time however very agreably. I know not what the winter may be, but I am enchanted with the beauty of this country in summer; bold, picturesque, romantic, nature reigns here in all her wanton luxuriance, adorned by a thousand wild graces which mock the cultivated beauties of Europe. The scenery about the town is infinitely lovely; the prospect extensive, and diversified by a variety of hills, woods, rivers, cascades, intermingled with smiling farms and cottages, and bounded by distant mountains which seem to scale the very Heavens.

The days are much hotter here than in England, but the heat is more supportable from the breezes which always spring up about noon; and the evenings are charming beyond expression. We have much thunder and lightening, but very few instances of their being fatal: the thunder is more magnificent and aweful than in Europe, and the lightening brighter and more beautiful; I have even seen it of a clear pale purple, resembling the gay tints of the morning.

The verdure is equal to that of England, and in the evening acquires an unspeakable beauty from the lucid splendor of the fire-flies sparkling like a thousand little stars on the trees and on the grass.

There are two very noble falls of water near Quebec, la Chaudiere and Montmorenci: the former is a prodigious sheet of water, rushing over the wildest rocks, and forming a scene grotesque, irregular, astonishing: the latter, less wild, less irregular, but more pleasing and more majestic, falls from an immense height, down the side of a romantic mountain into the river St Lawrence, opposite the most smiling part of the island of Orleans, to the cultivated charms of which it forms the most striking and agreable contrast.

The river of the same name, which supplies the cascade of Montmorenci, is the most lovely of all inanimate objects: but why do I call it inanimate? It almost breathes; I no longer wonder at the enthusiasm of Greece and Rome; 'twas from objects resembling this their mythology took its rise; it seems the residence of a thousand deities.

Paint to yourself a stupendous rock burst as it were in sunder by the hands of nature, to give passage to a small, but very deep and beautiful river; and forming on each side a regular and magnificent wall, crowned with the noblest woods that can be imagined; the sides of these romantic walls adorned with a variety of the gayest

[1]Brooke borrowed this name from the woman to whom Alexander Pope dedicated *The Rape of the Lock* (1712) and who served as a model for its central character, Belinda—the epitome of a mannered coquette. Brooke may also have liked the name because its eighteenth-century pronunciation—'Farmer'—would have made it, like 'Rivers', appropriate to her rustic setting. This letter is addressed to Lucy Rivers, Ed. Rivers' sister, who remains in London.

flowers, and in many places little streams of the purest water gushing through, and losing themselves in the river below: a thousand natural grottoes in the rock make you suppose yourself in the abode of the Nereids;[2] as a little island, covered with flowering shrubs, about a mile above the falls, where the river enlarges itself as to give it room, seems intended for the throne of the river goddess. Beyond this, the rapids, formed by the irregular projections of the rock, which in some places seem almost to meet, rival in beauty, as they excel in variety, the cascade itself, and close this little world of enchantment.

In short, the loveliness of this fairy scene alone more than pays the fatigues of my voyage; and, if I ever murmur at having crossed the Atlantic, remind me that I have seen the river Montmorenci.

I can give you a very imperfect account of the people here; I have only examined the landscape about Quebec, and have given very little attention to the figures; the French ladies are handsome, but as to the beaux, they appear to me not at all dangerous, and one might safely walk in a wood by moonlight with the most agreable Frenchman here. I am surprized the Canadian ladies take such pains to seduce our men from us; but I think it a little hard we have no temptation to make reprisals.

I am at present at an extreme pretty farm on the banks of the river St Lawrence; the house stands at the foot of a steep mountain covered with a variety of trees, forming a verdant sloping wall, which rises in a kind of regular confusion,

'Shade above shade, a woody theatre,'[3]

and has in front this noble river, on which the ships continually passing present to the delighted eye the most charming moving picture imaginable: I never saw a place so formed to inspire that pleasing lassitude, that divine inclination to saunter, which may not improperly be called, the luxurious indolence of the country. I intend to build a temple here to the charming goddess of laziness.

A gentleman is just coming down the winding path on the side of the hill, whom by his air I take to be your brother. Adieu! I must receive him: my father is at Quebec.

Yours,

Arabella Fermor

Your brother has given me a very pleasing piece of intelligence: my friend Emily Montague is at Montreal, and is going to be married to great advantage; I must write to her immediately, and insist on her making me a visit before she marries. She came to America two years ago, with her uncle Colonel Montague, who died here, and I imagined was gone back to England; she is however at Montreal with Mrs Melmoth, a distant relation of her mother's. Adieu! *ma très chére!*

---

[2]Sea-nymphs.

[3]Milton, *Paradise Lost*: 'Cedar, and pine, and fir, and branching palm,/A sylvan scene, and, as the ranks ascend/Shade above shade, a woody theatre/of stateliest view' (IV, 139-142).

LETTER 11
TO MISS RIVERS, CLARGES STREET
[FROM ED. RIVERS]

Quebec, September 10

I find, my dear, that absence and amusement are the best remedies for a beginning passion; I have passed a fortnight at the Indian village of Lorette,[1] where the novelty of the scene, and the enquiries I have been led to make into their antient religion and manners, have been of a thousand times more service to me than all the reflection in the world would have been.

I will own to you that I staid too long at Montreal, or rather at Major Melmoth's; to be six weeks in the same house with one of the most amiable, most pleasing of women, was a trying situation to a heart full of sensibility, and of a sensibility which has been hitherto, from a variety of causes, a good deal restrained. I should have avoided the danger from the first, had it appeared to me what it really was; but I thought myself secure in the consideration of her engagements, a defence however which I found grow weaker every day.

But to my savages: other nations talk of liberty, they possess it; nothing can be more astonishing than to see a little village of about thirty or forty families, the small remains of the Hurons, almost exterminated by long and continual war with the Iroquoise, preserve their independence in the midst of an European colony consisting of seventy thousand inhabitants; yet the fact is true of the savages of Lorette; they assert and they maintain that independence with a spirit truly noble. One of our company having said something which an Indian understood as a supposition that they had been *subjects* of France, his eyes struck fire, he stop'd him abruptly, contrary to their respectful and sensible custom of never interrupting the person who speaks. 'You mistake, brother,' said he; 'we are subject to no prince; a savage is free all over the world.' And he spoke only truth; they are not only free as a people, but every individual is perfectly so. Lord of himself, at once subject and master, a savage knows no superior, a circumstance which has a striking effect on his behaviour; unawed by rank or riches, distinctions unknown amongst his own nation, he would enter as unconcerned, would possess all his powers as freely in the palace of an oriental monarch, as in the cottage of the meanest peasant: 'tis the species, 'tis man, 'tis his equal he respects, without regarding the gaudy trappings, the accidental advantages, to which polished nations pay homage.

I have taken some pains to develop their present, as well as past, religious sentiments, because the Jesuit missionaries have boasted so much of their conversion; and find they have rather engrafted a few of the most plain and simple truths of Christianity on their ancient superstitions, than exchanged one faith for another; they are baptized, and even submit to what they themselves call the *yoke* of confession, and worship according to the outward forms of the Romish church, the drapery of which cannot but strike minds unused to splendor; but their belief is very little changed, except that the women seem to pay great reverence to the Virgin, perhaps because flattering to the sex. They anciently believed in one God, the ruler and creator of the universe, whom they called *The Great Spirit* and the *Master of Life*; in the sun as his image and representative; in a multitude of inferior spirits and demons;

[1]More properly Jeune Lorette, where the Hurons settled in 1697, having previously taken refuge from the Iroquois at Lorette a generation earlier.

and in a future state of rewards and punishments, or, to use their own phrase, in *a country of souls*. They reverenced the spirits of their departed heroes, but it does not appear that they paid them any religious adoration. Their morals were more pure, their manners more simple, than those of polished nations, except in what regarded the intercourse of the sexes: the young women before marriage were indulged in great libertinism, hid however under the most reserved and decent exterior. They held adultery in abhorrence, and with the more reason as their marriages were dissolvible at pleasure. The missionaries are said to have found no difficulty so great in gaining them to Christianity, as that of persuading them to marry for life: they regarded the Christian system of marriage as contrary to the laws of nature and reason; and asserted that, as the *Great Spirit* formed us to be happy, it was opposing his will, to continue together when otherwise.

The sex we have so unjustly excluded from power in Europe have a great share in the Huron government; the chief is chose by the matrons from amongst the nearest male relations, by the female line, of him he is to succeed; and is generally an aunt's or sister's son; a custom which, if we examine strictly into the principle on which it is founded, seems a little to contradict what we are told of the extreme chastity of the married ladies.

The power of the chief is extremely limited; he seems rather to advise his people as a father than command them as a master: yet, as his commands are always reasonable, and for the general good, no prince in the world is so well obeyed. They have a supreme council of ancients, into which every man enters of course at an age fixed, and another of assistants to the chief on common occasions, the members of which are like him elected by the matrons: I am pleased with this last regulation, as women are, beyond all doubt, the best judges of the merit of men; and I should be extremely pleased to see it adopted in England: canvassing for elections would then be the most agreeable thing in the world, and I am sure the ladies would give their votes on much more generous principles than we do. In the true sense of the word *we* are the savages, who so impolitely deprive you of the common rights of citizenship, and leave you no power but that of which we cannot deprive you, the resistless power of your charms. By the way, I don't think you are obliged in conscience to obey laws you have had no share in making; your plea would certainly be at least as good as that of the Americans, about which we every day hear so much.

The Hurons have no positive laws; yet being a people not numerous, with a strong sense of honor, and in that state of equality which gives no food to the most tormenting passions of the human heart, and the council of ancients having a power to punish atrocious crimes, which power however they very seldom find occasion to use, they live together in a tranquillity and order which appears to us surprizing.

In more numerous Indian nations, I am told, every village has its chief and its councils, and is perfectly independent on the rest; but on great occasions summon a general council, to which every village sends deputies.

Their language is at once sublime and melodious; but, having much fewer ideas, it is impossible it can be so copious as those of Europe: the pronunciation of the men is guttural, but that of the women extremely soft and pleasing; without understanding one word of the language, the sound of it is very agreeable to me. Their style even in speaking French is bold and metaphorical: and I am told is on important occasions extremely sublime. Even in common conversation they speak in figures, of which I have this moment an instance. A savage woman was wounded lately in defending an English family from the drunken rage of one of her nation. I asked her after her wound; 'It is well,' said she; 'my sisters at Quebec (meaning the English ladies) have been kind to me; and piastres,[2] you know, are very healing.'

They have no idea of letters, no alphabet, nor is their language reducible to rules: 'tis by painting they preserve the memory of the only events which interest them, or that they think worth recording, the conquests gained over their enemies in war.

When I speak of their paintings, I should not omit that, though extremely rude, they have a strong resemblance to the Chinese, a circumstance which struck me the more, as it is not the stile of nature. Their dances also, the most lively pantomimes I ever saw, and especially the dance of peace, exhibit variety of attitudes resembling the figures on Chinese fans; nor have their features and complexion less likeness to the pictures we see of the Tartars, as their wandering manner of life, before they became christians, was the same.

If I thought it necessary to suppose they were not natives of the country, and that America was peopled later than the other quarters of the world, I should imagine them the descendants of Tartars; as nothing can be more easy than their passage from Asia, from which America is probably not divided; or, if it is, by a very narrow channel. But I leave this to those who are better informed, being a subject on which I honestly confess my ignorance.

I have already observed, that they retain most of their antient superstitions. I should particularize their belief in dreams, of which folly even repeated disappointments cannot cure them: they have also an unlimited faith in their *powawers*, or conjurers, of whom there is one in every Indian village, who is at once physician, orator, and divine, and who is consulted as an oracle on every occasion. As I happened to smile at the recital a savage was making of a prophetic dream, from which he assured us of the death of an English officer whom I knew to be alive, 'You Europeans,' said he, 'are the most unreasonable people in the world; you laugh at our belief in dreams, and yet expect us to believe things a thousand times more incredible.'

Their general character is difficult to describe; made up of contrary and even contradictory qualities; they are indolent, tranquil, quiet, humane in peace; active, restless, cruel, ferocious in war: courteous, attentive, hospitable, and even polite, when kindly treated; haughty, stern, vindictive, when they are not; and their resentment is the more to be dreaded, as they hold it a point of honor to dissemble their sense of an injury[3] till they find an opportunity to revenge it.

They are patient of cold and heat, of hunger and thirst, even beyond all belief when necessity requires, passing whole days, and often three or four days together, without food, in the woods, when on the watch for an enemy, or even on their hunting parties; yet indulging themselves in their feasts even to the most brutal degree of intemperance. They despise death, and suffer the most excruciating tortures not only without a groan, but with an air of triumph; singing their death song, deriding their tormentors, and threatening them with the vengeance of their surviving friends: yet hold it honorable to fly before an enemy that appears the least superior in number or force.

Deprived by their extreme ignorance, and that indolence which nothing but their ardor for war can surmount, of all the conveniencies, as well as elegant refinements

[2]Coins.   [3]i.e., to pretend not to be insulted.

of polished life; strangers to the softer passions, love being with them on the same footing as amongst their fellow-tenants of the woods, their lives appear to me rather tranquil than happy: they have fewer cares, but they have also much fewer enjoyments, than fall to our share. I am told, however, that, though insensible to love, they are not without affections; are extremely awake to friendship, and passionately fond of their children.

They are of a copper color, which is rendered more unpleasing by a quantity of coarse red on their cheeks; but the children, when born, are of a pale silver white; perhaps their indelicate custom of greasing their bodies, and their being so much exposed to the air and sun even from infancy, may cause that total change of complexion, which I know not how otherwise to account for: their hair is black and shining, the women's very long, parted at the top, and combed back, tied behind, and often twisted with a thong of leather, which they think very ornamental: the dress of both sexes is a close jacket, reaching to their knees, with spatterdashes[4] all of coarse blue cloth, shoes of deer-skin, embroidered with porcupine quills, and sometimes with silver spangles; and a blanket thrown across their shoulders, and fastened before with a kind of bodkin,[5] with necklaces, and other ornaments of beads or shells.

They are in general tall, well made, and agile to the last degree; have a lively imagination, a strong memory; and, as far as their interests are concerned, are very dextrous politicians.

Their address is cold and reserved; but their treatment of strangers, and the unhappy, infinitely kind and hospitable. A very worthy priest, with whom I am acquainted at Quebec, was some years since shipwrecked in December on the island of Anticosti:[6] after a variety of distresses, not difficult to be imagined on an island without inhabitants, during the severity of a winter even colder than that of Canada; he, with the small remains of his companions who survived such complicated distress, early in the spring, reached the main land in their boat, and wandered to a cabbin of savages; the antient of which, having heard his story, bid him enter, and liberally supplied their wants: 'Approach, brother,' said he; 'the unhappy have a right to our assistance; we are men, and cannot but feel for the distresses which happen to men;' a sentiment which has a strong resemblance to a celebrated one in a Greek tragedy.[7]

You will not expect more from me on this subject, as my residence here has been short, and I can only be said to catch a few marking[8] features flying. I am unable to give you a picture at full length.

Nothing astonishes me so much as to find their manners so little changed by their intercourse with the Europeans; they seem to have learnt nothing of us but excess in drinking.

The situation of the village is very fine, on an eminence, gently rising to a thick wood at some distance, a beautiful little serpentine river in front, on which are a

[4]Leggings worn to protect the trousers or stockings from mud.
[5]A small pointed instrument.
[6]Ile d'Anticosti in the Gulf of St Lawrence.
[7]In fact this is a rather common sentiment in Greek tragedy, but the resemblance Brooke has in mind may well be to Theseus' first speech in Sophocles' *Oedipus at Colonus*:

> . . . *no wanderer shall come, as you do,*
> *And be denied my audience or aid.*
> *I know I am only a man; I have no more*
> *To hope for in the end than you have.*

[8]Characteristic.

bridge, a mill, and a small cascade, at such a distance as to be very pleasing objects from their houses; and a cultivated country, intermixed with little woods lying between them and Quebec, from which they are distant only nine very short miles.

What a letter have I written! I shall quit my post of historian to your friend Miss Fermor; the ladies love writing much better than we do; and I should perhaps be only just, if I said they write better.

Adieu!

Ed. Rivers

LETTER 49
TO MISS RIVERS, CLARGES STREET
[FROM ARABELLA FERMOR]

Silleri, Jan. 1

It is with difficulty I breathe, my dear; the cold is so amazingly intense as almost totally to stop respiration. I have business, the business of pleasure, at Quebec; but have not courage to stir from the stove.

We have had five days, the severity of which none of the natives remember to have ever seen equaled: 'tis said, the cold is beyond all the thermometers here, tho' intended for the climate.

The strongest wine freezes in a room which has a stove in it; even brandy is thickened to the consistence of oil: the largest wood fire, in a wide chimney, does not throw out its heat a quarter of a yard.

I must venture to Quebec to-morrow, or have company at home: amusements are here necessary to life; we must be jovial, or the blood will freeze in our veins.

I no longer wonder the elegant arts are unknown here; the rigour of the climate suspends the very powers of the understanding; what then must become of those of the imagination? Those who expect to see

'A new Athens rising near the pole,'[1]

will find themselves extremely disappointed. Genius will never mount high, where the faculties of the mind are benumbed half the year.

'Tis sufficient employment for the most lively spirit here to contrive how to preserve an existence, of which there are moments that one is hardly conscious: the cold really sometimes brings on a sort of stupefaction.

We had a million of beaux here yesterday, notwithstanding the severe cold: 'tis the Canadian custom, calculated I suppose for the climate, to visit all the ladies on New-year's-day, who sit dressed in form to be kissed: I assure you, however, our kisses could not warm them; but we were obliged, to our eternal disgrace, to call in rasberry brandy as an auxiliary.

You would have died to see the men; they look just like so many bears in their open carrioles,[2] all wrapped in furs from head to foot; you see nothing of the human form appear, but the tip of a nose.

[1]Adapted from a passage in Pope, 'Two Chorus's to the Tragedy of Brutus' (1717), about the Muses going into exile from ancient Greece to distant Britain, whereupon the island will:
See arts her savage sons controul,
And Athens *rising near the pole!*
[2]A kind of sleigh, usually for one person.

They have intire coats of beaver skin exactly like Friday's in Robinson Crusoe, and casques[3] on their heads like the old knights errant in romance; you never saw such tremendous figures; but without this kind of cloathing it would be impossible to stir out at present.

The ladies are equally covered up, tho' in a less unbecoming style; they have long cloth cloaks with loose hoods, like those worn by the market-women in the north of England. I have one in scarlet, the hood lined with sable, the prettiest ever seen here, in which I assure you I look amazingly handsome; the men think so, and call me the *Little red riding-hood*; a name which becomes me as well as the hood.

The Canadian ladies wear these cloaks in India silk in summer, which, fluttering in the wind, look really graceful on a fine woman.

Besides our riding-hoods, when we go out, we have a large buffaloe's skin under our feet, which turns up, and wraps round us almost to our shoulders; so that, upon the whole, we are pretty well guarded from the weather as well as the men.

Our covered carrioles too have not only canvas windows (we dare not have glass, because we often overturn), but cloth curtains to draw all around us; the extreme swiftness of these carriages also, which dart along like lightening, helps to keep one warm, by promoting the circulation of the blood.

I pity the Fitz;[4] no tiger was ever so hard-hearted as I am this weather: the little god[5] has taken his flight, like the swallows. I say nothing, but cruelty is no virtue in Canada; at least at this season.

I suppose Pygmalion's statue was some frozen Canadian gentlewoman, and a sudden warm day thawed her.[6] I love to expound ancient fables, and I think no exposition can be more natural than this.

Would you know what makes me chatter so this morning? Papa has made me take some excellent *liqueur*; 'tis the mode here; all the Canadian ladies take a little, which makes them so coquet and agreable. Certainly brandy makes a woman talk like an angel. Adieu!

Yours,

A. Fermor

[3]Helmets.
[4]Captain J. Fitzgerald, Arabella's suitor in Canada.
[5]Cupid.
[6]In Greek mythology Pygmalion was a sculptor who made a statue of such beauty that he fell in love with it. The goddess Aphrodite took pity on his plight and brought the statue to life.

LETTER 80
TO MISS RIVERS, CLARGES STREET
[FROM ARABELLA FERMOR]

Silleri, Feb. 25

Those who have heard no more of a Canadian winter than what regards the intenseness of its cold, must suppose it a very joyless season: 'tis, I assure you, quite otherwise; there are indeed some days here of the severity of which those who were never out of England can form no conception; but those days seldom exceed a dozen in a whole winter; nor do they come in succession, but at intermediate periods, as the winds set in from the North-West; which, coming some hundred leagues, from frozen lakes and rivers, over woods and mountains covered with snow, would be insupportable, were it not for the furs with which the country abounds, in such variety and plenty as to be within the reach of all its inhabitants.

Thus defended, the British belles set the winter of Canada at defiance; and the season of which you seem to entertain such terrible ideas, is that of the utmost chearfulness and festivity.

But what particularly pleases me is, there is no place where women are of such importance:[1] not one of the sex, who has the least share of attractions, is without a levee[2] of beaux interceding for the honor of attending her on some party, of which every day produces three or four.

I am just returned from one of the most agreable jaunts imagination can paint, to the island of Orleans, by the falls of Montmorenci; the latter is almost nine miles distant, across the great bason of Quebec; but as we are obliged to reach it in winter by the waving line, our direct road being intercepted by the inequalities of the ice, it is now perhaps a third more. You will possibly suppose a ride of this kind must want one of the greatest essentials to entertainment, that of variety, and imagine it only one dull whirl over an unvaried plain of snow; on the contrary, my dear, we pass hills and mountains of ice in the trifling space of these few miles. The bason of Quebec is formed by the conflux of the rivers St Charles and Montmorenci with the great river St Lawrence, the rapidity of whose flood-tide, as these rivers are gradually seized by the frost, breaks up the ice, and drives it back in heaps, till it forms ridges of transparent rock to an height that is astonishing, and of a strength which bids defiance to the utmost rage of the most furiously rushing tide.

This circumstance makes this little journey more pleasing than you can possibly conceive: the serene blue sky above, the dazzling brightness of the sun, and the colors from the refraction of its rays on the transparent part of these ridges of ice, the winding course these oblige you to make, the sudden disappearing of a train of fifteen or twenty carrioles, as these ridges intervene, which again discover themselves on your rising to the top of the frozen mount, the tremendous appearance both of the ascent and descent, which however are not attended with the least danger; all together give a grandeur and variety to the scene, which almost rise to enchantment.

Your dull foggy climate affords nothing that can give you the least idea of our frost pieces in Canada; nor can you form any notion of our amusements, of the agreableness of a covered carriole, with a sprightly fellow, rendered more sprightly by the keen air and romantic scene about him; to say nothing of the fair lady at his side.

Even an overturning has nothing alarming in it; you are laid gently down on a soft bed of snow, without the least danger of any kind; and an accident of this sort only gives a pretty fellow occasion to vary the style of his civilities, and shew a greater degree of attention.

But it is almost time to come to Montmorenci; to avoid, however, fatiguing you or myself, I shall refer the rest of our tour to another letter, which will probably accompany this: my meaning is, that two moderate letters are vastly better than one long one; in which sentiment I know you agree with

Yours,

A. Fermor

[1]In Letter 6 Brooke has Ed. Rivers say almost the same thing of the women he encounters among the French farmers: they play a civilizing role and 'Their conversation is lively and amusing, all the little knowledge of Canada is confined to the [female] sex. . . .'

[2]An assembly of visitors, especially but not necessarily in the morning.

LETTER 123
TO THE EARL OF——
[FROM CAPTAIN WM. FERMOR[1]]

Silleri, April 14

England, however populous, is undoubtedly, my Lord, too small to afford very large supplies of people to her colonies: and her people are also too useful, and of too much value, to be suffered to emigrate, if they can be prevented, whilst there is sufficient employment for them at home.

It is not only our interest to have colonies; they are not only necessary to our commerce, and our greatest and surest sources of wealth, but our very being as a powerful commercial nation depends on them: it is therefore an object of all others most worthy our attention, that they should be as flourishing and populous as possible.[2]

It is however equally our interest to support them at as little expence of our own inhabitants as possible: I therefore look on the acquisition of such a number of subjects as we found in Canada, to be a much superior advantage to that of gaining ten times the immense tract of land ceded to us, if uncultivated and destitute of inhabitants.

But it is not only contrary to our interest to spare many of our own people as settlers in America; it must also be considered, that, if we could spare them, the English are the worst settlers on new lands in the universe.

Their attachment to their native country, especially amongst the lower ranks of people, is so very strong, that few of the honest and industrious can be prevailed on to leave it; those therefore who go, are generally the dissolute and the idle, who are of no use any where.

The English are also, though industrious, active, and enterprizing, ill fitted to bear the hardships, and submit to the wants, which inevitably attend an infant settlement even on the most fruitful lands.

The Germans, on the contrary, with the same useful qualities, have a patience, a perseverance, and abstinence, which peculiarly fit them for the cultivation of new countries; too great encouragement therefore cannot be given to them to settle in our colonies: they make better settlers than our own people; and at the same time their numbers are an acquisition of real strength where they fix, without weakening the mother country.

It is long since the populousness of Europe has been the cause of her sending out colonies: a better policy prevails; mankind are enlightened; we are now convinced, both by reason and experience, that no industrious people can be too populous.

The northern swarms[3] were compelled to leave their respective countries, not because those countries were unable to support them, but because they were too idle to cultivate the ground: they were a ferocious, ignorant, barbarous people, averse to labor, attached to war, and, like our American savages, believing every employment

---

[1]Arabella's father. A Polonius-like character, he writes letters full of pompous statements and conventional wisdom. In Letter 133 [135] Fermor says: 'People who have no ideas out of the common road are, I believe, generally the greatest talkers.'

[2]Fermor's colonial attitude is expressed even more emphatically in Letter 131 [133]: 'Every advantage you give the North American trade centers at last in the mother, they are the bees, who roam abroad for that honey which enriches the paternal hive.'

[3]Fermor here apparently refers to the medieval migration of barbarians out of Northern Europe.

not relative to this favorite object, beneath the dignity of man.

Their emigrations therefore were less owing to their populousness, than to their want of industry, and barbarous contempt of agriculture and every useful art.

It is with pain I am compelled to say, the late spirit of encouraging the monopoly of farms, which, from a narrow, short-sighted policy, prevails amongst our landed men at home, and the alarming growth of celibacy amongst the peasantry, which is its necessary consequence, to say nothing of the same ruinous increase of celibacy in higher ranks, threatens us with such a decrease of population, as will probably equal that caused by the ravages of those scourges of heaven, the sword, the famine, and the pestilence.[4]

If this selfish policy continues to extend itself, we shall in a few years be so far from being able to send emigrants to America, that we shall be reduced to solicit their return, and that of their posterity, to prevent England's becoming in its turn an uncultivated desert.

But to return to Canada; this large acquisition of people is an invaluable treasure, if managed, as I doubt not it will be, to the best advantage; if they are won by the gentle arts of persuasion, and the gradual progress of knowledge, to adopt so much of our manners as tends to make them happier in themselves, and more useful members of the society to which they belong: if with our language, which they should by every means be induced to learn, they acquire the mild genius of our religion and laws, and that spirit of industry, enterprize, and commerce, to which we owe all our greatness.

* * *

Your Lordship enquires into the nature of this climate in respect to health. The air being uncommonly pure and serene, it is favorable to life beyond any I ever knew: the people live generally to a very advanced age; and are remarkably free from diseases of every kind, except consumptions, to which the younger part of the inhabitants are a good deal subject.

It is however a circumstance one cannot help observing, that they begin to look old much sooner than the people in Europe; on which my daughter observes, that it is not very pleasant for women to come to reside in a country where people have a short youth, and a long old age.

The diseases of cold countries are in general owing to want of perspiration; for which reason exercise, and even dissipation are here the best medicines.

The Indians therefore shewed their good sense in advising the French, on their first arrival, to use dancing, mirth, chearfulness, and content, as the best remedies against the inconveniences of the climate.

I have already swelled this letter to such a length, that I must postpone to another time my account of the peculiar natural productions of Canada; only observing, that one would imagine heaven intended a social intercourse between the most distant nations, by giving them productions of the earth so very different each from the other, and each more than sufficient for itself, that the exchange might be the means

---

[4]For much of the previous century, holdings of farmland in Britain had been becoming more and more concentrated among relatively few large landholders. The notion that the consequent displacement of farm families would result in a decline in fertility seems to have been a common—if unwarranted—fear of the time.

of spreading the bond of society and brotherhood over the whole globe.

In my opinion, the man who conveys, and causes to grow in any country, a grain, a fruit, or even a flower, it never possessed before, deserves more praise than a thousand heroes: he is a benefactor, he is in some degree a creator.

I have the honor to be,

My Lord,

Your Lordship's & c.

William Fermor

LETTER 127
TO JOHN TEMPLE, ESQ; PALL MALL
[FROM ARABELLA FERMOR]

Silleri, April 18

* * *

Cruel creature! why did you give me the idea of flowers? I now envy you your foggy climate: the earth with you is at this moment covered with a thousand lovely children of the spring; with us, it is an universal plain of snow.

Our beaux are terribly at a loss for similies: you have lilies of the valley for comparisons; we nothing but what with the idea of whiteness gives that of coldness too.

This is all the quarrel I have with Canada: the summer is delicious, the winter pleasant with all its severities; but alas! the smiling spring is not here; we pass from winter to summer in an instant, and lose the sprightly season of the Loves.

A letter from the God of my idolatry[1]—I must answer it instantly.

Adieu! Yours, &c.

A. Fermor

[1]Captain Fitzgerald.

LETTER 131
TO THE EARL OF——
[FROM WM. FERMOR]

Silleri, April 20, Evening

We are returned, my Lord, from having seen an object as beautiful and magnificent in itself, as pleasing from the idea it gives of renewing once more our intercourse with Europe.

Before I saw the breaking up of the vast body of ice, which forms what is here called *the bridge*, from Quebec to Point Levi, I imagined there could be nothing in it worth attention; that the ice would pass away, or dissolve gradually, day after day, as the influence of the sun, and warmth of the air and earth increased; and that we should see the river open, without having observed by what degrees it became so.

But I found *the great river*, as the savages with much propriety call it, maintain its dignity in this instance as in all others, and assert its superiority over those petty streams which we honor with the names of rivers in England. Sublimity is the characteristic of this western world; the loftiness of the mountains, the grandeur of the lakes and rivers, the majesty of the rocks shaded with a picturesque variety of beautiful trees and shrubs, and crowned with the noblest of the offspring of the forest, which form the banks of the latter, are as much beyond the power of fancy as that of description: a landscape-painter might here expand his imagination, and find ideas which he will seek in vain in our comparatively little world.

The object of which I am speaking has all the American magnificence.

The ice before the town, or, to speak in the Canadian stile, *the bridge*, being of a thickness not less than five feet, a league in length, and more than a mile broad, resists for a long time the rapid tide that attempts to force it from the banks.

We are prepared by many previous circumstances to expect something extraordinary in this event, if I may so call it: every increase of heat in the weather for near a month before the ice leaves the banks; every warm day gives you terror for those you see venturing to pass it in carrioles; yet one frosty night makes it again so strong, that even the ladies, and the timid amongst them, still venture themselves over in parties of pleasure; though greatly alarmed at their return, if a few hours of uncommon warmth intervene.

But, during the last fortnight, the alarm grows indeed a very serious one: the eye can distinguish, even at a considerable distance, that the ice is softened and detached from the banks; and you dread every step being death to those who have still the temerity to pass it, which they will continue always to do till one or more pay their rashness with their lives.

From the time the ice is no longer a bridge on which you see crowds driving with such vivacity on business or pleasure, every one is looking eagerly for its breaking away, to remove the bar to the continually wished and expected event, of the arrival of ships from that world from whence we have seemed so long in a manner excluded.

The hour is come; I have been with a crowd of both sexes, and all ranks, hailing the propitious moment: our situation, on the top of Cape Diamond, gave us a prospect some leagues above and below the town; above Cape Diamond the river was open, it was so below Point Levi, the rapidity of the current having forced a passage for the water under the transparent bridge, which for more than a league continued firm.

We stood waiting with all the eagerness of expectation; the tide came rushing with an amazing impetuosity; the bridge seemed to shake, yet resisted the force of the waters; the tide recoiled, it made a pause, it stood still, it returned with redoubled fury, the immense mass of ice gave way.

A vast plain appeared in motion; it advanced with solemn and majestic pace: the points of land on the banks of the river for a few moments stopped its progress; but the immense weight of so prodigious a body, carried along by a rapid current, bore down all opposition with a force irresistible.

There is no describing how beautiful the opening river appears, every moment gaining on the sight, till, in a time less than can possibly be imagined, the ice passing Point Levi, is hid in one moment by the projecting land, and all is once more a clear plain before you; giving at once the pleasing, but unconnected, ideas of that direct intercourse with Europe from which we have been so many months excluded, and of the earth's again opening her fertile bosom, to feast our eyes and imagination with her various verdant and flowery productions.

I am afraid I have conveyed a very inadequate idea of the scene which has just passed before me; it however struck me so strongly, that it was impossible for me not to attempt it.

If my painting has the least resemblance to the original, your Lordship will agree with me, that the very vicissitudes of season here partake of the sublimity which so strongly characterizes the country.

The changes of season in England, being slow and gradual, are but faintly felt; but being here sudden, instant, violent, afford to the mind, with the lively pleasure arising from meer change, the very high additional one of its being accompanied with grandeur. I have the honor to be,

My Lord,

Your Lordship's, &c.

William Fermor

LETTER 169
TO CAPTAIN FERMOR, AT SILLERI
[FROM ED. RIVERS[1]]

Aug. 6

I have been taking an exact survey of the house and estate with my mother, in order to determine on some future plan of life.

'Tis inconceivable what I felt on returning to a place so dear to me, and which I had not seen for many years; I ran hastily from one room to another; I traversed the garden with inexpressible eagerness: my eye devoured every object; there was not a tree, not a bush, which did not revive some pleasing, some soft idea.

I felt, to borrow a very pathetic expression of Thomson's,

'A thousand little tendernesses throb,'[2]

on revisiting those dear scenes of infant happiness; which were increased by having with me that estimable, that affectionate mother, to whose indulgence all my happiness had been owing.

*   *   *

The situation of the house is enchanting; and with all my passion for the savage luxuriance of America, I begin to find my taste return for the more mild and regular charms of my native country.

We have no Chaudieres, no Montmorencis, none of those magnificent scenes on which the Canadians have a right to pride themselves; but we excel them in the lovely, the smiling: in enameled meadows, in waving corn-fields, in gardens the boast of Europe; in every elegant art which adorns and softens human life; in all the riches and beauty which cultivation can give.

I begin to think I may be blest in the possession of my Emily, without betraying her into a state of want; we may, I begin to flatter myself, live with decency, in retirement; and, in my opinion, there are a thousand charms in retirement with those we love.

Upon the whole, I believe we shall be able to live, taking the word *live* in the

---

[1]After his return to England.

[2]Actually 'Ten thousand little tendernesses throb': James Thomson, *Agamemnon. A Tragedy* (1738), I, iii, 8.

sense of lovers, not of the *beau monde*, who will never allow a little country squire of four hundred pounds a year to *live*.[3]

Time may do more for us; at least, I am of an age and temper to encourage hope. All here are perfectly yours.

Adieu! my dear friend,
Your affectionate

Ed. Rivers

1769

[3] As in many works of the period that deal with marriage among the landed gentry on fixed incomes, the question of money plays an important role in the question of matrimony. The opposition in this passage between fashionable society (the *beau monde*) and a simple country life that embodies the pastoral ideal of moderation occurs several times in the book. Compare Letter 175 [177]: 'Upon the whole, I believe, the most agreable, as well as most free of all situations, to be that of a little country gentleman, who lives upon his income, and knows enough of the world not to envy his richer neighbours.' In her conclusion, however, Brooke places Ed. Rivers and his new wife beyond all financial constraints by having Emily turn out to be a lost heir.

Samuel Hearne

1745-1792

Samuel Hearne, a Londoner, served in the Royal Navy for nearly ten years before joining the Hudson's Bay Company as a seaman in 1766 at the age of twenty-one. After sailing for a time in Hudson Bay, Hearne demonstrated his ability to travel on foot by making an overland trip along the west coast of the Bay from Fort Prince of Wales (now Churchill, Man.) to York Factory and back. In 1769 he was given 'Orders and Instructions' to explore 'the Northern Indians Country, &c.'. In particular he was to find the Indian guide Matonabbee and, with him, seek out 'a river represented by the Indians to abound with copper ore, animals of the furr kind, &c., and which is said to be so far to the Northward, that in the middle of the Summer the Sun does not set. . . . And if the said river be likely to be of any utility, take possession of it on behalf of the Hudson's Bay Company.' A subsequent letter of instruction further describes him as being 'in quest of a North West Passage, Copper Mines, or any other thing that may be ser-

viceable to the British Nation in general, or the Hudson's Bay Company in particular.' The series of three journeys that Hearne made in fulfilment of his commission took him into difficult and previously uncharted territory. As he wrote in the introduction to his journals: 'I drew a Map on a large skin of parchment . . . but left the interior parts blank, to be filled up during my Journey.' In 1771-2 he found the Coppermine River and became the first European to reach the Arctic Ocean by travelling overland.

In 1774 Hearne founded Cumberland House, the Company's first inland post, and the next year he was made governor of Fort Prince of Wales. In 1782 he surrendered to a French expedition led by the Comte de Lapérouse, who destroyed the fort and returned Hearne's journals to him only after extracting a promise that Hearne would have them published. The fort was rebuilt in 1783 and Hearne returned as governor. In 1787 he retired to London, where he spent the rest of his life working on a final version of an account of his journeys. *A Journey from Prince of Wales's Fort in Hudson's Bay, to the northern ocean, undertaken by order of the Hudson's Bay Company, for the discovery of copper mines, a north west passage, &c. in the years 1769, 1770, 1771, & 1772,* which was not published until three years after his death, is one of the classic narratives of exploration, an understated chronicle of stoic endeavour. In his decision to live alone with the Indians, travelling in their nomadic fashion and depending on the land for sustenance, Hearne helped to pioneer an effective method of exploration, while his scrupulous concern for accuracy—as opposed to the fantastic quality of the travellers' tales that had previously come out of the New World wilderness—and the fullness of his records established his book as an important document. Although not free from cultural bias, Hearne provides coolly dispassionate accounts of the native peoples he encountered, which have remained valuable to ethnographers and stand in sharp contrast to earlier portrayals of Indians that idealized them or saw them as irredeemable savages. In addition he reveals himself as an excellent natural historian, with exceptional powers of memory and observation, in his careful descriptions of the animals and plants of the North.

From *A Journey from Prince of Wales's Fort in Hudson's Bay to the Northern Ocean*

[*Between 6 November and 11 December 1769 Samuel Hearne made an abortive journey from Fort Prince of Wales through the Barren Lands in search of copper and the Coppermine River. Hardships were increased by the perfidy of his first Indian guide, Chawchinahaw. In February 1770 he set out on a second attempt to find the Coppermine with a new guide, Conne-e-queese, who led him on a slow, uncertain trek during which Hearne became assimilated into the migratory life of his Indian companions.*]

JUNE 5TH-23RD 1770

The snow was by this time so soft as to render walking in snow-shoes very laborious; and though the ground was bare in many places, yet at times, and in particular places, the snow-drifts were so deep, that we could not possibly do without them. By the sixth, however, the thaws were so general, and the snows so much melted, that as our snow-shoes were attended with more trouble than service, we all consented to throw them away. Till the tenth, our sledges proved serviceable, particularly in crossing lakes and ponds on the ice; but that mode of travelling now growing dangerous on account of the great thaws, we determined to throw away our sledges, and every one to take a load on his back.

This I found to be much harder work than the winter carriage, as my part of the luggage consisted of the following articles, viz. the quadrant[1] and its stand, a trunk containing books, papers, &c. a land-compass, and a large bag containing all my wearing apparel; also a hatchet, knives, files, &c. beside several small articles, intended for presents to the natives. The aukwardness of my load, added to its great weight, which was upward of sixty pounds, and the excessive heat of the weather, rendered walking the most laborious task I had ever encountered; and what considerably increased the hardship, was the badness of the road, and the coarseness of our lodging, being, on account of the want of proper tents, exposed to the utmost severity of the weather. The tent we had with us was not

[1] An instrument used in navigation for measuring angles and taking bearings.

only too large, and unfit for barren ground service, where no poles were to be got, but we had been obliged to cut it up for shoes, and each person carried his own share. Indeed my guide behaved both negligently and ungenerously on this occasion; as he never made me, or my Southern Indians,[2] acquainted with the nature of pitching tents on the barren ground; which had he done, we could easily have procured a set of poles before we left the woods. He took care, however, to procure a set for himself and his wife; and when the tent was divided, though he made shift to get a piece large enough to serve him for a complete little tent, he never asked me or my Southern Indians to put our heads into it.

Beside the inconvenience of being exposed to the open air, night and day, in all weathers, we experienced real distress from the want of victuals. When provisions were procured, it often happened that we could not make a fire, so that we were obliged to eat the meat quite raw; which at first, in the article of fish particularly, was as little relished by my Southern companions as myself.

Notwithstanding these accumulated and complicated hardships, we continued in perfect health and good spirits; and my guide, though a perfect niggard of his provisions, especially in times of scarcity, gave us the strongest assurance of soon arriving at a plentiful country, which would not only afford us a certain supply of provisions, but where we should meet with other Indians, who probably would be willing to carry part of our luggage. This news naturally gave us great consolation; for at that time the weight of our constant loads was so great, that when Providence threw any thing in our way,[3] we could not carry above two days provisions with us, which indeed was the chief reason of our being so frequently in want.

From the twentieth to the twenty-third we walked every day near twenty miles, without any other subsistence than a pipe of tobacco, and a drink of water when we pleased: even partridges and gulls, which some time before were in great plenty, and easily procured, were now so scarce and shy, that we could rarely get one; and as to geese, ducks, &c. they had all flown to the Northward to breed and molt.

Early in the morning of the twenty-third, we set out as usual, but had not walked above seven or eight miles before we saw three musk-oxen grazing by the side of a small lake. The Indians immediately went in pursuit of them; and as some of them were expert hunters, they soon killed the whole of them. This was no doubt very fortunate; but, to our great mortification, before we could get one of them skinned, such a fall of rain came on, as to put it quite out of our power to make a fire; which, even in the finest weather, could only be made of moss, as we were near an hundred miles from any woods. This was poor comfort for people who had not broke their fast for four or five days. Necessity, however, has no law; and having been before initiated into the method of eating raw meat, we were the better prepared for this repast: but this was by no means so well relished, either by me or the Southern Indians, as either raw venison or raw fish had been: for the flesh of the musk-ox is not only coarse and tough, but smells and tastes so strong of musk as to make it very disagreeable when raw, though it is tolerable eating when properly cooked. The weather continued so remarkably

[2] The Cree, as opposed to the 'Northern' or Chipewyan Indians.
[3] i.e. when heaven provided game.

bad, accompanied with constant heavy rain, snow, and sleet, and our necessities were so great by the time the weather permitted us to make a fire, that we had nearly eat to the amount of one buffalo quite raw.

Notwithstanding I mustered up all my philosophy on this occasion, yet I must confess that my spirits began to fail me. Indeed our other misfortunes were greatly aggravated by the inclemency of the weather, which was not only cold, but so very wet that for near three days and nights I had not one dry thread about me. When the fine weather returned, we made a fire, though it was only of moss, as I have already observed; and having got my cloaths dry, all things seemed likely to go on in the old channel, though that was indifferent enough; but I endeavoured, like a sailor after a storm, to forget past misfortunes.

None of our natural wants, if we except thirst, are so distressing, or hard to endure, as hunger; and in wandering situations, like that which I now experienced, the hardship is greatly aggravated by the uncertainty with respect to its duration, and the means most proper to be used to remove it, as well as by the labour and fatigue we must necessarily undergo for that purpose, and the disappointments which too frequently frustrate our best concerted plans and most strenuous exertions: it not only enfeebles the body, but depresses the spirits, in spite of every effort to prevent it. Besides, for want of action, the stomach so far loses its digestive powers, that after long fasting it resumes its office with pain and reluctance. During this journey I have too frequently experienced the dreadful effects of this calamity, and more than once been reduced to so low a state by hunger and fatigue, that when Providence threw any thing in my way, my stomach has scarcely been able to retain more than two or three ounces, without producing the most oppressive pain. Another disagreeable circumstance of long fasting is, the extreme difficulty and pain attending the natural evacuations for the first time; and which is so dreadful, that of it none but those who have experienced can have an adequate idea.

To record in detail each day's fare since the commencement of this journey, would be little more than a dull repetition of the same occurrences. A sufficient idea of it may be given in a few words, by observing that it may justly be said to have been either all feasting, or all famine: sometimes we had too much, seldom just enough, frequently too little, and often none at all. It will be only necessary to say that we have fasted many times two whole days and nights; twice upwards of three days; and once, while at the She-than-nee,[4] near seven days, during which we tasted not a mouthful of any thing, except a few cranberries, water, scraps of old leather, and burnt bones. On those pressing occasions I have frequently seen the Indians examine their wardrobe, which consisted chiefly of skin-clothing, and consider what part could best be spared; sometimes a piece of an old, half-rotten deer skin, and at others a pair of old shoes, were sacrificed to alleviate extreme hunger. The relation of such uncommon hardships may perhaps gain little credit in Europe; while those who are conversant with the history of Hudson's Bay, and who are thoroughly acquainted with the distress which the natives of the country about it frequently endure, may consider them as no more

[4]A lake on the Seal River, not far from Fort Prince of Wales.

than the common occurrences of an Indian life, in which they are frequently driven to the necessity of eating one another.[5]

[*Hearne and Conne-e-queese eventually lost their way. His quadrant broken, Hearne turned back, arriving at the fort in November after nearly nine months of fruitless wandering—though on the last leg of this journey he met Matonabbee, the knowledgeable guide he had been searching for all along. Soon after his return; in December 1770, with Matonabbee and a company of Chipewyan Indians, Hearne set out on his third and longest journey. Under Matonabbee's leadership they drew near to the Coppermine River over six months later.*]

MAY 31ST 1771

Though it was so late when we left the women, we walked about ten miles that night before we stopped. In our way we saw many deer; several of which the Indians killed. To talk of travelling and killing deer in the middle of the night, may at first view have the appearance of romance; but our wonder will speedily abate, when it is considered that we were then to the Northward of 64° of North latitude, and that, in consequence of it, though the Sun did not remain the whole night above the horizon, yet the time it remained below it was so short, and its depression even at midnight so small at this season of the year, that the light, in clear weather, was quite sufficient for the purpose both of walking, and hunting any kind of game.

---

[5] 'It is the general opinion of the Southern Indians, that when any of their tribe have been driven to the necessity of eating human flesh, they become so fond of it, that no person is safe in their company. And though it is well known they are never guilty of making this horrid repast but when driven to it by necessity, yet those who have made it are not only shunned, but so universally detested by all who know them, that no Indians will tent with them, and they are frequently murdered slily. I have seen several of those poor wretches who, unfortunately for them, have come under the above description, and though they were persons much esteemed before hunger had driven them to this act, were afterward so universally despised and neglected, that a smile never graced their countenances: deep melancholy has been seated on their brows, while the eye most expressively spoke the dictates of the heart, and seemed to say, "Why do you despise me for my misfortunes? the period is probably not far distant, when you may be driven to the like necessity!"'

'In the Spring of the year 1775, when I was building Cumberland House, an Indian, whose name was Wapoos, came to the settlement, at a time when fifteen tents of Indians were on the plantations: they examined him very minutely, and found he had come a considerable way by himself, without a gun, or ammunition. This made many of them conjecture he had met with, and killed, some person by the way; and this was the more easily credited, from the care he took to conceal a bag of provisions, which he had brought with him, in a lofty pine-tree near the house.

'Being a stranger, I invited him in, though I saw he had nothing for trade; and during that interview, some of the Indian women examined his bag; and gave it as their opinion that the meat it contained was human flesh: in consequence, it was not without the interference of some principal Indians, whose liberality of sentiment was more extensive than that in the others, the poor creature saved his life. Many of the men cleaned and loaded their guns; others had their bows and arrows ready; and even the women took possession of the hatchets, to kill this poor inoffensive wretch, for no crime but that of travelling about two hundred miles by himself, unassisted by fire-arms for support in his journey' [Hearne's note].

It should have been observed, that during our stay at Clowey[1] a great number of Indians entered into a combination with those of my party to accompany us to the Copper-mine River; and with no other intent than to murder the Esquimaux, who are understood by the Copper Indians[2] to frequent that river in considerable numbers. This scheme, notwithstanding the trouble and fatigue, as well as danger, with which it must be obviously attended, was nevertheless so universally approved by those people, that for some time almost every man who joined us proposed to be of the party. Accordingly, each volunteer, as well as those who were properly of my party, prepared a target, or shield, before we left the woods of Clowey. Those targets were composed of thin boards, about three quarters of an inch thick, two feet broad, and three feet long; and were intended to ward off the arrows of the Esquimaux. Notwithstanding these preparations, when we came to leave the women and children, as has been already mentioned, only sixty volunteers would go with us; the rest, who were nearly as many more, though they had all prepared targets, reflecting that they had a great distance to walk, and that no advantage could be expected from the expedition, very prudently begged to be excused, saying, that they could not be spared for so long a time from the maintenance of their wives and families; and particularly, as they did not see any then in our company, who seemed willing to encumber themselves with such a charge. This seemed to be a mere evasion, for I am clearly of opinion that poverty on one side, and avarice on the other, were the only impediments to their joining our party; had they possessed as many European goods to squander away among their countrymen as Matonabbee and those of my party did, in all probability many might have been found who would have been glad to have accompanied us.

When I was acquainted with the intentions of my companions, and saw the warlike preparations that [they] were carrying on, I endeavoured as much as possible to persuade them from putting their inhuman design into execution; but so far were my intreaties from having the wished-for effect, that it was concluded I was actuated by cowardice; and they told me, with great marks of derision, that I was afraid of the Esquimaux. As I knew my personal safety depended in a great measure on the favourable opinion they entertained of me in this respect, I was obliged to change my tone, and replied, that I did not care if they rendered the name and race of the Esquimaux extinct; adding at the same time, that though I was no enemy to the Esquimaux, and did not see the necessity of attacking them without cause, yet if I should find it necessary to do it, for the protection of any one of my company, my own safety out of the question, so far from being afraid of a poor defenceless Esquimaux, whom I despised more than feared, nothing should be wanting on my part to protect all who were with me. This declaration was received with great satisfaction; and I never afterwards ventured to interfere with any of their war-plans. Indeed, when I came to consider seriously, I saw evidently that it was the highest folly for an individual like me, and in my situation, to attempt to turn the current of a national prejudice which had subsisted

[1] A small lake east of Great Slave Lake.
[2] Also known as the Yellowknives; like the Chipewyan, they were a band of Athapaskan Indians. Formerly widespread and powerful, they had been driven north and west at the beginning of the eighteenth century, when the Hudson's Bay Company's practice of supplying guns to the Chipewyan upset the historic balance among the bands.

between those two nations from the earliest periods, or at least as long as they had been acquainted with the existence of each other.

* * *

[*In July 1771 Hearne and his company at last 'arrived at that long wished-for spot, the Coppermine River', which turned out to be a much less impressive body of water than reports had led Hearne to expect. He began to map the river, though he quickly realized that it was not navigable.*]

JULY 15TH-17TH 1771

Early in the morning of the fifteenth, we set out, when I immediately began my survey, which I continued about ten miles down the river, till heavy rain coming on we were obliged to put up; and the place where we lay that night was the end, or edge of the woods, the whole space between it and the sea being entirely barren hills and wide open marshes. In the course of this day's survey, I found the river as full of shoals as the part which I had seen before; and in many places it was so greatly diminished in its width, that in our way we passed by two more capital falls.

Early in the morning of the sixteenth, the weather being fine and pleasant, I again proceeded with my survey, and continued it for ten miles farther down the river; but still found it the same as before, being every where full of falls and shoals. At this time (it being about noon) the three men who had been sent as spies met us on their return, and informed my companions that five tents of Esquimaux were on the west side of the river. The situation, they said, was very convenient for surprising them; and, according to their account, I judged it to be about twelve miles from the place we met the spies. When the Indians received this intelligence, no farther attendance or attention was paid to my survey, but their whole thoughts were immediately engaged in planning the best method of attack, and how they might steal on the poor Esquimaux the ensuing night, and kill them all while asleep. To accomplish this bloody design more effectually, the Indians thought it necessary to cross the river as soon as possible; and, by the account of the spies, it appeared that no part was more convenient for the purpose than that where we had met them, it being there very smooth, and at a considerable distance from any fall. Accordingly, after the Indians had put all their guns, spears, targets, &c. in good order, we crossed the river, which took up some time.

When we arrived on the West side of the river, each painted the front of his target or shield; some with the figure of the Sun, others with that of the Moon, several with different kinds of birds and beasts of prey, and many with the images of imaginary beings, which, according to their silly notions, are the inhabitants of the different elements, Earth, Sea, Air, &c.

On enquiring the reason of their doing so, I learned that each man painted his shield with the image of that being on which he relied most for success in the intended engagement. Some were contented with a single representation; while others, doubtful, as I suppose, of the quality and power of any single being, had their shields covered to the very margin with a group of hieroglyphics quite unintelligible to every one except the painter. Indeed, from the hurry in which this business was necessarily done, the want of every colour but red and black, and the deficiency of skill in the artist, most of those paintings had more the appearance of a number of accidental blotches, than 'of any thing that is on the earth, or in the water under the earth';[3] and though some few of them conveyed a tolerable idea of the thing intended, yet even these were many degrees worse than our country sign-paintings in England.

When this piece of superstition was completed, we began to advance toward the Esquimaux tents; but were very careful to avoid crossing any hills, or talking loud, for fear of being seen or overheard by the inhabitants; by which means the distance was not only much greater than it otherwise would have been, but, for the sake of keeping in the lowest grounds, we were obliged to walk through entire swamps of stiff marly clay, sometimes up to the knees. Our course, however, on this occasion, though very serpentine, was not altogether so remote from the river as entirely to exclude me from a view of it the whole way: on the contrary, several times (according to the situation of the ground) we advanced so near it, as to give me an opportunity of convincing myself that it was as unnavigable as it was in those parts which I had surveyed before, and which entirely corresponded with the accounts given of it by the spies.

It is perhaps worth remarking, that my crew, though an undisciplined rabble, and by no means accustomed to war or command, seemingly acted on this horrid occasion with the utmost uniformity of sentiment. There was not among them the least altercation or separate opinion; all were united in the general cause, and as ready to follow where Matonabbee led, as he appeared to be ready to lead, according to the advice of an old Copper Indian, who had joined us on our first arrival at the river where this bloody business was first proposed.

Never was reciprocity of interest more generally regarded among a number of people, than it was on the present occasion by my crew, for not one was a moment in want of any thing that another could spare; and if ever the spirit of disinterested friendship expanded the heart of a Northern Indian, it was here exhibited in the most extensive meaning of the word. Property of every kind that could be of general use now ceased to be private, and every one who had any thing which came under that description, seemed proud of an opportunity of giving it, or lending it to those who had none, or were most in want of it.

The number of my crew was so much greater than that which five tents could contain, and the warlike manner in which they were equipped so greatly superior to what could be expected of the poor Esquimaux, that no less than a total massacre of every one of them was likely to be the case, unless Providence should work a miracle for their deliverance.

The land was so situated that we walked under cover of the rocks and hills till we were within two hundred yards of the tents. There we lay in ambush for some time, watching the motions of the Esquimaux; and here the Indians would have advised me to stay till the fight was over, but to this I could by no means consent; for I considered that when the Esquimaux came to be surprised, they would try every way to escape, and if they found me alone, not knowing me from an enemy, they would probably proceed to violence against me when no person was near to assist. For this reason I determined to accompany them, telling them at

---

[3]A loose paraphrase of *Revelation* 5:13: 'And every creature which is in heaven, and on the earth, and under the earth, and such as are in the sea. . . .'

the same time, that I would not have any hand in the murder they were about to commit, unless I found it necessary for my own safety. The Indians were not displeased at this proposal; one of them immediately fixed me a spear, and another lent me a broad bayonet for my protection, but at that time I could not be provided with a target; nor did I want to be encumbered with such an unnecessary piece of lumber.

While we lay in ambush, the Indians performed the last ceremonies which were thought necessary before the engagement. These chiefly consisted in painting their faces; some all black, some all red, and others with a mixture of the two; and to prevent their hair from blowing into their eyes, it was either tied before and behind, and on both sides, or else cut short all round. The next thing they considered was to make themselves as light as possible for running; which they did, by pulling off their stockings, and either cutting off the sleeves of their jackets, or rolling them up close to their arm-pits; and though the muskettoes at that time were so numerous as to surpass all credibility, yet some of the Indians actually pulled off their jackets and entered the lists quite naked, except their breech-cloths and shoes. Fearing I might have occasion to run with the rest, I thought it also advisable to pull off my stockings and cap, and to tie my hair as close up as possible.

By the time the Indians had made themselves thus completely frightful, it was near one o'clock in the morning of the seventeenth; when finding all the Esquimaux quiet in their tents, they rushed forth from their ambuscade, and fell on the poor unsuspecting creatures, unperceived till close at the very eves of their tents, when they soon began the bloody massacre, while I stood neuter in the rear.

In a few seconds the horrible scene commenced; it was shocking beyond description; the poor unhappy victims were surprised in the midst of their sleep, and had neither time nor power to make any resistance; men, women, and children, in all upward of twenty, ran out of their tents stark naked, and endeavoured to make their escape; but the Indians having possession of all the land-side, to no place could they fly for shelter. One alternative only remained, that of jumping into the river; but, as none of them attempted it, they all fell a sacrifice to Indian barbarity!

The shrieks and groans of the poor expiring wretches were truly dreadful; and my horror was much increased at seeing a young girl, seemingly about eighteen years of age, killed so near me, that when the first spear was stuck into her side she fell down at my feet, and twisted round my legs, so that it was with difficulty that I could disengage myself from her dying grasps. As two Indian men pursued this unfortunate victim, I solicited very hard for her life; but the murderers made no reply till they had stuck both their spears through her body, and transfixed her to the ground. They then looked me sternly in the face, and began to ridicule me, by asking if I wanted an Esquimaux wife; and paid not the smallest regard to the shrieks and agony of the poor wretch, who was twining round their spears like an eel! Indeed, after receiving much abusive language from them on the occasion, I was at length obliged to desire that they would be more expeditious in dispatching their victim out of her misery, otherwise I should be obliged, out of pity, to assist in the friendly office of putting an end to the existence of a fellow-creature who was so cruelly wounded. On this request being made, one of the Indians hastily drew his spear from the place where it was first lodged, and pierced it through her breast near the heart. The love of life, however, even in this most miserable state, was so predominant, that though this might justly be called the most merciful act that could be done for the poor creature, it seemed to be unwelcome, for though much exhausted by pain and loss of blood, she made several efforts to ward off the friendly blow. My situation and the terror of my mind at beholding this butchery, cannot easily be conceived, much less described; though I summed up all the fortitude I was master of on the occasion, it was with difficulty that I could refrain from tears; and I am confident that my features must have feelingly expressed how sincerely I was affected at the barbarous scene I then witnessed; even at this hour I cannot reflect on the transactions of that horrid day without shedding tears.

[*Hearne reached the mouth of the Coppermine and found that the 'mine' he had heard about was a disappointment. His commission fulfilled, he turned back. During this final trek, the most difficult of all, several of the Indians died of sickness and starvation. Hearne did not arrive back at Fort Prince of Wales until a year and a half after he had left it. His account of his explorations concludes with these words: 'Though my discoveries are not likely to prove of any material advantage to the Nation at large, or indeed to the Hudson's Bay Company, yet I have the pleasure to think that I have fully complied with the orders of my Masters, and that it has put a final end to all disputes concerning a North West Passage through Hudson's Bay.'*]

1795

David Thompson

1770-1857

David Thompson was recruited from a London charity school at fourteen to become an apprentice clerk with the Hudson's Bay Company. Although he later wrote that when he arrived at Fort Prince of Wales (Churchill, Man.) in 1784, 'I bid a long and sad farewell to my . . . country, an exile for ever', Thompson seems to have been eager to learn what he could of the company's operations. Confined by a broken leg at nineteen, he spent almost a year at Cumberland House studying mathematics, astronomy, and field surveying, and made himself one of the best cartographers of his time. In twenty-eight years of exploring the West he managed to survey and map nearly two million square miles with such accuracy that maps at the beginning of this century were still based on his work. The explorer J.B. Tyrrell, who oversaw the first publication of Thompson's narrative, called him 'the greatest practical land geographer that the world had produced.'

In 1797 Thompson left the employ of the Hudson's Bay Company and went to the rival North West Company as a surveyor and map-maker, instructed to determine the position of company posts in relation to the recently established boundary at the forty-ninth parallel. Thompson travelled widely in the West and Northwest in the years that followed. He married Charlotte Small, the daughter of an English fur trader and an Indian mother. In 1815 Thompson and his wife retired to Williamstown, Upper Canada. However, he did not cease working. He served as Astronomer and Surveyor to the British Boundary Commission, establishing the United States-Canada boundary for Ontario and Quebec, and revised the maps he made on his trips of western exploration. In 1846 he began to write a narrative account of his travels based on journals that he had begun in 1789 (and that eventually ran to thirty-nine volumes). He laboured on this project for the next five years, but blindness brought it to a halt before it was completed. *David Thompson's Narrative of his Explorations in Western North America 1784-1812*, edited by J.B. Tyrrell, was published in 1916.

When he first arrived at Fort Prince of Wales, Thompson served under Hearne and disliked the older man, both for his supposed cowardice in surrendering the fort to the French and for being a free-thinker and follower of Voltaire. He may, however, have known Hearne's journals in manuscript; certainly in his narrative Thompson reveals the same strengths as the earlier writer-explorer. He was able to understand and be accepted by the Indians; he was a keen observer and diligent recorder who provided accounts that are both factual and anecdotal; and he expressed himself in an unaffected style that gives his writing authority and immediacy.

All Thompson's activities were governed by an intensely inquiring mind. He was never intimidated by harsh conditions in his determined effort to study and understand his environment, as may be seen in his description of crossing the Rockies by way of the Athabasca Pass:

The view now before us was an ascent of deep snow. . . . It was to me a most exhilarating sight, but to my uneducated men a dreadful sight. They had no scientific object in view, their feelings were of the place they were. . . . Many reflections came on my mind; a new world was in a manner before me.

From the
Narrative of His Explorations in Western North America, 1784-1812

CHAPTER VI
LIFE AMONG THE NAHATHAWAYS

* * *

It may now [be time to] say something of myself, and of the character the Natives and the French Canadians entertained of me, they were almost my only companions. My instruments for practical astronomy were a brass Sextant of ten inches radius, an achromatic Telescope[1] of high power for observing the Satellites of Jupiter and other phenomena, one of the same construction for common use, Parallel glasses and quicksilver horizon for double Altitudes; Compass, Thermometer, and other requisite instruments, which I was in the constant practice of using in clear weather for observations on the Sun, Moon, Planets and Stars to deter-

---

[1]An achromatic lens is one that does not introduce colour by breaking light into its constituent parts. In taking readings with his sextant, Thompson needed an artificial horizon since he could not, as mariners could, always see the true horizon; for this purpose mercury ('quicksilver') was carried in a flat rectangular tray, shielded from the wind by glass plates that had to have truly parallel faces so as not to introduce any distortion in the light passing through them (hence 'parallel glasses'). Position could then be calculated by taking the angle of an astronomical body, and of its reflection, in the horizontal surface of the mercury pool at rest (a 'double altitude').

mine the positions of the Rivers, Lakes, Mountains and other parts of the country I surveyed from Hudson Bay to the Pacific Ocean. Both Canadians and Indians often inquired of me why I observed the Sun, and sometimes the Moon, in the daytime, and passed whole nights with my instruments looking at the Moon and Stars. I told them it was to determine the distance and direction from the place I observed to other places. Neither the Canadians nor the Indians believed me; for both argued that if what I said was truth, I ought to look to the ground and over it and not to the Stars. Their opinions were that I was looking into futurity and seeing everybody and what they were doing [and that I knew] how to raise the wind, but did not believe I could calm it. This they argued from seeing me obliged to wait the calming of the wind on the great Lakes, to which the Indians added that I knew where the Deer were, and other superstitious opinions.

During my life I have always been careful not to pretend to any knowledge of futurity, and [said] that I knew nothing beyond the present hour. Neither argument nor ridicule had any effect and I had to leave them to their own opinions, and yet inadvertingly on my part several things happened to confirm their opinions. One fine evening in February two Indians came to the house to trade. The Moon rose bright and clear with the planet Jupiter a few degrees on its east side and the Canadians as usual predicted that Indians would come to trade in the direction of this star. To show them the folly of such predictions I told them the same bright star, the next night, would be as far from the Moon on its west side. This of course took place from the Moon's motion in her orbit and is the common occurence of almost every month, and yet all parties were persuaded I had done it by some occult power to falsify the predictions of the Canadians. Mankind are fond of the marvelous; it seems to heighten their character by relating they have seen such things.

I had always admired the tact of the Indian in being able to guide himself through the darkest pine forests to exactly the place he intended to go; his keen, constant attention on everything: the removal of the smallest stone, the bent or broken twig, a slight mark on the ground, all spoke plain language to him. I was anxious to acquire this knowledge, and often being in company with them, sometimes for several months, I paid attention to what they pointed out to me, and became almost equal to some of them, which became of great use to me. The North West Company of Furr Traders, from their Depot in Lake Superior sent off Brigades of Canoes loaded with about three Tons weight of Merchandise, Provisions and Baggage. Those for the most distant trading Posts are sent off first, with an allowance of two days' time between each Brigade to prevent incumbrances on the Carrying Places. I was in my first year in the third Brigade of six Canoes each and having nothing to do but sketch off my survey and make Observations. I was noticing how far we gained or lost ground on the Brigade before us by the fires they made, and other marks, as we were equally manned with five men to each canoe. In order to prevent the winter coming on us, before we reached our distant winter quarters, the Men had to work very hard from daylight to sunset, or later, and at night slept on the ground, constantly worried by Musketoes, and had no time to look about them. I found we gained very little on them. At the end of fifteen days we had to arrive at Lake Winipeg (that is the Sea Lake from its size) and for more than two days it had been blowing a northwest gale, which did not allow the Brigade before us to proceed; and I told the Guide that early the next morning we should see them. These Guides have charge of conducting the march and are all proud of coming up to the canoes ahead of them, and by dawn of day we entered the Lake now calm, and as the day came on us saw the Brigade that were before us only one Mile ahead of us. The Guide and the men shouted with joy, and when we came up to them told them of my wonderful predictions, and that I had pointed out every place they had slept at, and all by looking at the Stars. One party seemed delighted in being credulous, the other in exageration; such are ignorant men, who never give themselves a moment's reflection.

* * *

This section of the Stony Region is called the Musk Rat Country and contains an area of about 22,360 square miles, of which full two fifths of this surface is Rivers and Lakes, having phenomena distinct from the dry, elevated, distant, interior countries. The Natives are Nahathaway Indians, whose fathers from time, beyond any tradition, have hunted in these Lands. In conversing with them on their origin they appear never to have turned their minds to this subject; and [think] that mankind and the animals are in a constant state of succession; and the time of their great grandfathers is the extent of their actual knowledge of times past. Their tradition of the Deluge and of the Rainbow I have already mentioned;[2] yet their stories all refer to times when Men were much taller and stronger than at present, the animals more numerous, and many could converse with mankind, particularly, the Bear, Beaver, Lynx and Fox. Writers on the North American Indians always write as comparing them with themselves, who are all men of education, and of course [the Indians] lose by comparison. This is not fair. Let them be compared with those who are uneducated in Europe; yet even in this comparison the Indian has the disadvantage in not having the light of Christianity. Of course his moral character has not the firmness of Christian morality, but in practice he is fully equal to those of his class in Europe; living without law, they are a law to themselves. The Indian is said to be a creature of apathy. When he appears to be so he is in an assumed character to conceal what is passing in his mind, as he has nothing of the almost infinite diversity of things which interest and amuse the civilised man. His passions, desires and affections are strong, however appeared subdued, and engage the whole man. The law of retaliation, which is fully allowed, makes the life of man respected; and in general he abhors the sheding of blood, and should sad necessity compel him to it, which is sometimes the case, he is held to be an unfortunate man. But he who has committed wilful murder is held in abhorrence, as one with whom the life of no person is in safety, and possessed with an evil spirit.

When Hudson Bay was discovered, and the first trading settlement made, the Natives were far more numerous than at present. In the year 1782 the small pox

[2]Thompson earlier retells the Indian tale, widespread throughout North America, of the earth's being covered by a great deluge until Trickster (in this version called Weesaukajauk, the Flatterer) sends various animals diving beneath the flood to bring up some earth from which he recreates dry land. Thompson adds to this an instance of hearing an Indian say of the rainbow, 'Oh, there is a mark of life, we shall yet live'—to which Thompson replied, '. . . our books also call the rainbow the mark of life'.

from Canada extended to them and more than one half of them died; since which, although they had no enemies [and] their country [is] very healthy, yet their numbers increase very slowly. The Musk Rat country, of which I have given the area, may have ninety-two families, each of seven souls, giving to each family an area of two-hundred-and-forty-eight square miles of hunting grounds; or thirty-five square miles to each soul—a very thin population. A recent writer (Ballantyne)[3] talks of myriads of wild animals. Such writers talk at random; they have never counted nor calculated. The animals are by no means numerous, and only in sufficient numbers to give a tolerable subsistence to the Natives, who are too often obliged to live on very little food and sometimes all but perish with hunger. Very few Beaver are to be found, the Bears are not many, and all the furr-bearing animals an Indian can kill can scarcely furnish himself and family with the bare necessaries of life.

A strange Idea prevails among these Natives, and also of all the Indians to the Rocky Mountains, though unknown to each other, that when they were numerous, before they were destroyed by the Small Pox, all the animals of every species were also very numerous and more so in comparison of the number of Natives than at present; and this was confirmed to me by old Scotchmen in the service of the Hudson's Bay Company, and by the Canadians from Canada. The knowledge of the latter extended over all the interior countries, yet no disorder was known among the animals; the fact was certain, and nothing they knew of could account for it. It might justly be supposed the destruction of Mankind would allow the animals to increase, even to become formidable to the few Natives who survived, but neither the Bison, the Deer, nor the carnivorous animals increased, and as I have already remarked, are no more than sufficient for the subsistence of the Natives and Traders. The trading Houses over the whole country are situated on the banks of lakes of at least twenty miles in length by two or three miles in width . . . as it is only large and deep Lakes that have Fish sufficient to maintain the Trader and his Men, for the Indians at best can only afford a Deer now and then.

* * *

Formerly the Beavers were very numerous. The many Lakes and Rivers gave them ample space and the poor Indian had then only a pointed stick shaped and hardened in the fire, a stone Hatchet, Spear and Arrowheads of the same. Thus armed he was weak against the sagacious Beaver who, on the banks of a Lake, made itself a house of a foot thick or more, composed of earth and small flat stones, crossed and bound together with pieces of wood, upon which no impression could be made but by fire. But when the arrival of the White People had changed all their weapons from stone to iron and steel, and added the fatal Gun, every animal fell before the Indian. The Bear was no longer dreaded, and the Beaver became a desirable animal for food and clothing and the furr a valuable article of trade; and as the Beaver is a stationary animal, it could be attacked at any convenient time in all seasons, and thus their numbers soon became reduced.

[3]The Scottish writer R. M. Ballantyne (1825-94), who was employed by the Hudson's Bay Company from 1841 to 1847, began publishing his stories of life among Company fur traders around the time Thompson was writing his memoirs.

The old Indians, when speaking of their ancestors, wonder how they could live, as the Beaver was wiser and the Bear stronger than them, and confess that if they were deprived of the Gun they could not live by the Bow and Arrow and must soon perish.

The Beaver skin is the standard by which other Furrs are traded; and London prices have very little influence on this value of barter, which is more a matter of expedience and convenience to the Trader and the Native than of real value. The only Bears of this country are the small black Bear, with a chance Yellow Bear;[4] this latter has a fine furr and trades for three Beavers in barter when full grown. The Black Bear is common, and according to size passes for one or two Beavers. The young are often tamed by the Natives and are harmless and playful until near full grown, when they become troublesome and are killed or sent into the woods. While they can procure roots and berries they look for nothing else; but in the Spring, when they leave their winter dens, they can get neither the one nor the other, prowl about, and go to the Rapids where the Carp are spawning. Here Bruin lives in plenty; but not content with what it can eat, amuses itself with tossing ashore ten times more than it can devour, each stroke of its forepaw sending a fish eight or ten yards according to its size. The fish thus thrown ashore attract the Eagle and the Raven. The sight of these birds flying about leads the Indian to the place and Bruin loses his life and his skin. The meat of the Bear feeding on the roots and berries becomes very fat and good, and in this condition it enters its den for the winter, at the end of which the meat is still good, and has some fat; but [at] the very first meal of fish the taste of the meat is changed for the worse, and soon becomes disagreeable. When a Mahmees Dog in the winter season has discovered a den and the Natives go to kill the Bear, on uncovering the top of the den Bruin is found roused out of its dormant state and sitting ready to defend itself. The eldest man now makes a speech to it, reproaching the Bear and all its race with being the old enemies of Man, killing the children and women when it was large and strong, but now, since the Manito[5] has made him small and weak to what he was before, he has all the will, though not the power, to be as bad as ever; that he is treacherous and cannot be trusted; that although he has sense he makes bad use of it and must therefore be killed. Parts of the speech have many repetitions to impress its truth on the Bear, who all the time is grinning and growling, willing to fight, but more willing to escape, until the axe descends on its head, or [it] is shot—the latter more frequently, as the den is often under the roots of fallen trees and protected by the branches of the roots.

When a Bear thus killed was hauled out of its den I enquired of the Indian who made the speech whether he really thought the Bear understood him. He replied, 'How can you doubt it? Did you not see how ashamed I made him, and how he held down his head?' 'He might well hold down his head when you were flourishing a heavy axe over it, with which you killed him.' On this animal they have several superstitions, and he acts a prominent part in many of their tales.

* * *

[4] Actually a colour phase of the black bear.
[5] Or 'manitou': Thompson earlier records that the Nahathaway (or Cree) 'believe in the self existence of the Kee-che Kee-che Manito (the Great, Great Spirit). . . . He leaves the human race to their own conduct, but has placed all other living creatures under the care of manitos (or inferior angels).'

What is called Mirage is common on all these Lakes, but frequently [is] simply an elevation of the woods and shores that bound the horizon; yet at times draws attention to the change of scenery it exhibits, and on these Lakes has often kept me watching it for many minutes; and [I] would have stayed longer if the cold had permitted. The first and most changeable Mirage is seen in the latter part of February and the month of March, the weather clear, the wind calm, or light; the Thermometer from ten above to twelve degrees below zero, the time about ten in the morning. On one occasion, going to an Isle where I had two traps for Foxes, when about one mile distant the ice between me and the Isle appeared of a concave form, which, if I entered, I should slide into its hollow; [and although I was] sensible of the illusion, it had the power to perplex me. I found my snow shoes on a level and advanced slowly, as afraid to slide into it; in about ten minutes this mirage ceased, the ice became [distinct] and showed a level surface, and with confidence I walked to my traps, in one of which I found a red Fox. This sort of Mirage is not frequent. That most common elevates and depresses objects, and sometimes makes them appear to change places.

In the latter end of February at the Reed Lake, at its west end, a Mirage took place in one of its boldest forms. About three miles from me was the extreme shore of the Bay; the Lake was near three miles in width, in which was a steep Isle of rock and another of tall Pines; on the other side a bold Point of steep rock. The Mirage began slowly to elevate all objects, then gently to lower them, until the Isles and the Point appeared like black spots on the ice, and no higher than its surface. The above bold Bay Shore was a dark black curved line on the ice. In the time of three minutes they all arose to their former height and became elevated to twice their height. Beyond the Bay the rising grounds, distant eight miles, with all their woods appeared, and remained somewhat steady for a few minutes; the Isles and Point again disappeared. The Bay Shore with the distant Forests came rolling forward with an undulating motion, as if in a dance; the distant Forests became so near to me I could see their branches, then with the same motion retired to half distance. The Bay shore could not be distinguished; it was blended with the distant land, thus advancing and retiring with different elevations for about fifteen minutes when the distant Forests vanished, the Isles took their place, and the Lake shores their form. The whole wild scenery was a powerful illusion, too fleeting and changeful for any pencil.

This was one of the clearest and most distinct Mirages I had ever seen. There can be no doubt it is the effect of a cause which, perhaps, was waves of the atmosphere loaded with vapours, though not perceptible to the eye, between the beholder and the objects on which the mirage acts, with the Sun in a certain position. When the objects were seen on the ridge of the wave, it gave them their elevation; when in the hollow of the wave, their greatest depression; and viewed obliquely to the direction of the wave, the objects appeared to change places. There may be a better theory to account for the Mirage.

While the Mirage is in full action, the scenery is so clear and vivid, the illusion so strong, as to perplex the Hunter and the Traveller. It appears more like the power of magic than the play of nature. When enquiring of the Natives what they thought of it, they said it was Manito Korso—the work of a Manito—and with this argument they account for everything that is uncommon.

Although the climate and country of which I am writing is far better than that of Hudson's Bay, yet the climate is severe in Winter, the Thermometer often from thirty to forty degrees below Zero. The month of December is the coldest. The long absence of the Sun gives full effect to the action of the cold; the Snow increases in depth—it may be said to fall as dry as dust; the ice rapidly increases in thickness and the steady cold of the rest of winter adds but little to that of the end of this month. But its contraction by intense cold causes the ice to rend in many places with a loud rumbling noise, and through these rents water is often thrown out and flows over part of the ice, making bad walking. This month has very variable weather; sometimes a calm of several days, then Gales of wind with light snow, which from its lightness is driven about like dust. This dull month of long nights we wish to pass away. The country affords no tallow for candles nor fish oil for lamps; the light of the fire is what we have to work and read by. Christmas when it comes finds us glad to see it and pass; we have nothing to welcome it with.

In one of the calms of this month Tapahpahtum, a good hunter, came to us for some provisions and fish hooks. He said his three wives and his children had had very little to eat for nearly a whole Moon, adding, 'You may be sure that we suffer hunger when I come to beg fish, and get hooks for my women to angle with.' He took away about thirty pounds of fish, which he had to carry about twenty miles to his tent. I felt for him, for nothing but sad necessity can compel a Nahathaway hunter to carry away fish, and angle for them; this is too mean for a hunter. Meat he carries with pleasure, but fish is degradation. The calm still continued, and two days after Tapahpahtum came in the evening. He looked somewhat wild; he was a powerful man of strong passions. As usual I gave him a bit of Tobacco. He sat down and smoked, inhaling the smoke as if he would have drawn the tobacco through the pipe stem; then saying, 'Now I have smoked, I may speak. I do not come to you for fish. I hope never to disgrace myself again. I now come for a wind which you must give me.' In the mood he was in, to argue with him was of no use, and I said, 'Why did you not bring one of your women with you? She would have taken some fish to the tent.' 'My women are too weak. They snare a hare, or two every day, barely enough to keep them alive. I am come for a wind which you must give me.' 'You know as well as I do that the Great Spirit alone is master of the Winds; you must apply to him and not to me.' 'Ah, that is always your way of talking to us. When you will not hear us, then you talk to us of the Great Spirit. I want a Wind. I must have it. Now think on it and dream how I am to get it.' I lent him an old Bison Robe to sleep on, which was all we could spare. The next day was calm. He sat on the floor in a despondent mood, at times smoking his pipe, and saying to me, 'Be kind to me, be kind to me, give me a Wind that we may live.' I told him the Good Spirit alone could cause the wind to blow. And my French Canadians were as foolish as the poor Indian, saying to one another, 'It would be a good thing, and well done, if he got a wind. We should get meat to eat.'

The night was very fine and clear. I passed most of it observing the Moon and Stars as usual. The small meteors were very numerous, which indicated a Gale of Wind. The morning rose fine, and before the appearance of the Sun, tho' calm with us, the tops of the tall Pines were waving, all foretelling a heavy gale, which usually follows a long calm. All this was plain to everyone. Very early Tapah-pahtum said, 'Be kind and give me a strong wind.' Vexed with him, I told him to go and take care that the trees did not fall upon him. He shouted, 'I have got it', sprang from the floor, snatched his gun, whipt on his Snow Shoes, and dashed away at five miles an hour. The gale from North East came on as usual with snow and high drift and lasted three days. For the two first days we could not visit the nets, which sometimes happens; the third day the drift ceased, but the nets had been too long in the water without being washed, and we had to take them up. On this gale of wind, a common occurence, I learnt my men were more strangely foolish than the Indians. Something better than two months after this gale I sent three of the men with letters to another trading house and to bring some articles I wanted. Here these men related how I had raised a storm of wind for the Indian, but had made it so strong that for two days they got no fish from the nets, adding they thought I would take better care another time. In these distant solitudes, Men's minds seem to partake of the wildness of the country they live in. . . .

Wiskahoo was naturally a cheerful, good-natured, careless man, but hard times had changed him. He was a good Beaver worker and trapper, but an indif-ferent Moose Hunter, [though] now and then [he] killed one by chance. He had been twice so reduced by hunger as to be twice on the point of eating one of his children to save the others, when he was fortunately found and relieved by the other Natives. These sufferings had at times unhinged his mind, and made him dread being alone. He had for about a month been working Beaver and had now joined Tapahpahtum, and their Tents were together. He came to trade, and brought some meat the other had sent. It is usual when the Natives come to trade to give them a pint of grog, a liquor which I always used very sparingly. It was a bad custom, but could not be broken off. Wiskahoo, as soon as he got it, and while drinking of it, used to say in a thoughtful mood, 'Nee weet to go' 'I must be a Man eater.' This word seemed to imply, 'I am possessed of an evil spirit to eat human flesh', 'Wee tee go'[6] is the evil Spirit that devours humankind. When he had said this a few times, one of the Men used to tie him slightly and he soon became quiet. These sad thoughts at times came upon him from the dreadful dis-tress he had suffered; and at times took him in his tent, when he always allowed himself to be tied during this sad mood, which did not last long.

Three years afterwards this sad mood came upon him so often that the Natives got alarmed. They shot him and burnt his body to ashes to prevent his ghost remaining in this world.

Apistawahshish (the Dwarf) was of low stature, but strongly made and very active, a good Beaver worker, and a second rate hunter of Moose deer. He was careful and industrious. When the leaves of the trees had fallen, and winter was coming on, he had parted from the others to work Beaver. At first he was suc-cessful; but the third house he attacked, the beaver had worked many stones into it, [so] that he broke his ice chissel and blunted one of his axes useless; the other

---

[6]Now usually spelled 'Windigo': a cannibalistic monster, formerly a man. Thompson's is one of the earliest records of this important Indian myth, which seems to have functioned both to enunciate the prohibition of cannibalism and to serve as a warning against the abuses of power—especially among shamans and other powerful leaders who were said to have to guard themselves against becoming Windigoes (i.e. against using their strength to consume the essence of their companions).

was all they had to cut fire wood. The edges of the Lakes were frozen over and canoes could not be used. Distressing times came, and they were reduced to use as food the youngest child to save the others. They were so weak they could barely get a little wood for the fire. Sitting in sorrow and despair looking at the child next to lose its life, a Rein Deer came and stood a few yards from the tent door. He shot it and [it] became the means of saving them and recovering their strength; and for the winter he was a fortunate hunter. Both himself, his family, and the Natives believed that this Deer was sent by the Manito in pity to himself and family. He kept the skin, which I saw.

The Indians did not hold him culpable. They felt they were all liable to the same sad affliction; and the Manito sending him a Deer showed a mark of favor. As the strong affections of an Indian is centered in his children, for they may be said to be all he has to depend upon, they believe the dreadful distressed state of mind which necessity forces on them to take the life of one of their children to preserve the others leaves such sad indelible impressions that the parents are never again the same [as] they were before, and are liable to aberrations of mind. It is only on this Region and the Lakes westward to near the great plains where there are Horses that the Natives are subject to this distress of hunger. Their Dogs are starved and do them very little good. If the country contained but half the Deer and other animals some writers speak of, the Natives would not suffer as they do. Notwithstanding the hardships the Natives sometimes suffer, they are strongly attached to the country of Rivers, Lakes, and Forests.

[1846-51], 1916

Oliver Goldsmith

1794-1861

Oliver Goldsmith, Canadian grandnephew and namesake of the British author of *The Vicar of Wakefield* and *She Stoops To Conquer*, published *The Rising Village: A Poem* in London in 1825, in response to his great-uncle's long pastoral poem, *The Deserted Village* (1770). Where the earlier poem elegizes the vanishing rural life of the poet's childhood, *The Rising Village* counters by suggesting that the emergence of a Canadian agrarian society will compensate Britain for its loss of village society. Retaining, over fifty years later, the rhyming couplets, diction, and imagery of its model, *The Rising Village* was the first volume of Canadian verse to receive serious critical attention—mostly from British reviewers, whose

unflattering comparisons with *The Deserted Village* so dismayed the poet that he lost much of his interest in writing. Goldsmith did, however, eventually return to his poem to revise it, shortening it by twenty-two lines; the revision was published in New Brunswick in 1834.

Son of a British army officer who settled in Canada after fighting in the American Revolutionary War, Goldsmith was born in 1794 in Saint Andrews, N.B., and grew up in Halifax. After five years of false starts, he found at fifteen his permanent career with the Commissariat, the civilian supply branch of the British army, where he remained until his retirement in 1885. A life-long bachelor, he then moved to Liverpool to live with his sister and compose his *Autobiography*, in which he has recorded how he came to undertake his venture into poetry:

> . . . the celebrated Author of the 'Deserted Village' had pathetically displayed the Anguish of his Countrymen, on being forced, from various causes, to quit their native plains, endeared to them by so many delightful recollections, and seek a Refuge at that time but little known. . . . In my humble poem I, therefore, endeavoured to describe the sufferings they experienced in a new and uncultivated Country, the Difficulties they surmounted, the Rise and progress of a Village, and the prospects which promised Happiness to its future possessors.

Despite Goldsmith's description of his poem as being about progress and future happiness, there are many features of *The Rising Village* that give it an unresolved ironic tension. The melodramatic story of Albert and Flora forms an uneasy centre, and even before this episode the poet frequently adds afterthoughts to apparently innocent passages that make the pleasant aspects of village life seem ridiculous, or the benevolent ones dangerous. Lines 131-52 provide a good example of the way light social satire creeps unexpectedly into the poem, while the description of the emerging professions in the Rising Village is rather sinister: there may be something good about the openness of a new society, since it enables a wandering pedlar to become a prosperous merchant, but unfortunately it also allows poorly trained school teachers to instruct and inept doctors to practise without challenge. When the poem rises to its patriotic conclusion, invoking loyal homage to Britain, these discordant notes are stilled—but are they really?

The Rising Village

Thou dear companion of my early years,[1]
Partner of all my boyish hopes and fears,
To whom I oft addressed the youthful strain,
And sought no other praise than thine to gain;
Who oft hast bid me emulate his[2] fame
Whose genius formed the glory of our name;
Say, when thou canst, in manhood's ripened age,
With judgment scan the more aspiring page,
Wilt thou accept this tribute of my lay,
By far too small thy fondness to repay?   10
Say, dearest Brother, wilt thou now excuse
This bolder flight of my adventurous muse?
    If, then, adown your cheek a tear should flow
For Auburn's Village,[3] and its speechless woe;
If, while you weep, you think the 'lowly train'[4]
Their early joys can never more regain,
Come, turn with me where happier prospects rise,
Beneath the sternness of Acadian skies.
And thou, dear spirit! whose harmonious lay
Didst lovely Auburn's piercing woes display,   20
Do thou to thy fond relative impart

[1] The poet's brother Henry, to whom the poem is dedicated.
[2] The elder Oliver Goldsmith.
[3] The village of *The Deserted Village*.
[4] Compare *The Deserted Village*, 11. 251-2: 'Yes! let the rich deride, the proud disdain,/These simple blessings of the lowly train.'

Some portion of thy sweet poetic art;
Like thine, Oh! let my verse as gently flow,
While truth and virtue in my numbers glow:
And guide my pen with thy bewitching hand,
To paint the Rising Village of the land.
   How chaste and splendid are the scenes that lie
Beneath the circle of Britannia's sky!
What charming prospects there arrest the view,
How bright, how varied, and how boundless too!   30
Cities and plains extending far and wide,
The merchant's glory, and the farmer's pride.
Majestic palaces in pomp display
The wealth and splendour of the regal sway;
While the low hamlet and the shepherd's cot,
In peace and freedom mark the peasant's lot.
There nature's vernal bloom adorns the field,
And Autumn's fruits their rich luxuriance yield.
There men, in busy crowds, with men combine,
That arts may flourish, and fair science shine;   40
And thence, to distant climes their labours send,
As o'er the world their widening views extend.
Compar'd with scenes like these, how lone and drear
Did once Acadia's woods and wilds appear;
Where wandering savages, and beasts of prey,
Displayed, by turns, the fury of their sway.
What noble courage must their hearts have fired,
How great the ardour which their souls inspired,
Who leaving far behind their native plain,
Have sought a home beyond the Western main;[5]   50
And braved the perils of the stormy seas,
In search of wealth, of freedom, and of ease!
Oh! none can tell but they who sadly share
The bosom's anguish, and its wild despair,
What dire distress awaits the hardy bands,
That venture first on bleak and desert lands.
How great the pain, the danger, and the toil,
Which mark the first rude culture of the soil.
When, looking round, the lonely settler sees
His home amid a wilderness of trees: 60
How sinks his heart in those deep solitudes,
Where not a voice upon his ear intrudes;
Where solemn silence all the waste pervades,
Heightening the horror of its gloomy shades;
Save where the sturdy woodman's strokes resound,
That strew the fallen forest on the ground.
See! from their heights the lofty pines descend,
And crackling, down their pond'rous lengths extend.
Soon from their boughs the curling flames arise,

---

[5] In the last part of *The Deserted Village* the poet imagines the displaced villagers—too proud to beg—crossing the Atlantic to the New World, where they would unfortunately meet 'the various terrors of that horrid shore' (11. 337-46).

Mount into air, and redden all the skies;   70
And where the forest once its foliage spread,
The golden corn triumphant waves its head.
  How blest, did nature's ruggedness appear
The only source of trouble or of fear;
How happy, did no hardship meet his view,
No other care his anxious steps pursue;
But, while his labour gains a short repose,
And hope presents a solace for his woes,
New ills arise, new fears his peace annoy,
And other dangers all his hopes destroy.   80
Behold the savage tribes in wildest strain,
Approach with death and terror in their train;
No longer silence o'er the forest reigns,
No longer stillness now her power retains;
But hideous yells announce the murderous band,
Whose bloody footsteps desolate the land;
He hears them oft in sternest mood maintain,
Their right to rule the mountain and the plain;
He hears them doom the *white man's* instant death,
Shrinks from the sentence, while he gasps for breath,   90
Then, rousing with one effort all his might,
Darts from his hut, and saves himself by flight.
Yet, what a refuge! Here a host of foes,
On every side, his trembling steps oppose;
Here savage beasts around his cottage howl,
As through the gloomy wood they nightly prowl,
Till morning comes, and then is heard no more
The shouts of man, or beast's appalling roar;
The wandering Indian turns another way,
And brutes avoid the first approach of day.[6]   100
  Yet, tho' these threat'ning dangers round him roll,
Perplex his thoughts, and agitate his soul,
By patient firmness and industrious toil,
He still retains possession of the soil;
Around his dwelling scattered huts extend,
Whilst every hut affords another friend.
And now, behold! his bold aggressors fly,
To seek their prey beneath some other sky;
Resign the haunts they can maintain no more,
And safety in far distant wilds explore.   110
His perils vanished, and his fears o'ercome,

---

[6] With these lines about the terrors the first settlers found, compare *The Deserted Village,* 11. 349-56, in which the New World settler is imagined encountering
> *Those matted woods where birds forget to sing,*
> *But silent bats in drowsy cluster cling,*
> *Those poisonous fields with rank luxuriance crowned,*
> *Where the dark scorpion gathers death around;*
> *Where at each step the stranger fears to wake*
> *The rattling terrors of the vengeful snake;*
> *Where crouching tigers wait their hapless prey,*
> *And savage men, more murderous still than they.*

Sweet hope portrays a happy peaceful home.
On every side fair prospects charm his eyes,
And future joys in every thought arise.
His humble cot, built from the neighbouring trees,
Affords protection from each chilling breeze;
His rising crops, with rich luxuriance crowned,
In waving softness shed their freshness round;
By nature nourished, by her bounty blest,
He looks to Heaven, and lulls his cares to rest.   120
    The arts of culture now extend their sway,
And many a charm of rural life display.
Where once the pine upreared its lofty head,
The settlers' humble cottages are spread;
Where the broad firs once sheltered from the storm,
By slow degrees a neighbourhood they form:
And, as it bounds, each circling year, increase
In social life, prosperity, and peace,
New prospects rise, new objects too appear,
To add more comfort to its lowly sphere.   130
Where some rude sign or post the spot betrays,
The tavern first its useful front displays.[7]
Here, oft the weary traveller at the close
Of evening, finds a snug and safe repose.
The passing stranger here, a welcome guest,
From all his toil enjoys a peaceful rest;
Unless the host, solicitous to please,
With care officious mar his hope of ease,
With flippant questions to no end confined,
Exhaust his patience, and perplex his mind.   140
    Yet, let no one condemn with thoughtless haste,
The hardy settler of the dreary waste,
Who, far removed from every busy throng,
And social pleasures that to life belong,
Whene'er a stranger comes within his reach,
Will sigh to learn whatever he can teach.
To this, must be ascribed in great degree,
That ceaseless, idle curiosity,
Which over all the Western world prevails,
And every breast, or more or less, assails;   150
Till, by indulgence, so o'erpowering grown,
It seeks to know all business but its own.
Here, oft when winter's dreary terrors reign,
And cold, and snow, and storm, pervade the plain,
Around the birch-wood blaze the settlers draw,
To tell of all they felt, and all they saw.[8]

[7]Compare *The Deserted Village*, 11.220-1ff.:
  Where once the signpost caught the passing eye,
  Low lies that house where nut-brown draughts inspired.
[8]The elder Goldsmith says that the loss of Auburn is a great personal loss because, deprived of returning to his village at the end of his life, he will not be able to enjoy a time when he will 'around my fire
an evening group to draw,/And tell of all I felt, and all I saw' (11. 91-2).

When, thus in peace are met a happy few,
Sweet are the social pleasures that ensue.
What lively joy each honest bosom feels,
As o'er the past events his memory steals,   160
And to the listeners paints the dire distress,
That marked his progress in the wilderness;
The danger, trouble, hardship, toil, and strife,
Which chased each effort of his struggling life.
 In some lone spot of consecrated ground,
Whose silence spreads a holy gloom around,
The village church in unadorned array,
Now lifts its turret to the opening day.
How sweet to see the villagers repair
In groups to pay their adoration there;   170
To view, in homespun dress, each sacred morn,
The old and young its hallowed seats adorn,
While, grateful for each blessing God has given,
In pious strains, they waft their thanks to Heaven.
 Oh, heaven-born faith! sure solace of our woes,
How lost is he who ne'er thy influence knows,
How cold the heart thy charity ne'er fires,
How dead the soul thy spirit ne'er inspires!
When troubles vex and agitate the mind,
By gracious Heaven for wisest ends designed,   180
When dangers threaten, or when fears invade,
Man flies to thee for comfort and for aid;
The soul, impelled by thy all-powerful laws,
Seeks safety, only, in a Great First Cause![9]
If, then, amid the busy scene of life,
Its joy and pleasure, care, distrust, and strife;
Man, to his God for help and succour fly,
And on his mighty power to save, rely;
If, then, his thoughts can force him to confess
His errors, wants, and utter helplessness;   190
How strong must be those feelings which impart
A sense of all his weakness to the heart,
Where not a friend in solitude is nigh,
His home the wild, his canopy the sky;
And, far removed from every human arm,
His God alone can shelter him from harm.
 While now the Rising Village claims a name,
Its limits still increase, and still its fame.
The wandering Pedlar, who undaunted traced
His lonely footsteps o'er the silent waste;   200
Who traversed once the cold and snow-clad plain,
Reckless of danger, trouble, or of pain,
To find a market for his little wares,
The source of all his hopes, and all his cares,
Established here, his settled home maintains,

[9]Original cause or creator of the universe: God.

And soon a merchant's higher title gains.
Around his store, on spacious shelves arrayed,
Behold his great and various stock in trade.
Here, nails and blankets, side by side, are seen,
There, horses' collars, and a large tureen;   210
Buttons and tumblers, fish-hooks, spoons and knives,
Shawls for young damsels, flannel for old wives;
Woolcards and stockings, hats for men and boys,
Mill-saws and fenders, silks, and children's toys;
All useful things, and joined with many more,
Compose the well-assorted country store.
    The half-bred Doctor next then settles down,
And hopes the village soon will prove a town.
No rival here disputes his doubtful skill,
He cures, by chance, or ends each human ill;   220
By turns he physics,[1] or his patient bleeds,
Uncertain in what case each best succeeds.
And if, from friends untimely snatched away,
Some beauty fall a victim to decay;
If some fine youth, his parents' fond delight,
Be early hurried to the shades of night,
Death bears the blame, 'tis his envenomed dart
That strikes the suffering mortal to the heart.
    Beneath the shelter of a log-built shed
The country school-house next erects its head.   230
No 'man severe,'[2] with learning's bright display,
Here leads the opening blossoms into day;
No master here, in every art refined,
Through fields of science guides the aspiring mind;
But some poor wanderer of the human race,
Unequal to the task, supplies his place,
Whose greatest source of knowledge or of skill
Consists in reading, and in writing ill;
Whose efforts can no higher merit claim,
Than spreading Dilworth's great scholastic fame.[3]   240
No modest youths surround his awful chair,
His frowns to deprecate, or smiles to share,[4]
But all the terrors of his lawful sway
The proud despise, the fearless disobey;
The rugged urchins spurn at all control,

[1] To treat with medicine, especially with purgatives.
[2] Compare *The Deserted Village*, 11. 195ff.:
    There in his noisy mansion, skilled to rule,
    The Village master taught his little school;
    A man severe he was, and stern to view,
    I knew him well, and every truant knew.
[3] Thomas Dilworth was the author of several eighteenth-century school texts, including an arithmetic
and a spelling book.
[4] Compare *The Deserted Village*, 11. 201-4:
    Full well they laughed with counterfeited glee,
    At all his jokes, for many a joke had he;
    Full well the busy whisper circling round,
    Conveyed the dismal tidings when he frowned.

Which cramps the movements of the free-born soul,
Till, in their own conceit so wise they've grown,
They think their knowledge far exceeds his own.
    As thus the village each successive year
Presents new prospects, and extends its sphere,   250
While all around its smiling charms expand,
And rural beauties decorate the land.
The humble tenants, who were taught to know,
By years of suffering, all the weight of woe;
Who felt each hardship nature could endure,
Such pains as time alone could ease or cure,
Relieved from want, in sportive pleasures find
A balm to soften and relax the mind;
And now, forgetful of their former care,
Enjoy each sport, and every pastime share.   260
Beneath some spreading tree's expanded shade
Here many a manly youth and gentle maid,
With festive dances or with sprightly song
The summer's evening hours in joy prolong,
And as the young their simple sports renew,
The aged witness, and approve them too.
And when the Summer's bloomy charms are fled,
When Autumn's fallen leaves around are spread,
When Winter rules the sad inverted year,
And ice and snow alternately appear,   270
Sports not less welcome lightly they essay,
To chase the long and tedious hours away.
Here, ranged in joyous groups around the fire,
Gambols and freaks[5] each honest heart inspire;
And if some venturous youth obtain a kiss,
The game's reward, and summit of its bliss,
Applauding shouts the victor's prize proclaim,
And every tongue augments his well-earned fame;
While all the modest fair one's blushes tell
Success had crowned his fondest hopes too well.   280
Dear humble sports, Oh! long may you impart
A guileless pleasure to the youthful heart,
Still may your joys from year to year increase,
And fill each breast with happiness and peace.
    Yet, tho' these simple pleasures crown the year,
Relieve its cares, and every bosom cheer,
As life's gay scenes in quick succession rise,
To lure the heart and captivate the eyes;
Soon vice steals on, in thoughtless pleasure's train,
And spreads her miseries o'er the village plain.   290
Her baneful arts some happy home invade,
Some bashful lover, or some tender maid;
Until, at length, repressed by no control,
They sink, debase, and overwhelm the soul.

[5]Capers.

How many aching breasts now live to know
The shame, the anguish, misery and woe,
That heedless passions, by no laws confined,
Entail forever on the human mind.
Oh, Virtue! that thy powerful charms could bind
Each rising impulse of the erring mind.   300
That every heart might own thy sovereign sway,
And every bosom fear to disobey;
No father's heart would then in anguish trace
The sad remembrance of a son's disgrace;
No mother's tears for some dear child undone
Would then in streams of poignant sorrow run,
Nor could my verse the hapless story tell
Of one poor maid who loved—and loved too well.

   Among the youths that graced their native plain,
Albert was foremost of the village train;   310
The hand of nature had profusely shed
Her choicest blessings on his youthful head;
His heart seemed generous, noble, kind, and free,
Just bursting into manhood's energy.
Flora was fair, and blooming as that flower
Which spreads its blossom to the April shower;
Her gentle manners and unstudied grace
Still added lustre to her beaming face,
While every look, by purity refined,
Displayed the lovelier beauties of her mind.   320

   Sweet was the hour, and peaceful was the scene
When Albert first met Flora on the green;
Her modest looks, in youthful bloom displayed,
Then touched his heart, and there a conquest made
Nor long he sighed, by love and rapture fired,
He soon declared the passion she inspired.
In silence, blushing sweetly, Flora heard
His vows of love and constancy preferred;
And, as his soft and tender suit he pressed,
The maid, at length, a mutual flame confessed.   330

   Love now had shed, with visions light as air,
His golden prospects on this happy pair;
Those moments soon rolled rapidly away,
Those hours of joy and bliss that gently play
Around young hearts, ere yet they learn to know
Life's care or trouble, or to feel its woe.
The day was fixed, the bridal dress was made,
And time alone their happiness delayed,
The anxious moment that, in joy begun,
Would join their fond and faithful hearts in one.   340
'Twas now at evening's hour, about the time
When in Acadia's cold and northern clime
The setting sun, with pale and cheerless glow,
Extends his beams o'er trackless fields of snow,
That Flora felt her throbbing heart oppressed

By thoughts, till then, a stranger to her breast.
Albert had promised that his bosom's pride
That very morning should become his bride;
Yet morn had come and passed; and not one vow
Of his had e'er been broken until now.   350
But, hark! a hurried step advances near,
'Tis Albert's breaks upon her listening ear;
Albert's, ah, no! a ruder footstep bore,
With eager haste, a letter to the door;
Flora received it, and could scarce conceal
Her rapture, as she kissed her lover's seal.
Yet, anxious tears were gathered in her eye,
As on the note it rested wistfully;
Her trembling hands unclosed the folded page,
That soon she hoped would every fear assuage,   360
And while intently o'er the lines she ran,
In broken half breathed tones she thus began:
    'Dear Flora, I have left my native plain,
And fate forbids that we shall meet again:
'Twere vain to tell, nor can I now impart
The sudden motive to this change of heart.
The vows so oft repeated to thine ear
As tales of cruel falsehood must appear.
Forgive the hand that deals this treacherous blow,
Forget the heart that can afflict this woe;   370
Farewell! and think no more of Albert's name,
His weakness pity, now involved in shame.'
    Ah! who can paint her features as, amazed,
In breathless agony, she stood and gazed!
Oh, Albert, cruel Albert! she exclaimed,
Albert was all her faltering accents named.
A deadly feeling seized upon her frame,
Her pulse throbb'd quick, her colour went and came;
A darting pain shot through her frenzied head,
And from that fatal hour her reason fled!   380
    The sun had set; his lingering beams of light
From western hills had vanished into night.
The northern blast along the valley rolled,
Keen was that blast, and piercing was the cold,
When, urged by frenzy, and by love inspired,
For what but madness could her breast have fired!
Flora, with one slight mantle round her waved,
Forsook her home, and all the tempest braved.
Her lover's falsehood wrung her gentle breast,
His broken vows her tortured mind possessed;   390
Heedless of danger, on she bent her way
Through drifts of snow, where Albert's dwelling lay,
With frantic haste her tottering steps pursued
Amid the long night's darkness unsubdued;
Until, benumbed, her fair and fragile form
Yielded beneath the fury of the storm;

Exhausted nature could no further go,
And, senseless, down she sank amid the snow.
    Now as the morn had streaked the eastern sky
With dawning light, a passing stranger's eye,   400
By chance directed, glanced upon the spot
Where lay the lovely sufferer: To his cot
The peasant bore her, and with anxious care
Tried every art, till hope became despair.
With kind solicitude his tender wife
Long vainly strove to call her back to life;
At length her gentle bosom throbs again,
Her torpid limbs their wonted power obtain;
The loitering current now begins to flow,
And hapless Flora wakes once more to woe: 410
But all their friendly efforts could not find
A balm to heal the anguish of her mind.
    Come hither, wretch, and see what thou hast done,
Behold the heart thou hast so falsely won,
Behold it, wounded, broken, crushed and riven,
By thy unmanly arts to ruin driven;
Hear Flora calling on thy much loved name,
Which, e'en in madness, she forbears to blame.
Not all thy sighs and tears can now restore
One hour of pleasure that she knew before;   420
Not all thy prayers can now remove the pain,
That floats and revels o'er her maddened brain.
Oh, shame of manhood! that could thus betray
A maiden's hopes, and lead her heart away;
Oh, shame of manhood! that could blast her joy,
And one so fair, so lovely, could destroy.
    Yet, think not oft such tales of real woe
Degrade the land, and round the village flow.
Here virtue's charms appear in bright array,
And all their pleasing influence display;   430
Here modest youths, impressed in beauty's train,
Or captive led by love's endearing chain,
And fairest girls whom vows have ne'er betrayed,
Vows that are broken oft as soon as made,
Unite their hopes, and join their lives in one,
In bliss pursue them, as at first begun.
Then, as life's current onward gently flows,
With scarce one fault to ruffle its repose,
With minds prepared, they sink in peace to rest,
To meet on high the spirits of the blest.   440
    While time thus rolls his rapid years away,
The Village rises gently into day.
How sweet it is, at first approach of morn,
Before the silvery dew has left the lawn,
When warring winds are sleeping yet on high,
Or breathe as softly as the bosom's sigh,
To gain some easy hill's ascending height,

Where all the landscape brightens with delight,
And boundless prospects stretched on every side,
Proclaim the country's industry and pride.   450
Here the broad marsh extends its open plain,
Until its limits touch the distant main;
There verdant meads along the uplands spring,
And grateful odours to the breezes fling;
Here crops of grain in rich luxuriance rise,
And wave their golden riches to the skies;
There smiling orchards interrupt the scene,
Or gardens bounded by some fence of green;
The farmer's cottage, bosomed 'mong the trees,
Whose spreading branches shelter from the breeze;   460
The winding stream that turns the busy mill,
Whose clacking echos o'er the distant hill;
The neat white church, beside whose walls are spread
The grass-clad hillocks of the sacred dead,
Where rude cut stones or painted tablets tell,
In laboured verse, how youth and beauty fell;
How worth and hope were hurried to the grave,
And torn from those who had no power to save.
      Or, when the Summer's dry and sultry sun
Adown the West his fiery course has run;   470
When o'er the vale his parting rays of light
Just linger, ere they vanish into night,
How sweet to wander round the wood-bound lake,
Whose glassy stillness scarce the zephyrs wake;
How sweet to hear the murmuring of the rill,
As down it gurgles from the distant hill;
The note of Whip-poor-Will how sweet to hear,
When sadly slow it breaks upon the ear,
And tells each night, to all the silent vale,
The hopeless sorrows of its mournful tale.   480
Dear lovely spot! Oh may such charms as these,
Sweet tranquil charms, that cannot fail to please,
Forever reign around thee, and impart
Joy, peace, and comfort to each native heart.
      Happy Acadia! though around thy shore
Is heard the stormy wind's terrific roar;
Though round thee Winter binds his icy chain,
And his rude tempests sweep along thy plain,
Still Summer comes, and decorates thy land
With fruits and flowers from her luxuriant hand;   490
Still Autumn's gifts repay the labourer's toil
With richest products from thy fertile soil;
With bounteous store his varied wants supply,
And scarce the plants of other suns deny.
How pleasing, and how glowing with delight
Are now thy budding hopes! How sweetly bright
They rise to view! How full of joy appear
The expectations of each future year!

Not fifty Summers yet have blessed thy clime,
How short a period in the page of time!   500
Since savage tribes, with terror in their train,
Rushed o'er thy fields, and ravaged all thy plain.
But some few years have rolled in haste away
Since, through thy vales, the fearless beast of prey,
With dismal yell and loud appalling cry,
Proclaimed his midnight reign of terror nigh.
And now how changed the scene! the first, afar,
Have fled to wilds beneath the northern star;
The last has learned to shun man's dreaded eye,
And, in his turn, to distant regions fly.   510
While the poor peasant, whose laborious care
Scarce from the soil could wring his scanty fare;
Now in the peaceful arts of culture skilled,
Sees his wide barn with ample treasures filled;
Now finds his dwelling, as the year goes round,
Beyond his hopes, with joy and plenty crowned.
    Nor culture's arts, a nation's noblest friend,
Alone o'er Scotia's fields their power extend;
From all her shores, with every gentle gale,
Commerce expands her free and swelling sail;   520
And all the land, luxuriant, rich, and gay,
Exulting owns the splendour of their sway.
These are thy blessings, Scotia, and for these,
For wealth, for freedom, happiness, and ease,
Thy grateful thanks to Britain's care are due,
Her power protects, her smiles past hopes renew,
Her valour guards thee, and her councils guide,
Then, may thy parent ever be thy pride!
    Happy Britannia! though thy history's page
In darkest ignorance shrouds thine infant age,   530
Though long thy childhood's years in error strayed,
And long in superstition's bands delayed;
Matur'd and strong, thou shin'st in manhood's prime,
The first and brightest star of Europe's clime.
The nurse of science, and the seat of arts,
The home of fairest forms and gentlest hearts;
The land of heroes, generous, free, and brave,
The noblest conquerors of the field and wave;
Thy flag, on every sea and shore unfurled,
Has spread thy glory, and thy thunder hurled.   540
When, o'er the earth, a tyrant would have thrown
His iron chain, and called the world his own,
Thine arm preserved it, in its darkest hour,
Destroyed his hopes, and crushed his dreaded power,
To sinking nations life and freedom gave,
'Twas thine to conquer, as 'twas thine to save.
    Then blest Acadia! ever may thy name,
Like hers, be graven on the rolls of fame;
May all thy sons, like hers, be brave and free,

Possessors of her laws and liberty;   550
Heirs of her splendour, science, power, and skill,
And through succeeding years her children still.
And as the sun, with gentle dawning ray,
From night's dull bosom wakes, and leads the day,
His course majestic keeps, till in the height
He glows one blaze of pure exhaustless light;
So may thy years increase, thy glories rise,
To be the wonder of the Western skies;
And bliss and peace encircle all thy shore,
Till empires rise and sink, on earth, no more.   560

1825, rev. 1834

Anna Brownell Jameson

1794-1860

Anna Jameson had already established her reputation as an author in England before she came to Canada in 1836 to join her estranged husband. Her stay in Canada was brief—the attempted reconciliation was unsuccessful—but it provided her with the opportunity to write *Winter Studies and Summer Rambles in Canada* (London, 1838). This work, part of the vogue for books about journeys abroad that began in the eighteenth century, is the best-known early travel book about Canada. It has remained in print (usually in abridged form) ever since its publication.

Born in Dublin, Anna Brownell Murphy was a precocious reader who had read all of Shakespeare's plays between the ages of seven and ten. In 1806 she moved with her parents to London, where her father became a court painter of miniatures. She became governess for the Marquis of Winchester in 1810, and worked as a governess until she was thirty, eventually serving three families.

In 1821 Anna Murphy became engaged to Robert Jameson, with whom she shared interests in art and literature. Both strong-willed, they seem to have been temperamentally unsuited to one another, but although the original engagement was broken off, they married four years later. With Robert's encouragement, she published her first book, *A Lady's Diary* (1826; subsequently retitled *The Diary of an Ennuyée*), a sentimental, fictionalized version of a journey to the continent made with one of her employers. Though the book appeared anonymously, Mrs Jameson's authorship soon became known. After its success she became part of a group of writers whose work was regularly published in recently established magazines, such as *Blackwoods*. These new periodicals catered especially for women eager to acquire knowledge and culture, and Mrs Jameson's writing was valued in part because she dealt with the rights of women, emphasized the need for female education, and generally reflected attitudes aligned with the feminism developing in England in the years that followed the publication of Mary Wollstonecraft's *Vindication of the Rights of Women* (1792).

Mrs Jameson did not accompany her husband to the West Indies when he accepted a judgeship in 1829, nor did she join him immediately when, in 1833, he became attorney-general of Upper Canada. During this period she travelled on the continent and wrote five more books. Four were about women: *Memoirs of the Lovers of the Poets* (1829), *Memoirs of the Celebrated Female Sovereigns* (1831), *Memoirs of the Beauties of the Court of Charles II* (1831), and *Characteristics of Women* (1832). The last of these, a series of psychological studies of the female characters in Shakespeare's dramas (subsequently retitled *Shakespeare's Heroines*), is the book for which she became best known. She also completed a second travel diary, *Visits and Sketches at Home and Abroad* (1834).

When, at the urging of her husband, Mrs Jameson finally joined him in Canada, she deeply regretted leaving behind the culture and civilization of Europe. Her first entry in *Winter Studies and Summer Rambles*, for 20 Dec., 1836, records her disillusionment on arriving at her new home:

> What Toronto may be in summer, I cannot tell; they say it is a pretty place. At present its appearance to me, a stranger, is most strangely mean and melancholy. A little ill-built town on low land, at the bottom of a frozen bay, with one very ugly church, without tower or steeple; some government offices, built of staring red brick, in the most tasteless, vulgar style imaginable; three feet of snow all around; and the gray, sullen, wintry lake, and the dark gloom of the pine forest bounding the prospect; such seems Toronto to me now. I did not expect much; but for this I was not prepared.

Determined to provide a written record of her Canadian experience, she set about acquainting herself with Toronto society. In the 'Winter Studies' portion of her book she sets down her observations, intermixed with reflections on literature and life, and quotations from works of German literature that she was then reading. 'I know no better way of coming at the truth,' she wrote, 'than by observing and recording faithfully the impressions made by objects and characters on my own mind—or, rather, the impress they *receive* from my own mind.' She took particular interest in the condition of women in the province, observing, 'I have not often in my life met with contented and cheerful-minded women, but I never met with so many repining and discontented women as in Canada,' though she believed that 'really accomplished women, accustomed to what is called the best society, have more resources here, and manage better . . .'

In June 1837 Mrs Jameson decided that she wished to see more of Upper Canada, and embarked—over her husband's objections and in an age when a woman travelling without friends or escort was extremely unusual, especially in such primitive conditions—on the journey that was to provide materials for the 'summer rambles' section of her account.

> To undertake such a journey alone is rash perhaps—yet alone it must be achieved, I find, or not at all; I shall have neither companion nor manservant, nor femme de chambre, nor even a 'little foot-pages', to give notice of my fate, should I be swamped in a bog, or eaten up by a bear, or scalped, or disposed of in some strange way; but shall I leave this fine country without seeing anything of its great characteristic features?

The trip included visits to Niagara Falls (with which she expressed disappointment), Hamilton, London, and Port Talbot, and she eventually made her way through Detroit and as far north as what she called her 'Ultima Thule', Sault Ste Marie. Her curiosity about North American native peoples led her to call on Henry Schoolcraft (whose extensive collection of Indian lore later furnished material for Longfellow's *Hiawatha*) and to attend an Indian conclave at Manitoulin Island. In the more distant parts of her trip, Mrs Jameson travelled with only a few other passengers in small boats rowed by *voyageurs*, and she was the first European woman to pass through the rapids at the Sault. When she returned to Toronto in August, she recorded that 'the people here are in great enthusiasm about me and stare at me as if I had done some most wonderful thing; the most astonished of all is Mr Jameson.'

Anna Jameson returned to England in 1838, and the publication of *Winter Sketches and Summer Rambles* in that year proved timely, for many of her countrymen were especially interested in her observations of Canada since they were made on the eve of the 1837 Rebellion. Remaining separated from her husband, Mrs Jameson supported herself for the rest of her life through her writing—chiefly volumes of commentary on art. For some of these books she also prepared the illustrations; her drawings for *Winter Sketches and Summer Rambles* were omitted by its publisher, but they were eventually published on their own in 1958 as *Early Canadian Sketches*. Although, as she herself realized, Mrs Jameson's regrets about leaving behind a career in England gave a negative cast to her perceptions of Upper Canada, the scope and acuity of her observations are, given the brevity of her visit, admirable; particularly penetrating are her insights into the difficulties of forming a new society in Canada, which anticipate those of Susanna Moodie and of many later writers.

From *Winter Studies and Summer Rambles in Canada*

January 16.

Some philosopher has said or written, that our good and bad qualities, our virtues and our vices, depend more on the influence of climate, than the pride of civilised humanity would be willing to allow; and this is a truth or truism, which for my own part I cannot gainsay—yet which I do not much like to believe. Whatever may be the climate in which the human being is born or reared, can he not always by moral strength raise himself above its degrading, or benumbing, or exciting influence? and yet more, rather than less, easily, when, at a mature age and with habits formed, he is subjected accidentally to such influences? Is there most wisdom, in such a case, in passively assimilating ourselves, our habits, and our feelings, to external circumstances, or resisting and combating them, rather to defend the integrity of our own individual being, than with the hope of changing or controlling the physical or social influences around us?

How I might have settled this question with myself, long ago, when in possession of the health and energy and trusting spirit of my young years, I know—but now it is too late. I could almost wish myself a dormouse, or a she-bear, to sleep away the rest of this cold, cold winter, and wake only with the first green leaves, the first warm breath of the summer wind. I shiver through the day and through the night; and, like poor Harry Gill, 'my teeth they chatter, chatter still;'[1] and then at intervals I am burned up with a dry hot fever: this is what my maid, a good little Oxfordshire girl, calls the *hager* (the ague,) more properly the lake fever, or cold fever. From the particular situation of Toronto, the disorder is very prevalent here in the spring: being a stranger, and not yet *acclimatée*, it has attacked me thus unseasonably. Bark is the general and unfailing remedy.

The cold is at this time so intense, that the ink freezes while I write, and my fingers stiffen round the pen; a glass of water by my bed-side, within a few feet of the hearth, (heaped with logs of oak and maple kept burning all night long,) is a solid mass of ice in the morning. God help the poor emigrants who are yet unprepared against the rigour of the season!—yet this is nothing to the climate of the lower province, where, as we hear, the thermometer has been thirty degrees below zero. I lose all heart to write home, or to register a reflection or a feeling;—thought stagnates in my head as the ink in my pen—and this will never do!—I *must* rouse myself to occupation; and if I cannot find it without, I must create it from within. There are yet four months of winter and leisure to be disposed of. How?—I know not; but they *must* be employed, not wholly lost.

* * *

Toronto, February 7.

Mr B. gave me a seat in his sleigh, and after a rapid and very pleasant journey, during which I gained a good deal of information, we reached Toronto yesterday morning.

The road was the same as before, with one deviation however—it was found expe-

---

[1]Wordsworth's poem 'Goody Blake and Harry Gill: A True Story' (1798), recounts the legend of a man who beats a poor woman for gathering firewood from his hedge, and is thereafter cursed with feeling cold for the rest of his life. The poem opens: 'Oh! what's the matter? What's the matter?/ What is't that ails young Harry Gill?/ That evermore his teeth they chatter,/ Chatter, chatter, chatter still.'

dient to cross Burlington Bay on the ice, about seven miles over, the lake beneath being twenty, and five-and-twenty fathoms in depth. It was ten o'clock at night, and the only light was that reflected from the snow. The beaten track, from which it is not safe to deviate, was very narrow, and a man, in the worst, if not the last stage of intoxication, noisy and brutally reckless, was driving before us in a sleigh. All this, with the novelty of the situation, the tremendous cracking of the ice at every instant, gave me a sense of apprehension just sufficient to be exciting, rather than very unpleasant, though I will confess to a feeling of relief when we were once more on the solid earth.

B. is said to be a hard, active, clever, practical man. I liked him, and thought him intelligent and good-natured: we had much talk. Leaving his servant to drive, he would jump down, stand poised upon one of the runners, and, thus gliding smoothly along, we conversed.

It is a remarkable fact, with which you are probably acquainted, that when one growth of timber is cleared from the land, another of quite a different species springs up spontaneously in its place. Thus, the oak or the beech succeeds to the pine, and the pine to the oak or maple. This is not accounted for, at least I have found no one yet who can give me a reason for it. We passed by a forest lately consumed by fire, and I asked why, in clearing the woods, they did not leave groups of the finest trees, or even single trees, here and there, to embellish the country? But it seems that this is impossible—for the trees thus left standing, when deprived of the shelter and society to which they have been accustomed, uniformly perish—which, for mine own poor part, I thought very natural.

A Canadian settler *hates* a tree, regards it as his natural enemy, as something to be destroyed, eradicated, annihilated by all and any means. The idea of useful or ornamental is seldom associated here even with the most magnificent timber trees, such as among the Druids had been consecrated, and among the Greeks would have sheltered oracles and votive temples. The beautiful faith which assigned to every tree of the forest its guardian nymph, to every leafy grove its tutelary divinity, would find no votaries here. Alas! for the Dryads and Hamadryads of Canada![2]

There are two principal methods of killing trees in this country, besides the quick, unfailing destruction of the axe; the first by setting fire to them, which sometimes leaves the root uninjured to rot gradually and unseen, or be grubbed up at leisure, or, more generally, there remains a visible fragment of a charred and blackened stump, deformed and painful to look upon: the other method is slower, but even more effectual; a deep gash is cut through the bark into the stem, quite round the bole of the tree. This prevents the circulation of the vital juices, and by degrees the tree droops and dies. This is technically called *ringing* timber. Is not this like the two ways in which a woman's heart may be killed in this world of ours—by passion and by sorrow? But better far the swift fiery death than this 'ringing,' as they call it!

* * *

February 17.

'There is no *society* in Toronto,' is what I hear repeated all around me—even by those who compose the only society we have. 'But,' you will say, 'what could be expected in a remote town, which forty years ago was an uninhabited swamp, and twenty years ago only began to exist?' I really do not know what I expected, but I

[2]Wood nymphs.

will tell you what I did *not* expect. I did not expect to find here in this new capital of a new country, with the boundless forest within half a mile of us on almost every side,—concentrated as it were the worst evils of our old and most artificial social system at home, with none of its *agrémens*, and none of its advantages. Toronto is like a fourth or fifth rate provincial town, with the pretensions of a capital city. We have here a petty colonial oligarchy, a self-constituted aristocracy, based upon nothing real, nor even upon anything imaginary; and we have all the mutual jealousy and fear, and petty gossip, and mutual meddling and mean rivalship, which are common in a small society of which the members are well known to each other, a society composed, like all societies, of many heterogeneous particles; but as these circulate within very confined limits, there is no getting out of the way of what one most dislikes: we must necessarily hear, see, and passively endure much that annoys and disgusts any one accustomed to the independence of a large and liberal society, or the ease of continental life. It is curious enough to see how quickly a new fashion, or a new folly, is imported from the old country, and with what difficulty and delay a new idea finds its way into the heads of the people, or a new book into their hands. Yet, in the midst of all this, I cannot but see that good spirits and corrective principles are at work; that progress is making: though the march of intellect be not here in double quick time, as in Europe, it does not absolutely stand stock-still.

There reigns here a hateful factious spirit in political matters, but for the present no public or patriotic feeling, no recognition of general or generous principles of policy: as yet I have met with none of these. Canada is a colony, not a *country;* it is not yet identified with the dearest affections and associations, remembrances, and hopes of its inhabitants: it is to them an adopted, not a real mother. Their love, their pride, are not for poor Canada, but for high and happy England; but a few more generations must change all this.

We have here Tories, Whigs, and Radicals, so called; but these words do not signify exactly what we mean by the same designations at home.

You must recollect that the first settlers in Upper Canada were those who were obliged to fly from the United States during the revolutionary war, in consequence of their attachment to the British government, and the soldiers and non-commissioned officers who had fought during the war. These were recompensed for their losses, sufferings, and services, by grants of land in Upper Canada. Thus the very first elements out of which our social system was framed, were repugnance and contempt for the new institutions of the United States, and a dislike to the people of that country,—a very natural result of foregone causes; and thus it has happened that the slightest tinge of democratic, or even liberal principles in politics, was for a long time a sufficient impeachment of the loyalty, a stain upon the personal character, of those who held them. The Tories have therefore been hitherto the influential party; in their hands we find the government patronage, the principal offices, the sales and grants of land, for a long series of years.

Another party, professing the same boundless loyalty to the mother country, and the same dislike for the principles and institutions of their Yankee neighbours, may be called the Whigs of Upper Canada; these look with jealousy and scorn on the power and prejudices of the Tory families, and insist on the necessity of many reforms in the colonial government. Many of these are young men of talent, and professional men, who find themselves shut out from what they regard as their fair proportion of social consideration and influence, such as, in a small society like this, their superior education and character ought to command for them.

Another set are the Radicals, whom I generally hear mentioned as 'those scoundrels,' or 'those rascals,' or with some epithet expressive of the utmost contempt and disgust. They are those who wish to see this country erected into a republic, like the United States. A few among them are men of talent and education, but at present they are neither influential nor formidable.

There is among all parties a general tone of complaint and discontent—a mutual distrust—a languor and supineness—the causes of which I cannot as yet understand. Even those who are enthusiastically British in heart and feeling, who sincerely believe that it is the true interest of the colony to remain under the control of the mother country, are as discontented as the rest: they bitterly denounce the ignorance of the colonial officials at home, with regard to the true interests of the country: they ascribe the want of capital for improvement on a large scale to no mistrust in the resources of the country, but to a want of confidence in the measures of the government, and the security of property.

In order to understand something of the feelings which prevail here, you must bear in mind the distinction between the two provinces of Upper and Lower Canada. The project of uniting them once more into one legislature, with a central metropolis, is most violently opposed by those whose personal interests and convenience would suffer materially by a change in the seat of government. I have heard some persons go so far as to declare, that if the union of the two provinces were to be established by law, it were sufficient to absolve a man from his allegiance. On the other hand, the measure has powerful advocates in both provinces. It seems, on looking over the map of this vast and magnificent country, and reading its whole history, that the political division into five provinces,[3] each with its independent governor and legislature, its separate correspondence with the Colonial-office, its local laws, and local taxation, must certainly add to the amount of colonial patronage, and perhaps render more secure the subjection of the whole to the British crown; but may it not also have perpetuated local distinctions and jealousies—kept alive divided interests, narrowed the resources, and prevented the improvement of the country on a large and general scale?

But I had better stop here, ere I get beyond my depth. I am not one of those who opine sagely, that women have nothing to do with politics. On the contrary; but I do seriously think that no one, be it man or woman, ought to talk, much less write, on what they do not understand. Not but that I have my own ideas on these matters, though we were never able to make out, either to my own satisfaction or to yours, whether I am Whig or Tory or Radical. In politics I acknowledge but two parties,—those who hope and those who fear. In morals, but two parties—those who lie and those who speak truth: and all the world I divide into those who love, and those who hate. This comprehensive arrangement saves me a vast deal of trouble, and answers all my own purposes to admiration.

* * *

[3]'Viz. Upper Canada, Lower Canada, Nova Scotia, New Brunswick, and Prince Edward's Island' [Jameson's note].

February 18.

* * *

Here, as everywhere else, I find the women of the better class lamenting over the want of all society, except of the lowest grade in manners and morals. For those who have recently emigrated, and are settled more in the interior, there is absolutely no social intercourse whatever; it is quite out of the question. They seem to me perishing of ennui, or from the want of sympathy which they cannot obtain, and, what is worse, which they cannot feel: for being in general unfitted for out-door occupations, unable to comprehend or enter into the interests around them, and all their earliest prejudices and ideas of the fitness of things continually outraged in a manner exceedingly unpleasant, they may be said to live in a perpetual state of inward passive discord and fretful endurance—

> 'All too timid and reserved
> For onset, for resistance too inert—
> Too weak for suffering, and for hope too tame.'

A gentleman well known to me by name, who was not a resident in London, but passing through it on his way from a far western settlement up by Lake Huron, was one of my morning visitors. He had been settled in the bush for five years, had a beautiful farm, well cleared, well stocked. He was pleased with his prospects, his existence, his occupations: all he wanted was a wife, and on this subject he poured forth a most eloquent appeal.

'Where,' said he, 'shall I find such a wife as I could, with a safe conscience, bring into these wilds, to share a settler's fate, a settler's home? You, who know your own sex so well, point me out such a one, or tell me at least where to seek her. I am perishing and deteriorating, head and heart, for want of a companion—a wife, in short. I am becoming as rude and coarse as my own labourers, and as hard as my own axe. If I wait five years longer, no woman will be able to endure such a fellow as I shall be by that time—no woman, I mean, whom I could marry—for in this lies my utter unreasonableness. Habituated to seek in woman those graces and refinements which I have always associated with her idea, I must have them here in the forest, or dispense with all female society whatever. With some one to sympathise with me—to talk to—to embellish the home I return to at night—such a life as I now lead, with all the cares and frivolities of a too artificial society cast behind us, security and plenty all around us, and nothing but hope before us, a life of "cheerful yesterdays and confident to-morrows"[4]—were it not delicious? I want for myself nothing more, nothing better; but—perhaps it is a weakness, an inconsistency!—I could not love a woman who was inferior to all my preconceived notions of feminine elegance and refinement—inferior to my own mother and sisters. You know I was in England two years ago;—well, I have a vision of a beautiful creature, with the figure of a sylph and the head of a sibyl, bending over her harp, and singing "*A te, O cara*;"[5] and when I am logging in the woods with my men, I catch myself meditating on that vision, and humming *A te, O cara*, which somehow or other runs strangely in my head.

[4]From Wordsworth's *The Excursion* (1814), where a peasant seen by the poet is idealized as 'A Man . . . of cheerful yesterdays/ And confident to-morrows' (VII.557-58).
[5]The Italian song she sings begins, 'To you, O love'.

Now, what is to be done? What could I do with that fair vision here? Without cox-combry may I not say, that I need not entirely despair of winning the affections of an amiable, elegant woman, and might even persuade her to confront, for my sake, worse than all this? For what will not your sex do and dare for the sake of us men creatures, savages that we are? But even for that reason shall I take advantage of such sentiments? You know what this life is—this isolated life in the bush—and so do I; but by what words could I make it comprehensible to a fine lady? Certainly I might draw such a picture of it as should delight by its novelty and romance, and de-ceive even while it does not deviate from the truth. A cottage in the wild woods—solitude and love—the world forgetting, by the world forgot—the deer come skipping by—the red Indian brings game, and lays it at her feet—how pretty and how romantic! And for the first few months, perhaps the first year, all goes well; but how goes it the next, and the next? I have observed with regard to the women who come out, that they do well enough the first year, and some even the second; but the third is generally fatal: and the worst with you women—or the best shall I not say?—is, that you cannot, and do not, forget domestic ties left behind. We men go out upon our land, or to the chase, and the women, poor souls, sit, and sew, and *think*. You have seen Mrs A. and Mrs B., who came out here, as I well remember, full of health and bloom—what are they now? premature old women, sickly, care-worn, without nerve or cheerfulness:—and as for C , who brought his wife to his place by Lake Simcoe only three years ago, I hear the poor fellow must sell all off, or see his wife perish before his eyes. Would you have me risk the alternative? Or perhaps you will say, marry one of the women of the country—one of the daughters *of the bush*. No, I cannot; I must have something different. I may not have been par-ticularly fortunate, but the women I have seen are in general coarse and narrow-minded, with no education whatever, or with an education which apes all I most dis-like, and omits all I could admire in the fashionable education of the old country. What could I do with such women? In the former I might find an upper servant, but no companion—in the other, neither companionship nor help!'

To this discontented and fastidious gentleman I ventured to recommend two or three very amiable girls I had known at Toronto and Niagara; and I told him, too, that among the beautiful and spirited girls of New England he might also find what would answer his purpose. But with regard to Englishwomen of that grade in station and education, and personal attraction, which would content him, I could not well speak; not because I knew of none who united grace of person and lively talents with capabilities of strong affection, ay, and sufficient energy of character to meet trials and endure privations; but in women, as now educated, there is a strength of local habits and attachments, a want of cheerful self-dependence, a cherished physical delicacy, a weakness of temperament,—deemed, and falsely deemed, in deference to the pride of man, essential to feminine grace and refinement,—altogether unfit-ting them for a life which were otherwise delightful:—the active out-of-door life in which she must share and sympathise, and the in-door occupations which in England are considered servile; for a woman who cannot perform for herself and others all household offices, has no business here. But when I hear some men declare that they cannot endure to see women eat, and others speak of brilliant health and strength in young girls as being rude and vulgar, with various notions of the same kind too grossly absurd and perverted even for ridicule, I cannot wonder at any nonsensical affectations I meet with in my own sex; nor do otherwise than pity the mistakes and deficiencies of those who are sagely brought up with the one end and aim—to get married. As you always used to say, 'Let there be a demand for a better article, and a better article will be supplied.'

* * *

1838

Thomas Chandler Haliburton

1796-1865

In his humorous tales of a Yankee clock pedlar in Nova Scotia, Thomas Haliburton wrote sketches that united such Burkeian Tory principles as stability, respect for law, and fair-mindedness, with an appreciation of the attributes he most admired in New Englanders—their outspoken self-confidence, adaptability, and work ethic. This blend of Tory and Yankee values contains many of the contradictions that existed in Haliburton himself.

Born in Windsor, N.S., in 1796 of old Loyalist stock, Haliburton grew up in a colony that seemed to him a well-established society on the eve of its industrial age. He was eager to participate in Nova Scotia's future development and in righting its social inequities; his education at King's College in Windsor, the accepted preparation for a young Anglican Tory professional, was a means of readying himself for the role. After establishing a successful law practice in Annapolis Royal, Haliburton became a member of the Legislative Assembly and, in 1826, was arguing for various social and governmental reforms that were intended to perfect the strong colonial relationship with England. However, he lacked political effectiveness, because with his blunt and undiplomatic manner he alienated the Tories by supporting reforms and the reformers by wanting to maintain close ties with the Crown. He accepted a propitious call to the bench in 1829, taking the judgeship in the Court of Common Pleas recently vacated by his father's death.

Haliburton's first two books—*A General Description of Nova Scotia* (1823) and *An Historical and Statistical Account of Nova Scotia* (1829)—show his deep knowledge of the colony as well as the range of his interest in it. By becoming a circuit judge he was able to learn still more of the particulars of daily life as he travelled widely through Nova Scotia. This occupation was a good preparation for his creation of Sam Slick, another circuit rider. Indeed, it was in his first years as a judge, when he was disenchanted with politics and convinced that the only changes of real importance would come through a basic transformation in the character of his countrymen, who seemed to him to be apathetic, that Haliburton hit on the idea of writing satirical sketches that would hold up a mirror to Nova Scotians and goad them into action. To this end he created two principal characters, using their dialogues to debate his chief ideas. One of these characters, the Squire, embodied Haliburton's own Tory colonial ideals, but he plays a secondary and mollifying role to the more central figure of Sam Slick, the conniving Connecticut clock salesman who, while he cannot be trusted, still illuminates the valuable qualities of 'Industry, Enterprise, Economy'—virtues that can be summarized in a single phrase of Slick's: 'Go ahead'.

The Clockmaker sketches first appeared in 1835 in *The Nova Scotian*, a newspaper edited by Joseph Howe, a friend and a reformer with whom Haliburton had once been allied. In 1836 Howe gathered thirty-three of the sketches and published the first of what eventually became eleven volumes chronicling 'The Sayings and Doings of Samuel Slick, of Slickville'. Within fifty years of Slick's first appearance there were more than a hundred editions of these books. Haliburton was being read not only in Canada, England, and the United States, but in translation in France and Germany.

In 1841 Haliburton became Chief Justice of the Supreme Court of Nova Scotia, a position he held until his retirement in 1856. *The Old Judge, or Life in a Colony* (1849) is a sympathetic presentation of Nova Scotian life that comes out of this experience. Notable for its close observation, it is the only one of Haliburton's works without Sam Slick that is still occasionally read today.

Britain attracted Haliburton as he grew older, and he moved there after his retirement. In England he took up politics once more, becoming a Conservative M.P. at the end of his life, and often arguing in the British Parliament against the reforms he had once supported as a young man. In 1858 he became the first colonial to be given an honorary degree for literary merit by Oxford University.

With his irreverent tone, his use of broad dialect for comic effect, a narrative style that drew heavily on folk and oral tradition, and the creation of a character type known in nineteenth-century America as 'an original', Haliburton helped to establish a tradition in American humour—influencing Mark Twain among others. He edited two anthologies, *Traits of American Humour by Native Authors* (1852) and *The Americans at Home; or Byeways, Backwoods, and Prairies* (1854), that were widely read and helped perpetuate his kind of storytelling.

From *The Clockmaker* (First Series)

THE TROTTING HORSE

I was always well mounted. I am fond of a horse, and always piqued[1] myself on having the fastest trotter in the Province. I have made no great progress in the world. I feel doubly, therefore, the pleasure of not being surpassed on the road. I never feel so well or so cheerful as on horseback, for there is something exhilarating in quick motion; and, old as I am, I feel a pleasure in making any person whom I meet on the way put his horse to the full gallop, to keep pace with my trotter. Poor Ethiope! You recollect him, how he was wont to lay back his ears on his arched neck, and push away from all competition. He is done, poor fellow! The spavin[2] spoiled his speed, and he now roams at large upon 'my farm at Truro'. Mohawk never failed me till this summer.

I pride myself (you may laugh at such childish weaknesses in a man of my age), but still I pride myself in taking the conceit out of coxcombs I meet on the road, and on the ease with which I can leave a fool behind, whose nonsense disturbs my solitary musings.

On my last journey to Fort Lawrence, as the beautiful view of Colchester had just opened upon me, and as I was contemplating its richness and exquisite

[1] Prided.
[2] A bony tumour on a horse's leg that causes inflammation and pain.

scenery, a tall thin man, with hollow cheeks and bright twinkling black eyes, on a good bay horse, somewhat out of condition, overtook me; and drawing up, said, 'I say, stranger, I guess you started early this morning, didn't you?' 'I did sir,' I replied. 'You did not come from Halifax, I presume, sir, did you?' in a dialect too rich to be mistaken as genu*ine* Yankee. 'And which way may you be travelling?' asked my inquisitive companion. 'To Fort Lawrence.' 'Ah!' said he, 'so am I, it is *in my circuit.*'[3] The word *circuit* sounded so professional, I looked again at him to ascertain whether I had ever seen him before, or whether I had met with one of those nameless but innumerable limbs of the law who now flourish in every district of the Province. There was a keenness about his eye, and an acuteness of expression, much in favour of the law; but the dress, and general bearing of the man, made against the supposition. His was not the coat of a man who can afford to wear an old coat, nor was it one of 'Tempest and More's' that distinguish country lawyers from country boobies. His clothes were well made, and of good materials, but looked as if their owner had shrunk a little since they were made for him; they hung somewhat loose on him. A large brooch, and some superfluous seals and gold keys, which ornamented his outward man, looked 'New England' like. A visit to the States had, perhaps, I thought, turned this Colchester beau into a Yankee fop. Of what consequence was it to me who he was—in either case I had nothing to do with him, and I desired neither his acquaintance nor his company— still I could not but ask myself who can this man be? 'I am not aware,' said I, 'that there is a court sitting at this time at Cumberland?' 'Nor am I,' said my friend. What then could he have to do with the circuit? It occurred to me he must be a Methodist preacher. I looked again, but his appearance again puzzled me. His attire might do—the colour might be suitable—the broad brim not out of place; but there was a want of that staidness of look, that seriousness of countenance, that expression, in short, so characteristic of the clergy.

I could not account for my idle curiosity—a curiosity which, in him, I had the moment before viewed both with suspicion and disgust; but so it was—I felt a desire to know who he could be who was neither lawyer nor preacher, and yet talked of his *circuit* with the gravity of both. How ridiculous, I thought to myself, is this; I will leave him. Turning towards him, I said, I feared I should be late for breakfast, and must, therefore, bid him good morning. Mohawk felt the pressure of my knees, and away we went at a slapping pace. I congratulated myself on conquering my own curiosity, and on avoiding that of my travelling companion. This, I said to myself, this is the value of a good horse; I patted his neck—I felt proud of him. Presently I heard the steps of the unknown's horse— the clatter increased. Ah, my friend, thought I, it won't do; you should be well mounted if you desire my company; I pushed Mohawk faster, faster, faster—to his best. He outdid himself; he had never trotted so handsomely—so easily—so well.

'I guess that is a pretty considerable smart horse,' said the stranger as he came beside me, and apparently reined in, to prevent his horse passing me. 'There is not, I reckon, so spry a one on *my circuit.*'

---

[3]The regular journey through an area made by certain itinerant professionals such as preachers and judges.

Circuit, or no circuit, one thing was settled in my mind; he was a Yankee, and a very impertinent Yankee too. I felt humbled, my pride was hurt, and Mohawk was beaten. To continue this trotting contest was humiliating; I yielded, therefore, before the victory was palpable, and pulled up.

'Yes,' continued he, 'a horse of pretty considerable good action, and a pretty fair trotter, too, I guess.' Pride must have a fall—I confess mine was prostrate in the dust. These words cut me to the heart. What! is it come to this, poor Mohawk, that you, the admiration of all but the envious, the great Mohawk, the standard by which all other horses are measured—trots next to Mohawk, only yields to Mohawk, looks like Mohawk—that you are, after all, only a counterfeit, and pronounced by a straggling Yankee to be merely a 'pretty fair trotter'!

'If he was trained, I guess that he might be made to do a little more. Excuse me, but if you divide your weight between the knee and the stirrup, rather most on the knee, and rise forward on the saddle, so as to leave a little daylight between you and it, I hope I may never ride *this circuit again*, if you don't get a mile more an hour out of him.'

What! not enough, I mentally groaned, to have my horse beaten, but I must be told that I don't know how to ride him; and that, too, by a Yankee. Aye, there's the rub—a Yankee what? Perhaps a half-bred puppy, half yankee, half bluenose. As there is no escape, I'll try to make out my riding master. '*Your circuit*,' said I, my looks expressing all the surprise they were capable of—'your circuit, pray what may that be?' 'Oh,' said he, 'the eastern circuit—I am on the eastern circuit, sir.' 'I have heard,' said I, feeling that I now had a lawyer to deal with, 'that there is a great deal of business on this circuit—pray, are there many cases of importance?' 'There is a pretty fair business to be done, at least there has been,' said he, 'but the cases are of no great value—we don't make much out of them. We get them up very easy, but they don't bring much profit.' What a beast, thought I, is this; and what a curse to a country, to have such an unfeeling pettifogging rascal practising in it—a horse jockey,[4] too, what a finished character! I'll try him on that branch of his business.

'That is a superior animal you are mounted on,' said I. 'I seldom meet one that can keep pace with mine.' 'Yes,' said he coolly, 'a considerable fair traveller, and most particular good bottom.'[5] I hesitated: this man who talks with such unblushing effrontery of getting up cases, and making profit out of them, cannot be offended at the question—yes, I will put it to him. 'Do you feel an inclination to part with him?' 'I never part with a horse, sir, that suits me,' said he. 'I am fond of a horse—I don't like to ride in the dust after every one I meet, and I allow no man to pass me but when I choose.' Is it possible, I thought, that he can know me? that he has heard of my foible, and is quizzing[6] me, or have I this feeling in common with him? 'But,' continued I, 'you might supply yourself again.' 'Not on *this circuit*, I guess,' said he, 'nor yet in Campbell's circuit.' 'Campbell's circuit—pray, sir, what is that?' 'That,' said he, 'is the western—and Lampton rides the shore circuit; and as for the people on the shore, they know so little of horses that Lampton tells me a man from Aylesford once sold a hornless ox

[4] Horse trader.
[5] Physical endurance; strength.
[6] Mocking.

there, whose tail he had cut and nicked, for a horse of the Goliath breed.' 'I should think,' said I, 'that Mr Lampton must have no lack of cases among such enlightened clients.' 'Clients, sir!' said my friend, 'Mr Lampton is not a lawyer.' 'I beg pardon, I thought you said he rode the *circuit*.' 'We call it a circuit,' said the stranger, who seemed by no means flattered by the mistake. 'We divide the Province, as in the Almanack, into circuits, in each of which we separately carry on our business of manufacturing and selling clocks. There are few, I guess,' said the Clockmaker, 'who go upon *tick* as much as we do, who have so little use for lawyers. If attornies could wind a *man up again*, after he has been fairly *run down*, I guess they'd be a pretty harmless sort of folks.'

This explanation restored my good humour, and as I could not quit my companion, and he did not feel disposed to leave me, I made up my mind to travel with him to Fort Lawrence, the limit of *his circuit*.

THE CLOCKMAKER

I had heard of Yankee clock pedlars, tin pedlars, and bible pedlars, especially of him who sold Polyglot Bibles[1] (*all in English*) to the amount of sixteen thousand pounds. The house of every substantial farmer had three substantial ornaments, a wooden clock, a tin reflector, and a Polyglot Bible. How is it that an American can sell his wares, at whatever price he pleases, where a blue-nose[2] would fail to make a sale at all? I will inquire of the Clockmaker the secret of his success.

'What a pity it is, Mr *Slick*,' (for such was his name), 'what a pity it is,' said I, 'that you, who are so successful in teaching these people the value of *clocks*, could not also teach them the value of *time*.' 'I guess,' said he, 'they have got that ring to grow on their horns yet,[3] which every four-year-old has in our country. We reckon hours and minutes to be dollars and cents. They do nothin in these parts but eat, drink, smoke, sleep, ride about, lounge at taverns, make speeches at temperance meetings, and talk about *"House of Assembly"*. If a man don't hoe his corn, and he don't get a crop, he says it is all owin to the Bank; and if he runs into debt and is sued, why he says lawyers are a cuss to the country. They are a most idle set of folks, I tell *you*.'

'But how is it,' said I, 'that you manage to sell such an immense number of clocks (which certainly cannot be called necessary articles) among a people with whom there seems to be so great a scarcity of money?'

Mr Slick paused, as if considering the propriety of answering the question, and looking me in the face, said, in a confidential tone, 'Why I don't care if I do tell you, for the market is glutted, and I shall quit this circuit. It is done by a knowledge of *soft sawder* and *human natur*. But here is Deacon Flint's,' said he. 'I have but one clock left, and I guess I will sell it to him.'

At the gate of a most comfortable-looking farmhouse stood Deacon Flint, a

[1] Bibles published in several Biblical languages as well as in modern translation; used to settle textual disputes; 'tin reflector': a reflector placed behind a candle to allow it to serve as a lamp.
[2] Nova Scotians are 'known throughout America as Mr Blue Nose, a sobriquet acquired from a superior potato of that name' (Haliburton's Preface to *The Old Judge*).
[3] Cattle and oxen grow rings on their horns as they mature.

respectable old man, who had understood the value of time better than most of his neighbours, if one might judge from the appearance of everything about him. After the usual salutation, an invitation to 'alight' was accepted by Mr Slick, who said he wished to take leave of Mrs Flint before he left Colchester.

We had hardly entered the house before the Clockmaker pointed to the view from the window, and addressing himself to me, said, 'If I was to tell them in Connecticut there was such a farm as this away down east here in Nova Scotia, they wouldn't believe me—why there ain't such a location in all New England. The deacon has a hundred acres of dyke.'[4] 'Seventy,' said the Deacon, 'only seventy.' 'Well, seventy; but then there is your fine deep bottom. Why I could run a ramrod into it.' 'Interval, we call it,' said the Deacon, who, though evidently pleased at this eulogium,[5] seemed to wish the experiment of the ramrod to be tried in the right place. 'Well, interval if you please (though Professor Eleazer Cumstick, in his work on Ohio, calls them bottoms) is just as good as dyke. Then there is that water privilege,[6] worth 3,000 or 4,000 dollars, twice as good as what Governor Cass paid 15,000 dollars for.[7] I wonder, Deacon, you don't put up a carding mill[8] on it: the same works would carry a turning lathe, a shingle machine, a circular saw, grind bark, and—' 'Too old,' said the Deacon, 'too old for all those speculations.' 'Old,' repeated the Clockmaker, 'not you; why you are worth half a dozen of the young men we see now-a-days; you are young enough to have—' Here he said something in a lower tone of voice, which I did not distinctly hear; but whatever it was, the Deacon was pleased. He smiled, and said he did not think of such things now.

'But your beasts, dear me, your beasts must be put in and have a feed,' saying which he went out to order them to be taken to the stable.

As the old gentleman closed the door after him, Mr Slick drew near to me, and said in an undertone, 'Now that is what I call *"soft sawder"*. An Englishman would pass that man as a sheep passes a hog in a pastur, without lookin at him. Or,' said he, looking rather archly, 'if he was mounted on a pretty smart horse, I guess he'd trot away, *if he could*. Now I find—' Here his lecture on '*soft sawder*' was cut short by the entrance of Mrs Flint. 'Jist come to say goodbye, Mrs Flint.' 'What, have you sold all your clocks?' 'Yes, and very low, too, for money is scarce, and I wished to close the concarn.[9] No, I am wrong in saying all, for I have jist one left. Neighbour Steel's wife asked to have the refusal of it, but I guess I won't sell it, I had but two of them, this one and the feller of it that I sold Governor Lincoln.[1] General Green, the Secretary of State for Maine, said he'd give me 50 dollars for this here one—it has composition wheels and patent axles, it is a beautiful article—a real first chop[2]—no mistake. Genuine superfine. But I guess I'll take it back; and beside, Squire Hawk might think kinder harder

---

[4] Land built up to hold water back; a 'bottom' or an 'interval' is low-lying land, usually along a river.

[5] Formal expression of praise.

[6] Right to use water, especially running water to turn machinery.

[7] A governor of the territory of Michigan who paid $12,000 for 500 acres at the mouth of the Detroit River; though the sum was deemed exorbitant at the time, the property made the governor's personal fortune.

[8] Mill for combing and cleansing raw wool.

[9] Concern.

[1] Fourth governor of Maine, 1827-9.

[2] First-rate article.

that I didn't give him the offer.' 'Dear me,' said Mrs Flint, 'I should like to see it. Where is it?' 'It is in a chist of mine over the way, at Tom Tape's store. I guess he can ship it on to Eastport.' 'That's a good man,' said Mrs Flint, 'jist let's look at it.'

Mr Slick, willing to oblige, yielded to these entreaties, and soon produced the clock—a gawdy, highly varnished, trumpery looking affair. He placed it on the chimney-piece, where its beauties were pointed out and duly appreciated by Mrs Flint, whose admiration was about ending in a proposal, when Mr Flint returned from giving his directions about the care of the horses. The Deacon praised the clock. He too thought it a handsome one; but the Deacon was a prudent man, he had a watch—he was sorry, but he had no occasion for a clock. 'I guess you're in the wrong furrow this time, Deacon, it an't for sale,' said Mr Slick. 'And if it was, I reckon neighbour Steel's wife would have it, for she gives me no peace about it.' Mrs Flint said that Mr Steel had enough to do, poor man, to pay his interest, without buying clocks for his wife. 'It's no consarn of mine,' said Mr Slick, 'so long as he pays me what he has to do. But I guess I don't want to sell it, and besides it comes too high; that clock can't be made at Rhode Island under 40 dollars. Why it an't possible,' said the Clockmaker, in apparent surprise, looking at his watch, 'why as I'm alive, it is 4 o'clock, and if I hav'nt been two blessed hours here—how on airth shall I reach River Philip tonight? I'll tell you what, Mrs Flint, I'll leave the clock in your care till I return on my way to the States—I'll set it a goin, and put it to the right time.'

As soon as this operation was performed, he delivered the key to the Deacon with a sort of serio-comic injunction to wind up the clock every Saturday night, which Mrs Flint said she would take care should be done, and promised to remind her husband of it in case he should chance to forget it.

'That,' said the Clockmaker, as soon as we were mounted, 'that I call "human natur"! Now that clock is sold for 40 dollars—it cost me jist 6 dollars and 50 cents. Mrs Flint will never let Mrs Steel have the refusal—nor will the Deacon larn, until I call for the clock, that having once indulged in the use of a superfluity, how difficult it is to give it up. We can do without any article of luxury we have never had, but when once obtained, it isn't "in human natur" to surrender it voluntarily. Of fifteen thousand sold by myself and partners in this Province, twelve thousand were left in this manner, and only ten clocks were ever returned—when we called for them, they invariably bought them. We trust to "soft sawder" to get them into the house, and to "human natur" that they never come out of it.'

Catharine Parr Traill

1802-1899

Catharine Strickland was born in London into a large and literary family. As Catharine Parr Traill she became one of three siblings to write accounts of pioneer experience in nineteenth-century Canada. Her brother Samuel Strickland was the author of *Twenty-seven Years in Canada West* (1853), while her younger sister, Susanna Moodie, became famous as the author of *Roughing It in the Bush* (1852). It was through Susanna and her new husband, Lieut. John Moodie, that Catharine first met Lieut. Thomas Traill, a half-pay officer. The Traills were married in 1832, and both they and the Moodies emigrated to Upper Canada that year, departing within a week of one another. The Traills settled in Douro Township (near Peterborough), at Rice Lake; their farm was next to that of Samuel Strickland, who had preceded them there in 1825.

By the time she came to Canada, Catharine Traill had already written children's stories and a book on her future homeland—*The Young Emigrants; or, Pictures of Canada* (1826), based on the experiences of a family of her acquaintance. Four years after her arrival she published *The Backwoods of Canada* (1836), a work drawing on letters she had written home; it was undertaken, as she later said, 'with the view of preparing females of my own class . . . for the changes that awaited them in the life of a Canadian emigrant's wife.' In 1852 she published a children's book about her adopted country, *Canadian Crusoes*, which remains interesting both for its idealized treatment of the union in Canada of English and French, Scots and Indians, and because Crusoe has become—like Noah—an emblematic figure in Canadian writing: the individual who recreates the civilization from which he has been separated. In 1854 Traill published *The Female Emigrant's Guide* (reprinted as *The Canadian Settler's Guide*), a work that continues the project begun in *The Backwoods of Canada* of conveying to emigrating gentlewomen the knowledge Traill had won through hard experience. Already interested in nature, she displayed considerable talents as a naturalist once in Canada, collecting and cataloguing the plant life she found around her. Her chapter on flowers in *The Backwoods of Canada*, and such later studies as *Canadian Wild Flowers* (1869) and *Studies of Plant Life in Canada* (1885), are botanical landmarks. Traill, whose life spanned the nineteenth century, continued to write even into her nineties: *Pearls and Pebbles; or, Notes of an Old Naturalist* was published when she was ninety-two.

The Backwoods of Canada is often contrasted with Susanna Moodie's *Roughing It in the Bush*. Like her younger sister, Traill tells of many hardships, but her overall outlook is much more optimistic. Indeed, she so buoyed the despairing Susanna's spirits that Moodie writes midway through *Roughing It:* 'My conversation with her [Catharine] had quite altered the aspect of the country, and predisposed me to view things in the most favourable light.' Traill saw the pleasanter aspects of nature as expressing God's benevolence, and believed that in adversity the individual's duty to self and God lay in strong-willed determination: 'In cases of emergency, it is folly to fold one's hands and sit down to bewail in abject terror: it is better to be up and doing' (*The Female Emigrant's Guide*). Hers was clearly an attitude valuable to new pioneers; lacking it, they tended, as she observed, to 'blame the Colony for the failure of the individual.' In *The Diviners* (1974) Margaret Laurence has her central character enter into imaginary dialogues with Catharine Traill, even to the point of invoking her: 'Saint Catharine: Where are you now that we need you?'

From *The Backwoods of Canada*

LETTER IX

Lake House
April 18, 1833

But it is time that I should give you some account of our log-house, into which we moved a few days before Christmas. Many unlooked-for delays having hindered its completion before that time, I began to think it would never be habitable.

The first misfortune that happened was the loss of a fine yoke of oxen that were purchased to draw in the house-logs, that is, the logs for raising the walls of the house. Not regarding the bush as pleasant as their former master's cleared pastures, or perhaps foreseeing some hard work to come, early one morning they took into their heads to ford the lake at the head of the rapids, and march off, leaving no trace of their route excepting their footing at the water's edge. After many days spent in vain search for them, the work was at a stand, and for one month they were gone, and we began to give up all expectation of hearing any news of them. At last we learned they were some twenty miles off, in a distant township, having made their way through bush and swamp, creek and lake, back to their former owner, with an instinct that supplied to them the want of roads and compass.

Oxen have been known to traverse a tract of wild country to a distance of thirty or forty miles going in a direct line for their former haunts by unknown paths, where memory could not avail them. In the dog we consider it is scent as well as memory that guides him to his far-off home;—but how is this conduct of the oxen to be accounted for? They returned home through the mazes of interminable forests, where man, with all his reason and knowledge, would have been bewildered and lost.

It was the latter end of October before even the walls of our house were up. To effect this we called 'a bee'.[1] Sixteen of our neighbours cheerfully obeyed our summons; and though the day was far from favourable, so faithfully did our hive perform their tasks, that by night the outer walls were raised.

The work went merrily on with the help of plenty of Canadian nectar (whiskey), the honey that our *bees* are solaced with. Some huge joints of salt pork, a peck of potatoes, with a rice-pudding, and a loaf as big as an enormous Cheshire cheese, formed the feast that was to regale them during the raising. This was spread out in the shanty,[2] in a *very rural style*. In short, we laughed, and called it a *pic-nic in the backwoods;* and rude as was the fare, I can assure you, great was the satisfaction expressed by all the guests of every degree, our 'bee' being considered as very well conducted. In spite of the difference of rank among those that assisted at the bee, the greatest possible harmony prevailed, and the party separated well pleased with the day's work and entertainment.

The following day I went to survey the newly-raised edifice, but was sorely puzzled, as it presented very little appearance of a house. It was merely an oblong square of logs raised one above the other, with open spaces between every

[1] Any gathering for communal work.
[2] Used here in its French-Canadian sense: 'workshop'.

row of logs. The spaces for the doors and windows were not then chopped out, and the rafters were not up. In short, it looked a very queer sort of a place, and I returned home a little disappointed, and wondering that my husband should be so well pleased with the progress that had been made. A day or two after this I again visited it. The *sleepers*[3] were laid to support the floors, and the places for the doors and windows cut out of the solid timbers, so that it had not quite so much the look of a bird-cage as before.

After the roof was shingled, we were again at a stand, as no boards could be procured nearer than Peterborough, a long day's journey through horrible roads. At that time no saw-mill was in progress; now there is a fine one building within a little distance of us. Our flooring-boards were all to be sawn by hand, and it was some time before any one could be found to perform this necessary work, and that at high wages—six-and-sixpence per day. Well, the boards were at length down, but of course of unseasoned timber: this was unavoidable; so as they could not be planed we were obliged to put up with their rough unsightly appearance, for no better were to be had. I began to recall to mind the observation of the old gentleman with whom we travelled from Cobourg to Rice Lake.[4] We console ourselves with the prospect that by next summer the boards will all be seasoned, and then the house is to be turned topsy-turvy, by having the floors all relaid, jointed, and smoothed.

The next misfortune that happened, was, that the mixture of clay and lime that was to plaster the inside and outside of the house between the chinks of the logs was one night frozen to stone. Just as the work was about half completed, the frost suddenly setting in, put a stop to our proceeding for some time, as the frozen plaster yielded neither to fire nor to hot water, the latter freezing before it had any effect on the mass, and rather making bad worse. Then the workman that was hewing the inside walls to make them smooth, wounded himself with the broad axe, and was unable to resume his work for some time.

I state these things merely to show the difficulties that attend us in the fulfilment of our plans, and this accounts in a great measure for the humble dwellings that settlers of the most respectable description are obliged to content themselves with at first coming to this country,—not, you may be assured, from inclination, but necessity: I could give you such narratives of this kind as would astonish you. After all, it serves to make us more satisfied than we should be on casting our eyes around to see few better off than we are, and many not half so comfortable, yet of equal, and, in some instances, superior pretensions as to station and fortune.

Every man in this country is his own glazier; this you will laugh at: but if he does not wish to see and feel the discomfort of broken panes, he must learn to put

[3] Supporting beams.

[4] "If you go into the backwoods your house must necessarily be a log-house," said an elderly gentleman, who had been a settler many years in the country, "for you will most probably be out of the way of a saw-mill, and you will find so much to do, and so many obstacles to encounter, for the first two or three years, that you will hardly have opportunity for carrying these improvements into effect.

' "There is an old saying," he added . . . . " 'first creep and then go.' Matters are not carried on quite so easily here as at home. . . . At the end of ten or fifteen years you may begin to talk of these pretty improvements and elegancies and you will then be able to see a little what you are about. . . ." ' (Letter V).

them in his windows with his own hands. Workmen are not easily to be had in the backwoods when you want them, and it would be preposterous to hire a man at high wages to make two days' journey to and from the nearest town to mend your windows. Boxes of glass of several different sizes are to be bought at a very cheap rate in the stores. My husband amused himself by glazing the windows of the house preparatory to their being fixed in.[5]

To understand the use of carpenter's tools, I assure you, is no despicable or useless kind of knowledge here. I would strongly recommend all young men coming to Canada to acquire a little acquaintance with this valuable art, as they will often be put to great inconvenience for the want of it.

I was once much amused with hearing the remarks made by a very fine lady, the reluctant sharer of her husband's emigration, on seeing the son of a naval officer of some rank in the service busily employed in making an axe-handle out of a piece of rock-elm.

'I wonder that you allow George to degrade himself so,' she said, addressing his father.

The captain looked up with surprise. 'Degrade himself! In what manner, madam? My boy neither swears, drinks whiskey, steals, nor tells lies.'

'But you allow him to perform tasks of the most menial kind. What is he now better than a hedge carpenter;[6] and I suppose you allow him to chop, too?'

'Most assuredly I do. That pile of logs in the cart there was all cut by him after he had left study yesterday,' was the reply,

'I would see my boys dead before they should use an axe like common labourers.'

'Idleness is the root of all evil,' said the captain. 'How much worse might my son be employed if he were running wild about the streets with bad companions.'

'You will allow this is not a country for gentlemen or ladies to live in,' said the lady.

'It is the country for gentlemen that will not work and cannot live without, to starve in,' replied the captain bluntly; 'and for that reason I make my boys early accustom themselves to be usefully and actively employed.'

'My boys shall never work like common mechanics,'[7] said the lady, indignantly.

'Then, madam, they will be good for nothing as settlers; and it is a pity you dragged them across the Atlantic.'

'We were forced to come. We could not live as we had been used to do at home, or I never would have come to this horrid country.'

'Having come hither you would be wise to conform to circumstances. Canada is not the place for idle folks to retrench a lost fortune in. In some parts of the country you will find most articles of provision as dear as in London, clothing much dearer, and not so good, and a bad market to choose in.'

'I should like to know, then, who Canada is good for?' said she, angrily.

'It is a good country for the honest, industrious artisan. It is a fine country for

---

[5] That is, he placed the glass in the window-frames before putting the frames in place.
[6] Fence repairer.
[7] Manual labourers.

the poor labourer, who, after a few years of hard toil, can sit down in his own log-house, and look abroad on his own land, and see his children well settled in life as independent freeholders.[8] It is a grand country for the rich speculator, who can afford to lay out a large sum in purchasing land in eligible situations; for if he have any judgment, he will make a hundred per cent. as interest for his money after waiting a few years. But it is a hard country for the poor gentleman, whose habits have rendered him unfit for manual labour. He brings with him a mind unfitted to his situation; and even if necessity compels him to exertion, his labour is of little value. He has a hard struggle to live. The certain expenses of wages and living are great, and he is obliged to endure many privations if he would keep within compass, and be free of debt. If he have a large family, and brings them up wisely, so as to adapt themselves early to a settler's life, why he does well for them, and soon feels the benefit on his own land; but if he is idle himself, his wife extravagant and discontented, and the children taught to despise labour, why, madam, they will soon be brought down to ruin. In short, the country is a good country for those to whom it is adapted; but if people will not conform to the doctrine of necessity and expediency, they have no business in it. It is plain Canada is not adapted to every class of people.'

'It was never adapted for me or my family,' said the lady, disdainfully.

'Very true,' was the laconic reply; and so ended the dialogue.

But while I have been recounting these remarks, I have wandered far from my original subject, and left my poor log-house quite in an unfinished state. At last I was told it was in a habitable condition, and I was soon engaged in all the bustle and fatigue attendant on removing our household goods. We received all the assistance we required from ____, who is ever ready and willing to help us. He laughed and called it a '*moving* bee'; I said it was a 'fixing bee'; and my husband said it was a 'settling bee'; I know we were unsettled enough till it was over. What a din of desolation is a small house, or any house under such circumstances. The idea of chaos must have been taken from a removal or a setting to rights, for I suppose the ancients had their *flitting*,[9] as the Scotch call it, as well as the moderns.

Various were the valuable articles of crockery-ware that perished in their short but rough journey through the woods. Peace to their manes.[1] I had a good helper in my Irish maid, who soon roused up famous fires, and set the house in order.

We have now got quite comfortably settled, and I shall give you a description of our little dwelling. What is finished is only a part of the original plan; the rest must be added next spring, or fall, as circumstances may suit.

A nice small sitting-room with a store closet, a kitchen, pantry, and bed-chamber form the ground floor; there is a good upper floor that will make three sleeping-rooms.

'What a nut-shell!' I think I hear you exclaim. So it is at present; but we purpose adding a handsome frame front as soon as we can get boards from the mill, which will give us another parlour, long hall, and good spare bed-room. The windows and glass door of our present sitting-room command pleasant lake-

[8]Those that own land without restrictions on its sale or use.
[9]Moving from place to place.
[1]Spirits (Latin: the deified souls of departed ancestors).

views to the west and south. When the house is completed, we shall have a verandah in front; and at the south side, which forms an agreeable addition in the summer, being used as a sort of outer room, in which we can dine, and have the advantage of cool air, protected from the glare of the sunbeams. The Canadians call these verandahs 'stoups'. Few houses, either log or frame, are without them. The pillars look extremely pretty, wreathed with the luxuriant hop-vine, mixed with the scarlet creeper and 'morning glory', the American name for the most splendid of major convolvuluses. These stoups are really a considerable ornament, as they conceal in a great measure the rough logs, and break the barnlike form of the building.

Our parlour is warmed by a handsome Franklin stove with brass galley, and fender. Our furniture consists of a brass-railed sofa, which serves upon occasion for a bed, Canadian painted chairs, a stained pine table, green and white curtains, and a handsome Indian mat that covers the floor. One side of the room is filled up with our books. Some large maps and a few good prints nearly conceal the rough walls, and form the decoration of our little dwelling. Our bed-chamber is furnished with equal simplicity. We do not, however, lack comfort in our humble home; and though it is not exactly such as we could wish, it is as good as, under existing circumstances, we could have.

*   *   *

LETTER X

Lake House
May the 9th, 1833

*   *   *

Though the Canadian winter has its disadvantages, it also has its charms. After a day or two of heavy snow the sky brightens, and the air becomes exquisitely clear and free from vapour; the smoke ascends in tall spiral columns till it is lost: seen against the saffron-tinted sky of an evening, or early of a clear morning, when the hoar-frost sparkles on the trees, the effect is singularly beautiful.

I enjoy a walk in the woods of a bright winter-day, when not a cloud, or the faint shadow of a cloud, obscures the soft azure of the heavens above; when but for the silver covering of the earth I might look upwards to the cloudless sky and say, 'It is June, sweet June.' The evergreens, as the pines, cedars, hemlock, and balsam firs, are bending their pendent branches, loaded with snow, which the least motion scatters in a mimic shower around, but so light and dry is it that it is shaken off without the slightest inconvenience.

The tops of the stumps look quite pretty, with their turbans of snow; a blackened pine-stump, with its white cap and mantle, will often startle you into the belief that some one is approaching you thus fancifully attired. As to ghosts or spirits they appear totally banished from Canada. This is too matter-of-fact country for such supernaturals to visit. Here there are no historical associations, no legendary tales of those that came before us. Fancy would starve for lack of marvellous food to keep her alive in the backwoods. We have neither fay nor fairy, ghost nor bogle,[1] satyr nor wood-nymph; our very forests disdain to shelter

[1] Goblin; 'dryad' and 'hamadryad': wood nymphs; 'naiad': water nymph; 'Druid': primitive Celtic priest.

dryad or hamadryad. No naiad haunts the rushy margin of our lakes, or hallows with her presence our forest-rills. No Druid claims our oaks; and instead of poring with mysterious awe among our curious limestone rocks, that are often singularly grouped together, we refer them to the geologist to exercise his skill in accounting for their appearance: instead of investing them with the solemn characters of ancient temples or heathen altars, we look upon them with the curious eye of natural philosophy alone.

Even the Irish and Highlanders of the humblest class seem to lay aside their ancient superstitions on becoming denizens of the woods of Canada. I heard a friend exclaim, when speaking of the want of interest this country possessed, 'It is the most unpoetical of all lands; there is no scope for imagination; here all is new—the very soil seems newly formed; there is no hoary ancient grandeur in these woods; no recollections of former deeds connected with the country. The only beings in which I take any interest are the Indians, and they want the warlike character and intelligence that I had pictured to myself they would possess.'

This was the lamentation of a poet. Now, the class of people to whom this country is so admirably adapted are formed of the unlettered and industrious labourers and artisans. They feel no regret that the land they labour on has not been celebrated by the pen of the historian or the lay of the poet. The earth yields her increase to them as freely as if it had been enriched by the blood of heroes. They would not spare the ancient oak from feelings of veneration, nor look upon it with regard for any thing but its use as timber. They have no time, even if they possessed the taste, to gaze abroad on the beauties of Nature, but their ignorance is bliss.

After all, these are imaginary evils, and can hardly be considered just causes for dislike to the country. They would excite little sympathy among every-day men and women, though doubtless they would have their weight with the more refined and intellectual members of society, who naturally would regret that taste, learning, and genius should be thrown out of its proper sphere.

For myself, though I can easily enter into the feelings of the poet and the enthusiastic lover of the wild and the wonderful of historic lore, I can yet make myself very happy and contented in this country. If its volume of history is yet a blank, that of Nature is open, and eloquently marked by the finger of God; and from its pages I can extract a thousand sources of amusement and interest whenever I take my walks in the forest or by the borders of the lakes.

1836

Susanna Moodie

1803-1885

Susanna Moodie, like her older sister Catharine Parr Traill, began her literary career early, publishing her first novel by the time she was nineteen. She continued writing and published a collection of her poetry in 1831, the year she married John Dunbar Moodie, a retired army officer from the Orkneys. The couple immigrated to Canada in 1832, settling near Cobourg. After two difficult years they relocated in Douro Township to be closer to Susanna's brother Samuel Strickland and her sister Catharine. Farming was still so difficult, however, that only when Dunbar Moodie was recalled to active service because of the Rebellion of 1837 did the family gain some measure of financial security. When, in 1839, Mr Moodie was appointed Sheriff of Victoria District (later Hastings County), it was with relief that the couple moved to Belleville, abandoning forever their attempts at managing a bush farm.

Once Mrs Moodie left rural life behind, she was able to return to her faltering literary career. Between 1839 and 1851 she contributed seventy-five poems and twenty pieces of prose to various magazines, including *The Canadian Literary Magazine, The North American Review*, and *The Literary Garland*. She integrated several of her published sketches into a larger narrative recounting her years of struggle as a farm wife, entitling it *Roughing It in the Bush; or, Forest Life in Canada;* it appeared in 1852. In Moodie's lifetime, this book was republished in several editions, the contents of which varied somewhat; later some versions deleted whole chapters. (In 1988, the Centre for Editing Early Canadian Texts brought out a scholarly edition of *Roughing It in the Bush*.) A sequel, *Life in the Clearings versus the Bush*, appeared the next year. There she explained that while *Roughing It* was intended 'to point out the error of gentlemen bringing delicate women and helpless children to toil in the woods', she nevertheless affirmed 'the REAL benefits to be derived from a judicious choice of settlement in this great and rising country.' Moodie wrote very

rapidly in the years that followed, turning out several novels and helping to fill the pages of *The Literary Garland* and other magazines. Most of what she wrote is little read today except *Roughing It*, to which is sometimes added *Life in the Clearings* and the Introduction to her novel *Mark Hurdlestone* for its account of literary activity in Canada in 1853.

Roughing It in the Bush, originally published in London, was not immediately popular here: it was not published in Canada until 1871. In a preface to that edition the author expressed her hard-won affection for her adopted country. Perhaps because of those comments, or because the events were now sufficiently distant, the book gained its Canadian readership. It has maintained one since, even though Moodie's real purpose in writing was to warn unwary immigrants about the deceptive appearances they would find in Canada. In fact, Moodie has become a mythic figure for modern Canadians—so much so that Margaret Atwood responded to her Canadian chronicles with a collection of poems, *The Journals of Susanna Moodie* (1970), that in its own way has become as much of a classic as *Roughing It*.

Moodie's book is made up of a series of anecdotes that reveal its author as a practised storyteller. She had a remarkable ability to convey the variety of characters she met in the bush by using their colourful, idiomatic speech in lively dialogue. As a whole, *Roughing It* takes the form of a complaint, so that a speech in Chapter 19 by an acquaintance seems almost to capture its essence: 'Bah!—The only consolation one feels for such annoyances is to complain. Oh, the woods!—the cursed woods!—how I wish I were out of them.' In her Afterword to the *Journals* Atwood sees Moodie as 'divided down the middle'—an emblem of the 'violent duality' of Canada itself. Indeed, what most engages the modern reader is that although Moodie reveals herself as melancholy, inflexible, and proud to the point of condescension, she still continues to struggle against the perpetual defeat of her hopes, all the while giving vent to a confused mixture of feelings. Combining in her narrative the perspective of the time of the events described with the 'reconciled' viewpoint of the older woman recalling those events, she shows us her exhilaration in small victories, a degree of pleasure in enduring painful experiences, and the tearful sadness even she felt at leaving the scene of her hardships. It is in watching Moodie make her choice and achieve—even if almost despite herself—her reconciliation with the land that the greatest attraction of her story lies.

From *Roughing It in the Bush*

INTRODUCTION TO THE THIRD EDITION

In most instances, emigration is a matter of necessity, not of choice; and this is more especially true of the emigration of persons of respectable connections, or of any station or position in the world. Few educated persons, accustomed to the refinements and luxuries of European society, ever willingly relinquish those advantages, and place themselves beyond the protective influence of the wise and revered institutions of their native land, without the pressure of some urgent cause. Emigration may, indeed, generally be regarded as an act of severe duty, performed at the expense of personal enjoyment, and accompanied by the sacrifice of those local attachments which stamp the scenes amid which our childhood grew, in imperishable characters, upon the heart. Nor is it until adversity has pressed sorely upon the proud and wounded spirit of the well-educated sons and daughters of old but impoverished families, that they gird up the loins of the mind, and arm themselves with fortitude to meet and dare the heart-breaking conflict.

The ordinary motives for the emigration of such persons may be summed up in a few brief words;—the emigrant's hope of bettering his condition, and of escaping from the vulgar sarcasms too often hurled at the less wealthy by the purse-proud, common-place people of the world. But there is a higher motive still, which has its origin in that love of independence which springs up spontaneously in the breasts of the high-souled children of a glorious land. They cannot labour in a menial capacity in the country where they were born and educated to command. They can trace no difference between themselves and the more fortunate individuals of a race whose blood warms their veins, and whose name they bear. The want of wealth alone places an impassable barrier between them and the more favoured offspring of the same parent stock; and they go forth to make for themselves a new name and to find another country, to forget the past and to live in the future, to exult in the prospect of their children being free and the land of their adoption great.

The choice of the country to which they devote their talents and energies depends less upon their pecuniary means than upon the fancy of the emigrant or the popularity of a name. From the year 1826 to 1829, Australia and the Swan River were all the rage. No other portions of the habitable globe were deemed worthy of notice. These were the *El Dorados*[1] and lands of Goshen to which all respectable emigrants eagerly flocked. Disappointment, as a matter of course, followed their high-raised expectations. Many of the most sanguine of these adventurers returned to their native

---

[1] A fabled city of gold sought by early Spanish explorers of the New World. Goshen was the fertile land alloted the Israelites in Egypt, in which there was light during the plague of darkness; hence, a land of light and plenty.

shores in a worse condition than when they left them. In 1830, the great tide of emigration flowed westward. Canada became the great land-mark for the rich in hope and poor in purse. Public newspapers and private letters teemed with the unheard-of advantages to be derived from a settlement in this highly-favoured region.

Its salubrious climate, its fertile soil, commercial advantages, great water privileges, its proximity to the mother country, and last, not least, its almost total exemption from taxation—that bugbear which keeps honest John Bull in a state of constant ferment—were the theme of every tongue, and lauded beyond all praise. The general interest, once excited, was industriously kept alive by pamphlets, published by interested parties, which prominently set forth all the *good* to be derived from a settlement in the Backwoods of Canada; while they carefully concealed the toil and hardship to be endured in order to secure these advantages. They told of lands yielding forty bushels to the acre, but they said nothing of the years when these lands, with the most careful cultivation, would barely return fifteen; when rust and smut, engendered by the vicinity of damp over-hanging woods, would blast the fruits of the poor emigrant's labour, and almost deprive him of bread. They talked of log houses to be raised in a single day, by the generous exertions of friends and neighbours, but they never ventured upon a picture of the disgusting scenes of riot and low debauchery exhibited during the raising, or upon a description of the dwellings when raised—dens of dirt and misery, which would, in many instances, be shamed by an English pig-sty. The necessaries of life were described as inestimably cheap; but they forgot to add that in remote bush settlements, often twenty miles from a market town, and some of them even that distance from the nearest dwelling, the necessaries of life which would be deemed indispensable to the European, could not be procured at all, or, if obtained, could only be so by sending a man and team through a blazed forest road,—a process far too expensive for frequent repetition.

Oh, ye dealers in wild lands—ye speculators in the folly and credulity of your fellow-men—what a mass of misery, and of misrepresentation productive of that misery, have ye not to answer for! You had your acres to sell, and what to you were the worn-down frames and broken hearts of the infatuated purchasers? The public believed the plausible statements you made with such earnestness, and men of all grades rushed to hear your hired orators declaim upon the blessings to be obtained by the clearers of the wilderness.

Men who had been hopeless of supporting their families in comfort and independence at home, thought that they had only to come out to Canada to make their fortunes; almost even to realize the story told in the nursery, of the sheep and oxen that ran about the streets, ready roasted, and with knives and forks upon their backs. They were made to believe that if it did not actually rain gold, that precious metal could be obtained, as is now stated of California and Australia, by stooping to pick it up.

The infection became general. A Canada mania pervaded the middle ranks of British society; thousands and tens of thousands, for the space of three or four years, landed upon these shores. A large majority of the higher class were officers of the army and navy, with their families—a class perfectly unfitted by their previous habits and education for contending with the stern realities of emigrant life. The hand that has long held the sword, and been accustomed to receive implicit obedience from those under its control, is seldom adapted to wield the spade and guide the plough, or try its strength against the stubborn trees of the forest. Nor will such persons submit cheerfully to the saucy familiarity of servants, who, republicans in spirit, think themselves as good as their employers. Too many of these brave and honourable men were easy dupes to the designing land-speculators. Not having counted the cost, but only looked upon the bright side of the picture held up to their admiring gaze, they fell easily into the snares of their artful seducers.

To prove their zeal as colonists, they were induced to purchase large tracts of wild land in remote and unfavourable situations. This, while it impoverished and often proved the ruin of the unfortunate immigrant, possessed a double advantage to the seller. He obtained an exorbitant price for the land which he actually sold, while the residence of a respectable settler upon the spot greatly enhanced the value and price of all other lands in the neighbourhood.

It is not by such instruments as those I have just mentioned, that Providence works when it would reclaim the waste places of the earth, and make them subservient to the wants and happiness of its creatures. The Great Father of the souls and bodies of men knows the arm which wholesome labour from infancy has made strong, the nerves which have become iron by patient endurance, by exposure to weather, coarse fare, and rude shelter; and he chooses such, to send forth into the forest to hew out the rough paths for the advance of civilisation. These men become wealthy and prosperous, and form the bones and sinews of a great and rising country. Their labour is wealth, not exhaustion; its produce independence and content, not home-sickness and despair. What the Backwoods of Canada are to the industrious and ever-to-be-honoured sons of honest poverty, and what they are to the refined and accomplished gentleman, these simple sketches will endeavour to portray. They are drawn principally from my own experience, during a sojourn of nineteen years in the colony.

In order to diversify my subject, and make it as amusing as possible, I have between the sketches introduced a few small poems, all written during my residence in Canada, and descriptive of the country.

In this pleasing task I have been assisted by my husband, J.W. Dunbar Moodie, author of 'Ten Years in South Africa'.[2]

BELLEVILLE, UPPER CANADA

1854

[2]Published in 1835, the story of Dunbar Moodie's years (1819-29) with his brother at his farm near Sellendam, South Africa.

I. A VISIT TO GROSSE ISLE

* * *

As the sun rose above the horizon, all these matter-of-fact circumstances were gradually forgotten and merged in the surpassing grandeur of the scene that rose majestically before me. The previous day had been dark and stormy; and a heavy fog had concealed the mountain chain, which forms the stupendous background to this sublime view, entirely from our sight. As the clouds rolled away from their grey, bald brows, and cast into denser shadow the vast forest belt that girdled them round, they loomed out like mighty giants—Titans of the earth, in all their rugged and awful beauty—a thrill of wonder and delight pervaded my mind. The spectacle floated dimly on my sight—my eyes were blinded with tears—blinded with the excess of beauty. I turned to the right and to the left, I looked up and down the glorious river; never had I beheld so many striking objects blended into one mighty whole! Nature had lavished all her noblest features in producing that enchanting scene.

The rocky isle in front, with its neat farm-houses at the eastern point, and its high bluff at the western extremity, crowned with the telegraph—the middle space occupied by tents and sheds for the cholera patients, and its wooded shores dotted over with motley groups—added greatly to the picturesque effect of the land scene. Then the broad glittering river, covered with boats darting to and fro, conveying passengers from twenty-five vessels, of various size and tonnage, which rode at anchor, with their flags flying from the mast-head, gave an air of life and interest to the whole. Turning to the south side of the St Lawrence, I was not less struck with its low fertile shores, white houses, and neat churches, whose slender spires and bright tin roofs shone like silver as they caught the first rays of the sun. As far as the eye could reach, a line of white buildings extended along the bank; their background formed by the purple hue of the dense, interminable forest. It was a scene unlike any I had ever beheld, and to which Britain contains no parallel. Mackenzie, an old Scotch dragoon, who was one of our passengers, when he rose in the morning and saw the parish of St Thomas for the first time, exclaimed: 'Weel, it beats a'! Can thae white clouts[1] be a' houses? They look like claes hung out to drie!' There was some truth in this odd comparison, and for some minutes I could scarcely convince myself that the white patches scattered so thickly over the opposite shore could be the dwellings of a busy, lively population.

'What sublime views of the north side of the river those *habitans* of St Thomas must enjoy,' thought I. Perhaps familiarity with the scene has rendered them indifferent to its astonishing beauty.

Eastward, the view down the St Lawrence towards the Gulf is the finest of all, scarcely surpassed by anything in the world. Your eye follows the long range of lofty mountains until their blue summits are blended and lost in the blue of the sky. Some of these, partially cleared round the base, are sprinkled over with neat cottages, and the green slopes that spread around them are covered with flocks and herds. The surface of the splendid river is diversified with islands of every size and shape, some in wood, others partially cleared, and adorned with orchards and white farm-houses. As the early sun streamed upon the most prominent of these, leaving the others in deep shade, the effect was strangely novel and imposing. In more remote regions, where the forest has never yet echoed to the woodman's axe, or received the impress of civilisation, the first approach to the shore inspires a melancholy awe which becomes painful in its intensity.

[1]Cloths; 'claes', clothes.

Land of vast hills, and mighty streams,
The lofty sun that o'er thee beams
On fairer clime sheds not his ray,
When basking in the noon of day
Thy waters dance in silver light,
And o'er them frowning, dark as night,
Thy shadowy forests, soaring high,
Stretch forth beyond the aching eye,
And blend in distance with the sky.

And silence—awful silence broods
Profoundly o'er these solitudes;
Not but the lapsing of the floods
Breaks the deep stillness of the woods;
A sense of desolation reigns
O'er these unpeopled forest plains
Where sounds of life ne'er wake a tone
Of cheerful praise round Nature's throne,
Man finds himself with God—alone.

My daydreams were dispelled by the return of the boat, which brought my husband and the captain from the island.

'No bread,' said the latter, shaking his head; 'you must be content to starve a little longer. Provision-ship not in till four o'clock.' My husband smiled at the look of blank disappointment with which I received these unwelcome tidings. 'Never mind, I have news which will comfort you. The officer who commands the station sent a note to me by an orderly, inviting us to spend the afternoon with him. He promises to show us everything worthy of notice on the island. Captain —— claims acquaintance with me; but I have not the least recollection of him. Would you like to go?'

'Oh, by all means. I long to see the lovely island. It looks a perfect paradise at this distance.'

The rough sailor-captain screwed his mouth on one side, and gave me one of his comical looks; but he said nothing until he assisted in placing me and the baby in the boat.

'Don't be too sanguine, Mrs Moodie; many things look well at a distance which are bad enough when near.'

I scarcely regarded the old sailor's warning, so eager was I to go on shore—to put my foot upon the soil of the new world for the first time. I was in no humour to listen to any depreciation of what seemed so beautiful.

It was four o'clock when we landed on the rocks, which the rays of an intensely scorching sun had rendered so hot that I could scarcely place my foot upon them. How the people without shoes bore it I cannot imagine. Never shall I forget the extraordinary spectacle that met our sight the moment we passed the low range of bushes which formed a screen in front of the river. A crowd of many hundred Irish emigrants had been landed during the present and former day and all this motley crew—men, women, and children, who were not confined by sickness to the sheds (which greatly resembled cattle-pens)—were employed in washing clothes or spreading them out on the rocks and bushes to dry.

The men and boys were *in* the water, while the women, with their scanty garments tucked above their knees, were tramping their bedding in tubs or in holes in the rocks, which the retiring tide had left half full of water. Those who did not possess washing tubs, pails, or iron pots, or could not obtain access to a hole in the rocks, were running to and fro, screaming and scolding in no measured terms. The confusion of Babel was among them. All talkers and no hearers—each shouting and yelling in his or her uncouth dialect, and all accompanying their vociferations with violent and extraordinary gestures, quite incomprehensible to the uninitiated. We were literally stunned by the strife of tongues. I shrank, with feelings almost akin to fear, from the hard-featured, sun-burnt harpies as they elbowed rudely past me.

I had heard and read much of savages, and have since seen, during my long residence in the bush, somewhat of uncivilised life; but the Indian is one of Nature's gentlemen—he never says or does a rude or vulgar thing. The vicious, uneducated barbarians, who form the surplus of overpopulous European countries, are far behind the wild man in delicacy of feeling or natural courtesy. The people who covered the island appeared perfectly destitute of shame, or even a sense of common decency. Many were almost naked, still more but partially clothed. We turned in disgust from the revolting scene, but were unable to leave the spot until the captain had satisfied a noisy group of his own people, who were demanding a supply of stores.

And here I must observe that our passengers, who were chiefly honest Scotch labourers and mechanics from the vicinity of Edinburgh, and who while on board ship had conducted themselves with the greatest propriety, and appeared the most quiet, orderly set of people in the world, no sooner set foot upon the island than they became infected by the same spirit of insubordination and misrule, and were just as insolent and noisy as the rest.

While our captain was vainly endeavouring to satisfy the unreasonable demands of his rebellious people, Moodie had discovered a woodland path that led to the back of the island. Sheltered by some hazel-bushes from the intense heat of the sun, we sat down by the cool, gushing river, out of sight, but, alas! not out of hearing of the noisy, riotous crowd. Could we have shut out the profane sounds which came to us on every breeze, how deeply should we have enjoyed an hour amid the tranquil beauties of that retired and lovely spot!

* * *

VIII. UNCLE JOE AND HIS FAMILY

Ay, your rogue is a laughing rogue, and not a whit the less dangerous for the smile on his lip, which comes not from an honest heart, which reflects the light of the soul through the eye. All is hollow and dark within; and the contortion of the lip, like the phosphoric glow upon decayed timber, only serves to point out the rottenness within.

Uncle Joe! I see him now before me, with his jolly red face, twinkling black eyes, and rubicund nose. No thin, weasel-faced Yankee was he, looking as if he had lived upon 'cute[1] ideas and speculations all his life; yet Yankee he was by birth, ay, and in mind, too; for a more knowing fellow at a bargain never crossed the lakes to abuse

---

[1] Acute, cunning.

British institutions and locate himself comfortably among the despised Britishers. But, then, he had such a good-natured, fat face, such a mischievous, mirth-loving smile, and such a merry, roguish expression in those small, jet-black, glittering eyes, that you suffered yourself to be taken in by him, without offering the least resistance to his impositions.

Uncle Joe's father had been a New England loyalist, and his doubtful attachment to the British government had been repaid by a grant of land in the township of H——. He was the first settler in that township, and chose his location in a remote spot, for the sake of a beautiful natural spring, which bubbled up in a small stone basin in the green bank at the back of the house.

'Father might have had the pick of the township,' quoth Uncle Joe; 'but the old coon preferred that sup of good water to the site of a town. Well, I guess it's seldom I trouble the spring; and whenever I step that way to water the horses, I think what a tarnation fool the old one was, to throw away such a chance of making his fortune for such cold lap.'[2]

'Your father was a temperance man?'[3]

'Temperance!—He had been fond enough of the whiskey bottle in his day. He drank up a good farm in the United States, and then he thought he could not do better than turn loyal, and get one here for nothing. He did not care a cent, not he, for the King of England. He thought himself as good, anyhow. But he found that he would have to work hard here to scratch along, and he was mightily plagued with the rheumatics, and some old woman told him that good spring water was the best cure for that; so he chose this poor, light, stony land on account of the spring, and took to hard work and drinking cold water in his old age.'

'How did the change agree with him?'

'I guess better than could have been expected. He planted that fine orchard, and cleared his hundred acres, and we got along slick enough as long as the old fellow lived.'

'And what happened after his death, that obliged you to part with your land?'

'Bad times—bad crops,' said Uncle Joe, lifting his shoulders. 'I had not my father's way of scraping money together. I made some deuced clever speculations, but they all failed. I married young, and got a large family; and the women critters ran up heavy bills at the stores, and the crops did not yield enough to pay them; and from bad we got to worse, and Mr C —— put in an execution,[4] and seized upon the whole concern. He sold it to your man for double what it cost him; and you got all that my father toiled for during the last twenty years of his life for less than half the cash he laid out upon clearing it.'

'And had the whiskey nothing to do with this change?' said I, looking him in the face suspiciously.

'Not a bit! When a man gets into difficulties, it is the only thing to keep him from sinking outright. When your husband has had as many troubles as I have had, he will know how to value the whiskey bottle.'

---

[2]Weak drink.

[3]A man advocating abstinence from liquor, or one who has sworn to abstain.

[4]The seizure of goods under law in default of payment.

This conversation was interrupted by a queer-looking urchin of five years old, dressed in a long-tailed coat and trowsers, popping his black shock head in at the door, and calling out,

'Uncle Joe!—You're wanted to hum.'[5]

'Is that your nephew?'

'No! I guess 'tis my woman's eldest son,' said Uncle Joe, rising, 'but they call me Uncle Joe. 'Tis a spry chap that—as cunning as a fox. I tell you what it is—he will make a smart man. Go home, Ammon, and tell your ma that I am coming.'

'I won't,' said the boy; 'you may go hum and tell her yourself. She has wanted wood cut this hour, and you'll catch it!'

Away ran the dutiful son, but not before he had applied his forefinger significantly to the side of his nose, and, with a knowing wink, pointed in the direction of home.

Uncle Joe obeyed the signal, drily remarking that he could not leave the barn door without the old hen clucking him back.

At this period we were still living in Old Satan's log house, and anxiously looking out for the first snow to put us in possession of the good substantial log dwelling occupied by Uncle Joe and his family, which consisted of a brown brood of seven girls, and the highly-prized boy who rejoiced in the extraordinary name of Ammon.

Strange names are to be found in this free country. What think you, gentle reader, of *Solomon Sly, Reynard Fox*, and *Hiram Dolittle*; all veritable names, and belonging to substantial yeomen? After Ammon and Ichabod, I should not be at all surprised to meet with Judas Iscariot, Pilate, and Herod. And then the female appellations! But the subject is a delicate one, and I will forbear to touch upon it. I have enjoyed many a hearty laugh over the strange affectations which people designate here *very handsome names*. I prefer the old homely Jewish names, such as that which it pleased my godfather and godmothers to bestow upon me, to one of those high-sounding christianities, the Minervas, Cinderellas, and Almerias of Canada. The love of singular names is here carried to a marvellous extent. It is only yesterday that, in passing through one busy village, I stopped in astonishment before a tombstone headed thus:—'Sacred to the memory of *Silence* Sharman, the beloved wife of Asa Sharman.' Was the woman deaf and dumb, or did her friends hope by bestowing upon her such an impossible name to still the voice of Nature, and check, by an admonitory appellative, the active spirit that lives in the tongue of woman? Truly, Asa Sharman, if thy wife was silent by name as well as by nature, thou wert a fortunate man!

But to return to Uncle Joe. He made many fair promises of leaving the residence we had bought, the moment he had sold his crops and could remove his family. We could see no interest which could be served by his deceiving us, and therefore we believed him, striving to make ourselves as comfortable as we could in the meantime in our present wretched abode. But matters are never so bad but that they may be worse. One day when we were at dinner, a waggon drove up to the door, and Mr —— alighted, accompanied by a fine-looking, middle-aged man, who proved to be Captain S ——, who had just arrived from Demerara[6] with his wife and family. Mr ——, who had purchased the farm of Old Satan, had brought Captain S —— over to

[5]At home.
[6]British Guiana.

inspect the land, as he wished to buy a farm, and settle in that neighbourhood. With some difficulty, I contrived to accommodate the visitors with seats, and provide them with a tolerable dinner. Fortunately, Moodie had brought in a brace of fine fat partridges that morning; these the servant transferred to a pot of boiling water, in which she immersed them for the space of a minute—a novel but very expeditious way of removing the feathers, which then come off at the least touch. In less than ten minutes they were stuffed, trussed, and in the bake-kettle; and before the gentlemen returned from walking over the farm, the dinner was on the table.

To our utter consternation, Captain S —— agreed to purchase, and asked if we could give him possession in a week!

'Good heavens!' cried I, glancing reproachfully at Mr ——, who was discussing[7] his partridge with stoical indifference. 'What will become of us? Where are we to go?'

'Oh, make yourself easy; I will force that old witch, Joe's mother, to clear out.'

'But 'tis impossible to stow ourselves into that pig-sty.'

'It will only be for a week or two, at farthest. This is October; Joe will be sure to be off by the first of sleighing.'

'But if she refuses to give up the place?'

'Oh, leave her to me. I'll talk her over,' said the knowing land speculator. 'Let it come to the worst,' he said, turning to my husband, 'she will go out for the sake of a few dollars. By-the-by, she refused to bar the dower[8] when I bought the place; we must cajole her out of that. It is a fine afternoon; suppose we walk over the hill, and try our luck with the old nigger?'

I felt so anxious about the result of the negotiation, that, throwing my cloak over my shoulders, and tying on my bonnet without the assistance of a glass, I took my husband's arm, and we walked forth.

It was a bright, clear afternoon, the first week in October, and the fading woods, not yet denuded of their gorgeous foliage, glowed in a mellow, golden light. A soft, purple haze rested on the bold outline of the Haldimand hills, and in the rugged beauty of the wild landscape I soon forgot the purport of our visit to the old woman's log hut.

On reaching the ridge of the hill, the lovely valley in which our future home lay smiled peacefully upon us from amidst its fruitful orchards, still loaded with their rich, ripe fruit.

'What a pretty place it is!' thought I, for the first time feeling something like a local interest in the spot springing up in my heart. 'How I wish those odious people would give us possession of the home which for some time has been our own!'

The log hut that we were approaching, and in which the old woman, H ——, resided, by herself—having quarrelled years ago with her son's wife—was of the smallest dimensions, only containing one room, which served the old dame for kitchen, and bed-room, and all. The open door, and a few glazed panes, supplied it with light and air; while a huge hearth, on which crackled two enormous logs—which are tech-

---

[7]Consuming (humorous).

[8]Void her right to legal tenancy. Joe had inherited the land from his father, but his mother had use of it during her lifetime.

nically termed a front and a back stick—took up nearly half the domicile; and the old woman's bed, which was covered with an unexceptionally clean patched quilt, nearly the other half, leaving just room for a small home-made deal[9] table, of the rudest workmanship, two basswood-bottomed chairs, stained red, one of which was a rocking-chair, appropriated solely to the old woman's use, and a spinning-wheel. Amidst this muddle of things—for, small as was the quantum of furniture, it was all crowded into such a tiny space that you had to squeeze your way through it in the best manner you could—we found the old woman, with a red cotton handkerchief tied over her grey locks, hood-fashion, shelling white bush-beans into a wooden bowl. Without rising from her seat, she pointed to the only remaining chair. 'I guess, miss, you can sit there; and if the others can't stand, they can make a seat of my bed.'

The gentlemen assured her that they were not tired, and could dispense with seats. Mr —— then went up to the old woman, and proffering his hand, asked after her health in his blandest manner.

'I'm none the better for seeing you, or the like of you,' was the ungracious reply. 'You have cheated my poor boy out of his good farm; and I hope it may prove a bad bargain to you and yours.'

'Mrs H ——,' returned the land speculator, nothing ruffled by her unceremonious greeting, 'I could not help your son giving way to drink, and getting into my debt. If people will be so imprudent, they cannot be so stupid as to imagine that others can suffer for their folly.'

'*Suffer!*' repeated the old woman, flashing her small, keen black eyes upon him with a glance of withering scorn. 'You suffer! I wonder what the widows and orphans you have cheated would say to that! My son was a poor, weak, silly fool to be sucked in by the like of you. For a debt of eight hundred dollars—the goods never cost you four hundred—you take from us our good farm; and these, I s'pose,' pointing to my husband and me, 'are the folk you sold it to. Pray, miss,' turning quickly to me, 'what might your man give for the place?'

'Three hundred pounds in cash.'

'Poor sufferer!' again sneered the hag. 'Four hundred dollars is a very *small* profit in as many weeks. Well, I guess, you beat the Yankees hollow. And pray, what brought you here to-day, scenting about you like a carrion-crow? We have no more land for you to seize from us.'

Moodie now stepped forward, and briefly explained our situation, offering the old woman anything in reason to give up the cottage and reside with her son until he removed from the premises; which, he added, must be in a very short time.

The old dame regarded him with a sarcastic smile. 'I guess, Joe will take his own time. The house is not built which is to receive him; and he is not a man to turn his back upon a warm hearth to camp in the wilderness. You were *green* when you bought a farm of that man, without getting along with it the right of possession.'[1]

'But, Mrs H ——, your son promised to go out the first of sleighing.'

'Wheugh!' said the old woman. 'Would you have a man give away his hat and

---

[9]Pine wood.
[1]Right of occupancy as distinguished from ownership.

leave his own head bare? It's neither the first snow nor the last frost that will turn Joe out of his comfortable home. I tell you all that he will stay here, if it is only to plague you.'

Threats and remonstrances were alike useless, the old woman remained inexorable; and we were just turning to leave the house, when the cunning old fox exclaimed, 'And now, what will you give me to leave my place?'

'Twelve dollars, if you give us possession next Monday,' said my husband.

'Twelve dollars! I guess you won't get me out for that.'

'The rent would not be worth more than a dollar a month,' said Mr ——, pointing with his cane to the dilapidated walls. 'Mr Moodie has offered you a year's rent for the place.'

'It may not be worth a cent,' returned the woman, 'for it will give everybody the rheumatism that stays a week in it—but it is worth that to me, and more nor[2] double that just now to him. But I will not be hard with him,' continued she, rocking herself to and fro. 'Say twenty dollars, and I will turn out on Monday.'

'I dare say you will,' said Mr ——, 'and who do you think would be fool enough to give you such an exorbitant sum for a ruined old shed like this?'

'Mind your own business, and make your own bargains,' returned the old woman, tartly. 'The devil himself could not deal with you, for I guess he would have the worst of it. What do you say, sir?' and she fixed her keen eyes upon my husband, as if she would read his thoughts. 'Will you agree to my price?'

'It is a very high one, Mrs H ——; but as I cannot help myself, and you take advantage of that, I suppose I must give it.'

''Tis a bargain,' cried the old crone, holding out her hard, bony hand. 'Come, cash down!'

'Not until you give me possession on Monday next; or you might serve me as your son has done.'

'Ha!' said the old woman, laughing and rubbing her hands together; 'you begin to see daylight, do you? In a few months, with the help of him,' pointing to Mr ——, 'you will be able to go alone; but have a care of your teacher, for it's no good that you will learn from him. But will you *really* stand to your word, mister?' she added, in a coaxing tone, 'if I go out on Monday?'

'To be sure I will; I never break my word.'

'Well, I guess you are not so clever as our people, for they only keep it as long as it suits them. You have an honest look; I will trust you; but I will not trust him,' nodding to Mr ——, 'he can buy and sell his word as fast as a horse can trot. So on Monday I will turn out my traps. I have lived here six-and-thirty years; 'tis a pretty place, and it vexes me to leave it,' continued the poor creature, as a touch of natural feeling softened and agitated her world-hardened heart. 'There is not an acre in cultivation but I helped to clear it, nor a tree in yonder orchard but I held it while my poor man, who is dead and gone, planted it; and I have watched the trees bud from year to year, until their boughs over-shadowed the hut, where all my children, but Joe, were born. Yes, I came here young, and in my prime; and must leave it in age and poverty. My children and husband are dead, and their bones rest beneath the turf in

2Than.

the burying-ground on the side of the hill. Of all that once gathered about my knees, Joe and his young ones alone remain. And it is hard, very hard, that I must leave their graves to be turned by the plough of a stranger.

I felt for the desolate old creature—the tears rushed to my eyes; but there was no moisture in hers. No rain from the heart could filter through that iron soil.

'Be assured, Mrs H ——,' said Moodie, 'that the dead will be held sacred; the place will never be disturbed by me.'

'Perhaps not; but it is not long that you will remain here. I have seen a good deal in my time; but I never saw a gentleman from the old country make a good Canadian farmer. The work is rough and hard, and they get out of humour with it, and leave it to their hired helps, and then all goes wrong. They are cheated on all sides, and in despair take to the whiskey bottle, and that fixes them. I tell you what it is, mister—I give you just three years to spend your money and ruin yourself; and then you will become a confirmed drunkard, like the rest.'

The first part of her prophecy was only too true. Thank God! the last has never been fulfilled, and never can be.

Perceiving that the old woman was not a little elated with her bargain, Mr —— urged upon her the propriety of barring the dower. At first, she was outrageous, and very abusive, and rejected all his proposals with contempt; vowing that she would meet him in a certain place below, before she would sign away her right to the property.

'Listen to reason, Mrs H ——,' said the land speculator. 'If you will sign the papers before the proper authorities, the next time that your son drives you to C ——, I will give you a silk gown.'

'Pshaw! Buy a shroud for yourself; you will need it before I want a silk gown,' was the ungracious reply.

'Consider, woman; a black silk of the best quality.'

'To mourn in for my sins, or for the loss of the farm?'

'Twelve yards,' continued Mr ——, without noticing her rejoinder, 'at a dollar a yard. Think what a nice church-going gown it will make.'

'To the devil with you! I never go to church.'

'I thought as much,' said Mr ——, winking to us. 'Well, my dear madam, what will satisfy you?'

'I'll do it for twenty dollars,' returned the old woman, rocking herself to and fro in her chair; her eyes twinkling, and her hands moving convulsively, as if she already grasped the money so dear to her soul.

'Agreed,' said the land speculator. 'When will you be in town?'

'On Tuesday, if I be alive. But, remember, I'll not sign till I have my hand on the money.'

'Never fear,' said Mr ——, as we quitted the house; then, turning to me, he added, with a peculiar smile, 'That's a devilish smart woman. She would have made a clever lawyer.'

Monday came, and with it all the bustle of moving, and, as is generally the case on such occasions, it turned out a very wet day. I left Old Satan's hut without regret, glad, at any rate, to be in a place of my own, however humble. Our new habitation, though small, had a decided advantage over the one we were leaving. It stood on a gentle slope; and a narrow but lovely stream, full of speckled trout, ran murmuring under the little window; the house, also, was surrounded by fine fruit trees.

I know not how it was, but the sound of that tinkling brook, for ever rolling by, filled my heart with a strange melancholy, which for many nights deprived me of rest. I loved it, too. The voice of waters, in the stillness of night, always had an extraordinary effect upon my mind. Their ceaseless motion and perpetual sound convey to me the idea of life—eternal life; and looking upon them, glancing and flashing on, now in sunshine, now in shade, now hoarsely chiding with the opposing rock, now leaping triumphantly over it,—creates within me a feeling of mysterious awe of which I never could wholly divest myself.

A portion of my own spirit seemed to pass into that little stream. In its deep wailings and fretful sighs, I fancied myself lamenting for the land I had left for ever; and its restless and impetuous rushings against the stones which choked its passage, were mournful types of my own mental struggles against the strange destiny which hemmed me in. Through the day the stream still moaned and travelled on,—but, engaged in my novel and distasteful occupations, I heard it not; but whenever my winged thoughts flew homeward, then the voice of the brook spoke deeply and sadly to my heart, and my tears flowed unchecked to its plaintive and harmonious music.

In a few hours I had my new abode more comfortably arranged than the old one, although its dimensions were much smaller. The location was beautiful, and I was greatly consoled by this circumstance. The aspect of Nature ever did, and I hope ever will, continue—

'To shoot marvellous strength into my heart.'

As long as we remain true to Divine Mother, so long will she remain faithful to her suffering children.

At that period my love for Canada was a feeling very nearly allied to that which the condemned criminal entertains for his cell—his only hope of escape being through the portals of the grave.

The fall rains had commenced. In a few days the cold wintry showers swept all the gorgeous crimson from the trees, and a bleak and desolate waste presented itself to the shuddering spectator. But, in spite of wind and rain, my little tenement was never free from the intrusion of Uncle Joe's wife and children. Their house stood about a stone's-throw from the hut we occupied, in the same meadow, and they seemed to look upon it still as their own, although we had literally paid for it twice over. Fine strapping girls they were, from five years old to fourteen, but rude and unnurtured as so many bears. They would come in without the least ceremony, and, young as they were, ask me a thousand impertinent questions; and when I civilly requested them to leave the room, they would range themselves upon the door-step, watching my motions, with their black eyes gleaming upon me through their tangled, uncombed locks. Their company was a great annoyance, for it obliged me to put a painful restraint upon the thoughtfulness in which it was so delightful to me to indulge. Their visits were not visits of love, but of mere idle curiosity, not unmingled with malicious hatred.

The simplicity, the fond, confiding faith of childhood is unknown in Canada. There are no children here. The boy is a miniature man—knowing, keen, and wide awake; as able to drive a bargain and take an advantage of his juvenile companion as the grown-up, world-hardened man. The girl, a gossipping flirt, full of vanity and affectation, with a premature love of finery, and an acute perception of the advantages to be derived from wealth, and from keeping up a certain appearance in the world.

The flowers, the green grass, the glorious sunshine, the birds of the air, and the young lambs gambolling down the verdant slopes, which fill the heart of a British child with a fond ecstacy, bathing the young spirit in Elysium, would float unnoticed before the vision of a Canadian child; while the sight of a dollar, or a new dress, or a gay bonnet, would swell its proud bosom with self-importance and delight. The glorious blush of modest diffidence, the tear of gentle sympathy, are so rare on the cheek, or in the eye of the young, that their appearance creates a feeling of surprise. Such perfect self-reliance in beings so new to the world is painful to a thinking mind. It betrays a great want of sensibility and mental culture, and a melancholy knowledge of the arts of life.

For a week I was alone, my good Scotch girl having left me to visit her father. Some small baby-articles were needed to be washed, and after making a great preparation, I determined to try my unskilled hand upon the operation. The fact is, I knew nothing about the task I had imposed upon myself, and in a few minutes rubbed the skin off my wrists without getting the clothes clean.

The door was open, as it generally was, even during the coldest winter days, in order to let in more light, and let out the smoke, which otherwise would have enveloped us like a cloud. I was so busy that I did not perceive that I was watched by the cold, heavy, dark eyes of Mrs Joe, who, with a sneering laugh, exclaimed,

'Well, thank God! I am glad to see you brought to work at last. I hope you may have to work as hard as I have. I don't see, not I, why you, who are no better than me, should sit still all day, like a lady!'

'Mrs H ——,' said I, not a little annoyed at her presence, 'what concern is it of yours whether I work or sit still? I never interfere with you. If you took it into your head to lie in bed all day, I should never trouble myself about it.'

'Ah, I guess you don't look upon us as fellow-critters, you are so proud and grand. I s'pose you Britishers are not made of flesh and blood, like us. You don't choose to sit down at meat with your helps. Now, I calculate, we think them a great deal better nor you.'

'Of course,' said I, 'they are more suited to you than we are; they are uneducated, and so are you. This is no fault in either; but it might teach you to pay a little more respect to those who are possessed of superior advantages. But, Mrs H ——, my helps, as you call them, are civil and obliging, and never make unprovoked and malicious speeches. If they could so far forget themselves, I should order them to leave the house.'

'Oh, I see what you are up to,' replied the insolent dame; 'you mean to say that if I were your help, you would turn me out of your house; but I'm a free-born American, and I won't go at your bidding. Don't think I come here out of regard to you. No, I hate you all; and I rejoice to see you at the wash-tub, and I wish that you may be brought down upon your knees to scrub the floors.'

This speech only caused a smile, and yet I felt hurt and astonished that a woman whom I had never done anything to offend should be so gratuitously spiteful.

In the evening she sent two of her brood over to borrow my 'long iron', as she called an Italian iron.[3] I was just getting my baby to sleep, sitting upon a low stool by the fire. I pointed to the iron upon the shelf, and told the girl to take it. She did so, but stood beside me, holding it carelessly in her hand, and staring at the baby, who had just sunk to sleep upon my lap.

The next moment the heavy iron fell from her relaxed grasp, giving me a severe blow upon my knee and foot; and glanced so near the child's head that it drew from me a cry of terror.

'I guess that was nigh braining the child,' quoth Miss Amanda, with the greatest coolness, and without making the least apology. Master Ammon burst into a loud laugh. 'If it had, Mandy, I guess we'd have cotched it.' Provoked at their insolence, I told them to leave the house. The tears were in my eyes, for I felt certain that had they injured the child, it would not have caused them the least regret.

The next day, as we were standing at the door, my husband was greatly amused by seeing fat Uncle Joe chasing the rebellious Ammon over the meadow in front of the house. Joe was out of breath, panting and puffing like a small steam-engine, and his face flushed to deep red with excitement and passion.

'You —— young scoundrel!' he cried, half choked with fury, 'if I catch up to you, I'll take the skin off you!'

'You —— old scoundrel, you may have my skin if you can get at me,' retorted the precocious child, as he jumped up upon the top of the high fence, and doubled his fist in a menacing manner at his father.

'That boy is growing too bad,' said Uncle Joe, coming up to us out of breath, the perspiration streaming down his face. 'It is time to break him in, or he'll get the master of us all.'

'You should have begun that before,' said Moodie. 'He seems a hopeful pupil.'

'Oh, as to that, a little swearing is manly,' returned the father; 'I swear myself, I know, and as the old cock crows, so crows the young one. It is not his swearing that I care a pin for, but he will not do a thing I tell him to.'

'Swearing is a dreadful vice,' said I, 'and, wicked as it is in the mouth of a grown-up person, it is perfectly shocking in a child; it painfully tells he has been brought up without the fear of God.'

'Pooh! pooh! that's all cant; there is no harm in a few oaths, and I cannot drive oxen and horses without swearing. I dare say that you can swear, too, when you are riled, but you are too cunning to let us hear you.'

I could not help laughing outright at this supposition, but replied very quietly, 'Those who practice such iniquities never take any pains to conceal them. The concealment would infer a feeling of shame; and when people are conscious of their guilt, they are in the road to improvement.' The man walked whistling away, and the wicked child returned unpunished to his home.

The next minute the old woman came in. 'I guess you can give me a piece of silk for a hood,' said she, 'the weather is growing considerable cold.'

[3]Iron of a special shape for pressing clothes. In Chapter 5, 'Our First Settlement, & the Borrowing System', Moodie describes how this woman perpetually borrowed items: 'Day after day I was tormented by this importunate creature; she borrowed of me tea, sugar, candles, starch, blueing, irons, pots, bowls—in short, every article in common domestic use—while it was with utmost difficulty we could get them returned. . . . This method of living upon their neighbours is a most convenient one to unprincipled people.'

'Surely it cannot well be colder than it is at present,' said I, giving her the rocking-chair by the fire.

'Wait a while; you know nothing of a Canadian winter. This is only November; after the Christmas thaw, you'll know something about cold. It is seven-and-thirty years ago since I and my man left the U-ni-ted States. It was called the year of the great winter. I tell you, woman, that the snow lay so deep on the earth, that it blocked up all the roads, and we could drive a sleigh whither we pleased, right over the snake fences.[4] All the cleared land was one wide white level plain; it was a year of scarcity, and we were half starved; but the severe cold was far worse nor the want of provisions. A long and bitter journey we had of it; but I was young then, and pretty well used to trouble and fatigue; my man stuck to the British government. More fool he! I was an American born, and my heart was with the true cause. But his father was English, and, says he, "I'll live and die under their flag." So he dragged me from my comfortable fireside to seek a home in the far Canadian wilderness. Trouble! I guess you think you have your troubles; but what are they to mine?' She paused, took a pinch of snuff, offered me the box, sighed painfully, pushed the red handkerchief from her high, narrow, wrinkled brow, and continued:—'Joe was a baby then, and I had another helpless critter in my lap—an adopted child. My sister had died from it, and I was nursing it at the same breast with my boy. Well, we had to perform a journey of four hundred miles in an ox-cart, which carried, besides me and the children, all our household stuff. Our way lay chiefly through the forest, and we made but slow progress. Oh! what a bitter cold night it was when we reached the swampy woods where the city of Rochester now stands. The oxen were covered with icicles, and their breath sent up clouds of steam. "Nathan," says I to my man, "you must stop and kindle a fire; I am dead with cold, and I fear the babes will be frozen." We began looking about for a good spot to camp in, when I spied a light through the trees. It was a lone shanty, occupied by two French lumberers. The men were kind; they rubbed our frozen limbs with snow, and shared with us their supper and buffalo skins. On that very spot where we camped that night, where we heard nothing but the wind soughing amongst the trees, and the rushing of the river, now stands the great city of Rochester. I went there two years ago, to the funeral of a brother. It seemed to me like a dream. Where we foddered our beasts by the shanty fire, now stands the largest hotel in the city; and my husband left this fine growing country to starve here.'

I was so much interested in the old woman's narrative—for she was really possessed of no ordinary capacity, and, though rude and uneducated might have been a very superior person under different circumstances—that I rummaged among my stores, and soon found a piece of black silk, which I gave her for the hood she required.

The old woman examined it carefully over, smiled to herself, but, like all her people, was too proud to return a word of thanks. One gift to the family always involved another.

'Have you any cotton-batting, or black sewing-silk, to give me, to quilt it with?'

'No.'

'Humph!' returned the old dame, in a tone which seemed to contradict my asser-

---

[4]Zigzag fences made of split rails.

tion. She then settled herself in her chair, and, after shaking her foot a while, and fixing her piercing eyes upon me for some minutes, she commenced the following list of interrogatories:—

'Is your father alive?'

'No; he died many years ago, when I was a young girl.'

'Is your mother alive?'

'Yes.'

'What is her name?' I satisfied her on this point.

'Did she ever marry again?'

'She might have done so, but she loved her husband too well, and preferred living single.'

'Humph! We have no such notions here. What was your father?'

'A gentleman, who lived upon his own estate.'

'Did he die rich?'

'He lost the greater part of his property from being surety for another.'[5]

'That's a foolish business. My man burnt his fingers with that. And what brought you out to this poor country—you, who are no more fit for it than I am to be a fine lady?'

'The promise of a large grant of land, and the false statements we heard regarding it.'

'Do you like the country?'

'No; and I fear I never shall.'

'I thought not; for the drop is always on your cheek, the children tell me; and those young ones have keen eyes. Now, take my advice: return while your money lasts; the longer you remain in Canada the less you will like it; and when your money is all spent, you will be like a bird in a cage; you may beat your wings against the bars, but you can't get out.' There was a long pause. I hoped that my guest had sufficiently gratified her curiosity, when she again commenced:—

'How do you get your money? Do you draw it from the old country, or have you it with you in cash?'

Provoked by her pertinacity, and seeing no end to her cross-questioning, I replied very impatiently, 'Mrs H ——, is it the custom in your country to catechize strangers whenever you meet with them?'

'What do you mean?' she said, colouring, I believe, for the first time in her life.

'I mean,' quoth I, 'an evil habit of asking impertinent questons.'

The old woman got up, and left the house without speaking another word.

[During the winter of 1833 the Moodies finally moved into their new house. When spring came they brought in a man and his wife to help work the farm in return for a share of the produce. These people unfortunately proved not to be trustworthy. With them, Mrs Moodie writes, 'commenced that long series of losses and troubles to which their conduct formed the prelude.']

[5]Guaranteeing a loan by becoming responsible for the debt.

XI. BRIAN, THE STILL-HUNTER

O'er memory's glass I see his shadow flit,
Though he was gathered to the silent dust
Long years ago. A strange and wayward man,
That shunn'd companionship, and lived apart;
The leafy covert of the dark brown woods,
The gleamy lakes, hid in their gloomy depths,
Whose still, deep waters never knew the stroke
Of cleaving oar, or echoed to the sound
Of social life, contained for him the sum
Of human happiness. With dog and gun
Day after day he track'd the nimble deer
Through all the tangled mazes of the forest.

It was early day. I was alone in the old shanty, preparing breakfast, and now and then stirring the cradle with my foot, when a tall, thin, middle-aged man walked into the house, followed by two large, strong dogs.

Placing the rifle he had carried on his shoulder in a corner of the room, he advanced to the hearth, and, without speaking, or seemingly looking at me, lighted his pipe, and commenced smoking. The dogs, after growling and snapping at the cat, who had not given the strangers a very courteous reception, sat down on the hearthstone on either side of their taciturn master, eyeing him from time to time, as if long habit had made them understand all his motions. There was a great contrast between the dogs. The one was a brindled bull dog of the largest size, a most formidable and powerful brute; the other a stag hound, tawny, deep-chested, and strong-limbed. I regarded the man and his hairy companions with silent curiosity.

He was between forty and fifty years of age; his head, nearly bald, was studded at the sides with strong, coarse, black curling hair. His features were high, his complexion brightly dark, and his eyes, in size, shape, and colour, greatly resembling the eyes of a hawk. The face itself was sorrowful and taciturn; and his thin, compressed lips looked as if they were not much accustomed to smile, or often to unclose to hold social communion with any one. He stood at the side of the huge hearth, silently smoking, his eyes bent on the fire, and now and then he patted the heads of his dogs, reproving their exuberant expressions of attachment with—'Down, Music; down, Chance!'

'A cold, clear morning,' said I, in order to attract his attention and draw him into conversation.

A nod, without raising his head, or withdrawing his eyes from the fire, was his only answer; and, turning from my unsociable guest, I took up the baby, who just then awoke, sat down on a low stool by the table, and began feeding her. During this operation, I once or twice caught the stranger's hawk-eye fixed upon me and the child, but word spoke he none; and presently, after whistling to his dogs, he resumed his gun, and strode out.

When Moodie and Monaghan[1] came in to breakfast, I told them what a strange visitor I had had; and Moodie laughed at my vain attempt to induce him to talk.

'He is a strange being,' I said; 'I must find out who and what he is.'

In the afternoon an old soldier, called Layton, who had served during the American war, and got a grant of land about a mile in the rear of our location, came in to

[1]The Moodies' new hired man.

trade for a cow. Now, this Layton was a perfect ruffian; a man whom no one liked, and whom all feared. He was a deep drinker, a great swearer, in short, a perfect reprobate; who never cultivated his land, but went jobbing about from farm to farm, trading horses and cattle, and cheating in a pettifogging way. Uncle Joe had employed him to sell Moodie a young heifer, and he had brought her over for him to look at. When he came in to be paid, I described the stranger of the morning; and as I knew that he was familiar with every one in the neighbourhood, I asked if he knew him.

'No one should know him better than myself,' he said, "'tis old Brian B——, the still-hunter,[2] and a near neighbour of your'n. A sour, morose, queer chap he is, and as mad as a March hare! He's from Lancashire, in England, and came to this country some twenty years ago, with his wife, who was a pretty young lass in those days, and slim enough then, though she's so awfully fleshy now. He had lots of money, too, and he bought four hundred acres of land, just at the corner of the concession line, where it meets the main road. And excellent land it is; and a better farmer, while he stuck to his business, never went into the bush, for it was all bush here then. He was a dashing, handsome fellow, too, and did not hoard the money either; he loved his pipe and his pot too well; and at last he left off farming, and gave himself to them altogether. Many a jolly booze he and I have had, I can tell you. Brian was an awful passionate man, and, when the liquor was in, and the wit was out, as savage and as quarrelsome as a bear. At such times there was no one but Ned Layton dared go near him. We once had a pitched battle, in which I was conqueror, and ever arter he yielded a sort of sulky obedience to all I said to him. Arter being on the spree for a week or two, he would take fits of remorse, and return home to his wife; would fall down at her knees, and ask her forgiveness, and cry like a child. At other times he would hide himself up in the woods, and steal home at night, and get what he wanted out of the pantry, without speaking a word to any one. He went on with these pranks for some years, till he took a fit of the blue devils.

' "Come away, Ned, to the —— lake, with me," said he; "I am weary of my life, and I want a change."

' "Shall we take the fishing-tackle?" says I. "The black bass are in prime season, and F—— will lend us the old canoe. He's got some capital rum up from Kingston. We'll fish all day, and have a spree at night."

' "It's not to fish I'm going," says he.

' "To shoot, then? I've bought Rockwood's new rifle."

' "It's neither to fish nor to shoot, Ned; it's a new game I'm going to try; so come along."

'Well, to the —— lake we went. The day was very hot, and our path lay through the woods, and over those scorching plains, for eight long miles. I thought I should have dropped by the way; but during our long walk my companion never opened his lips. He strode on before me, at a half-run, never once turning his head.

' "The man must be a devil!" says I, "and accustomed to a warmer place, or he must feel this. Hollo, Brian! Stop there! Do you mean to kill me?"

' "Take it easy," says he; "you'll see another day arter this—I've business on hand and cannot wait."

---

[2]One who hunts game on foot or in a quiet or stealthy manner.

'Well, on we went, at the same awful rate, and it was midday when we got to the little tavern on the lake shore, kept by one F——, who had a boat for the convenience of strangers who came to visit the place. Here we got our dinner, and a glass of rum to wash it down. But Brian was moody, and to all my jokes he only returned a sort of grunt; and while I was talking with F ——, he steps out, and a few minutes arter we saw him crossing the lake in the old canoe.

' "What's the matter with Brian?" says F ——; "all does not seem right with him, Ned. You had better take the boat and look arter him."

' "Pooh!" says I; "he's often so, and grows so glum now-a-days that I will cut his acquaintance altogether if he does not improve."

' "He drinks awful hard," says F ——; "maybe he's got a fit of the delirium-tremulous. There is no telling what he may be up to at this minute."

'My mind misgave me too, so I e'en takes the oars, and pushes out, right upon Brian's tracks; and by the Lord Harry! if I did not find him, upon my landing on the opposite shore, lying wallowing in his blood, with his throat cut. "Is that you, Brian?" says I, giving him a kick with my foot, to see if he was alive or dead. "What upon earth tempted you to play me and F —— such a dirty, mean trick, as to go and stick yourself like a pig, bringing such a discredit upon the house?—and you so far from home and those who should nurse you."

'I was so mad with him, that (saving your presence, ma'am) I swore awfully, and called him names that would be ondacent to repeat here; but he only answered with groans and a horrid gurgling in his throat. "It's a choking you are," said I; "but you shan't have your own way and die so easily either, if I can punish you by keeping you alive." So I just turned him upon his stomach, with his head down the steep bank; but he still kept choking and growing black in the face.'

Layton then detailed some particulars of his surgical practice which it is not necessary to repeat. He continued—

'I bound up his throat with my handkerchief, and took him neck and heels, and threw him into the bottom of the boat. Presently he came to himself a little, and sat up in the boat; and—would you believe it?—made several attempts to throw himself into the water. "This will not do," says I; "you've done mischief enough already by cutting your weasand![3] If you dare to try that again, I will kill you with the oar." I held it up to threaten him; he was scared, and lay down as quiet as a lamb. I put my foot upon his breast. "Lie still, now! or you'll catch it." He looked piteously at me; he could not speak, but his eyes seemed to say, "Have pity upon me, Ned; don't kill me."

'Yes, ma'am, this man, who had just cut his throat, and twice arter that had tried to drown himself, was afraid that I should knock him on the head and kill him. Ha! ha! I never shall forget the work that F —— and I had with him arter I got him up to the house.

'The doctor came and sewed up his throat; and his wife—poor crittur!—came to nurse him. Bad as he was, she was mortal fond of him! He lay there, sick and unable to leave his bed, for three months, and did nothing but pray to God to forgive him, for he thought the devil would surely have him for cutting his own throat; and when he got about again, which is now twelve years ago, he left off drinking entirely, and

---

[3]Windpipe or throat.

wanders about the woods with his dogs, hunting. He seldom speaks to any one, and his wife's brother carries on the farm for the family. He is so shy of strangers that 'tis a wonder he came in here. The old wives are afraid of him; but you need not heed him—his troubles are to himself, he harms no one.'

Layton departed, and left me brooding over the sad tale which he had told in such an absurd and jesting manner. It was evident from the account he had given of Brian's attempt at suicide, that the hapless hunter was not wholly answerable for his conduct—that he was a harmless maniac.

The next morning, at the very same hour, Brian again made his appearance; but instead of the rifle across his shoulder, a large stone jar occupied the place, suspended by a stout leather thong. Without saying a word, but with a truly benevolent smile that flitted slowly over his stern features, and lighted them up like a sunbeam breaking from beneath a stormy cloud, he advanced to the table, and unslinging the jar, set it down before me, and in a low and gruff, but by no means an unfriendly, voice, said, 'Milk, for the child,' and vanished.

'How good it was of him! How kind!' I exclaimed, as I poured the precious gift of four quarts of pure new milk out into a deep pan. I had not asked him—had never said that the poor weanling wanted milk. It was the courtesy of a gentleman—of a man of benevolence and refinement.

For weeks did my strange, silent friend steal in, take up the empty jar, and supply its place with another replenished with milk. The baby knew his step, and would hold out her hands to him and cry, 'Milk!' and Brian would stoop down and kiss her, and his two great dogs lick her face.

'Have you any children, Mr B ——?'

'Yes, five; but none like this.'

'My little girl is greatly indebted to you for your kindness.'

'She's welcome, or she would not get it. You are strangers; but I like you all. You look kind, and I would like to know more about you.'

Moodie shook hands with the old hunter, and assured him that we should always be glad to see him. After this invitation, Brian became a frequent guest. He would sit and listen with delight to Moodie while he described to him elephant-hunting at the Cape;[4] grasping his rifle in a determined manner, and whistling an encouraging air to his dogs. I asked him one evening what made him so fond of hunting.

''Tis the excitement,' he said; 'it drowns thought, and I love to be alone. I am sorry for the creatures, too, for they are free and happy; yet I am led by an instinct I cannot restrain to kill them. Sometimes the sight of their dying agonies recalls painful feelings; and then I lay aside the gun, and do not hunt for days. But 'tis fine to be alone with God in the great woods—to watch the sunbeams stealing through the thick branches, the blue sky breaking in upon you in patches, and to know that all is bright and shiny above you, in spite of the gloom that surrounds you.'

After a long pause, he continued, with much solemn feeling in his look and tone—

'I lived a life of folly for years, for I was respectably born and educated, and had seen something of the world, perhaps more than was good, before I left home for the woods; and from the teaching I had received from kind relatives and parents I should have known how to have conducted myself better. But, madam, if we associ-

[4]Cape of Good Hope, South Africa.

ate long with the depraved and ignorant, we learn to become even worse than they. I felt deeply my degradation—felt that I had become the slave to low vice, and in order to emancipate myself from the hateful tyranny of evil passions, I did a very rash and foolish thing. I need not mention the manner in which I transgressed God's holy laws; all the neighbours know it, and must have told you long ago. I could have borne reproof, but they turned my sorrow into indecent jests, and, unable to bear their coarse ridicule, I made companions of my dogs and gun, and went forth into the wilderness. Hunting became a habit. I could no longer live without it, and it supplies the stimulant which I lost when I renounced the cursed whiskey-bottle.

'I remember the first hunting excursion I took alone in the forest. How sad and gloomy I felt! I thought that there was no creature in the world so miserable as myself. I was tired and hungry, and I sat down upon a fallen tree to rest. All was still as death around me, and I was fast sinking to sleep, when my attention was aroused by a long, wild cry. My dog, for I had not Chance then, and he's no hunter, pricked up his ears, but instead of answering with a bark of defiance, he crouched down, trembling, at my feet. "What does this mean?" I cried, and I cocked my rifle and sprang upon the log. The sound came nearer upon the wind. It was like the deep baying of a pack of hounds in full cry. Presently a noble deer rushed past me, and fast upon his trail—I see them now, like so many black devils—swept by a pack of ten or fifteen large, fierce wolves, with fiery eyes and bristling hair, and paws that seemed hardly to touch the ground in their eager haste. I thought not of danger, for, with their prey in view, I was safe; but I felt every nerve within me tremble for the fate of the poor deer. The wolves gained upon him at every bound. A close thicket intercepted his path, and, rendered desperate, he turned at bay. His nostrils were dilated, and his eyes seemed to send forth long streams of light. It was wonderful to witness the courage of the beast. How bravely he repelled the attacks of his deadly enemies, how gallantly he tossed them to the right and left, and spurned them from beneath his hoofs; yet all his struggles were useless, and he was quickly overcome and torn to pieces by his ravenous foes. At that moment he seemed more unfortunate even than myself, for I could not see in what manner he had deserved his fate. All his speed and energy, his courage and fortitude, had been exerted in vain. I had tried to destroy myself; but he, with every effort vigorously made for self-preservation, was doomed to meet the fate he dreaded! Is God just to his creatures?'

With this sentence on his lips, he started abruptly from his seat and left the house.

One day he found me painting some wild flowers, and was greatly interested in watching the progress I made in the group. Late in the afternoon of the following day he brought me a large bunch of splendid spring flowers.

'Draw these,' said he; 'I have been all the way to the —— lake plains to find them for you.'

Little Katie, grasping them one by one, with infantile joy, kissed every lovely blossom.

'These are God's pictures,' said the hunter, 'and the child, who is all nature, understands them in a minute. Is it not strange that these beautiful things are hid away in the wilderness, where no eyes but the birds of the air, and the wild beasts of the wood, and the insects that live upon them, ever see them? Does God provide, for the pleasure of such creatures, these flowers? Is His benevolence gratified by the admiration of animals whom we have been taught to consider as having neither thought nor reflection? When I am alone in the forest, these thoughts puzzle me.'

Knowing that to argue with Brian was only to call into action the slumbering fires of his fatal malady, I turned the conversation by asking him why he called his favourite dog Chance?

'I found him,' he said, 'forty miles back in the bush. He was a mere skeleton. At first I took him for a wolf, but the shape of his head undeceived me. I opened my wallet,[5] and called him to me. He came slowly, stopping and wagging his tail at every step, and looking me wistfully in the face. I offered him a bit of dried venison, and he soon became friendly, and followed me home, and has never left me since. I called him Chance, after the manner I happened with him; and I would not part with him for twenty dollars.'

Alas, for poor Chance! he had, unknown to his master, contracted a private liking for fresh mutton, and one night he killed no less than eight sheep that belonged to Mr D ——, on the front road; the culprit, who had been long suspected, was caught in the very act, and this *mischance* cost him his life. Brian was sad and gloomy for many weeks after his favourite's death.

'I would have restored the sheep fourfold,' he said, 'if he would but have spared the life of my dog.'

My recollections of Brian seem more particularly to concentrate in the adventures of one night, when I happened to be left alone, for the first time since my arrival in Canada. I cannot now imagine how I could have been such a fool as to give way for four-and-twenty hours to such childish fears; but so it was, and I will not disguise my weakness from my indulgent reader.

* * *

[5]Knapsack.

XXIII. THE FIRE

> Now, Fortune, do thy worst! For many years,
> Thou, with relentless and unsparing hand,
> Hast sternly pour'd on our devoted heads
> The poison'd phials of thy fiercest wrath.

The early part of the winter of 1837, a year never to be forgotten in the annals of Canadian history, was very severe. During the month of February, the thermometer often ranged from eighteen to twenty-seven degrees below zero. Speaking of the coldness of one particular day, a genuine brother Jonathan[1] remarked, with charming simplicity, that it was thirty degrees below zero that morning, and it would have been much colder if the thermometer had been longer.

The morning of the seventh was so intensely cold that everything liquid froze in the house. The wood that had been drawn for the fire was green, and it ignited too slowly to satisfy the shivering impatience of women and children; I vented mine in audibly grumbling over the wretched fire, at which I in vain endeavoured to thaw frozen bread, and to dress crying children.

It so happened that an old friend, the maiden lady before alluded to, had been

[1]Typical Yankee.

staying with us for a few days. She had left us for a visit to my sister, and as some relatives of hers were about to return to Britain, by the way of New York, and had offered to convey letters to friends at home, I had been busy all the day before preparing a packet for England.

It was my intention to walk to my sister's with this packet, directly the important affair of breakfast had been discussed; but the extreme cold of the morning had occasioned such delay, that it was late before the breakfast-things were cleared away.

After dressing, I found the air so keen that I could not venture out without some risk to my nose, and my husband kindly volunteered to go in my stead.

I had hired a young Irish girl the day before. Her friends were only just located in our vicinity, and she had never seen a stove until she came to our house. After Moodie left, I suffered the fire to die away in the Franklin stove in the parlour, and went into the kitchen to prepare bread for the oven.

The girl, who was a good-natured creature, had heard me complain bitterly of the cold, and the impossibility of getting the green wood to burn, and she thought that she would see if she could not make a good fire for me and the children, against[2] my work was done. Without saying one word about her intention, she slipped out through a door that opened from the parlour into the garden, ran round to the woodyard, filled her lap with cedar chips, and, not knowing the nature of the stove, filled it entirely with the light wood.

Before I had the least idea of my danger, I was aroused from the completion of my task by the crackling and roaring of a large fire, and a suffocating smell of burning soot. I looked up at the kitchen cooking-stove. All was right there. I knew I had left no fire in the parlour stove; but not being able to account for the smoke and smell of burning, I opened the door, and, to my dismay, found the stove red-hot, from the front plate to the topmost pipe that let out the smoke through the roof.

My first impulse was to plunge a blanket, snatched from the servant's bed, which stood in the kitchen, into cold water. This I thrust into the stove, and upon it I threw water, until all was cool below. I then ran up to the loft, and, by exhausting all the water in the house, even to that contained in the boilers upon the fire, contrived to cool down the pipes which passed through the loft. I then sent the girl out of doors to look at the roof, which, as a very deep fall of snow had taken place the day before, I hoped would be completely covered, and safe from all danger of fire.

She quickly returned, stamping, and tearing her hair, and making a variety of uncouth outcries, from which I gathered that the roof was in flames.

This was terrible news, with my husband absent, no man in the house, and a mile and a quarter from any other habitation. I ran out to ascertain the extent of the misfortune, and found a large fire burning in the roof between the two stove-pipes. The heat of the fires had melted off all the snow, and a spark from the burning pipe had already ignited the shingles. A ladder, which for several months had stood against the house, had been moved two days before to the barn, which was at the top of the hill near the road; there was no reaching the fire through that source. I got out the dining-table, and tried to throw water upon the roof by standing on a chair placed upon it, but I only expended the little water that remained in the boiler, without reaching the fire. The girl still continued weeping and lamenting.

[2]Until.

'You must go for help,' I said. 'Run as fast as you can to my sister's, and fetch your master.'

'And lave you, ma'arm, and the childher alone wid the burnin' house?'

'Yes, yes! Don't stay one moment.'

'I have no shoes, ma'arm, and the snow is so deep.'

'Put on your master's boots; make haste, or we shall be lost before help comes.'

The girl put on the boots and started, shrieking 'Fire!' the whole way. This was utterly useless, and only impeded her progress by exhausting her strength. After she had vanished from the head of the clearing into the wood, and I was left quite alone, with the house burning over my head, I paused one moment to reflect what had best be done.

The house was built of cedar logs; in all probability it would be consumed before any help could arrive. There was a brisk breeze blowing up from the frozen lake, and the thermometer stood at eighteen degrees below zero. We were placed between the two extremes of heat and cold, and there was as much danger to be apprehended from the one as the other. In the bewilderment of the moment, the direful extent of the calamity never struck me; we wanted but this to put the finishing stroke to our misfortunes, to be thrown naked, houseless, and penniless, upon the world. *'What shall I save first?'* was the thought just then uppermost in my mind. Bedding and clothing appeared the most essentially necessary, and, without another moment's pause, I set to work with a right good will to drag all that I could from my burning home.

While little Agnes, Dunbar, and baby Donald filled the air with their cries, Katie, as if fully conscious of the importance of exertion, assisted me in carrying out sheets and blankets, and dragging trunks and boxes some way up the hill, to be out of the way of the burning brands when the roof should fall in.

How many anxious looks I gave to the head of the clearing as the fire increased, and large pieces of burning pine began to fall through the boarded ceiling about the lower rooms where we were at work. The children I had kept under a large dresser in the kitchen, but it now appeared absolutely necessary to remove them to a place of safety. To expose the young, tender things to the direful cold, was almost as bad as leaving them to the mercy of the fire. At last I hit upon a plan to keep them from freezing. I emptied all the clothes out of a large, deep chest of drawers, and dragged the empty drawers up the hill; these I lined with blankets, and placed a child in each drawer, covering it well over with the bedding, giving to little Agnes the charge of the baby to hold between her knees, and keep well covered until help should arrive. Ah, how long it seemed coming!

The roof was now burning like a brush-heap, and, unconsciously, the child and I were working under a shelf upon which were deposited several pounds of gunpowder, which had been procured for blasting a well, as all our water had to be brought uphill from the lake. This gunpowder was in a stone jar, secured by a paper stopper; the shelf upon which it stood was on fire, but it was utterly forgotten by me at the time, and even afterwards, when my husband was working on the burning loft over it.

I found that I should not be able to take many more trips for goods. As I passed out of the parlour for the last time, Katie looked up at her father's flute, which was suspended upon two brackets, and said,

'Oh, dear mamma! do save papa's flute; he will be so sorry to lose it.'

God bless the dear child for the thought! the flute was saved; and, as I succeeded in dragging out a heavy chest of clothes, and looked up once more despairingly to the road, I saw a man running at full speed. It was my husband. Help was at hand, and my heart uttered a deep thanksgiving as another and another figure came upon the scene.

I had not felt the intense cold, although without cap, or bonnet, or shawl; with my hands bare and exposed to the bitter, biting air. The intense excitement, the anxiety to save all I could, had so totally diverted my thoughts from myself, that I had felt nothing of the danger to which I had been exposed; but now that help was near, my knees trembled under me, I felt giddy and faint, and dark shadows seemed dancing before my eyes.

The moment my husband and brother-in-law entered the house, the latter exclaimed,

'Moodie, the house is gone; save what you can of your winter stores and furniture.'

Moodie thought differently. Prompt and energetic in danger, and possessing admirable presence of mind and coolness when others yield to agitation and despair, he sprang upon the burning loft and called for water. Alas, there was none!

'Snow, snow; hand me pailfuls of snow!'

Oh! it was bitter work filling those pails with frozen snow; but Mr T —— and I worked at it as fast as we were able.

The violence of the fire was greatly checked by covering the boards of the loft with this snow. More help had now arrived. Young B —— and S —— had brought the ladder down with them from the barn, and were already cutting away the burning roof, and flinging the flaming brands into the deep snow.

'Mrs Moodie, have you any pickled meat?'

'We have just killed one of our cows and salted it for winter stores.'

'Well, then, fling the beef into the snow, and let us have the brine.'

This was an admirable plan. Wherever the brine wetted the shingles, the fire turned from it, and concentrated into one spot.

But I had not time to watch the brave workers on the roof. I was fast yielding to the effects of over excitement and fatigue, when my brother's team dashed down the clearing, bringing my excellent old friend, Miss B ——, and the servant-girl.

My brother sprang out, carried me back into the house, and wrapped me up in one of the large blankets scattered about. In a few minutes I was seated with the dear children in the sleigh, and on the way to a place of warmth and safety.

Katie alone suffered from the intense cold. The dear little creature's feet were severely frozen, but were fortunately restored by her uncle discovering the fact before she approached the fire, and rubbing them well with snow.

In the meanwhile, the friends we had left so actively employed at the house, succeeded in getting the fire under before it had destroyed the walls. The only accident that occurred was to a poor dog that Moodie had called Snarleyowe. He was struck by a burning brand thrown from the house, and crept under the barn and died.

Beyond the damage done to the building, the loss of our potatoes and two sacks of flour, we had escaped in a manner almost miraculous. This fact shows how much can be done by persons working in union, without bustle and confusion, or running in each other's way. Here were six men, who, without the aid of water, succeeded in saving a building, which, at first sight, almost all of them had deemed past hope. In after-years, when entirely burnt out in a disastrous fire that consumed almost all we were worth in the world, some four hundred persons were present, with a fire-engine to second their endeavours, yet all was lost. Every person seemed in the way; and though the fire was discovered immediately after it took place, nothing was done beyond saving some of the furniture.

* * *

[After the fire, circumstances improved for the Moodies, so much so that Mrs Moodie writes of that time: 'We were always cheerful, and sometimes contented and happy.' The Rebellion of 1837 brought this period to a sudden close.]

* * *

XXV. ADIEU TO THE WOODS

Reader! it is not my intention to trouble you with the sequel of our history. I have given you a faithful picture of a life in the backwoods of Canada, and I leave you to draw from it your own conclusions. To the poor, industrious working man it presents many advantages; to the poor gentleman, *none!* The former works hard, puts up with coarse, scanty fare, and submits, with a good grace, to hardships that would kill a domesticated animal at home. Thus he becomes independent, inasmuch as the land that he has cleared finds him in the common necessaries of life; but it seldom, if ever, in remote situations, accomplishes more than this. The gentleman can neither work so hard, live so coarsely, nor endure so many privations as his poorer but more fortunate neighbour. Unaccustomed to manual labour, his services in the field are not of a nature to secure for him a profitable return. The task is new to him, he knows not how to perform it well; and, conscious of his deficiency, he expends his little means in hiring labour, which his bush-farm can never repay. Difficulties increase, debts grow upon him, he struggles in vain to extricate himself, and finally sees his family sink into hopeless ruin.

If these sketches should prove the means of deterring one family from sinking their property, and shipwrecking all their hopes, by going to reside in the backwoods of Canada, I shall consider myself amply repaid for revealing the secrets of the prison-house, and feel that I have not toiled and suffered in the wilderness in vain.

1852

Charles Sangster

1822-1893

Called in his own time 'Canada's national bard' and the 'first important national poet', Charles Sangster became, by virtue of two books published in his thirties, the unofficial poet laureate of his day. He was born at the Navy Yard in Kingston, Upper Canada, in 1822; his father died while he was still an infant. At fifteen he went to work full time at Fort Henry, where he was employed to make cartridges. After two years there his job changed to one in which, as he later said, he was 'ranked as a messenger, received the pay of a labourer, and did the duty of a clerk.' Of the loss of schooling, which might have given him better preparation for a career as a poet, he wrote:

. . . like many leading Canadians, [I am] a self-made man . . . I have not the advantages of a classical education. All that I possess mentally has been acquired by careful reading of the best authors (chiefly Fiction), properly directed thought, and a tolerable share of industry. . . . Even as a boy my ear seems to have been tuned to the harmony of sounds. I would have read more in my younger days, but books were not to be had—the Bible, and the 'Citizen of the World' in two volumes, constituted my library for many years. That I have read the former attentively is apparent from my poems.

Having begun to write poems for newspapers and magazines such as The Literary Garland and The Anglo-American Review, Sangster quit Fort Henry in 1849 to become the editor of the Courier at Amherstburg. Unfortunately the paper collapsed when its publisher died, and in 1850 he took more menial employment with the Kingston British Whig, remaining for the next fourteen years. Despite the arduousness of his tasks there, he managed to write The St Lawrence and the Saguenay and Other Poems (1856) and Hesperus, and Other Poems, and Lyrics (1860). The presence of love poetry in each reminds us that the two books coincided with Sangster's two marriages—the first to Mary Kilborne, whose death eighteen months later greatly saddened the poet; the second to Henrietta Meagher. In 1864 Sangster became a reporter for the Kingston Daily News, and in

1868 he joined the newly formed federal post office in Ottawa as a clerk; he remained in this position until a nervous breakdown forced his retirement in 1886. He had hoped to ready for publication two more volumes of his poetry, but was unable to do so. He died in Kingston.

Sangster was the first Canadian poet to achieve recognition in Canada in his lifetime. Edward Hartley Dewart, in his introduction to Selections from Canadian Poets (1864), stated that Sangster occupied 'first place' among his peers. In 1882 Sangster became a charter member of the Royal Society of Canada and in 1890 an honorary member of the Society of Canadian Literature. Sangster, choosing to work in the tradition of the English Romantic poets, attempted to respond to his immediate landscape rather than writing in the more formalized neo-classic mode of his predecessors. Although Sangster attempted to depict a Canadian landscape in 'The St Lawrence and the Saguenay', a work indebted to Wordsworth's late sonnet sequence 'The River Duddon', Sir Daniel Wilson pointed out that it was not true to its Canadian environment and to the creation of a native idiom:

Were we to transport the scene to the firth of Clyde, or any other islanded home river, and change only a single term; that of the Red Man for the old Pict . . . there is nothing in the description that would betray its new-world parentage. At best it is no true Indian, but only the white man dressed in his attire; strip him of his paint and feathers, and it is our old-world familiar acquaintance. . . . However much taste and refinement may be displayed in such echoes of the old thought and fancy of Europe, the path to success lies not in this direction for the poet of the new world. [Wilson, The Canadian Journal of Industry, Science, and Art (January 1985)]

Wilson's argument, one that has often been made since, may have had an effect on Sangster, because the poems in Sonnets Written in the Orillia Woods suffer much less from these defects: they begin to evoke the Canadian experience and to leave behind an artifically imposed poetics.

From *The St Lawrence and the Saguenay*[1] — islands,
* * *   stately

The bark leaps love-fraught from the land; the sea
Lies calm before us. Many an isle is there,[2]   20
Clad with soft verdure; many a stately tree
Uplifts its leafy branches through the air;
The amorous current bathes the islets fair,
As we skip, youth-like, o'er the limpid waves;
White cloudlets speck the golden atmosphere,
Through which the passionate sun looks down, and graves
His image on the pearls that boil from the deep caves,

And bathe the vessel's prow. Isle after isle
Is passed, as we glide tortuously through
The opening vistas, that uprise and smile   30
Upon us from the ever-changing view.
Here nature, lavish of her wealth, did strew
Her flocks of panting islets on the breast
Of the admiring River, where they grew,
Like shapes of Beauty, formed to give a zest
To the charmed mind, like waking Visions of the Blest.

The silver-sinewed arms of the proud Lake,
Love-wild, embrace each islet tenderly,
The zephyrs kiss the flowers when they wake
At morn, flushed with a rare simplicity;   40
See how they bloom around yon birchen tree,
And smile along the bank, by the sandy shore,
In lovely groups—a fair community!
The embossed rocks glitter like golden ore,
And here, the o'erarching trees form a fantastic bower.

Red walls of granite rise on either hand,
Rugged and smooth; a proud young eagle soars
Above the stately evergreens, that stand
Like watchful sentinels on these God-built towers;
And near yon beds of many-colored flowers   50
Browse two majestic deer, and at their side
A spotted fawn all innocently cowers;
In the rank brushwood it attempts to hide,
While the strong-antlered stag steps forth with lordly stride,

And slakes his thirst, undaunted, at the stream.
Isles of o'erwhelming beauty! surely here
The wild enthusiast might live, and dream

[1]Stanzas 3 to 11.   [2]The setting of this first section is the Thousand Islands.

His life away. No Nymphic trains appear,
To charm the pale Ideal Worshipper
Of Beauty; nor Neriads[3] from the deeps below;   60
Nor hideous Gnomes, to fill the breast with fear;
But crystal streams through endless landscapes flow,
And o'er the clustering Isles the softest breezes blow.

LYRIC TO THE ISLES

Here the Spirit of Beauty keepeth
Jubilee for evermore;
Here the Voice of Gladness leapeth,
Echoing from shore to shore.
O'er the hidden watery valley,
O'er each buried wood and glade,
Dances our delighted galley,   70
Through the sunlight and the shade—
Dances o'er the granite cells,
Where the Soul of Beauty dwells:

Here the flowers are ever springing,
While the summer breezes blow;
Here the Hours are ever clinging,
Loitering before they go;
Playing round each beauteous islet,
Loath to leave the sunny shore,
Where, upon her couch of violet,   80
Beauty sits for evermore—
Sits and smiles by day and night,
Hand in hand with pure Delight.

Here the Spirit of Beauty dwelleth
In each palpitating tree,
In each amber wave that welleth
From its home, beneath the sea;
In the moss upon the granite,
In each calm, secluded bay,
With the zephyr trains that fan it   90
With their sweet breaths all the day—
On the waters, on the shore,
Beauty dwelleth evermore!

Yes, here the Genius[4] of Beauty truly dwells.
I worship Truth and Beauty in my soul.
The pure prismatic globule that upwells

[3]Water nymphs.   [4]Guardian spirit.

From the blue deep; the psalmy waves that roll
Before the hurricane; the outspread scroll
Of heaven, with its written tomes of stars;
The dew-drop on the leaf: These I extol,   100
And all alike—each one a Spirit-Mars,
Guarding my Victor-Soul above Earth's prison bars.

There was a stately Maiden once, who made
These Isles her home. Oft has her lightsome skiff
Toyed with the waters; and the velvet glade,
The shadowy woodland, and the granite cliff,
Joyed at her footsteps. Here the Brigand Chief,
Her father, lived, an outlaw. Her soul's pride
Was ministering to his wants. In brief,
The wildest midnight she would cross the tide,   110
Full of a daughter's love, to hasten to his side.

Queen of the Isles! she well deserved the name:
In look, in action, in repose a Queen!
Some Poet-Muse may yet hand down to fame
Her woman's courage, and her classic mien;
Some Painter's skill immortalize the scene,
And blend with it that Maiden's history;
Some Sculptor's hand from the rough marble glean
An eloquent Thought, whose truthfulness shall be
The expounder of her worth and moral dignity.   120

On, through the lovely Archipelago,
Glides the swift bark. Soft summer matins ring
From every isle. The wild fowl come and go,
Regardless of our presence. On the wing,
And perched upon the boughs, the gay birds sing
Their loves: This is their summer paradise;
From morn till night their joyous caroling
Delights the ear, and through the lucent skies
Ascends the choral hymn in softest symphonies.

          *   *   *

1856

From *Sonnets Written in the Orillia Woods*

IV

The birds are singing merrily, and here
A squirrel claims the lordship of the woods,
And scolds me for intruding. At my feet
The tireless ants all silently proclaim

The dignity of labour. In my ear
The bee hums drowsily; from sweet to sweet
Careering, like a lover weak in aim.
I hear faint music in the solitudes;
A dreamlike melody that whispers peace
Imbues the calmy forest, and sweet rills   10
Of pensive feeling murmur through my brain,
Like ripplings of pure water down the hills
That slumber in the moonlight. Cease, oh, cease!
Some day my weary heart will coin these into pain.

VII

Our life is like a forest, where the sun
Glints down upon us through the throbbing leaves;
The full light rarely finds us. One by one,
Deep rooted in our souls, there springeth up
Dark groves of human passion, rich in gloom,
At first no bigger than an acorn-cup.
Hope threads the tangled labyrinth, but grieves
Till all our sins have rotted in their tomb,
And made the rich loam of each yearning heart
To bring forth fruits and flowers to new life.   10
We feel the dew from heaven, and there start
From some deep fountain little rills whose strife
Is drowned in music. Thus in light and shade
We live, and move, and die, through all this earthly glade.

XIII

I've almost grown a portion of this place;
I seen familiar with each mossy stone;
Even the nimble chipmunk passes on,
And looks, but never scolds me. Birds have flown
And almost touched my hand; and I can trace
The wild bees to their hives. I've never known
So sweet a pause from labour. But the tone
Of a past sorrow, like a mournful rill
Threading the heart of some melodious hill,
Or the complainings of the whippoorwill,   10
Passes through every thought, and hope, and aim.
It has its uses; for it cools the flame
Of ardent love that burns my being up—
Love, life's celestial pearl, diffused through all its cup.

1860

Isabella Valancy Crawford

1850-1887

In the twentieth century Isabella Valancy Crawford has gained critical recognition, but she never achieved either the financial success or the readership she longed for in her own time. Instead, she lived out a brief and difficult life against a background of family tragedy. Her father, a physician, and her mother left Crawford's birthplace, Dublin, to immigrate to North America, eventually settling in Paisley, Canada West (near the Bruce Peninsula), in 1858. Dr Crawford's practice was never profitable enough there, nor in Lakefield, to which they moved in 1863, to keep the family from the poverty that was a result of his heavy drinking, and of being paid mostly in barter. A move to Peterborough around 1870 did not help Dr Crawford, by that time elderly; he died there in 1875. Nine of Valancy Crawford's eleven siblings had already died in the early years, possibly because of a congenital heart condition that may have been aggravated by malnutrition. The remaining sister died in 1876 as a young woman, either 'from consumption' or of heart failure. A brother had already gone north to seek his own livelihood, and Crawford was left alone to care for her mother.

Valancy Crawford never attended school. Her parents educated her at home, instructing her in Latin and French as well as English; Horace and Dante were said to be her favourite poets. Having formed an early ambition to write, she moved with her mother to Toronto around 1876 to be close to newspapers and publishers. She hoped to succeed as a commercial writer, and most of what she wrote was intended for newspapers and periodicals. She discovered, however, that her poems earned her little or nothing. The collection she issued at her own expense, '*Old Spookses' Pass*', '*Malcolm's Katie*' *and Other Poems* (1884), sold few copies—although it received good reviews in Canada and Britain. Her fiction was more successful. She won a prize for a story in 1873 ($500, of which she received only $100), and in Toronto she saw the serialization of at least two novels: one in the *Evening Globe* in 1885-6 and another in a journal called *The Fireside Weekly*. Only a single chapter of the *Globe* novel now survives; the other novel has been entirely lost. She died of heart failure at the age of thirty-six. *The Collected Poems of Isabella Valancy Crawford*, edited by John Garvin, was published in 1905.

Crawford's rich imagination was shaped by the classics and by contemporary English and French literature. Her poetry has affinities with that of the Pre-Raphaelites, but Crawford brought to that tradition a Canadian background, from which she drew native imagery and a native mythology. She so imbues nature with life that her settings often become animistic, and her poems have a quality so sensual that some modern critics have offered Freudian interpretations. She shows remarkable control over a wide range of forms, including long narrative poems, such as her famous 'Malcolm's Katie', song-like lyrics, poems in dialect, and dramatic monologues. Her vision is repeatedly one of a world of forces in opposition. In its starkest manifestation this becomes—as in 'A Battle' and 'The Dark Stag'—a cosmic struggle between darkness and light. Northrop Frye has called hers 'the most remarkable mythopoeic imagination in Canadian poetry'; it was also the first.

A Battle

Slowly the Moon her banderoles[1] of light
Unfurls upon the sky; her fingers drip
Pale, silvery tides; her armoured warriors
Leave Day's bright tents of azure and of gold,
Wherein they hid them, and in silence flock
Upon the solemn battlefield of Night
To try great issues with the blind old king,
The Titan Darkness, who great Pharoah fought
With groping hands, and conquered for a span.[2]

The starry hosts with silver lances prick   10
The scarlet fringes of the tents of Day,
And turn their crystal shields upon their breasts,
And point their radiant lances, and so wait
The stirring of the giant in his caves.

The solitary hills send long, sad sighs
As the blind Titan grasps their locks of pine
And trembling larch to drag him toward the sky,
That his wild-seeking hands may clutch the Moon
From her war-chariot, scythed[3] and wheeled with light,
Crush bright-mailed stars, and so, a sightless king,   20
Reign in black desolation! Low-set vales
Weep under the black hollow of his foot,
While sobs the sea beneath his lashing hair
Of rolling mists, which, strong as iron cords,
Twine round tall masts and drag them to the reefs.

Swifter rolls up Astarte's[4] light-scythed car;
Dense rise the jewelled lances, groves of light;
Red flouts Mars' banner in the voiceless war
(The mightiest combat is the tongueless one);
The silvery dartings of the lances prick   30
His fingers from the mountains, catch his locks
And toss them in black fragments to the winds,
Pierce the vast hollow of his misty foot,
Level their diamond tips against his breast,
And force him down to lair within his pit
And thro' its chinks thrust down his groping hands
To quicken Hell with horror—for the strength
That is not of the Heavens is of Hell.

1874, 1905

[1]Ornamental silver streamers, here like those on the lance of a knight.
[2]That is, the giant god Darkness fought and conquered the Pharoah when Moses called down the plague of darkness on Egypt (Exodus 10:21-9).
[3]Roman war-chariots were sometimes 'scythed' by having carved blades attached to their wheels.
[4]Phoenician goddess of the moon; 'car': chariot.

The Camp of Souls[1]

My white canoe, like the silvery air
 O'er the River of Death that darkly rolls
When the moons of the world are round and fair,
 I paddle back from the 'Camp of Souls'.
When the wishton-wish[2] in the low swamp grieves
Come the dark plumes of red 'Singing Leaves'.[3]

Two hundred times have the moons of spring
 Rolled over the bright bay's azure breath
Since they decked me with plumes of an eagle's wing,
 And painted my face with the 'paint of death',   10
And from their pipes o'er my corpse there broke
The solemn rings of the blue 'last smoke'.

Two hundred times have the wintry moons
 Wrapped the dead earth in a blanket white;
Two hundred times have the wild sky loons
 Shrieked in the flush of the golden light
Of the first sweet dawn, when the summer weaves
Her dusky wigwam of perfect leaves.

Two hundred moons of the falling leaf
 Since they laid my bow in my dead right hand   20
And chanted above me the 'song of grief'
 As I took my way to the spirit land;
Yet when the swallow the blue air cleaves
Come the dark plumes of red 'Singing Leaves'.

White are the wigwams in that far camp,
 And the star-eyed deer on the plains are found;
No bitter marshes or tangled swamp
 In the Manitou's happy hunting-ground!
And the moon of summer forever rolls
Above the red men in their 'Camp of Souls'.   30

Blue are its lakes as the wild dove's breast,
 And their murmurs soft as her gentle note;
As the calm, large stars in the deep sky rest,
 The yellow lilies upon them float;
And canoes, like flakes of the silvery snow,
Thro' the tall, rustling rice-beds come and go.

[1] The place of afterlife (Indian).
[2] Whippoorwill.
[3] The name of the spirit-narrator of the poem.

Green are its forests; no warrior wind
   Rushes on war trail the dusk grove through,
With leaf-scalps of tall trees mourning behind;
   But South Wind, heart friend of Great Manitou,   40
When ferns and leaves with cool dews are wet,
Blows flowery breaths from his red calumet.[4]

Never upon them the white frosts lie,
   Nor glow their green boughs with the 'paint of death';
Manitou smiles in the crystal sky,
   Close breathing above them His life-strong breath;
And He speaks no more in fierce thunder sound,
So near is His happy hunting-ground.

Yet often I love, in my white canoe,
   To come to the forests and camps of earth: 50
'Twas there death's black arrow pierced me through;
   'Twas there my red-browed mother gave me birth;
There I, in the light of a young man's dawn,
Won the lily heart of dusk 'Springing Fawn'.

And love is a cord woven out of life,
   And dyed in the red of the living heart;
And time is the hunter's rusty knife,
   That cannot cut the red strands apart:
And I sail from the spirit shore to scan
Where the weaving of that strong cord began.   60

But I may not come with a giftless hand,
   So richly I pile, in my white canoe,
Flowers that bloom in the spirit land,
   Immortal smiles of Great Manitou.
When I paddle back to the shores of earth
I scatter them over the white man's hearth.

For love is the breath of the soul set free;
   So I cross the river that darkly rolls,
That my spirit may whisper soft to thee
   Of *thine* who wait in the 'Camp of Souls'.   70
When the bright day laughs, or the wan night grieves,
Come the dusky plumes of red 'Singing Leaves'.

1880, 1905

---

[4]Peace pipe.

The Dark Stag[1]

A startled stag, the blue-grey Night,
   Leaps down beyond black pines.
Behind—a length of yellow light—
   The hunter's arrow shines:
His moccasins are stained with red,
   He bends upon his knee,
From covering peaks his shafts are sped,
The blue mists plume his mighty head,—
   Well may the swift Night flee!

The pale, pale Moon, a snow-white doe,   10
   Bounds by his dappled flank:
They beat the stars down as they go,
   Like wood-bells growing rank.
The winds lift dewlaps from the ground,
   Leap from the quaking reeds;
Their hoarse bays shake the forests round,
With keen cries on the track they bound,—
   Swift, swift the dark stag speeds!

Away! his white doe, far behind,
   Lies wounded on the plain;   20
Yells at his flank the nimblest wind,
   His large tears fall in rain;
Like lily-pads, small clouds grow white
   About his darkling way;
From his bald nest upon the height
The red-eyed eagle sees his flight;
He falters, turns, the antlered Night,—
   The dark stag stands at bay!

His feet are in the waves of space;
   His antlers broad and dun   30
He lowers; he turns his velvet face
   To front the hunter, Sun;
He stamps the lilied clouds, and high
   His branches fill the west.
The lean stork sails across the sky,
The shy loon shrieks to see him die,
   The winds leap at his breast.

Roar the rent lakes as thro' the wave
   Their silver warriors plunge,
As vaults from core of crystal cave   40
   The strong, fierce muskallunge;[2]

[1] Dorothy Livesay's discovery of an unfinished manuscript suggests that this poem and one called 'The Lily Bed' were intended as part of a long narrative, an edition of which has now been edited by Glenn Clever under the title *Hugh and Ion* (1977).
[2] Pike.

Red torches of the sumach glare,
    Fall's council-fires are lit;
The bittern, squaw-like, scolds the air;
The wild duck splashes loudly where
    The rustling rice-spears knit.

Shaft after shaft the red Sun speeds:
    Rent the stag's dappled side,
His breast, fanged by the shrill winds, bleeds,
    He staggers on the tide;   50
He feels the hungry waves of space
    Rush at him high and blue;
Their white spray smites his dusky face,
Swifter the Sun's fierce arrows race
    And pierce his stout heart thro'.

His antlers fall; once more he spurns
    The hoarse hounds of the day;
His blood upon the crisp blue burns,
    Reddens the mounting spray;
His branches smite the wave—with cries   60
    The loud winds pause and flag—
He sinks in space—red glow the skies,
The brown earth crimsons as he dies,
    The strong and dusky stag.

1883, 1905

Said the Canoe[1]

My masters twain made me a bed
Of pine-boughs resinous, and cedar;
Of moss, a soft and gentle breeder
Of dreams of rest; and me they spread
With furry skins and, laughing, said:
'Now she shall lay her polished sides
As queens do rest, or dainty brides,
Our slender lady of the tides!'

My masters twain their camp-soul[2] lit;
Streamed incense from the hissing cones;   10
Large crimson flashes grew and whirled;
Thin golden nerves of sly light curled
Round the dun camp; and rose faint zones,
Half way about each grim bole knit,
Like a shy child that would bedeck
With its soft clasp a Brave's red neck,
Yet sees the rough shield on his breast,

[1]Originally titled 'The Canoe'.
[2]i.e. the campfire.

The awful plumes shake on his crest,
And, fearful, drops his timid face,
Nor dares complete the sweet embrace.   20

Into the hollow hearts of brakes—
Yet warm from sides of does and stags
Passed to the crisp, dark river-flags—
Sinuous, red as copper-snakes,
Sharp-headed serpents, made of light,
Glided and hid themselves in night.

My masters twain the slaughtered deer
Hung on forked boughs with thongs of leather:
Bound were his stiff, slim feet together,
His eyes like dead stars cold and drear.   30
The wandering firelight drew near
And laid its wide palm, red and anxious,
On the sharp splendour of his branches,
On the white foam grown hard and sere
    On flank and shoulder.
Death—hard as breast of granite boulder—
    Under his lashes
Peered thro' his eyes at his life's grey ashes.

My masters twain sang songs that wove—
As they burnished hunting-blade and rifle—   40
A golden thread with a cobweb trifle,
Loud of the chase and low of love:

'O Love! art thou a silver fish,
Shy of the line and shy of gaffing,
Which we do follow, fierce, yet laughing,
Casting at thee the light-winged wish?
And at the last shall we bring thee up
From the crystal darkness, under the cup
    Of lily folden
    On broad leaves golden?   50

'O Love! art thou a silver deer
With feet as swift as wing of swallow,
While we with rushing arrows follow?
And at the last shall we draw near
And o'er thy velvet neck cast thongs
Woven of roses, stars and songs—
    New chains all moulden
    Of rare gems olden?'

They hung the slaughtered fish like swords
    On saplings slender; like scimitars,   60
    Bright, and ruddied from new-dead wars,
Blazed in the light the scaly hordes.

They piled up boughs beneath the trees,
   Of cedar web and green fir tassel.
   Low did the pointed pine tops rustle,
The camp-fire blushed to the tender breeze.

The hounds laid dewlaps on the ground
   With needles of pine, sweet, soft and rusty,
   Dreamed of the dead stag stout and lusty;
A bat by the red flames wove its round.   70

The darkness built its wigwam walls
   Close round the camp, and at its curtain
   Pressed shapes, thin, woven and uncertain
As white locks of tall waterfalls.

1884

Sir Charles G.D. Roberts

1860-1945

Charles G.D. Roberts, his cousin Bliss Carman, Archibald Lampman, and Duncan Campbell Scott are often called the 'Poets of the Confederation': their prominence between 1867 and the Great War, their concern with nationalism, and their interrelated lives make them truly members of a school of poetry. The oldest and the first to publish (*Orion and Other Poems*, 1880), Roberts seemed to his fellow poets their founding father. A famous essay by Lampman suggests his importance:

It was almost ten years ago, and I was very young, an undergraduate at college. One May evening somebody lent me Orion *and Other Poems, then recently published. Like most of the young fellows about me I had been under the depressing conviction that we were situated hopelessly on the outskirts of civilization, where no art and no literature could be, and it was useless to expect that anything great could be done by any of our companions, still more useless to expect that we could do it ourselves. I sat up all night reading and re-reading* Orion *in a state of the wildest excitement and when I went to bed I could not sleep. It seemed to me a wonderful thing that such work could be done by a Canadian, by a young man, one of ourselves.* ('*Two Canadian Poets: A Lecture*', 1891)

Roberts' youth, the resource out of which much of his best poetry is constructed, combined many of the common elements of Confederation life: an English and Loyalist background, a rural boyhood in close contact with the wilderness, and a broad classical education given him by his parents. When Roberts was fourteen, his father, an Anglican clergyman, accepted a new post at Fredericton, moving the boy away from the Tantramar region of New Brunswick, where he had spent his childhood and which he loved, into a larger world. At Fredericton Collegiate School, where he first met his cousin Bliss Carman, he expanded his classical education to include recent British poets; later, at the University of New Brunswick, he added philosophy and political economy to his studies. While completing his degree he began writing poetry. By the time he was twenty-three Roberts had not only married and been head of two schools, but had published three books of verse. The first of these, *Orion*, received international praise and Matthew Arnold among others saw it as distinctively Canadian; at home, however, it was criticized as being too regional. Roberts took this criticism to heart and by 1886 was calling for a more national approach in the writing of Canadian poetry: 'We must forget to ask of a work whether it is Nova Scotian or British Columbian, of Ontario, or of New Brunswick, until we have inquired if it be broadly and truly Canadian.' This changed attitude was partly due to his having come in contact with the Canada First Movement, a loose union of people who were intent on developing national pride by celebrating Anglo-Canadian history, encouraging Canadian arts, and strengthening Canada politically.

In 1883 Roberts became literary editor of the *Week*, a Toronto periodical founded by Goldwin Smith (who was active in the Canada First Movement). During his brief association with the *Week* Roberts used it as a forum to encourage young writers, and he himself became more involved with the literary community. In 1885 he returned to teaching, accepting a post at King's College, Windsor, N.S., and during his ten years there he wrote prolifically. Shortly after he left teaching in 1895, he also left his wife and family and became an expatriate for many years, working as an editor and writing numerous books, including collections of highly popular animal stories, historical romances, works of non-fiction, and further collections of verse. He lived in New York until 1907, and in London from 1912 to 1925, when he returned to Canada for a triumphant and extended lecture tour. He became active in the Canadian literary scene once more and settled permanently in Toronto. He was knighted in 1935 and died ten years later at eighty-five.

Like many of his contemporaries, Roberts was marked by contradictions. A man of letters, at various times in his life he earned most of his income through commercial writing; a nationalist who wrote patriotic verse and a history of Canada, he lived in exile for an extended period. Though he preached the primacy of nation over region, his best poems—like the sonnet sequence in *Songs of the Common Day* (1893)—are early ones that portray manifestations of nature in New Brunswick from season to season. And though he owes a considerable debt to the pre-Raphaelite tradition and to Transcendentalism, a surprisingly modern vision pervades other early poems, such as 'The Tantramar Revisited', in which man's belief in permanence is seen as an illusion in a world dominated by 'chance and change'. (In 'A Note on Modernism', which first ap-peared in *Open House*, 1931, a collection of his essays, Roberts recognizes the transitional role that he and the other Confederation poets played in breaking the ground in Canada for the modernist movement.)

Roberts' vision of continual flux informed his poetry until his death and is also central in the animal stories to which Roberts turned once he began to support himself through his writing. Collected in *The Kindred of the Wild* (1902) and many other books, these stories, told from the animals' point of view, express a Darwinian vision. Every creature lives in danger from what one story calls 'all the foraging world', and survival is often a matter of luck as much as of fitness. Even man himself, in 'When Twilight Falls on the Stump Lots', becomes no more than one of the larger beasts of prey. Late in life, however, Roberts found harmony in the chaos of existence, for in 'As Down the Woodland Ways' death is 'but a travail-pang of life,/Destruction but a name.'

The Sower[1]

A brown, sad-coloured hillside, where the soil
    Fresh from the frequent harrow, deep and fine,
    Lies bare; no break in the remote sky-line,
Save where a flock of pigeons streams aloft,
Startled from feed in some low-lying croft,
    Or far-off spires with yellow of sunset shine;
    And here the Sower, unwittingly divine,
Exerts the silent forethought of his toil.

Alone he treads the glebe,[2] his measured stride
    Dumb in the yielding soil; and though small joy   10
    Dwell in his heavy face, as spreads the blind
Pale grain from his dispensing palm aside,
    This plodding churl grows great in his employ;—
    God-like, he makes provision for mankind.

1866

[1]Roberts had a print of Millet's painting *The Sower* in his study.
[2]Field (poetic), especially land assigned to a clergyman.

Tantramar Revisited[1]

Summers and summers have come, and gone with the flight of the swallow;
Sunshine and thunder have been, storm, and winter, and frost;
Many and many a sorrow has all but died from remembrance,
Many a dream of joy fall'n in the shadow of pain.
Hands of chance and change have marred, or moulded, or broken,
Busy with spirit or flesh, all I most have adored;
Even the bosom of Earth is strewn with heavier shadows,—
Only in these green hills, aslant to the sea, no change!
Here where the road that has climbed from the inland valleys and woodlands,
Dips from the hill-tops down, straight to the base of the hills,—   10
Here, from my vantage-ground, I can see the scattering houses,
Stained with time, set warm in orchards, and meadows, and wheat,
Dotting the broad bright slopes outspread to southward and eastward,
Wind-swept all day long, blown by the south-east wind.

Skirting the sunbright uplands stretches a riband[2] of meadow.
Shorn of the labouring grass, bulwarked well from the sea.
Fenced on its seaward border with long clay dikes from the turbid
Surge and flow of the tides vexing the Westmoreland shores.
Yonder, toward the left, lie broad the Westmoreland marshes,—
Miles on miles they extend, level, and grassy, and dim,   20
Clear from the long red sweep of flats to the sky in the distance,
Save for the outlying heights, green-rampired[3] Cumberland Point;
Miles on miles outrolled, and the river-channels divide them,—
Miles on miles of green, barred by the hurtling gusts.

Miles on miles beyond the tawny bay is Minudie.
There are the low blue hills; villages gleam at their feet.
Nearer a white sail shines across the water, and nearer
Still are the slim, grey masts of fishing boats dry on the flats.
Ah, how well I remember those wide red flats, above tide-mark
Pale with scurf[4] of the salt, seamed and baked in the sun!   30
Well I remember the piles of blocks and ropes, and the net-reels
Wound with the beaded nets, dripping and dark from the sea!
Now at this season the nets are unwound; they hang from the rafters
Over the fresh-stowed hay in upland barns, and the wind
Blows all day through the chinks, with the streaks of sunlight and sways them
Softly at will; or they lie heaped in the gloom of a loft.

Now at this season the reels are empty and idle; I see them
Over the lines of the dikes, over the gossiping grass.
Now at this season they swing in the long strong wind, thro' the lonesome
Golden afternoon, shunned by the foraging gulls.   40

[1] The Tantramar is a tidal river that empties into the Cumberland Basin of the Bay of Fundy. The region includes the village of Westcock in Westmoreland County, N.B., and the fertile farmlands, tidal flats, and marshes that slope down to the river. Cumberland Point, now called Dorchester, is a village west of Westcock; Minudie is a village that lies across the bay in Nova Scotia.
[2] Ribbon.
[3] Barricaded. 'Green-rampired' refers to the natural fortification of the sloping land.
[4] Scaly flakes.

Near about sunset the crane will journey homeward above them;
Round them, under the moon, all the calm night long,
Winnowing soft grey wings of marsh-owls wander and wander,
Now to the broad, lit marsh, now to the dusk of the dike.
Soon, thro' their dew-wet frames, in the live keen freshness of morning,
Out of the teeth of the dawn blows back the awakening wind.
Then, as the blue day mounts, and the low-shot shafts of the sunlight
Glance from the tide to the shore, gossamers jewelled with dew
Sparkle and wave, where late sea-spoiling fathoms of drift-net
Myriad-meshed, uploomed sombrely over the land.   50

Well I remember it all. The salt, raw scent of the margin;
While, with men at the windlass, groaned each reel, and the net,
Surging in ponderous lengths, uprose and coiled in its station;
Then each man to his home,—well I remember it all!

Yet, as I sit and watch, this present peace of the landscape,—
Stranded boats, these reels empty and idle, the hush,
One grey hawk slow-wheeling above yon cluster of haystacks,—
More than the old-time stir this stillness welcomes me home.
Ah, the old-time stir, how once it stung me with rapture,—
Old-time sweetness, the winds freighted with honey and salt!   60
Yet will I stay my steps and not go down to the marshland,—
Muse and recall far off, rather remember than see,—
Lest on too close sight I miss the darling illusion,
Spy at their task even here the hands of chance and change.

1886

The Winter Fields

Winds here, and sleet, and frost that bites like steel.
   The low bleak hill rounds under the low sky.
   Naked of flock and fold the fallows lie,
Thin streaked with meagre drift. The gusts reveal
By fits the dim grey snakes of fence, that steal
   Through the white dusk. The hill-foot poplars sigh,
   While storm and death with winter trample by,
And the iron fields ring sharp, and blind lights reel.
Yet in the lonely ridges, wrenched with pain,
   Harsh solitary hillocks, bound and dumb,   10
Grave glebes[1] close-lipped beneath the scourge and chain,
   Lurks hid the germ of ecstacy—the sum
Of life that waits on summer, till the rain
   Whisper in April and the crocus come.

1893

[1]Fields.

The Flight of the Geese

I hear the low wind wash the softening snow,
  The low tide loiter down the shore. The night,
  Full filled with April forecast, hath no light.
The salt wave on the sedge-flat[1] pulses slow.
Through the hid furrows lisp in murmurous flow
  The thaw's shy ministers; and hark! The height
  Of heaven grows weird and loud with unseen flight
Of strong hosts prophesying as they go!

High through the drenched and hollow night their wings
  Beat northward hard on Winter's trail. The sound   10
Of their confused and solemn voices, borne
Athwart the dark to their long Arctic morn,
  Comes with a sanction and an awe profound,
A boding of unknown, foreshadowed things.

1893

[1] A flat terrain covered with rushes or rough grasses.

The Skater

My glad feet shod with the glittering steel
I was the god of the wingèd heel.

The hills in the far white sky were lost;
The world lay still in the wide white frost;

And the woods hung hushed in their long white dream
By the ghostly, glimmering, ice-blue stream.

Here was a pathway, smooth like glass,
Where I and the wandering wind might pass

To the far-off palaces, drifted deep,
Where Winter's retinue rests in sleep.   10

I followed the lure, I fled like a bird,
Till the startled hollows awoke and heard

A spinning whisper, a sibilant twang,
As the stroke of the steel on the tense ice rang;

And the wandering wind was left behind
As faster, faster I followed my mind;

Till the blood sang high in my eager brain,
And the joy of my flight was almost pain.

Then I stayed the rush of my eager speed
And silently went as a drifting seed,—   20

Slowly, furtively, till my eyes
Grew big with the awe of a dim surmise,

And the hair of my neck began to creep
At hearing the wilderness talk in sleep.

Shapes in the fir-gloom drifted near.
In the deep of my heart I heard my fear.

And I turned and fled, like a soul pursued,
From the white, inviolate solitude.

1901

As Down the Woodland Ways

As down the woodland ways I went
    With every wind asleep
I felt the surge of endless life
    About my footsteps creep.

I felt the urge of quickening mould
    That had been once a flower
Mount with the sap to bloom again
    At its appointed hour.

I saw gray stumps go crumbling down
    In sodden, grim decay,   10
To soar in pillared green again
    On some remoter day.

I saw crushed beetles, mangled grubs,
    All crawling, perished things,
Whirl up in air, an ecstasy
    Of many-coloured wings.

Through weed and world, through worm and star,
    The sequence ran the same:—
Death but the travail-pang of life,
    Destruction but a name.   20

1937

When Twilight Falls on the Stump Lots

The wet, chill first of the spring, its blackness made tender by the lilac wash of the afterglow, lay upon the high, open stretches of the stump lots. The winter-whitened stumps, the sparse patches of juniper and bay just budding, the rough-mossed hillocks, the harsh boulders here and there up-thrusting from the soil, the swampy hollows wherein a coarse grass began to show green, all seemed anointed, as it were, to an ecstasy of peace by the chrism[1] of that paradisal colour. Against the lucid immensity of the April sky the thin tops of five or six soaring ram-pikes[2] aspired like violet flames. Along the skirts of the stump lots a fir wood reared a ragged-crested wall of black against the red amber of the horizon.

Late that afternoon, beside a juniper thicket not far from the centre of the stump lots, a young black and white cow had given birth to her first calf. The little animal had been licked assiduously by the mother's caressing tongue till its colour began to show of a rich dark red. Now it had struggled to its feet, and, with its disproportionately long, thick legs braced wide apart, was beginning to nurse. Its blunt wet muzzle and thick lips tugged eagerly, but somewhat blunderingly as yet, at the unaccustomed teats; and its tail lifted, twitching with delight, as the first warm streams of mother milk went down its throat. It was a pathetically awkward, unlovely little figure, not yet advanced to that youngling winsomeness which is the heritage, to some degree and at some period, of the infancy of all the kindreds that breathe upon the earth. But to the young mother's eyes it was the most beautiful of things. With her head twisted far around, she nosed and licked its heaving flanks as it nursed; and between deep, ecstatic breathings she uttered in her throat low murmurs, unspeakably tender, of encouragement and caress. The delicate but pervading flood of sunset colour had the effect of blending the ruddy-hued calf into the tones of the landscape; but the cow's insistent blotches of black and white stood out sharply, refusing to harmonise. The drench of violet light was of no avail to soften their staring contrasts. They made her vividly conspicuous across the whole breadth of the stump lots, to eyes that watched her from the forest coverts.

The eyes that watched her—long, fixedly, hungrily—were small and red. They belonged to a lank she-bear, whose gaunt flanks and rusty coat proclaimed a season of famine in the wilderness. She could not see the calf, which was hidden by a hillock and some juniper scrub; but its presence was very legibly conveyed to her by the mother's solicitous watchfulness. After a motionless scrutiny from behind the screen of fir branches, the lean bear stole noiselessly forth from the shadows into the great wash of violet light. Step by step, and very slowly, with the patience that endures because confident of its object, she crept toward that oasis of mothering joy in the vast emptiness of the stump lots. Now crouching, now crawling, turning to this side and to that, taking advantage of every hollow, every thicket, every hillock, every aggressive stump, her craft succeeded in eluding even the wild and menacing watchfulness of the young mother's eyes.

The spring had been a trying one for the lank she-bear. Her den, in a dry tract

---

[1] Sacramental balm or unguent.
[2] Decaying trees or stumps.

of hemlock wood some furlongs back from the stump lots, was a snug little cave under the uprooted base of a lone pine, which had somehow grown up among the alien hemlocks only to draw down upon itself at last, by its superior height, the fury of a passing hurricane. The winter had contributed but scanty snowfall to cover the bear in her sleep; and the March thaws, unseasonably early and ardent, had called her forth to activity weeks too soon. Then frosts had come with belated severity, sealing away the budding tubers, which are the bear's chief dependence for spring diet; and worst of all, a long stretch of intervale[3] meadow by the neighbouring river, which had once been rich in ground-nuts, had been ploughed up the previous spring and subjected to the producing of oats and corn. When she was feeling the pinch of meagre rations, and when the fat which a liberal autumn of blueberries had laid up about her ribs was getting as shrunken as the last snow in the thickets, she gave birth to two hairless and hungry little cubs. They were very blind, and ridiculously small to be born of so big a mother; and having so much growth to make during the next few months, their appetites were immeasurable. They tumbled, and squealed, and tugged at their mother's teats, and grew astonishingly, and made huge haste to cover their bodies with fur of a soft and silken black; and all this vitality of theirs made a strenuous demand upon their mother's milk. There were no more bee trees left in the neighbourhood. The long wanderings which she was forced to take in her search for roots and tubers were in themselves a drain upon her nursing powers. At last, reluctant though she was to attract the hostile notice of the settlement, she found herself forced to hunt on the borders of the sheep pastures. Before all else in life was it important to her that these two tumbling little ones in the den should not go hungry. Their eyes were open now—small and dark and whimsical, their ears quaintly large and inquiring for their roguish little faces. Had she not been driven by the unkind season to so much hunting and foraging, she would have passed near all her time rapturously in the den under the pine root, fondling those two soft miracles of her world.

With the killing of three lambs—at widely scattered points, so as to mislead retaliation—things grew a little easier for the harassed bear; and presently she grew bolder in tampering with the creatures under man's protection. With one swift, secret blow of her mighty paw she struck down a young ewe which had strayed within reach of her hiding-place. Dragging her prey deep into the wood, she fared well upon it for some days, and was happy with her growing cubs. It was just when she had begun to feel the fasting which came upon the exhaustion of this store that, in a hungry hour, she sighted the conspicuous markings of the black and white cow.

It is altogether unusual for the black bear of the eastern woods to attack any quarry so large as a cow, unless under the spur of fierce hunger or fierce rage. The she-bear was powerful beyond her fellows. She had the strongest possible incentive to bold hunting, and she had lately grown confident beyond her wont. Nevertheless, when she began her careful stalking of this big game which she coveted, she had no definite intention of forcing a battle with the cow. She had observed that cows, accustomed to the protection of man, would at times leave their calves asleep and stray off some distance in their pasturing. She had even

[3]Low land, generally beside a river.

seen calves left all by themselves in a field, from morning till night, and had wondered at such negligence in their mothers. Now she had a confident idea that sooner or later the calf would lie down to sleep, and the young mother roam a little wide in search of the scant young grass. Very softly, very self-effacingly, she crept nearer step by step, following up the wind, till at last, undiscovered, she was crouching behind a thick patch of juniper, on the slope of a little hollow not ten paces distant from the cow and the calf.

By this time the tender violet light was fading to a grayness over hillock and hollow; and with the deepening of the twilight the faint breeze, which had been breathing from the northward, shifted suddenly and came in slow, warm pulsations out of the south. At the same time the calf, having nursed sufficiently, and feeling his baby legs tired of the weight they had not yet learned to carry, laid himself down. On this the cow shifted her position. She turned half round, and lifted her head high. As she did so a scent of peril was borne in upon her fine nostrils. She recognised it instantly. With a snort of anger she sniffed again; then stamped a challenge with her fore hoofs, and levelled the lance-points of her horns toward the menace. The next moment her eyes, made keen by the fear of love, detected the black outline of the bear's head through the coarse screen of the juniper. Without a second's hesitation, she flung up her tail, gave a short bellow, and charged.

The moment she saw herself detected, the bear rose upon her hindquarters; nevertheless she was in a measure surprised by the sudden blind fury of the attack. Nimbly she swerved to avoid it, aiming at the same time a stroke with her mighty forearm, which, if it had found its mark, would have smashed her adversary's neck. But as she struck out, in the act of shifting her position, a depression of the ground threw her off her balance. The next instant one sharp horn caught her slantingly in the flank, ripping its way upward and inward, while the mad impact threw her upon her back.

Grappling, she had her assailant's head and shoulders in a trap, and her gigantic claws cut through the flesh and sinew like knives; but at the desperate disadvantage of her position she could inflict no disabling blow. The cow, on the other hand, though mutilated and streaming with blood, kept pounding with her whole massive weight, and with short tremendous shocks crushing the breath from her foe's ribs.

Presently, wrenching herself free, the cow drew off for another battering charge; and as she did so the bear hurled herself violently down the slope, and gained her feet behind a dense thicket of bay shrub. The cow, with one eye blinded and the other obscured by blood, glared around for her in vain, then, in a panic of mother terror, plunged back to her calf.

Snatching at the respite, the bear crouched down, craving that invisibility which is the most faithful shield of the furtive kindred. Painfully, and leaving a drenched red trail behind her, she crept off from the disastrous neighbourhood. Soon the deepening twilight sheltered her. But she could not make haste; and she knew that death was close upon her.

Once within the woods, she struggled straight toward the den that held her young. She hungered to die licking them. But destiny is as implacable as iron to the wilderness people, and even this was denied her. Just a half score of paces from the lair in the pine root, her hour descended upon her. There was a sudden redder and fuller gush upon the trail; the last light of longing faded out of her eyes; and she lay down upon her side.

The merry little cubs within the den were beginning to expect her, and getting restless. As the night wore on, and no mother came, they ceased to be merry. By morning they were shivering with hunger and desolate fear. But the doom of the ancient wood was less harsh than its wont, and spared them some days of starving anguish; for about noon a pair of foxes discovered the dead mother, astutely estimated the situation, and then, with the boldness of good appetite, made their way into the unguarded den.

As for the red calf, its fortune was ordinary. Its mother, for all her wounds, was able to nurse and cherish it through the night; and with morning came a searcher from the farm and took it, with the bleeding mother, safely back to the settlement. There it was tended and fattened, and within a few weeks found its way to the cool marble slabs of a city market.

1902

Bliss Carman

1861-1929

Bliss Carman grew up in Fredericton, N.B., and experienced an adolescence similar to that of his cousin Charles G.D. Roberts, attending Fredericton Collegiate and the University of New Brunswick. Upon graduation—unlike Roberts—Carman began to have serious difficulties establishing his independence owing to his indecisiveness. He was unable to leave home permanently until after the death of his parents, unable to choose a profession, and unable to complete the advanced degrees he began at various universities in Britain (at Oxford, Edinburgh, London), and in the United States (at Harvard). After the death of his father in 1885 and of his mother the next year, Carman left Canada, returning periodically but never permanently. In 1890 he moved to New York to take an editorial job on a religious weekly, *The Independent*, where he stayed for over two years, his longest term of employment. After leaving that position he supported himself through various short-lived journalistic positions as well as, in later years, by lecturing and reading his poetry on tour. From 1892 Carman lived as a visitor with friends and relatives, often with Roberts, moving cyclically with the seasons; yet even without the normal expenses of living, his income was never sufficient. Finally, in 1908, he found a home with Dr and Mrs King of Connecticut, with whom he lived until his death.

Carman was an extremely popular as well as a critically acclaimed poet in his day. While he published much of his verse only in periodicals, he still produced over fifty books and chapbooks, the first and best of which is *Low Tide on Grand Pré* (N.Y., 1893). His most popular work, the Vagabondia series, was begun in 1894 and ran to four volumes by 1912. Their success encouraged another series, the Pipes of Pan (five volumes, 1902-5). All these books of light verse, celebrating a nostalgic, carefree world in which the landscape remains pastoral and life simple, appealed to the late-Victorian reader. Carman's ability to create an Edenic setting was obscured in later volumes, however, by his increasing interest in quasi-reli-gious philosophies, especially the pantheism of Dr King's wife, Mary.

From the beginning of his adulthood Carman suffered from depressions, which were often interspersed with manic joy. His most effective poetry, regardless of its date of composition, is that which reflects this emotional flux. In harmony with the kind of romanticism he encouraged in his youth and the Transcendentalism of his distant kinsman, Emerson—but unlike Lampman and Roberts—Carman writes of feelings, not thoughts, and gives impressions, not descriptions. Carman's poetry at its best captures the ephemeral quality of a melancholic dream, a glimpse of a world always remote, yet never far away. Carman's verse has not worn well for modern readers. A.J.M. Smith voiced a frequent complaint when he said of the poems: 'too many of them trail away after a fine beginning into a glib and tenuous vacuity.'

The Eavesdropper

In a still room at hush of dawn,
   My Love and I lay side by side
And heard the roaming forest wind
   Stir in the paling autumn-tide.

I watched her earth-brown eyes grow glad
   Because the round day was so fair;
While memories of reluctant night
   Lurked in the blue dusk of her hair.

Outside, a yellow maple tree,
   Shifting upon the silvery blue   10
With tiny multitudinous sound,
   Rustled to let the sunlight through.

The livelong day the elvish leaves
   Danced with their shadows on the floor;
And the lost children of the wind
   Went straying homeward by our door.

And all the swarthy afternoon
   We watched the great deliberate sun
Walk through the crimsoned hazy world,
   Counting his hilltops one by one.   20

Then as the purple twilight came
   And touched the vines along our eaves,

Another Shadow stood without
    And gloomed the dancing of the leaves.

The silence fell on my Love's lips;
    Her great brown eyes were veiled and sad
With pondering some maze of dream,
    Though all the splendid year was glad.

Restless and vague as a gray wind
    Her heart had grown, she knew not why.   30
But hurrying to the open door,
    Against the verge of western sky

I saw retreating on the hills,
    Looming and sinister and black,
The stealthy figure swift and huge
    Of One who strode and looked not back.

1893

Low Tide on Grand Pré[1]

The sun goes down, and over all
    These barren reaches by the tide
Such unelusive glories fall,
    I almost dream they yet will bide
    Until the coming of the tide.

And yet I know that not for us,
    By any ecstasy of dream,
He lingers to keep luminous
    A little while the grievous stream,
    Which frets, uncomforted of dream—   10

A grievous stream, that to and fro
    Athrough the fields of Acadie
Goes wandering, as if to know
    Why one beloved face should be
    So long from home and Acadie.

Was it a year or lives ago
    We took the grasses in our hands,
And caught the summer flying low
    Over the waving meadow lands,
    And held it there between our hands?   20

[1] Marshlands on Minas Basin at the mouth of the Gaspéreau River in Nova Scotia; when dyked by the Acadians they became rich farmlands. In 1755 the Acadians were expelled from the village of Grand Pré by the British. It is near Windsor, N.S., where Carman stayed several summers with Roberts.

The while the river at our feet—
  A drowsy inland meadow stream—
At set of sun the after-heat
  Made running gold, and in the gleam
  We freed our birch upon the stream.

There down along the elms at dusk
  We lifted dripping blade to drift,
Through twilight scented fine like musk,
  Where night and gloom awhile uplift,
  Nor sunder soul and soul adrift.   30

And that we took into our hands
  Spirit of life or subtler thing—
Breathed on us there, and loosed the bands
  Of death, and taught us, whispering,
  The secret of some wonder-thing.

Then all your face grew light, and seemed
  To hold the shadow of the sun;
The evening faltered, and I deemed
  That time was ripe, and years had done
  Their wheeling underneath the sun.   40

So all desire and all regret,
  And fear and memory, were naught;
One to remember or forget
  The keen delight our hands had caught;
  Morrow and yesterday were naught.

The night has fallen, and the tide . . .
  Now and again comes drifting home,
Across these aching barrens wide,
  A sigh like driven wind or foam:
  In grief the flood is bursting home.   50

1893

Morning in the Hills

How quiet is the morning in the hills!
The stealthy shadows of the summer clouds
Trail through the cañon,[1] and the mountain stream
Sounds his sonorous music far below
In the deep-wooded wind-enchanted clove.[2]

Hemlock and aspen, chestnut, beech, and fir
Go tiering down from storm-worn crest and ledge,
While in the hollows of the dark ravine
See the red road emerge, then disappear
Towards the wide plain and fertile valley lands.   10

My forest cabin half-way up the glen
Is solitary, save for one wise thrush,
The sound of falling water, and the wind
Mysteriously conversing with the leaves.

Here I abide unvisited by doubt,
Dreaming of far-off turmoil and despair,
The race of men and love and fleeting time,
What life may be, or beauty, caught and held
For a brief moment at eternal poise.

What impulse now shall quicken and make live   20
This outward semblance and this inward self?
One breath of being fills the bubble world,
Colored and frail, with fleeting change on change.

Surely some God contrived so fair a thing
In the vast leisure of uncounted days,
And touched in with the breath of living joy,
Wondrous and fair and wise! It must be so.

1912

[1] Canyon.
[2] Ravine.

Sara Jeannette Duncan

1861-1922

Born Sarah Janet Duncan, in Brantford, Canada West, she used many versions of her name and other pseudonyms before settling on the name by which she is now remembered. After her marriage, the name that most often appeared on the cover of her books was Mrs Everard Cotes (though she continued to be identified parenthetically as Sara Jeannette Duncan on the title page).

Almost as various as her pen-names were the roles Duncan played and the voices she adopted in her writing. Trained to be a school teacher, she established herself in her twenties as a breezy, colloquial journalist, and her first books—light fiction made up of loosely linked sketches—are written in her casual journalistic style. She soon abandoned the masculine pseudonym 'Garth' that she had found necessary in order to be taken seriously in the journalistic world of her day, and adopted the role of a late nineteenth-century 'American girl'—an emancipated, brash, slangy young woman—often emphasizing this characterization by playing it off against British national stereotypes, as in *A Social Departure: How Orthodocia and I Went Round the World by Ourselves* (1890), *An American Girl in London* (1891), and *A Voyage of Consolation* (1898). A restless traveller, Duncan chronicled in her early journalism and books her visit to New Orleans in 1884 (where she met the flamboyant American poet Joaquin Miller, with whom, along with other 'Bohemians', she eventually travelled to Florida in search of the Fountain of Youth); her brief sojourn in British Honduras; and her world-tour with fellow Canadian journalist Lily Lewis, a trip that took them through Western Canada on the recently completed Canadian Pacific Railway—they rode the cowcatcher of their train through the Rockies—as well as to Japan and India.

After failing to secure a staff position at the Toronto *Globe* in 1885 (she later complained of the conservatism of Canadian journalism with regard to employing wom-

en), Duncan accepted a job at the Washington *Post*. In the following year, however, she was hired by the *Globe* and placed in charge of the 'Woman's World' section, becoming the first woman to hold a full-time position in Canadian journalism. Always interested in politics, she went to the Montreal *Star* as parliamentary correspondent in 1888.

Between 1886 and 1888 Duncan also contributed columns and book reviews to Goldwin Smith's important Canadian journal of ideas *The Week*, in which she struck a more elevated and intellectual (and sometimes more rhetorical) tone than that of her other journalism. Her interest in literary fiction had begun early in her career, and *The Week* gave her an opportunity to discuss questions of Canadian culture. Duncan became one of the earliest writers to stress the need for Canada to move beyond colonial self-definition:

> In our character as colonists we find the root of all our sins of omission in letters. . . . Our enforced political humility is the distinguishing characteristic of every phase of our national life. We are ignored, and we ignore ourselves. . . . So long as Canada remains in political obscurity, content to thrive only at the roots, so long will the leaves and blossoms of art and literature be scanty and stunted products of our national energy. . . . A national literature cannot be looked for as an outcome of anything less than a complete national existence. [1886]

She was nevertheless convinced that 'national literature cannot be wholly evoked from within' and took a lively interest in the novelists then emerging in America, particularly Henry James and W.D. Howells (whom she met in Washington), and in the controversies that arose from Howells' advocacy of realism.

Although she continued to write in a popular vein throughout her life, Duncan undertook serious fiction as well after moving, in 1891, to India, where she married Everard

Cotes (whom she had met during her earlier trip). *The Simple Adventures of a Mem-Sahib* (1893) tells of a young English woman's difficult entry into the somewhat cloistered world of the Anglo-Indians; *A Daughter of To-Day* (1894) is an account of a nonconformist woman who leaves America for a career as an expatriate artist and writer in Europe but eventually commits suicide over her lack of success; *His Honour, and a Lady* (1896), an acutely observed portrait of Anglo-Indian politics, shows Duncan's continued interest in women who play untraditional roles.

In 1901 Duncan published *On the Other Side of the Latch*, an affecting memoir that describes a summer of convalescence from tuberculosis, probably brought on by conditions in India. Her only short fiction, three novellas and the short story printed below, all dealing with the emotions suppressed beneath the formal surfaces of the highly mannered Anglo-Indian community, were written around this time; they were collected in *The Pool in the Desert* (1903). In an introduction to a recent reissue of this book, Rosemary Sullivan writes:

While Duncan may rehearse in her female characters the problems of frustration and unfulfilment, she is nowhere strident. Her stories are not simply displacements of some personal confusion, nor are they written in a way that implies self-pity. In fact, she is a master ironist, and the failure to live one's true potential is seen as the general human lot. Her stories are fused with an elegiac sense of diminishment, an ironic resignation to the human capacity for self-deception, and a longing for the self to be deeply moved.

In the way the subtle psychological nuances of the situation outweigh the external events of the story and in the careful control of a highly-subjective character through whom the narrative is filtered, 'The Pool in the Desert' shows the influence of Henry James on Duncan. She is the first Canadian writer to make use of these Jamesian techniques, so important to early literary modernism.

Although initially attracted by its exoticism, Duncan came to feel that India was, as she wrote in a letter, 'too far out upon the periphery of the Empire'. She increasingly depended upon her earnings as a writer to allow her to make return visits to Canada and to live for extended periods in London, where her health seemed better. She published two books that deal extensively with Canada, *The Imperialist* (1904) and *Cousin Cinderella: A Canadian Girl in London* (1908). *The Imperialist*—a gently satirical tale of the fictional town of Elgin, Ontario, and of a brother and a sister who become involved in an election in which the strengthening of Canada's ties to England is an issue—was not well received at the time of its publication; a reprint edition in 1961 found a new audience for the book, which is now generally regarded as Duncan's best. (The coolness of its initial reception seems to have stemmed from a lack of interest in Canada among readers in England and a feeling, among Canadian reviewers, that a woman was not a shrewd enough political observer to carry off this kind of novel.)

Duncan's later career, which was increasingly spent in England, saw the production of a Kensington memoir, *Two in a Flat* (1908), several more novels, most of which rework the 'international theme' that preoccupied James, and popular plays. She died in England in 1922, the author of twenty books, numerous plays, and a great quantity of journalism.

The Pool in the Desert

I knew Anna Chichele and Judy Harbottle so well, and they figured so vividly at one time against the rather empty landscape of life in a frontier station, that my affection for one of them used to seem little more, or less, than a variant upon my affection for the other. That recollection, however, bears examination badly; Judy was much the better sort, and it is Judy's part in it that draws me into telling the story. Conveying Judy is what I tremble at: her part was simple. Looking back—and not so very far—her part has the relief of high comedy with the proximity of tears; but looking closely, I find that it is mostly Judy, and what she did is entirely second, in my untarnished picture, to what she was. Still I do not think I can dissuade myself from putting it down.

They would, of course, inevitably have found each other sooner or later, Mrs Harbottle and Mrs Chichele, but it was I who actually introduced them; my palmy veranda in Rawul Pindi; where the tea-cups used to assemble, was the scene of it. I presided behind my samovar over the early formalities that were almost at once to drop from their friendship, like the sheath of some bursting flower. I deliberately brought them together, so the birth was not accidental, and my interest in it quite legitimately maternal. We always had tea in the veranda in Rawul Pindi, the drawing-room was painted blue, blue for thirty feet up to the whitewashed cotton ceiling; nothing of any value in the way of a human relation, I am sure, could have originated there. The veranda was spacious and open, their mutual observation had room and freedom; I watched it to and fro. I had not long to wait for my reward; the beautiful candour I expected between them was not ten minutes in coming. For the sake of it I had taken some trouble, but when I perceived it revealing I went and sat down beside Judy's husband, Robert Harbottle, and talked about Pharoah's split hoof. It was only fair; and when next day I got their impressions of one another, I felt single-minded and deserving.

I knew it would be a satisfactory sort of thing to do, but perhaps it was rather more for Judy's sake than for Anna's that I did it. Mrs Harbottle was only twenty-seven then and Robert a major, but he had brought her to India out of an episode too colour-flushed to tone with English hedges;[1] their marriage had come, in short, of his divorce, and as too natural a consequence. In India it is well known that the eye becomes accustomed to primitive pigments and high lights; the aesthetic consideration, if nothing else, demanded Robert's exchange. He was lucky to get a Piffer[2]

[1] That is, they have left England and settled in India because they had soiled their reputation. The paragraph that follows and alludes to this event is a model of the over-refined indirection of speech that the narrator resorts to when conveying certain delicate matters. Contemporary readers, partly because they are unused to the customs referred to, may find the passage puzzling. Judy Thynne, who attracted from an early age the enmity of her cousin, the wife of Robert Harbottle, came to Paris to study art. There she formed an 'attachment' with Robert, which the narrator insists was innocent but which, because of her old animosity, provoked Mrs Harbottle into a divorce proceeding that named Judy as co-respondent for having alienated Robert's affections. Robert and Judy chose not to contest the action or protest her innocence because Robert, desirous of his freedom, feared winning the case; Judy's reputation was therefore sacrificed. Thus although, as the narrator observes, it was not an unusual practice at that time for a 'blameless' individual to serve as co-respondent (or for other causes to be invented) in order to mitigate the difficulties of divorce, this particular occurrence was 'the reversal of the modern situation'.

[2] Punjab Frontier Force.

regiment, and the Twelfth were lucky to get him; we were all lucky, I thought, to get Judy. It was an opinion, of course, a good deal challenged, even in Rawul Pindi, where it was thought, especially in the beginning, that acquiescence was the most the Harbottles could hope for. That is not enough in India; cordiality is the common right. I could not have Judy preserving her atmosphere at our tea-parties and gymkhanas.[3] Not that there were two minds among us about 'the case'; it was a preposterous case, sentimentally undignified, from some points of view deplorable. I chose to reserve my point of view, from which I saw it, on Judy's behalf, merely quixotic, preferring on Robert's just to close my eyes. There is no doubt that his first wife was odious to a degree which it is simply pleasanter not to recount, but her malignity must almost have amounted to a sense of humour. Her detestation of her cousin Judy Thynne dated much further back than Robert's attachment. That began in Paris, where Judy, a young widow, was developing a real vein at Julian's.[4] I am entirely convinced that there was nothing, as people say, 'in it,' Judy had not a thought at that time that was not based on Chinese white[5] and permeated with goodfellowship; but there was a good deal of it, and no doubt the turgid imagination of the first Mrs Harbottle dealt with it honestly enough. At all events, she saw her opportunity, and the depths of her indifference to Robert bubbled up venomously into the suit. That it was undefended was the senseless mystery; decency ordained that he and Judy should have made a fight, even in the hope that it would be a losing one. The reason it had to be a losing one—the reason so immensely criticized—was that the petitioning lady obstinately refused to bring her action against any other set of circumstances than those to which, I have no doubt, Judy contributed every indiscretion. It is hard to imagine Robert Harbottle refusing her any sort of justification that the law demands short of beating her, but her malice would accept nothing of which the account did not go for final settlement to Judy Thynne. If her husband wanted his liberty, he should have it, she declared, at that price and no other. Major Harbottle did indeed deeply long for his liberty, and his interesting friend, Mrs Thynne, had, one can only say, the most vivid commiseration for his bondage. Whatever chance they had of winning, to win would be, for the end they had at heart, to lose, so they simply abstained, as it were, from comment upon the detestable procedure which terminated in the rule absolute. I have often wondered whether the whole business would not have been more defensible if there had been on Judy's part any emotional spring for the leap they made. I offer my conviction that there was none, that she was only extravagantly affected by the ideals of the Quarter[6]—it is a transporting atmosphere—and held a view of comradeship which permitted the reversal of the modern situation filled by a blameless co-respondent. Robert, of course, was tremendously in love with her; but my theory is that she married him as the logical outcome of her sacrifice and by no means the smallest part of it.

It was all quite unimaginable, as so many things are, but the upshot of it brought Judy to Rawul Pindi, as I have said, where I for one thought her mistake insignifi-

[3]Sports recreations (Anglo-Indian).
[4]The Académie Julien, an art school in Paris; its women's class attracted some of the important women artists of the late nineteenth century.
[5]A fine white pigment; i.e., her thoughts were pure.
[6]The Latin Quarter, the Paris district associated with students and artists and known for its Bohemian mores.

cant compared with her value. It would have been great, her value, anywhere; in the middle of the Punjab it was incalculable. To explain why would be to explain British India, but I hope it will appear; and I am quite willing, remember, to take responsibility if it does not.

Somers Chichele, Anna's son, it is absurd to think, must have been about fifteen then, reflecting at Winchester with the other 'men' upon the comparative merits of tinned sardines and jam roll, and whether a packet of real Egyptians was not worth the sacrifice of either. His father was colonel of the Twelfth; his mother was still charming. It was the year before Dick Forsyth came down from the neighbourhood of Sheikhbudin with a brevet[7] and a good deal of personal damage. I mention him because he proved Anna's charm in the only conclusive way before the eyes of us all; and the station, I remember, was edified to observe that if Mrs Chichele came out of the matter 'straight'—one relapses so easily into the simple definitions of those parts—which she undoubtedly did, she owed it in no small degree to Judy Harbottle. This one feels to be hardly a legitimate reference, but it is something tangible to lay hold upon in trying to describe the web of volitions which began to weave itself between the two that afternoon on my veranda and which afterward became so strong a bond. I was delighted with the thing; its simplicity and sincerity stood out among our conventional little compromises at friendship like an ideal. She and Judy had the assurance of one another; they made upon one another the finest and often the most unconscionable demands. One met them walking at odd hours in queer places, of which I imagine they were not much aware. They would turn deliberately off the Maidan[8] and away from the band-stand to be rid of our irrelevant bows; they did their duty by the rest of us, but the most egregious among us, the Deputy-Commissioner for selection, could see that he hardly counted. I thought I understood, but that may have been my fatuity; certainly when their husbands inquired what on earth they had been talking of, it usually transpired that they had found an infinite amount to say about nothing. It was a little worrying to hear Colonel Chichele and Major Harbottle describe their wives as 'pals,' but the fact could not be denied, and after all we were in the Punjab. They were pals too, but the terms were different.

People discussed it according to their lights, and girls said in pretty wonderment that Mrs Harbottle and Mrs Chichele were like men, they never kissed each other. I think Judy prescribed these conditions. Anna was far more a person who did as the world told her. But it was a poor negation to describe all that they never did; there was no common little convention of attachment that did not seem to be tacitly omitted between them. I hope one did not too cynically observe that they offered these to their husbands instead; the redeeming observation was their husbands' complete satisfaction. This they maintained to the end. In the natural order of things Robert Harbottle should have paid heavily for interfering as he did in Paris between a woman and what she was entitled to live for. As a matter of fact he never paid anything at all; I doubt whether he ever knew himself a debtor. Judy kept her temperament under like a current and swam with the tides of the surface, taking refreshing dips only now and then which one traced in her eyes and her hair when she and Robert came back from leave. That sort of thing is lost in the sands of India, but it makes

[7]An Army document conferring nominal rank (without corresponding pay).
[8]Parade-ground (Anglo-Indian).

an oasis as it travels, and it sometimes seemed to me a curious pity that she and Anna should sit in the shade of it together, while Robert and Peter Chichele, their titular companions, blundered on in the desert. But after all, if you are born blind—and the men were both immensely liked, and the shooting was good.

Ten years later Somers joined. The Twelfth were at Peshawur. Robert Harbottle was Lieutenant-Colonel by that time and had the regiment. Distinction had incrusted, in the Indian way, upon Peter Chichele, its former colonel; he was General Commanding the District and K.C.B.[9] So we were all still together in Peshawur. It was great luck for the Chicheles, Sir Peter's having the district, though his father's old regiment would have made it pleasant enough for the boy in any case. He came to us, I mean, of course, to two or three of us, with the interest that hangs about a victim of circumstances; we understood that he wasn't a 'born soldier.' Anna had told me on the contrary that he was a sacrifice to family tradition made inevitable by the General's unfortunate investments. Bellona's bridegroom[1] was not a role he fancied, though he would make a kind of compromise as best man; he would agree, she said, to be a war correspondent and write picturesque specials for the London halfpenny press. There was the humour of the poor boy's despair in it, but she conveyed it, I remember, in exactly the same tone with which she had said to me years before that he wanted to drive a milk-cart. She carried quite her half of the family tradition, though she could talk of sacrifice and make her eyes wistful, contemplating for Somers the limitations of the drill-book and the camp of exercise, proclaiming and insisting upon what she would have done if she could only have chosen for him. Anna Chichele saw things that way. With more than a passable sense of all that was involved, if she could have made her son an artist in life or a commander-in-chief, if she could have given him the seeing eye or the Order of the Star of India, she would not have hesitated for an instant. Judy, with her single mind, cried out, almost at sight of him, upon them both, I mean both Anna and Sir Peter. Not that the boy carried his condemnation badly, or even obviously; I venture that no one noticed it in the mess; but it was naturally plain to those of us who were under the same. He had put in his two years with a British regiment at Meerut—they nurse subalterns that way for the Indian army—and his eyes no longer played with the tinsel vision of India; they looked instead into the arid stretch beyond. This preoccupation conveyed to the Surgeon-Major's wife the suggestion that Mr Chichele was the victim of a hopeless attachment. Mrs Harbottle made no such mistake; she saw simply, I imagine, the beginnings of her own hunger and thirst in him, looking back as she told us across a decade of dusty sunsets to remember them. The decade was there, close to the memory of all of us; we put, from Judy herself downward, an absurd amount of confidence in it.

She looked so well the night she met him. It was English mail day; she depended a great deal upon her letters, and I suppose somebody had written her a word that brought her that happy, still excitement that is the inner mystery of words. He went straight to her with some speech about his mother having given him leave, and for twenty minutes she patronized him on a sofa as his mother would not have dreamed of doing.

[9]Knight Commander of the Bath; i.e., he had been knighted for his service.
[1]Bellona is the Roman goddess of war; in *Macbeth* (I.ii.54), Macbeth refers to himself as 'Bellona's bridegroom', i.e., married to war.

Anna Chichele, from the other side of the room, smiled on the pair.

'I depend on you and Judy to be good to him while we are away,' she said. She and Sir Peter were going on leave at the end of the week to Scotland, as usual, for the shooting.

Following her glance I felt incapable of the proportion she assigned me. 'I will see after his socks with pleasure,' I said. 'I think, don't you, we may leave the rest to Judy?'

Her eyes remained upon the boy, and I saw the passion rise in them, at which I turned mine elsewhere. Who can look unperturbed upon such a privacy of nature as that?

'Poor old Judy!' she went on. 'She never would be bothered with him in all his dear hobble-dehoy time; she resented his claims, the unreasonable creature, used to limit me to three anecdotes a week; and now she has him on her hands, if you like. See the pretty air of deference in the way he listens to her! He has nice manners, the villain, if he is a Chichele!'

'Oh, you have improved Sir Peter's,' I said kindly.

'I do hope Judy will think him worth while. I can't quite expect that he will be up to her, bless him, she is so much cleverer, isn't she, than any of us? But if she will just be herself with him it will make such a difference.'

The other two crossed the room to us at that, and Judy gaily made Somers over to his mother, trailing off to find Robert in the billiard-room.

'Well, what has Mrs Harbottle been telling you?' Anna asked him.

The young man's eye followed Judy, his hand went musingly to his moustache.

'She was telling me,' he said, 'that people in India were sepulchers of themselves, but that now and then one came who could roll away another's stone.'

'It sounds promising,' said Lady Chichele to me.

'It sounds cryptic,' I laughed to Somers, but I saw that he had the key.

I can not say that I attended diligently to Mr Chichele's socks, but the part corresponding was freely assigned me. After his people went I saw him often. He pretended to find qualities in my tea, implied that he found them in my talk. As a matter of fact it was my inquiring attitude that he loved, the knowledge that there was no detail that he could give me about himself, his impressions and experiences, that was unlikely to interest me. I would not for the world imply that he was egotistical or complacent, absolutely the reverse, but he possessed an articulate soul which found its happiness in expression, and I liked to listen. I feel that these are complicated words to explain a very simple relation, and I pause to wonder what is left to me if I wished to describe his commerce with Mrs Harbottle. Luckily there is an alternative; one needn't do it. I wish I had somewhere on paper Judy's own account of it at this period, however. It is a thing she would have enjoyed writing and more enjoyed communicating, at this period.

There was a grave reticence in his talk about her which amused me in the beginning. Mrs Harbottle had been for ten years important enough to us all, but her serious significance, the light and the beauty in her, had plainly been reserved for the discovery of this sensitive and intelligent person not very long from Sandhurst and exactly twenty-six. I was barely allowed a familiar reference, and anything approaching a flippancy was met with penetrating silence. I was almost rebuked for lightly suggesting that she must occasionally find herself bored in Peshawur.

'I think not anywhere,' said Mr Chichele; 'Mrs Harbottle is one of the few people who sound the privilege of living.'

This to me, who had counted Mrs Harbottle's yawns on so many occasions! It became presently necessary to be careful, tactful, in one's implications about Mrs Harbottle, and to recognize a certain distinction in the fact that one was the only person with whom Mr Chichele discussed her at all.

The day came when we talked of Robert; it was bound to come in the progress of any understanding and affectionate coloquy which had his wife for inspiration. I was familiar, of course, with Somer's opinion that the Colonel was an awfully good sort; that had been among the preliminaries and become understood as the base of all references. And I liked Robert Harbottle very well myself. When his adjutant called him a born leader of men, however, I felt compelled to look at the statement consideringly.

'In a tight place,' I said—dear me, what expressions had the freedom of our little frontier drawing-rooms!—'I would as soon depend on him as on anybody. But as for leadership—'

'He is such a good fellow that nobody here does justice to his soldierly qualities,' said Mr Chichele, 'except Mrs Harbottle.'

'Has she been telling you about them?' I inquired.

'Well,' he hesitated, 'she told me about the Mulla Nulla affair. She is rather proud of that. Any woman would be.'

'Poor dear Judy!' I mused.

Somers said nothing, but looked at me, removing his cigarette, as if my words would be the better of explanation.

'She has taken refuge in them—in Bob Harbottle's soldierly qualities—ever since she married him,' I continued.

'Taken refuge,' he repeated, coldly, but at my uncompromising glance his eyes fell.

'Well?' I said.

'You mean—'

'Oh, I mean what I say,' I laughed. 'Your cigarette has gone out—have another.'

'I think her devotion to him splendid.'

'Quite splendid. Have you seen the things he brought her from the Simla Art Exhibition? He said they were nice bits of colour, and she has hung them in the drawing-room, where she will have to look at them every day. Let us admire her—dear Judy.'

'Oh,' he said, with a fine air of detachment, 'do you think they are so necessary, those agreements?'

'Well,' I replied, 'we see that they are not indispensable. More sugar? I have only given you one lump. And we know, at all events,' I added, unguardedly, 'that she could never have had an illusion about him.'

The young man looked up quickly. 'Is that story true?' he asked.

'There was a story, but most of us have forgotten it. Who told you?'

'The doctor.'

'The Surgeon-Major,' I said, 'has an accurate memory and a sense of proportion. As I suppose you were bound to get it from somebody, I am glad you got it from him.'

I was not prepared to go on, and saw with some relief that Somers was not either. His silence, as he smoked, seemed to me deliberate; and I had oddly enough at this moment for the first time the impression that he was a man and not a boy. Then the Harbottles themselves joined us, very cheery after a gallop from the Wazir-Bagh. We talked of old times, old friendships, good swords that were broken, names that had carried far, and Somers effaced himself in the perfect manner of the British subaltern. It was a long, pleasant gossip, and I thought Judy seemed rather glad to let her husband dictate its level, which, of course, he did. I noticed when the three rode away together that the Colonel was beginning to sit down rather solidly on his big New Zealander; and I watched the dusk come over from the foot-hills for a long time thinking more kindly than I had spoken of Robert Harbottle.

I have often wondered how far happiness is contributed to a temperament like Judy Harbottle's, and how far it creates its own; but I doubt whether, on either count, she found as much in any other winter of her life except perhaps the remote ones by the Seine. Those ardent hours of hers, when everything she said was touched with the flame of her individuality, came oftener; she suddenly cleaned up her palate and began to translate in one study after another the language of the frontier country, that spoke only in stones and in shadows under the stones and in sunlight over them. There is nothing in the Academy[2] of this year, at all events, that I would exchange for the one she gave me. She lived her physical life at a pace which carried us all along with her; she hunted and drove and danced and dined with such sincere intention as convinced us all that in hunting and driving and dancing and dining there were satisfactions that had been somehow overlooked. The Surgeon-Major's wife said it was delightful to meet Mrs Harbottle, she seemed to enjoy everything so thoroughly; the Surgeon-Major looked at her critically and asked her if she were quite sure she hadn't a night temperature. He was a Scotchman. One night Colonel Harbottle, hearing her give away the last extra,[3] charged her with renewing her youth.

'No, Bob,' she said, 'only imitating it.'

Ah, that question of her youth. It was so near her—still, she told me once, she heard the beat of its flying, and the pulse in her veins answered the false signal. That was afterward, when she told the truth. She was not so happy when she indulged herself otherwise. As when she asked one to remember that she was a middle-aged woman, with middle-aged thoughts and satisfactions.

'I am now really happiest,' she declared, 'when the Commissioner takes me in to dinner, when the General Commanding leads me to the dance.'

She did her best to make it an honest conviction. I offered her a recent success not crowned by the Academy, and she put it down on the table. 'By and by,' she said. 'At present I am reading Pascal and Bossuet.'[4] Well, she was reading Pascal and Bossuet. She grieved aloud that most of our activities in India were so indomitably youthful, owing to the accident that most of us were always so young. 'There is no

---

[2]The Annual Exhibition of the Royal Academy of Painting, Sculpture, and Architecture (in England).
[3]At a ball 'extras' are dances added to those on the program.
[4]Blaise Pascal (1623-62) and Jacques Bénigne Bossuet (1627-1704) were French religious philosophers. Pascal also contributed to mathematical theory, particularly in the field of probability.

dignified distraction in this country,' she complained, 'for respectable ladies nearing forty.' She seemed to like to make these declarations in the presence of Somers Chichele, who would look at her with a little queer smile—a bad translation, I imagine, of what he felt.

She gave herself so generously to her seniors that somebody said Mrs Harbottle's girdle was hung with brass hats. It seems flippant to add that her complexion was as honest as the day, but the fact is that the year before Judy had felt compelled, like the rest of us, to repair just a little the ravages of the climate. If she had never done it one would not have looked twice at the absurdity when she said of the powder-puff in the dressing-room, 'I have raised that thing to the level of an immorality,' and sailed in to dance with an uncompromising expression and a face uncompromised. I have not spoken of her beauty; for one thing it was not always there, and there were people who would deny it altogether, or whose considered comment was, 'I wouldn't call her plain.' They, of course, were people in whom she declined to be interested, but even for those of us who could evoke some demonstration of her vivid self her face would not always light in correspondence. When it did there was none that I liked better to look at; and I envied Somers Chichele his way to make it the pale, shining thing that would hold him lifted, in return, for hours together, with I know not what mystic power of a moon upon the tide. And he? Oh, he was dark and delicate, by nature simple, sincere, delightfully intelligent. His common title to charm was the rather sweet seriousness that rested on his upper lip, and a certain winning gratification in his attention; but he had a subtler one in his eyes, which must be always seeking and smiling over what they found; those eyes of perpetual inquiry for the exquisite which ask so little help to create it. A personality to button up in a uniform, good heavens!

As I begin to think of them together I remember how the maternal note appeared in her talk about him.

'His youth is pathetic,' she told me, 'but there is nothing that he does not understand.'

'Don't apologize, Judy,' I said. We were so brusque on the frontier. Besides, the matter still suffered a jocular presentment. Mrs Harbottle and Mr Chichele were still 'great friends'; we could still put them next each other at our dinner-parties without the feeling that it would be 'marked.' There was still nothing unusual in the fact that when Mrs Harbottle was there Mr Chichele might be taken for granted. We were so broad-minded also, on the frontier.

It grew more obvious, the maternal note. I began positively to dread it, almost as much, I imagine, as Somers did. She took her privileges all in Anna's name, she exercised her authority quite as Lady Chichele's proxy. She went to the very limit. 'Anna Chichele,' she said actually in his presence, 'is a fortunate woman. She has all kinds of cleverness, and she has her tall son. I have only one little talent, and I have no tall son.' Now it was not in nature that she could have had a son as tall as Somers, nor was that desire in her eyes. All civilization implies a good deal of farce, but this was a poor refuge, a cheap device; I was glad when it fell away from her sincerity, when the day came on which she looked into my fire and said simply, 'An attachment like ours has no terms.'

'I wonder,' I said.

'For what comes and goes,' she went on dreamily, 'how could there be a formula?'

'Look here, Judy,' I said, 'you know me very well. What if the flesh leaps with the spirit?'

She looked at me, very white. 'Oh no,' she said, 'no.'

I waited, but there seemed nothing more that she could say; and in the silence the futile negative seemed to wander round the room repeating itself like an echo. 'Oh no, no.' I poked the fire presently to drown the sound of it. Judy sat still, with her feet crossed and her hands thrust into the pockets of her coat, staring into the coals.

'Can you live independently, satisfied with your interests and occupations?' she demanded at last. 'Yes, I know you can. I can't. I must exist more than half in other people. It is what they think and feel that matters to me, just as much as what I think and feel. The best of life is in that communication.'

'It has always been a passion with you, Judy,' I replied. 'I can imagine how much you must miss—'

'Whom?'

'Anna Chichele,' I said softly.

She got up and walked about the room, fixing here and there an intent regard upon things which she did not see. 'Oh, I do,' she said at one point, with the effect of pulling herself together. She took another turn or two, and then finding herself near the door she went out. I felt as profoundly humiliated for her as if she had staggered.

The next night was one of those that stand out so vividly, for no reason that one can identify, in one's memory. We were dining with the Harbottles, a small party, for a tourist they had with them. Judy and I and Somers and the traveller had drifted out into the veranda, where the scent of Japanese lilies came and went on the spring wind to trouble the souls of any taken unawares. There was a brightness beyond the foot-hills where the moon was coming, and I remember how one tall clump swayed out against it, and seemed in passionate perfume to lay a burden on the breast. Judy moved away from it and sat clasping her knees on the edge of the veranda. Somers, when his eyes were not upon her, looked always at the lily.

Even the spirit of the globe-trotter was stirred, and he said, 'I think you Anglo-Indians live in a kind of little paradise.'

There was an instant's silence, and then Judy turned her face into the lamplight from the drawing-room. 'With everything but the essentials,' she said.

We stayed late; Mr Chichele and ourselves were the last to go. Judy walked with us along the moonlit drive to the gate, which is so unnecessary a luxury in India that the servants always leave it open. She swung the stiff halves together.

'Now,' she said, 'it is shut.'

'And I,' said Somers Chichele, softly and quickly, 'am on the other side.'

Even over that depth she could flash him a smile. 'It is the business of my life,' she gave him in return, 'to keep this gate shut.' I felt as if they had forgotten us. Somers mounted and rode off without a word; we were walking in a different direction. Looking back, I saw Judy leaning immoveable on the gate, while Somers turned in his saddle, apparently to repeat the form of lifting his hat. And all about them stretched the stones of Kabul valley, vague and formless in the tide of the moonlight . . .

Next day a note from Mrs Harbottle informed me that she had gone to Bombay for a fortnight. In a postscript she wrote, 'I shall wait for the Chicheles there, and come back with them.' I remember reflecting that if she could not induce herself to take a passage to England in the ship that brought them, it seemed the right thing to do.

She did come back with them. I met the party at the station. I knew Somers would meet them, and it seemed to me, so imminent did disaster loom, that some one else should be there, some one to offer a covering movement or a flank support wherever it might be most needed. And among all our smiling faces disaster did come, or the cold premonition of it. We were all perfect, but Somers's lip trembled. Deprived for a fortnight he was eager for the draft, and he was only twenty-six. His lip trembled, and there, under the flickering station-lamps, suddenly stood that of which there never could be again any denial, for those of us who saw.

Did we make, I wonder, even a pretense of disguising the consternation that sprang up among us, like an armed thing, ready to kill any further suggestion of the truth? I don't know. Anna Chichele's unfinished sentence dropped as if someone had given her a blow upon the mouth. Coolies were piling the luggage into a hired carriage at the edge of the platform. She walked mechanically after them, and would have stepped in with it but for the sight of her own gleaming landau drawn up within a yard or two, and the General waiting. We all got home somehow, taking it with us, and I gave Lady Chichele twenty-four hours to come to me with her face all one question and her heart all one fear. She came in twelve.

'Have you seen it—long?' Prepared as I was her directness was demoralizing.

'It isn't a mortal disease.'

'Oh, for Heaven's sake—'

'Well, not with certainty, for more than a month.'

She made a little spasmodic movement with her hands, then dropped them pitifully. 'Couldn't you do *anything*?'

I looked at her, and she said at once, 'No, of course you couldn't.'

For a moment or two I took my share of the heavy sense of it, my trivial share, which yet was an experience sufficiently exciting. 'I am afraid it will have to be faced,' I said.

'What will happen?' Anna cried. 'Oh, what will happen?'

'Why not the usual thing?' Lady Chichele looked up quickly as if at a reminder. 'The ambiguous attachment of the country,' I went on, limping but courageous, 'half declared, half admitted, that leads vaguely nowhere, and finally perishes as the man's life enriches itself—the thing we have seen so often.'

'Whatever Judy is capable of it won't be the usual thing. You know that.'

I had to confess in silence that I did.

'It flashed at me—the difference in her—in Bombay.' She pressed her lips together and then went on unsteadily. 'In her eyes, her voice. She was mannered, extravagant, elaborate. With me! All the way up I wondered and worried. But I never thought—' She stopped; her voice simply shook itself into silence. I called a servant.

'I am going to give you a good stiff peg,' I said. I apologize for the 'peg,' but not for the whisky and soda. It is a beverage on the frontier, of which the vulgarity is lost in the value. While it was coming I tried to talk of other things, but she would only nod absently in the pauses.

'Last night we dined with him, it was guest night at the mess, and she was there. I watched her, and she knew it. I don't know whether she tried, but anyway, she failed. The covenant between them was written on her forehead whenever she looked at him, though that was seldom. She dared not look at him. And the little conversation that they had—you would have laughed—it was a comedy of stutters. The facile Mrs Harbottle!'

'You do well to be angry, naturally,' I said; 'but it would be fatal to let yourself go, Anna.'

'Angry? Oh, I am *sick*. The misery of it! The terror of it! If it were anybody but Judy! Can't you imagine the passion of a temperament like that in a woman who has all these years been feeding on herself? I tell you she will take him from my very arms. And he will go—to I dare not imagine what catastrophe! Who can prevent it? Who can prevent it?'

'There is you,' I said.

Lady Chichele laughed hysterically. 'I think you ought to say, "There are you." I—what can I do? Do you realize that it's *Judy*? My friend—my other self? Do you think we can drag all that out of it? Do you think a tie like that can be broken by an accident—by a misfortune? With it all I *adore* Judy Harbottle. I love her, as I have always loved her, and—it's damnable, but I don't know whether, whatever happened, I wouldn't go on loving her.'

'Finish your peg,' I said. She was sobbing.

'Where I blame myself most,' she went on, 'is for not seeing in him all that makes him mature to her—that makes her forget the absurd difference between them, and take him simply and sincerely as I know she does, as the contemporary of her soul if not of her body. I saw none of that. Could I, as his mother? Would he show it to me? I thought him just a charming boy, clever, too, of course, with nice instincts and well plucked; we were always proud of that, with his delicate physique. Just a boy! I haven't yet stopped thinking how different he looks without his curls. And I thought she would be just kind and gracious and delightful to him because he was my son.'

'There, of course,' I said, 'is the only chance.'

'Where—what?'

'He is your son.'

'Would you have me appeal to her? Do you know I don't think I could?'

'Dear me, no. Your case must present itself. It must spring upon her and grow before her out of your silence, and if you can manage it, your confidence. There is a great deal, after all, remember, to hold her in that. I can't somehow imagine her failing you. Otherwise—'

Lady Chichele and I exchanged a glance of candid admission.

'Otherwise she would be capable of sacrificing everything—everything. Of gathering her life into an hour. I know. And do you know if the thing were less impossible, less grotesque, I should not be so much afraid? I mean that the *absolute* indefensibility of it might bring her a recklessness and a momentum which might—'

'Send her over the verge,' I said. 'Well, go home and ask her to dinner.'

There was a good deal more to say, of course, than I have thought proper to put down here, but before Anna went I saw that she was keyed up to the heroic part. This was none the less to her credit because it was the only part, the dictation of a sense of expediency that despaired while it dictated. The noble thing was her capacity to take it, and, amid all that warred in her, to carry it out on the brave high lines of her inspiration. It seemed a literal inspiration, so perfectly calculated that it was hard not to think sometimes, when one saw them together, that Anna had been lulled into a simple resumption of the old relation. Then from the least thing possible—the lift of an eyelid—it flashed upon one that between these two every moment was dramatic, and one took up the word with a curious sense of detachment and futility, but with one's heart beating like a trip-hammer with the mad excitement of it. The acute thing was the splendid sincerity of Judy Harbottle's response. For days she was profoundly on her guard, then suddenly she seemed to become practically, vividly aware of what I must go on calling the great chance, and passionately to fling herself upon it. It was the strangest co-operation without a word or a sign to show it conscious—a playing together for stakes that could not be admitted, a thing to hang upon breathless. It was there between them—the tenable ground of what they were to each other: they occupied it with almost an equal eye upon the tide that threatened, while I from my mainland tower also made an anguished calculation of the chances. I think in spite of the menace, they found real beatitudes; so keenly did they set about the business that it brought them moments finer than any they could count in the years that were behind them, the flat and colourless years that were gone. Once or twice the wild idea even visited me that it was, after all, the projection of his mother in Somers that had so seized Judy Harbottle, and that the original was all that was needed to help the happy process of detachment. Somers himself at the time was a good deal away on escort duty: they had a clear field.

I can not tell exactly when—between Mrs Harbottle and myself—it became a matter for reference more or less overt, I mean her defined problem, the thing that went about between her and the sun. It will be imagined that it did not come up like the weather; indeed, it was hardly ever to be envisaged and never to be held; but it was always there, and out of our joint consciousness it would sometimes leap and pass, without shape or face. It might slip between two sentences, or it might remain, a dogging shadow, for an hour. Or a week would go by while, with a strong hand, she held it out of sight altogether and talked of Anna—always of Anna. Her eyes shone with the things she told me then: she seemed to keep herself under the influence of them as if they had the power of narcotics. At the end of a time like this she turned to me in the door as she was going and stood silent, as if she could neither go nor stay. I had been able to make nothing of her that afternoon: she had seemed preoccupied with the pattern of the carpet which she traced continually with her riding crop, and finally I, too, had relapsed. She sat haggard, with the fight forever in her eyes, and the day seemed to sombre about her in her corner. When she turned in the door, I looked up with sudden prescience of a crisis.

'Don't jump,' she said, 'it was only to tell you that I have persuaded Robert to apply for furlough. Eighteen months. From the first of April. Don't touch me.' I suppose I made a movement towards her. Certainly I wanted to throw my arms about her; with the instinct, I suppose, to steady her in her great resolution.

'At the end of that time, as you know, he will be retired. I had some trouble, he is so keen on the regiment, but I think—I have succeeded. You might mention it to Anna.'

'Haven't you?' sprang past my lips.

'I can't. It would be like taking an oath to tell her, and—I can't take an oath to go. But I mean to.'

'There is nothing to be said,' I brought out, feeling indeed that there was not. 'But I congratulate you, Judy.'

'No, there is nothing to be said. And you congratulate me, no doubt!'

She stood for a moment quivering in the isolation she made for herself; and I felt a primitive angry revolt against the delicate trafficking of souls that could end in such ravage and disaster. The price was too heavy; I would have denuded her, at the moment, of all that had led her into this, and turned her out a clod with fine shoulders like fifty other women in Peshawur. Then, perhaps, because I held myself silent and remote and she had no emotion of fear from me, she did not immediately go.

'It will beat itself away, I suppose, like the rest of the unreasonable pain of the world,' she said at last; and that, of course, brought me to her side. 'Things will go back to their proportions. This,' she touched an open rose, 'will claim its beauty again. And life will become—perhaps—what it was before.' Still I found nothing to say, I could only put my arm in hers and walk with her to the edge of the veranda where the syce[5] was holding her horse. She stroked the animal's neck. 'Everything in me answered him,' she informed me, with the grave intelligence of a patient who relates a symptom past. As she took the reins she turned to me again. 'His spirit came to mine like a homing bird,' she said, and in her smile even the pale reflection of happiness was sweet and stirring. It left me hanging in imagination over the source and the stream, a little blessed in the mere understanding.

Too much blessed for confidence, or any safe feeling that the source was bound. Rather I saw it leaping over every obstacle, flashing to its destiny. As I drove to the Club next day I decided that I would not tell Anna Chichele of Colonel Harbottle's projected furlough. If to Judy telling her would be like taking an oath that they would go, to me it would at least be like assuming sponsorship for their intention. That would be heavy indeed. From the first of April—we were then in March. Anna would hear it soon enough from the General, would see it soon enough, almost, in the *Gazette*, when it would have passed into irrecoverable fact. So I went by her with locked lips, kept out of the way of those eyes of the mother that asked and asked, and would have seen clear to any depth, any hiding-place of knowledge like that. As I pulled up at the Club I saw Colonel Harbottle talking concernedly to the wife of our Second-in-Command, and was reminded that I had not heard for some days how Major Watkins was going on. So I, too, approached Mrs Watkins in her victoria[6] to ask. Robert Harbottle kindly forestalled her reply. 'Hard luck, isn't it? Watkins has been ordered home at once. Just settled into their new house, too—last of the kit came up from Calcutta yesterday, didn't it, Mrs Watkins? But it's sound to go—Peshawur is the worst hole in Asia to shake off dysentery in.'

We agreed upon this and discussed the sale-list of her new furniture that Mrs Watkins would have to send round the station, and considered the chances of a trooper—to the Watkinses with two children and not a penny but his pay it did make it easier not to have to go by a liner—and Colonel Harbottle and I were half-way to the reading-room before the significance of Major Watkin's sick-leave flashed upon me.

'But this,' I cried, 'will make a difference to your plans. You won't—'

'Be able to ask for that furlough Judy wants. Rather not. I'm afraid she's disappointed—she was tremendously set on going—but it doesn't matter tuppence to me.'

[5]Groom (Anglo-Indian).
[6]A light four-wheeled carriage.

I sought out Mrs Harbottle, at the end of the room. She looked radiant; she sat on the edge of the table and swung a light-hearted heel. She was talking to people who in themselves were a witness to high spirits, Captain the Hon. Freddy Gisborne, Mrs Flamboys.

At sight of me her face clouded, fell suddenly into the old weary lines. It made me feel somehow a little sick; I went back to my cart and drove home.

For more than a week I did not see her except when I met her riding with Somers Chichele along the peach-bordered road that leads to the Wazir-Bagh. The trees were all in blossom and made a picture that might well catch dreaming hearts into a beatitude that would correspond. The air was full of spring and the scent of violets, those wonderful Peshawur violets that grow in great clumps, tall and double. Gracious clouds came and trailed across the frontier barrier; blue as an idyll it rose about us; the city smiled in her gardens.

She had it all in her face, poor Judy, all the spring softness and more, the morning she came, intensely controlled, to announce her defeat. I was in the drawing-room doing the flowers; I put them down to look at her. The wonderful telegram from Simla arrived—that was the wonderful part—at the same time; I remembered how the red, white, and blue turban of the telegraph peon bobbed up behind her shoulder in the veranda. I signed and laid it on the table; I suppose it seemed hardly likely that anything could be important enough to interfere at the moment with my impression of what love, unbound and victorious, could do with a face I thought I knew. Love sat there careless of the issue, full of delight. Love proclaimed that between him and Judith Harbottle it was all over—she had met him, alas, in too narrow a place—and I marvelled at the paradox with which he softened every curve and underlined every vivid note of personality in token that it had just begun. He sat there in great serenity, and though I knew that somewhere behind lurked a vanquished woman, I saw her through such a radiance that I could not be sure of seeing her at all . . .

She went back to the very first of it; she seemed herself intensely interested in the facts; and there is no use in pretending that, while she talked, the moral consideration was at all present with me either; it wasn't. Her extremity was the thing that absorbed us; she even, in tender thoughtfulness, diagnosed it from its definite beautiful beginning.

'It was there, in my heart, when I woke one morning, exquisite and strange, the assurance of a gift. How had it come there, while I slept? I assure you when I closed my eyes it did not exist for me. . . . Yes, of course, I had seen him, but only somewhere at dinner. . . . As the day went on it changed—it turned into a clear pool, into a flower. And I—think of my not understanding! I was pleased with it! For a long time, for days, I never dreamed that it could be anything but a little secret joy. Then, suddenly—oh, I had not been perceiving enough!—It was in all my veins, a tide, an efflorescence, a thing of my very life.

'Then—it was a little late—I understood, and since—

'I began by hating it—being furious, furious—and afraid, too. Sometimes it was like a low cloud, hovering and travelling always with me, sometimes like a beast of prey that went a little way off and sat looking at me. . .

'I have—done my best. But there is nothing to do, to kill, to abolish. How can I say, 'I will not let you in,' when it is already there? How can I assume indifference when this thing is imposed upon every moment of my day? And it has grown so sweet—the longing—that—isn't it strange?—I could more willingly give him up than the desire of him. That seems as impossible to part with as life itself.'

She sat reflective for a moment, and I saw her eyes slowly fill.

'Don't—don't *cry*, Judy,' I faltered, wanting to horribly, myself.

She smiled them dry.

'Not now. But I am giving myself, I suppose, to many tears.'

'God help you,' I said. What else was there to say?

'There is no such person,' she replied, gaily. 'There is only a blessed devil.'

'Then you go all the way—to the logical conclusion?'

She hardly hesitated. 'To the logical conclusion. What poor words!'

'May I ask—when?'

'I should like to tell you that quite definitely, and I think I can. The English mail leaves tonight.'

'And you have arranged to take it?'

'We have arranged nothing. Do you know'—she smiled as if at the fresh colours of an idyll—'we have not even come to the admission? There has been between us no word, no vision. Ah, we have gone in bonds, and dumb! Hours we have had, exquisite hours of the spirit, but never a moment of the heart, a moment confessed. It was mine to give—that moment, and he has waited—I know—wondering whether perhaps it would ever come. And today—we are going for a ride today, and I do not think we shall come back.'

'O Judy,' I cried, catching at her sleeve, 'he is only a boy!'

'There were times when I thought that conclusive. Now the misery of it has gone to sleep; don't waken it. It pleases me to believe that the years are a convention. I never had any dignity, you know, and I seem to have missed the moral deliverance. I only want—oh, you know what I want. Why don't you open your telegram?'

I had been folding and fingering the brown envelope as if it had been a scrap of waste-paper.

'It is probably from Mrs Watkins about the victoria,' I said, feeling its profound irrelevance. 'I wired an offer to her in Bombay. However'—and I read the telegram, the little solving telegram from Army Headquarters. I turned my back on her to read it again, and then I replaced it very carefully and put it in my pocket. It was a moment to take hold of with both hands, crying on all one's gods for steadiness.

'How white you look!' said Mrs Harbottle, with concern. 'Not bad news?'

'On the contrary, excellent news. Judy, will you stay to lunch?'

She looked at me, hesitating. 'Won't it seem rather a compromise on your part? When you ought to be rousing the city—'

'I don't intend to rouse the city,' I said.

'I have given you the chance.'

'Thank you,' I said, grimly, 'but the only real favour you can do me is to stay and lunch.' It was then just on one.

'I'll stay,' she said, 'if you will promise not to make any sort of effort. I shouldn't mind, but it would distress you.'

'I promise absolutely,' I said, and ironical joy rose up in me, and the telegram burned in my pocket.

She would talk of it, though I found it hard to let her go on, knowing and knowing and knowing as I did that for that day at least it could not be. There was very little about herself that she wanted to tell me; she was there confessed a woman whom joy had overcome; it was understood that we both accepted that situation. But in the details which she asked me to take charge of it was plain that she also kept a watchful eye upon fate—matters of business.

We were in the drawing-room. The little round clock in its Amritsar[7] case marked half-past three. Judy put down her coffee-cup and rose to go. As she glanced at the clock the light deepened in her eyes, and I, with her hand in mine, felt like an agent of the Destroyer—for it was half-past three—consumed myself with fear lest the blow had miscarried. Then as we stood, suddenly, the sound of hoofs at a gallop on the drive, and my husband threw himself off at the door and tore through the hall to his room; and in the certainty that overwhelmed me even Judy, for an instant, stood dim and remote.

'Major Jim seems to be in a hurry,' said Mrs Harbottle, lightly. 'I have always liked your husband. I wonder whether he will say tomorrow that he always liked me.'

'Dear Judy, I don't think he will be occupied with you tomorrow.'

'Oh, surely, just a little, if I go tonight.'

'You won't go tonight.'

She looked at me helplessly. I felt as if I were insisting upon her abasement instead of her salvation. 'I wish— '

'You're not going—you're not! You can't! Look!'

I pulled it out of my pocket and thrust it at her—the telegram. It came, against every regulation, from my good friend the Deputy Adjutant-General, in Simla, and it read, '*Row Khurram 12th probably ordered front three hours' time.*'

Her face changed—how my heart leaped to see it change!—and that took command there which will command trampling, even in the women of the camp, at news like this.

'What luck that Bob couldn't take his furlough!' she exclaimed, single- thoughted. 'But you have known this for hours'—there was even something of the Colonel's wife, authority, incisiveness. 'Why didn't you tell me? Ah—I see.'

I stood before her abashed, and that was ridiculous, while she measured me as if I presented in myself the woman I took her to be. 'It wasn't like that,' she said. I had to defend myself. 'Judy,' I said, 'if you weren't in honour bound to Anna, how could I know that you would be in honour bound to the regiment? There was a train at three.'

'I beg to assure you that you have overcalculated,' said Mrs Harbottle. Her eyes were hard and proud. 'And I am not sure'—a deep red swept over her face, a man's blush—'in the light of this I am not sure that I am not in honour bound to Anna.'

We had reached the veranda, and at her signal her coachman drove quickly up. 'You have kept me here three hours when there was the whole of Bob's kit to see to,' she said, as she flung herself in; 'you might have thought of that.'

It was a more than usually tedious campaign, and Colonel Robert Harbottle was ambushed and shot in a place where one must believe pure boredom induced him to

[7]A city in Northwest India. It is the site of the Golden Temple, set in the centre of a lake, a place especially sacred to Sikhs.

take his men. The incident was relieved, the newspapers said—and they are seldom so clever in finding relief for such incidents—by the dash and courage shown by Lieutenant Chichele, who, in one of those feats which it has lately been the fashion to criticize, carried the mortally wounded body of his Colonel out of range at conspicuous risk of depriving the Queen of another officer. I helped Judy with her silent packing; she had forgiven me long before that; and she settled almost at once into the flat in Chelsea which has since been credited with so delightful an atmosphere, went back straight into her own world. I have always kept her first letters about it, always shall. For months after, while the expedition still raged after snipers and rifle-thieves, I discussed with Lady Chichele the probable outcome of it all. I have sometimes felt ashamed of leaping as straight as I did with Anna to what we thought the inevitable. I based no calculation on all Mrs Harbottle had gone back to, just as I had based no calculation on her ten years' companionship in arms when I kept her from the three o'clock train. This last was a retrospection in which Anna naturally could not join me; she never knew, poor dear, how fortunate as to its moment was the campaign she deplored, and nothing to this day can have disturbed her conviction that the bond she was at such magnificent pains to strengthen, held against the strain, as long, happily, as the supreme need existed. 'How right you were!' she often said. 'She did, after all, love me best, dear, wonderful Judy!' Her distress about poor Robert Harbottle was genuine enough, but one could not be surprised at a certain ambiguity; one tear for Robert, so to speak, and two for her boy. It could hardly be, for him, a marriage after his mother's heart. And she laid down with some emphasis that Somers was brilliantly entitled to all he was likely to get—which was natural, too. . . .

I had been from the beginning so much 'in it' that Anna showed me, a year later, though I don't believe she liked doing it, the letter in part of which Mrs Harbottle shall finally excuse herself.

'Somers will give you this,' I read, 'and with it take back your son. You will not find, I know, anything grotesque in the charming enthusiasm with which he has offered his life to me; you understand too well, you are too kind. And if you wonder that I can so render up a dear thing which I might keep and would once have taken, think how sweet in the desert is the pool, and how barren was the prospect from Balclutha.'

It was like her to abandon in pride a happiness that asked so much less humiliation; I don't know why, but it was like her. And of course, when one thought of it, she had consulted all sorts of high expediencies. But I sat silent with remembrance, quieting a pang in my heart, trying not to calculate how much it had cost Judy Harbottle to take her second chance.

1903

Pauline Johnson

1861-1913

Pauline Johnson was born in 'Chiefswood', a mansion built on the Six Nations Reserve in the Grand River valley near Brantford, Ont., by her Mohawk father (Chief George Henry Martin Johnson) for his English bride, Emily Susanna Howells. Johnson's early learning was derived from stories told by her grandfather, John Smoke Johnson, and from her governesses. Although her formal education was limited—she spent two years at a school on the reserve and two more at Central Collegiate in Brantford (1875-7)—her mother introduced her to the work of Longfellow, Byron, Shakespeare, and Emerson. Johnson also read the important poets and prose writers of her day. At school, she pursued her interest in the performing arts, and learned the rhetorical skills that would be the cornerstone of her career.

After her return to Chiefswood, Johnson began to write poetry. In 1886 she adopted the Mohawk name 'Tekahionwake' (or 'Double Wampum'), and published her first poem that year, after reading it at the unveiling of the Joseph Brant Statue in Brantford's Victoria Park. In 1892, her reading of 'A Cry from an Indian Wife' at the Young Liberals' Club in Toronto was so well received that it launched her career as a poet-performer. She toured as the 'Mohawk Princess', wearing a buckskin costume when reading Indian poems, and evening dress for the remainder of her performance. She performed with the comedian and musician Owen Smiley (until 1897) and with Walter McRaye (after 1901), whose discussion of her career is recorded in *Pauline Johnson and her Friends* (1947). In 1909 she retired to Vancouver, where she learned, in 1910, that she had cancer. She died in Bute hospital after a long illness.

Johnson's reputation as a poet was established when two of her poems were included in the anthology, *Songs of the Great Dominion* (London, 1889). By the time her first collection of poetry, *The White Wampum*, was published in Britain in 1895

she was already a popular performer both there and in North America. This collection and her next, *Canadian Born* (1903), increased the interest in her performances. Her last collection, *Flint and Feather* (1912), published just before her death, is drawn principally from the two previous volumes. After 1904, however, Johnson had begun to concentrate on writing prose, and published three collections of short fiction: *Legends of Vancouver* (1911), based on stories told to her by Chief Joe Capilano of the Squamish Indians; and *The Shagganappi* (1913) and *The Moccasin Maker* (1913), both of which were published posthumously.

In the Foreword to *Flint and Feather*, Johnson explains that she chose this title because it represented the twin emphases of her work. 'Flint suggests the Red man's weapons of war; it is the arrow tip, the heart-quality of mine own people; let it therefore apply to those poems that touch upon Indian life and love. The lyrical verse herein is as a "Skyward floating feather, / Sailing on summer air." And yet that feather may be the eagle plume that crests the head of a warrior chief; so both flint and feather bear the hallmark of my Mohawk blood.'

The tension in Johnson's work resulting from her twin heritages—Mohawk and British—is most clear in 'A Cry from an Indian Wife'. Although she makes use of her Mohawk heritage for both the content and the perspective of the poem, which conveys an Indian wife's thoughts on the North-West rebellion of 1869-70 led by Louis Riel, Johnson also draws heavily on her knowledge of the conventions of English verse. (The speaker's hesitations, for instance, are more reminiscent of a Shakespeare soliloquy than of the oral tradition of Johnson's Mohawk ancestors.) But this was the key to Johnson's charm for contemporary audiences: this 'Mohawk Princess' communicated the unfamiliar in a way wholly familiar to them. In 'Silhouette', for example—part of the Smiley-Johnson performance routine called 'There and Back' (first published in *Canadian Born* under the title 'Silhouetted')—Johnson uses a variation of the familiar ballad to paint a picture of a noble and endangered way of life, and to make it readily accessible to her audience.

Despite the use of a specifically Canadian landscape—the maples and the maize of 'The Flight of the Wild Crows'—the antecedents of Johnson's lyric verse are in the poetry of the British Romantics. No wonder Pauline Johnson was so well received in England in 1894 and again in 1906, and that her first book was published by the British house of Bodley Head. When she moved away from that tradition, as she did in 1894

with the publication in the Toronto *Globe* of 'His Majesty the West Wind'—an uncharacteristically frank criticism of her own popular poem, 'The Song My Paddle Sings'—she made even her Canadian audiences uncomfortable (*Beaver*, December 1986/January 1987):

I never thought when grinding out those
stanzas
I'd have to swallow specks of prairie dust,
That I'd deny my old extravaganzas
And wish His Majesty distinctly—cussed!

The spark of humour in this poem shows a side of Johnson that was rarely seen; but her refusal to reprint the poem reveals how well she understood her public image.

His Majesty the West Wind

Once in a fit of mental aberration
I wrote some stanzas to the western wind,
A very stupid, maudlin invocation
That into ears of audiences I've dinned.

A song about a sail, canoe and paddle
Recited by a sailor flannel dressed,
And when they heard it, people would skedaddle,
Particularly those who had been west.

For they alas had knowledge I was missing
To write of something I had never known,   10
That I had never experienced the driving
Of western winds across a prairie blown.

I never thought when grinding out those stanzas
I'd have to swallow specks of prairie dust,
That I'd deny my old extravaganzas
And wish His Majesty distinctly — cussed!

[1894]

A Cry from an Indian Wife

My Forest Brave, my Red-skin love, farewell;
We may not meet to-morrow; who can tell
What mighty ills befall our little band,

Or what you'll suffer from the white man's hand?
Here is your knife! I thought 'twas sheathed for aye.
No roaming bison calls for it to-day;
No hide of prairie cattle will it maim;
The plains are bare, it seeks a nobler game:
'Twill drink the life-blood of a soldier host.
Go; rise and strike, no matter what the cost.   10
Yet stay. Revolt not at the Union Jack,
Nor raise Thy hand against this stripling pack
Of white-faced warriors, marching West to quell
Our fallen tribe that rises to rebel.
They all are young and beautiful and good;
Curse to the war that drinks their harmless blood.
Curse to the fate that brought them from the East
To be our chiefs—to make our nation least
That breathes the air of this vast continent.
Still their new rule and council is well meant.   20
They but forget we Indians owned the land
From ocean unto ocean; that they stand
Upon a soil that centuries agone
Was our sole kingdom and our right alone.
They never think how they would feel to-day,
If some great nation came from far away,
Wresting their country from their hapless braves,
Giving what they gave us—but wars and graves.
Then go and strike for liberty and life,
And bring back honour to your Indian wife.   30
Your wife? Ah, what of that, who cares for me?
Who pities my poor love and agony?
What white-robed priest prays for your safety here,
As prayer is said for every volunteer
That swells the ranks that Canada sends out?
Who prays for vict'ry for the Indian scout?
Who prays for our poor nation lying low?
None—therefore take your tomahawk and go.
My heart may break and burn into its core,
But I am strong to bid you go to war.   40
Yet stay, my heart is not the only one
That grieves the loss of husband and of son;
Think of the mothers o'er the inland seas;
Think of the pale-faced maiden on her knees;
One pleads her God to guard some sweet-faced child
That marches on toward the North-West wild.
The other prays to shield her love from harm,
To strengthen his young, proud uplifted arm.
Ah, how her white face quivers thus to think,
Your tomahawk his life's best blood will drink.   50

She never thinks of my wild aching breast,
Nor prays for your dark face and eagle crest
Endangered by a thousand rifle balls,
My heart the target if my warrior falls.
O! coward self I hesitate no more;
Go forth, and win the glories of the war.
Go forth, nor bend to greed of white men's hands,
By right, by birth we Indians own these lands,
Though starved, crushed, plundered, lies our nation low . . .
Perhaps the white man's God has willed it so.   60

1895   1892

The Flight of the Crows

The autumn afternoon is dying o'er
    The quiet western valley where I lie
Beneath the maples on the river shore,
    Where tinted leaves, blue waters and fair sky
    Environ all; and far above some birds are flying by

To seek their evening haven in the breast
    And calm embrace of silence, while they sing
Te Deums to the night, invoking rest
    For busy chirping voice and tired wing—
    And in the hush of sleeping trees their sleeping
        cradles swing.   10

In forest arms the night will soonest creep,
    Where sombre pines a lullaby intone,
Where Nature's children curl themselves to sleep,
    And all is still at last, save where alone
    A band of black, belated crows arrive from lands
        unknown.

Strange sojourn has been theirs since waking day,
    Strange sights and cities in their wanderings blend
With fields of yellow maize, and leagues away
    With rivers where their sweeping waters wend
    Past velvet banks to rocky shores, in cañons bold
        to end.   20

O'er what vast lakes that stretch superbly dead,
    Till lashed to life by storm-clouds, have they
        flown?
In what wild lands, in laggard flight have led

Their aërial career unseen, unknown,
'Till now with twilight come their cries in lonely
   monotone?

The flapping of their pinions in the air
   Dies in the hush of distance, while they light
Within the fir tops, weirdly black and bare,
   That stand with giant strength and peerless
     height,
   To shelter fairy, bird and beast throughout the
     closing night.   30

Strange black and princely pirates of the skies,
   Would that your wind-tossed travels I could
     know!
Would that my soul could see, and, seeing, rise
   To unrestricted life where ebb and flow
   Of Nature's pulse would constitute a wider life
     below!

Could I but live just here in Freedom's arms,
   A kingly life without a sovereign's care!
Vain dreams! Day hides with closing wings her
     charms,
   And all is cradled in repose, save where
   Yon band of black, belated crows still frets the
     evening air.   40

1895

The Song My Paddle Sings

West wind, blow from your prairie nest,
Blow from the mountains, blow from the west
The sail is idle, the sailor too ;
O ! wind of the west, we wait for you.
Blow, blow !
I have wooed you so,
But never a favour you bestow.
You rock your cradle the hills between,
But scorn to notice my white lateen.

I stow the sail, unship the mast :   10
I wooed you long but my wooing's past ;
My paddle will lull you into rest.
O ! drowsy wind of the drowsy west,
Sleep, sleep,
By your mountain steep,

Or down where the prairie grasses sweep !
Now fold in slumber your laggard wings,
For soft is the song my paddle sings.

August is laughing across the sky,
Laughing while paddle, canoe and I,   20
Drift, drift,
Where the hills uplift
On either side of the current swift.

The river rolls in its rocky bed ;
My paddle is plying its way ahead ;
Dip, dip,
While the waters flip
In foam as over their breast we slip.

And oh, the river runs swifter now;
The eddies circle about my bow.   30
Swirl, swirl !
How the ripples curl
In many a dangerous pool awhirl !

And forward far the rapids roar,
Fretting their margin for evermore.
Dash, dash,
With a mighty crash,
They seethe, and boil, and bound, and splash.

Be strong, O paddle ! be brave, canoe !
The reckless waves you must plunge into.   40
Reel, reel.
On your trembling keel,
But never a fear my craft will feel.

We've raced the rapid, we're far ahead !
The river slips through its silent bed.
Sway, sway,
As the bubbles spray
And fall in tinkling tunes away.

And up on the hills against the sky,
A fir tree rocking its lullaby,   50
Swings, swings,
Its emerald wings,
Swelling the song that my paddle sings.

1895   1891-2

Silhouette

The sky-line melts from russet into blue,
Unbroken the horizon, saving where
A wreath of smoke curls up the far, thin air,
And points the distant lodges of the Sioux.

Etched where the lands and cloudlands touch and die
A solitary Indian tepee stands,
The only habitation of these lands,
That roll their magnitude from sky to sky.

The tent poles lift and loom in thin relief,
The upward floating smoke ascends between,   10
And near the open doorway, gaunt and lean,
And shadow-like, there stands an Indian Chief.

With eyes that lost their lustre long ago,
With visage fixed and stern as fate's decree,
He looks towards the empty west, to see
The never-coming herd of buffalo.

Only the bones that bleach upon the plains,
Only the fleshless skeletons that lie
In ghastly nakedness and silence, cry
Out mutely that naught else to him remains.   20

1903   1892

'Through Time and Bitter Distance'[1]

Unknown to you, I walk the cheerless shore.
    The cutting blast, the hurl of biting brine
May freeze, and still, and bind the waves at war,
    Ere you will ever know, O! Heart of mine,
That I have sought, reflected in the blue
    Of these sea depths, some shadow of your eyes;
Have hoped the laughing waves would sing of you,
    But this is all my starving sight descries—

                    I
            Far out at sea a sail
                Bends to the freshening breeze,
            Yields to the rising gale   10
                That sweeps the seas;

[1]For this title the author is indebted to Mr Charles G.D. Roberts. It occurs in his sonnet, 'Rain'.

II

Yields, as a bird wind-tossed,
    To saltish waves that fling
Their spray, whose rime and frost
    Like crystals cling

III

To canvas, mast and spar,
    Till, gleaming like a gem,
She sinks beyond the far
    Horizon's hem.   20

IV

Lost to my longing sight,
    And nothing left to me
Save an oncoming night,—
    An empty sea.

1903

Archibald Lampman

1861-1899

Archibald Lampman—like Roberts and Carman—was born into a Loyalist Anglican family. Although he grew up on the edge of the wilderness, his education and career carried him into the increasingly urban world of the emerging Canadian nation. Born in Morpeth, a village in Canada West on Lake Erie, Lampman spent his childhood in the Rice Lake district, first at Gore's Landing—where he met the Strickland sisters, Susanna Moodie and Catharine Parr Traill—and then, after a brief time in Cobourg, where his clergyman father had taken a new parish, as a boarder at Trinity College School, Port Hope. He won a Foundation scholarship at Trinity College, Toronto, but his pursuit of the less academic side of undergraduate life there cost him a first-class degree and an academic career. After realizing that he disliked high-school teaching, he settled into a permanent position in the civil service, working as a clerk in the Post Office Department. In 1887 Lampman married Maud Playter, against her family's wishes; the union was apparently unhappy for both partners. However, he found a group of people, members of the Ottawa Literary and Scientific Society, who shared his national and intellectual interests; among them were two other poets and civil servants, Wilfred Campbell and Duncan Campbell Scott.

Scott and Lampman became close friends, for they shared a love of the wilderness, joining in many canoeing expeditions while they discussed their real work, the writing of poetry. As a naturalist poet Lampman learned to employ vivid yet simple images and diction, to build poems out of the sounds, the motion, and even the colours of the wilderness. A poet in the Romantic tradition, Lampman saw himself as being a manifestation of Keats—even saying 'I have an idea that he has found a sort of faint reincarnation in me'—but his importance lies in his attempts to capture a uniquely Canadian landscape, for he believed that 'climate and scenic conditions have much to do with the molding of national character'. Like other Romantics, Lampman feared that the city was a threat to nature, yet because he considered Canada to be 'still in the house-building, land-breaking stage', he believed that the growth and materialism of the new Confederation were necessary in order for future generations to have the leisure to create a balanced culture.

Lampman's writing was well received in his time, appearing in various journals in Canada and the United States. He had, however, to publish his first volume of poetry, *Among the Millet* (Ottawa, 1888), at his own expense. Though he was unable to interest anyone in a book of sonnets, Lampman found an American publisher who accepted a volume of nature lyrics, *Lyrics of the Earth* (Boston, 1895). Around this time Lampman's health began to deteriorate rapidly, partly because the effects of rheumatic fever in childhood were made more acute by a depression following the deaths of his son (1894) and his father (1897). He died of heart disease at thirty-seven, before a third volume, *Alcyone*, reached the printing stage. Shortly after Lampman's death, D.C. Scott ordered a printing of twelve copies. As Lampman's literary executor, Scott published a memorial collection of his friend's poems in 1900. In 1943 Scott and E.K. Brown discovered 'At the Long Sault' in manuscript and published it in a new edition of Lampman's poems. Among other unpublished poems Lampman left behind when he died were a group of love poems inspired by his close friendship with Katherine Waddell, a fellow civil servant. Suppressed by Scott—except for six sonnets that appeared in *At the Long Sault and Other New Poems* (1943)—they were finally published in *Lampman's Kate* (1975) edited by Margaret Coulby Whitridge.

Roberts and Lampman present an informative contrast. Where Roberts found change at the heart of things, Lampman saw change as existing only in the superficialities of appearance, and he sought instead the vision (he often called it a dream) of the true and unchanging reality that lies beneath the surface. His poetry, which records those moments of intense experience with nature that give man glimpses of eternal truth, may therefore be said to look back to the English Romantics in a way that Robert's poetry does not—but its expression is so effective that Lampman is now generally thought of

as the best of the Confederation poets. His description of how Emerson responded to the 'cosmic sympathy' of the universe might well be applied to himself: 'He is drawn to nature because in the energy of his own soul he is aware of a kinship to the forces of nature, and feels with an elemental joy as if it were a part of himself the eternal movement of life' ('At the Mermaid Inn', 22 April 1893).

Heat

From plains that reel to southward, dim,
   The road runs by me white and bare;
Up the steep hill it seems to swim
   Beyond, and melt into the glare.
Upward half-way, or it may be
   Nearer the summit, slowly steals
A hay-cart, moving dustily
   With idly clacking wheels.

By his cart's side the wagoner
   Is slouching slowly at his ease,   10
Half-hidden in the windless blur
   Of white dust puffing to his knees.
This wagon on the height above,
   From sky to sky on either hand,
Is the sole thing that seems to move
   In all the heat-held land.

Beyond me in the fields the sun
   Soaks in the grass and hath his will;
I count the marguerites[1] one by one;
   Even the buttercups are still.   20
On the brook yonder not a breath
   Disturbs the spider or the midge.
The water-bugs draw close beneath
   The cool gloom of the bridge.

Where the far elm-tree shadows flood
   Dark patches in the burning grass,
The cows, each with her peaceful cud,
   Lie waiting for the heat to pass.
From somewhere on the slope near by
   Into the pale depth of the noon   30
A wandering thrush slides leisurely
   His thin revolving tune.

[1] Daisies.

In intervals of dreams I hear
 The cricket from the droughty ground;
The grasshoppers spin into mine ear
 A small innumerable sound.
I lift mine eyes sometimes to gaze:
 The burning sky-line blinds my sight:
The woods far off are blue with haze:
 The hills are drenched in light.   40

And yet to me not this or that
 Is always sharp or always sweet;
In the sloped shadow of my hat
 I lean at rest, and drain the heat;
Nay more, I think some blessèd power
 Hath brought me wandering idly here:
In the full furnace of this hour
 My thoughts grow keen and clear.

1888

The Frogs

I

Breathers of wisdom won without a quest,
Quaint uncouth dreamers, voices high and strange;
Flutists of lands where beauty hath no change,
And wintry grief is a forgotten guest,
Sweet murmurers of everlasting rest,
For whom glad days have ever yet to run,
And moments are as aeons, and the sun
But ever sunken half-way toward the west.

Often to me who heard you in your day,
With close rapt ears, it could not choose but seem 10
That earth, our mother, searching in what way
Men's hearts might know her spirit's inmost dream;
Ever at rest beneath life's change and stir,
Made you her soul, and bade you pipe for her.

II

In those mute days when spring was in her glee,
And hope was strong, we knew not why or how,
And earth, the mother, dreamed with brooding brow,
Musing on life, and what the hours might be,
When love should ripen to maternity,
Then like high flutes in silvery interchange 20
Ye piped with voices still and sweet and strange,
And ever as ye piped, on every tree

The great buds swelled; among the pensive woods
The spirits of first flowers awoke and flung
From buried faces the close-fitting hoods,
And listened to your piping till they fell,
The frail spring-beauty[1] with her perfumed bell,
The wind-flower, and the spotted adder-tongue.

III

All the day long, wherever pools might be
Among the golden meadows, where the air   30
Stood in a dream, as it were moorèd there
For ever in a noon-tide reverie,
Or where the birds made riot of their glee
In the still woods, and the hot sun shone down,
Crossed with warm lucent shadows on the brown
Leaf-paven pools, that bubbled dreamily,

Or far away in whispering river meads[2]
And watery marshes where the brooding noon,
Full with the wonder of its own sweet boon,
Nestled and slept among the noiseless reeds,   40
Ye sat and murmured, motionless as they,
With eyes that dreamed beyond the night and day.

IV

And when day passed and over heaven's height,
Thin with the many stars and cool with dew,
The fingers of the deep hours slowly drew
The wonder of the ever-healing night,
No grief or loneliness or rapt delight
Or weight of silence ever brought to you
Slumber or rest; only your voices grew
More high and solemn; slowly with hushed flight   50

Ye saw the echoing hours go by, long-drawn,
Nor ever stirred, watching with fathomless eyes,
And with your countless clear antiphonies
Filling the earth and heaven, even till dawn,
Last-risen, found you with its first pale gleam,
Still with soft throats unaltered in your dream.

V

And slowly as we heard you, day by day,
The stillness of enchanted reveries
Bound brain and spirit and half-closed eyes,
In some divine sweet wonder-dream astray;   60
To us no sorrow or upreared dismay

[1]A common spring wildflower (*Claytonia virginica*) having small white or pinkish flowers; 'windflow-er': an anemone, a flower of the buttercup family; 'adder-tongue': a spring flower with mottled leaves, also known as the dogtooth violet or trout lily.
[2]Meadows.

Nor any discord came, but evermore
The voices of mankind, the outer roar,
Grew strange and murmurous, faint and far away.

Morning and noon and midnight exquisitely,
Rapt with your voices, this alone we knew,
Cities might change and fall, and men might die,
Secure were we, content to dream with you
That change and pain are shadows faint and fleet,
And dreams are real, and life is only sweet.   70

1888

The City of the End of Things

Beside the pounding cataracts
Of midnight streams unknown to us
'Tis builded in the leafless tracts
And valleys huge of Tartarus.[1]
Lurid and lofty and vast it seems;
It hath no rounded name that rings,
But I have heard it called in dreams
The City of the End of Things.

Its roofs and iron towers have grown
None knoweth how high within the night,   10
But in its murky streets far down
A flaming terrible and bright
Shakes all the stalking shadows there,
Across the walls, across the floors,
And shifts upon the upper air
From out a thousand furnace doors;
And all the while an awful sound
Keeps roaring on continually,
And crashes in the ceaseless round
Of a gigantic harmony.   20
Through its grim depths re-echoing
And all its weary height of walls,
With measured roar and iron ring,
The inhuman music lifts and falls.
Where no thing rests and no man is,
And only fire and night hold sway;
The beat, the thunder and the hiss
Cease not, and change not, night nor day.

---

[1]Infernal abyss below Hades; true hell where Zeus threw rebel Titans.

And moving at unheard commands,
The abysses and vast fires between,   30
Flit figures that with clanking hands
Obey a hideous routine;
They are not flesh, they are not bone,
They see not with the human eye,
And from their iron lips is blown
A dreadful and monotonous cry;
And whoso of our mortal race
Should find that city unaware,
Lean Death would smite him face to face,
And blanch him with its venomed air: 40
Or caught by the terrific spell,
Each thread of memory snapt and cut,
His soul would shrivel and its shell
Go rattling like an empty nut.

It was not always so, but once,
In days that no man thinks upon,
Fair voices echoed from its stones,
The light above it leaped and shone:
Once there were multitudes of men,
That built that city in their pride,   50
Until its might was made, and then
They withered age by age and died.
But now of that prodigious race,
Three only in an iron tower,
Set like carved idols face to face,
Remain the masters of its power;
And at the city gate a fourth,
Gigantic and with dreadful eyes,
Sits looking toward the lightless north,
Beyond the reach of memories;   60
Fast rooted to the lurid floor,
A bulk that never moves a jot,
In his pale body dwells no more,
Or mind or soul,—an idiot!
But sometimes in the end those three
Shall perish and their hands be still,
And with the master's touch shall flee
Their incommunicable skill.
A stillness absolute as death
Along the slacking wheels shall lie,   70
And, flagging at a single breath,
The fires shall moulder out and die.
The roar shall vanish at its height,
And over that tremendous town
The silence of eternal night
Shall gather close and settle down.
All its grim grandeur, tower and hall,
Shall be abandoned utterly,

And into rust and dust shall fall
From century to century;   80
Nor ever living thing shall grow,
Nor trunk of tree, nor blade of grass;
No drop shall fall, no wind shall blow,
Nor sound of any foot shall pass:
Alone of its accursèd state,
One thing the hand of Time shall spare,
For the grim Idiot at the gate
Is deathless and eternal there.

1895

At the Long Sault: May, 1660[1]

Under the day-long sun there is life and mirth
    In the working earth,
And the wonderful moon shines bright
    Through the soft spring night,
The innocent flowers in the limitless woods are springing
    Far and away
With the sound and the perfume of May,
And ever up from the south the happy birds are winging,
    The waters glitter and leap and play
    While the gray hawk soars.   10

But far in an open glade of the forest set
    Where the rapid plunges and roars,
Is a ruined fort with a name that men forget,—
    A shelterless pen
    With its broken palisade,
    Behind it, musket in hand,
    Beyond message or aid
    In this savage heart of the wild,
    Mere youngsters, grown in a moment to men,
    Grim and alert and arrayed,   20
    The comrades of Daulac stand.
    Ever before them, night and day,
    The rush and skulk and cry
    Of foes, not men but devils, panting for prey;
    Behind them the sleepless dream
Of the little frail-walled town,[2] far away by the plunging stream.
    Of maiden and matron and child,
With ruin and murder impending, and none but they
To beat back the gathering horror

[1]On 1 May 1660 Adam Dollard des Ormeaux (sometimes called Daulac), with sixteen companions and forty-four Hurons and Algonkins, laid an ambush for some Iroquois at an abandoned fort on the Ottawa River. The Iroquois were joined by a reinforcement of 500, but it took them ten days to vanquish the Frenchmen and their allies. Until fairly recently this event was considered to have saved the colony of Montreal from Iroquois attack, and the Frenchmen were considered martyrs for the faith.
[2]Montreal.

Deal death while they may,   30
    And then die.

Day and night they have watched while the little plain
Grew dark with the rush of the foe, but their host
Broke ever and melted away, with no boast
But to number their slain;
And now as the days renew
Hunger and thirst and care
Were they never so stout, so true,
Press at their hearts; but none
Falters or shrinks or utters a coward word,   40
Though each setting sun
Brings from the pitiless wild new hands to the Iroquois horde,
And only to them despair.

Silent, white-faced, again and again
Charged and hemmed round by furious hands,
Each for a moment faces them all and stands
In his little desperate ring; like a tired bull moose
Whom scores of sleepless wolves, a ravening pack,
Have chased all night, all day
Through the snow-laden woods, like famine let loose;   50
And he turns at last in his track
Against a wall of rock and stands at bay;
Round him with terrible sinews and teeth of steel
They charge and recharge; but with many a furious plunge and wheel,
Hither and thither over the trampled snow,
He tosses them bleeding and torn;
Till, driven, and ever to and fro
Harried, wounded, and weary grown,
His mighty strength gives way
And all together they fasten upon him and drag him down.   60

So Daulac turned him anew
With a ringing cry to his men
In the little raging forest glen,
And his terrible sword in the twilight whistled and slew.
And all his comrades stood
With their backs to the pales,[3] and fought
Till their strength was done;
The thews that were only mortal flagged and broke
Each struck his last wild stroke,
And they fell one by one,   70
And the world that had seemed so good
Passed like a dream and was naught.

And then the great night came
With the triumph-songs of the foe and the flame
Of the camp-fires.

[3]Row of spiked wooden poles, here the walls of the fort.

Out of the dark the soft wind woke,
The song of the rapid rose alway
And came to the spot where the comrades lay,
Beyond help or care,
With none but the red men round them   80
To gnash their teeth and stare.

All night by the foot of the mountain
    The little town lieth at rest,
The sentries are peacefully pacing;
    And neither from East nor from West
Is there rumor of death or of danger;
    None dreameth tonight in his bed
That ruin was near and the heroes
    That met it and stemmed it are dead.

But afar in the ring of the forest,   90
    Where the air is so tender with May
And the waters are wild in the moonlight
    They lie in their silence of clay.

The numberless stars out of heaven
    Look down with a pitiful glance;
And the lilies asleep in the forest
    Are closed like the lilies of France. [4]

1943

[4] That is, the fleur-de-lis, the emblematic flower of France, often appearing as a heraldic emblem on the shields of warriors.

A Summer Dream [1]

Once in a dream, between two troubled slips
Of sleep, I saw you in your brightest guise.
Methought you stood, but tears were in your eyes,
Softer than rain or any dew that drips.
On my cold hand you laid your finger tips
And I, touched by a sudden sweet surprise,
Caught you in both mine arms with sobs and sighs
And kissed your brow, beloved, and your lips.

And you—ah yes! even you, upon my breast
Leaned for a moment, with cheeks wet and wan,   10
Then smiled and vanished; but for many hours
I wandered in a speechless dream, caressed
By winds from such a magic summer dream
As never wantoned over earthly flowers.

[1896], 1975

[1] One of the poems addressed to Katherine Waddell that remained in manuscript until 1975.

Voices of Earth

We have not heard the music of the spheres,[1]
The song of star to star, but there are sounds
More deep than human joy and human tears,
That Nature uses in her common rounds;
The fall of streams, the cry of winds that strain
The oak, the roaring of the sea's surge, might
Of thunder breaking afar off, or rain
That falls by minutes in the summer night.
These are the voices of earth's secret soul,
Uttering the mystery from which she came.   10
To him who hears them grief beyond control,
Or joy inscrutable without a name,
Wakes in his heart thoughts bedded there, impearled,
Before the birth and making of the world.

1899

[1]Cosmic harmonies, supposed to be produced by the movement of heavenly bodies.

Winter Evening

Tonight the very horses springing by
Toss gold from whitened nostrils. In a dream
The streets that narrow to the westward gleam
Like rows of golden palaces; and high
From all the crowded chimneys tower and die
A thousand aureoles. Down in the west
The brimming plains beneath the sunset rest,
One burning sea of gold. Soon, soon shall fly
The glorious vision, and the hours shall feel
A mightier master; soon from height to height,   10
With silence and the sharp unpitying stars,
Stern creeping frosts, and winds that touch like steel,
Out of the depth beyond the eastern bars,
Glittering and still shall come the awful night.

1899

To a Millionaire

The world in gloom and splendor passes by,
And thou in the midst of it with brows that gleam,
A creature of that old distorted dream
That makes the sound of life an evil cry.
Good men perform just deeds, and brave men die,
And win not honor such as gold can give,
While the vain multitudes plod on, and live,
And serve the curse that pins them down: But I
Think only of the unnumbered broken hearts,
The hunger and the mortal strife for bread,   10
Old age and youth alike mistaught, misfed,
By want and rags and homelessness made vile,
The griefs and hates, and all the meaner parts
That balance thy one grim misgotten pile.

1900

Duncan Campbell Scott

1862-1947

The writing of Duncan Campbell Scott, like that of the other Confederation poets, developed out of a profound response to the Canadian landscape and its people, and was influenced as well by mid-nineteenth-century British and American thought. Born in Ottawa and raised in villages in Ontario and Quebec, where his father served as a Methodist minister, Scott became interested as a boy in the life and customs of the Indian tribes, the frontier lumbermen, and the French-Canadian *habitants*—all of which became important subjects in his writing.

Unlike the other Confederation writers, however, Scott was unable to attend university for financial reasons. In 1879, after an interview with the prime minister, Sir John A. Macdonald, he accepted a clerkship at $1.50 a day in the Department of Indian Affairs, where he remained for over fifty years, eventually assuming that department's highest permanent office. He began to write in the mid-1880s, when he met Archibald Lampman, another civil servant. As Roberts had earlier inspired Lampman, now Lampman supplied Scott with the confidence he needed. Within the next few years Scott's stories and poems began to appear in periodicals. He published his first book of poetry, *The Magic House and Other Poems*, in 1893, and in 1896 his first volume of short stories, *In the Village of Viger*, appeared. In 1892 Scott and Lampman had joined another civil servant, Wilfred Campbell, in writing 'At the Mermaid Inn', for the Toronto *Globe*, a column in which they commented on the Canadian cultural milieu and developed their own literary theories. Scott also continued his interest in wilderness life, taking long recreational canoe trips with Lampman, as well as making an increasing number of professional expeditions to visit Indian tribes. In his second book of verse, *Labour and the Angel* (1898), Scott began to move away from the shadowy, lush poetry of his earlier volume and introduced the first of the Indian poems that distinguished him from the other Confederation poets. In this book Scott's depiction of large conflicts between contrasting forces—producing a dialectic that recurs throughout his work—first emerges. For him the natural struggle often resolves itself in moments of beauty and serenity that are, like those in 'The Height of Land' (1916), 'deeper than peace'. As well as continuing to write poetry and prose throughout his lifetime, Scott edited several volumes of Lampman's verse after his friend died in 1899.

While Scott continued to work for the more conservative traditions of Confederation poetry, in 1922 he helped to open the doors of what had become a staid literary establishment to the post-war writers, many of whom were proponents of modernism. In a speech he gave as President of the Royal Society he condemned the static condition of Canadian writing and recommended new voices:

It is the mission of new theories in the arts, and particularly of new theories that come to us illustrated by practice, to re-examine the grounds of our preferences, and to retest our accepted dogmas. . . . We require more rage of our poets. We should like them to put to the proof that saying of William Blake: 'The tigers of wrath are wiser than the horses of instruction.'

Scott's request for poetic rage may derive from his strong sense of man in confrontation with a violent universe. His answer to that violence was often what Desmond Pacey called 'gay fatalism'—an affirmation of death as a part of life. In 'At the Cedars' the lumberman Isaac Dufour, swept along by forces beyond his control, keeps his balance and sings; when, inevitably, neither his skill nor his nonchalance can continue to protect him, he makes a gesture of graceful acceptance: 'And when he was there/In the air, /Kissed his hand/To the land.' Similarly the heroic Chipewa woman in 'The Forsaken' not only stays alive by fishing with her flesh, but later accepts her inevitable death unflinchingly as she meets the 'silence deeper than silence'.

At the Cedars

You had two girls—Baptiste—
One is Virginie—
Hold hard—Baptiste!
Listen to me.

The whole drive was jammed
In that bend at the Cedars,
The rapids were dammed
With the logs tight rammed
And crammed; you might know
The Devil had clinched them below.   10

We worked three days—not a budge,
'She's as tight as a wedge, on the ledge,'
Says our foreman;
'Mon Dieu! boys, look here,
We must get this thing clear.'
He cursed at the men
And we went for it then;
With our cant-dogs[1] arow,

[1] Hooked tools that bite into logs.

We just gave he-yo-ho;
When she gave a big shove   20
From above.

The gang yelled and tore
For the shore,
The logs gave a grind
Like a wolf's jaws behind,
And as quick as a flash,
With a shove and a crash,
They were down in a mash,
But I and ten more,
All but Isaàc Dufour,   30
Were ashore.

He leaped on a log in the front of the rush,
And shot out from the bind
While the jam roared behind;
As he floated along
He balanced his pole
And tossed us a song.
But just as we cheered,
Up darted a log from the bottom,
Leaped thirty feet square and fair,   40
And came down on his own.

He went up like a block
With the shock,
And when he was there
In the air,
Kissed his hand
To the land;
When he dropped
My heart stopped,
For the first logs had caught him   50
And crushed him;
When he rose in his place
There was blood on his face.

There were some girls, Baptiste,
Picking berries on the hillside,
Where the river curls, Baptiste,
You know—on the still side
One was down by the water,
She saw Isaàc
Fall back.   60

She did not scream, Baptiste,
She launched her canoe;
It did seem, Baptiste,
That she wanted to die too,

For before you could think
The birch cracked like a shell
In that rush of hell,
And I saw them both sink—

Baptiste!—
He had two girls,   70
One is Virginie,
What God calls the other
Is not known to me.

1893

The Onondaga[1] Madonna

She stands full-throated and with careless pose,
This woman of a weird and waning race,
The tragic savage lurking in her face,
Where all her pagan passion burns and glows;
Her blood is mingled with her ancient foes,
And thrills with war and wildness in her veins;
Her rebel lips are dabbled with the stains
Of feuds and forays and her father's woes.

And closer in the shawl about her breast,
The latest promise of her nation's doom,   10
Paler than she her baby clings and lies,
The primal warrior gleaming from his eyes;
He sulks, and burdened with his infant gloom,
He draws his heavy brows and will not rest.

1898

---

[1] An Iroquois tribe.

Night Hymns on Lake Nipigon

Here in the midnight, where the dark mainland and island
Shadows mingle in shadow deeper, profounder,
Sing we the hymns of the churches, while the dead water
    Whispers before us.

Thunder is travelling slow on the path of the lightning;
One after one the stars and the beaming planets
Look serene in the lake from the edge of the storm-cloud,
    Then have they vanished.

While our canoe, that floats dumb in the bursting thunder,
Gathers her voice in the quiet and thrills and whispers,   10
Presses her prow in the star-gleam, and all her ripple
    Lapses in blackness.

Sing we the sacred ancient hymns of the churches,
Chanted first in old-world nooks of the desert,
While in the wild, pellucid Nipigon reaches
    Hunted the savage.

Now have the ages met in the Northern midnight,
And on the lonely, loon-haunted Nipigon reaches
Rises the hymn of triumph and courage and comfort,
    Adeste Fideles.   20

Tones that were fashioned when the faith brooded in darkness,
Joined with sonorous vowels in the noble Latin,
Now are married with the long-drawn Ojibwa,
    Uncouth and mournful.

Soft with the silver drip of the regular paddles
Falling in rhythm, timed with the liquid, plangent
Sounds from the blades where the whirlpools break and are carried
    Down into darkness;

Each long cadence, flying like a dove from her shelter
Deep in the shadow, wheels for a throbbing moment,   30
Poises in utterance, returning in circles of silver
    To nest in the silence.

All wild nature stirs with the infinite, tender
Plaint of a bygone age whose soul is eternal,
Bound in the lonely phrases that thrill and falter
    Back into quiet.

Back they falter as the deep storm overtakes them,
Whelms them in splendid hollows of booming thunder,
Wraps them in rain, that, sweeping, breaks and onrushes
    Ringing like cymbals.   40

1905

The Forsaken

I

Once in the winter
Out on a lake
In the heart of the north-land,
Far from the Fort
And far from the hunters,
A Chippewa woman
With her sick baby,
Crouched in the last hours
Of a great storm.
Frozen and hungry,   10
She fished through the ice
With a line of the twisted
Bark of the cedar,
And a rabbit-bone hook
Polished and barbed;
Fished with the bare hook
All through the wild day,
Fished and caught nothing;
While the young chieftain
Tugged at her breasts,   20
Or slept in the lacings
Of the warm *tikanagan*.[1]
All the lake-surface
Streamed with the hissing
Of millions of iceflakes,
Hurled by the wind;
Behind her the round
Of a lonely island
Roared like a fire
With the voice of the storm   30
In the deeps of the cedars.
Valiant, unshaken,
She took of her own flesh,
Baited the fish-hook,
Drew in a grey-trout,
Drew in his fellows,
Heaped them beside her,
Dead in the snow.
Valiant, unshaken,
She faced the long distance,   40
Wolf-haunted and lonely,
Sure of her goal
And the life of her dear one;
Tramped for two days,
On the third in the morning,
Saw the strong bulk
Of the Fort by the river,

[1] Moss-filled cradle board.

Saw the wood-smoke
Hang soft in the spruces,
Heard the keen yelp   50
Of the ravenous huskies
Fighting for whitefish:
Then she had rest.

II

Years and years after,
When she was old and withered,
When her son was an old man
And his children filled with vigour,
They came in their northern tour on the verge of winter,
To an island on a lonely lake.
There one night they camped, and on the morrow   60
Gathered their kettles and birch-bark²
Their rabbit-skin robes and their mink-traps,
Launched their canoes and slunk away through the islands,
Left her alone forever,
Without a word of farewell,
Because she was old and useless,
Like a paddle broken and warped,
Or a pole that was splintered.
Then, without a sigh,
Valiant, unshaken,   70
She smoothed her dark locks under her kerchief,
Composed her shawl in state,
Then folded her hands ridged with sinews and corded with veins,
Folded them across her breasts spent with the nourishing of children,
Gazed at the sky past the tops of the cedars,
Saw two spangled nights arise out of the twilight,
Saw two days go by filled with the tranquil sunshine,
Saw, without pain, or dread, or even a moment of longing:
Then on the third great night there came thronging and thronging
Millions of snowflakes out of a windless cloud;   80
They covered her close with a beautiful crystal shroud,
Covered her deep and silent.
But in the frost of the dawn,
Up from the life below,
Rose a column of breath
Through a tiny cleft in the snow,
Fragile, delicately drawn,
Wavering with its own weakness,
In the wilderness a sign of the spirit,
Persisting still in the sight of the sun   90
Till day was done.
Then all light was gathered up by the hand of God and hid in His breast,
Then there was born a silence deeper than silence,
Then she had rest.
1905

²Waterproof birch-bark bowls or buckets.

The Height of Land[1]

Here is the height of land:
The watershed on either hand
Goes down to Hudson Bay
Or Lake Superior;
The stars are up, and far away
The wind sounds in the wood, wearier
Than the long Ojibwa cadence
In which Potàn the Wise[2]
Declares the ills of life
And Chees-que-ne-ne makes a mournful sound   10
Of acquiescence. The fires burn low
With just sufficient glow
To light the flakes of ash that play
At being moths, and flutter away
To fall in the dark and die as ashes:
Here there is peace in the lofty air,
And Something comes by flashes
Deeper than peace;—
The spruces have retired a little space
And left a field of sky in violet shadow   20
With stars like marigolds in a water-meadow.

Now the Indian guides are dead asleep;
There is no sound unless the soul can hear
The gathering of the waters in their sources.

We have come up through the spreading lakes
From level to level,—
Pitching our tents sometimes over a revel
Of roses that nodded all night,
Dreaming within our dreams,
To wake at dawn and find that they were captured   30
With no dew on their leaves;
Sometimes mid sheaves
Of bracken and dwarf-cornel,[3] and again
On a wide blueberry plain
Brushed with the shimmer of a bluebird's wing;
A rocky islet followed
With one lone poplar and a single nest
Of white-throat-sparrows that took no rest
But sang in dreams or woke to sing,—
To the last portage and the height of land—:   40
Upon one hand
The lonely north enlaced with lakes and streams,
And the enormous targe[4] of Hudson Bay,

[1] Here, the Arctic water-shed; north of that point all rivers flow into the Arctic Ocean.
[2] The name of one of the two Indian guides who led the speaker into the wilderness in Scott's poem 'Spring on Mattagami'; Chees-que-ne-ne, or Jeesekeewinini is a shaman who is able to summon supernatural powers or beings.
[3] 'Cornel': one of a group of trees or shrubs similar to the dogwood and the cherry.
[4] Shield.

Glimmering all night
In the cold arctic light;
On the other hand
The crowded southern land
With all the welter of the lives of men.
But here is peace, and again
That Something comes by flashes   50
Deeper than peace,—a spell
Golden and inappellable[5]
That gives the inarticulate part
Of our strange being one moment of release
That seems more native than the touch of time,
And we must answer in chime;
Though yet no man may tell
The secret of that spell
Golden and inappellable.

Now are there sounds walking in the wood,   60
And all the spruces shiver and tremble,
And the stars move a little in their courses.
The ancient disturber of solitude
Breathes a pervasive sigh,
And the soul seems to hear
The gathering of the waters at their sources;
Then quiet ensues and pure starlight and dark;
The region-spirit murmurs in meditation,
The heart replies in exaltation
And echoes faintly like an inland shell   70
Ghost tremors of the spell;
Thought reawakens and is linked again
With all the welter of the lives of men.
Here on the uplands where the air is clear
We think of life as of a stormy scene,—
Of tempest, of revolt and desperate shock;
And here, where we can think, on the bright uplands
Where the air is clear, we deeply brood on life
Until the tempest parts, and it appears
As simple as to the shepherd seems his flock: 80
A Something to be guided by ideals—
That in themselves are simple and serene—
Of noble deed to foster noble thought,
And noble thought to image noble deed,
Till deed and thought shall interpenetrate,
Making life lovelier, till we come to doubt
Whether the perfect beauty that escapes
Is beauty of deed or thought or some high thing
Mingled of both, a greater boon than either:
Thus we have seen in the retreating tempest   90
The victor-sunlight merge with the ruined rain,
And from the rain and sunlight spring the rainbow.

[5] From which there can be no appeal.

The ancient disturber of solitude
Stirs his ancestral potion in the gloom,
And the dark wood
Is stifled with the pungent fume
Of charred earth burnt to the bone
That takes the place of air.
Then sudden I remember when and where,—
The last weird lakelet foul with weedy growths   100
And slimy viscid things the spirit loathes,
Skin of vile water over viler mud
Where the paddle stirred unutterable stenches,
And the canoes seemed heavy with fear,
Not to be urged toward the fatal shore
Where a bush fire, smouldering, with sudden roar
Leaped on a cedar and smothered it with light
And terror.   It had left the portage-height
A tangle of slanted spruces burned to the roots,
Covered still with patches of bright fire   110
Smoking with incense of the fragrant resin
That even then began to thin and lessen
Into the gloom and glimmer of ruin.

'Tis overpast.[6]   How strange the stars have grown;
The presage of extinction glows on their crests
And they are beautied with impermanence;
They shall be after the race of men
And mourn for them who snared their fiery pinions,
Entangled in the meshes of bright words.

A lemming stirs the fern and in the mosses   120
Eft-minded things feel the air change, and dawn
Tolls out from the dark belfries of the spruces.
How often in the autumn of the world
Shall the crystal shrine of dawning be rebuilt
With deeper meaning!   Shall the poet then,
Wrapped in his mantle on the height of land,
Brood on the welter of the lives of men
And dream of his ideal hope and promise
In the blush sunrise?   Shall he base his flight
Upon a more compelling law than Love   130
As Life's atonement; shall the vision
Of noble deed and noble thought immingled
Seem as uncouth to him as the pictograph
Scratched on the cave side by the cave-dweller
To us of the Christ-time?   Shall he stand
With deeper joy, with more complex emotion,
In closer commune with divinity,
With the deep fathomed, with the firmament charted,
With life as simple as a sheep-boy's song,

[6] Over, ended.

What lies beyond a romaunt[7] that was read   140
Once on a morn of storm and laid aside
Memorious with strange immortal memories?
Or shall he see the sunrise as I see it
In shoals of misty fire the deluge-light
Dashes upon and whelms with purer radiance,
And feel the lulled earth, older in pulse and motion,
Turn the rich lands and the inundant[8] oceans
To the flushed colour, and hear as now I hear
The thrill of life beat up the planet's margin
And break in the clear susurrus[9] of deep joy   150
That echoes and reëchoes in my being?
O Life is intuition the measure of knowledge
And do I stand with heart entranced and burning
At the zenith of our wisdom when I feel
The long light flow, the long wind pause, the deep
Influx of spirit, of which no man may tell
The Secret, golden and inappellable?

1916

[7] Romantic tale or poem.
[8] Flooding.
[9] Whispering.

Stephen Leacock

1869-1944

Stephen Leacock once explained his having left England at six in this way: 'My parents migrated to Canada in 1876, and I decided to go with them.' We recognize in this line the ironic and often self-mocking quality that characterizes much of Leacock's best writing—the sense of deflation that comes when individuals try to assert more control over their fate than they can ever really have. Perhaps it was Leacock's early years that led him to regard the world as an unreliable place: after coming to Canada he grew up on a farm (near Lake Simcoe, Ont.) that, as a result of his father's mismanagement, teetered continually on the edge of financial collapse. Although Leacock's mother provided the family with stability, she may also have sharpened his sense of the absurd as she engaged in her constant struggle to instil into eleven children the manners of a distant British aristocracy. The Leacock family's insecure life never reached the point of complete disaster only because occasional assistance from England kept the family afloat, even allowing Stephen to attend Upper Canada College, Toronto, as a boarder.

As an adult Leacock lived two lives: he was first an academic, and only later a humorist. He began his teaching career at Upper Canada College while completing a B.A. at the University of Toronto. He later left UCC to pursue graduate work at the University of Chicago, where he studied economics under Thorstein Veblen. His Ph.D. completed, he joined the Department of Economics and Political Science at McGill University in 1903. He gained distinction as an engaging classroom lecturer, and his first book, *Elements of Political Science* (1906), which earned him a reputation for clarity of thought and vigour of expression, soon became a standard text. In 1907, at the request of the Governor General, Leacock undertook a year-long tour of the British Empire to speak on Imperial unity; and upon his return he was placed in charge of his department.

Leacock began his second career in 1910 when—against the advice of a friend who thought he would harm his scholarly reputation—he collected the occasional pieces of humour he had written for magazines and published them at his own expense as *Literary Lapses*. An immediate success, the collection was reprinted in England and America, as well as in Canada. Leacock quickly followed it with *Nonsense Novels* (1911), a book that gave the world his famous description of the young man who 'flung himself upon his horse and rode madly off in all directions'. His third book of humour, *Sunshine Sketches of a Little Town*, was published in 1912, after appearing as a series in the Montreal *Star*.

Sunshine Sketches was based on Leacock's experience of Orillia, near which, in 1908, he had bought a farm for his annual summer holidays. His friend B.K. Sandwell later observed of the book that 'It was the only really large-scale commission ever received [by Leacock] for a fictional job to be done for a purely Canadian audience . . . he had a wealth of material not too suitable for his American buyers.' Leacock's decision to write this book for a Canadian readership was probably the reason the book never achieved the international, nor therefore the commercial, success of his others, although it is now generally regarded as his best as well as his most unified work. In 1914 Leacock made use in a similar fashion of recent events and scenes drawn from Montreal life

for *Arcadian Adventures with the Idle Rich*, a companion volume to *Sunshine Sketches* —but he transposed the setting of that work to an American city.

For the rest of his career Leacock worked at an intense pace, averaging a book of humour a year, as well as writing biographies, social commentary, and popular histories. The quality of his humorous writing suffered as a result of this industry, which was impelled by a strong drive for money and prestige. In addition, in 1921 he was instrumental in organizing the Canadian Authors' Association as a means of working out a satisfactory agreement on Canadian copyright. After his enforced retirement from McGill at sixty-five, Leacock, already a popular public speaker, embarked on a lecture tour of western Canada that led to *My Discovery of the West* (1937), the book for which he won a Governor General's Award in the second year of these awards.

Despite its satire and comedy, *Sunshine Sketches* is Leacock's adaptation of the 'regional idyll' that, according to Desmond Pacey, was the dominant literary form in Canada between 1900 and 1920. Although many Orillia citizens were angered by Leacock's failure to disguise the identities of the people on whom he modelled his characters, there is an evident fondness in the book for the fictional town of 'Mariposa'—an affection most evident in the nostalgic sketch that closes the work, 'L'Envoi: The Train to Mariposa'. There he writes of how we all dream of returning to that 'little Town in the Sunshine that once we knew':

Look from the window as you go. The city is far behind now and right and left of you there are trim farms with elms and maples near them and with tall windmills beside the old barns that you can still see in the gathering dusk. There is a dull red light from the windows of the farmstead. It must be comfortable there after the roar and clatter of the city, and only think of the still quiet of it. . . .

What? It feels nervous and strange to be coming here again after all these years? It must indeed. No, don't bother to look at the reflection of your face in the window-pane shadowed by the night outside. Nobody could tell you now after all these years. Your face has changed in these long years of money-getting in the city. Perhaps if you had come back now and again, just at odd times, it wouldn't have been so.

The Marine Excursion of the Knights of Pythias

Half-past six on a July morning! The *Mariposa Belle* is at the wharf, decked in flags, with steam up ready to start.

Excursion day!

Half-past six on a July morning, and Lake Wissanotti lying in the sun as calm as glass. The opal colours of the morning light are shot from the surface of the water.

Out on the lake the last thin threads of the mist are clearing away like flecks of cotton wool.

The long call of the loon echoes over the lake. The air is cool and fresh. There is in it all the new life of the land of the silent pine and the moving waters. Lake Wissanotti in the morning sunlight! Don't talk to me of the Italian lakes, or the Tyrol or the Swiss Alps. Take them away. Move them somewhere else. I don't want them.

Excursion Day, at half-past six of a summer morning! With the boat all decked in flags and all the people in Mariposa on the wharf, and the band in peaked caps with big cornets tied to their bodies ready to play at any minute! I say! Don't tell me about the Carnival of Venice and the Delhi Durbar. Don't! I wouldn't look at them. I'd shut my eyes! For light and colour give me every time an excursion out of Mariposa down the lake to the Indian's Island out of sight in the morning mist. Talk of your Papal Zouaves and your Buckingham Palace Guard! I want to see the Mariposa band in uniform and the Mariposa Knights of Pythias with their aprons and their insignia and their picnic baskets and their five-cent cigars!

Half-past six in the morning, and all the crowd on the wharf and the boat due to leave in half an hour. Notice it!—in half an hour. Already she's whistled twice (at six, and at six fifteen), and at any minute now, Christie Johnson will step into the pilot house and pull the string for the warning whistle that the boat will leave in half an hour. So keep ready. Don't think of running back to Smith's Hotel for the sandwiches. Don't be fool enough to try to go up to the Greek Store, next to Netley's, and buy fruit. You'll be left behind for sure if you do. Never mind the sandwiches and the fruit! Anyway, here comes Mr Smith himself with a huge basket of provender that would feed a factory. There must be sandwiches in that. I think I can hear them clinking. And behind Mr Smith is the German waiter from the caff with another basket—undubitably lager beer; and behind him, the bartender of the hotel, carrying nothing, as far as one can see. But of course if you know Mariposa you will understand that why he looks so nonchalant and empty-handed is because he has two bottles of rye whisky under his linen duster. You know, I think, the peculiar walk of a man with two bottles of whisky in the inside pockets of a linen coat. In Mariposa, you see, to bring beer to an excursion is quite in keeping with public opinion. But, whisky—well, one has to be a little careful.

Do I say that Mr Smith is here? Why, everybody's here. There's Hussell, the editor of the *Newspacket*, wearing a blue ribbon on his coat, for the Mariposa Knights of Pythias are, by their constitution, dedicated to temperance; and there's Henry Mullins, the manager of the Exchange Bank, also a Knight of Pythias, with a small flask of Pogram's Special in his hip pocket as a sort of amendment to the constitution. And there's Dean Drone, the Chaplain of the Order, with a fishing-rod (you never saw such green bass as lie among the rocks at Indian's Island), and with a trolling line in case of maskinonge, and a landing-net in case of pickerel, and with his eldest daughter, Lilian Drone, in case of young men. There never was such a fisherman as the Rev. Rupert Drone.

* * *

Perhaps I ought to explain that when I speak of the excursion as being of the Knights of Pythias, the thing must not be understood in any narrow sense. In Mariposa practically everybody belongs to the Knights of Pythias just as they do to everything else. That's the great thing about the town and that's what makes it so different from the city. Everybody is in everything.

You should see them on the seventeenth of March, for example, when everybody wears a green ribbon and they're all laughing and glad—you know what the Celtic nature is—and talking about Home Rule.

On St Andrew's Day every man in town wears a thistle and shakes hands with everybody else, and you see the fine old Scotch honesty beaming out of their eyes.

And on St George's Day!—well, there's no heartiness like the good old English spirit, after all; why shouldn't a man feel glad that he's an Englishman?

Then on the Fourth of July there are stars and stripes flying over half the stores in town, and suddenly all the men are seen to smoke cigars, and to know all about Roosevelt and Bryan and the Philippine Islands. Then you learn for the first time that Jeff Thorpe's people came from Massachusetts and that his uncle fought at Bunker Hill (anyway Jefferson will swear it was in Dakota all right enough); and you find that George Duff has a married sister in Rochester and that her husband is all right; in fact, George was down there as recently as eight years ago. Oh, it's the most American town imaginable is Mariposa—on the fourth of July.

But wait, just wait, if you feel anxious about the solidity of the British connexion, till the twelfth of the month, when everybody is wearing an orange streamer in his coat and the Orangemen (every man in town) walk in the big procession. Allegiance! Well, perhaps you remember the address they gave to the Prince of Wales on the platform of the Mariposa station as he went through on his tour to the west. I think that pretty well settled that question.

So you will easily understand that of course everybody belongs to the Knights of Pythias and the Masons and Oddfellows, just as they all belong to the Snow Shoe Club and the Girls' Friendly Society.

And meanwhile the whistle of the steamer has blown again for a quarter to seven—loud and long this time, for anyone not here now is late for certain, unless he should happen to come down in the last fifteen minutes.

What a crowd upon the wharf and how they pile onto the steamer! It's a wonder that the boat can hold them all. But that's just the marvellous thing about the *Mariposa Belle*.

I don't know—I have never known—where the steamers like the *Mariposa Belle* come from. Whether they are built by Harland and Wolff of Belfast, or whether, on the other hand, they are not built by Harland and Wolff of Belfast, is more than one would like to say offhand.

The *Mariposa Belle* always seems to me to have some of those strange properties that distinguish Mariposa itself. I mean, her size seems to vary so. If you see her there in the winter, frozen in the ice beside the wharf with a snowdrift against the windows of the pilot house, she looks a pathetic little thing the size of a butternut.

But in the summer time, especially after you've *been* in Mariposa for a month or two, and have paddled alongside of her in a canoe, she gets larger and taller, and with a great sweep of black sides, till you see no difference between the *Mariposa Belle* and the *Lusitania*. Each one is a big steamer and that's all you can say.

Nor do her measurements help you much. She draws about eighteen inches forward, and more than that—at least half an inch more, astern, and when she's loaded down with an excursion crowd she draws a good two inches'more. And above the water—why, look at all the decks on her! There's the deck you walk onto, from the wharf, all shut in, with windows along it, and the after cabin with the long table, and above that the deck with all the chairs piled upon it, and the deck in front where the band stand round in a circle, and the pilot house is higher than that, and above the pilot house is the board with the gold name and the flag pole and the steel ropes and the flags; and fixed in somewhere on the different levels is the lunch counter where they sell the sandwiches, and the engine room, and down below the deck level, beneath the water line, is the place where the crew sleep. What with steps and stairs and passages and piles of cordwood for the engine—oh, no, I guess Harland and Wolff didn't build her. They couldn't have.

Yet even with a huge boat like the *Mariposa Belle*, it would be impossible for her to carry all of the crowd that you see in the boat and on the wharf. In reality, the crowd is made up of two classes—all of the people in Mariposa who are going on the excursion and all those who are not. Some come for the one reason and some for the other.

The two tellers of the Exchange Bank are both there standing side by side. But one of them—the one with the cameo pin and the long face like a horse—is going, and the other—with the other cameo pin and the face like another horse—is not. In the same way, Hussell of the *Newspacket* is going, but his brother, beside him, isn't. Lilian Drone is going, but her sister can't; and so on all through the crowd.

* * *

And to think that things should look like that on the morning of a steamboat accident.

How strange life is!

To think of all these people so eager and anxious to catch the steamer, and some of them running to catch it, and so fearful that they might miss it—the morning of a steamboat accident. And the captain blowing his whistle, and warning them so severely that he would leave them behind—leave them out of the accident! And everybody crowding so eagerly to be in the accident.

Perhaps life is like that all through.

Strangest of all to think, in a case like this, of the people who were left behind, or in some way or other prevented from going, and always afterwards told of how they had escaped being on board the *Mariposa Belle* that day!

Some of the instances were certainly extraordinary.

Nivens, the lawyer, escaped from being there merely by the fact that he was away in the city.

Towers, the tailor, only escaped owing to the fact that, not intending to go on the excursion he had stayed in bed till eight o'clock and so had not gone. He narrated afterwards that waking up that morning at half-past five, he had thought of the excursion and for some unaccountable reason had felt glad that he was not going.

* * *

The case of Yodel, the auctioneer, was even more inscrutable. He had been to the Oddfellows' excursion on the train the week before and to the Conservative picnic the week before that, and had decided not to go on this trip. In fact, he had not the least intention of going. He narrated afterwards how the night before someone had stopped him on the corner of Nippewa and Tecumseh Streets (he indicated the very spot) and asked: 'Are you going to take in the excursion tomorrow?' and he had said, just as simply as he was talking when narrating it: 'No.' And ten minutes after that, at the corner of Dalhousie and Brock Streets (he offered to lead a party of verification to the precise place) somebody else had stopped him and asked: 'Well, are you going on the steamer trip tomorrow?' Again he had answered: 'No,' apparently almost in the same tone as before.

He said afterwards that when he heard the rumour of the accident it seemed like the finger of Providence, and he fell on his knees in thankfulness.

There was the similar case of Morison (I mean the one in Glover's hardware store that married one of the Thompsons). He said afterwards that he had read so much in the papers about accidents lately—mining accidents, and aeroplanes and gasoline—that he had grown nervous. The night before his wife had asked him at supper: 'Are you going on the excursion?' He had answered: 'No, I don't think I feel like it,' and had added: 'Perhaps your mother might like to go.' And the next evening just at dusk, when the news ran through the town, he said the first thought that flashed through his head was: 'Mrs Thompson's on that boat.'

He told this right as I say it—without the least doubt or confusion. He never for a moment imagined she was on the *Lusitania* or the *Olympic* or any other boat. He knew she was on this one. He said you could have knocked him down where he stood. But no one had. Not even when he got halfway down—on his knees, and it would have been easier still to knock him down or kick him. People do miss a lot of chances.

Still, as I say, neither Yodel nor Morison nor anyone thought about there being an accident until just after sundown when they—

Well, have you ever heard the long booming whistle of a steamboat two miles out on the lake in the dusk, and while you listen and count and wonder, seen the crimson rockets going up against the sky and then heard the fire bell ringing right there beside you in the town, and seen the people running to the town wharf?

That's what the people of Mariposa saw and felt that summer evening as they watched the Mackinaw lifeboat go plunging out into the lake with seven sweeps to a side and the foam clear to the gunwale with the lifting stroke of fourteen men!

But, dear me, I am afraid that this is no way to tell a story. I suppose the true art would have been to have said nothing about the accident till it happened. But when you write about Mariposa, or hear of it, if you know the place, it's all so vivid and real, that a thing like the contrast between the excursion crowd in the morning and the scene at night leaps into your mind and you must think of it.

* * *

But never mind about the accident—let us turn back again to the morning.

The boat was due to leave at seven. There was no doubt about the hour—not only seven, but seven sharp. The notice in the *Newspacket* said: 'The boat will leave sharp at seven'; and the advertising posters on the telegraph poles on Missinaba Street that began, 'Ho, for Indian's Island!' ended up with the words: 'Boat leaves at seven sharp.' There was a big notice on the wharf that said: 'Boat leaves sharp on time.'

So at seven, right on the hour, the whistle blew loud and long, and then at seven-fifteen three short peremptory blasts, and at seven-thirty one quick angry call—just one—and very soon after that they cast off the last of the ropes and the *Mariposa Belle* sailed off in her cloud of flags, and the band of the Knights of Pythias, timing it to a nicety, broke into the 'Maple Leaf for Ever!'

I suppose that all excursions when they start are much the same. Anyway, on the *Mariposa Belle* everybody went running up and down all over the boat with deck chairs and camp stools and baskets, and found places, splendid places to sit, and then got scared that there might be better ones and chased off again. People hunted for places out of the sun and when they got them swore that they weren't going to freeze to please anybody; and the people in the sun said that they hadn't paid fifty cents to get roasted. Others said that they hadn't paid fifty cents to get covered with cinders, and there were still others who hadn't paid fifty cents to get shaken to death with the propeller.

Still, it was all right presently. The people seemed to get sorted out into the places on the boat where they belonged. The women, the older ones, all gravitated into the cabin on the lower deck and by getting round the table with needlework, and with all the windows shut, they soon had it, as they said themselves, just like being at home.

All the young boys and the toughs and the men in the band got down on the lower deck forward, where the boat was dirtiest and where the anchor was and the coils of rope.

And upstairs on the after deck there were Lilian Drone and Miss Lawson, the high-school teacher, with a book of German poetry—Gothey I think it was—and the bank teller and the young men.

In the centre, standing beside the rail, were Dean Drone and Dr Gallagher, looking through binocular glasses at the shore.

Up in front on the little deck forward of the pilot house was a group of the older men, Mullins and Duff and Mr Smith in a deck chair, and beside him Mr Golgotha Gingham, the undertaker of Mariposa, on a stool. It was part of Mr Gingham's principles to take in an outing of this sort, a business matter, more or less—for you never know what may happen at these water parties. At any rate, he was there in a neat suit of black, not, of course, his heavier or professional suit, but a soft clinging effect as of burnt paper that combined gaiety and decorum to a nicety.

* * *

'Yes,' said Mr Gingham, waving his black glove in a general way towards the shore, 'I know the lake well, very well. I've been pretty much all over it in my time.'

'Canoeing?' asked somebody.

'No,' said Mr Gingham, 'not in a canoe.' There seemed a peculiar and quiet meaning in his tone.

'Sailing, I suppose,' said somebody else.

'No,' said Mr Gingham. 'I don't understand it.'

'I never knowed that you went onto the water at all, Gol,' said Mr Smith, breaking in.

'Ah, not now,' explained Mr Gingham; 'it was years ago, the first summer I came to Mariposa. I was on the water practically all day. Nothing like it to give a man an appetite and keep him in shape.'

'Was you camping?' asked Mr Smith.

'We camped at night,' assented the undertaker, 'but we put in practically the whole day on the water. You see, we were after a party that had come up here from the city on his vacation and gone out in a sailing canoe. We were dragging. We were up every morning at sunrise, lit a fire on the beach and cooked breakfast, and then we'd light our pipes and be off with the net for a whole day. It's a great life,' concluded Mr Gingham wistfully.

'Did you get him?' asked two or three together.

There was a pause before Mr Gingham answered.

'We did,' he said '—down in the reeds past Horseshoe Point. But it was no use. He turned blue on me right away.'

After which Mr Gingham fell into such a deep reverie that the boat had steamed another half-mile down the lake before anybody broke the silence again. Talk of this sort—and after all what more suitable for a day on the water?—beguiled the way.

*　*　*

Down the lake, mile by mile over the calm water, steamed the *Mariposa Belle*. They passed Poplar Point where the high sand-banks are with all the swallows' nests in them, and Dean Drone and Dr Gallagher looked at them alternately through the binocular glasses, and it was wonderful how plainly one could see the swallows and the banks and the shrubs—just as plainly as with the naked eye.

And a little farther down they passed the Shingle Beach, and Dr Gallagher, who knew Canadian history, said to Dean Drone that it was strange to think that Champlain had landed there with his French explorers three hundred years ago; and Dean Drone, who didn't know Canadian history, said it was stranger still to think that the hand of the Almighty had piled up the hills and rocks long before that; and Dr Gallagher said it was wonderful how the French had found their way through such a pathless wilderness; and Dean Drone said that it was wonderful also to think that the Almighty had placed even the smallest shrub in its appointed place. Dr Gallagher said it filled him with admiration. Dean Drone said it filled him with awe. Dr Gallagher said he'd been full of it ever since he was a boy and Dean Drone said so had he.

Then a little further, as the *Mariposa Belle* steamed on down the lake, they passed the Old Indian Portage where the great grey rocks are; and Dr Gallagher drew Dean Drone's attention to the place where the narrow canoe track wound up from the shore to the woods, and Dean Drone said he could see it perfectly well without the glasses.

Dr Gallagher said that it was just here that a party of five hundred French had made their way with all their baggage and accoutrements across the rocks of the divide and down to the Great Bay. And Dean Drone said that it reminded him of Xenophon leading his ten thousand Greeks over the hill passes of Armenia down to the sea. Dr Gallagher said that he had often wished he could have seen and spoken to Champlain, and Dean Drone said how much he regretted to have never known Xenophon.

And then after that they fell to talking of relics and traces of the past, and Dr Gallagher said that if Dean Drone would come round to his house some night he would show him some Indian arrow heads that he had dug up in his garden. And Dean Drone said that if Dr Gallagher would come round to the rectory any afternoon he would show him a map of Xerxes' invasion of Greece. Only he must come some time between the Infant Class and the Mothers' Auxiliary.

So presently they both knew that they were blocked out of one another's houses for some time to come, and Dr Gallagher walked forward and told Mr Smith, who had never studied Greek, about Champlain crossing the rock divide.

Mr Smith turned his head and looked at the divide for half a second and then said he had crossed a worse one up north back of the Wahnipitae and that the flies were Hades—and then went on playing freezeout poker with the two juniors in Duff's bank.

So Dr Gallagher realized that that's always the way when you try to tell people things, and that as far as gratitude and appreciation goes one might as well never read books or travel anywhere or do anything.

In fact, it was at this very moment that he made up his mind to give the arrows to the Mariposa Mechanics' Institute—they afterwards became, as you know, the Gallagher Collection. But, for the time being, the doctor was sick of them and wandered off round the boat and watched Henry Mullins showing George Duff how to make a John Collins without lemons, and finally went and sat down among the Mariposa band and wished that he hadn't come.

So the boat steamed on and the sun rose higher and higher, and the freshness of the morning changed into the full glare of noon, and pretty soon the *Mariposa Belle* had floated out onto the lake again and they went on to where the lake began to narrow in at its foot, just where the Indian's Island is—all grass and trees and with a log wharf running into the water. Below it the Lower Ossawippi runs out of the lake, and quite near are the rapids, and you can see down among the trees the red brick of the power house and hear the roar of the leaping water.

The Indian's Island itself is all covered with trees and tangled vines, and the water about it is so still that it's all reflected double and looks the same either way up. Then when the steamer's whistle blows as it comes into the wharf, you hear it echo among the trees of the island, and reverberate back from the shores of the lake.

The scene is all so quiet and still and unbroken, that Miss Cleghorn—the sallow girl in the telephone exchange, that I spoke of—said she'd like to be buried there. But all the people were so busy getting their baskets and gathering up their things that no one had time to attend to it.

I mustn't even try to describe the landing and the boat crunching against the wooden wharf and all the people running to the same side of the deck and Christie Johnson calling out to the crowd to keep to the starboard and nobody being able to find it. Everyone who has been on a Mariposa excursion knows all about that.

Nor can I describe the day itself and the picnic under the trees. There were speeches afterwards, and Judge Pepperleigh gave such offence by bringing in Conservative politics that a man called Patriotus Canadiensis wrote and asked for some of the invaluable space of the *Mariposa Times-Herald* and exposed it.

I should say that there were races too, on the grass on the open side of the island, graded mostly according to ages—races for boys under thirteen and girls over nine-teen and all that sort of thing. Sports are generally conducted on that plan in Mari-posa. It is realized that a woman of sixty has an unfair advantage over a mere child.

Dean Drone managed the races and decided the ages and gave out the prizes; the Wesleyan minister helped, and he and the young student, who was relieving in the Presbyterian Church, held the string at the winning point.

They had to get mostly clergymen for the races because all the men had wandered off, somehow, to where they were drinking lager beer out of two kegs stuck on pine logs among the trees.

But if you've ever been on a Mariposa excursion you know all about these details anyway.

So the day wore on and presently the sun came through the trees on a slant and the steamer whistle blew with a great puff of white steam and all the people came straggling down to the wharf and pretty soon the *Mariposa Belle* had floated out onto the lake again and headed for the town, twenty miles away.

* * *

I suppose you have often noticed the contrast there is between an excursion on its way out in the morning and what it looks like on the way home.

In the morning everybody is so restless and animated and moves to and from all over the boat and asks questions. But coming home, as the afternoon gets later and later and the sun sinks beyond the hills, all the people seem to get so still and quiet and drowsy.

So it was with the people on the *Mariposa Belle*. They sat there on the benches and the deck chairs in little clusters, and listened to the regular beat of the propeller and almost dozed off asleep as they sat. Then when the sun set and the dusk drew on, it grew almost dark on the deck and so still that you could hardly tell there was anyone on board.

And if you had looked at the steamer from the shore or from one of the islands, you'd have seen the row of lights from the cabin windows shining on the water and the red glare of the burning hemlock from the funnel, and you'd have heard the soft thud of the propeller miles away over the lake.

Now and then, too, you could have heard them singing on the steamer—the voices of the girls and the men blended into unison by the distance, rising and falling in long-drawn melody: '*O—Can-a-da—O—Can-a-da.*'

You may talk as you will about the intoning choirs of your European cathedrals, but the sound of '*O Can-a-da*', borne across the waters of a silent lake at evening is good enough for those of us who know Mariposa.

I think that it was just as they were singing like this: '*O—Can-a-da*', that word went round that the boat was sinking.

If you have ever been in any sudden emergency on the water, you will understand the strange psychology of it—the way in which what is happening seems to become known all in a moment without a word being said. The news is transmitted from one to the other by some mysterious process.

At any rate, on the *Mariposa Belle* first one and then the other heard that the steamer was sinking. As far as I could ever learn the first of it was that George Duff, the bank manager, came very quietly to Dr Gallagher and asked him if he thought that the boat was sinking. The doctor said no, that he had thought so earlier in the day but that he didn't now think that she was.

After that Duff, according to his own account, had said to Macartney, the lawyer, that the boat was sinking, and Macartney said that he doubted it very much.

Then somebody came to Judge Pepperleigh and woke him up and said that there was six inches of water in the steamer and that she was sinking. And Pepperleigh said it was perfect scandal and passed the news on to his wife and she said that they had no business to allow it and that if the steamer sank that was the last excursion she'd go on.

So the news went all round the boat and everywhere the people gathered in groups and talked about it in the angry and excited way that people have when a steamer is sinking on one of the lakes like Lake Wissanotti.

Dean Drone, of course, and some others were quieter about it, and said that one must make allowances and that naturally there were two sides to everything. But most of them wouldn't listen to reason at all. I think, perhaps, that some of them were frightened. You see the last time but one that the steamer had sunk, there had been a man drowned and it made them nervous.

What? Hadn't I explained about the depth of Lake Wissanotti? I had taken it for granted that you knew; and in any case parts of it are deep enough, though I don't suppose in this stretch of it from the big reed beds up to within a mile of the town wharf, you could find six feet of water in it if you tried. Oh, pshaw! I was not talking about a steamer sinking in the ocean and carrying down its screaming crowds of people into the hideous depths of green water. Oh, dear me, no! That kind of thing never happens on Lake Wissanotti.

But what does happen is that the *Mariposa Belle* sinks every now and then, and sticks there on the bottom till they get things straightened up.

On the lakes round Mariposa, if a person arrives late anywhere and explains that the steamer sank, everybody understands the situation.

You see when Harland and Wolff built the *Mariposa Belle*, they left some cracks in between the timbers that you fill up with cotton waste every Sunday. If this is not attended to, the boat sinks. In fact, it is part of the law of the province that all the steamers like the *Mariposa Belle* must be properly corked—I think that is the word—every season. There are inspectors who visit all the hotels in the province to see that it is done.

So you can imagine now that I've explained it a little straighter, the indignation of the people when they knew that the boat had come uncorked and that they might be stuck out there on a shoal or a mud-bank half the night.

I don't say either that there wasn't any danger; anyway, it doesn't feel very safe when you realize that the boat is settling down with every hundred yards that she goes, and you look over the side and see only the black water in the gathering night.

Safe! I'm not sure now that I come to think of it that it isn't worse than sinking in the Atlantic. After all, in the Atlantic there is wireless telegraphy, and a lot of trained sailors and stewards. But out on Lake Wissanotti—far out, so that you can only just see the lights of the town away off to the south—when the propeller comes to a stop—and you can hear the hiss of steam as they start to rake out the engine fires to prevent an explosion—and when you turn from the red glare that comes from the furnace doors as they open them, to the black dark that is gathering over the lake—and there's a night wind beginning to run among the rushes—and you see the men going forward to the roof of the pilot house to send up the rockets to rouse the town—safe? Safe yourself, if you like; as for me, let me once get back into Mariposa again, under the night shadow of the maple trees, and this shall be the last, last time I'll go on Lake Wissanotti.

Safe! Oh, yes! Isn't it strange how safe other people's adventures seem after they happen? But you'd have been scared, too, if you'd been there just before the steamer sank, and seen them bringing up all the women on to the top deck.

I don't see how some of the people took it so calmly; how Mr Smith, for instance, could have gone on smoking and telling how he'd had a steamer 'sink on him' on Lake Nipissing and a still bigger one, a side-wheeler, sink on him in Lake Abbitibbi.

Then, quite suddenly, with a quiver, down she went. You could feel the boat sink, sink—down, down—would it never get to the bottom? The water came flush up to the lower deck, and then—thank heaven—the sinking stopped and there was the *Mariposa Belle* safe and tight on a reed bank.

Really, it made one positively laugh! It seemed so queer and, anyway, if a man has a sort of natural courage, danger makes him laugh. Danger? pshaw! fiddlesticks! everybody scouted the idea. Why, it is just the little things like this that give zest to a day on the water.

Within half a minute they were all running round looking for sandwiches and cracking jokes and talking of making coffee over the remains of the engine fires.

* * *

I don't need to tell at length how it all happened after that.

I suppose the people on the *Mariposa Belle* would have had to settle down there all night or till help came from the town, but some of the men who had gone forward and were peering out into the dark said that it couldn't be more than a mile across the water to Miller's Point. You could almost see it over there to the left—some of them, I think, said 'off on the port bow,' because you know when you get mixed up in these marine disasters, you soon catch the atmosphere of the thing.

So pretty soon they had the davits swung out over the side and were lowering the old lifeboat from the top deck into the water.

There were men leaning out over the rail of the *Mariposa Belle* with lanterns that threw the light as they let her down, and the glare fell on the water and the reeds. But when they got the boat lowered, it looked such a frail, clumsy thing as one saw it from the rail above, that the cry was raised: 'Women and children first!' For what was the sense, if it should turn out that the boat wouldn't even hold women and children, of trying to jam a lot of heavy men into it?

So they put in mostly women and children and the boat pushed out into the darkness so freighted down it would hardly float.

In the bow of it was the Presbyterian student who was relieving the minister, and he called out that they were in the hands of Providence. But he was crouched and ready to spring out of them at the first moment.

So the boat went and was lost in the darkness except for the lantern in the bow that you could see bobbing on the water. Then presently it came back and they sent another load, till pretty soon the decks began to thin out and everybody got impatient to be gone.

It was about the time that the third boat-load put off that Mr Smith took a bet with Mullins for twenty-five dollars, that he'd be home in Mariposa before the people in the boats had walked round the shore.

No one knew just what he meant, but pretty soon they saw Mr Smith disappear down below the lowest part of the steamer with a mallet in one hand and a big bundle of marline in the other.

They might have wondered more about it, but it was just at this time that they heard the shouts from the rescue boat—the big Mackinaw lifeboat—that had put out from the town with fourteen men at the sweeps when they saw the first rockets go up.

I suppose there is always something inspiring about a rescue at sea, or on the water.

After all, the bravery of the lifeboat man is the true bravery—expended to save life, not to destroy it.

Certainly they told for months after of how the rescue boat came out to the *Mariposa Belle.*

I suppose that when they put her in the water the lifeboat touched it for the first time since the old Macdonald Government placed her on Lake Wissanotti.

Anyway, the water poured in at every seam. But not for a moment—even with two miles of water between them and the steamer—did the rowers pause for that.

By the time they were halfway there the water was almost up to the thwarts, but they drove her on. Panting and exhausted (for mind you, if you haven't been in a fool boat like that for years, rowing takes it out of you), the rowers stuck to their task. They threw the ballast over and chucked into the water the heavy cork jackets and lifebelts that encumbered their movements. There was no thought of turning back. They were nearer to the steamer than the shore.

'Hang to it, boys,' called the crowd from the steamer's deck, and hang they did.

They were almost exhausted when they got them; men leaning from the steamer threw them ropes and one by one every man was hauled aboard just as the lifeboat sank under their feet.

Saved! by heaven, saved by one of the smartest pieces of rescue work ever seen on the lake.

There's no use describing it; you need to see rescue work of this kind by lifeboats to understand it.

Nor were the lifeboat crew the only ones that distinguished themselves.

Boat after boat and canoe after canoe had put out from Mariposa to the help of the steamer. They got them all.

Pupkin, the other bank teller with a face like a horse, who hadn't gone on the excursion—as soon as he knew that the boat was signalling for help and that Miss Lawson was sending up rockets—rushed for a row boat, grabbed an oar (two would have hampered him)—and paddled madly out into the lake. He struck right out into the dark with the crazy skiff almost sinking beneath his feet. But they got him. They rescued him. They watched him, almost dead with exhaustion, make his way to the steamer, where he was hauled up with ropes. Saved! Saved!

*　*　*

They might have gone on that way half the night, picking up the rescuers, only, at the very moment when the tenth load of people left for the shore—just as suddenly and saucily as you please, up came the *Mariposa Belle* from the mud bottom and floated.

Floated?

Why, of course she did. If you take a hundred and fifty people off a steamer that has sunk, and if you get a man as shrewd as Mr Smith to plug the timber seams with mallet and marline, and if you turn ten bandsmen of the Mariposa band onto your hand pump on the bow of the lower decks—float? why, what else can she do?

Then, if you stuff in hemlock into the embers of the fire that you were raking out, till it hums and crackles under the boiler, it won't be long before you hear the propeller thud—thudding at the stern again, and before the long roar of the steam whistle echoes over to the town.

And so the *Mariposa Belle*, with all steam up again and with the long train of sparks careering from the funnel, is heading for the town.

But no Christie Johnson at the wheel in the pilot house this time.

'Smith! Get Smith!' is the cry.

Can he take her in? Well, now! Ask a man who has had steamers sink on him in half the lakes from Temiscaming to the Bay, if he can take her in? Ask a man who has run a York boat down the rapids of the Moose when the ice is moving, if he can grip the steering wheel of the *Mariposa Belle*? So there she steams safe and sound to the town wharf!

Look at the lights and the crowds! If only the federal census taker could count us now! Hear them calling and shouting back and forward from the deck to the shore! Listen! There is the rattle of the shore ropes as they get them ready, and there's the Mariposa band—actually forming in a circle on the upper deck just as she docks, and the leader with his baton—one—two—ready now—

'O CAN-A-DA!'

1912

Frederick Philip Grove

1879-1948

The man we call Grove created a fictional version of his life so tangled that a great deal of effort had to be devoted to uncovering the truth hidden there. *A Search for America* (1927) and *In Search of Myself* (1946), long regarded as generally accurate autobiographical accounts, are now recognized as having more affinities with fiction than with fact.

According to *In Search of Myself* Grove was born in 1871 in Russia, the son of a wealthy Swedish landowner, and came to North America in 1891, working for some months as a waiter in Toronto. From there he began an odyssey that carried him across the North American continent in a twenty-year search for place. In *A Search for America* Grove describes how this became a quest for an idealized 'America' that finally led him to choose Canada as the place in North America where the agrarian order he valued still endured.

Opposed to these accounts is Douglas O. Spettigue's reconstruction of Grove's early life in *F.P.G.: The European Years*. Spettigue identifies Grove with Felix Paul Greve, a German national who as a young man was a writer, translator, minor conman, and womanizer. Perpetually in trouble, Greve spent over a year in prison before finally faking a suicide in 1909 in order to escape his debts and personal entanglements. After fleeing Europe, he emerged in his new identity of Frederick Philip Grove in northern Manitoba around 1912, married soon after, and became a stable member of the community. He worked as a school teacher, and for a time was principal of a high school in Gladstone, where he began to write. In 1929 Grove quit teaching and left Manitoba, settling for a year in Ottawa and then on a farm north of Simcoe, Ont.

In his commitment to a realistic, unsentimental treatment of prairie and, later, Ontario life, Grove became one of the important founders of the modern tradition in Canada. His two early works of non-fiction,

Over Prairie Trails (1922) and *The Turn of the Year* (1923), describe Grove's northern milieu in a way that demonstrates their author's inquiring mind and observant eye—traits that served him well in his four prairie novels that followed: *Settlers of the Marsh* (1925), *Our Daily Bread* (1928), *Yoke of Life* (1930), and *Fruits of the Earth* (1933). As with early realists elsewhere, the frankness of his fiction got Grove into trouble with the moral arbiters of his time, and *Settlers of the Marsh* was condemned as pornographic. The part of the novel considered most offensive—a striking passage about a prairie wife who deliberately induces abortions by engaging in punishing work—can now be seen simply as one of the many instances in which Grove was responding compassionately to the terrible suffering and deprivation endured by women on lonely northern farms.

In his depiction of pioneer men Grove was more ambivalent, for in the monumental task of clearing the land there lay the possibility of acts of noble stoicism and even grandeur, as well as of great folly. In recording the prairie farmer's struggles, Grove showed that the common materials of daily rural life could be given epic sweep, and even take on mythic dimensions.

All of Grove's writing deals in some ways with change—from the changing aspects of the natural cycle that seem central to his experience of Manitoba, to the tremendous social and technological transformations that were affecting the whole social fabric around him. In his later Ontario novels (*Two Generations*, 1939, and *The Master of the Mill*, 1944) it is change itself rather than the gruelling demands of pioneer life that disrupts the family and produces social conflicts.

Grove's last novel, *Consider Her Ways* (1947), a social satire in the form of an allegory about ants, is a departure from his realistic mode. His early essays and speeches were collected in *It Needs to be Said* (1929);

a selection of his short stories, *Tales from the Margin*, was edited by Desmond Pacey in 1971. Grove received some official recognition before he died in the form of a Governor General's Award for *In Search of Myself*.

The selection that follows is one of the seven sketches in *Over Prairie Trails*. Each sketch in that work is the story of one of Grove's weekend trips from the school where he taught to the house where his wife and daughter waited, some thirty-four miles away.

From *Over Prairie Trails*

SNOW[1]

The blizzard started on Wednesday morning. It was that rather common, truly western combination of a heavy snowstorm with a blinding northern gale—such as piles the snow in hills and mountains and makes walking next to impossible.

I cannot exactly say that I viewed it with unmingled joy. There were special reasons for that. It was the second week in January; when I had left 'home'[2] the Sunday before, I had been feeling rather bad; so my wife would worry a good deal, especially if I did not come at all. I knew there was such a thing as its becoming quite impossible to make the drive. I had been lost in a blizzard once or twice before in my lifetime. And yet, so long as there was the least chance that horse-power and human will-power combined might pull me through at all, I was determined to make or anyway to try it.

At noon I heard the first dismal warning. For some reason or other I had to go down into the basement of the school. The janitor, a highly efficient but exceedingly bad-humoured cockney, who was dissatisfied with all things Canadian because 'in the old country we do things differently'—whose sharp tongue was feared by many, and who once remarked to a lady teacher in the most casual way, 'If you *was* a lidy, I'd wipe my boots on you!'—this selfsame janitor, standing by the furnace, turned slowly around, showed his pale and hollow-eyed face, and smiled a withering and commiserating smile. 'Ye won't go north this week,' he remarked—not without sympathy, for somehow he had taken a liking to me, which even prompted him off and on to favour me with caustic expressions of what he thought of the school board and the leading citizens of the town. I, of course, never encouraged him in his communicativeness which seemed to be just what he would expect, and no rebuff ever goaded him into the slightest show of resentment. 'We'll see,' I said briefly. 'Well, Sir,' he repeated apodeictically,[3] 'ye won't.' I smiled and went out.

But in my classroom I looked from the window across the street. Not even in broad daylight could you see the opposite houses or trees. And I knew that, once a storm like that sets in, it is apt to continue for days at a stretch. It was one of those orgies in which Titan Wind indulges ever so often on our western prairies. I certainly needed something to encourage me, and so, before leaving the build-

[1] 'Snow', the fourth sketch in *Over Prairie Trails*, is entirely different from the often-reprinted Grove short story of the same title.
[2] Grove explains in his preface how his school teaching kept him 'in a small country town' during the week while his wife looked after a rural school and lived with their daughter in its residence some thirty-four miles away, 'in the southern fringe of the great northern timber expanse, not very far from the western shore of a great lake.'
[3] As if based on incontrovertible evidence.

ing, I went upstairs to the third story and looked through a window which faced north. But, though I was now above the drifting layer, I could not see very far here either; the snowflakes were small and like little round granules, hitting the panes of the windows with little sounds of 'ping-ping'; and they came, driven by a relentless gale, in such numbers that they blotted out whatever was more than two or three hundred yards away.

The inhabitant of the middle latitudes of this continent has no data to picture to himself what a snowstorm in the north may be. To him snow is something benign that comes soft-footedly over night, and on the most silent wings like an owl, something that suggests the sleep of Nature rather than its battles. The further south you go, the more, of course, snow loses of its aggressive character.

At the dinner table in the hotel I heard a few more disheartening words. But after four I defiantly got my tarpaulin out and carried it to the stable. If I had to run the risk of getting lost, at least I was going to prepare for it. I had once stayed out, snow-bound, for a day and a half, nearly without food and altogether without shelter; and I was not going to get thus caught again. I also carefully over-hauled my cutter.[4] Not a bolt but I tested it with a wrench; and before the stores were closed, I bought myself enough canned goods to feed me for a week should through any untoward accident the need arise. I always carried a little alcohol stove, and with my tarpaulin I could convert my cutter within three minutes into a windproof tent. Cramped quarters, to be sure, but better than being given over to the wind at thirty below!

More than any remark on the part of friends or acquaintances one fact depressed me when I went home. There was not a team in town which had come in from the country. The streets were deserted: the stores were empty. The north wind and the snow had the town to themselves.

On Thursday the weather was unchanged. On the way to the school I had to scale a snowdrift thrown up to a height of nearly six feet, and, though it was beginning to harden, from its own weight and the pressure of the wind, I still broke in at every step and found the task tiring in the extreme. I did my work, of course, as if nothing oppressed me, but in my heart I was beginning to face the possibility that, even if I tried, I might fail to reach my goal. The day passed by. At noon the school-children, the teachers, and a few people hurrying to the post-office for their mail lent a fleeting appearance of life to the streets. It nearly cheered me; but soon after four the whole town again took on that deserted look which reminded me of an abandoned mining camp. The lights in the store windows had something artificial about them, as if they were merely painted on the canvas-wings of a stage-setting. Not a team came in all day.

On Friday morning the same. Burroughs[5] would have said that the weather had gone into a rut. Still the wind whistled and howled through the bleak, dark, hollow dawn; the snow kept coming down and piling up, as if it could not be any otherwise. And as if to give notice of its intentions, the drift had completely closed up my front door. I fought my way to the school and thought things over. My wife and I had agreed, if ever the weather should be so bad that there was

[4]A light horse-drawn sleigh.
[5]John Burroughs (1837-1921), a popular and prolific American nature writer to whom Grove alludes several times in *Over Prairie Trails*.

danger in going at night, I was to wait till Saturday morning and go by daylight. Neither one of us ever mentioned the possibility of giving the attempt up altogether. My wife probably understood that I would not bind myself by any such promise. Now even on this Friday I should have liked to go by night, if for no other reason, then for the experience's sake; but I reflected that I might get lost and not reach home at all. The horses knew the road—so long as there was any road; but there was none now. I felt it would not be fair to wife and child. So, reluctantly and with much hesitation, but definitely at last, I made up my mind that I was going to wait till morning. My cutter was ready—I had seen to that on Wednesday. As soon as the storm had set in, I had instinctively started to work in order to frustrate its designs.

At noon I met in front of the post-office a charming lady who with her husband and a young Anglican curate constituted about the only circle of real friends I had in town. 'Why!' I exclaimed, 'what takes you out into this storm, Mrs ——?' 'The desire,' she gasped against the wind and yet in her inimitable way, as if she were asking a favour, 'to have you come to our house for tea, my friend. You surely are not going this week?' 'I am going to go to-morrow morning at seven,' I said. 'But I shall be delighted to have tea with you and Mr ——.' I read her at a glance. She knew that in not going out at night I should suffer—she wished to help me over the evening, so I should not feel too much thwarted, too helpless, and too lonesome. She smiled. 'You really want to go? But I must not keep you. At six, if you please.' And we went our ways without a salute, for none was possible at this gale-swept corner.

After four o'clock I took word to the stable to have my horses fed and harnessed by seven in the morning. The hostler had a tale to tell. 'You going out north?' he enquired although he knew perfectly well I was. 'Of course,' I replied. 'Well,' he went on, 'a man came in from ten miles out; he was half dead; come, look at his horses! He says, in places the snow is over the telephone posts.' 'I'll try it anyway,' I said. 'Just have the team ready. I know what I can ask my horses to do. If it cannot be done, I shall turn back, that is all.'

When I stepped outside again, the wind seemed bent upon shaking the strongest faith. I went home to my house across the bridge and dressed. As soon as I was ready, I allowed myself to be swept past stable, past hotel and post-office till I reached the side street which led to the house where I was to be the guest.

How sheltered, homelike and protected everything looked inside. The hostess, as usual, was radiantly amiable. The host settled back after supper to talk old country. The Channel Islands, the French Coast, Kent and London—those were from common knowledge our most frequently recurring topics. Both host and hostess, that was easy to see, were bent upon beguiling the hours of their rather dark-humoured guest. But the howling gale outside was stronger than their good intentions. It was not very long before the conversation got around—reverted, so it seemed—to stories of storms, of being lost, of nearly freezing. The boys were sitting with wide and eager eyes, afraid they might be sent to bed before the feast of yarns was over. I told one or two of my most thrilling escapes, the host contributed a few more, and even the hostess had had an experience, driving on top of a railroad track for several miles, I believe, with a train, snowbound, behind her. I leaned over. 'Mrs——,' I said, 'do not try to dissuade me. I am sorry to say it, but it is useless. I am bound to go.' 'Well,' she said, 'I wish you would not.' 'Thanks,' I replied and looked at my watch. It was two o'clock. 'There is only one thing wrong with coming to have tea in this home,' I continued and smiled; 'it is so hard to say good-bye.'

I carefully lighted my lantern and got into my wraps. The wind was howling dismally outside. For a moment we stood in the hall, shaking hands and paying the usual compliments; then one of the boys opened the door for me; and in step-ping out I had one of the greatest surprises. Not far from the western edge of the world there stood the setting half-moon in a cloudless sky; myriads of stars were dusted over the vast, dark blue expanse, twinkling and blazing at their liveliest. And though the wind still whistled and shrieked and rattled, no snow came down, and not much seemed to drift. I pointed to the sky, smiled, nodded and closed the door. As far as the drifting of the snow went, I was mistaken, as I found out when I turned to the north, into the less sheltered street, past the post-office, hotel and stable. In front of a store I stopped to read a thermometer which I had found halfways reliable the year before. It read minus thirty-two degrees. . . .[6]

It was still dark, of course, when I left the house on Saturday morning to be on my way. Also, it was cold, bitterly cold, but there was very little wind. In cross-ing the bridge which was swept nearly clean of snow I noticed a small, but some-how ominous-looking drift at the southern end. It had such a disturbed, lashed-up appearance. The snow was still loose, yet packed just hard enough to have a cer-tain degree of toughness. You could no longer swing your foot through it: had you run into it at any great speed, you would have fallen; but as yet it was not hard enough to carry you. I knew that kind of a drift; it is treacherous. On a later drive one just like it, only built on a vastly larger scale, was to lead to the first of a series of little accidents which finally shattered my nerve. That was the only time that my temerity failed me. I shall tell you about that drive later on.[7]

At the stable I went about my preparations in a leisurely way. I knew that a supreme test was ahead of myself and the horses, and I meant to have daylight for tackling it. Once more I went over the most important bolts; once more I felt and pulled at every strap in the harness. I had a Clark footwarmer[8] and made sure that it functioned properly. I pulled the flaps of my military fur cap down over neck, ears and cheeks. I tucked a pillow under the sweater over my chest and made sure that my leggings clasped my furlined moccasins well. Then, to pre-vent my coat from opening even under the stress of motion, just before I got into the cutter, I tied a rope around my waist.

The hostler brought the horses into the shed. They pawed the floor and snorted with impatience. While I rolled my robes about my legs and drew the canvas cur-tain over the front part of the box, I weighed Dan with my eyes. I had no fear for Peter, but Dan would have to show to-day that he deserved the way I had fed and nursed him. Like a chain, the strength of which is measured by the strength of its

[6]The ellipsis mark is frequently used by Grove to punctuate these sketches. There are no editorial de-letions.
[7]In the seventh and concluding sketch, 'Skies and Scares', Grove tells this story of how 'the cumula-tive effect of three mishaps, one following the other', combined with 'the aspect of the skies' and 'broke my nerve that night'.
[8]A kind of metal box containing coal.

weakest link, my team was measured by Dan's pulling power and endurance. But he looked good to me as he danced across the pole and threw his head, biting back at Peter who was teasing him.

The hostler was morose and in a biting mood. Every motion of his seemed to say, 'What is the use of all this? No teamster would go out on a long drive in this weather, till the snow has settled down; and here a schoolmaster wants to try it.'

At last he pushed the slide doors aside, and we swung out. I held the horses tight and drove them into that little drift at the bridge to slow them down right from the start.

The dawn was white, but with a strictly localised angry glow where the sun was still hidden below the horizon. In a very few minutes he would be up, and I counted on making that first mile just before he appeared.

This mile is a wide, well levelled road, but ever so often, at intervals of maybe fifty to sixty yards, steep and long promontories of snow had been flung across— some of them five to six feet high. They started at the edge of the field to the left where a rank growth of shrubby weeds gave shelter for the snow to pile in. Their base, alongside the fence, was broad, and they tapered across the road, with a perfectly flat top, and with concave sides of a most delicate, smooth, and finished looking curve, till at last they ran out into a sharp point, mostly beyond the road on the field to the right.

The wind plays strange pranks with snow; snow is the most plastic medium it has to mould into images and symbols of its moods. Here one of these promontories would slope down, and the very next one would slope upward as it advanced across the open space. In every case there had been two walls, as it were, of furious blow, and between the two a lane of comparative calm, caused by the shelter of a clump of brush or weeds, in which the snow had taken refuge from the wind's rough and savage play. Between these capes of snow there was an occasional bare patch of clean swept ground. Altogether there was an impression of barren, wild, bitter-cold windiness about the aspect that did not fail to awe my mind; it looked inhospitable, merciless, and cruelly playful.

As yet the horses seemed to take only delight in dashing through the drifts, so that the powdery crystals flew aloft and dusted me all over. I peered across the field to the left, and a curious sight struck me. There was apparently no steady wind at all, but here and there, and every now and then a little whirl of snow would rise and fall again. Every one of them looked for all the world like a rabbit reconnoitring in deep grass. It jumps up on its hindlegs, while running, peers out, and settles down again. It was as if the snow meant to have a look at me, the interloper at such an early morning hour. The snow was so utterly dry that it obeyed the lightest breath; and whatever there was of motion in the air, could not amount to more than a cat's-paw's sudden reach.

At the exact moment when the snow where it stood up highest became suffused with a rose-red tint from the rising sun, I arrived at the turn to the correction line.[9] Had I been a novice at the work I was engaged in, the sight that met

---

[9]A correction made along the longitudinal line of a survey to compensate for the curvature of the earth. On the Prairies, roads are generally laid out along survey lines; north-south roads, therefore, turn east-west for a short distance along the correction line.

my eye might well have daunted me. Such drifts as I saw here should be broken by drivers who have short hauls to make before the long distance traveller attempts them. From the fence on the north side of the road a smoothly curved expanse covered the whole of the road allowance and gently sloped down into the field at my left. Its north edge stood like a cliff, the exact height of the fence, four feet I should say. In the centre it rose to probably six feet and then fell very gradually, whaleback fashion, to the south. Not one of the fence posts to the left was visible. The slow emergence of the tops of these fence posts became during the following week, when I drove out here daily, a measure for me of the settling down of the drift. I believe I can say from my observations that if no new snow falls or drifts in, and if no very considerable evaporation takes place, a newly piled snowdrift, undisturbed except by wind-pressure, will finally settle down to about from one third to one half of its original height, according to the pressure of the wind that was behind the snow when it first was thrown down. After it has, in this contracting process, reached two thirds of its first height, it can usually be relied upon to carry horse and man.

The surface of this drift, which covered a ditch besides the grade and its grassy flanks, showed that curious appearance that we also find in the glaciated surfaces of granite rock and which, in them, geologists call exfoliation. In the case of rock it is the consequence of extreme changes in temperature. The surface sheet in expanding under sudden heat detaches itself in large, leaflike layers. In front of my wife's cottage up north there lay an exfoliated rock in which I watched the process for a number of years. In snow, of course, the origin of this appearance is entirely different; snow is laid down in layers by the waves in the wind. 'Adfoliation' would be a more nearly correct appellation of the process. But from the analogy of the appearance I shall retain the more common word and call it exfoliation. Layers upon layers of paperlike sheets are superimposed upon each other, their edges often 'cropping out' on sloping surfaces; and since these edges, according to the curvatures of the surfaces, run in wavy lines, the total aspect is very often that of 'moire' silk.

I knew the road as well as I had ever known a road. In summer there was a grassy expanse some thirty feet wide to the north; then followed the grade, flanked to the south by a ditch; and the tangle of weeds and small brush beyond reached right up to the other fence. I had to stay on or rather above the grade; so I stood up and selected the exact spot where to tackle it. Later, I knew, this drift would be harmless enough; there was sufficient local traffic here to establish a well-packed trail. At present, however, it still seemed a formidable task for a team that was to pull me over thirty-three miles more. Besides it was a first test for my horses; I did not know yet how they would behave in snow.

But we went at it. For a moment things happened too fast for me to watch details. The horses plunged wildly and reared on their hind feet in a panic, straining against each other, pulling apart, going down underneath the pole, trying to turn and retrace their steps. And meanwhile the cutter went sharply up at first, as if on the crest of a wave, then toppled over into a hole made by Dan, and altogether behaved like a boat tossed on a stormy sea. Then order returned into the chaos. I had the lines short, wrapped double and treble around my wrists; my feet stood braced in the corner of the box, knees touching the dashboard; my robes slipped down. I spoke to the horses in a soft, quiet, purring voice; and at last I pulled in. Peter hated to stand. I held him. Then I looked back. This first wild plunge had taken us a matter of two hundred yards into the drift. Peter pulled and champed at the bit; the horses were sinking nearly out of sight. But I knew that many and many a time in the future I should have to go through just this and that from the beginning I must train the horses to tackle it right. So, in spite of my aching wrists I kept them standing till I thought that they were fully breathed. Then I relaxed my pull the slightest bit and clicked my tongue. 'Good,' I thought, 'they are pulling together!' And I managed to hold them in line. They reared and plunged again like drowning things in their last agony, but they no longer clashed against nor pulled away from each other. I measured the distance with my eye. Another two hundred yards or thereabout, and I pulled them in again. Thus we stopped altogether four times. The horses were steaming when we got through this drift which was exactly half a mile long; my cutter was packed level full with slabs and clods of snow; and I was pretty well exhausted myself.

'If there is very much of this,' I thought for the moment, 'I may not be able to make it.' But then I knew that a north-south road will drift in badly only under exceptional circumstances. It is the east-west grades that are most apt to give trouble. Not that I minded my part of it, but I did not mean to kill my horses. I had sized them up in their behaviour towards snow. Peter, as I had expected, was excitable. It was hard to recognize in him just now, as he walked quietly along, the uproar of playing muscle and rearing limbs that he had been when we first struck the snow. That was well and good for a short, supreme effort; but not even for Peter would it do in the long, endless drifts which I had to expect. Dan was quieter, but he did not have Peter's staying power; in fact, he was not really a horse for the road. Strange, in spite of his usual keenness on the level road, he seemed to show more snow sense in the drift. This was to be amply confirmed in the future. Whenever an accident happened, it was Peter's fault. As you will see if you read on, Dan once lay quiet when Peter stood right on top of him.

On this road north I found the same 'promontories' that had been such a feature of the first one, flung across from the northwest to the southeast. Since the clumps of shrubs to the left were larger here, and more numerous, too, the drifts occasionally also were larger and higher; but not one of them was such that the horses could not clear it with one or two leaps. The sun was climbing, the air was winter-clear and still. None of the farms which I passed showed the slightest sign of life. I had wrapped up again and sat in comparative comfort and at ease, enjoying the clear sparkle and glitter of the virgin snow. It was not till considerably later that the real significance of the landscape dawned upon my consciousness. Still there was even now in my thoughts a speculative undertone. Subconsciously I wondered what might be ahead of me.

We made Bell's corner[1] in good time. The mile to the west proved easy. There were drifts, it is true, and the going was heavy, but at no place did the snow for

---

[1] The corner of a farm that served Grove as a landmark, signalling the completion of the first leg of his journey, a distance of about six miles from town. Later in this sketch he mentions other landmarks by which he judges his progress, such as the 'hovel', 'half-way farm', and the 'White Range Line House'.

any length of time reach higher than the horses' hocks. We turned to the north again, and here, for a while, the road was very good indeed; the underbrush to the left, on those expanses of wild land, had fettered, as it were, the feet of the wind. The snow was held everywhere, and very little of it had drifted. Only one spot I remember where a clump of Russian willow close to the trail had offered shelter enough to allow the wind to fill in the narrow roadgap to a depth of maybe eight or nine feet; but here it was easy to go around to the west. Without any further incident we reached the point where the useless, supernumerary fence post had caught my eye on my first trip out. I had made nearly eight miles now.

But right here I was to get my first inkling of sights that might shatter my nerve. You may remember that a grove of tall poplars ran to the east, skirted along its southern edge by a road and a long line of telephone posts. Now here, in this shelter of the poplars, the snow from the more or less level and unsheltered spaces to the northwest had piled in indeed. It sloped up to the east; and never shall I forget what I beheld.

The first of the posts stood a foot in snow; at the second one the drift reached six or seven feet up; the next one looked only half as long as the first one, and you might have imagined, standing as it did on a sloping hillside, that it had intentionally been made so much shorter than the others; but at the bottom of the visible part the wind, in sweeping around the pole, had scooped out a funnel-shaped crater which seemed to open into the very earth like a sinkhole. The next pole stood like a giant buried up to his chest and looked singularly helpless and footbound; and the last one I saw showed just its crossbar with three glassy, green insulators above the mountain of snow. The whole surface of this gigantic drift showed again that 'exfoliated' appearance which I have described. Strange to say, this very exfoliation gave it something of a quite peculiarly desolate aspect. It looked so harsh, so millennial-old, so antediluvian and pre-adamic! I still remember with particular distinctness the slight dizziness that overcame me, the sinking feeling in my heart, the awe, and the foreboding that I had challenged a force in Nature which might defy all tireless effort and the most fearless heart.

So the hostler had not been fibbing after all!

But not for a moment did I think of turning back. I am fatalistic in temperament. What is to be, is to be, that is not my outlook.[2] If at last we should get bound up in a drift, well and good, I should then see what the next move would have to be. While the wind blows, snow drifts; while my horses could walk and I was not disabled, my road led north, not south. Like the snow I obeyed the laws of my nature. So far the road was good, and we swung along.

Somewhere around here a field presented a curious view. Its crop had not been harvested; it still stood in stooks. But from my side I saw nothing of the sheaves—it seemed to be flax, for here and there a flag of loose heads showed at the top. The snow had been blown up from all directions, so it looked, by the counter-currents that set up in the lee of every obstacle. These mounds presented one and all the appearance of cones or pyramids of butter patted into shape by upward strokes made with a spoon. There were the sharp ridges, irregular and

[2]The sense of this passage seems to call for this sentence to conclude with the words, '. . . that is my outlook', but Grove's original manuscript does not support an emendation.

erratic, and there were the hollows running up their flanks—exactly as such a cone of butter will show them. And the whole field was dotted with them, as if there were so many fresh graves.

I made the twelve-mile bridge—passing through the cottonwood gate—reached the 'hovel', and dropped into the wilderness again. Here the bigger trees stood strangely bare. Winter reveals the bark and the 'habit'[3] of trees. All ornaments and unessentials have been dropped. The naked skeletons show. I remember how I was more than ever struck by that dappled appearance of the bark of the balm:[4] an olive-green, yellowish hue, ridged and spotted with the black of ancient, overgrown leaf-scars; there was actually something gay about it; these poplars are certainly beautiful winter trees. The aspens were different. Although their stems stood white on white in the snow, that greenish tinge in their white gave them a curious look. From the picture that I carry about in my memory of this morning I cannot help the impression that they looked as if their white were not natural at all; they looked whitewashed! I have often since confirmed this impression when there was snow on the ground.

In the copses of saplings the zigzagging of the boles from twig to twig showed very distinctly, more so, I believe, than to me it had ever done before. How slender and straight they look in their summer garb—now they were stripped, and bone and sinew appeared.

We came to the 'half way farms', and the marsh lay ahead. I watered the horses, and I do not know what made me rest them for a little while, but I did. On the yard of the farm where I had turned in there was not a soul to be seen. Barns and stables were closed—and I noticed that the back door of the dwelling was buried tight by the snow. No doubt everybody preferred the neighbourhood of the fire to the cold outside. While stopping, I faced for the first time the sun. He was high in the sky by now—it was half-past ten—and it suddenly came home to me that there was something relentless, inexorable, cruel, yes, something of a sneer in the pitiless way in which he looked down on the infertile waste around. Unaccountably two Greek words formed on my lips: Homer's Pontos atrygetos—the barren sea.[5] Half an hour later I was to realize the significance of it.

I turned back to the road and north again. For another half mile the fields continued on either side; but somehow they seemed to take on a sinister look. There was more snow on them than I had found on the level land further south; the snow lay more smoothly, again under those 'exfoliated' surface sheets which here, too, gave it an inhuman, primeval look; in the higher sun the vast expanse looked, I suppose, more blindingly white; and nowhere did buildings or thickets seem to emerge. Yet, so long as the grade continued, the going was fair enough.

Then I came to the corner which marked half the distance, and there I stopped. Right in front, where the trail had been and where a ditch had divided off the marsh, a fortress of snow lay now: a seemingly impregnable bulwark, six or seven feet high, with rounded top, fitting descriptions which I had read of the underground bombproofs around Belgian strongholds—those forts which were

[3]In botany, the characteristic growth and appearance of a plant.
[4]Balsam poplar.
[5]A common Homeric formula in *The Odyssey*.

hammered to pieces by the Germans in their first, heartbreaking forward surge in 1914. There was not a wrinkle in this inverted bowl. There it lay, smooth and slick—curled up in security, as it were, some twenty, thirty feet across; and behind it others, and more of them to the right and to the left. This had been a stretch, covered with brush and bush, willow and poplar thickets; but my eye saw nothing except a mammiferous[6] waste, cruelly white, glittering in the heatless, chuckling sun, and scoffing at me, the intruder. I stood up again and peered out. To the east it seemed as if these buttes of snow were a trifle lower; but maybe the ground underneath also sloped down. I wished I had travelled here more often by daytime, so I might know. As it was, there was nothing to it; I had to tackle the task. And we plunged in.

I had learned something from my first experience in the drift one mile north of town, and I kept my horses well under control. Still, it was a wild enough dash. Peter lost his footing two or three times and worked himself into a mild panic. But Dan—I could not help admiring the way in which, buried over his back in snow, he would slowly and deliberately rear on his hindfeet and take his bound. For fully five minutes I never saw anything of the horses except their heads. I inferred their motions from the dusting snowcloud that rose above their bodies and settled on myself. And then somehow we emerged. We reached a stretch of ground where the snow was just high enough to cover the hocks of the horses. It was a hollow scooped out by some freak of the wind. I pulled in, and the horses stood panting. Peter no longer showed any desire to fret and to jump. Both horses apparently felt the wisdom of sparing their strength. They were all white with the frost of their sweat and the spray of the snow. . . .

While I gave them their time, I looked around, and here a lesson came home to me. In the hollow where we stood, the snow did not lie smoothly. A huge obstacle to the northwest, probably a buried clump of brush, had made the wind turn back upon itself, first downward, then, at the bottom of the pit, in a direction opposite to that of the main current above, and finally slantways upward again to the summit of the obstacle, where it rejoined the parent blow. The floor of the hollow was cleanly scooped out and chiselled in low ridges; and these ridges came from the southeast, running their points to the northwest. I learned to look out for this sign, and I verily believe that, had I not learned that lesson right now, I should never have reached the creek which was still four or five miles distant.

The huge mound in the lee of which I was stopping was a matter of two hundred yards away; nearer to it the snow was considerably deeper; and since it presented an appearance very characteristic of Prairie bush-drifts, I shall describe it in some detail. Apparently the winds had first bent over all the stems of the clump; for whenever I saw one of them from the north, it showed a smooth, clean upward sweep. On the south side the snow first fell in a sheer cliff; then there was a hollow which was partly filled by a talus-shaped[7] drift thrown in by the counter currents from the southern pit in which we were stopping; the sides of this talus again showed the marks that reminded of those left by the spoon when butter is roughly stroked into the shape of a pyramid. The interesting parts of the

---

[6] Breast-like.
[7] Like a sloping wall in a fortification, wider at its base than at its top.

structure consisted in the beetling brow of the cliff and the roof of the cavity underneath. The brow had a honeycombed appearance; the snow had been laid down in layers of varying density (I shall discuss this more fully in the next chapter when we are going to look in on the snow while it is actually at work); and the counter currents that here swept upward in a slanting direction had bitten out the softer layers, leaving a fine network of little ridges which reminded strangely of the delicate fretwork-tracery in wind-sculptured rock—as I had seen it in the Black Hills in South Dakota. This piece of work of the wind is exceedingly short-lived in snow, and it must not be confounded with the honeycombed appearance of those faces of snow cliffs which are 'rotting' by reason of their exposure to the heat of the noonday sun. These latter are coarse, often dirty, and nearly always have something bristling about them which is entirely absent in the sculptures of the wind. The under side of the roof in the cavity looked very much as a very stiff or viscid treacle would look when spread over a meshy surface, as, for instance, over a closely woven netting of wire. The stems and the branches of the brush took the place of the wire, and in their meshes the snow had been pressed through by its own weight, but held together by its curious ductility or tensile strength of which I was to find further evidence soon enough. It thus formed innumerable, blunted little stalactites, but without the corresponding stalagmites which you find in limestone caves or on the north side of buildings when the snow from the roof thaws and forms icicles and slender cones of ice growing up to meet them from the ground where the trickling drops fall and freeze again.

By the help of these various tokens I had picked my next resting place before we started up again. It was on this second dash that I understood why those Homeric words had come to my lips a while ago. This was indeed like nothing so much as like being out on rough waters and in a troubled sea, with nothing to brace the storm with but a wind-tossed nutshell of a one-man sailing craft. I knew that experience for having outridden many a gale in the mouth of the mighty St Lawrence River. When the snow reached its extreme in depth, it gave you the feeling which a drowning man may have when fighting his desperate fight with the salty waves. But more impressive than that was the frequent outer resemblance. The waves of the ocean rise up and reach out and batter against the rocks and battlements of the shore, retreating again and ever returning to the assault, covering the obstacles thrown in the way of their progress with thin sheets of licking tongues at least. And if such a high crest wave had suddenly been frozen into solidity, its outline would have mimicked to perfection many a one of the snow shapes that I saw around.

Once the horses had really learned to pull exactly together—and they learned it thoroughly here—our progress was not too bad. Of course, it was not like going on a grade, be it ever so badly drifted in. Here the ground underneath, too, was uneven and overgrown with a veritable entanglement of brush in which often the horses' feet would get caught. As for the road, there was none left, nothing that even by the boldest stretch of imagination could have been considered even as the slightest indication of one. And worst of all, I knew positively that there would be no trail at any time during the winter. I was well aware of the fact that, after it once snowed up, nobody ever crossed this waste between the 'half-way farms' and the 'White Range Line House'. This morning it took me two and a half solid hours to make four miles.

But the ordeal had its reward. Here where the fact that there was snow on the ground, and plenty of it, did no longer need to be sunk into my brain—as soon as it had lost its value as a piece of news and a lesson, I began to enjoy it just as the hunter in India will enjoy the battle of wits when he is pitted against a yellow-black tiger. I began to catch on to the ways of this snow; I began, as it were, to study the mentality of my enemy. Though I never kill, I am after all something of a sportsman. And still another thing gave me back that mental equilibrium which you need in order to see things and to reason calmly about them. Every dash of two hundred yards or so brought me that much nearer to my goal. Up to the 'half-way farms' I had, as it were, been working uphill: there was more ahead than behind. This was now reversed: there was more behind than ahead, and as yet I did not worry about the return trip.

Now I have already said that snow is the only really plastic element in which the wind can carve the vagaries of its mood and leave a record of at least some permanency. The surface of the sea is a wonderful book to be read with a lightning-quick eye; I do not know anything better to do as a cure for ragged nerves—provided you are a good sailor. But the forms are too fleeting, they change too quickly—so quickly, indeed, that I have never succeeded in so fixing their record upon my memory as to be able to develop one form from the other in descriptive notes. It is that very fact, I believe, upon which hinges the curative value of the sight: you are so completely absorbed by the moment, and all other things fall away. Many and many a day have I lain on my deck chair on board a liner and watched the play of the waves; but the pleasure, which was very great indeed, was momentary; and sometimes, when in an unsympathetic mood, I have since impatiently wondered in what that fascination may have consisted. It was different here. Snow is very nearly as yielding as water and, once it fully responds in its surface to the carving forces of the wind, it stays—as if frozen into the glittering marble image of its motion. I know few things that are as truly fascinating as the sculptures of the wind in snow; for here you have time and opportunity a-plenty to probe not only into the what, but also into the why. Maybe that one day I shall write down a fuller account of my observations. In this report I shall have to restrict myself to a few indications, for this is not the record of the whims of the wind, but merely the narrative of my drives.

In places, for instance, the rounded, 'bomb-proof' aspect of the expanses would be changed into the distinct contour of gigantic waves with a very fine, very sharp crest-line. The upsweep from the northwest would be ever so slightly convex, and the downward sweep into the trough was always very distinctly concave. This was not the ripple which we find in beach sand. That ripple was there, too, and in places it covered the wide backs of these huge waves all over; but never was it found on the concave side. Occasionally, but rarely, one of these great waves would resemble a large breaker with a curly crest. Here the onward sweep from the northwest had built the snow out, beyond the supporting base, into a thick overhanging ledge which here and there had sagged; but by virtue of that tensile strength and cohesion in snow which I have mentioned already, it still held together and now looked convoluted and ruffled in the most deceiving way.

I believe I actually listened for the muffled roar which the breaker makes when its subaqueous part begins to sweep the upward sloping beach. To make this illusion complete, or to break it by the very absurdity and exaggeration of a comparison drawn out too far—I do not know which—there would, every now and then, from the crest of one of these waves, jut out something which closely resembled the wide back of a large fish diving down into the concave side towards the trough. This looked very much like porpoises or dolphins jumping in a heaving sea; only that in my memory picture the real dolphins always jump in the opposite direction, against the run of the waves, bridging the trough.

In other places a fine, exceedingly delicate crest-line would spring up from the high point of some buried obstacle and sweep along in the most graceful curve as far as the eye would carry. I particularly remember one of them, and I could discover no earthly reason for the curvature in it.

Again there would be a triangular—or should I say 'tetrahedral'?—up-sweep from the direction of the wind, ending in a sharp, perfectly plane down-sweep on the south side; and the point of this three-sided but oblique pyramid would hang over like the flap of a tam. There was something of the consistency of very thick cloth about this overhanging flap.

Or an up-slope from the north would end in a long, nearly perpendicular cliff-line facing south. And the talus formation which I have mentioned would be perfectly smooth; but it did not reach quite to the top of the cliff, maybe to within a foot of it. The upsloping layer from the north would hang out again, with an even brow; but between this smooth cornice and the upper edge of the talus the snow looked as if it had been squeezed out by tremendous pressure from above, like an exceedingly viscid liquid—cooling glue, for instance, which is being squeezed out from between the core and the veneer in a veneering press.

Once I passed close to and south of, two thickets which were completely buried by the snow. Between them a ditch had been scooped out in a very curious fashion. It resembled exactly a winding river bed with its water drained off; it was two or three feet deep, and wherever it turned, its banks were undermined on the 'throw' side by the 'wash' of the furious blow. The analogy between the work of the wind and the work of flowing water constantly obtrudes, especially where this work is one of 'erosion'.

But as flowing water will swing up and down in the most surprising forms where the bed of the river is rough with rocks and throws it into choppy waves which do not seem to move, so the snow was thrown up into the most curious forms where the frozen swamp ground underneath had bubbled, as it were, into phantastic shapes. I remember several places where a perfect circle was formed by a sharp crestline that bounded an hemispherical, crater-like hollow. When steam bubbles up through thick porridge, in its leisurely and impeded way, and the bubble bursts with a clucking sound, then for a moment a crater is formed just like these circular holes; only here in the snow they were on a much larger scale, of course, some of them six to ten feet in diameter.

And again the snow was thrown up into a bulwark, twenty and more feet high, with that always repeating cliff-face to the south, resembling a miniature Gibraltar, with many smaller ones of most curiously similar form on its back: bulwarks upon bulwarks, all lowering to the south. In these the aggressive nature of storm-flung snow was most apparent. They were formidable structures; formidable and intimidating, more through the suggestiveness of their shape than through mere size.

I came to places where the wind had had its moments of frolicsome humour, where it had made grim fun of its own massive and cumbersome and yet so pliable and elastic majesty. It had turned around and around, running with breathless speed, with its tongue lolling out, as it were, and probably yapping and snapping in mocking mimicry of a pup trying to catch its tail; and it had scooped out a spiral trough with overhanging rim. I felt sorry that I had not been there to watch it, because after all, what I saw, was only the dead record of something that had been very much alive and vociferatingly noisy. And in another place it had reared and raised its head like a boa constrictor, ready to strike at its prey; up to the flashing, forked tongue it was there. But one spot I remember, where it looked exactly as if quite consciously it had attempted the outright ludicrous: it had thrown up the snow into the semblance of some formidable animal—more like a gorilla than anything else it looked, a gorilla that stands on its four hands and raises every hair on its back and snarls in order to frighten that which it is afraid of itself—a leopard maybe.

And then I reached the 'White Range Line House'. Curiously enough, there it stood, sheltered by its majestic bluff to the north, as peaceful looking as if there were no such a thing as that record, which I had crossed, of the uproar and fury of one of the forces of Nature engaged in an orgy. And it looked so empty, too, and so deserted, with never a wisp of smoke curling from its flue-pipe, that for a moment I was tempted to turn in and see whether maybe the lonely dweller was ill. But then I felt as if I could not be burdened with any stranger's worries that day.

The effective shelter of the poplar forest along the creek made itself felt. The last mile to the northeast was peaceful driving. I felt quite cheered, though I walked the horses over the whole of the mile since both began to show signs of wear. The last four miles had been a test to try any living creature's mettle. To me it had been one of the culminating points in that glorious winter, but the horses had lacked the mental stimulus, and even I felt rather exhausted.

On the bridge I stopped, threw the blankets over the horses, and fed. Somehow this seemed to be the best place to do it. There was no snow to speak of, and I did not know yet what might follow. The horses were drooping, and I gave them an additional ten minutes' rest. Then I slowly made ready. I did not really expect any serious trouble.

We turned at a walk, and the chasm of the bush road opened up. Instantly I pulled the horses in. What I saw, baffled me for a moment so completely that I just sat there and gasped. There was no road. The trees to both sides were not so overly high, but the snow had piled in level with their tops; the drift looked like a gigantic barricade. It was that fleeting sight of the telephone posts over again, though on a slightly smaller scale; but this time it was in front. Slowly I started to whistle and then looked around. I remembered now. There was a newly cut-out road running north past the school which lay embedded in the bush. It had offered a lane to the wind; and the wind, going there, in cramped space, at a doubly furious stride, had picked up and carried along all the loose snow from the grassy glades in its path. The road ended abruptly just north of the drift, where the east-west grade sprang up. When the wind had reached this end of the lane, where the bush ran at right angles to its direction, it had found itself in something like a blind alley, and, sweeping upward, to clear the obstacle, it had dropped every bit of its load into the shelter of the brush, gradually, in the course of three long days, building up a ridge that buried underbrush and trees. I might have known it, of course. I knew enough about snow; all the conditions for an exceptionally large drift were provided for here. But it had not occurred to me, especially after I had found the northern fringe of the marsh so well sheltered. Here I felt for a moment as if all the snow of the universe had piled in. As I said, I was so completely baffled that I could have turned the horses then and there.

But after a minute or two my eyes began to cast about. I turned to the south, right into the dense underbrush and towards the creek which here swept south in a long, flat curve. Peter was always intolerant of anything that moved underfoot. He started to bolt when the dry and hard-frozen stems snapped and broke with reports resembling pistol shots. But since Dan kept quiet, I held Peter well in hand. I went along the drift for maybe three to four hundred yards, reconnoitring. Then the trees began to stand too dense for me to proceed without endangering my cutter. Just beyond I saw the big trough of the creek bed, and though I could not make out how conditions were at its bottom, the drift continued on its southern bank, and in any case it was impossible to cross the hollow. So I turned; I had made up my mind to try the drift.

About a hundred and fifty yards from the point where I had turned off the road there was something like a fold in the flank of the drift. At its foot I stopped. For a moment I tried to explain that fold to myself. This is what I arrived at. North of the drift, just about where the new cut-out joined the east-west grade, there was a small clearing caused by a bush fire which a few years ago had penetrated thus far into this otherwise virgin corner of the forest. Unfortunately it stood so full of charred stumps that it was impossible to get through there. But the main currents of the wind would have free play in this opening, and I knew that, when the blizzard began, it had been blowing from a more northerly quarter than later on, when it veered to the northwest. And though the snow came careering along the lane of the cut-out, that is, from due north, its 'throw' and therefore, the direction of the drift would be determined by the direction of the wind that took charge of it on this clearing. Probably, then, a first, provisional drift whose long axis lay nearly in a north-south line, had been piled up by the first, northerly gale. Later a second, larger drift had been superimposed upon it at an angle, with its main axis running from the northwest to the southeast. The fold marked the point where the first, smaller drift still emerged from the second larger one. This reasoning was confirmed by a study of the clearing itself which I came to make two or three weeks after.

Before I called on the horses to give me their very last ounce of strength, I got out of my cutter once more and made sure that my lines were still sound. I trusted my ability to guide the horses even in this crucial test, but I dreaded nothing so much as that the lines might break; and I wanted to guard against any accident. I should mention that, of course, the top of my cutter was down, that the traces of the harness were new, and that the cutter itself during its previous trials had shown an exceptional stability. Once more I thus rested my horses for five minutes; and they seemed to realize what was coming. Their heads were up, their ears were cocked. When I got back into my cutter, I carefully brushed the snow from moccasins and trousers, laid the robe around my feet, adjusted my knees against the dashboard, and tied two big loops into the lines to hold them by.

Then I clicked my tongue. The horses bounded upward in unison. For a moment it looked as if they intended to work through, instead of over, the drift. A wild shower of angular snow-slabs swept in upon me. The cutter reared up and plunged and reared again—and then the view cleared. The snow proved harder than I had anticipated—which bespoke the fury of the blow that had piled it. It did not carry the horses, but neither—once we had reached a height of five or six feet—did they sink beyond their bellies and out of sight. I had no eye for anything except them. What lay to right or left, seemed not to concern me. I watched them work. They went in bounds, working beautifully together. Rhythmically they reared, and rhythmically they plunged. I had dropped back to the seat, holding them with a firm hand, feet braced against the dashboard; and whenever they got ready to rear, I called to them in a low and quiet voice, 'Peter—Dan—now!' And their muscles played with the effort of desperation. It probably did not take more than five minutes, maybe considerably less, before we had reached the top, but to me it seemed like hours of nearly fruitless endeavour. I did not realize at first that we were high. I shall never forget the weird kind of astonishment when the fact came home to me that what snapped and crackled in the snow under the horses' hoofs, were the tops of trees. Nor shall the feeling of estrangement, as it were—as if I were not myself, but looking on from the outside at the adventure of somebody who yet was I—the feeling of other-worldliness, if you will pardon the word, ever fade from my memory—a feeling of having been carried beyond my depth where I could not swim—which came over me when with two quick glances to right and left I took in the fact that there were no longer any trees to either side, that I was above that forest world which had so often engulfed me.

Then I drew my lines in. The horses fought against it, did not want to stand. But I had to find my way, and while they were going, I could not take my eyes from them. It took a supreme effort on my part to make them obey. At last they stood, but I had to hold them with all my strength, and with not a second's respite. Now that I was on top of the drift, the problem of how to get down loomed larger than that of getting up had seemed before. I knew I did not have half a minute in which to decide upon my course; for it became increasingly difficult to hold the horses back, and they were fast sinking away.

During this short breathing spell I took in the situation. We had come up in a northeast direction, slanting along the slope. Once on top, I had instinctively turned to the north. Here the drift was about twenty feet wide, perfectly level and with an exfoliated surface layer. To the east the drift fell steeply, with a clean, smooth cliff-line marking off the beginning of the descent; this line seemed particularly disconcerting, for it betrayed the concave curvature of the down-sweep. A few yards to the north I saw below, at the foot of the cliff, the old logging-trail, and I noticed that the snow on it lay as it had fallen, smooth and sheer, without a ripple of a drift. It looked like mockery. And yet that was where I had to get down.

The next few minutes are rather a maze in my memory. But two pictures were photographed with great distinctness. The one is of the moment when we went over the edge. For a second Peter reared up, pawing the air with his forefeet; Dan tried to back away from the empty fall. I had at this excruciating point no purchase whatever on the lines. Then apparently Peter sat or fell down, I do not know which, on his haunches and began to slide. The cutter lurched to the left as if it were going to spill all it held. Dan was knocked off his hind feet by the draw-bar—and we plunged. . . . We came to with a terrific jolt that sent me in a heap against the dash board. One jump, and I stood on the ground. The cutter—and this is the second picture which is etched clearly on the plate of my memory—stood on its pole, leaning at an angle of forty-five degrees against the drift. The horses were as if stunned. 'Dan, Peter!' I shouted, and they struggled to their feet. They were badly winded, but otherwise everything seemed all right. I looked wistfully back and up at the gully which we had torn into the flank of the drift.

I should gladly have breathed the horses again, but they were hot, the air was at zero or colder, the rays of the sun had begun to slant. I walked for a while alongside the team. They were drooping sadly. Then I got in again, driving them slowly till we came to the crossing of the ditch. I had no eye for the grade ahead. On the bush road the going was good—now and then a small drift, but nothing alarming anywhere. The anti-climax had set in. Again the speckled trunks of the balm poplars struck my eye, now interspersed with the scarlet stems of the red osier dogwood. But they failed to cheer me—they were mere facts, unable to stir moods. . . .

I began to think. A few weeks ago I had met that American settler with the French sounding name who lived alongside the angling dam further north. We had talked snow, and he had said, 'Oh, up here it never is bad except along this grade,'—we were stopping on the last east-west grade, the one I was coming to—'there you cannot get through. You'd kill your horses. Level with the tree-tops.' Well, I had had just that a little while ago—I could not afford any more of it. So I made up my mind to try a new trail, across a section which was fenced. It meant getting out of my robes twice more, to open the gates, but I preferred that to another tree-high drift. To spare my horses was now my only consideration. I should not have liked to take the new trail by night, for fear of missing the gates; but that objection did not hold just now. Horses and I were pretty well spent. So, instead of forking off the main trail to the north we went straight ahead.

In due time I came to the bridge which I had to cross in order to get up on the dam. Here I saw—in an absent-minded, half unconscious, and uninterested way—one more structure built by architect wind. The deep master ditch from the north emptied here, to the left of the bridge, into the grade ditch which ran east and west. And at the corner the snow had very nearly bridged it—so nearly that you could easily have stepped across the remaining gap. But below it was hol-low—nothing supported the bridge—it was a mere arch, with a vault underneath that looked temptingly sheltered and cosy to wearied eyes.

The dam was bare, and I had to pull off to the east, on to the swampy plain. I gave my horses the lines, and slowly, slowly they took me home! Even had I not always lost interest here, to-day I should have leaned back and rested. Although the horses had done all the actual work, the strain of it had been largely on me. It was the after-effect that set in now.

I thought of my wife, and of how she would have felt had she been able to follow the scenes in some magical mirror through every single vicissitude of my drive. And once more I saw with the eye of recent memory the horses in that long, endless plunge through the corner of the marsh. Once more I felt my muscles a-quiver with the strain of that last wild struggle over that last, inhuman drift. And slowly I made up my mind that the next time, the very next day, on my return trip, I was going to add another eleven miles to my already long drive and to take a different road. I knew the trail over which I had been coming so far was closed for the rest of the winter—there was no traffic there—no trail would be kept open. That other road of which I was thinking and which lay further west was the main cordwood trail to the towns in the south. It was out of my way, to be sure, but I felt convinced that I could spare my horses and even save time by making the detour.

Being on the east side of the dam, I could not see school or cottage till I turned up on the correction line. But when at last I saw it, I felt somewhat as I had felt coming home from my first big trip overseas. It seemed a lifetime since I had started out. I seemed to be a different man.

Here, in the timber land, the snow had not drifted to any extent. There were signs of the gale, but its record was written in fallen tree trunks, broken branches, a litter of twigs—not in drifts of snow. My wife would not surmise what I had gone through.

She came out with a smile on her face when I pulled in on the yard. It was characteristic of her that she did not ask why I came so late; she accepted the fact as something for which there were no doubt compelling reasons. 'I was giving our girl a bath,' she said; 'she cannot come.' And then she looked wistfully at my face and at the horses. Silently I slipped the harness off their backs. I used to let them have their freedom for a while on reaching home. And never yet but Peter at least had had a kick and a caper and a roll before they sought their mangers. To-day they stood for a moment knock-kneed, without moving, then shook themselves in a weak, half-hearted way and went with drooping heads and weary limbs straight to the stable.

'You had a hard trip?' asked my wife; and I replied with as much cheer as I could muster, 'I have seen sights to-day that I did not expect to see before my dying day.' And taking her arm, I looked at the westering sun and turned towards the house.

1922

E.J. Pratt

1882-1964

The publication in 1923 of Pratt's *Newfoundland Verse* marked a turning-point in Canadian literary history. The short poems collected in that volume initiated the Canadian modernist movement that would eventually include Robert Finch and Dorothy Livesay in Toronto and A.J.M. Smith, F.R. Scott, Leo Kennedy, and A.M. Klein in Montreal. Pratt himself, however, was never a member of any school or movement but a poet who went his own way in creating a distinctive body of work. Unlike his contemporaries, he generally worked in longer poetic forms—even moulding two narratives, *Brébeuf and His Brethren* (1940) and *Towards the Last Spike* (1952), into national epics. Indeed, Pratt's long poems have sometimes overshadowed the short ones, many of which are important in their own right. The polished, epigrammatic quality of 'From Stone to Steel' and the density and complex dramatic construction of 'Come Away, Death' make them among the most memorable poems in our literature.

E.J. Pratt—'Ned' to the many friends who still remember with affection his personal warmth and conviviality—was born in 1882 in Western Bay, Nfld, a village on Conception Bay. Growing up on the Newfoundland coast gave him an intense feeling for the sea, especially as a place where man is tested by nature; confrontations with the elements later became a frequent subject of his poetry. As a young man Pratt prepared himself to follow his father into the Methodist ministry, and after his education at St John's Methodist College he served as both a student-minister and a teacher in several small Newfoundland communities. In 1907 he came to Canada to continue his education, enrolling in Victoria College, University of Toronto, where he studied theology, philosophy, and psychology. Although he completed his Bachelor of Divinity and was ordained in 1913, he remained at the university, becoming a demonstrator for the Department of Psychology and completing a

Ph.D. thesis on the eschatology of St Paul. In 1919 Pelham Edgar, the chairman of the Department of English and a staunch supporter of Canadian poetry, provided Pratt with an alternative to a religious career by making him an Associate Professor of English at Victoria, largely on the strength of his promise as a poet. Pratt remained there until he retired as Professor Emeritus in 1953.

Pratt's choice not to enter the ministry was apparently the result of a crisis of faith not uncommon in the late-Victorian era that produced him; but it also had its roots in his childhood encounters with the tragedies of Newfoundland seafaring life. As he later wrote, he was puzzled by 'the ironic enigma of Nature in relation to the Christian view of the world'. In one of his earliest poems, 'Clay' (never published), Pratt gave voice to this puzzlement:

What Shepherd, this, that so attends his
*   flocks,*
As lead them out into the wilderness,
*   What Father, this*
Who cares so little for his children's fate,
That though he holds the sea within his
*   hands,*
He pours its floods upon their heads, lets
*   loose*
His lightnings, blasts and stalking
*   pestilences.*

. . .

*   Named you him, Father?*
God? No. Rather a Potter with some clay.

The Darwinism that dominated the intellectual climate of Pratt's formative years seemed to offer more comprehensive explanations of the natural world and man's place in it than those Pratt found in religion; and, although Christianity continued to provide him with a rich store of images, his poetry came to express what Sandra Djwa has called an 'evolutionary vision'. The philosophical position implied in this poetry is not, however, entirely clear, for it variously commends humanism, Stoic heroism, and aspects of Christianity. Perhaps the closest Pratt ever came to synthesizing his beliefs was in a statement he made, in a radio broadcast, about the self-sacrificing heroism shown in the sea-rescue that was the subject of *The Roosevelt and the Antinoe* (1930): 'Science in league with good will; individual courage and humanity behind the machine. It's that sort of thing that's the hope of the world.'

Newfoundland Verse was followed by *The Witches' Brew* (1925), a comic saga about the intoxication of the ocean's creatures that demonstrates the exuberant humour often found in Pratt's writing. The next year Pratt published *Titans*, a volume made up of two long poems: 'The Cachalot', about a hunt for a great whale, and 'The Great Feud', a fable of prehistoric war among the animals that ends in a holocaust survived only by the anthropoid ape that began the conflict. In these two poems Pratt shows not only his preoccupation with the natural struggle but also the fascination with themes and subjects of epic magnitude that came to dominate his poetry. Later the sinking of the *Titanic* offered him what he called a 'study in irony, probably the greatest single illustration of the ironic in marine history', and inspired one of his most famous poems, *The Titanic* (1935). From the vast patterns of conflict in the Second World War Pratt drew the material for *Dunkirk* (1941) and *Behind the Log* (1947). He then turned to Canadian history for two narrative poems that are extended considerations of crucial episodes in the nation's development: *Brébeuf and His Brethren*, the story of seventeenth-century Jesuit missionaries to the Hurons, and *Towards the Last Spike*, about the building of the CPR. (Both won Governor General's awards.)

Pratt gives these poems an epic quality—even utilizing a twelve-part structure in *Brébeuf*—and his version of the sinking of the *Titanic* suggests classic and Renaissance tragic drama. He does not, however, follow the epic or tragic convention of unifying his action around a single hero. Instead individuals are inextricably part of a larger social unit, subjected not only to the powerful influence of natural forces but to the shaping influence of their own technology or culture as well. The assimilation of historical details in these poems (Pratt was a painstaking researcher) makes them examples of what Dorothy Livesay has called a new kind of poetry that is 'neither epic nor narrative, but documentary' ('The Documentary Poem: A Canadian Genre', 1971). This documentary quality in Pratt's poetry—especially striking in *The Titanic*, with its journalistic style, extracts of dramatic dialogue, and fragmented form—derives not only from subject matter but also from its specialized language, full of technical names, precise bits of knowledge, and arcane facts, all of which cohere in such a way as to confirm Northrop Frye's observation in *The Bush Garden* that Pratt took on the role of epic bard in Canada, like a 'poet of an oral and pre-literate society', transforming the history and scientific knowledge of a culture into a heroic and mythic whole.

From Stone to Steel

From stone to bronze, from bronze to steel
Along the road-dust of the sun,
Two revolutions of the wheel
From Java[1] to Geneva run.

The snarl Neanderthal[2] is worn
Close to the smiling Aryan lips,
The civil polish of the horn
Gleams from our praying finger tips.

The evolution of desire
Has but matured a toxic wine,   10
Drunk long before its heady fire
Reddened Euphrates or the Rhine.

Between the temple and the cave
The boundary lies tissue-thin:
The yearlings still the altars crave
As satisfaction for a sin.

The road goes up, the road goes down—
Let Java or Geneva be—
But whether to the cross or crown,
The path lies through Gethsemane.[3]   20

1932

[1]Site of the discovery of fossils of one of the oldest types of man: 'Java man'. 'Geneva': the city most associated with man's attempts to check his war-like tendencies. The Geneva Convention of 1864 established rules for humane conduct in wartime; the League of Nations had its headquarters in Geneva after the Great War; the site of a world disarmament conference in 1927, Geneva is also a theological centre and was the seat of the Protestant Reformation in the sixteenth century.
[2]Neanderthal man, a paleolithic cave-dweller who preceded modern man. 'Aryan': although Hitler did not come to power until 1933, the racist doctrines of the Nazis (who gained control of the German parliament in 1932) were already well known: according to them, non-Jewish Germans, especially those of Nordic stock, were classified as Aryans and regarded as superior to other races.
[3]The garden of Gethsemane, outside Jerusalem, is the place where, just before the crucifixion, Christ retired and prayed: 'Let this cup pass from me'; while he was there, Peter and two others who should have been standing guard fell asleep, allowing Judas to betray Christ by bringing soldiers there to arrest him.

The Prize Cat

Pure blood domestic, guaranteed,
Soft-mannered, musical in purr,
The ribbon had declared the breed,
Gentility was in the fur.

Such feline culture in the gads[1]
No anger ever arched her back—
What distance since those velvet pads
Departed from the leopard's track!

And when I mused how Time had thinned
The jungle strains within the cells,   10
How human hands had disciplined
Those prowling optic parallels;

I saw the generations pass
Along the reflex of a spring,
A bird had rustled in the grass,
The tab had caught it on the wing:

Behind the leap so furtive-wild
Was such ignition in the gleam,
I thought an Abyssinian child
Had cried out in the whitethroat's[2] scream.   20

1937

---

[1] Claws.
[2] Sparrow.

Come Away, Death[1]

Willy-nilly, he comes or goes, with the clown's logic,
Comic in epitaph, tragic in epithalamium,[2]
And unseduced by any mused rhyme.
However blow the winds over the pollen,
Whatever the course of the garden variables,
He remains the constant,
Ever flowering from the poppy seeds.

There was a time he came in formal dress,
Announced by Silence tapping at the panels
In deep apology.   10
A touch of chivalry in his approach,
He offered sacramental wine,
And with acanthus[3] leaf
And petals of the hyacinth
He took the fever from the temples
And closed the eyelids,
Then led the way to his cool longitudes
In the dignity of the candles.

His mediaeval grace is gone—
Gone with the flame of the capitals[4]   20
And the leisured turn of the thumb
Leafing the manuscripts,
Gone with the marbles
And the Venetian mosaics,
With the bend of the knee
Before the rose-strewn feet of the Virgin.
The *paternosters* of his priests,
Committing clay to clay,

[1] In Shakespeare's *Twelfth Night* a clown sings an 'old and plain' song that begins:
> Come away, come away, death
>   And in sad cypress let me be laid
> Fly away, fly away, breath,
>   I am slain by a fair cruel maid
> My shroud of white, stuck all with yew,
>   Oh, prepare it!
> My part of death, no one so true
>   Did share it!

Sandra Djwa (in *The E.J. Pratt Symposium*, 1977) has pointed out that in the opening there is a further echo of one of Shakespeare's clowns: 'If a man . . . drown himself, it is, will he, nill he, he goes' (the gravedigger in *Hamlet*, V. i. 16-17).

[2] A formal poem on the occasion of a wedding.

[3] A herb once in wide use for its supposed mollifying properties. Hyacinth petals were associated with the ancient festival honouring the mythic youth Hyacinthus, who was turned into a hyacinth after his death at the hands of Apollo; the festival began with funeral offerings and lamentations, but ended with songs of joy for his achievement of immortality.

[4] That is, the illustrated letters that begin passages in illuminated medieval manuscripts; but with a possible pun on capital cities.

Have rattled in their throats
Under the gride[5] of his traction tread.   30

One night we heard his footfall—one September night—
In the outskirts of a village near the sea.
There was a moment when the storm
Delayed its fist, when the surf fell
Like velvet on the rocks—a moment only;
The strangest lull we ever knew!
A sudden truce among the oaks
Released their fratricidal arms;
The poplars straightened to attention
As the winds stopped to listen   40
To the sound of a motor drone—
And then the drone was still.[6]
We heard the tick-tock on the shelf,
And the leak of valves in our hearts.
A calm condensed and lidded
As at the core of a cyclone ended breathing.
This was the monologue of Silence
Grave and unequivocal.

What followed was a bolt
Outside the range and target of the thunder,   50
And human speech curved back upon itself
Through Druid runways[7] and the Piltdown scarps,
Beyond the stammers of the Java caves,
To find its origins in hieroglyphs
On mouths and eyes and cheeks
Etched by a foreign stylus never used
On the outmoded page of the Apocalypse.[8]

1943

---

[5]Grating sound; perhaps also with its alternate meaning of a spasm of pain. The whole line refers to the introduction of tanks in modern warfare.

[6]The reference here is to the German bombs that fell during the Battle of Britain in 1940. (Pratt's poem was first published in April 1941.) After the planes passed over, there was a moment before the explosion of the bombs.

[7]The paths that form a part of primitive religious monuments such as those at Avebury and Stonehenge, which were formerly believed to be the work of the Druids (early Celtic priests). 'Piltdown', 'Java': when Pratt wrote the poem, Piltdown man and Java man were believed to be among the most primitive ancestors of modern man (the fossil evidence for Piltdown man was subsequently discovered to be fraudulent).

[8]Another name for Revelation, the last book of the Bible, which predicts the events leading up to the end of the world, including Armageddon—the final battle between good and evil.

The Truant[1]

'What have you there?' the great Panjandrum[2] said
To the Master of the Revels[3] who had led
A bucking truant with a stiff backbone
Close to the foot of the Almighty's throne.

'Right Reverend, most adored,
And forcibly acknowledged Lord
By the keen logic of your two-edged sword!
This creature has presumed to classify
Himself—a biped, rational, six feet high
And two feet wide; weighs fourteen stone;   10
Is guilty of a multitude of sins.
He has abjured his choric origins,
And like an undomesticated slattern,
Walks with tangential step unknown
Within the weave of the atomic pattern.
He has developed concepts, grins
Obscenely at your Royal bulletins,
Possesses what he calls a will
Which challenges your power to kill.'

'What is his pedigree?'   20

'The base is guaranteed, your Majesty—
Calcium, carbon, phosphorus, vapour
And other fundamentals spun
From the umbilicus[4] of the sun,
And yet he says he will not caper
Around your throne, nor toe the rules
For the ballet of the fiery molecules.'

'His concepts and denials—scrap them, burn them—
To the chemists with them promptly.'

                              'Sire,   30
The stuff is not amenable to fire.
Nothing but their own kind can overturn them.
The chemists have sent back the same old story—
"With our extreme gelatinous apology,
We beg to inform your Imperial Majesty,
Unto whom be dominion and power and glory,
There still remains that strange precipitate

---

[1]For the intellectual debate that provides the context for this poem, see Djwa, *E.J. Pratt: The Evolutionary Vision* (1974), pp. 114-20. Of this poem Pratt himself wrote to Desmond Pacey: 'My own profession of faith was expressed in "The Truant", a comparatively late poem. . . . It is an indictment of absolute power without recognition of moral ends.'
[2]A pompous and pretentious official; here, God, not as traditionally conceived, but as a deity embodying mechanistic theories of the universe as a set of explicable scientific principles.
[3]Formerly, a person appointed to organize merry-making; here a satanic figure.
[4]Core (literally, 'navel').

Which has the quality to resist
Our oldest and most trusted catalyst.
It is a substance we cannot cremate   40
By temperatures known to our Laboratory.'' '

And the great Panjandrum's face grew dark—
'I'll put those chemists to their annual purge,
And I myself shall be the thaumaturge[5]
To find the nature of this fellow's spark.
Come, bring him nearer by yon halter rope:
I'll analyse him with the cosmoscope.'

Pulled forward with his neck awry,
The little fellow six feet short,
Aware he was about to die,   50
Committed grave contempt of court
By answering with a flinchless stare
The Awful Presence seated there.

The ALL HIGH swore until his face was black.
He called him a coprophagite,[6]
A genus *homo*, egomaniac,
Third cousin to the family of worms,
A sporozoan[7] from the ooze of night,
Spawn of a spavined troglodyte:
He swore by all the catalogue of terms   60
Known since the slang of carboniferous[8] Time.
He said that he could trace him back

To pollywogs and earwigs in the slime.
And in his shrillest tenor he began
Reciting his indictment of the man,
Until he closed upon this capital crime—
'You are accused of singing out of key,
(A foul unmitigated dissonance)
Of shuffling in the measures of the dance,
Then walking out with that defiant, free   70
Toss of your head, banging the doors,
Leaving a stench upon the jacinth[9] floors.
You have fallen like a curse
On the mechanics of my Universe.

'Herewith I measure out your penalty—
Hearken while you hear, look while you see:
I send you now upon your homeward route

[5] Miracle-worker.
[6] Feces-eater.
[7] A parasitic protozoan, a primitive form of life; 'spavined': lame; 'troglodyte': prehistoric cave-dweller.
[8] The Carboniferous period, in the latter part of the Paleozoic era, began about 345 million years ago.
[9] Reddish-orange gem.

Where you shall find
Humiliation for your pride of mind.
I shall make deaf the ear, and dim the eye,   80
Put palsy in your touch, make mute
Your speech, intoxicate your cells and dry
Your blood and marrow, shoot
Arthritic needles through your cartilage,
And having parched you with old age,
I'll pass you wormwise through the mire;
And when your rebel will
Is mouldered, all desire
Shrivelled, all your concepts broken,
Backward in dust I'll blow you till   90
You join my spiral festival of fire.[1]
Go, Master of the Revels—I have spoken.'

And the little genus *homo,* six feet high,
Standing erect, countered with this reply—
'You dumb insouciant invertebrate,
You rule a lower than a feudal state—
A realm of flunkey decimals that run,
Return; return and run; again return,
Each group around its little sun,
And every sun a satellite.   100
There they go by day and night,
Nothing to do but run and burn,
Taking turn and turn about,
Light-year in and light-year out,
Dancing, dancing in quadrillions,[2]
Never leaving their pavillions.

'Your astronomical conceit
Of bulk and power is anserine.[3]
Your ignorance so thick,
You did not know your own arithmetic.   110
We flung the graphs about your flying feet;
We measured your diameter—
Merely a line
Of zeros prefaced by an integer.
Before we came
You had no name.
You did not know direction or your pace;
We taught you all you ever knew
Of motion, time and space.
We healed you of your vertigo   120
And put you in our kindergarten show,
Perambulated you through prisms, drew

---

[1]An allusion to Dante's *Divina Commedia.* The poem is divided into three sections, which describe Dante's winding descent into Hell (the 'Inferno'), followed by his ascent, via the 'spiral stairs' alluded to at l. 138, through Purgatory (the 'Purgatorio') to the earthly Paradise (the 'Paradiso').

[2]10^{15}; with a pun on 'quadrille', a square-dance for four couples.   [3]Goose-like, foolish.

Your mileage through the Milky Way,
Lassoed your comets when they ran astray,
Yoked Leo, Taurus, and your team of Bears
To pull our kiddy cars of inverse squares.

'Boast not about your harmony,
Your perfect curves, your rings
Of *pure and endless light*[4]—'Twas we
Who pinned upon your Seraphim their wings,   130
And when your brassy heavens rang
With joy that morning while the planets sang
Their choruses of archangelic lore,
'Twas we who ordered the notes upon their score
Out of our winds and strings.
Yes! all your shapely forms
Are ours—parabolas of silver light,
Those blueprints of your spiral stairs
From nadir depth to zenith height,
Coronas, rainbows after storms,   140
Auroras on your eastern tapestries
And constellations over western seas.

'And when, one day, grown conscious of your age,
While pondering an eolith,[5]
We turned a human page
And blotted out a cosmic myth
With all its baby symbols to explain
The sunlight in Apollo's eyes,[6]
Our rising pulses and the birth of pain,   150
Fear, and that fern-and-fungus breath
Stalking our nostrils to our cave of death—
That day we learned how to anatomize
Your body, calibrate your size
And set a mirror up before your face
To show you what you really were—a rain
Of dull Lucretian atoms[7] crowding space,
A series of concentric waves which any fool
Might make by dropping stones within a pool,

---

[4]From the opening lines of 'The World' by the seventeenth-century mystical poet Henry Vaughan:

I saw Eternity the other night
Like a great Ring *of pure and endless light.*

[5]Stone-age artifact.
[6]Apollo, especially under his epithet Phoebus (The Bright One), was identified as the god of the sun by early writers.
[7]Lucretius (96?-55 B.C.) was a Roman poet and philosopher and one of the early atomists; he believed that the universe was made up of primordial 'seeds' of infinitesimal size dropping through a void.

Or an exploding bomb forever in flight[8]
Bursting like hell through Chaos and Old Night. 160

'You oldest of the hierarchs
Composed of electronic sparks,
We grant you speed,
We grant you power, and fire
That ends in ash, but we concede
To you no pain nor joy nor love nor hate,
No final tableau of desire,
No causes won or lost, no free
Adventure at the outposts—only
The degradation of your energy[9] 170
When at some late
Slow number of your dance your sergeant-major Fate
Will catch you blind and groping and will send
You reeling on that long and lonely
Lockstep of your wave-lengths towards your end.

'We who have met
With stubborn calm the dawn's hot fusillades;
Who have seen the forehead sweat
Under the tug of pulleys on the joints,
Under the liquidating tally[1] 180
Of the cat-and-truncheon[2] bastinades;
Who have taught our souls to rally
To mountain horns and the sea's rockets
When the needle ran demented through the points;
We who have learned to clench
Our fists and raise our lightless sockets
To morning skies after the midnight raids,
Yet cocked our ears to bugles on the barricades,
And in cathedral rubble found a way to quench
A dying thirst within a Galilean[3] valley— 190
No! by the Rood, we will not join your ballet.'

1943

---

[8]The concept of the universe as beginning with an explosion from a single point and continuing to expand as matter moves away from this point was first formulated in the 1920s and became a well-established scientific theory during the 1930s. 'Chaos and Old Night': In Milton's *Paradise Lost* the fallen angels give 'A shout that tore Hell's Concave, and beyond/Frighted the Reign of *Chaos* and old Night' (I. 542-3). 'Old night' or 'eldest night', the outer limit of the universe in Milton's cosmology, was the eternal uncreated aspect of God out of which God derived Chaos—undifferentiated inchoate matter; God then produced Creation from Chaos.
[9]A reference to the concept of entropy, the idea—implicit in the second law of thermodynamics—that the universe is running down because of a continuing loss of available energy.
[1]Record or score, but with a possible pun on the original meaning of 'tally', a notched stick, because 'bastinade' is a beating with a stick.
[2]Whip (cat-o'-nine-tails) and club.
[3]Of Galilee (in northern Palestine); 'Rood': the cross.

Towards the Last Spike

It was the same world then as now—the same,
Except for little differences of speed
And power, and means to treat myopia
To show an axe-blade infinitely sharp
Splitting things infinitely small, or else
Provide the telescopic sight to roam
Through curved dominions never found in fables.
The same, but for new particles of speech—
Those algebraic substitutes for nouns
That sky cartographers would hang like signboards   10
Along the trespass of our thoughts to stop
The stutters of our tongues with their equations.

As now, so then, blood kept its ancient colour,
And smoothly, roughly, paced its banks; in calm
Preserving them, in riot rupturing them.
Wounds needed bandages and stomachs food:
The hands outstretched had joined the lips in prayer—
'Give us our daily bread, give us our pay.'
The past flushed in the present and tomorrow
Would dawn upon today: only the rate   20
To sensitize or numb a nerve would change;
Only the quickening of a measuring skill
To gauge the onset of a birth or death
With the precision of micrometers.
Men spoke of acres then and miles and masses,
Velocity and steam, cables that moored
Not ships but continents, world granaries,
The east-west cousinship, a nation's rise,
Hail of identity, a world expanding,
If not the universe: the feel of it   30
Was in the air—*'Union required the Line.'* [1]
The theme was current at the banquet tables,
And arguments profane and sacred rent
God-fearing families into partisans.
Pulpit, platform and floor were sounding-boards;
Cushions beneath the pounding fists assumed
The hues of western sunsets; nostrils sniffed
The prairie tang; the tongue rolled over texts:
Even St Paul was being invoked to wring
The neck of Thomas in this war of faith   40
With unbelief. [2] Was ever an adventure

[1] When British Columbia was admitted into Confederation in 1871 it was with the promise that a railway would be built within ten years to connect that province with eastern Canada. Sir John A. Macdonald and his Conservative party argued in Parliament that Canada's hold on the West and Northwest depended on the fulfilment of that promise, and that an all-Canadian route was essential to future national unity.

[2] St Paul preached a doctrine of faith. The unbelievers are like the apostle Thomas who, before acknowledging the resurrected Christ, required physical proof (hence doubting 'Thomas'). Pratt is

Without its cost? Analogies were found
On every page of history or science.
A nation, like the world, could not stand still.
What was the use of records but to break them?
The tougher armour followed the new shell;
The newer shell the armour; lighthouse rockets
Sprinkled their stars over the wake of wrecks.
Were not the engineers at work to close
The lag between the pressures and the valves?   50
The same world then as now thirsting for power
To crack those records open, extra pounds
Upon the inches, extra miles per hour.
The mildewed static schedules which before
Had like asbestos been immune to wood
Now curled and blackened in the furnace coal.
This power lay in the custody of men
From down-and-outers needing roofs, whose hands
Were moulded by their fists, whose skins could feel
At home incorporate with dolomite,[3]   60
To men who with the marshal instincts in them,
Deriving their authority from wallets,
Directed their battalions from the trestles.

THE GATHERING

(*'Oats—a grain which in England is generally given to horses,
but in Scotland supports the people.'—Dr Samuel Johnson.*
'True, but where will you find such horses, where such men?'—
Lord Elibank's reply as recorded by Sir Walter Scott.)

Oatmeal was in their blood and in their names.
Thrift was the title of their catechism.
It governed all things but their mess of porridge
Which, when it struck the hydrochloric acid
With treacle and skim-milk, became a mash.
Entering the duodenum, it broke up
Into amino acids: then the liver   70
Took on its natural job as carpenter:
Foreheads grew into cliffs, jaws into juts.
The meal, so changed, engaged the follicles:
Eyebrows came out as gorse, the beards as thistles,
And the chest-hair the fell[4] of Grampian rams.
It stretched and vulcanized the human span:
Nonagenarians worked and thrived upon it.
Out of such chemistry run through by genes,
The food released its fearsome racial products:—
The power to strike a bargain like a foe,   80
To win an argument upon a burr,

also playfully alluding to the fact that the men who built the CPR gained their railroad experience revi-
talizing the St Paul and Pacific Railway (see p. 218, note 7).
[3] An important mineral in building, found in much limestone and some marble.
[4] Fleece; the Grampians are the principal mountains of Scotland.

Invest the language with a Bannockburn,[5]
Culloden or the warnings of Lochiel,
Weave loyalties and rivalries in tartans,
Present for the amazement of the world
Kilts and the civilized barbaric Fling,
And pipes which, when they acted on the mash,
Fermented lullabies to *Scots wha hae*.[6]

Their names were like a battle-muster—Angus[7]
(He of the Shops) and Fleming (of the Transit),   90
Hector (of the *Kicking Horse*), Dawson,
'Cromarty' Ross, and Beatty (Ulster Scot),
Bruce, Allan, Galt and Douglas, and the 'twa'—
Stephen (Craigellachie) and Smith (Strathcona)—
Who would one day climb from their Gaelic hide-outs,
Take off their plaids and wrap them round the mountains.
And then the everlasting tread of the Macs,
Vanguard, centre and rear, their roving eyes
On summits, rivers, contracts, beaver, ledgers;
Their ears cocked to the skirl of Sir John A.,   100
The general of the patronymic march.[8]

[5] The English were beaten back by the Scots at the Battle of Bannockburn in 1314. In 1746 the forces of Bonnie Prince Charlie were defeated at Culloden, a celebrated battle that marked the break-up of the Highland Clans. Donald Cameron of Lochiel was a famous Highland chieftain allied with Charles Stuart; in 'Lochiel's Warning' (1802) the poet Thomas Campbell tells of a wizard appearing to Lochiel and forecasting the coming defeat.

[6] A reference to 'Robert Bruce's March to Bannockburn' by Robert Burns (1759-1796), a warlike patriotic song beginning, 'Scots wha hae wi' Wallace bled, / Scots, wham Bruce has aften led, / Welcome to your gory bed / Or to Victorie!'

[7] Richard B. Angus (1821-1922) became general manager in 1879 of the St Paul and Pacific Railway following its purchase in 1877 by Donald Smith, George Stephen, Jim Hill, John S. Kennedy, Duncan McIntyre, and Norman Kittson; in 1880 Angus became part of the syndicate—with Smith, Stephen, McIntyre, and Henry Beatty—that was formed for the construction of the Canadian Pacific Railway (see lines 658-66). He later established shops in Montreal for the building of railway equipment. Sandford Fleming (1827-1915) was appointed engineer-in-chief for the CPR in 1871 and made the original surveys through the mountain ranges that presented the greatest obstacle between east and west. (A transit is a surveyor's instrument.) James Hector (1834-1907), geologist, discovered the Kicking Horse Pass through the Rocky Mountains, the pass eventually chosen over the more northerly Yellowhead Pass favoured by Fleming. Simon James Dawson (1820-1902), a civil engineer, first opened communications with the Red River country by means of the 'Dawson Route', and therefore was an important forerunner of the railway builders. James Ross (1848-1913), born in Cromarty, Scotland, took charge of the CPR west of Winnipeg in 1883. Randolph Bruce (1863-1942) was an engineer on surveys investigating alternate passes through the Rockies in 1891. Sir Hugh Allen (1810-1882), one of the original projectors of the CPR, was given the initial contract for its construction in 1872; subsequent revelations of financial improprieties resulted in the fall of the Macdonald government and the loss of the contract. Alexander Galt (1817-1893), one of the chief architects of the British North America Act, was an early railroad builder in Canada, associated with the Grand Trunk Railway. Sir James Douglas (1803-77) was the first governor of British Columbia (1858-64). George Stephen (1829-1921) was president of the syndicate formed to build the CPR and one of its two most important members along with Donald Smith (1820-1914), later Baron Strathcona. It was Smith who drove the last spike in 1885 symbolizing the completion of the laying of tracks. In 1884 Stephen, who had gone to England to raise funds to keep the railway solvent in a period of financial crisis, sent a famous cable to Smith with the message 'Stand Fast, Craigellachie'—the defiant war-cry of the Clan Grant, which refers to a sentinel rock in the Scottish countryside familiar to both men. All of the men named in these lines came from Scotland except for Galt, who was born in England but was the son of the Scottish novelist John Galt.

[8] That is, many of those involved in the railroad had the patronymic prefix 'Mac' on their names, chief among them Sir John A. Macdonald.

(Sir John revolving round the Terms of Union with British Columbia. Time, late at night.)

Insomnia had ripped the bed-sheets from him
Night after night. How long was this to last?
Confederation had not played this kind
Of trickery on him. That was rough indeed,
So gravelled,[9] that a man might call for rest
And take it for a life accomplishment.
It was his laurel though some of the leaves
Had dried. But this would be a longer tug
Of war which needed for his team thick wrists   110
And calloused fingers, heavy heels to dig
Into the earth and hold—men with bull's beef
Upon their ribs. Had he himself the wind,
The anchor-waist to peg at the rope's end?
'Twas bad enough to have these questions hit
The waking mind: 'twas much worse when he dozed;
For goblins had a way of pinching him,
Slapping a nightmare on to dwindling snoozes.
They put him and his team into a tug
More real than life. He heard a judge call out—   120
'Teams settle on the rope and take the strain!'
And with the coaches' *heave,* the running welts
Reddened his palms, and then the gruelling *backlock*
Inscribed its indentations on his shoulders.
This kind of burn he knew he had to stand;
It was the game's routine; the other fire
Was what he feared the most for it could bake him—
That white dividing rag tied to the rope
Above the centre pole had with each heave
Wavered with chances equal. With the backlock,   130
Despite the legs of Tupper[1] and Cartier,
The western anchor dragged; the other side
Remorselessly was gaining, holding, gaining.
No sleep could stand this strain and, with the nightmare
Delivered of its colt, Macdonald woke.

Tired with the midnight toss, lock-jawed with yawns,
He left the bed and, shuffling to the window,
He opened it. The air would cool him off
And soothe his shoulder burns. He felt his ribs:
Strange, nothing broken—how those crazy drowses   140
Had made the fictions tangle with the facts!
He must unscramble them with steady hands.
Those Ranges pirouetting in his dreams
Had their own knack of standing still in light,

---

[9]Perplexed.
[1]Charles Tupper (1821-1915) and George Etienne Cartier (1811-73) were Macdonald's staunchest allies in Parliament during the 1871 debate with Alexander Mackenzie's Liberals over the proposed transcontinental railway.

Revealing peaks whose known triangulation
Had to be read in prose severity.
Seizing a telescope, he swept the skies,
The north-south drift, a self-illumined chart.
Under Polaris was the Arctic Sea
And the sub-Arctic gates well stocked with names: 150
Hudson, Davis, Baffin, Frobisher;[2]
And in his own day Franklin, Ross and Parry
Of the Canadian Archipelago;
Kellett, McClure, McClintock, of *The Search*.
Those straits and bays had long been kicked by keels,
And flags had fluttered on the Capes that fired
His youth, making familiar the unknown.
What though the odds were nine to one against,
And the Dead March was undertoning trumpets,
There was enough of strychnine[3] in the names   160
To make him flip a penny for the risk,
Though he had palmed the coin reflectively
Before he threw and watched it come down *heads*.
That stellar path looked too much like a road map
Upon his wall—the roads all led to market—
The north-south route. He lit a candle, held
It to a second map full of blank spaces
And arrows pointing west. Disturbed, he turned
The lens up to the zenith, followed the course
Tracked by a cloud of stars that would not keep   170
Their posts—Capella,[4] Perseus, were reeling;
Low in the north-west, Cassiopeia
Was qualmish, leaning on her starboard arm-rest,
And Aries was chasing, butting Cygnus,
Just diving. Doubts and hopes struck at each other.
Why did those constellations look so much
Like blizzards? And what lay beyond the blizzards?

'Twas chilly at the window. He returned
To bed and savoured soporific terms:
Superior, the *Red River, Selkirk, Prairie,*   180
Port Moody and *Pacific.* Chewing them,
He spat out *Rocky* grit before he swallowed.
Selkirk![5] This had the sweetest taste. Ten years

[2]That is, these early explorers gave their names to Hudson Bay, Davis Strait, Baffin Bay, and Frobisher Bay. John Franklin made three famous expeditions into the Arctic archipelago between 1819 and 1846; John Ross accompanied by Edward Parry in 1818, and Parry in 1819, made voyages that added vastly to knowledge about the region. After Franklin was lost on his third voyage a huge reward was offered for information about his fate, and a famous search was mounted for him that lasted from 1848 to 1859; Henry Kellett, Robert McClure, and Leopold McClintock were among those who took part.
[3]Although highly toxic, strychnine was formerly used for its properties as a stimulant.
[4]Brightest star in the constellation Auriga, which is one of the prominent constellations of the northern celestial hemisphere, with Perseus, Cassiopeia, Aries, and Cygnus.
[5]The town founded by the Red River settlers. The lines that follow recapitulate the progress of these distressed Highlanders who came to Canada under the leadership of Lord Selkirk (1771-1820) as they journeyed to the Red River to found a settlement there, on land granted to Selkirk by the Hudson's

Before, the Highland crofters had subscribed
Their names in a memorial[6] for the Rails.
Sir John reviewed the story of the struggle,
That four months' journey from their native land—
The Atlantic through the Straits to Hudson Bay,
Then the Hayes River to Lake Winnipeg
Up to the Forks of the Assiniboine.   190
He could make use of that—just what he needed,
A Western version of the Arctic daring,
Romance and realism, double dose.
How long ago? Why, this is '71.
Those fellows came the time Napoleon
Was on the steppes.[7] For sixty years they fought
The seasons, 'hoppers, drought, hail, wind and snow;
Survived the massacre at Seven Oaks,
The 'Pemmican War' and the Red River floods.
They wanted now the Road—those pioneers   200
Who lived by spades instead of beaver traps.
Most excellent word that, pioneers! Sir John
Snuggled himself into his sheets, rolling
The word around his tongue, a theme for song,
Or for a peroration to a speech.

THE HANGOVER AT DAWN

He knew the points that had their own appeal.
These did not bother him: the patriot touch,
The Flag, the magnetism of explorers,
The national unity. These could burn up
The phlegm in most of the provincial throats.   210
But there was one tale central to his plan
(The focus of his headache at this moment),
Which would demand the limit of his art—
The ballad of his courtship in the West:
Better reveal it soon without reserve.

THE LADY OF BRITISH COLUMBIA

Port Moody and Pacific! He had pledged
His word the Line should run from sea to sea.
'*From sea to sea*', a hallowed phrase.[8] Music

Bay Company; crucial events in the history of the Settlement are mentioned in lines 186-99. The
massacre at Seven Oaks took place in 1816 when the governor of the colony and twenty of his men
were killed by Métis; this hostility had been prompted by the North West Company, which found that
the location of the Red River Settlement cut off its vital supply of pemmican (preserved buffalo
meat); the union in 1821 of the rival Hudson's Bay Company with the North West Company ended
that conflict, but flooding in 1826 (and again in 1852) brought new hardship to the Selkirk settlers.
[6]Petition.
[7]Napoleon invaded Russia in 1812 (the year the Red River Settlement was founded), although he
never actually reached the steppes, southeast of Moscow.
[8]'Hallowed' because its original source is Psalm 72:8: 'He shall have dominion also from sea to sea';
the phrase was adopted as Canada's national motto in 1866, when 'dominion' was chosen to designate Canada.

Was in that text if the right key were struck,
And he must strike it first, for, as he fingered   220
The clauses of the pledge, rough notes were rasping—
'*No Road, No Union*', and the converse true.
East-west against the north-south run of trade,
For California like a sailor-lover
Was wooing over-time. He knew the ports.
His speech was as persuasive as his arms,
As sinuous as Spanish arias—
Tamales, Cazadero, Mendecino,
Curling their baritones around the Lady.
Then Santa Rosa, Santa Monica,   230
Held absolution in their syllables.
But when he saw her stock of British temper
Starch at ironic sainthood in the whispers—
'*Rio de nuestra señora de buena guia,*'[9]
He had the tact to gutturalize the liquids,
Steeping the tunes to drinking songs, then take
Her on a holiday where she could watch
A roving sea-born Californian pound
A downy chest and swear by San Diego.

Sir John, wise to the tricks, was studying hard,   240
A fresh proposal for a marriage contract.[1]
He knew a game was in the ceremony.
That southern fellow had a healthy bronze
Complexion, had a vast estate, was slick
Of manner. In his ardour he could tether
Sea-roses to the blossoms of his orchards,
And for his confidence he had the prime
Advantage of his rival—*he was there.*

THE LONG-DISTANCE PROPOSAL

A game it was, and the Pacific lass
Had poker wisdom on her face. Her name   250
Was rich in values—*British;* this alone
Could raise Macdonald's temperature: so could
Columbia[2] with a different kind of fever,
And in between the two, *Victoria.*
So the *Pacific* with its wash of letters
Could push the Fahrenheit another notch.
She watched for bluff on those Disraeli features,[3]
Impassive but for arrowy chipmunk eyes,
Engaged in fathoming a contract time.

---

[9]'River of Our Lady of Safe Conduct' (Pratt's note).
[1]Pratt's image of British Columbia as a prospective bride has its source in popular journalism of the period; for example, on 2 January 1871 the *British Colonist* wrote: 'clad in bridal attire, she is about to unite her destinies with a country which is prepared to do much for her.'
[2]A name used to personify the United States.
[3]Benjamin Disraeli (1804-88) was prime minister of England in 1868 (and again in 1874-80). Both Macdonald and Disraeli were thought of as being physically unattractive, with prominent noses.

With such a dowry she could well afford   260
To take the risk of tightening the terms—
'Begin the Road in two years, end in ten' [4]—
Sir John, a moment letting down his guard,
Frowned at the Rocky skyline, but agreed.

(The Terms ratified by Parliament, British Columbia enters Confederation July, 1871, Sandford Fleming being appointed engineer-in-chief of the proposed Railway, Walter Moberly[5] to cooperate with him in the location of routes. 'Of course, I don't know how many millions you have, but it is going to cost you money to get through those canyons.'—Moberly to Macdonald.)

THE PACIFIC SCANDAL[6]

(Huntingdon's charges of political corruption based on correspondence and telegrams rifled from the offices of the solicitor of Sir Hugh Allan, Head of the Canada Pacific Company; Sir John's defence; and the appearance of the Honourable Edward Blake[7] who rises to reply to Sir John at 2 a.m.)

BLAKE IN MOOD

Of all the subjects for debate here was
His element. His soul as clean as surf,
No one could equal him in probing cupboards
Or sweeping floors and dusting shelves, finding
A skeleton inside an overcoat;
Or shaking golden eagles[8] from a pocket   270
To show the copper plugs within the coins.
Rumours he heard had gangrened into facts—
Gifts nuzzling at two-hundred-thousand dollars,
Elections on, and with a contract pending.
The odour of the bills had blown his gorge.

---

[4]The first clause of the agreement negotiated with British Columbia in 1870 read: 'The Government of the Dominion undertake to secure the commencement simultaneously, within two years from the date of the union, of the construction of a railway, from the Pacific towards the Rocky Mountains, and from such point as may be selected, east of the Rocky Mountains towards the Pacific, to connect the seaboard of British Columbia with the railway system of Canada, and further, to secure the completion of such railway within ten years from the date of such union.'

[5](1852-1915); Moberly had had extensive experience in railway construction prior to taking charge of the difficult Rocky Mountain and British Columbia surveys in 1871.

[6]Name given the general charges of bribery, corruption, and underhand dealing that were brought by Liberal M.P. L. S. Huntingdon in 1872 against Macdonald and Hugh Allan. The charges, based on correspondence and papers stolen from Allan's office, suggested that Allan had paid Macdonald and Cartier for railway contracts. Subsequent investigation showed that at the very least the Prime Minister had acted unwisely in accepting substantial campaign contributions from Allan. On 3 November 1873 Macdonald defended himself in Parliament in a famous speech that lasted five hours.

[7]Although Alexander Mackenzie was the formally chosen leader of the Liberals, Blake (1833-1912)—famous for his intellectual capacity and for his long and meticulously argued orations—was regarded as the party's real leader. He responded to Macdonald's speech for about half an hour immediately after it was over, and then for a further four hours the next day. The Macdonald government fell on 5 November 1873.

[8]U.S. gold coins worth $10; profiteers sometimes debased such currency by removing their centres and replacing them with copper.

His appetitie, edged by a moral hone,
Could surfeit only on the Verities.

November 3, 1873

A Fury[9] rode him to the House. He took
His seat, and with a stoic gloom he heard
The Chieftain's great defence and noted well   280
The punctuation of the cheers. He needed all
The balance of his mind to counterpoise
The movements of Macdonald as he flung
Himself upon the House, upon the Country,
Upon posterity, upon his conscience.
That plunging played the devil with Blake's tiller,
Threatened the set of his sail. To save the course,
To save himself, in that five hours of gale,
He had to jettison his meditation,
His brooding on the follies of mankind,   290
Clean out the wadding from his tortured ears:
That roaring mob before him could be quelled
Only by action; so when the last round
Of the applause following the peroration
Was over, slowly, weightily, Blake rose.

A statesman-chancellor now held the Floor.
He told the sniffing Commons that a sense
Keener than smell or taste must be invoked
To get the odour. Leading them from facts
Like telegrams and stolen private letters,   300
He soared into the realm of principles
To find his scourge; and then the men involved,
Robed like the Knights of Malta,[1] Blake undressed,
Their cloaks inverted to reveal the shoddy,
The tattered lining and bare-threaded seams.
He ripped the last stitch from them—by the time
Recess was called, he had them in the dock
As brigands in the Ministry of Smells,
Naked before the majesty of Heaven.

For Blake recesses were but sandwiches   310
Provided merely for cerebral luncheons—
No time to spread the legs under the table,
To chat and chaff a while, to let the mind
Roam, like a goblet up before the light
To bask in natural colour, or by whim
Of its own choice to sway luxuriously
In tantalizing arcs before the nostrils.
A meal was meant by Nature for nutrition—

[9]One of the avenging spirits of classical mythology, concerned with the punishment of crimes, especially violations of the social contracts on which civilization depends.
[1]Military religious order that wore black capes.

A sorry farinaceous business scaled
Exactly to caloric grains and grams 320
Designed for intellectual combustion,
For energy directed into words
Towards proof. Abuse was overweight. He saw
No need for it; no need for caricature,
And if a villainous word had to be used,
'Twas for a villain—keen upon the target.
Irrelevance was like a moral lesion
No less within a speech than in a statute.
What mattered it who opened up the files,
Sold for a bid the damning correspondence— 330
That Montreal-Chicago understanding?[2]
A dirty dodge, so let it be conceded.
But *here* the method was irrelevant.
Whether by legal process or by theft,
The evidence was there unalterable.
So with the House assembled, he resumed
Imperial indictment of the bandits.
The logic left no loopholes in the facts.
Figures that ran into the hundred-thousands
Were counted up in pennies, each one shown 340
To bear the superscription of debasement.

Again recess, again the sandwiches,
Again the invocation of the gods:
Each word, each phrase, each clause went to position,
Each sentence regimented like a lockstep.
The only thing that would not pace was time;
The hours dragged by until the thrushes woke—
Two days, two nights—someone opened a window,
And members of the House who still were conscious
Uncreaked their necks to note that even Sir John 350
Himself had put his fingers to his nose.

*(The appeal to the country: Macdonald defeated: Mackenzie
assumes power, 1874.)*

A change of air, a drop in temperature!
The House had rarely known sobriety
Like this. No longer clanged the *'Westward Ho!'*
And quiet were the horns upon the hills.
Hard times ahead.[3] The years were rendering up

---

[2]Allan's original Montreal-based syndicate had included several Americans who were suspected of joining only to delay the building of a Canadian railroad. Allan was told by Macdonald that he had to exclude his American associates; he appeared to comply, but continued to strike secret bargains with his U.S. investors.
[3]The whole of Alexander Mackenzie's term as prime minister (1873-8) coincided with a period of serious economic depression. Mackenzie and his Liberal party had always advocated a go-slow policy on the building of the railroad in any case; only a few sections, those that were easiest to construct, were built during his term, although extensive new surveys of the passes through the mountains were undertaken. While the Conservatives had argued that settlement would follow the railroad, the Liberals argued that the railroad should follow the settlers.

Their fat. Measured and rationed was the language
Directed to the stringency of pockets.
The eye must be convinced before the *vision.*
'But one step at a time,' exclaimed the feet.   360
It was the story of the hen or egg;
Which came before the other? *"Twas the hen,'*
Cried one; *'undoubtedly the hen must lay*
The egg, hatch it and mother it.' *'Not so,'*
Another shouted, *"Twas the egg or whence*
The hen?' For every one who cleared his throat
And called across the House with Scriptural passion—
'The Line is meant to bring the loaves and fishes,' [4]
A voting three had countered with the question—
'Where are the multitudes that thirst and hunger?'   370
Passion became displaced by argument.
Till now the axles justified their grease,
Taught coal a lesson in economy.
All doubts here could be blanketed with facts,
With phrases smooth as actuarial velvet.

For forty years in towns and cities men
Had watched the Lines baptized with charters, seen
Them grown, marry and bring forth children.
Parades and powder had their uses then
For gala days; and bands announced arrivals,   380
Betrothals, weddings and again arrivals.
Champagne brimmed in the font as they were named
With titles drawn from the explorers' routes,
From Saints and Governors, from space and seas
And compass-points—Saints Andrew, Lawrence, Thomas,
Louis and John; Champlain, Simcoe; Grand Trunk,
Intercolonial, the Canadian Southern,
Dominion-Atlantic, the Great Western—names
That caught a continental note and tried
To answer it. Half-gambles though they were,   390
Directors built those Roads and heard them run
To the sweet silver jingle in their minds.

The airs had long been mastered like old songs
The feet could tap to in the galleries.
But would they tap to a new rhapsody,
A harder one to learn and left unfinished?
What ear could be assured of absolute pitch
To catch this kind of music in the West?
The far West? Men had used this flattering name
For East or but encroachment on the West.   400

---

[4]According to the gospels, Jesus miraculously fed a hungry multitude by dividing up 'five loaves, and two fishes' (Matthew 14: 15-21). *'Where are the multitudes that thirst and hunger?'* is an ironic recasting of the line from the Sermon on the Mount in which Christ, 'seeing the multitudes', said to them, 'Blessed are they which do hunger and thirst after righteousness: for they shall be filled' (Matthew 5:6).

And was not Lake Superior still the East,
A natural highway which ice-ages left,
An unappropriated legacy?
There was no discord in the piston-throbs
Along this Road. This was old music too.
That northern spine of rock, those western mountains,
Were barriers built of God and cursed of Blake.
Mild in his oaths, Mackenzie would avoid them.
He would let contracts for the south and west,
Push out from settlement to settlement.   410
This was economy, just plain horse-sense.
The Western Lines were there—American.
He would link up with them, could reach the Coast.
The Eagle and the Lion were good friends:
At least the two could meet on sovereign terms
Without a sign of fur and feathers flying.
As yet, but who could tell? So far, so good.
Spikes had been driven at the boundary line,
From Emerson across the Red to Selkirk,[5]
And then to Thunder Bay—to Lake Superior;   420
Across the prairies in God's own good time,
His plodding, patient, planetary time.

Five years' delay: surveys without construction;
Short lines suspended, discord in the Party.
The West defrauded of its glittering peaks,
The public blood was stirring and protesting
At this continuous dusk upon the mountains.
The old conductor off the podium,
The orchestra disbanded at the time
The daring symphony was on the score,   430
The audience cupped their ears to catch a strain:
They heard a plaintive thinning oboe-A
That kept on thinning while slow feeble steps
Approached the stand. Was this the substitute
For what the auditorium once knew—
The maestro who with tread of stallion hoofs
Came forward shaking platforms and the rafters,
And followed up the concert pitch with sound
Of drums and trumpets and the organ blasts
That had the power to toll out apathy   440
And make snow peaks ring like Cathedral steeples?
Besides, accompanying those bars of music,
There was an image men had not forgotten,
The shaggy chieftain standing at his desk,
That last-ditch fight when he was overthrown,
That desperate five hours. At least they knew
His personal pockets were not lined with pelf,
Whatever loot the others grabbed. The words

[5] Track was laid north from the U.S.-Canada border at Emerson, Man., as part of the reorganized St Paul and Pacific Railway, the forerunner of the CPR syndicate.

British, the West instead of South, the Nation,
The all-Canadian route—these terms were singing   450
Fresher than ever while the grating tones
Under the stress of argument had faded
Within the shroud of their monotony.

(Sir John returns to power in 1878 with a National Policy of Protective Tariff and the Transcontinental.)

Two years of tuning up: it needed that
To counterpoint Blake's eloquence or lift
Mackenzie's non-adventurous common sense
To the ignition of an enterprise.
The pace had to be slow at first, a tempo
Cautious, simple to follow. Sections strewn
Like amputated limbs along the route   460
Were sutured. This appealed to sanity.
No argument could work itself to sweat
Against a prudent case, for the terrain
Looked easy from the Lake to the Red River.
To stop with those suspensions was a waste
Of cash and time. But the huge task announced
Ten years before had now to start afresh—
The moulding of men's minds was harder far
Than moulding of the steel and prior to it.
It was the battle of ideas and words   470
And kindred images called by the same name,
Like brothers who with temperamental blood
Went to it with their fists. Canyons and cliffs
Were precipices down which men were hurled,
Or something to be bridged and sheared and scaled.
Likewise the Pass had its ambiguous meaning.[6]
The leaders of the factions in the House
And through the country spelled the word the same:
The way they got their tongue around the word
Was different, for some could make it hiss   480
With sound of blizzards screaming over ramparts:
The Pass—the Yellowhead, the Kicking Horse—
Or jam it with *coureur-de-bois*[7] romance,
Or join it to the empyrean. Eagles,
In flight banking their wings above a fish-stream,
Had guided the explorers to a route
And given the Pass the title of their wings.[8]

---

[6] Because the choice of which passes would be used through the Rockies, and the mountains to their west, remained a matter of intense debate until the last possible moment. The choice of a pass through the Rockies was finally between the Yellowhead Pass, favoured by Sandford Fleming, which would mean a northerly route, and the Kicking Horse Pass, which would make for a more direct southern route but would mean steeper gradients. The CPR eventually chose the Kicking Horse.
[7] An unlicensed trapper or fur-trader of New France who first opened up the Northwest, literally 'runner of the woods'; 'empyrean': of the highest heaven.
[8] Eagle Pass, through the Gold Range, was discovered and named by Walter Moberly after he pursued a flight of eagles, knowing that they usually followed streams and would therefore show him an opening between the mountains.

The stories lured men's minds up to the mountains
And down along the sandbars of the rivers.
Rivalling the *'brown and barren'* on the maps,   490
Officially *'not fit for human life'*,
Were vivid yellows flashing in the news—
'Gold in the Cariboo,' 'Gold in the Fraser.' [9]
The swish of gravel in the placer-cradles
Would soon be followed by the spluttering fuses,
By thunder echoing thunder; for one month
After Blake's Ottawa roar would Onderdonk[1]
Roar back from Yale by ripping canyon walls
To crash the tons by millions in the gorges.

The farther off, as by a paradox   500
Of magnets, was the golden lure the stronger:
Two thousand miles away, imagined peaks
Had the vacation pull of mountaineering,
But with the closer vision would the legs
Follow the mind? 'Twas Blake who raised the question
And answered it. Though with his natural eyes
Up to this time he had not sighted mountains,
He was an expert with the telescope.

THE ATTACK

Sir John was worried. The first hour of Blake
Was dangerous, granted the theme. Eight years   510
Before, he had the theme combined with language.
Impeachment—word with an historic ring,
Reserved for the High Courts of Parliament,
Uttered only when men were breathing hard
And when the vertebrae were musket-stiff:
High ground was that for his artillery,
And *there*, despite the hours the salvoes lasted.

But *here* this was a theme less vulnerable
To fire, Macdonald thought, to Blake's gunfire,
And yet he wondered what the orator   520
Might spring in that first hour, what strategy
Was on the Bench. He did not mind the close
Mosaic of the words—too intricate,
Too massive in design. Men might admire
The speech and talk about it, then forget it.
But few possessed the patience or the mind
To tread the mazes of the labyrinth.

---

[9]It was the rush for gold after its discovery in the Fraser River in 1857 and, later, in the Cariboo Mountains, that brought settlers to British Columbia and led to its creation as a province.
[1]Andrew Onderdonk (1848-1905) supervised the building of the B.C. section of the CPR. On 14 May 1880, at Yale, B.C., the first shot of dynamite was fired on that construction. In April of that year Blake had spoken for five hours in Parliament demanding that Onderdonk be stopped and that there be no construction west of the Rockies.

Once in a while, however, would Blake's logic
Stumble upon stray figures that would leap
Over the walls of other folds and catch   530
The herdsmen in their growing somnolence.
The waking sound was not—*'It can't be done'*;
That was a dogma, anyone might say it.
It was the following burning corollary:
'To build a Road over that sea of mountains.' [2]
This carried more than argument. It was
A flash of fire which might with proper kindling
Consume its way into the public mind.
The House clicked to the ready and Sir John,
Burying his finger-nails into his palms,   540
Muttered—*'God send us no more metaphors
Like that—except from Tory factories.'*

Had Blake the lift of Chatham[3] as he had
Burke's wind and almost that sierra span
Of mind, he might have carried the whole House
With him and posted it upon that sea
Of mountains with sub-zeros on their scalps,
Their glacial ribs waiting for warmth of season
To spring an avalanche. Such similes
Might easily glue the members to their seats   550
With frost in preparation for their ride.
Sir John's *'from sea to sea'* was Biblical;
It had the stamp of reverent approval;
But Blake's was pagan, frightening, congealing.
The chieftain's lips continued as in prayer,
A fiercely secular and torrid prayer—
*'May Heaven intervene to stop the flow
Of such unnatural images and send
The rhetorician back to decimals,
Back to his tessellated[4] subtleties.'*   560
The prayer was answered for High Heaven did it.
The second hour entered and passed by,
A third, a fourth. Sir John looked round the House,
Noticed the growing shuffle of the feet,
The agony of legs, the yawn's contagion.
Was that a snore? Who was it that went out?
He glanced at the Press Gallery. The pens
Were scratching through the languor of the ink
To match the words with shorthand and were failing.
He hoped the speech would last another hour,   570

[2]On 30 October 1874, in a speech at Aurora, Ont., Blake had said that 'until we have found the least impracticable route through that inhospitable country, that "sea of mountains", it is folly to talk of commencing the work of construction'. The phrase had its source in a book by George Munro Grant, *Ocean to Ocean: Sandford Fleming's expedition through Canada in 1872* (1873).
[3]William Pitt (1708-78), Earl of Chatham, and Edmund Burke (1729-97) were both British statesmen famous for their oratorical powers.
[4]Made of small bits that combine to form a larger pattern; mosaic-like.

And still another. Well within the law,
This homicidal master of the opiates
Loosened the hinges of the Opposition:
The minds went first; the bodies sagged; the necks
Curved on the benches and the legs sprawled out.
And when the Fundy Tide had ebbed, Sir John,
Smiling, watched the debris upon the banks,
For what were yesterday grey human brains
Had with decomposition taken on
The texture and complexion of red clay.   580

*(In 1880 Tupper[5] lets contract to Onderdonk for survey and con-
struction through the Pacific Section of the mountains. Sir John,
Tupper, Pope, and McIntyre go to London to interest capital but
return without a penny.)*

Failing to make a dent in London dams,
Sir John set out to plumb a reservoir
Closer in reach. He knew its area,
Its ownership, the thickness of its banks,
Its conduits—if he could get his hands
Upon the local stopcocks, could he turn them?
The reservoir was deep. Two centuries
Ago it started filling when a king
Had in a furry moment scratched a quill
Across the bottom of His Royal Charter—   590
*'Granting the Governor and His Company
Of Gentlemen Adventurers the right
Exclusive to one-third a continent.'*[6]
Was it so easy then? A scratch, a seal,
A pinch of snuff tickling the sacred nostrils,
A puff of powder and the ink was dry.
Sir John twisted his lips: he thought of London.
Empire and wealth were in that signature
For royal, princely, ducal absentees,
For courtiers to whom the parallels   600
Were nothing but chalk scratches on a slate.
For them wild animals were held in game
Preserves, foxes as quarry in a chase,
And hills were hedges, river banks were fences,
And cataracts but fountains in a garden
Tumbling their bubbles into marble basins.
Where was this place called Hudson Bay? Some place
In the Antipodes?[7] Explorers, traders,

---

[5]Charles Tupper (1821-1915) was Macdonald's minister of railways and canals from 1879 to 1884;
John Henry Pope (1824-89) was minister of agriculture (he later succeeded Tupper). When they trav-
elled to England with Macdonald in July 1880, Duncan McIntyre, the head of the Canada Central
Railway, accompanied them unofficially.
[6]The charter of the Hudson's Bay Company, 1670, signed by Charles II in 1670, granted 'the sole
Trade and Commerce' of Rupert's Land to 'the Governor and Company of Adventurers of England
Trading into Hudsons Bay'.
[7]The other end of the earth, especially the region of Australia.

Would bring their revenues over that signet.
Two centuries—the new empire advanced,   610
Was broken, reunited, torn again.
The *fleur-de-lis* went to half-mast, the *Jack*
To the mast-head, but fresher rivalries
Broke out—Nor'-Westers at the Hudson's throat
Over the pelts, over the pemmican;
No matter what—the dividends flowed in
As rum flowed out like the Saskatchewan.

The twist left Sir John's lips and he was smiling.
Though English in ambition and design,
This reservoir, he saw there in control   620
Upon the floodgates not a Londoner
In riding breeches but, red-flannel-shirted,
Trousered in homespun, streaked and blobbed with seal-oil,
A Scot with smoke of peat fire on his breath—
Smith?[8] Yes: but christened Donald Alexander
And loined through issue from the Grants and Stuarts.

To smite the rock and bring forth living water,
Take lead or tin and transmute both to silver,
Copper to gold, betray a piece of glass
To diamonds, fabulize a continent,   630
Were wonders once believed, scrapped and revived;
For Moses, Marco Polo, Paracelsus,[9]
Fell in the same retort and came out *Smith*.
A miracle on legs, the lad had left
Forres and Aberdeen, gone to Lachine—
'*Tell Mr Smith to count and sort the rat-skins.*'
Thence Tadoussac and Posts off Anticosti;
From there to Rigolet in Labrador,
A thousand miles by foot, snowshoe and dog-sled.
He fought the climate like a weathered yak,   640
And conquered it, ripping the stalactites
From his red beard, thawing his feet, and wringing
Salt water from his mitts; but most of all
He learned the art of making change. Blankets,
Ribbons and beads, tobacco, guns and knives,
Were swapped for muskrat, marten, fox and beaver.
And when the fur trade thinned, he trapped the salmon,
Canned it; hunted the seal, traded its oil
And fertilized the gardens with the carcass.
Even the melons grew in Labrador.   650
What could resist this touch? Water from rock!

---

[8] Donald Smith joined the Hudson's Bay Company as a young man in 1838, and was stationed in Labrador from 1848 until becoming Governor of the Company in 1869. In lines 634-8 Pratt traces Smith's path from his native Scotland to temporary postings in Quebec (at Lachine, Tadoussac, and near Ile d'Anticosti), and then to Rigolet on the coast of Labrador. 'Rat-skins': muskrat pelts.
[9] Sixteenth-century Swiss physician who pioneered the use of therapeutic drugs.

Why not? No more a myth than pelts should be
Thus fabricated into bricks of gold.

If rat-skins, why not tweeds? If looms could take
Raw wool and twill it into selling shape,
They could under the draper's weaving mind
Be patterning gold braid:
So thought George Stephen.[1]

His legs less sturdy than his cousin Donald's,
His eyes were just as furiously alert,   660
His line of vision ran from the north-west
To the Dutch-held St Paul-Pacific Railway.
Allied with Smith, Kitson and Kennedy,
Angus, Jim Hill and Duncan McIntyre,
Could he buy up this semi-bankrupt Road
And turn the northern traffic into it?
Chief bricklayer of all the Scotian clans,
And foremost as a banking metallurgist,
He took the parchments at their lowest level
And mineralized them, roasted them to shape,   670
Then mortared them into the pyramid,
Till with the trowel-stretching exercise
He grew so Atlas-strong that he could carry
A mountain like a namesake on his shoulders.[2]

*(The Charter granted to The Canadian Pacific Railway, February
17, 1881, with George Stephen as first President . . . One William Cornelius Van Horne[3] arrives in Winnipeg, December 31,
1881, and there late at night, forty below zero, gives vent to a
soliloquy.)*

Stephen had laid his raw hands on Van Horne,
Pulled him across the border, sent him up
To get the feel of northern temperatures.
He knew through Hill[4] the story of his life
And found him made to order. Nothing less
Than geologic space his field of work,   680
He had in Illinois explored the creeks
And valleys, brooded on the rocks and quarries.
Using slate fragments, he became a draughtsman,
Bringing to life a landscape or a cloud,
Turning a tree into a beard, a cliff
Into a jaw, a creek into a mouth

---

[1]See above, p. 218, n. 7.
[2]Van Horne named Mount Stephen in the Rockies after him, and in 1891 George Stephen became
Baron Mount Stephen.
[3](1843-1915); Van Horne, an American, became general manager of the CPR in 1881.
[4]James Hill (1838-1916), the Canadian-born American investor who was responsible for the formation of the Canadian group (which included George Stephen) that purchased the St Paul and Pacific
Railway in 1877, recommended Van Horne to Stephen as 'a man of great mental and physical power
to carry this line through'.

With banks for lips. He loved to work on shadows.
Just now the man was forcing the boy's stature,
The while the youth tickled the man within.
Companioned by the shade of Agassiz,[5]   690
He would come home, his pockets stuffed with fossils—
Crinoids and fish-teeth—and his tongue jabbering
Of the earth's crust before the birth of life,
Prophetic of the days when he would dig
Into Laurentian rock. The morse-key tick
And tape were things mesmeric—space and time
Had found a junction. Electricity
And rock, one novel to the coiling hand,
The other frozen in the lap of age,
Were playthings for the boy, work for the man.   700
As man he was the State's first operator;[6]
As boy he played a trick upon his boss
Who, cramped with current, fired him on the instant;
As man at school, escaping Latin grammar,
He tore the fly-leaf from the text to draw
The contour of a hill; as boy he sketched
The principal, gave him flapdoodle ears,
Bristled his hair, turned eyebrows into quills,
His whiskers into flying buttresses,
His eye-tusks into rusted railroad spikes,   710
And made a truss between his nose and chin.
Expelled again, he went back to the keys,
To bush and rock and found companionship
With quarry-men, stokers and station-masters,
Switchmen and locomotive engineers.

Now he was transferred to Winnipeg.
Of all the places in an unknown land
Chosen by Stephen for Van Horne, this was
The pivot on which he could turn his mind.
Here he could clap the future on the shoulder   720
And order Fate about as his lieutenant,
For he would take no nonsense from a thing
Called Destiny—the stars had to be with him.
He spent the first night in soliloquy,
Like Sir John A. but with a difference.
Sir John wanted to sleep but couldn't do it:
Van Horne could sleep but never wanted to.
It was a waste of time, his bed a place
Only to think or dream with eyes awake.
Opening a jack-knife, he went to the window,   730

[5]Jean-Louis Agassiz (1807-73) was a Swiss-American naturalist who greatly added to the knowledge of North American zoology and geology; 'Crinoids': small plant-like sea animals; 'crinoid' means 'lily-shaped'.

[6]Van Horne became a telegraph operator on the Illinois Central Railway when he was fourteen, thereby beginning a lifelong association with railroads; but he lost that first job because he set up a ground plate that would give a mild shock to anyone who stepped on it.

Scraped off the frost. Great treks ran through his mind,
East-west. Two centuries and a half gone by,
One trek had started from the Zuyder Zee
To the new Amsterdam.[7] 'Twas smooth by now,
Too smooth. His line of grandsires and their cousins
Had built a city from Manhattan dirt.
Another trek to Illinois; it too
Was smooth, but this new one it was his job
To lead, then build a highway which men claimed
Could not be built. Statesmen and engineers   740
Had blown their faces blue with their denials:
The men who thought so were asylum cases
Whose monomanias harmless up to now
Had not swept into cells. His bearded chin
Pressed to the pane, his eyes roved through the west.
He saw the illusion at its worst—the frost,
The steel precision of the studded heavens,
Relentless mirror of a covered earth.
His breath froze on the scrape: he cut again
And glanced at the direction west-by-south.   750
That westward trek was the American,
Union-Pacific—easy so he thought,
Their forty million stacked against his four.
Lonely and desolate this. He stocked his mind
With items of his task: the simplest first,
Though hard enough, the Prairies, then the Shore
North of the Lake—a quantity half-guessed.
Mackenzie like a balky horse had shied
And stopped at this. Van Horne knew well the reason,
But it was vital for the all-land route.   760
He peered through at the South. Down there Jim Hill
Was whipping up his horses on a road[8]
Already paved. The stations offered rest
With food and warmth, and their well-rounded names
Were tossed like apples to the public taste.

He made a mental note of his three items.
He underlined the Prairies, double-lined
The Shore and triple-lined *Beyond the Prairies,*
Began counting the Ranges—first the Rockies;
The Kicking Horse ran through them, this he knew;   770
The Selkirks? Not so sure. Some years before
Had Moberly and Perry[9] tagged a route

[7]i.e., New York City.
[8]The St Paul and Pacific Railway.
[9]Albert Perry accompanied Moberly on his 1866 search for a pass through the Selkirk Mountains. Though the quest was unsuccessful then, and also when Moberly returned in 1871-2, Major A. B. Rogers later found in Moberly's journal a description of a valley that was partially investigated by Perry in 1866. Acting on that lead, Rogers eventually found the pass (named after him) that would take the CPR from the Kicking Horse Pass in the Rockies through the Selkirks. The Columbia River system forms a large, elliptical loop in the Selkirks, with Rogers Pass lying in the middle. An aneroid barometer measures elevation.

Across the lariat loop of the Columbia.
Now Rogers was traversing it on foot,
Reading an aneroid and compass, chewing
Sea-biscuit and tobacco. Would the steel
Follow this trail? Van Horne looked farther west.
There was the Gold Range, there the Coastal Mountains.
He stopped, putting a period to the note,
As rivers troubled nocturnes in his ears.   780
His plans must not seep into introspection—
Call it a night, for morning was at hand,
And every hour of daylight was for work.

(Van Horne goes to Montreal to meet the Directors.)

He had agenda staggering enough
To bring the sweat even from Stephen's face.
As daring as his plans, so daring were
His promises. To build five hundred miles
Upon the prairies in one season: this
Was but a cushion for the jars ahead.
The Shore—he had to argue, stamp and fight   790
For this. The watercourses had been favoured,
The nation schooled to that economy.[1]
He saw that Stephen, after wiping beads
From face and forehead, had put both his hands
Deep in his pockets—just a habit merely
Of fingering change—but still Van Horne went on
To clinch his case: the north shore could avoid
The over-border route—a national point
If ever there was one. He promised this
As soon as he was through with buffalo-grass.   800
And then the little matter of the Rockies:
This must be swallowed without argument,
As obvious as space, clear as a charter.
But why the change in Fleming's survey? Why
The Kicking Horse and not the Yellowhead?
The national point again. The Kicking Horse
Was shorter, closer to the boundary line;
No rival road would build between the two.
He did not dwell upon the other Passes.
He promised all with surety of schedule,   810
And with a self-imposed serenity
That dried the sweat upon the Board Room faces.

NUMBER ONE

Oak Lake to Calgary. Van Horne took off
His coat. The North must wait, for that would mean
His shirt as well. First and immediate

---

[1]Many opponents of a transcontinental railway system thought that freight should be shipped across
Lake Superior by boat, believing that a mixed transportation system of rail and water would avoid the
difficulties of laying track on the North Shore.

This prairie pledge—five hundred miles,[2] and it
Was winter. Failure of this trial promise
Would mean—no, it must not be there for meaning.
An order from him carried no repeal:
It was as final as an execution.   820
A cable started rolling mills in Europe:
A tap of Morse sent hundreds to the bush,
Where axes swung on spruce and the saws sang,
Changing the timber into pyramids
Of poles and sleepers. Clicks, despatches, words,
Like lanterns in a night conductor's hands,
Signalled the wheels: a nod put Shaughnessy[3]
In Montreal: supplies moved on the minute.
Thousands of men and mules and horses slipped
Into their togs and harness night and day.   830
The grass that fed the buffalo was turned over,
The black alluvial mould laid bare, the bed
Levelled and scraped. As individuals
The men lost their identity; as groups,
As gangs, they massed, divided, subdivided,
Like numerals only—sub-contractors, gangs
Of engineers, and shovel gangs for bridges,
Culverts, gangs of mechanics stringing wires,
Loading, unloading and reloading gangs,
Gangs for the fish-plates[4] and the spiking gangs,   840
Putting a silver polish on the nails.
But neither men nor horses ganged like mules:
Wiser than both they learned to unionize.
Some instinct in their racial nether regions
Had taught them how to sniff the five-hour stretch
Down to the fine arithmetic of seconds.
They tired out their rivals and they knew it.
They'd stand for overwork, not overtime.
Faster than workmen could fling down their shovels,
They could unhinge their joints, unhitch their tendons;   850
Jumping the foreman's call, they brayed *'Unhook'*
With a defiant, corporate instancy.
The promise which looked first without redemption
Was being redeemed. From three to seven miles
A day the parallels were being laid,
Though Eastern throats were hoarse with the old question—
Where are the settlements? And whence the gift
Of tongues which could pronounce place-names that purred
Like cats in relaxation after kittens?
Was it a part of the same pledge to turn   860
A shack into a bank for notes renewed;

---

[2] When Van Horne became manager of the CPR he promised the directors that he would lay 500 miles
of track in the 1882 season.
[3] Thomas Shaughnessy (1853-1933), known for his organizing ability, joined the CPR in 1882 as its
purchasing agent.
[4] Connecting metal plates, bolted alongside two rails where they meet to make them stable.

To call a site a city when men saw
Only a water-tank? This was an act
Of faith indeed—substance of things unseen—
Which would convert preachers to miracles,
Lure teachers into lean-to's for their classes.
And yet it happened that while labourers
Were swearing at their blisters in the evening
And straightening out their spinal kinks at dawn,
The tracks joined up Oak Lake to Calgary.   870

NUMBER TWO

On the North Shore a reptile[5] lay asleep—
A hybrid that the myths might have conceived,
But not delivered, as progenitor
Of crawling, gliding things upon the earth.
She lay snug in the folds of a huge boa
Whose tail had covered Labrador and swished
Atlantic tides, whose body coiled itself
Around the Hudson Bay, then curled up north
Through Manitoba and Saskatchewan
To Great Slave Lake. In continental reach   880
The neck went past the Great Bear Lake until
Its head was hidden in the Arctic Seas.
This folded reptile was asleep or dead:
So motionless, she seemed stone dead—just seemed:
She was too old for death, too old for life,[6]
For as if jealous of all living forms
She had lain there before bivalves began
To catacomb their shells on western mountains.
Somewhere within this life-death zone she sprawled,
Torpid upon a rock-and-mineral mattress.   890
Ice-ages had passed by and over her,
But these, for all their motion, had but sheared
Her spotty carboniferous hair or made
Her ridges stand out like the spikes of molochs.[7]
Her back grown stronger every million years,
She had shed water by the longer rivers
To Hudson Bay and by the shorter streams
To the great basins to the south, had filled
Them up, would keep them filled until the end
Of Time.   900

          Was this the thing Van Horne set out
To conquer? When Superior lay there

---

[5]Pratt uses two images of reptiles as personifications of the Laurentian Shield. The first, a sleeping reptile, is a female lizard that corresponds to the area of the shield along the North Shore of Lake Superior; it lies 'snug' against a larger reptile, a huge boa constrictor that represents the full extent of the Laurentian Shield itself.

[6]Because the Shield is composed of rock from the Precambrian period, dating mostly from before the advent of recorded life on earth.

[7]Spiny-backed lizard of Australia, said to be the most grotesque of living reptiles; also the name of one of Satan's company in John Milton's *Paradise Lost*.

With its inviting levels? Blake, Mackenzie,
Offered this water like a postulate.
'Why those twelve thousand men sent to the North?
Nonsense and waste with utter bankruptcy.'
And the Laurentian monster at the first
Was undisturbed, presenting but her bulk
To the invasion. All she had to do
Was lie there neither yielding nor resisting.   910
Top-heavy with accumulated power
And overgrown survival without function,
She changed her spots as though brute rudiments
Of feeling foreign to her native hour
Surprised her with a sense of violation
From an existence other than her own—
Or why take notice of this unknown breed,
This horde of bipeds that could toil like ants,
Could wake her up and keep her irritated?
They tickled her with shovels, dug pickaxes,   920
Into her scales and got under her skin,
And potted holes in her with drills and filled
Them up with what looked like fine grains of sand,
Black sand. It wasn't noise that bothered her,
For thunder she was used to from her cradle—
The head-push and nose-blowing of the ice,
The height and pressure of its body: these
Like winds native to clime and habitat
Had served only to lull her drowsing coils.
It was not size or numbers that concerned her.   930
It was their foreign build, their gait of movement.
They did not crawl—nor were they born with wings.
They stood upright and walked, shouted and sang;
They needed air—that much was true—their mouths
Were open but the tongue was alien.
The sounds were not the voice of winds and waters,
Nor that of any beasts upon the earth.
She took them first with lethargy, suffered
The rubbing of her back—those little jabs
Of steel were like the burrowing of ticks   940
In an elk's hide needing an antler point,
Or else left in a numb monotony.
These she could stand but when the breed
Advanced west on her higher vertebrae,
Kicking most insolently at her ribs,
Pouring black powder in her cavities,
And making not the clouds but her insides
The home of fire and thunder, then she gave
Them trial of her strength: the trestles tottered;
Abutments, bridges broke; her rivers flooded: 950
She summoned snow and ice, and then fell back
On the last weapon in her armoury—
The first and last—her passive corporal bulk,
To stay or wreck the schedule of Van Horne.

NUMBER THREE

The big one was the mountains—seas indeed!
With crests whiter than foam: they poured like seas,
Fluting the green banks of the pines and spruces.
An eagle-flight above they hid themselves
In clouds. They carried space upon their ledges.
Could these be overridden frontally,   960
Or like typhoons outsmarted on the flanks?
And what were on the flanks? The troughs and canyons,
Passes more dangerous to the navigator
Than to Magellan when he tried to read
The barbarous language of his Strait by calling
For echoes from the rocky hieroglyphs
Playing their pranks of hide-and-seek in fog:
As stubborn too as the old North-West Passage,
More difficult, for ice-packs could break up;
And as for bergs, what polar architect   970
Could stretch his compass points to draught such peaks
As kept on rising there beyond the foothills?
And should the bastions of the Rockies yield
To this new human and unnatural foe,
Would not the Selkirks stand? This was a range
That looked like some strange dread outside a door
Which gave its name but would not show its features,
Leaving them to the mind to guess at. This
Meant tunnels—would there be no end to boring?
There must be some day. Fleming and his men   980
Had nosed their paths like hounds; but paths and trails,
Measured in every inch by chain and transit,
Looked easy and seductive on a chart.
The rivers out there did not flow: they tumbled.
The cataracts were fed by glaciers;
Eddies were thought as whirlpools in the Gorges,
And gradients had paws that tore up tracks.

Terror and beauty like twin signal flags
Flew on the peaks for men to keep their distance.
The two combined as in a storm at sea—   990
'Stay on the shore and take your fill of breathing,
But come not to the decks and climb the rigging.'
The Ranges could put cramps in hands and feet
Merely by the suggestion of the venture.
They needed miles to render up their beauty,
As if the gods in high aesthetic moments,
Resenting the profanity of touch,
Chiselled this sculpture for the eye alone.

(Van Horne in momentary meditation at the Foothills.)

His name was now a legend. The North Shore,
Though not yet conquered, yet had proved that he   1000
Could straighten crooked roads by pulling at them,

Shear down a hill and drain a bog or fill
A valley overnight. Fast as a bobcat,
He'd climb and run across the shakiest trestle
Or, with a locomotive short of coal,
He could supply the head of steam himself.
He breakfasted on bridges, lunched on ties;
Drinking from gallon pails, he dined on moose.
He could tire out the lumberjacks; beat hell
From workers but no more than from himself.   1010
Only the devil or Paul Bunyan shared
With him the secret of perpetual motion,
And when he moved among his men they looked
For shoulder sprouts upon the Flying Dutchman.[8]

But would his legend crack upon the mountains?
There must be no retreat: his bugles knew
Only one call—the summons to advance
Against two fortresses: the mind, the rock.
To prove the first defence was vulnerable,
To tap the treasury at home and then   1020
Untie the purse-strings of the Londoners,
As hard to loosen as salt-water knots—
That job was Stephen's, Smith's, Tupper's, Macdonald's.
He knew its weight: had heard, as well as they,
Blake pumping at his pulmonary bellows,
And if the speeches made the House shock-proof
Before they ended, they could still peal forth
From print more durable than spoken tones.
Blake had returned to the attack and given
Sir John the ague with another phrase   1030
As round and as melodious as the first:
'The Country's wealth, its millions after millions
Squandered—LOST IN THE GORGES OF THE FRASER':[9]
A beautiful but ruinous piece of music
That could only be drowned with drums and fifes.
Tupper, fighting with fists and nails and toes,
Had taken the word *scandal* which had cut
His master's ballots, and had turned the edge
With his word *slander,* but Blake's *sea,* how turn
That edge? Now this last devastating phrase!   1040
But let Sir John and Stephen answer this
Their way. Van Horne must answer it in his.

---

[8]The ghostly captain of a legendary ship doomed to sail the seas forever.
[9]On 15-16 April 1880 Blake delivered his long speech opposing construction west of the Rockies, concluding in part: 'All that we can raise by taxes or loans, all that we can beg or borrow, is to be sunk in the gorges of the Fraser. . . . do not by your present action based on airy dreams and vain imaginings risk the ruin of your country.'

INTERNECINE STRIFE

The men were fighting foes which had themselves
Waged elemental civil wars and still
Were hammering one another at this moment.
The peaks and ranges flung from ocean beds
Had wakened up one geologic morning
To find their scalps raked off, their lips punched in,
The colour of their skins charged with new dyes.
Some of them did not wake or but half-woke;   1050
Prone or recumbent with the eerie shapes
Of creatures that would follow them. Weather
Had acted on their spines and frozen them
To stegosaurs[1] or, taking longer cycles,
Divining human features, had blown back
Their hair and, pressing on their cheeks and temples,
Bestowed on them the gravity of mummies.
But there was life and power which belied
The tombs. Guerrilla evergreens were climbing
In military order: at the base   1060
The *ponderosa* pine; the fir backed up
The spruce; and it the Stoney Indian lodge-poles;[2]
And these the white-barks; then, deciduous,
The outpost suicidal Lyell larches[3]
Aiming at summits, digging scraggy roots
Around the boulders in the thinning soil,
Till they were stopped dead at the timber limit—
Rock *versus* forest with the rock prevailing.
Or with the summer warmth it was the ice,
In treaty with the rock to hold a line   1070
As stubborn as a Balkan boundary,
That left its caves to score the Douglases,[4]
And smother them with half a mile of dirt,
And making snow-sheds, covering the camps,
Futile as parasols in polar storms.
One enemy alone had battled rock
And triumphed: searching levels like lost broods,
Keen on their ocean scent, the rivers cut
The quartzite, licked the slate and softened it,
Till mud solidified was mud again,   1080
And then, digesting it like earthworms, squirmed
Along the furrows with one steering urge—
To navigate the mountains in due time
Back to their home in worm-casts on the tides.

Into this scrimmage came the fighting men,

---

[1]Dinosaurs with a double row of upright bony plates along their backs.
[2]The lodge-pole pine, characterized by slim, straight trunks; 'white-barks': the white-bark pine.
[3]Or subalpine larch, which thrives at the timberline. The larch is the only tree with needlelike leaves that sheds them, hence it is deciduous.
[4]Douglas firs.

And all but rivers were their enemies.
Whether alive or dead the bush resisted:
Alive, it must be slain with axe and saw,
If dead, it was in tangle at their feet.
The ice could hit men as it hit the spruces.   1090
Even the rivers had betraying tricks,
Watched like professed allies across a border.
They smiled from fertile plains and easy runs
Of valley gradients: their eyes got narrow,
Full of suspicion at the gorges where
They leaped and put the rickets in the trestles.
Though natively in conflict with the rock,
Both leagued against invasion. At Hell's Gate[5]
A mountain laboured and brought forth a bull
Which, stranded in mid-stream, was fighting back   1100
The river, and the fight turned on the men,
Demanding from this route their bread and steel.
And there below the Gate was the Black Canyon
With twenty-miles-an-hour burst of speed.

(ONDERDONK BUILDS THE 'SKUZZY'[6] TO FORCE THE PASSAGE.)

'Twas more than navigation: only eagles
Might follow up this run; the spawning salmon
Gulled by the mill-race had returned to rot
Their upturned bellies in the canyon eddies.
Two engines at the stern, a forrard[7] winch,
Steam-powered, failed to stem the cataract.   1110
The last resource was shoulders, arms and hands.
Fifteen men at the capstan,[8] creaking hawsers,
Two hundred Chinese tugging at shore ropes
To keep her bow-on from the broadside drift,
The *Skuzzy* under steam and muscle took
The shoals and rapids, and warped through the Gate,
Until she reached the navigable water—
The adventure was not sailing: it was climbing.

As hard a challenge were the precipices
Worn water-smooth and sheer a thousand feet.   1120
Surveyors from the edges looked for footholds,
But, finding none, they tried marine manoeuvres.
Out of a hundred men they drafted sailors
Whose toes as supple as their fingers knew
The wash of reeling decks, whose knees were hardened

---

[5]The most treacherous section of the Fraser canyon.
[6]A small, sturdy steamboat that Onderdonk had built when he became unhappy with the cost of hauling freight ('bread and steel') over the wagon road. Few believed that the boat would be able to navigate the treacherous rapids.
[7]Forward.
[8]Vertical revolving barrel onto which the cables ('hawsers') were wound; it was turned by men walking around it, pushing on horizontal levers. This was used to supplement the steam-driven forward winch.

Through tying gaskets⁹ at the royal yards:
They lowered them with knotted ropes and drew them
Along the face until the lines were strung
Between the juts. Barefooted, dynamite
Strapped to their waists, the sappers¹ followed, treading   1130
The spider films and chipping holes for blasts,
Until the cliffs delivered up their features
Under the civil discipline of roads.

RING, RING THE BELLS

Ring, ring the bells, but not the engine bells:
Today only the ritual of the steeple
Chanted to the dull tempo of the toll.
Sorrow is stalking through the camps, speaking
A common mother-tongue. 'Twill leave tomorrow
To turn that language on a Blackfoot tepee,
Then take its leisurely Pacific time   1140
To tap its fingers on a coolie's door.
Ring, ring the bells but not the engine bells:
Today only that universal toll,
For granite, mixing dust with human lime,
Had so compounded bodies into boulders
As to untype the blood, and, then, the Fraser,
Catching the fragments from the dynamite,
Had bleached all birthmarks from her swirling dead.

Tomorrow and the engine bells again!

THE LAKE OF MONEY

(The appeal to the Government for a loan of twenty-two-and-a-
half million, 1883.)

Sir John began to muse on his excuses.   1150
Was there no bottom to this lake? One mile
Along that northern strip had cost—how much?
Eleven dollars to the inch. The Road
In all would measure up to ninety millions,
And diverse hands were plucking at his elbow.
The Irish and the Dutch he could outface,
Outquip. He knew Van Horne and Shaughnessy
Had little time for speeches—one was busy
In grinding out two thousand miles; the other
Was working wizardry on creditors,   1160
Pulling rabbits from hats, gold coins from sleeves
In Montreal. As for his foes like Blake,
He thanked his household gods the Irishman

---

⁹A small rope that secures a furled sail to its supporting yard-arm.
¹Men who dig tunnels or trenches for blasting to undermine the mountain walls; 'films': filaments, fine threads, i.e., the men climbing down the rock walls on ropes are like spiders walking along their webs.

Could claim only a viscous brand of humour,
Heavy, impenetrable till the hour
To laugh had taken on a chestnut colour.
But Stephen was his friend, hard to resist.
And there was Smith. He knew that both had pledged
Their private fortunes as security
For the construction of the Road. But that   1170
Was not enough. Sir John had yet to dip
And scrape farther into the public pocket,
Explore its linings: his, the greater task;
His, to commit a nation to the risk.
How could he face the House with pauper hands?
He had to deal with Stephen first—a man
Laconic, nailing points and clinching them.
Oratory, the weapon of the massed assemblies
Was not the weapon here—Scot meeting Scot.
The burr was hard to take; and Stephen had   1180
A Banffshire-cradled r.[2] Drilling the ear,
It paralysed the nerves, hit the red cells.
The logic in the sound, escaping print,
Would seep through channels and befog the cortex.

Sir John counted the exits of discretion:
Disguise himself? A tailor might do much;
A barber might trim down his mane, brush back
The forelock, but no artist of massage,
Kneading that face from brow to nasal tip,
Could change a chunk of granite into talc.   1190
His rheumatism? Yet he still could walk.
Neuralgia did not interfere with speech.
The bronchial tubing needed softer air?
Vacations could not cancel all appointments.
Men saw him in the flesh at Ottawa.
He had to speak this week, wheedling committees,
Much easier than to face a draper's clerk,[3]
Tongue-trained on Aberdonian bargain-counters.
He raised his closed left hand to straighten out
His fingers one by one—four million people.[4]   1200
He had to pull a trifle on that fourth,
Not so resilient as the other three.
Only a wrench could stir the little finger
Which answered with a vicious backward jerk.

The dollar fringes of one hundred million
Were smirching up the blackboard of his mind.
But curving round and through them was the thought

[2]That is, Stephen, born in Dufftown in Banffshire, Scotland, did not have the rough burr to his r that characterized the speech of the Glasgow-born Macdonald—whose accent was the kind, as Pratt says earlier, that allowed men to 'win an argument upon a burr' (line 81).
[3]Stephen, who had worked in a dry-goods store in Aberdeen before coming to Canada in 1850.
[4]The approximate population of Canada.

He could not sponge away. Had he not fathered
The Union? Prodigy indeed it was
From Coast to Coast. Was not the Line essential?   1210
What was this fungus sprouting from his rind
That left him at the root less clear a growth
Than this Dutch immigrant, William Van Horne?
The name suggested artificial land
Rescued from swamp by bulging dikes and ditches;
And added now to that were bogs and sloughs
And that most cursèd diabase⁵ which God
Had left from the explosions of his wrath.
And yet this man was challenging his pride.
North-Sea ancestral moisture on his beard,   1220
Van Horne was now the spokesman for the West,
The champion of an all-Canadian route,
The Yankee who had come straight over, linked
His name and life with the Canadian nation.
Besides, he had infected the whole camp.
Whether acquired or natural, the stamp
Of faith had never left his face. Was it
The artist's instinct which had made the Rockies
And thence the Selkirks, scenes of tourist lure,
As easy for the passage of an engine   1230
As for the flight of eagles? Miracles
Became his thought: the others took their cue
From him. They read the lines upon his lips.
But miracles did not spring out of air.
Under the driving will and sweltering flesh
They came from pay-cars loaded with the cash.
So that was why Stephen had called so often—
Money—that lake of money, bonds, more bonds.

(The Bill authorizing the loan stubbornly carries the House.)

DYNAMITE ON THE NORTH SHORE

The lizard was in sanguinary mood.
She had been waked again: she felt her sleep   1240
Had lasted a few seconds of her time.
The insects had come back—the ants, if ants
They were—dragging *those* trees, *those* logs athwart
Her levels, driving in *those* spikes; and how
The long grey snakes unknown within her region
Wormed from the east, unstriped, sunning themselves
Uncoiled upon the logs and then moved on,
Growing each day, ever keeping abreast!
She watched them, waiting for a bloody moment,
Until the borers halted at a spot,   1250
The most unvulnerable of her whole column,
Drove in that iron, wrenched it in the holes,

⁵A form of basalt, a hard rock formed from crystallized lava.

Hitting, digging, twisting. Why that spot?
Not this the former itch. That sharp proboscis
Was out for more than self-sufficing blood
About the cuticle:[6] 'twas out for business
In the deep layers and the arteries.
And this consistent punching at her belly
With fire and thunder slapped her like an insult,
As with the blasts the caches of her broods   1260
Broke—nickel, copper, silver and fool's gold,
Burst from their immemorial dormitories
To sprawl indecent in the light of day.
Another warning—this time different.

Westward above her webs she had a trap—
A thing called muskeg, easy on the eyes
Stung with the dust of gravel. Cotton grass,
Its white spires blending with the orchids,
Peeked through green table-cloths of sphagnum moss.
Carnivorous bladder-wort studded the acres,   1270
Passing the water-fleas through their digestion.
Sweet-gale and sundew[7] edged the dwarf black spruce;
And herds of cariboo had left their hoof-marks,
Betraying visual solidity,
But like the thousands of the pitcher plants,
Their downward-pointing hairs alluring insects,
Deceptive—and the men were moving west!
Now was her time. She took three engines, sank them
With seven tracks down through the hidden lake
To the rock bed, then over them she spread   1280
A counterpane of leather-leaf[8] and slime.
A warning, that was all for now. 'Twas sleep
She wanted, sleep, for drowsing was her pastime
And waiting through eternities of seasons.
As for intruders bred for skeletons—
Some day perhaps when ice began to move,
Or some convulsion ran fires through her tombs,
She might stir in her sleep and far below
The reach of steel and blast of dynamite,
She'd claim their bones as her possessive right   1290
And wrap them cold in her pre-Cambrian folds.

---

[6]Here, the epidermis, i.e., the surface.
[7]A shrub and a flower that, like the other plants mentioned in this passage, attests to the bog-like quality of the apparently solid muskeg. The sundew, like the bladder-wort and the pitcher plant, is carnivorous, trapping and consuming insects in its sticky leaves.
[8]A low evergreen shrub, so called because of the texture of its leaves.

THREATS OF SECESSION[9]

The Lady's face was flushed. Thirteen years now
Since that engagement ring adorned her finger!
Adorned? Betrayed. She often took it off
And flung it angrily upon the dresser,
Then took excursions with her sailor-lover.
Had that man[1] with a throat like Ottawa,
That tailored suitor in a cut-away,
Presumed compliance on her part? High time
To snub him for delay—for was not time   1300
The marrow of agreement? At the mirror
She tried to cream a wrinkle from her forehead,
Toyed with the ring, replaced it and removed it.
Harder, she thought, to get it on and off—
This like the wrinkle meant but one thing, age.
So not too fast; play safe. Perhaps the man
Was not the master of his choice. Someone
Within the family group might well contest
Exotic marriage. Still, her plumes were ruffled
By Blake's two-nights' address before the Commons: 1310
Three lines inside the twenty-thousand words
Had maddened her. She searched for hidden meanings—
'Should she insist on those preposterous terms
And threaten to secede, then let her go,
Better than ruin the country.' [2] *'Let her go,'*
And *'ruin'*—language this to shake her bodice.
Was this indictment of her character,
Or worse, her charm? Or was it just plain dowry?[3]
For this last one at least she had an answer.
Pay now or separation[4]—this the threat.   1320
Dipping the ring into a soapy lather,[5]
She pushed it to the second knuckle, twirled
It past. Although the diamond was off-colour,
She would await its partner ring of gold—
The finest carat; yes, by San Francisco!

---

[9]By 1875 British Columbia—discouraged by the lack of progress on the railway and by the Liberal repudiation of the agreed-upon deadline—began to threaten to sever its alliance with the Dominion; this threat was repeated even after Macdonald returned to power in 1878, and as late as 1881 when discontent in Victoria over the question of a rail link to Vancouver Island came to a head. It was not until 1883 that all differences were finally resolved.

[1]Macdonald.

[2]Paraphrased from Blake's speech of 15-16 April 1880; Blake had expressed such sentiments as early as his speech of 3-4 November 1873 (see p. 223, note 7) and had repeated them in the Aurora speech (see p. 230 note 2).

[3]Here, the gift given by a man to his bride: British Columbia fears that her dowry is Blake's constant attacks.

[4]As a result of Lord Carnarvon's attempts to find an equitable resolution of the differences between British Columbia and Ottawa, the Liberals offered $750,000 in cash to the province as compensation for delays in completing the railroad. British Columbia initially declined the offer because it seemed to be compensating for future delays as well as past ones, but in 1881 the province demanded the money.

[5]Possibly an allusion to the fact that at that time Victoria—the heart of secessionist feeling—had a soap factory prominently located near the harbour.

BACK TO THE MOUNTAINS

As grim an enemy as rock was time.
The little men from five-to-six feet high,
From three-to-four score years in lease of breath,
Were flung in double-front against them both
In years a billion strong; so long was it   1330
Since brachiapods[6] in mollusc habitats
Were clamping shells on weed in ocean mud.
Now only yesterday had Fleming's men,
Searching for toeholds on the sides of cliffs,
Five thousand feet above sea-level, set
A tripod's leg upon a trilobite.[7]
And age meant pressure, density. Sullen
With aeons, mountains would not stand aside;
Just block the path—morose but without anger,
No feeling in the menace of their frowns,   1340
Immobile for they had no need of motion;
Their veins possessed no blood—they carried quartzite.
Frontal assault! To go through them direct
Seemed just as inconceivable as ride
Over their peaks. But go through them the men
Were ordered and their weapons were their hands
And backs, pickaxes, shovels, hammers, drills
And dynamite—against the rock and time;
For here the labour must be counted up
In months subject to clauses of a contract   1350
Distinguished from the mortgage-run an age
Conceded to the trickle of the rain
In building river-homes. The men bored in,
The mesozoic rock arguing the inches.

This was a kind of surgery unknown
To mountains or the mothers of the myths.
These had a chloroform in leisured time,
Squeezing a swollen handful of light-seconds,
When water like a wriggling casuist[8]
Had probed and found the areas for incision.   1360
Now time was rushing labour—inches grew
To feet, to yards: the drills—the single jacks,
The double jacks—drove in and down; the holes
Gave way to excavations, these to tunnels,
Till men sodden with mud and roof-drip steamed
From sunlight through the tar-black to the sunlight.

[6]A bivalve mollusc that Darwin singled out as an example of a life-form that had not changed much
from a remote geological epoch; usually spelled 'brachiopod'.
[7]Fossil, one of the earliest anthropoids, extinct since the Paleozoic period.
[8]Here, one who specializes in quibbling, convoluted arguments.

HOLLOW ECHOES FROM THE TREASURY VAULT

Sir John was tired as to the point of death.
His chin was anchored to his chest. Was Blake
Right after all? And was Mackenzie right?
Superior could be travelled on. Besides,   1370
It had a bottom, but those northern bogs
Like quicksands could go down to the earth's core.
Compared with them, quagmires of ancient legend
Were backyard puddles for old ducks. To sink
Those added millions down that wallowing hole!
He thought now through his feet. Many a time
When argument cemented opposition,
And hopeless seemed his case, he could think up
A tale to laugh the benches to accord.
No one knew better, when a point had failed   1380
The brain, how to divert it through the ribs.
But now his stock of stories had run out.
This was exhaustion at its coma level.
Or was he sick? Never had spots like these
Assailed his eyes. He could not rub them out—
Those shifting images—was it the sunset
Refracted through the bevelled window edges?
He shambled over and drew down the blind;
Returned and slumped; it was no use; the spots
Were there. No light could ever shoot this kind   1390
Of orange through a prism, or this blue,
And what a green! The spectrum was ruled out;
Its bands were too inviolate. He rubbed
The lids again—a brilliant gold appeared
Upon a silken backdrop of pure white,
And in the centre, red—a scarlet red,
A dancing, rampant and rebellious red
That like a stain spread outward covering
The vision field. He closed his eyes and listened:
Why, what was that? 'Twas bad enough that light   1400
Should play such pranks upon him, but must sound
Crash the Satanic game, reverberate
A shot fifteen years after it was fired,
And culminate its echoes with the thud
Of marching choruses outside his window:

'We'll hang Riel up the Red River,
And he'll roast in hell forever,
We'll hang him up the River
With a yah-yah-yah.'

The noose was for the shot: 'twas blood for blood;   1410
The death of Riel for the death of Scott.[9]
What could not Blake do with that on the Floor,
Or that young, tall, bilingual advocate[1]
Who with the carriage of his syllables
Could bid an audience like an orchestra
Answer his body swaying like a reed?
Colours and sounds made riot of his mind—
White horses in July processional prance,
The blackrobe's swish, the Métis' sullen tread,
And out there in the rear the treaty-wise   1420
Full-breeds with buffalo wallows on their foreheads.

This he could stand no longer, sick indeed:
Send for his doctor, the first thought, then No;
The doctor would advise an oculist,
The oculist return him to the doctor,
The doctor would see-saw him to another—
A specialist on tumours of the brain,
And he might recommend close-guarded rest
In some asylum—Devil take them all,
He had his work to do. He glanced about   1430
And spied his medicine upon the sideboard;
Amber it was, distilled from Highland springs,
That often had translated age to youth
And boiled his blood on a victorious rostrum.
Conviction seized him as he stood, for here
At least he was not cut for compromise,
Nor curried to his nickname Old Tomorrow.
Deliberation in his open stance,
He trenched[2] a deep one, gurgled and sat down.
What were those paltry millions after all?   1440
They stood between completion of the Road
And bankruptcy of both Road and Nation.
Those north-shore gaps must be closed in by steel.
It did not need exhilarated judgment
To see the sense of that. To send the men
Hop-skip-and-jump upon lake ice to board

---

[9]During the Red River Rebellion of 1870 the Irish-Canadian Thomas Scott was taken prisoner by Louis Riel and executed for attempting to raise armed resistance against Riel's Provisional Government. Though the passing of the Manitoba Act resolved the immediate crisis, there was much festering bitterness on both sides: Riel—who spent many of the next fifteen years in flight or in exile—thought that he had been cheated of a promised immunity; public opinion in Ontario was that Scott's murder had gone unpunished. When, in 1885, Riel led a new armed uprising in Saskatchewan, Canadian troops were rushed into the area by means of the newly completed railway and the rebels were quickly defeated. Late in that year Riel was hanged—as much for the Scott killing as for his later acts. French Quebec viewed the dispute between Macdonald's Conservative government and the Riel-led Métis as one that had race and religion as its real issues, and in consequence permanently shifted its political allegiance away from the Conservatives.
[1]Wilfrid Laurier (1841-1919), who became a member of Parliament in 1874 and subsequently served in Mackenzie's cabinet; he later succeeded Blake as leader of the Liberal opposition (1887).
[2]Drained.

The flatcars was a revelry for imps.
And all that cutting through the mountain rock,
Four years of it and more, and all for nothing,
Unless those gaps were spanned, bedded and railed.   1450
To quit the Road, to have the Union broken
Was irredeemable. He rose, this time
Invincibility carved on his features,
Hoisted a second, then drew up the blind.
He never saw a sunset just like this.
He lingered in the posture of devotion:
That sun for sure was in the west, or was it?
Soon it would be upholstering the clouds
Upon the Prairies, Rockies and the Coast:
He turned and sailed back under double-reef,[3]   1460
Cabined himself inside an armchair, stretched
His legs to their full length under the table.
Something miraculous had changed the air—
A chemistry that knew how to extract
The iron from the will: the spots had vanished
And in their place an unterrestrial nimbus[4]
Circled his hair: the jerks had left his nerves:
The millions kept on shrinking or were running
From right to left: the fourth arthritic digit
Was straight, and yes, by heaven, the little fifth   1470
Which up to now was just a calcium hook
Was suppling in the Hebridean warmth.[5]
A blessèd peace fell like a dew upon him,
And soon, in trance, drenched in conciliation,
He hiccuped gently—'Now let S-S-Stephen come!'

(The Government grants the Directors the right to issue
$35,000,000, guarantees $20,000,000, the rest to be issued by
the Railway Directors.[6] Stephen goes to London, and Lord Revelstoke, speaking for the House of Baring, takes over the issue.)

SUSPENSE IN THE MONTREAL BOARD ROOM

Evening had settled hours before its time
Within the Room and on the face of Angus.
Dejection overlaid his social fur,
Rumpled his side-burns, left moustache untrimmed.
The vision of his Bank, his future Shops,   1480

[3]With his sails reduced by two reefs or folds; i.e., ready for rough weather.
[4]Celestial aura; halo.
[5]Lines 1469 ff. may be paraphrased: Macdonald's fourth finger, previously difficult to straighten
(lines 1201-2), is now more flexible, as is the little finger (see lines 1203-4), which no longer seems
to be a hook of 'calcium' (i.e., bone); both have been made supple by the effects of the Scotch
whisky ('Hebridean warmth') drunk in lines 1430-4.
[6]On 20 July 1885 the Canadian Pacific Bill was passed, narrowly averting the bankruptcy of the company and its principals; thirty-five million dollars of unsaleable stock was cancelled and replaced by
bonds, of which the government took twenty million dollars' worth. Through the influence of Tupper, the London firm of Baring and Glyn, headed by Lord Revelstoke, took the remainder of the
issue.

Was like his outlook for the London visit.
Van Horne was fronting him with a like visage
Except for two spots glowing on his cheeks—
Dismay and anger at those empty pay-cars.
His mutterings were indistinct but final
As though he were reciting to himself
The Athanasian[7] damnatory clauses.
He felt the Receiver's[8] breath upon his neck:
To come so near the end, and then this hurdle!

Only one thing could penetrate that murk—   1490
A cable pledge from London, would it come?
Till now refusal or indifference
Had met the overtures. Would Stephen turn
The trick?
                A door-knock and a telegram
With Stephen's signature! Van Horne ripped it
Apart. Articulation failed his tongue,
But Angus got the meaning from his face
And from a noisy sequence of deductions:—
An inkstand coasted through the office window,   1500
Followed by shredded maps and blotting-pads,
Fluttering like shad-flies in a summer gale;
A bookshelf smitten by a fist collapsed;
Two chairs flew to the ceiling—one retired,
The other roosted on the chandelier.
Some thirty years erased like blackboard chalk,
Van Horne was in a school at Illinois.
Triumphant over his two-hundred weight,
He leaped and turned a cartwheel on the table,
Driving heel sparables[9] into the oak,   1510
Came down to teach his partner a Dutch dance;
And in the presence of the messenger,
Who stared immobilized at what he thought
New colours in the managerial picture,
Van Horne took hold of Angus bodily,
Tore off his tie and collar, mauled his shirt,
And stuffed a Grand Trunk folder down his breeches.

*(The last gap in the mountains—between the Selkirks and
Savona's Ferry—is closed.)*

The Road itself was like a stream that men
Had coaxed and teased or bullied out of Nature.
As if watching for weak spots in her codes,   1520
It sought for levels like the watercourses.
It sinuously took the bends, rejoiced

---

[7]The Athanasian Creed, a profession of faith found in the Book of Common Prayer, contains warnings for the man who does not 'hold fast' and 'keep whole' his faith: 'without doubt he will perish eternally.'
[8]Person appointed by the court to administer property after bankruptcy.
[9]The nails that fastened his heels to his shoes.

In plains and easy grades, found gaps, poured through them,
But hating steep descents avoided them.
Unlike the rivers which in full rebellion
Against the canyons' hydrophobic slaver[1]
Went to the limit of their argument:
Unlike again, the stream of steel had found
A way to climb, became a mountaineer.
From the Alberta plains it reached the Summit,   1530
And where it could not climb, it cut and curved,
Till from the Rockies to the Coastal Range
It had accomplished what the Rivers had,
Making a hundred clean Caesarian cuts,
And bringing to delivery in their time
Their smoky, lusty-screaming locomotives.

THE SPIKE

Silver or gold? Van Horne had rumbled 'Iron'.
No flags or bands announced this ceremony,
No Morse in circulation through the world,
And though the vital words like Eagle Pass,   1540
Craigellachie,[2] were trembling in their belfries,
No hands were at the ropes. The air was taut
With silences as rigid as the spruces
Forming the background in November mist.
More casual than camera-wise, the men
Could have been properties upon a stage,[3]
Except for road maps furrowing their faces.

Rogers, his both feet planted on a tie,
Stood motionless as ballast. In the rear,
Covering the scene with spirit-level eyes,   1550
Predestination on his chin, was Fleming.
The only one groomed for the ritual
From smooth silk hat and well-cut square-rig beard
Down through his Caledonian[4] longitude,
He was outstaturing others by a foot,
And upright as the mainmast of a brig.
Beside him, barely reaching to his waist,
A water-boy had wormed his way in front
To touch this last rail with his foot, his face
Upturned to see the cheek-bone crags of Rogers.   1560
The other side of Fleming, hands in pockets,
Eyes leaden-lidded under square-crowned hat,

[1]That is, the canyons' walls seem to drool as would a rabid dog.
[2]The driving of the last spike signifying the completion of the CPR (which was deliberately done without the elaborate ritual that marked the completion of the Union Pacific in the States) took place in the Eagle Pass; the place was called Craigellachie because of the name's significance for Smith and Stephen (see p. 218, conclusion of n. 7).
[3]The lines that follow are based on the famous photograph of the driving of the last spike.
[4]Scottish (poetic).

And puncheon-bellied[5] under overcoat,
Unsmiling at the focused lens—Van Horne.
Whatever ecstasy played round that rail
Did not leap to his face. Five years had passed,
Less than five years—so well within the pledge.

The job was done. Was this the slouch of rest?
Not to the men he drove through walls of granite.
The embers from the past were in his soul,   1570
Banked for the moment at the rail and smoking,
Just waiting for the future to be blown.

At last the spike and Donald with the hammer!
His hair like frozen moss from Labrador
Poked out under his hat, ran down his face
To merge with streaks of rust in a white cloud.
What made him fumble the first stroke?[6] Not age:
The snow belied his middle sixties. Was
It lapse of caution or his sense of thrift,
That elemental stuff which through his life   1580
Never pockmarked his daring but had made
The man the canniest trader of his time,
Who never missed a rat-count, never failed
To gauge the size and texture of a pelt?
Now here he was caught by the camera,
Back bent, head bowed, and staring at a sledge,
Outwitted by an idiotic nail.
Though from the crowd no laughter, yet the spike
With its slewed[7] neck was grinning up at Smith.
Wrenched out, it was replaced. This time the hammer   1590
Gave a first tap as with apology,
Another one, another, till the spike
Was safely stationed in the tie and then
The Scot, invoking his ancestral clan,
Using the hammer like a battle-axe,
His eyes bloodshot with memories of Flodden,[8]
Descended on it, rammed it to its home.

The stroke released a trigger for a burst
Of sound that stretched the gamut of the air.
The shouts of engineers and dynamiters,   1600
Of locomotive-workers and explorers,
Flanking the rails, were but a tuning-up
For a massed continental chorus. Led
By Moberly (of the Eagles and *this* Pass)

---

[5]Pot-bellied (a puncheon is a large cask of liquor).
[6]Smith bent the first spike and had to drive a second.
[7]Twisted.
[8]Famous battle in which the English defeated the Scots (1513).

And Rogers (of *his own*), followed by Wilson,[9]
And Ross (charged with the Rocky Mountain Section),
By Egan (general of the Western Lines),
Cambie and Marcus Smith, Harris of Boston,
The roar was deepened by the bass of Fleming,
And heightened by the laryngeal fifes   1610
Of Dug McKenzie and John H. McTavish.
It ended when Van Horne spat out some phlegm
To ratify the tumult with *'Well Done'* [1]
Tied in a knot of monosyllables.

Merely the tuning up! For on the morrow
The last blow on the spike would stir the mould
Under the drumming of the prairie wheels,
And make the whistles from the steam out-crow
The Fraser. Like a gavel it would close
Debate, making Macdonald's *'sea to sea'*   1620
Pour through two oceanic megaphones—
Three thousand miles of *Hail* from port to port;
And somewhere in the middle of the line
Of steel, even the lizard heard the stroke.
The breed had triumphed after all. To drown
The traffic chorus, she must blend the sound
With those inaugural, narcotic notes
Of storm and thunder which would send her back
Deeper than ever in Laurentian sleep.
1952

[9]All the men named in this passage were present at the driving of the last spike: Tom Wilson had served as Rogers' guide in the Kicking Horse surveys; John Egan was general superintendant of the CPR western division under Van Horne; Henry J. Cambie was a government engineer who supervised a difficult section of the road in the Fraser Canyon; Marcus Smith took over the B.C. surveys in 1873; George Harris was a Boston financier and company director; John H. McTavish was the CPR land commissioner.

[1]Van Horne's famous speech at the driving of the last spike was brief and to the point: 'All I can say is that the work has been done well in every way.'

Marjorie Pickthall

1883-1922

Born in Middlesex, England, Marjorie Lowry Christie Pickthall immigrated with her parents to Toronto in 1889. She attended Saint Mildred's Girls' School and the Bishop Strachan School for Girls, selling her first story, 'Two Ears', to the Toronto *Globe* in 1898. After her mother's death in 1910 (an event that upset her greatly), she became an assistant librarian at Victoria College. In 1912 she returned to England to live with relatives, in an attempt to improve her failing health. There she contributed to the war effort as much as her health permitted, working as an ambulance driver, farm labourer, and assistant librarian in a meteorological office. She returned briefly to Toronto in 1919, before moving to Victoria and then to Vancouver, where she died of complications following heart surgery.

Although Pickthall had turned more towards prose at the time of her death (she was working on a novel, *The Beaten Man*), she was known primarily in Canada as a poet. Only two collections of poetry, however, were published during her lifetime: *The Drift of Pinions* (1913), and *The Lamp of Poor Souls* (1916). The others were published posthumously: *Mary Tired* (a Christmas remembrance; 1922), *The Woodcarver's Wife and Other Poems* (a one-act verse drama; 1922), *Two Poems* ('Vision' and 'Ebb Tide'; 1923), *Little Songs* (1925), and *The Naiad and Five Other Poems* (1931). *The Complete Poems of Marjorie Pickthall* (1925), collected by her father, Arthur C. Pickthall, saw a series of editions.

A prolific writer, Pickthall supported herself by working in a variety of forms and publishing her work in well-known magazines, both in North America and in England. Twenty-four of her many short stories were collected in *Angels' Shoes* (1922). As well, she wrote three juvenile novels— *Dick's Desertion; a Boy's Adventures in Canadian Forests* (1905), *The Straight Road* (1906), and *Billy's Hero; or The Valley of Gold* (1908)—and two adult novels, *Little Hearts* (1915) and *The Bridge; a Story of the*

Great Lakes (1921). *The Bridge* appeared both in *Everybody's* (New York) and *Sphere* (London, England); the juvenile novels were published serially in *East and West*, a paper sponsored by the Presbyterian Church.

In her day, Pickthall received both popular and critical acclaim, earning great praise from such influential critics as Archibald MacMechan, Andrew Macphail, and Lorne Pierce (who wrote her biography in 1925). The Montreal Branch of the Canadian Authors' Association noted at the time of her death that 'her place is secure, not only as the first poet of Canada, but one of the first poets of the English language' (23 April). Condemned, however, in the 1940s by E.K. Brown, and then in the 1950s by Desmond Pacey, her poetry fell out of fashion at a time when literary tastes favoured irony over reverie, and a realistic vision over a stylized romantic one.

Ironically, Pickthall's early success may have contributed to her decline in popularity. She received public recognition even before the publication of her first collection of poetry because of winning the Christmas poetry competition sponsored by the *The Mail and Empire* in 1900, and because of her many smaller publications in prominent magazines across North America. The poems in her first volume were collected at the suggestion of Sir Andrew Macphail, which guaranteed its success; the first edition of 1000 copies sold out in ten days. Because of the early praise she received she was never pushed to develop beyond the lyric conventions she inherited from the English Romantic poets and from the Confederation poets, her literary forebears in Canada. It is unfortunate that her career was cut short by her untimely death, because there is evidence in her poetry to suggest that she was beginning to question her use of these lyric conventions. As Diana Relke points out, Pickthall, as a female poet, has difficulty locating herself in a lyric tradition that deals with the relationship between man and nature

(*Canadian Literature* 1987). Her discomfort is evident in 'The Sleep-Seekers', for example, where the poetic voice, striving to identify itself in terms of 'there/here' and 'you/we', finally affirms a dream world beyond life and nature.

Much of Pickthall's poetry deals with this mystical and imaginative space, characterized by the colour silver, and accessible only through a kind of artistic reverie. The doctor in 'Modern Endymion', for instance, cannot make the imaginative leap into the speaker's dream of escape. This poetic dream world provided Pickthall with a refuge—in her early work, from the painful memory of her mother's death, and in later work, from a modern war-stricken world. In 'Made in His Image', she expresses some of her concerns about a God who may be all-powerful, even all-knowing, but ultimately unfeeling. This troubled tone in her work led a contempo-

rary essayist, John Daniel Logan, to describe her as not 'a natural, happy poet of Nature' but as a 'wistful, sorrowing poet of the Spirit' torn between a naturally 'pagan' spirit and a learned Christian 'asceticism' that did not wholly satisfy her (*Marjorie Pickthall: Her Poetic Genius and Art*, 1922).

The speaker's discomfort with her subject is echoed in the halting repetitions and alliterations of 'Made in His Image'. Unlike the flowing internal rhymes of 'The Sleep-Seekers', which inspired Archibald MacMehan to mourn the loss of 'the truest, sweetest singing voice ever heard in Canada', the play with rhythm and repetition in such poems as 'Modern Endymion', 'Made in His Image', and 'The Bird in the Room' demonstrates the range and variety of Pickthall's skill. In these poems her challenge to poetic convention lies as much in their form as in their content.

The Sleep-seekers

Lift thou the latch whereon the wild rose clings,
Touch the green door to which the briar has grown.
If you seek sleep, she dwells not with these things,—
The prisoned wood, the voiceless reed, the stone.
But where the day yields to one star alone,
Softly Sleep cometh on her brown owl-wings,
Sliding above the marshes silently
To the dim beach between the black pines and the sea.

There; or in one leaf-shaken loveliness
Of birchen light and shadow, deep she dwells,   10
Where the song-sparrow and the thrush are heard,
And once a wandering flute-voiced mocking-bird,
Where, when the year was young,
Grew sweet faint bloodroot, and the adder-tongue
Lifting aloft her spire of golden bells.

Here shall we lift our lodge against the rain,
Walling it deep
With tamarac branches and the balsam fir,
Sweet even as sleep,
And aspen boughs continually astir   20
To make a silver-gleaming,—
Here shall we lift our lodge and find again
A little space for dreaming.

1925

The Bird in the Room

Last autumn when they aired the house
A bird got in, and died in this room.
Here it fluttered
Close to the shuttered
Window, and beat in the airless gloom,
No space for its wing, no drop for its mouth,—
A swallow, flying south.

And the velvet-creeping unsleeping mouse
Trampled that swiftness where it fell
On the dusty border   10
Pattern'd in order
With a citron flower and a golden shell,—
But it might not fly and it might not drink,
On the carpet's sunless brink.

A thought of you beat into my mind,
Empty and shuttered, dark, and spread
With dusty sheeting
To hide the beating
Tread of the hours. But the thought was dead
When I opened the door of that room, to find   20
If the Spring
Had left me anything—

1936

Modern Endymion[1]

IN THE ASYLUM GARDEN

You!—
You stealing violets where the snail-tracks glisten
In the dew.
And little secret roses when the doctor's back is turned,—
Listen!
Listen, and I'll tell you how my window burned!

Burning silver ran about the pane in fires,
Piercing silver fires, and their points went creeping
All along the sidewalks and the branches and the wires

[1]Endymion: a beautiful shepherd with whom Selene, the goddess of the moon, falls in love when she sees him sleeping. So as to enjoy his beauty more fully, she causes him to sleep forever.

And the chimneys of the houses where the smoke was sleeping   10
O, white, white, white,
Was my window of the night,
And the glass was dripping in the old cold flame,
And soon, soon, soon,
Underneath the little bars that barricade it black,
With the whiteness and the brightness dripping from her back,
The bare moon came,
Came the moon!

They cannot keep her out, O my secret, O my white
Silver-throated goddess of the night, of the night.   20
They may stifle me all day, but by night I am free,
Waiting for the goddess to climb the walnut tree
In the gray asylum grounds
Where the watchman goes his rounds.
He never sees her mounting, limb by silver limb.
He never sees her counting the stairway of the stars
With her bright hair twining,—
She's just the moon to him,
Shining,—
Shining through my window with the black strong bars.   30

And close, close, close,
Closer than the dew-shine to the rose,
And near, near, near
I am holding her all night, my terrible, my dear.
And the four gray walls
Run a drowning sluice of silver, and it falls
Where it will,—
Falls
Fierce and still,
Fierce and still—   40

Hush!
The little doctor's coming to take away your flowers!
If you run, run, run
Round the candleberry bush
In the pathway of the sun,
Maybe he won't find you, he won't follow you for hours.
But he can't touch me.
He can't find her, he can't feel her, he can't see, see, see
Her climbing to my window by the silver fruited tree.

1936

Made in His Image

Between the archangels and the old eclipse
Of glory on perfect glory, does He feel
A vision, thin as frost at midnight, steal
And lay a nameless shadow on His lips?
Does He, Who gave the power, endure the pain?—
Look down the hollow'd universe, and see
His works, His worlds, choiring Him endlessly,—
His worlds, His works, all made, and made in vain?
Then does He bid all heaven beneath His hand,
In blossom of worship, flame on flame of praise,   10
And taste their thunders, and grow sick, and gaze
At some gray silence that He had not planned,
And shiver among His stars, and nurse each spark
That wards Him from the uncreated dark?

1936

Ethel Wilson

1888-1980

Ethel Davis Bryant Wilson, a daughter of a Methodist missionary, was born in South Africa and raised in England until her parents' death in 1898. At the age of ten she went to live with relatives in Vancouver who sent her to schools there and in Britain. She taught school until 1920, when she married a distinguished Vancouver physician, Dr Wallace Wilson. The two lived in various countries before returning home to Vancouver and the province they loved.

While Wilson's first short story was published in England in 1937, her wartime work—the editing of a Red Cross magazine—curtailed her serious writing for almost ten years. In 1947 Wilson, nearing sixty, published her first novel, *Hetty Dorval*. Over the next fourteen years she produced three more novels: *The Innocent Traveller* (1949), *Swamp Angel* (1954), and *Love and Salt Water* (1956); two novellas, which were combined in *The Equations of Love* (1952); and a collection of her previously published short fiction: *Mrs Golightly and Other Stories* (1961). A posthumous volume, *Ethel Wilson: Stories, Essays and Letters*, edited by David Stouck (1987), includes a number of previously unpublished stories.

Wilson's elegant, balanced style, with its seemingly artless surfaces, belies the complex structures of her narratives. The effect on the reader of Wilson's stories—simple tales of slightly absurd characters who live in a dream-like world—is achieved through the imposition of a comic, even biting, vision upon what is otherwise a meticulously realistic presentation. This yoking of literary modes allows her to examine two of the most important topics to emerge in Canadian literature: the universe as a tricky, unreliable place, and society as an increasingly dehumanized milieu. 'The Window' deals with both of these themes. Hugo McPherson has observed that 'its title image, the window framing by day the empty scene and mirroring by night the sterile life of the protagonist, is central not only to her but to much modern Canadian fiction.'

The Window

The great big window must have been at least twenty-five feet wide and ten feet high. It was constructed in sections divided by segments of something that did not interfere with the view; in fact the eye by-passed these divisions and looked only at the entrancing scenes beyond. The window, together with a glass door at the western end, composed a bland shallow curve and formed the entire transparent north-west (but chiefly north) wall of Mr Willy's living-room.

Upon his arrival from England Mr Willy had surveyed the various prospects of living in the quickly growing city of Vancouver with the selective and discarding characteristics which had enabled him to make a fortune and retire all of a sudden from business and his country in his advanced middle age. He settled immediately upon the very house. It was a small old house overlooking the sea between Spanish Banks and English Bay. He knocked out the north wall and made the window. There was nothing particular to commend the house except that it faced immediately on the sea-shore and the view. Mr Willy had left his wife and her three sisters to play bridge together until death should overtake them in England. He now paced from end to end of his living-room, that is to say from east to west, with his hands in his pockets, admiring the northern view. Sometimes he stood with his hands behind him looking through the great glass window, seeing the wrinkled or placid sea and the ships almost at his feet and beyond the sea the mountains, and seeing sometimes his emancipation. His emancipation drove him into a dream, and sea sky mountains swam before him, vanished, and he saw with immense release his wife in still another more repulsive hat. He did not know, nor would he have cared, that much discussion went on in her world, chiefly in the afternoons, and that he was there alleged to have deserted her. So he had, after providing well for her physical needs which were all the needs of which she was capable. Mrs Willy went on saying '. . . and he would come home my dear and never speak a word I can't tell you my dear how *frightful* it was night after night I might say for *years* I simply can't tell you . . .' No, she could not tell but she did, by day and night. Here he was at peace, seeing out of the window the crimped and wrinkled sea and the ships which passed and passed each other, the seabirds and the dream-inducing sky.

At the extreme left curve of the window an island appeared to slope into the sea. Behind this island and to the north, the mountains rose very high. In the summer time the mountains were soft, deceptive in their innocency, full of crags and crevasses and arêtes and danger. In the winter they lay magnificent, white and much higher, it seemed, than in the summer time. They tossed, static, in almost visible motion against the sky, inhabited only by eagles and—so a man had told Mr Willy, but he didn't believe the man—by mountain sheep and some cougars, bears, wild cats and, certainly, on the lower slopes, deer, and now a ski camp far out of sight. Mr Willy looked at the mountains and regretted his past youth and his present wealth. How could he endure to be old and rich and able only to look at these mountains which in his youth he had not known and did not climb. Nothing, now, no remnant of his youth would come and enable him to climb these mountains. This he found hard to believe, as old people do. He was shocked at the newly realized decline of his physical powers which had proved good enough on the whole for his years of success, and by the fact that now he had, at last, time and could not swim (heart), climb mountains (heart and legs), row a boat in a rough enticing sea (call that old age). These things have happened to other people, thought Mr Willy, but not to us, now, who have been so young, and yet it will happen to those who now are young.

Immediately across the water were less spectacular mountains, pleasant slopes which in winter time were covered with invisible skiers. Up the dark mountain at night sprang the lights of the ski-lift, and ceased. The shores of these mountains were strung with lights, littered with lights, spangled with lights, necklaces, bracelets, constellations, far more beautiful as seen through this window across the dark water than if Mr Willy had driven his car across the Lions' Gate Bridge and westwards among those constellations which would have disclosed only a shopping centre, people walking in the streets, street lights, innumerable cars and car lights like anywhere else and, up the slopes, peoples' houses. Then, looking back to the south across the dark water towards his own home and the great lighted window which he would not have been able to distinguish so far away, Mr Willy would have seen lights again, a carpet of glitter thrown over the slopes of the city.

Fly from one shore to the other, fly and fly back again, fly to a continent or to an island, but you are no better off than if you stayed all day at your own window (and such a window), thought Mr Willy pacing back and forth, then into the kitchen to put the kettle on for a cup of tea which he will drink beside the window, back for a glass of whisky, returning in time to see a cormorant flying level with the water, not an inch too high not an inch too low, flying out of sight. See the small ducks lying on the water, one behind the other, like beads on a string. In the mornings Mr Willy drove into town to see his investment broker and perhaps to the bank or round the park. He lunched, but not at a club. He then drove home. On certain days a woman called Mrs Ogden came in to 'do' for him. This was his daily life, very simple, and a routine was formed whose pattern could at last be discerned by an interested observer outside the window.

One night Mr Willy beheld a vast glow arise behind the mountains. The Arctic world was obviously on fire—but no, the glow was not fire glow, flame glow. The great invasion of colour that spread up and up the sky was not red, was not rose, but of a synthetic cyclamen colour. This cyclamen glow remained steady from mountain to zenith and caused Mr Willy, who had never seen the Northern Lights, to believe that these were not Northern Lights but that something had occurred for which one must be prepared. After about an hour, flanges of green as of putrefaction, and a melodious yellow arose and spread. An hour later the Northern Lights faded, leaving Mr Willy small and alone.

Sometimes as, sitting beside the window, he drank his tea, Mr Willy thought that nevertheless it is given to few people to be as happy (or contented, he would say), as he was, at his age, too. In his life of decisions, men, pressures, more men, antagonisms, fusions, fissions and Mrs Willy, in his life of hard success, that is, he had sometimes looked forward but so vaguely and rarely to a time when he would not only put this life down; he would leave it. Now he had left it and here he was by his window. As time went on, though, he had to make an effort to summon this happiness, for it seemed to elude him. Sometimes a thought or a shape (was it?), gray, like wood ash that falls in pieces when it is touched, seemed to be behind his chair, and this shape teased him and communicated to him that he had left humanity behind, that a man needs humanity and that if he ceases to be in touch with man and is not in touch with God, he does not matter. 'You do not matter any more,' said the spectre like wood ash before it fell to pieces, 'because you are no longer in touch with any one and so you do not exist. You are in a vacuum and so you are nothing.' Then Mr Willy, at first uneasy, became satisfied again for a time after being made uneasy by the spectre. A storm would get up and the wind, howling well, would lash the window sometimes carrying the salt spray from a very high tide which it flung against the great panes of glass. That was a satisfaction to Mr Willy and within him something stirred and rose and met the storm and effaced the spectre and other phantoms which were really vague regrets. But the worst that happened against the window was that from time to time a little bird, sometimes but not often a seabird, flung itself like a stone against the strong glass of the window and fell, killed by the passion of its flight. This grieved Mr Willy, and he could not sit unmoved when the bird flew at the clear glass and was met by death. When this happened, he arose from his chair, opened the glass door at the far end of the window, descended three or four steps and sought in the grasses for the body of the bird. But the bird was dead, or it was dying, its small bones were smashed, its head was broken, its beak split, it was killed by the rapture of its flight. Only once Mr Willy found the bird a little stunned and picked it up. He cupped the bird's body in his hands and carried it into the house.

Looking up through the grasses at the edge of the rough terrace that descended to the beach, a man watched him return into the house, carrying the bird. Still looking obliquely through the grasses the man watched Mr Willy enter the room and vanish from view. Then Mr Willy came again to the door, pushed it open, and released the bird which flew away, who knows where. He closed the door, locked it, and sat down on the chair facing east beside the window and began to read his newspaper. Looking over his paper he saw, to the east, the city of Vancouver deployed over rising ground with low roofs and high buildings and at the apex the tall Electric Building which at night shone like a broad shaft of golden light.

This time, as evening drew on, the man outside went away because he had other business.

Mr Willy's investment broker was named Gerald Wardho. After a time he said to Mr Willy in a friendly but respectful way, 'Will you have lunch with me at the Club tomorrow?' and Mr Willy said he would. Some time later Gerald Wardho said, 'Would you like me to put you up at the Club?'

Mr Willy considered a little the life which he had left and did not want to re-enter and also the fact that he had only last year resigned his membership in three clubs, so he said, 'That's very good of you, Wardho, but I think not. I'm enjoying things as they are. It's a novelty, living in a vacuum . . . I like it, for a time anyway.'

'Yes, but,' said Gerald Wardho, 'you'd be some time on the waiting list. It wouldn't hurt—'

'No,' said Mr Willy, 'no.'

Mr Willy had, Wardho thought, a distinguished appearance or perhaps it was an affable accustomed air, and so he had. When Mrs Wardho said to her husband, 'Gerry, there's not an extra man in this town and I need a man for Saturday,' Gerald Wardho said, 'I know a man. There's Willy.'

Mrs Wardho said doubtfully, 'Willy? Willy who? Who's Willy?'

Her husband said, 'He's fine, he's okay, I'll ask Willy.'

'How old is he?'

'About a hundred . . . but he's okay.'

'Oh-h-h,' said Mrs Wardho, 'isn't there anyone anywhere unattached young any more? Does he play bridge?'

'I'll invite him, I'll find out,' said her husband, and Mr Willy said he'd like to come to dinner.

'Do you care for a game of bridge, Mr Willy?' asked Gerald Wardho.

'I'm afraid not,' said Mr Willy kindly but firmly. He played a good game of bridge but had no intention of entering servitude again just yet, losing his freedom, and being enrolled as what is called a fourth. Perhaps later; not yet. 'If you're having bridge I'll come another time. Very kind of you, Wardho.'

'No no no,' said Gerald Wardho, 'there'll only be maybe a table of bridge for anyone who wants to play. My wife would be disappointed.'

'Well thank you very much. Black tie?'

'Yes. Black tie,' said Gerald Wardho.

And so, whether he would or no, Mr Willy found himself invited to the kind of evening parties to which he had been accustomed and which he had left behind, given by people younger and more animated than himself, and he realized that he was on his way to becoming old odd man out. There was a good deal of wood ash at these parties—that is, behind him the spectre arose, falling to pieces when he looked at it, and said 'So this is what you came to find out on this coast, so far from home, is it, or is there something else. What else is there?' The spectre was not always present at these parties but sometimes awaited him at home and said these things.

One night Mr Willy came home from an evening spent at Gerald Wardho's brother-in-law's house, a very fine house indeed. He had left lights burning and began to turn out the lights before he went upstairs. He went into the living-room and before turning out the last light gave a glance at the window which had in the course of the evening behaved in its accustomed manner. During the day the view through the window was clear or cloudy, according to the weather or the light or absence of light in the sky; but there it was—the view—never quite the same though, and that is owing to the character of oceans or of any water, great or small, and of light. Both water and light have so great an effect on land observed on any scene, rural, urban or wilderness, that one begins to think that life, that a scene, is an illusion produced by influences such as water and light. At all events, by day the window held this fine view as in a frame, and the view was enhanced by ships at sea of all kinds, but never was the sea crowded, and by birds, clouds, and even aeroplanes in the sky—no people to spoil this fine view. But as evening approached, and moonless night, all the view (illusion again) vanished slowly. The window, which was not illusion, only the purveyor of illusion, did not vanish, but became a mirror which reflected against the blackness every detail of the shallow living-room. Through this clear reflection of the whole room, distant lights from across the water intruded, and so chains of light were thrown across the reflected mantel-piece, or a picture, or a human face, enhancing it. When Mr Willy had left his house to dine at Gerald Wardho's brother-in-law's house the view through the window was placidly clear, but when he returned at 11:30 the window was dark and the room was reflected from floor to ceiling against the blackness. Mr Willy saw himself entering the room like a stranger, looking at first debonair with such a gleaming shirt front and then—as he approached himself—a little shabby, his hair perhaps. He advanced to the window and stood looking at himself with the room in all its detail behind him.

Mr Willy was too often alone, and spent far too much time in that space which lies between the last page of the paper or the turning-off of the radio in surfeit, and sleep. Now as he stood at the end of the evening and the beginning of the night, looking at himself and the room behind him, he admitted that the arid feeling which he had so often experienced lately was probably what is called loneliness. And yet he did not want another woman in his life. It was a long time since he had seen a woman whom he wanted to take home or even to see again. Too much smiling. Men were all right, you talked to them about the market, the emergence of the Liberal Party, the impossibility of arriving anywhere with those people while that fellow was in office, nuclear war (instant hells opened deep in everyone's mind and closed again), South Africa where Mr Willy was born, the Argentine where Mr Wardho's brother-in-law had spent many years—and then everyone went home.

Mr Willy, as the months passed by, was dismayed to find that he had entered an area of depression unknown before, like a tundra, and he was a little frightened of this tundra. Returning from the dinner party he did not at once turn out the single last light and go upstairs. He sat down on a chair beside the window and at last bowed his head upon his hands. As he sat there, bowed, his thoughts went very stiffly (for they had not had much exercise in that direction throughout his life), to some area that was not tundra but that area where there might be some meaning in creation which Mr Willy supposed must be the place where some people seemed to find a God, and perhaps a personal God at that. Such theories, or ideas, or passions had never been of interest to him, and if he had thought of such theories, or ideas, or passions he would have dismissed them as invalid and having no bearing on life as it is lived, especially when one is too busy. He had formed the general opinion that people who hold such beliefs were either slaves to an inherited convention, hypocrites, or nitwits. He regarded such people without interest, or at least he thought them negligible as he returned to the exacting life in hand. On the whole, though, he did not like them. It is not easy to say why Mr Willy thought these people were hypocrites or nit-wits because some of them, not all, had a strong religious faith, and why he was not a hypocrite or nit-wit because he had not a strong religious faith; but there it was.

As he sat on and on looking down at the carpet with his head in his hands he did not think of these people, but he underwent a strong shock of recognition. He found himself looking this way and that way out of his aridity for some explanation or belief beyond the non-explanation and non-belief that had always been sufficient and had always been his, but in doing this he came up against a high and solid almost visible wall of concrete or granite, set up between him and a religious belief. This wall had, he thought, been built by him through the period of his long life, or perhaps he was congenitally unable to have a belief; in that case it was no fault of his and there was no religious belief possible to him. As he sat there he came to have the conviction that the absence of a belief which extended beyond the visible world had something to do with his malaise; yet the malaise might possibly be cirrhosis of the liver or a sort of delayed male menopause. He recognized calmly that death was as inevitable as tomorrow morning or even tonight and he had a rational absence of fear of death. Nevertheless his death (he knew) had begun, and had begun—what with his awareness of age and this malaise of his—to assume a certainty that it had not had before. His death did not trouble him as much as the increasing tastelessness of living in this tundra of mind into which a belief did not enter.

The man outside the window had crept up through the grasses and was now watching Mr Willy from a point rather behind him. He was a morose man and strong. He had served two terms for robbery with violence. When he worked, he worked up the coast. Then he came to town and if he did not get into trouble it was through no fault of his own. Last summer he had lain there and, rolling over, had looked up through the grasses and into—only just into—the room where this guy was who seemed to live alone. He seemed to be a rich guy because he wore good clothes and hadn't he got this great big window and—later, he discovered—a high-price car. He had lain in the grasses and because his thoughts always turned that way, he tried to figger out how he could get in there. Money was the only thing that was any good to him and maybe the old guy didn't keep money or even carry it but he likely did. The man thought quite a bit about Mr Willy and then went up the coast and when he came down again he remembered the great big window and one or two nights he went around and about the place and figgered how he'd work it. The doors was all locked, even that glass door. That was easy enough to break but he guessed he'd go in without warning when the old guy was there so's he'd have a better chance of getting something off of him as well. Anyways he wouldn't break in, not that night, but if nothing else offered he'd do it some time soon.

Suddenly Mr Willy got up, turned the light out, and went upstairs to bed. That was Wednesday.

On Sunday he had his first small party. It seemed inevitable if only for politeness. Later he would have a dinner party if he still felt sociable and inclined. He invited the Wardhos and their in-laws and some other couples. A Mrs Lessways asked if she might bring her aunt and he said yes. Mrs Wardho said might she bring her niece who was arriving on Saturday to meet her fiancé who was due next week from Hong Kong, and the Wardhos were going to give the two young people a quiet wedding, and Mr Willy said 'Please do.' Another couple asked if they could bring another couple.

Mr Willy, surveying his table, thought that Mrs Ogden had done well. 'Oh I'm so glad you think so,' said Mrs Ogden, pleased. People began to arrive. 'Oh!' they exclaimed without fail, as they arrived, 'what a beautiful view!' Mrs Lessways' aunt who had blue hair fell delightedly into the room, turning this way and that way, acknowledging smiles and tripping to the window. 'Oh,' she cried turning to Mr Willy in a fascinating manner, 'isn't that just lovely! Edna says you're quite a recluse! I'm sure I don't blame you! Don't you think that's the

loveliest view Edna . . . oh how d'you do how d'you do, isn't that the loveliest
view? . . .' Having paid her tribute to the view she turned away from the window
and did not see it again. The Aunt twirled a little bag covered with iridescent
beads on her wrist. 'Oh!' and 'Oh!' she exclaimed, turning, 'My dear how *lovely*
to see you! I didn't even know you were back! Did you have a good time?' She
reminded Mr Willy uneasily of his wife. Mr and Mrs Wardho arrived accompanied by their niece Sylvia.

A golden girl, thought Mr Willy taking her hand, but her young face surrounded by sunny curls was stern. She stood, looking from one to another, not
speaking, for people spoke busily to each other and the young girl stood apart,
smiling only when need be and wishing that she had not had to come to the party.
She drifted to the window and seemed (and was) forgotten. She looked at the
view as at something seen for the first and last time. She inscribed those notable
hills on her mind because had she not arrived only yesterday? And in two days
Ian would be here and she would not see them again.

A freighter very low laden emerged from behind a forest and moved slowly
into the scene. So low it was that it lay like an elegant black line upon the water
with great bulkheads below. Like an iceberg, thought Sylvia, and her mind
moved along with the freighter bound for foreign parts. Someone spoke to her
and she turned. 'Oh thank you!' she said for her cup of tea.

Mr Willy opened the glass door and took with him some of the men who had
expressed a desire to see how far his property ran. 'You see, just a few feet, no
distance,' he said.

After a while day receded and night came imperceptibly on. There was not any
violence of reflected sunset tonight and mist settled down on the view with only
distant dim lights aligning the north shore. Sylvia, stopping to respond to ones
and twos, went to the back of the shallow room and sat down behind the out-jut
of the fireplace where a wood fire was burning. Her mind was on two levels. One
was all Ian and the week coming, and one—no thicker than a crust on the surface—was this party and all these people talking, the Aunt talking so busily that
one might think there was a race on, or news to tell. Sylvia, sitting in the shadow
of the corner and thinking about her approaching lover, lost herself in this reverie, and her lips, which had been so stern, opened slightly in a tender smile. Mr
Willy who was serving drinks from the dining-room where Mrs Ogden had left
things ready, came upon her and, struck by her beauty, saw a different sunny
girl. She looked up at him. She took her drink from him with a soft and tender
smile that was grateful and happy and was only partly for him. He left her, with a
feeling of beauty seen.

Sylvia held her glass and looked towards the window. She saw, to her surprise, so quickly had black night come, that the end of the room which had been
a view was now a large black mirror which reflected the glowing fire, the few
lights, and the people unaware of the view, its departure, and its replacement by
their own reflections behaving to each other like people at a party. Sylvia
watched Mr Willy who moved amongst them, taking a glass and bringing a
glass. He was removed from the necessities, now, of conversation, and looked
very sad. Why does he look sad, she wondered and was young enough to think,
he shouldn't look sad, he is well off. She took time off to like Mr Willy and to
feel sorry that he seemed melancholy.

People began to look at their watches and say good-bye. The Aunt redoubled her vivacity. The women all thanked Mr Willy for his tea party and for the beautiful beautiful view. They gave glances at the window but there was no view.

When all his guests had gone, Mr Willy, who was an orderly man, began to collect glasses and take them into the kitchen. In an armchair lay the bag covered with iridescent beads belonging to the Aunt. Mr Willy picked it up and put it on a table, seeing the blue hair of the Aunt. He would sit down and smoke for awhile. But he found that when, lately, he sat down in the evening beside the window and fixed his eyes upon the golden shaft of the Electric Building, in spite of his intention of reading or smoking, his thoughts turned towards this subject of belief which now teased him, eluded, yet compelled him. He was brought up, every time, against the great stone wall, how high, how wide he knew, but not how thick. If he could, in some way, break through the wall which bounded the area of his aridity and his comprehension, he knew without question that there was a light (not darkness) beyond, and that this light could in some way come through to him and alleviate the sterility and lead him, lead him. If there were some way, even some conventional way—although he did not care for convention—he would take it in order to break the wall down and reach the light so that it would enter his life; but he did not know the way. So fixed did Mr Willy become in contemplation that he looked as though he were graven in stone.

Throughout the darkened latter part of the tea party, the man outside had lain or crouched near the window. From the sands, earlier, he had seen Mr Willy open the glass door and go outside, followed by two or three men. They looked down talking, and soon went inside again together. The door was closed. From anything the watcher knew, it was not likely that the old guy would turn and lock the door when he took the other guys in. He'd just close it, see.

As night came on the man watched the increased animation of the guests preparing for departure. Like departing birds they moved here and there in the room before taking flight. The man was impatient but patient because when five were left, then three, then no one but the old guy who lived in the house, he knew his time was near. (How gay and how meaningless the scene had been, of these well-dressed persons talking and talking, like some kind of a show where nothing happened—or so it might seem, on the stage of the lighted room from the pit of the dark shore.)

The watcher saw the old guy pick up glasses and take them away. Then he came back into the room and looked around. He took something out of a chair and put it on a table. He stood still for a bit, and then he found some kind of a paper and sat down in the chair facing eastward. But the paper drooped in his hand and then it dropped to the floor as the old guy bent his head and then he put his elbows on his knees and rested his head in his hands as if he was thinking, or had some kind of a headache.

The watcher, with a sort of joy and a feeling of confidence that the moment had come, moved strongly and quietly to the glass door. He turned the handle expertly, slid inside, and slowly closed the door so that no draught should warn his victim. He moved cat-like to the back of Mr Willy's chair and quickly raised his arm. At the selfsame moment that he raised his arm with a short blunt weapon in his hand, he was aware of the swift movement of another person in the room. The man stopped still, his arm remained high, every fear was aroused. He turned instantly and saw a scene clearly enacted beside him in the dark mirror of the window. At the moment and shock of turning, he drew a sharp intake of breath and it was this that Mr Willy heard and that caused him to look up and around and see in the dark mirror the intruder, the danger, and the victim who was himself. At that still moment, the telephone rang shrilly, twice as loud in that still moment, on a small table near him.

It was not the movement of that figure in the dark mirror, it was not the bell ringing close at hand and insistently. It was an irrational and stupid fear lest his action, reproduced visibly beside him in the mirror, was being faithfully registered in some impossible way that filled the intruder with fright. The telephone ringing shrilly, Mr Willy now facing him, the play enacted beside him, and this irrational momentary fear caused him to turn and bound towards the door, to escape into the dark, banging the glass door with a clash behind him. When he got well away from the place he was angry—everything was always against him, he never had no luck, and if he hadn'ta lost his head it was a cinch he coulda done it easy.

'Damn you!' shouted Mr Willy in a rage, with his hand on the telephone, 'you might have broken it! Yes?' he said into the telephone, moderating the anger that possessed him and continuing within himself a conversation that said It was eighteen inches away, I was within a minute of it and I didn't know, it's no use telephoning the police but I'd better do that, it was just above me and I'd have died not knowing. 'Yes? Yes?' he said impatiently, trembling a little.

'Oh,' said a surprised voice, 'it *is* Mr Willy, isn't it? Just for a minute it didn't sound like you Mr Willy that was the *loveliest* party and what a lovely view and I'm sorry to be such a nuisance I kept on ringing and ringing because I thought you couldn't have gone out so soon' (tinkle tinkle) 'and you couldn't have gone to bed so soon but I do believe I must have left my little bead bag it's not the *value* but . . .' Mr Willy found himself shaking more violently now, not only with death averted and the rage of the slammed glass door but with the powerful thoughts that had usurped him and were interrupted by the dangerous moment which was now receding, and the tinkling voice on the telephone.

'I have it here. I'll bring it tomorrow,' he said shortly. He hung up the telephone and at the other end the Aunt turned and exclaimed, 'Well if he isn't the rudest man I never was treated like that in my whole life d'you know what he . . .'

Mr Willy was in a state of abstraction.

He went to the glass door and examined it. It was intact. He turned the key and drew the shutter down. Then he went back to the telephone in this state of abstraction. Death or near-death was still very close, though receding. It seemed to him at that moment that a crack had been coming in the great wall that shut him off from the light but perhaps he was wrong. He dialled the police, perfunctorily not urgently. He knew that before him lay the hardest work of his life—in his life but out of his country. He must in some way and very soon break the great wall that shut him off from whatever light there might be. Not for fear of death oh God not for fear of death but for fear of something else.

1961

F.R. Scott

1899-1985

Francis Reginald Scott was a second-generation Canadian poet, the son of Frederick George Scott (1861-1944), one of the lesser-known Confederation poets. Born in Quebec City, where his father was rector of St Matthew's Church, Frank Scott received a traditional Anglican upbringing. After attending the private High School of Quebec, and his father's *alma mater*, Bishop's College, he won a Rhodes Scholarship to Oxford University in 1920 and read history at Magdalen College. As Scott once said, 'I spent three blissful years at Oxford soaking up everything I could learn about the past and paying very little attention to the present.' On his return to Canada in 1923 he taught for a brief period at Lower Canada College before enrolling in law at McGill University. He was called to the bar in 1927 and was made a professor in the Faculty of Law in 1928; he served as its dean from 1961 to 1964 and retired in 1968.

The influence of his father had nurtured Scott's interest in poetry, both as a reader and a writer, but before 1925 this interest had progressed little beyond reading the Georgian poets and writing sonnets. At McGill he was befriended by A.J.M. Smith, who introduced him to the new American poets, including Pound and Eliot. Together Scott and Smith founded the *McGill Fortnightly Review* (1925-7), for which they wrote so prolifically that it became necessary for them to invent pseudonyms.

As the modernist poets changed Scott's conception of poetry, so the social decay of the Depression altered his ideas about politics and economics. He rejected not only the romantic poetry of his father's generation but its capitalism as well. He became a social reformer and a socialist, an authority on constitutional law, and a defender of civil liberties and social justice. He assisted in the formation of the Co-operative Commonwealth Federation (CCF), of which he was national chairman from 1942 to 1950; in the 1950s he fought three celebrated court cases in Quebec: against Premier Duplessis' pad-

lock law, against the censorship of Lawrence's *Lady Chatterley's Lover*, and a famous civil-liberties case, Roncarelli v. Duplessis. In the 1960s he was a member of the Royal Commission on Bilingualism and Biculturalism.

Frank Scott's poetry always reflected his social consciousness. As early as 1928 he joined other writers in helping to found the *Canadian Mercury*, a literary magazine that gave voice to three members of the 'Montreal Group', Leo Kennedy, A.M. Klein, and Scott himself. Though members of this group each wrote distinctly different poetry, they all wrote about the present in new ways that freed them from traditional forms. With Smith, Scott edited an anthology of this 'new' poetry, *New Provinces* (1936, reissued 1976), which served as a public manifesto that Canadian poetry was indeed changing. Over the years Scott continued to be interested in helping to provide a public outlet for new voices, often by his support of literary magazines. He helped to found *Preview* in 1942 which, like the *Canadian Mercury* and the *McGill Fortnightly Review* before it, gave a new generation of writers a public forum.

Scott's poems have been collected in *Overture* (1945), *Events and Signals* (1954), *The Eye of the Needle: Satires, Sorties, Sundries* (1957), *Signature* (1964), and *The Dance is One* (1973). His *Selected Poems* appeared in 1966, and his *Collected Poems*, which won a Governor General's Award, was published in 1981. In another collaboration with A.J.M. Smith, Scott compiled a popular anthology, *The Blasted Pine: An Anthology of Satire, Invective and Disrespectful Verse: Chiefly by Canadian Writers* (1957; rev. 1967).

Scott's poetry has often been divided into 'public' and 'private' poems, or grouped into the predominating modes and subjects of nature, satire, social and humanitarian idealism, and love. But even the public satire of 'The Canadian Authors Meet' is not without a personal voice. In his poetry we can see the best aspects of modernism: a penetrating vision expressed in a spare and precise style. To this Scott adds his own special qualities of grace and wit, so that his treatment of such subjects as social injustice or the artifacts of technology are given force and memorability by means of elegant diction and sharp satire. His is a comprehensive poetry that can unite the mythic nature of the land with the reality of personal experience, that can scrutinize the trivialities of a self-indulgent society while also seeing a lakeshore with the eye of a visionary. He writes of man's mediocrity as well as of his ultimate promise. His poetry depends not so much on metaphor as on verbal wit and word-play, and frequently on echoing allusions that can force the reader to look at the world both in terms of the past and with reference to the kind of future it suggests. A.J.M. Smith's poem commemorating his friend's seventieth birthday, 'To Frank Scott, Esq.', brings together many aspects of Scott. It begins:

Poet and Man of Law—O brave anomaly!—
dove wise and serpent-tongued for Song
  or Plea—
a parti-coloured animal, committed,
  parti-pris
but not a party man, a Man, and free.

The Canadian Authors¹ Meet

Expansive puppets percolate self-unction
Beneath a portrait of the Prince of Wales.
Miss Crotchet's muse has somehow failed to function,
Yet she's a poetess. Beaming, she sails

From group to chattering group, with such a dear
Victorian saintliness, as is her fashion,
Greeting the other unknowns with a cheer—
Virgins of sixty who still write of passion.

The air is heavy with Canadian topics,
And Carman, Lampman, Roberts, Campbell, Scott,   10
Are measured for their faith and philanthropics,
Their zeal for God and King, their earnest thought.

The cakes are sweet, but sweeter is the feeling
That one is mixing with the *literati*;
It warms the old, and melts the most congealing.
Really, it is a most delightful party.

Shall we go round the mulberry bush, or shall
We gather at the river, or shall we

¹The Canadian Authors' Association, founded in 1921, appeared to Scott to be a self-congratulatory and self-indulgent group that was mostly a refuge for poetasters and that celebrated safely established poets while ignoring modern innovators. He wrote this poem after attending a meeting of the CAA in the spring of 1925.

Appoint a Poet Laureate this fall,[2]
Or shall we have another cup of tea?   20

O Canada, O Canada, Oh can
A day go by without new authors springing
To paint the native maple, and to plan
More ways to set the selfsame welkin[3] ringing?[4]

1927, 1945

[2]At the meeting Scott attended the appointment of a poet laureate was seriously discussed.
[3]Sky (poetic archaism).
[4]When first published in the *McGill Fortnightly Review* (27 April 1927), this poem concluded with the additional stanza:

> *Far in a corner sits (though none would know it)*
> *The very picture of disconsolation,*
> *A rather lewd and most ungodly poet*
> *Writing these verses, for his soul's salvation.*

Trans Canada

Pulled from our ruts by the made-to-order gale
We sprang upward into a wider prairie
And dropped Regina below like a pile of bones.[1]

Sky tumbled upon us in waterfalls,
But we were smarter than a Skeena salmon
And shot our silver body over the lip of air
To rest in a pool of space
On the top storey of our adventure.

A solar peace
And a six-way choice.[2]   10

Clouds, now, are the solid substance,
A floor of wool roughed by the wind
Standing in waves that halt in their fall.
A still of troughs.

The plane, our planet,
Travels on roads that are not seen or laid
But sound in instruments on pilots' ears,
While underneath

[1]Early settlers' name for Regina.
[2]In that 'up and down' have been added to the usual four points of the compass.

The sure wings
Are the everlasting arms of science.   20

Man, the lofty worm, tunnels his latest clay,
And bores his new career.

This frontier, too, is ours.
This everywhere whose life can only be led
At the pace of a rocket
Is common to man and man,
And every country below is an I land.

The sun sets on its top shelf,
And stars seem farther from our nearer grasp.

I have sat by night beside a cold lake   30
And touched things smoother than moonlight on still water,
But the moon on this cloud sea is not human,
And here is no shore, no intimacy,
Only the start of space, the road to suns.

1945

Lakeshore — *Evolution*

The lake is sharp along the shore
Trimming the bevelled edge of land
To level curves; the fretted sands
Go slanting down through liquid air
Till stones below shift here and there
Floating upon their broken sky
All netted by the prism wave
And rippled where the currents are.

I stare through windows at this cave
Where fish, like planes, slow-motioned, fly.   10
Poised in a still of gravity
The narrow minnow, flicking fin,
Hangs in a paler, ochre sun,
His doorways open everywhere.

And I am a tall frond that waves
Its head below its rooted feet
Seeking the light that draws it down
To forest floors beyond its reach
Vivid with gloom and eerie dreams.

The water's deepest colonnades   20
Contract the blood, and to this home
That stirs the dark amphibian
With me the naked swimmers come
Drawn to their prehistoric womb.

They too are liquid as they fall
Like tumbled water loosed above
Until they lie, diagonal,
Within the cool and sheltered grove
Stroked by the fingertips of love.

Silent, our sport is drowned in fact   30
Too virginal for speech or sound
And each is personal and laned
Along his private aqueduct.

Too soon the tether of the lungs
Is taut and straining, and we rise
Upon our undeveloped wings
Toward the prison of our ground
A secret anguish in our thighs
And mermaids in our memories.

This is our talent, to have grown   40
Upright in posture, false-erect,
A landed gentry, circumspect,
Tied to a horizontal soil
The floor and ceiling of the soul;
Striving, with cold and fishy care
To make an ocean of the air.

Sometimes, upon a crowded street,
I feel the sudden rain come down
And in the old, magnetic sound
I hear the opening of a gate   50
That loosens all the seven seas.
Watching the whole creation drown
I muse, alone, on Ararat.[1]

1954

---

[1]The mountain on which Noah landed after the flood.

its place. If I write 'ostrich'
, never seen the bird see it
.n the sand and its plumes fluffed with the wind
.zie King talking on Freedom of Trade.

h.   /rite 'holocaust', and 'nightingales',
I start. the insurance agents and the virgins
Who belong, by this alchemy, in the same category,
Since both are very worried about their premiums.

A rose and a rose are two roses; a rose is a rose is a rose.[1]
Sometimes I have walked down a street marked No Outlet   10
Only to find that what was blocking my path
Was a railroad track roaring away to the west.

So I know it will survive. Not even the decline of reading
And the substitution of advertising for genuine pornography
Can crush the uprush of the mushrooming verb
Or drown the overtone of the noun on its own.

1954

[1]This alludes to a line from Gertrude Stein's poem 'Sacred Emily' (1913)—'Rose is a rose is a rose is
a rose'—that has come to exemplify her particular brand of difficult modern writing.

Laurentian Shield

Hidden in wonder and snow, or sudden with summer,
This land stares at the sun in a huge silence
Endlessly repeating something we cannot hear.
Inarticulate, arctic,
Not written on by history, empty as paper,
It leans away from the world with songs in its lakes
Older than love, and lost in the miles.

This waiting is wanting.
It will choose its language
When it has chosen its technic,   10
A tongue to shape the vowels of its productivity.

A language of flesh and of roses. [1]

[1]A line from an essay by Stephen Spender ('The Making of a Poem', from a book of the same title,
1955), which he uses to discuss the process of making poetry. This line, never developed into a
poem, came to Spender upon seeing the man-made landscape of mining country, ' a landscape of pits
and pit-heads, artificial mountains, jagged yellow wounds in the earth'. This landscape, and similar
creations of 'man's mind', seemed to Spender 'a kind of language of our inner wishes and thoughts'.
He found himself 'thinking that if the phenomena created by humanity are really like words in a language, what kind of language do we really aspire to?' His answer was 'a language of flesh and roses'.
Scott developed Spender's ideas in 'Laurentian Shield' to come to his own terms with the effect of
human beings on the land and of the land on its inhabitants, as well as with his own theory of poetry-
making.

Now there are pre-words,
Cabin syllables,
Nouns of settlement
Slowly forming, with steel syntax,
The long sentence of its exploitation.

The first cry was the hunter, hungry for fur,
And the digger for gold, nomad, no-man, a particle;
Then the bold commands of monopoly, big with machines,   20
Carving its kingdoms out of the public wealth;
And now the drone of the plane, scouting the ice,
Fills all the emptiness with neighbourhood
And links our future over the vanished pole.

But a deeper note is sounding, heard in the mines,
The scattered camps and the mills, a language of life,
And what will be written in the full culture of occupation
Will come, presently, tomorrow,
From millions whose hands can turn this rock into children.

1954

All the Spikes But the Last[1]

Where are the coolies in your poem, Ned?
Where are the thousands from China who swung
    their picks with bare hands at forty below?

Between the first and the million other spikes
    they drove, and the dressed-up act of
    Donald Smith,[2] who has sung their story?

Did they fare so well in the land they helped to
    unite? Did they get one of the 25,000,000 CPR acres?

Is all Canada has to say to them written in the Chinese
    Immigration Act?[3]   10

1957

[1]A response to E.J. ['Ned'] Pratt's poem, *Towards the Last Spike*. (see p. 216). Some 6,000 Chinese labourers, imported because of their willingness to accept low wages, endured brutal conditions while playing a vital role in the completion of the CPR in British Columbia.
[2]Donald Smith (1820-1913) was recognized for his role in the building of the CPR by being chosen to drive the last spike in 1885, a ritual he performed in frock-coat and high hat.
[3]The Chinese Immigration Act, more commonly known as the Chinese Exclusion Act, was passed in 1923. A late outgrowth of continued reaction against this imported labour, it virtually prohibited further entry into Canada by Chinese. The act was repealed in 1947.

A.J.M. Smith

1902-1980

Arthur James Marshall Smith had a profound effect on modern Canadian poetry. Poet, anthologist, critic, and teacher, he was one of the founders of the modernist literary movement in Canada. He was born in Montreal and in 1921 entered McGill, where he completed an undergraduate degree in science before taking an M.A. in literature. During this time he began two literary publications: the *Literary Supplement* of the *McGill Daily* (1924-5), which lasted less than a year, and, with F.R. Scott, the *McGill Fortnightly Review* (1925-7), which published poetry of the nascent 'Montreal group' (F.R. Scott, Leo Kennedy, and Smith himself, among others), along with Smith's early critical statements about the need for a modernist poetry in Canada. His well-known and influential critical article, 'Wanted—Canadian Criticism', appeared around this time in the *Canadian Forum* (April 1928).

In 1927 Smith married and left Montreal for Edinburgh, where he worked on his Ph.D. under the seventeenth-century poetry scholar, H.J.C. Grierson. While in Scotland, Smith contributed to the *Canadian Mercury* (1928-9), which in its brief lifetime continued the policies that had guided the *McGill Fortnightly*. In 1929 he returned to Montreal, but, unable to obtain a university position in Canada, he went to the United States to seek one. Although he could not find a permanent teaching post during the Depression years, he did complete his doctorate and finally, in 1938, was given an appointment at Michigan State University in Lansing, where he remained until his retirement in 1972. His deep interest in, and editorial efforts on behalf of, Canadian literature continued despite his American residence. From 1940 on Smith spent a great deal of time in Canada as a visiting professor and on leave preparing new anthologies, and at the beginning of each summer he and his family returned to their cottage near Magog, Qué.

In the thirties Smith and Scott compiled *New Provinces* (1936; reissued 1976), an anthology of 'new' Canadian poets. Containing poems by four members of the now-dispersed 'Montreal group' (Kennedy, A.M. Klein, Scott, and Smith), and by E.J. Pratt and Robert Finch of Toronto, this collection can now be seen as the volume that announced the existence of Canadian modernism. Its publication was clouded, however, by the rejection of Smith's Preface, both by Hugh Eayrs of Macmillan, the publisher, and by Finch and Pratt. They objected to the way Smith characterized romantic poetry of feeling as being inferior to an impersonal one of intellect, considering this preference an attack on earlier poets and seeing in it an implicit suggestion that worthwhile Canadian poetry began with the *New Provinces* writers. Scott wrote a less-controversial Preface and Smith's was not published until 1965.

In the Preface to *The Book of Canadian Poetry* (1943; rev. 1948, 1957) Smith made a controversial distinction between 'cosmopolitan' and 'native' verse that was much debated in subsequent discussions of Canadian poetry. For him the 'cosmopolitan' poet responded to what Canadian life 'had in common with life everywhere', while the 'native' poet 'concentrated on what is individual and unique in Canadian life.' Historically Smith saw the 'native' poet as trying to 'come to terms with an environment that is only now ceasing to be colonial'; the 'cosmopolitan' writer, on the other hand, 'from the very beginning has made a heroic effort to transcend colonialism by entering into the universal, civilizing culture of ideas.' For Smith colonialism, which he equated with parochialism, was a threat to Canadian writing.

This Preface to the 1943 anthology began a dispute between Smith and the poets who appeared in *First Statement* and particularly its editor, John Sutherland. In *Other Canadians: Anthology of the New Poetry in Canada: 1940-1946* (1947), Sutherland defended the 'hardfisted' proletarian writers who valued not the civilized poetry of 'cosmopolitanism' but verse that was 'racy and vigorous', 'healthy and masculine'—poets like Layton, Dudek, and Souster who wrote another sort of native poetry, one no longer focused on the physical world but on the people within it, a poetry 'of the common man'.

Smith continued to play an important role as an anthologist, becoming one of those who helped to shape the Canadian literary canon. The collections of poetry and prose he compiled include *The Oxford Book of Canadian Verse: In English and French* (1960), *Modern Canadian Verse: In English and French* (1967); (with F.R. Scott) *The Blasted Pine: An Anthology of Satire, Invective and Disrespectful Verse; Chiefly by Canadian Writers* (1957; rev. 1967); and the critical anthologies *Masks of Fiction* (1961) and *Masks of Poetry* (1962). His own critical essays were collected in *Towards a View of Canadian Poetry: Selected Critical Essays 1928-1971* (1973) and *On Poetry and Poets: Selected Essays* (1977).

Although Smith published his own verse steadily—most of it in periodicals such as the *Canadian Forum*—he refrained for many years from collecting it in book form. His first volume of poems, *News of the Phoenix*, which won a Governor General's Award, did not appear until 1943. There followed *A Sort of Ecstasy* (1954), *Collected Poems* (1963), *Poems: New and Collected* (1967), and *The Classic Shade: Selected Poems* (1978).

There is a powerful and witty tension in Smith's poetry that is produced by his assured command of form which controls his intricate allusions; by a style that can incorporate, within a single poem, a convoluted syntax derived from seventeenth-century poetry ('How all men wrongly death to dignify/Conspire. I tell') and the colloquial speech rhythms of the jazz world ('a worth/Beyond all highfalutin' woes or shows'); and by the ability to make the reader see the wry humour in even the most serious topic ('Plot Against Proteus'). A severe critic of his own efforts, and a constant reviser, Smith believed that a poem should be 'a highly organized, complex, and unified re-creation of experience in which the maximum use of meaning and suggestion in the sounds of words has been achieved with the minimum essential outlay of words. A poem is not the description of an experience, it is itself an experience, and it awakens in the mind of the alert and receptive reader a new experience analogous to the one in the mind of the poet ultimately responsible for the creation of the poem' ('The Refining Fire: The Meaning and Use of Poetry', 1954).

The Lonely Land[1]

Cedar and jagged fir
uplift sharp barbs
against the gray
and cloud-piled sky;
and in the bay
blown spume and windrift
and thin, bitter spray
snap
at the whirling sky;
and the pine trees   10
lean one way.

A wild duck calls
to her mate,
and the ragged
and passionate tones
stagger and fall,
and recover,
and stagger and fall,
on these stones—
are lost   20
in the lapping of water
on smooth, flat stones.

This is a beauty
of dissonance,
this resonance
of stony strand,
this smoky cry
curled over a black pine
like a broken
and wind-battered branch   30
when the wind
bends the tops of the pines
and curdles the sky
from the north.

This is the beauty
of strength
broken by strength
and still strong.

1936

---

[1]Originally subtitled 'Group of Seven' (in the *McGill Fortnightly Review*, 1926), this poem was revised for two other periodical publications, in 1927 and again in 1929.

Far West

Among the cigarettes and the peppermint creams
Came the flowers of fingers, luxurious and bland,
Incredibly blossoming in the little breast.
And in the Far West
The tremendous cowboys in goatskin pants
Shot up the town of her ignorant wish.

In the gun flash she saw the long light shake
Across the lake,[1] repeating that poem
At Finsbury Park.
But the echo was drowned in the roll of the trams—   10
Anyway, who would have heard? Not a soul.
Not one noble and toxic like Buffalo Bill.

In the holy name *bang! bang!* the flowers came
With the marvellous touch of fingers
Gentler than the fuzzy goats
Moving up and down up and down as if in ecstasy
As the cowboys rode their skintight stallions
Over the barbarous hills of California.

1943

---

[1] An allusion to Tennyson's 'The Princess', iv, Introductory Song:

> *The splendour falls on castle walls*
> *And snowy summits old in story:*
> *The long light shakes across the lakes,*
> *And the wild cataract leaps in glory.*
> *Blow, bugle, blow, set the wild echoes flying,*
> *Blow, bugle; answer, echoes, dying, dying, dying.*

'Finsbury Park' is an area in northwest London. The movie theatre in the poem is apparently located there.

...liff

Wave on wave
and green on rock
and white between
the splash and black
the crash and hiss
of the feathery fall,
the snap and shock
of the water wall
and the wall of rock:

after—   10
after the ebb-flow,
wet rock,
high—
high over the slapping green,
water sliding away
and the rock abiding,
new rock riding
out of the spray.

1943

The Plot Against Proteus[1]

This is a theme for muted coronets
To dangle from debilitated heads
Of navigation, kings, or riverbeds
That rot or rise what time the seamew[2] sets
Her course by stars among the smoky tides
Entangled, Old saltencrusted Proteus treads
Once more the watery shore that water weds
While rocking fathom bell rings round and rides.

Now when the blind king of the water thinks
The sharp hail of the salt out of his eyes   10
To abdicate,[3] run thou, O Prince,[4] and fall
Upon him. This cracked walrus skin that stinks
Of the rank sweat of a mermaid's thighs
Cast off, and nab him; when you have him, call.

1943

[1]Prophetic sea god who tended Poseidon's sea animals. When out-wrestled—a difficult achievement because he could change shape at will—he would foretell one's future.
[2]Sea gull.
[3]That is, to get rid of the salt in his eyes; to do so Proteus climbs out of the water and sleeps among the animals.
[4]Menelaus, husband of Helen of Troy, who offended Athena on his return home after the Trojan war. Wanting Proteus to tell him if it was possible to make amends, Menelaus waited under a seal skin for an opportunity to overpower him.

The Wisdom of Old Jelly Roll[1]

How all men wrongly death to dignify
Conspire, I tell. Parson, poetaster, pimp,
Each acts or acquiesces. They prettify,
Dress up, deodorize, embellish, primp,
And make a show of Nothing. Ah, but met-
aphysics laughs; she touches, tastes, and smells
—Hence knows—the diamond holes that make a net.
Silence resettled testifies to bells.
'Nothing' depends on 'Thing', which is or was:
So death makes life or makes life's worth, a worth   10
Beyond all highfalutin' woes or shows
To publish and confess, 'Cry at the birth,
Rejoice at the death,' old Jelly Roll said,
Being on whiskey, ragtime, chicken, and the scriptures fed.

1962

[1]Ferdinand Joseph La Menthe ('Jelly Roll') Morton (1885-1941), American jazz pianist and composer.

Morley Callaghan

1903-1990

While Morley Callaghan's fiction, like Ethel Wilson's, seems innocent of design, each narrative is actually a carefully planned structure in which a character faces a crisis that will determine the course of his life. The crossroads in each story is not merely a melodramatic device, but an index to the didactic role Callaghan (a committed Catholic) assumed, for he saw himself as a writer who, in the course of giving 'a shape and form to human experience', had 'become a moralist'.

Born and educated in Toronto, Callaghan as a boy pursued a wide variety of interests. During high school he was not only active in sports and debating, but he also made his first attempts to write fiction. Although he took a general B.A. from St Michael's College, University of Toronto in 1925, and completed law school in 1928, his real training as a writer came from the part-time jobs he held while a student; they supplied him with material for his stories and, when he worked as a reporter on the Toronto *Daily Star*, with confidence in his abilities. In 1923 Callaghan met Ernest Hemingway when the American writer was briefly employed by the *Star*. Hemingway encouraged Callaghan to continue writing and later passed his stories on to editors of Paris literary magazines and presses. As a result, Callaghan's first published story, 'A Girl with Ambition', came out in *This Quarter* in 1926. Hemingway's editor at Scribner's, Maxwell Perkins, accepted Callaghan's novel, *Strange Fugitive* (1928), as well as a collection of stories, *A Native Argosy* (1929).

In 1929 Callaghan and his wife travelled to Paris, where he met writers in the expatriate community there. (He wrote a memoir of this visit, *That Summer in Paris*, 1963, the best-known episode of which describes his victory in a boxing match with Hemingway.) Returning to North America later in the year, the Callaghans lived for a short time in the States before settling in Toronto.

During the thirties, stories by Callaghan frequently appeared in *The New Yorker*, and he had seven volumes of fiction published in eight years: *It's Never Over* (1930), *No Man's Meat* (1931), *A Broken Journey* (1932), *Such Is My Beloved* (1934), *They Shall Inherit the Earth* (1935), *Now That April's Here and Other Stories* (1936), and *More Joy in Heaven* (1937). In 1938, however, Callaghan entered a decade that he described as a 'period of spiritual dryness' during which he produced little new fiction. Instead he worked as a journalist, a scriptwriter, and even as a moderator and panelist on CBC radio. In 1948 he returned to writing; among his later works are *The Loved and the Lost* (1951), *Morley Callaghan's Stories* (1959), *A Passion in Rome* (1961), *A Fine and Private Place* (1975), and *A Wild Old Man on the Road* (1988).

While Callaghan received early international recognition, praise in Canada was not always forthcoming. It was not until the fifties that he received a Governor General's Award (1951); this was followed by the Lorne Pierce Medal in 1960 and in 1970 by the Molson Prize and the Royal Bank Award. Callaghan was criticized at home by both academics and newspaper reviewers for universalizing his characters and settings, a strategy they saw his having developed in order to gain an international market at the denial of his own 'Canadianness'. Callaghan's tendency to blur or make transparent particular features was not limited only to Canadian locales, however, for as the American critic Edmund Wilson, a long-time admirer, observed, Callaghan—in contrast to Fitzgerald and Hemingway — removed even his own individual presence from his writing: 'Callaghan is so much interested in moral character as exhibited in other people's behavior that, unlike his two exhibitionistic friends, he never shows himself at all.' In choosing to obscure both himself and his environment, Callaghan took the same option as A.J.M. Smith's 'cosmopolitan' writers. This choice runs counter to much twentieth-century Canadian prose that, resembling 'native' poetry, has often centred on the need to establish a Canadian identity.

Certainly Callaghan's tendency to generalize was consistent with his interest in 'timeless' issues. His novels are concerned with the universal problem of mankind's imperfect condition. While his early fiction considered social realism and Marxism as possible responses to man's difficulties, since the mid-thirties he found his solution in Christian humanism. Following his meetings in 1933 with the French philosopher, Jacques Maritain, Callaghan continued to develop the view that in an increasingly oppressive society the individual needs to control not so much his physical destiny as his personal salvation. This position resulted, in Callaghan's fiction, in a preoccupation with a particular kind of 'criminality' that sets itself in opposition to moral codes and social laws: his hero is often a criminal saint, a social martyr of individual conscience.

Nowhere is the extremity of the individual's situation more evident than in Callaghan's short stories, where the conflict is internalized inside a single character, one who often must choose between personal relationships and his desire to be part of an impersonal society. The merits of Callaghan's novels have been debated, but the quality of his stories has always been evident. They are crystallizations of man's sense of loss, of his longing for Edens no longer attainable. In the short stories especially, Callaghan's laconic style suggests objectivity, an unemotional mirroring of life. At the same time, beneath this surface detachment a homiletic voice sounds a warning against a dehumanized world and a law that has largely forgotten morality.

Watching and Waiting

Whenever Thomas Hilliard, the lawyer, watched his young wife dancing with men of her own age, he was very sad, for she seemed to glow with a laughter and elation that didn't touch her life with him at all. He was jealous, he knew; but his jealousy at that time made him feel humble. It gave him the fumbling tenderness of a young boy. But as time passed and he saw that his humility only added to her feeling of security, he grew sullen and furtive and began to spy on her.

At times he realized that he was making her life wretched, and in his great shame he struggled hard against the distrust of her that was breaking the peace of his soul. In his longing to be alone with her, so that he would be free to offer her whatever goodness there was in him, he insisted that they move out to the country and renovate the old farmhouse on the lake where he had been born. There they lived like two scared prisoners in the house that was screened from the lane by three old oak trees. He went into the city only three days a week and his business was soon ruined by such neglect.

One evening Thomas Hilliard was putting his bag in the car, getting ready to return to the city. He was in a hurry, for the sky was darkening; the wind had broken the surface of the lake into choppy little waves with whitecaps, and soon it would rain. A gust of wind slammed an open window. Above the noise of the water on the beach, he heard his wife's voice calling, rising eagerly as it went farther away from the house.

She was calling, 'Just a minute, Joe,' and she was running down to the gate by the lane, with the wind blowing her short fair hair back from her head as she ran.

At the gate a young man was getting out of a car, waving his hand to her like an old friend, and calling: 'Did you want to speak to me, Mrs Hilliard?'

'I wanted to ask you to do something for me,' she said.

The young man, laughing, lifted a large green bass from a pail in the back of his car, and he said: 'I caught it not more than half an hour ago. Will you take it, Mrs Hilliard?'

'Isn't it a beauty!' she said, holding it out at arm's length on the stick he had thrust through the jaws. 'You shouldn't be giving such a beauty away.' And she laughed, a free careless laugh that was carried up to the house on the wind.

For a while there was nothing Thomas Hilliard could hear but the murmur of his wife's voice mixed with the murmur of the young man's voice; but the way the laughter had poured out of her, and the look of pleasure on the young man's face, made him tense with resentment. He began to feel sure he had been actually thinking of that one man for months without ever naming him, that he had even been wondering about him while he was packing his bag and thinking of the drive into the city. Why was the young man so friendly that first time he had stopped them, on the main street of the town, when they were doing their week-end shopping, to explain that his name was Joe Whaley and he was their neighbour? That was something he had been wondering about for a long time. And every afternoon when Joe Whaley was off shore in his motorboat, he used to stand up and wave to them, the length of his lean young body outlined against the sky. It was as though all these things had been laid aside in Thomas Hilliard's head, to be given a sudden meaning now in the eager laughter of his wife, in her voice calling, and the pleasure on the young man's face.

He became so excited that he started to run down to the gate; and as he ran, his face was full of yearning and despair. They watched him coming, looking at each other doubtfully. When his wife saw how old and broken he looked, she suddenly dropped the fish in the dust of the road.

'Hey, there! Wait a minute,' he was calling to the young man, who had turned away awkwardly.

'Did you want to speak to me, Mr Hilliard?' Joe Whaley said.

'Is there something you want?' Hilliard asked.

'I just stopped a moment to give you people the fish.'

'I'd like to know, that's all,' Hilliard said, and he smiled foolishly.

The young man, who was astonished, mumbled some kind of an apology and got into his car. He drove up the lane with the engine racing, and the strong wind from the lake whirling the dust in a cloud across the fields.

Speaking quietly, as if nothing had happened to surprise her, Mrs Hilliard began, 'Did you think there was something the matter, Tom?' But then her voice broke, and she cried out: 'Why did you come running down here like that?'

'I heard the way you laughed,' he said.

'What was the matter with the way I laughed?'

'Don't you see how it would strike me? I haven't heard you laugh like that for such a long time.'

'I was only asking him if he'd be passing by the station tonight. I was going to ask him if he'd bring my mother here, if she was on the night train.'

'I don't believe that. You're making up a story,' he shouted.

It was the first time he had openly accused her of deceit; and when she tried to smile at him, her eyes were full of terror. It was as though she knew she was helpless at last, and she said slowly: 'I don't know why you keep staring at me. You're frightening me. I can't bear the way you watch me. It's been going on for such a long time. I've got to speak to someone—can't you see? It's dreadfully lonely here.'

She was staring out over the choppy wind-swept water: she turned and looked up with a child's wonder at the great oak trees that shut the house off from the road. 'I can't stand it any longer,' she said, her voice soft and broken. 'I've been a good wife. I had such an admiration for you when we started. There was nothing I wouldn't have trusted you with. And now—I don't know what's happened to us.' This was the first time she had ever tried to tell him of her hidden desolation; but all he could see was that her smile as she pleaded with him was pathetically false.

'You're lying. You're scared of what might happen,' he shouted.

'I've known how you've been watching me, and I've kept asking myself what the both of us have been waiting for,' she said. As the wind, driving through the leaves of the trees, rattled a window on the side of the house, and the last of the light faded from the lake, she cried out: 'What are we waiting for, day after day?'

'I'm not waiting any more,' he shouted. 'I'm going. You don't need to worry about me watching you any more. I'll not come back this time.' He felt crazy as he started to run over to the car.

Running after him, she cried out: 'I've kept hoping something would happen to make it different, something that would save us. I've prayed for it at night, just wanting you to be like you were three years ago.'

But he had started the car, and it came at her so suddenly that she had to jump out of the way. When the car lurched up the lane, he heard her cry out, but the words were blown away on the wind. He looked back, and saw her standing stiff by the gate, with both hands up to her head.

He drove up to the highway, swinging the car around so wildly at the turn by the grocery-store that the proprietor shouted at him. He began to like the way the car dipped at high speed down the deep valleys, and rose and fell with him always rigid and unthinking. When he reached the top of the highest hill in the country, the first of the rain whipped across his face, slashing and cutting at him in the way they slap the face of a fighter who has been beaten and is coming out of a stupor. His arms were trembling so he stopped the car; and there he sat for a long time, looking out over the hills in the night rain, at the low country whose roll and rise could be followed by the line of lights curving around the lake through the desolation of the wooded valleys and the rain-swept fields of this country of his boyhood, a gleaming line of light leading back to the farm and his wife.

There was a flash of lightning, and the fields and pasture-land gleamed for a moment in the dark. Then he seemed to hear her voice crying out above the wind: 'I've been waiting for so long!' And he muttered: 'How lost and frightened she'll be alone there on a night like this.' He knew then that he could go no farther. With his heart full of yearning for the tenderness he knew she had offered to him, he kept repeating: 'I can't leave her. I can't ever leave her. I'll go back and ask her to forgive me.'

So he sighed and was ashamed; and he drove back slowly along the way he had come, making up in his head fine little speeches that would make his wife laugh and forgive him.

But when he had turned off the highway and was going down the lane that led to the house, he suddenly thought it could do no harm if he stopped the car before it was heard, and went up to the house quietly to make sure no one else was there.

Such a notion made him feel terribly ashamed. As the car rocked in the ruts and puddles of the dirt road, and the headlights gleamed on the wet leaves from overhanging branches, he was filled with a profound sadness, as if he knew instinctively that no matter how he struggled, he would not be able to stop himself from sneaking up to the house like a spy. Stopping the car, he sat staring at the shuttered windows through which the light hardly filtered, mumbling: 'I've got a heart like a snake's nest. I've come back to ask her to forgive me.' Yet as he watched the strips of light on the shutters, he found himself thinking it could do no harm to make sure she was alone, that this would be the last time he would ever spy on her.

As he got out of the car, he stood a while in the road, getting soaking wet, assuring himself he had no will to be evil. And then as he started to drag his feet through the puddles, he knew he was helpless against his hunger to justify his lack of faith in her.

Swinging open the gate and crossing the grass underneath the oak tree, he stopped softly on the veranda and turned the door-knob slowly. When he found that the door was locked, his heart began to beat unevenly, and he went to pound the door with his fist. Then he grew very cunning. Jumping down to the grass, he went cautiously around to the side of the house, pressed his head against the shutters and listened. The rain streamed down his face and ran into his open mouth.

He heard the sound of his wife's voice, and though he could not make out the words, he knew she was talking earnestly to someone. Her voice seemed to be breaking; she seemed to be sobbing, pleading that she be comforted. His heart began to beat so loud he was sure they would be able to hear it. He grabbed at the shutter and tried to pry it open with his hand, but his fingers grew numb, and the back of his hand began to bleed. Stepping back from the house, he looked around wildly for some heavy stick or piece of iron. He remembered where there was an old horseshoe imbedded in the mud by the gate, and running there, he got down on his knees and scraped with his fingers, and he grinned in delight when he tugged the old horseshoe out of the mud.

But when he had inserted the iron prongs of the shoe between the shutters, and had started to use his weight, he realized that his wife was no longer talking. She was coming over to the window. He heard her gasp and utter a little cry. He heard her running from the room.

Full of despair, as though he were being cheated of the discovery he had been patiently seeking for years, he stepped back from the house, trembling with eagerness. The light in the room where he had loosened the shutter was suddenly turned out. He turned and ran back up the lane to the car, and got his flashlight.

This time he went round to the other side of the house, listening for the smallest sounds which might tell him where they were hiding, but it was hard to hear anything above the noise of the wind in the trees and the roll of the waves on the shore. At the kitchen window at the back of the house he pulled at the shutter. He heard them running out of the room.

The longing to look upon the face of the one who was with his wife became so great that he could hardly think of his wife at all. 'They probably went upstairs to the bedroom. That's where they'll be. I think I heard them going up the stairs.' He went over to the garage and brought out the ladder they had used to paint the house, and put it up against the bedroom window and started to climb on the slippery rungs with the flashlight clutched in his hand, eager for the joy that would be his if he could see without being seen.

The voices he heard as he lay against the ladder were broken with fright; he began to feel all the terror that grew in them as they ran from room to room and whispered and listened and hid in the darkness and longed to cry out.

But they must have heard some noise he made at the window, for before he was ready to use the flashlight, they ran from the room; they hurried downstairs in a way that showed they no longer cared what noise they made, they fled as though they intended to keep on going out of the front door and up the lane.

If he had taken the time to climb down the ladder, they might have succeeded; but instead of doing that, he wrapped his arms and legs around the wet rails and slid to the ground; he got over to the oak tree, and was hidden, his flashlight pointed at the door, before they came out.

As they came running from the house, he kept hidden and flashed the light on them, catching his wife in the strong beam of light, and making her stop dead and scream. She was carrying the rifle he used for hunting in the fall.

With a crazy joy he stepped out and swung the light on the other one; it was his wife's mother, stooped in horror. They were both held in the glare of the light, blinking and cringing in terror, while he tried to remember that the mother was to come to the house. And then his wife shrieked and pointed the gun into the darkness at the end of the beam of light, and fired: and he called out helplessly: 'Marion—'

But it was hurting him on his breast. The light dropped from his hand as he sank to the ground and began to cough.

Then his wife snatched up the light and let it shine on his face: 'Oh, Tom, Tom! Look what I've done,' she moaned.

The mother was still on her knees, stiff with fright.

His hand held against his breast was wet with warm blood; and as his head sank back on the grass he called out jerkily to the mother: 'Go on—hurry! Get someone—for Marion. I'm dying. I want to tell them how it happened.'

The mother, shrieking, hobbled over to the lane, and her cries for help were carried away on the wind.

With his weeping wife huddled over him, he lay dying in the rain. But when he groped with his hand and touched her head, his soul was suddenly overwhelmed by an agony of remorse for his lack of faith in her: in these few moments he longed to be able to show her all the comforting tenderness she had missed in the last three years. 'Forgive me,' he whispered. 'It was my fault—if only you could forgive me.' He wanted to soothe the fright out of her before the others came running up from the lane.

1959

Earle Birney

b. 1904

Born in Alberta, Alfred Earle Birney was raised there and in rural British Columbia, on small frontier farms and in the developing town of Banff. As a boy and young man Birney worked to help support his family and to earn enough money to attend university. The jobs he held—'chain-and-rod man with a Waterton survey party, pick-and-shovel and sledge-hammer man on a road crew, mountain guide, fossil hunter, axeman and oiler in a mosquito-control project', as well as suburban newspaper editor—influenced his poetry. In 1926 he graduated with a first-class honours B.A. in English literature from the University of British Columbia. Going on to study Old and Middle English at the University of Toronto, he worked on a Ph.D. thesis on Chaucer's irony while he held temporary positions at UBC and the University of California and studied at the University of London. After completing his degree in 1936 he accepted a teaching post at University College, Toronto, and remained there until he joined the army as a personnel officer in 1942. Invalided out of the war in 1945, Birney worked briefly for the CBC in Montreal before accepting a professorship in medieval literature at UBC. Since his retirement from that university in 1965 he has been writer-in-residence at the Universities of Toronto (1965-7), Waterloo (1967-8), and Western Ontario (1981-2), as well as Regents Professor at the University of California. Birney has received wide recognition: he won Governor General's Awards for poetry in 1942 and 1945, the Leacock Medal for Humour in 1949 for his novel *Turvey*, the Lorne Pierce Medal for Literature from the Royal Society of Canada, and in 1968 the Canada Council Medal 'for outstanding achievement'.

An extensive traveller, he has given readings of his work throughout the world under Canada Council grants and fellowships. Geographical location even became the organizing principle of his *Collected Poems* (1975). Believing that geography links man to his history, Birney takes pains in his poetry to mark, document, and define the significance of being in a particular place at a specific time.

No mere observer, Birney is a maker of new pathways in Canadian writing. Although he deprecates his role as innovator, he was the first writer in Canada to emphasize a metrics based on normal speech rhythms rather than artificial cadences; out of his 'doodles' (Birney's description of his visual poems) came the beginnings of concrete poetry, and out of his need to write down 'the particular sound of my own voice' the first sound poems in Canada. Birney also helped to provide Canadian writers with new outlets for publication, both as literary editor of the *Canadian Forum* (1936-40) and as editor of the *Canadian Poetry Magazine* (1946-8). He further contributed to Canadian writing by organizing one of the first creative-writing courses in Canada (at the University of Toronto in 1941) and the first department of creative writing (at the University of British Columbia in 1963). Out of this teaching experience came *The Creative Writer* (1966) and a book in which he discusses the composition of his own poems, *The Cow Jumped Over the Moon* (1972).

Around the time Birney began to edit and to teach creative writing, he also made a serious commitment to his own poetry. His first book, *David and Other Poems*, was published in 1942, and his second, *Now Is Time*, in 1945. He has since published some fifteen volumes of verse, as well as two novels, *Turvey* (1949) and *Down the Long Table* (1955). He has also written widely on poetry and poetics; some of his essays have been collected in *Spreading Time: 1904-1949* (1980).

Birney's poetry reflects a range of interests, from political beliefs (in the thirties and early forties he was an active Trotskyite) to Anglo-Saxon poetics; but despite the seriousness of many of his poems, they are rarely without a sense of playfulness. Always a public poet, Birney has sought his own path, reacting both to A.J.M. Smith's notion of 'cosmopolitanism' and to the more radical theories of the leftist poets of the forties in setting forth his ideas for a Canadian poetics:

A revolutionary approach to the world today is somehow associated with a revolt against syntax and the beauties of lucidity. In all this what is lost sight of is that the true cosmopolite in poetry, the great world figure, always had his roots deep in the peculiar soil of his own country, and made himself international because he spoke from his own nation even when he spoke for and to the world. . . . *The most cosmopolitan service a Canadian poet can do is to make himself . . . a clear and memorable and passionate interpreter of Canadians themselves, in the language of Canada . . . [for then he will] have eyes equally alert to the pages of* Pravda *and the exact shade of fuzz on a prairie poplar leaf.*—'Has Poetry a Future in Canada?' (1946).

In the last two decades Birney's poetry has become more personal, yet no less universal. A significant and original Canadian poet, Birney is a territory unto himself.

Vancouver Lights

About me the night   moonless   wimples the mountains
wraps ocean   land   air   and mounting
sucks at the stars   The city   throbbing below
webs the sable peninsula   The golden
strands overleap the seajet[1]   by bridge and buoy
vault the shears of the inlet   climb the woods
toward me   falter   and halt   Across to the firefly
haze of a ship on the gulf's erased horizon
roll the lambent spokes of a lighthouse

Through the feckless years we have come to the time   10
when to look on this quilt of lamps is a troubling delight
Welling from Europe's bog   through Africa flowing
and Asia   drowning the lonely lumes[2] on the oceans
tiding up over Halifax   now to this winking
outpost comes flooding the primal ink[3]

On this mountain's brutish forehead with terror of space
I stir   of the changeless night and the stark ranges

[1] Black sea.
[2] Lights.
[3] In this stanza Birney describes the progress of the Axis powers in the Second World War, which had caused 'the blackouts spreading from Europe through North Africa, over to Halifax, and [was] now threatening the lights of Vancouver'. (Birney, *The Cow Jumped Over the Moon*, hereafter abbreviated as *CJOM*.)

of nothing   pulsing down from beyond and between
the fragile planets   We are a spark beleaguered
by darkness   this twinkle we make in a corner of emptiness   20
how shall we utter our fear that the black Experimentress[4]
will never in the range of her microscope find it?   Our Phoebus
himself is a bubble that dries on Her slide   while the Nubian
wears for an evening's whim a necklace of nebulae

Yet we must speak   we the unique glowworms
Out of the waters and rocks of our little world
we conjured these flames   hooped these sparks
by our will   From blankness and cold we fashioned stars
to our size   and signalled Aldebaran[5]
This must we say   whoever may be to hear us   30
if murk devour   and none weave again in gossamer:

                    These rays were ours
we made and unmade them   Not the shudder of continents
doused us   the moon's passion   nor crash of comets
In the fathomless heat of our dwarfdom   our dream's combustion
we contrived the power   the blast that snuffed us
No one bound Prometheus   Himself he chained
and consumed his own bright liver[6]   O stranger
Plutonian   descendant   or beast in the stretching night—
there was light   40

1942[7]   1941

[4]Night, and the larger concept of the cosmic void, are personified as a black woman, a Nubian, whose experiment is the universe. Our sun, Phoebus, is only a small star or bubble to her; the nebulae or galaxies are but a necklace she has casually chosen to wear. This myth of a female progenitrix of the universe recalls the Orphic legend of creation.

[5]One of the twenty brightest stars in the sky, Aldebaran is used for navigation.

[6]When Prometheus stole divine fire for mankind, Zeus punished him by having him chained to a rock where a vulture perpetually devoured his liver. 'Plutonian': (i) pertaining to the god of the dead; (ii) of the planet Pluto.

[7]Birney revised many of his poems for *Selected Poems* (1966), mostly by replacing traditional punctuation with spaces.

Anglosaxon Street[1]

Dawn drizzle ended   dampness steams from
blotching brick and   blank plasterwaste
Faded housepatterns   hoary and finicky
unfold stuttering   stick like a phonograph

Here is a ghetto   gotten for goyim
O with care denuded   of nigger and kike

[1]This poem utilizes conventions of Old English, or Anglo-Saxon, poetry, including a caesura that breaks each line in two; single and double alliteration connecting the two halves; accented speech rhythms; kennings (metaphoric compounds substituted for ordinary words—E.G. 'learninghall' for school and 'whistleblow' for the end of the workday); and litotes (ironic understatement by negation—'not humbly' for proudly).

No coonsmell rankles   reeks only cellarrot
Ottar[2] of carexhaust   catcorpse and cookinggrease
Imperial hearts   heave in this haven
Cracks across windows   are welded with slogans   10
There'll Always Be An England   enhances geraniums
and V's for Victory   vanquish the housefly

Ho! with climbing sun   march the bleached beldames
festooned with shopping bags   farded[3] flatarched
bigthewed Saxonwives   stepping over buttrivers
waddling back wienerladen   to suckle smallfry

Hoy! with sunslope   shrieking over hydrants
flood from learninghall   the lean fingerlings
Nordic nobblecheeked[4]   not all clean of nose
leaping Commandowise   into leprous lanes   20

What! after whistleblow!   spewed from wheelboat
after daylight doughtiness   dire handplay
in sewertrench or sandpit   come Saxonthegns[5]
Junebrown Jutekings   jawslack for meat

Sit after supper   on smeared doorsteps
not humbly swearing   hatedeeds on Huns[6]
profiteers politicians   pacifists Jews

Then by twobit magic   to muse in movie
unlock picturehoard   or lope to alehall
soaking bleakly   in beer skittleless   30

Home again to hotbox   and humid husbandhood
in slumbertrough adding   sleepily to Anglekin
Alongside in lanenooks   carling[7] and leman
caterwaul and clip[8]   careless of Saxonry
with moonglow and haste   and a higher heartbeat

Slumbers now slumtrack   unstinks cooling
waiting brief for milkmaid   mornstar and worldrise

                  Toronto 1942

rev. 1966

[2]Attar: fragrant essence, usually rose-like.
[3]Rouged.
[4]Pimpled. Compare Chaucer's description of the Summoner who could not find an ointment to cure him of the 'knobbes sittynge on his cheeks' ('General Prologue' to *The Canterbury Tales* 1.633).
[5]Freemen who provided military services for the Saxon lords; 'Jute kings' refers to the Jutes, the German tribe which, invading England in the fifth century, spearheaded the Anglo-Saxon conquest.
[6]The savage Asiatic people who invaded Europe in the fourth century; also a modern term of contempt for Germans.
[7]Churl; 'leman': lover.   [8]Embrace.

The Ebb Begins from Dream

The stars like stranded starfish pale and die
and tinted sands of dawning dry
The ebb begins from dream   leaving a border
of morning papers on the porches

From crusted reefs of homes   from unkempt shores
the workers slip reluctant   half-asleep
lapse back into the city's deep
The waves of factory hands and heads   of salesman
eyes and waiting waitress faces
slide soughing out from night's brief crannies   10
suck back along the strand of streets
rattling pebbled smalltalk

O then the curves and curls
of girl stenographers
the loops and purls[1]
of children foaming in the ooze
that by the ceaseless moon of living moves
through heaving flats of habit down the day

And late   from tortuous coves   remoter bays
there sets the sinuous undertow   20
of brokers   and the rolling politicians flow
to welter in the one pelagic[2] motion

Housewives   beached like crabs in staling pools
crisscross   are swashed in search of food
down to the midtown breakers' booming

At last with turning earth   relentless moon
slow but flooding comes the swell once more
with gurge[3] and laughter's plash and murmur
back to the fraying rocks   far-freighted now
with briny flotsam of each morning vow   30
a wrack of deeds that dulls with neaping[4]
dead thoughts that float again to sea
salt evening weeds that lie
and rot between the cracks of life
and hopes that waterlogged will never link
with land   but will be borne until they sink

Now tide is full and sighing creeps
into the clean sought coigns[5] of sleep

[1] Murmuring ripples.
[2] Of the open sea.
[3] Whirlpool.
[4] The coming of neap tide (here synonymous with ebbing).
[5] Corners.

And yet in sleep begins to stir
to mutter in the dark its yearning   40
and to the round possessive mother turning
dreams of vaster wellings
makes the last cliff totter
cradles all the globe in swaying water

The ebb begins from dream. . . .

Toronto 1945/Eaglecliff 1947

rev. 1966

Bushed

He invented a rainbow but lightning struck it
shattered it into the lake-lap of a mountain
so big his mind slowed when he looked at it

Yet he built a shack on the shore
learned to roast porcupine belly and
wore the quills on his hatband

At first he was out with the dawn
whether it yellowed bright as wood-columbine
or was only a fuzzed moth in a flannel of storm
But he found the mountain was clearly alive   10
sent messages whizzing down every hot morning
boomed proclamations at noon and spread out
a white guard of goat
before falling asleep on its feet at sundown

When he tried his eyes on the lake   ospreys
would fall like valkyries
choosing the cut-throat[1]
He took then to waiting
till the night smoke rose from the boil of the sunset

But the moon carved unknown totems   20
out of the lakeshore
owls in the beardusky woods derided him
moosehorned cedars circled his swamps and tossed
their antlers up to the stars
then he knew   though the mountain slept   the winds

---

[1]Cut-throat: 1. B.C. trout that osprey prey upon; 2. the slain upon the field of battle who are gathered up by the Valkyries, the spirit-guides to the afterlife (Valkyries take the form of both women and birds of prey).

were shaping its peak to an arrowhead
poised

And now he could only
bar himself in and wait
for the great flint to come singing into his heart   30
                              Wreck Beach 1951

1952

Can. Lit.
(or *them able leave her ever*[1])

since we'd always sky about
when we had eagles they flew out
leaving no shadow bigger than wren's
to trouble even our broodiest hens

too busy bridging loneliness
to be alone
we hacked in railway ties
what Emily[2] etched in bone

we French&English never lost
our civil war   10
endure it still
a bloody civil bore

the wounded sirened off
no Whitman wanted
it's only by our lack of ghosts
we're haunted
                      Spanish Banks, Vancouver 1947/1966

1962, rev. 1966

---

[1]Word play on 'The Maple Leaf Forever'.   [2]Emily Dickinson.

A Walk in Kyoto

all week   the maid tells me   bowing
her doll's body at my mat   is Boys' Day[1]
also please Mans' Day   and gravely
bends deeper   the magnolia sprig in my alcove
is it male   the old discretions of Zen[2]
were not shaped for my phallic western eye
there is so much discretion
in this small bowed body of an empire
(the wild hair of waterfalls combed straight
in the ricefields   the inn-maid retreating   10
with the face of a shut flower)   i stand hunched
and clueless   like a castaway in the shoals of my room

when i slide my parchment door to stalk awkward
through lilliput gardens framed & untouchable
as watercolours   the streets look much as everywhere
men are pulled past on the strings
of their engines   the legs of boys
are revolved by a thousand pedals
& all the faces are taut & unfestive as Moscow's
or Toronto's   or mine   20

Lord Buddha help us all there is vigour enough
in these islands & in all islands reefed & resounding
with cities   but the pitch is high   high as the ping
of cicadas (those small strained motors concealed
in the propped pines by the dying river) & only male
as the stretched falsetto of actors mincing the roles
of kabuki women[3]   or female only as the lost heroes
womanized in the Ladies' Opera—
where in these alleys jammed with competing waves
of signs in two tongues & three scripts[4]   30
can the simple song of a man be heard?

by the shoguns' palace   the Important Cultural Property[5]

---

[1] Boys' Festival, now calendared as Children's Day, is an ancient celebration giving thanks for healthy boys and prayers for their continued protection from sickness and evil. Many of the traditions of the holiday stem from martial eras in which boys' play was directed toward ensuring manliness and warrior-like skills. One such game is kite-fighting, in which a boy lets his kite or kite-line entangle with another's to make it fall. The kites are usually made in the shape of a golden carp, a symbol of virility.

[2] Zen Buddhism, as well as other Japanese religious philosophies, tends to divide the universe into masculine and feminine components; an ideal world results when they are in balance. The 'magnolia sprig', or the meaning of its arrangement, may seem male to a Japanese but not to a westerner.

[3] In the Kabuki, the classical theatre of Japan, male actors play women's roles as well as men's, while in Takarazuka or 'ladies' opera', women play both male and female roles.

[4] The two tongues are Japanese and Chinese: written Japanese employs Chinese characters, to which are added two separate Japanese scripts.

[5] 'The surviving castles [of the feudal shogun lords that have been] turned to museums, are often labelled Important Cultural Property under a law designed to protect art objects from vandalism' (CJOM).

stripped for tiptoeing schoolgirls   i stare
at the staring penned carp that flail
on each others backs to the shrunk pools edge
for the crumb this non-fish tossed
is this the Day's one parable
or under that peeling pagoda the 500 tons
of hermaphrodite Word?[6]

at the inn i prepare to surrender again   40
my defeated shoes to the bending maid   but suddenly
the closed lotus opens to a smile & she points
to where   over my shoulder   above the sagging tiles
tall in the bare sky & huge as Gulliver
a carp is rising   golden & fighting
thrusting its paper body up from the fist
of a small boy on an empty roof   higher
& higher   into the endless winds of the world

                                              1958

1962

[6]Statue of Buddha.

The Bear on the Delhi Road

Unreal   tall as a myth
by the road the Himalayan bear
is beating the brilliant air
with his crooked arms
About him two men   bare
spindly as locusts   leap

One pulls on a ring
in the great soft nose   His mate
flicks   flicks with a stick
up at the rolling eyes   10

They have not led him here
down from the fabulous hills
to this bald alien plain
and the clamorous world   to kill
but simply to teach him to dance

They are peaceful both   these spare
men of Kashmir   and the bear
alive is their living   too
If   far on the Delhi way
around him galvanic they dance   20
it is merely to wear   wear
from his shaggy body the tranced

wish forever to stay
only an ambling bear
four-footed in berries

It is no more joyous for them
in this hot dust to prance
out of reach of the praying claws
sharpened to paw for ants
in the shadows of deodars[1]
It is not easy to free   30
myth from reality
or rear this fellow up
to lurch   lurch with them
in the tranced dancing of men

> Srinagar 1958/Île des Porquerolles 1959
1962

[1] A Himalayan cedar tree; the name means 'divine tree of the gods'.

El Greco: *Espolio*[1]

The carpenter is intent on the pressure of his hand

on the awl   and the trick of pinpointing his strength
through the awl to the wood   which is tough
He has no effort to spare for despoilings
or to worry if he'll be cut in on the dice
His skill is vital to the scene   and the safety of the state
Anyone can perform the indignities   It's his hard arms
and craft that hold the eyes of the convict's women
There is the problem of getting the holes exact
(in the middle of this elbowing crowd)   10
and deep enough to hold the spikes
after they've sunk through those bared feet
and inadequate wrists he knows are waiting behind him

He doesn't sense perhaps that one of the hands
is held in a curious gesture over him—
giving   or asking   forgiveness?—
but he'd scarcely take time to be puzzled by poses
Criminals come in all sorts
as anyone knows who makes crosses
are as mad or sane as those who decide on their killings   20
Our one at least has been quiet so far
though they say he talked himself into this trouble
a carpenter's son who got notions of preaching

[1] *Espolio* [is] an imagining of the scene when Christ waited on the Hill of Calvary before his execution. Meantime he endured the Espolio or "spoliation" (latin *expolio*, that is "despoiling"), a tearing away of his clothes by greedy spectators who would then gamble for the strips. In [El Greco's] painting, there is a prominent figure in the right foreground, in workmen's clothes, whom I take to be the carpenter; he is busy putting holes in the cross' *(CJOM)*.

Well here's a carpenter's son who'll have carpenter sons
God willing   and build what's wanted
temples or tables   mangers or crosses
and shape them decently
working alone in that firm and profound abstraction
which blots out the bawling of rag-snatchers
To construct with hands   knee-weight   braced thigh   30
keeps the back turned from death

But it's too late now for the other carpenter's boy
to return to this peace before the nails are hammered
Point Grey 1960

1962, rev. 1966

Sinclair Ross

b. 1908

Although his short story collections were not brought out until much later, almost all of Sinclair Ross's short fiction was originally published between 1934 and 1952, chiefly in *Queen's Quarterly*. Most of these stories were gathered in *The Lamp at Noon and Other Stories* (1968). The uncollected stories and two newer ones were subsequently published as *The Race and Other Stories* (1982). In these pieces and in his first novel, *As for Me and My House* (1941), Ross has given his readers a moving, if darkly monochromatic, picture of prairie life, a vision of human suffering and endurance that has earned him a permanent place in Canadian literature.

Born the youngest of three children on his parents' homestead near Prince Albert, Sask., Ross's first experiences were of a prairie farm life like that described in his stories. While working on the farm Ross's father was severely injured when thrown from a horse and, after the accident, drew apart from his family and finally left his wife around the time Ross was six. After the breakup of his home, Ross stayed with his mother, who moved from place to place while she worked on various farms as a housekeeper. Their finances forced Ross to leave school at sixteen, after completing grade eleven, and take a job with the Union Bank of Canada (later part of the Royal Bank). Except for four years in the Royal Canadian Ordinance Corps during the Second World War, he remained with the Royal Bank until he retired in 1968. He left Canada in that year, spending the next three years in Greece and a decade in Spain. He returned in 1981 to settle in Montreal.

Ross's experience working in the banks of three small Saskatchewan towns (between 1924 and 1933), and later in Winnipeg (1933-42) and Montreal (1946-68), seems to have given him an opportunity to learn a great deal about the aspirations and disappointments of those around him. Perhaps because he witnessed the economic failure of so many farmers in the thirties, victims not only of the Depression but of the disastrous weather that characterized the decade, his stories are imbued with a sense of desolation. As Margaret Laurence observed, the world of Ross's short fiction is one in which 'The farms stand far apart. . . . The human community is, for the most of the time reduced to its smallest unit, one family. The isolation is virtually complete' (Preface to *The Lamp at Noon*).

This isolation is not limited to the countryside. In *As for Me and My House* Mrs Bentley, the novel's narrator, describes the gulf that separates her from the other residents of Horizon, and from her husband, who has come to this small town as minister. The understated pathos of that book makes it, like 'A Field of Wheat', a moving experience for the reader; but the emotional bleakness generated by the soul-destroying landscape may have limited its initial readership. Now, however, it is recognized as one of the classics of Canadian fiction. In the two less-successful novels that followed, *The Well* (1958) and *Whir of Gold* (1970), Ross investigates both the modern prairies and the big city. More recently, in *Sawbones Memorial* (1974), he effectively portrays a small town similar to Horizon. But here his vision is less grim: 'a little humour in the face of the inscrutable' now seems appropriate.

Ross was one of the first modernists in Canadian fiction. His stories, like those of Callaghan, were innovative in their use of a restricted point of view: these third-person narratives develop within the consciousness of one character only. In *As for Me and My House* and in some of his stories, Ross went still further in his exploration of technique by using first-person narrators who do not fully understand the experiences they describe: the reader must discern the ultimate significance of their stories.

Although in its complex use of multiple points of view *Sawbones Memorial* also explores narrative technique, none of Ross's last three works achieve the impact of his early fiction, with its powerful delineations not only of landscape but of individuals working out a private destiny: 'Ross's characters grapple with their lives and their fate, a fate partly imposed upon them by an uncaring and fickle natural order and partly compelled by [their] own spiritual inheritance, the pride and determination which enable them to refuse defeat' (Laurence). Again and again they make the kind of discovery that comes to the farm wife in 'The Painted Door', who is 'roused by the whip and batter of the storm to retaliative anger':

For a moment her impulse was to face the wind and strike back blow for blow; then, as suddenly as it had come, her frantic strength gave way to limpness and exhaustion. Suddenly, a comprehension so clear and terrifying that it struck all thoughts . . . from her mind, she realized in such a storm her puniness. And the realization gave her new strength, stilled this time to a desperate persistence.

There are many such passages in which the individual, pitted against the natural world, moves between the extremes of hope and despair; yet a 'desperate persistence' to endure ultimately emerges. In his fiction Ross—himself one of the most solitary figures in Canadian writing—shows deep insight not only into the loneliness of the human soul but also in its capacity to carry on.

A Field of Wheat

It was the best crop of wheat that John had ever grown; sturdy, higher than the knee, the heads long and filling well; a still, heat-hushed mile of it, undulating into a shimmer of summer-colts and crushed horizon blue. Martha finished pulling the little patch of mustard that John had told her about at noon, stood a minute with her shoulders strained back to ease the muscles that were sore from bending, then bunched up her apron filled with the yellow-blossomed weeds and started towards the road. She walked carefully, placing her feet edgeways between the rows of wheat to avoid trampling and crushing the stalks. The road was only a few rods distant, but several times she stopped before reaching it, holding her apron with one hand and with the other stroking the blades of grain that pressed close against her skirts, luxuriant and tall. Once she looked back, her eyes shaded, across the wheat to the dark fallow land beside it. John was there; she could see the long, slow-settling plume of dust thrown up by the horses and the harrow-cart. He was a fool for work, John. This year he was farming the whole section of land without help, managing with two outfits of horses, one for the morning and one for the afternoon; six, and sometimes even seven hours a shift.

It was John who gave such allure to the wheat. She thought of him hunched black and sweaty on the harrow-cart, twelve hours a day, smothering in dust, shoulders sagged wearily beneath the glare of sun. Her fingers touched the stalks of grain again and tightened on a supple blade until they made it squeak like a mouse. A crop like this was coming to him. He had had his share of failures and set-backs, if ever a man had, twenty times over.

Martha was thirty-seven. She had clinched with the body and substance of life; had loved, borne children—a boy had died—and yet the quickest aches of life, travail, heartbrokenness, they had never wrung as the wheat wrung. For the wheat allowed no respite. Wasting and unending it was struggle, struggle against wind and insects, drought and weeds. Not an heroic struggle to give a man courage and resolve, but a frantic, unavailing one. They were only poor, taunted, driven things; it was the wheat that was invincible. They only dreaded, built bright futures; waited for the first glint of green, watched timorous and eager while it thickened, merged, and at last leaned bravely to a ripple in the wind; then followed every slip of cloud into the horizon, turned to the wheat and away again. And it died tantalizingly sometimes, slowly: there would be a cool day, a pittance of rain.

Or perhaps it lived, perhaps the rain came, June, July, even into August, hope climbing, wish-patterns painted on the future. And then one day a clench and tremble to John's hand; his voice faltering, dull. Grasshoppers perhaps, sawflies or rust; no matter, they would grovel for a while, stand back helpless, then go on again. Go on in bitterness and cowardice, because there was nothing else but going-on.

She had loved John, for these sixteen years had stood close watching while he died—slowly, tantalizingly, as the parched wheat died. He had grown unkempt, ugly, morose. His voice was gruff, contentious, never broke into the deep, strong laughter that used to make her feel she was living at the heart of things. John was gone, love was gone; there was only wheat.

She plucked a blade; her eyes travelled hungrily up and down the field. Serene now, all its sting and torment sheathed. Beautiful, more beautiful than Annabelle's poppies, than her sunsets. Theirs—all of it. Three hundred acres ready to give perhaps a little of what it had taken from her—John, his love, his lips unclenched.

Three hundred acres. Bushels, thousands of bushels, she wouldn't even try to think how many. And prices up this year. It would make him young again, lift his head, give him spirit. Maybe he would shave twice a week as he used to when they were first married, buy new clothes, believe in himself again.

She walked down the road towards the house, her steps quickening to the pace of her thoughts until the sweat clung to her face like little beads of oil. It was the children now, Joe and Annabelle: this winter perhaps they could send them to school in town and let them take music lessons. Annabelle, anyway. At a pinch Joe could wait a while; he was only eight. It wouldn't take Annabelle long to pick up her notes; already she played hymn tunes by ear on the organ. She was bright, a real little lady for manners; among town people she would learn a lot. The farm was no place to bring her up. Running wild and barefoot, what would she be like in a few years? Who would ever want to marry her but some stupid country lout?

John had never been to school himself; he knew what it meant to go through life with nothing but his muscles to depend upon; and that was it, dread that Annabelle and Joe would be handicapped as he was, that was what had darkened him, made him harsh and dour. That was why he breasted the sun and dust a frantic, dogged fool, to spare them, to help them to a life that offered more than sweat and debts. Martha knew. He was a slow, inarticulate man, but she knew. Sometimes it even vexed her, brought a wrinkle of jealousy, his anxiety about the children, his sense of responsibility where they were concerned. He never seemed to feel that he owed her anything, never worried about her future. She could sweat, grow flat-footed and shapeless, but that never bothered him.

Her thoughts were on their old, trudging way, the way they always went; but then she halted suddenly, and with her eyes across the wheat again found freshening promise in its quiet expanse. The children must come first, but she and John—mightn't there be a little of life left for them too? A man was young at thirty-nine. And if she didn't have to work so hard, if she could get some new clothes, maybe some of the creams and things that other women had. . . .

As she passed through the gate, Annabelle raced across the yard to meet her. 'Do you know what Joe's done? He's taken off all his clothes and he's in the trough with Nipper!' She was a lanky girl, sunburned, barefoot, her face oval and regular, but spoiled by an expression that strained her mouth and brows into a reproachful primness. It was Martha who had taught her the expression, dinning manners and politeness into her, trying to make her better than the other girls who went to the country school. She went on, her eyes wide and aghast, 'And when I told him to come out he stood right up, all bare, and I had to come away.'

'Well, you tell him he'd better be out before I get there.'

'But how can I tell him? He's all bare.'

Then Joe ran up, nothing on but little cotton knee-pants, strings of green scum from the water-trough still sticking to his face and arms. 'She's been peekin'.' He pointed at Annabelle. 'Nipper and me just got into the trough to get cooled off, and she wouldn't mind her own business.'

'Don't you tell lies about me.' Annabelle pounced on him and slapped his bare back. 'You're just a dirty little pig anyway, and the horses don't want to drink after you've been in the trough.'

Joe squealed, and excited by the scuffle Nipper yelped and spattered Martha with a spray of water from his coat and tail. She reached out to cuff him, missed, and then to satisfy the itch in her fingers seized Joe and boxed his ears. 'You put your shirt on and then go and pick peas for supper. Hurry now, both of you, and only the fat ones, mind. No, not you, Annabelle.' There was something about Annabelle's face, burned and countrified, that changed Martha's mind. 'You shell the peas when he gets them. You're in the sun too much as it is.'

'But I've got a poppy out and if he goes to the garden by himself he'll pick it— just for spite.' Annabelle spun round, and leaving the perplexity in her voice behind her, bolted for the garden. The next minute, before Martha had even reached the house, she was back again triumphant, a big fringed pink and purple poppy in her hand. Sitting down on the doorstep to admire the gaudy petals, she complained to herself, 'They go so fast—the first little wind blows them all away.' On her face, lengthening it, was bitten deeply the enigma of the flowers and the naked seed-pods. Why did the beauty flash and the bony stalks remain?

Martha had clothes to iron, and biscuits to bake for supper; Annabelle and Joe quarrelled about the peas until she shelled them herself. It was hot—heat so intense and breathless that it weighed like a solid. An ominous darkness came with it, gradual and unnoticed. All at once she turned away from the stove and stood strained, inert. The silence seemed to gather itself, hold its breath. She tried to speak to Nipper and the children, all three sprawled in a heap alongside the house, but the hush over everything was like a raised finger, forbidding her.

A long immobile minute; suddenly a bewildering awareness that the light was choked; and then, muffled, still distant, but charged with resolution, climaxing the stillness, a slow, long brooding heave of thunder.

Martha darted to the door, stumbled down the step and around the corner of the house. To the west there was no sky, only a gulf of blackness, so black that the landscape seemed slipping down the neck of a funnel. Above, almost over-head, a heavy, hard-lined bank of cloud swept its way across the sun-white blue in august, impassive fury.

'Annabelle!' She wanted to scream a warning, but it was a bare whisper. In front of her the blackness split—an abrupt, unforked gash of light as if angry hands had snatched to seal the rent.

'Annabelle! Quick—inside—!' Deep in the funnel shaggy thunder rolled, emerged and shook itself, then with hurtling strides leaped up to drum and burst itself on the advancing peak of cloud.

'Joe, come back here!' He was off in pursuit of Nipper, who had broken away from Annabelle when she tried to pull him into the house. 'Before I warm you!'

Her voice broke. She stared into the blackness. There it was—the hail again— the same white twisting little cloud against the black one—just as she had seen it four years ago.

She craned her neck, looking to see whether John was coming. The wheat, the acres and acres of it, green and tall, if only he had put some insurance on it. Damned mule—just work and work. No head himself and too stubborn to listen to anyone else.

There was a swift gust of wind, thunder in a splintering avalanche, the ragged hail-cloud low and close. She wheeled, with a push sent Annabelle toppling into the house, and then ran to the stable to throw open the big doors. John would turn the horses loose—surely he would. She put a brace against one of the doors, and bashed the end into the ground with her foot. Surely—but he was a fool—such a fool at times. It would be just like him to risk a runaway for the sake of getting to the end of the field.

The first big drops of rain were spitting at her before she reached the house. Quietly, breathing hard, she closed the door, numb for a minute, afraid to think or move. At the other side of the kitchen Annabelle was tussling with Joe, trying to make him go down cellar with her. Frightened a little by her mother's excitement, but not really able to grasp the imminence of danger, she was set on exploiting the event; and to be compelled to seize her little brother and carry him down cellar struck her imagination as a superb way of crystallizing for all time the dreadfulness of the storm and her own dramatic part in it. But Martha shouted at her hoarsely, 'Go and get pillows. Here, Joe, quick, up on the table.' She snatched him off his feet and set him on the table beside the window. 'Be ready now when the hail starts, to hold the pillow tight against the glass. You, Annabelle, stay upstairs at the west window in my room.'

The horses were coming, all six at a break-neck gallop, terrified by the thunder and the whip stripes John had given them when he turned them loose. They swept past the house, shaking the earth, their harness jangling tinny against the brattle[1] of thunder, and collided headlong at the stable door.

John, too; through Joe's legs Martha caught sight of his long, scarecrow shape stooped low before the rain. Distractedly, without purpose, she ran upstairs two steps at a time to Annabelle. 'Don't be scared, here comes your father!' Her own voice shook, craven. 'Why don't you rest your arms? It hasn't started yet.'

As she spoke there was a sharp, crunching blow on the roof, its sound abruptly dead, sickening, like a weapon that has sunk deep into flesh. Wildly she shook her hands, motioning Annabelle back to the window, and started for the stairs. Again the blow came; then swiftly a stuttered dozen of them.

She reached the kitchen just as John burst in. With their eyes screwed up against the pommelling roar of the hail they stared at each other. They were deafened, pinioned, crushed. His face was a livid blank, one cheek smeared with blood where a jagged stone had struck him. Taut with fear, her throat aching, she turned away and looked through Joe's legs again. It was like a furious fountain, the stones bouncing high and clashing with those behind them. They had buried the earth, blotted out the horizon; there was nothing but their crazy spew of whiteness. She cowered away, put her hands to her ears.

Then the window broke, and Joe and the pillow tumbled off the table before the howling inrush of the storm. The stones clattered on the floor and bounded up to the ceiling, lit on the stove and threw out sizzling steam. The wind whisked pots and kettles off their hooks, tugged at and whirled the sodden curtains, crashed down a shelf of lamps and crockery. John pushed Martha and Joe into the next room and shut the door. There they found Annabelle huddled at the foot of the stairs, round-eyed, biting her nails in terror. The window she had been holding was broken too; and she had run away without closing the bedroom door, leaving a wild tide of wind upstairs to rage unchecked. It was rocking the whole

[1]Sharp rattling sound as of a series of blows or of something bursting.

house, straining at the walls. Martha ran up to close the door, and came down whimpering.

There was hail heaped on the bed, the pictures were blown off the walls and broken, the floor was swimming; the water would soak through and spoil all the ceilings.

John's face quietened her. They all crowded together, silent, averting their eyes from one another. Martha wanted to cry again, but dared not. Joe, awed to calmness, kept looking furtively at the trickle of blood on his father's face. Annabelle's eyes went wide and glassy as suddenly she began to wonder about Nipper. In the excitement and terror of the storm they had all forgotten him.

When at last they could go outside they stumbled over his body on the step. He had run away from Joe before the storm started, crawled back to the house when he saw John go in, and crouching down against the door had been beaten lifeless. Martha held back the children, while John picked up the mangled heap and hurried away with it to the stable.

Neither Joe nor Annabelle cried. It was too annihilating, too much like a blow. They clung tightly to Martha's skirts, staring across the flayed yard and garden. The sun came out, sharp and brilliant on the drifts of hail. There was an icy wind that made them shiver in their thin cotton clothes. 'No, it's too cold on your feet.' Martha motioned them back to the step as she started towards the gate to join John. 'I want to go with your father to look at the wheat. There's nothing anyway to see.'

Nothing but the glitter of sun on hailstones. Nothing but their wheat crushed into little rags of muddy slime. Here and there an isolated straw standing bolt upright in headless defiance. Martha and John walked to the far end of the field. There was no sound but their shoes slipping and rattling on the pebbles of ice. Both of them wanted to speak, to break the atmosphere of calamity that hung over them, but the words they could find were too small for the sparkling serenity of wasted field. Even as waste it was indomitable. It tethered them to itself, so that they could not feel or comprehend. It had come and gone, that was all; before its tremendousness and havoc they were prostrate. They had not yet risen to cry out or protest.

It was when they were nearly back to the house that Martha started to whimper. 'I can't go on any longer; I can't, John. There's no use, we've tried.' With one hand she clutched him and with the other held her apron to her mouth. 'It's driving me out of my mind. I'm so tired—heart-sick of it all. Can't you see?'

He laid his big hands on her shoulders. They looked at each other for a few seconds, then she dropped her head weakly against his greasy smock. Presently he roused her. 'Here come Joe and Annabelle!' The pressure of his hands tightened. His bristly cheek touched her hair and forehead. 'Straighten up, quick, before they see you!'

It was more of him than she had had for years. 'Yes, John, I know—I'm all right now.' There was a wistful little pull in her voice as if she would have had him hold her there, but hurriedly instead she began to dry her eyes with her apron. 'And tell Joe you'll get him another dog.'

Then he left her and she went back to the house. Mounting within her was a resolve, a bravery. It was the warming sunlight, the strength and nearness of John, a feeling of mattering, belonging. Swung far upwards by the rush and swell of recaptured life, she was suddenly as far above the desolation of the storm as a little while ago she had been abject before it. But in the house she was alone; there was no sunlight, only a cold wind through the broken window; and she crumpled again.

She tried to face the kitchen, to get the floor dried and the broken lamps swept up. But it was not the kitchen; it was tomorrow, next week, next year. The going on, the waste of life, the hopelessness.

Her hands fought the broom a moment, twisting the handle as if trying to unscrew the rusted cap of a jar; then abruptly she let it fall and strode outside. All very fine for John: he'd talk about education for Joe and Annabelle, and she could worry where the clothes were to come from so that they could go clean and decent even to the country school. It made no difference that she had wanted to take out hail insurance. He was the one that looked after things. She was just his wife; it wasn't for her to open her mouth. He'd pat her shoulder and let her come back to this. They'd be brave, go on again, forget about the crop. Go on, go on— next year and the next—go on till they were both ready for the scrap-heap. But she'd had enough. This time he'd go on alone.

Not that she meant it. Not that she failed to understand what John was going through. It was just rebellion. Rebellion because their wheat was beaten to the ground, because there was this brutal, callous finish to everything she had planned, because she had will and needs and flesh, because she was alive. Rebellion, not John at all—but how rebel against a summer storm, how find the throat of a cloud?

So at a jerky little run she set off for the stable, for John. Just that she might release and spend herself, no matter against whom or what, unloose the fury that clawed within her, strike back a blow for the one that had flattened her.

The stable was quiet, only the push of hay as the horses nosed through the mangers, the lazy rub of their flanks and hips against the stall partitions; and before its quietness her anger subsided, took time for breath. She advanced slowly, almost on tiptoe, peering past the horses' rumps for a glimpse of John. To the last stall, back again. And then there was a sound different from the stable sounds. She paused.

She had not seen him the first time she passed because he was pressed against one of the horses, his head pushed into the big deep hollow of its neck and shoulder, one hand hooked by the fingers in the mane, his own shoulders drawn up and shaking. She stared, thrust out her head incredulously, moved her lips, but stood silent. John sobbing there, against the horse. It was the strangest, most frightening moment of her life. He had always been so strong and grim; had just kept on as if he couldn't feel, as if there were a bull's hide over him, and now he was beaten.

She crept away. It would be unbearable to watch his humiliation if he looked up and saw her. Joe was wandering about the yard, thinking about Nipper and disconsolately sucking hailstones, but she fled past him, head down, stricken with guilty shame as if it were she who had been caught broken and afraid. He had always been so strong, a brute at times in his strength, and now—

Now—why now that it had come to this, he might never be able to get a grip of himself again. He might not want to keep on working, not if he were really beaten. If he lost heart, if he didn't care about Joe and Annabelle any more. Weeds and pests, drought and hail—it took so much fight for a man to hold his own against them all, just to hold his own, let alone make headway.

'Look at the sky!' It was Annabelle again, breathless and ecstatic. 'The far one—look how it's opened like a fan!'

Withdrawn now in the eastern sky the storm clouds towered, gold-capped and flushed in the late sunlight, high still pyramids of snowiness and shadow. And one that Annabelle pointed to, apart, the farthest away of them all, this one in bronzed slow splendour spread up mountains high to a vast, plateau-like summit.

Martha hurried inside. She started the fire again, then nailed a blanket over the broken window and lit the big brass parlour lamp—the only one the storm had spared. Her hands were quick and tense. John would need a good supper tonight. The biscuits were water-soaked, but she still had the peas. He liked peas. Lucky that they had picked them when they did. This winter they wouldn't have so much as an onion or potato.

1935, 1968

A.M. Klein

1909-1972

Abraham Moses Klein was one of twin sons (his brother died in his first year). Born to Russian-emigré parents four years after they arrived in the Jewish ghetto of Montreal, to which they came seeking freedom from persecution, Klein received an orthodox upbringing. He supplemented his lessons in Montreal's English Protestant schools with instruction in Hebrew, and in the Torah (the five books of scripture attributed to Moses) and the Talmud (commentaries on the Torah). A natural scholar from his early days, Klein steeped himself in the Talmudic tradition of textual study and learned commentary, and also became fluent in five languages (English, Yiddish, Hebrew, French, Latin). He graduated from McGill University in 1930, then took a law degree at the University of Montreal. He was called to the bar in 1933 and in 1939 established his own firm.

Klein began his studies at McGill in the last year of publication of the *McGill Fortnightly Review* (1925-7), and seems to have been deeply affected by the poetic fervour he found there. Although it is said that his only submission to the *McGill Fortnightly* was not accepted, when the *Canadian Mercury* (1928-9) was created to take its place, Klein was one of the first contributors. Within twelve months Klein had published thirty poems in periodicals ranging from the *Canadian Mercury* and the *Canadian Forum* through the *Menorah Journal* to the prestigious *Poetry* (Chicago). As Desmond Pacey remarked: '. . . never before or since has a Canadian poet made such a sudden, dramatic, and prolific beginning. . . . he had established himself before his twenty-first birthday in the very vanguard of Canadian poetry.' Seven years later, when *New Provinces* (1936) belatedly affirmed the existence of modern poetry in Canada, Klein was one of the six poets represented in that volume.

In the decade that followed, Klein, while continuing to practise law and write poetry, became increasingly active in the Jewish community, and especially in the Zionist movement. From 1936 to 1937 he edited the *Canadian Zionist*, and in 1939 he became the editor of the *Canadian Jewish Chronicle*, a position he held for the next fifteen years. In 1948, combining his Zionism with political activism, Klein unsuccessfully campaigned as a CCF candidate for civic office.

Klein's poetry passed through two stages. The first comprises poems published between 1929 and 1944—most of which were collected in *Hath Not a Jew* . . . (1940) and *Poems* (1944). These draw heavily on his Jewish background and are written in a style that owes something to Biblical rhetoric on the one hand and to such varied English influences as the Renaissance poets and T.S. Eliot on the other. In 1944 Klein also published the *Hitleriad*, a satire on Nazism, written in a form and style derived from Alexander Pope. The growing anti-Semitism of the era must have been extremely painful for a man who has been described as 'easily bruised', and his poetry often reflects his struggle to understand a world that permits evil and injustice. Even when the poems depict a grim existence, however, their irony and humour save them from being despairing. What Irving Layton wrote of the sequence of Psalms that opens *Poems* might be said about much of Klein's work up to this time.

. . . *they wonderfully express the Jew's attitude towards his God, an attitude which is a rich and puzzling alloy of self-abasement and pride, of humility and defiance; it is one of accepting the heavenly scourge while establishing at the same time his human dignity by questioning its necessity or its timing.* (First Statement, *II, No. 12*).

The second stage of Klein's poetry coincided with the emergence in the forties of a new and vigorous poetry in Montreal, centring on the journals *Preview* and *First Statement*, both of which Klein was in con-

tact with. The influence of the poets in these groups—which included F.R. Scott, P.K. Page, Patrick Anderson, Layton, and Louis Dudek—and his appointment from 1945 to 1947 as Visiting Lecturer in English at McGill University, encouraged Klein to experiment with a more broadly based poetry and a somewhat simpler style. A collection of this new poetry, *The Rocking Chair and Other Poems* (1948), won a Governor General's Award. For these poems Klein turned mostly to the milieu of French Quebec for inspiration. As he explained in a letter to the American poet Karl Shapiro: 'Two books I wrote, both stemming out of my ancestral traditions; both praised ancient virtues; when I looked around for those virtues in the here and now, I found them in Quebec. . . . here was a minority, like my own, which led a compact life; continued, unlike my own, an ancient tradition, preserved inherited values, felt that it "belonged". . . .'

After *The Rocking Chair* Klein devoted most of his creative energies to a novel, *The Second Scroll*, and to a study of Joyce's *Ulysses*, a book that had long preoccupied him. The first three chapters of his Joyce study, appearing in journals between 1949 and 1951, are detailed and insightful critiques of the textual complexities of Joyce's elaborate, mythic fiction. They, along with Klein's other critical pieces, are reprinted in *Literary Essays and Reviews* (1987). In its own way Klein's novel, published in 1951, is, like *Ulysses*, a radical departure from the conventions of storytelling. The tale of a young Jew in quest of his heroic and mysterious uncle, *The Second Scroll* combines traditional narrative with poetry, essay, and even drama, and casts the whole into a complicated structure based on the Torah and its Talmudic commentaries.

Around 1954 Klein suffered a breakdown from which he never fully recovered. He retired from active life and gave up writing, leaving his work on Joyce unfinished. In 1957 he was awarded the Lorne Pierce Medal by the Royal Society of Canada. Two years after his death Miriam Waddington edited *The Collected Poems of A.M. Klein* (1974), a volume that brings together his four books of poetry as well as the previously uncollected poems that appeared in periodicals and in *The Second Scroll*. In the over three-hundred poems contained in that collection, the reader can discover how well

Klein fulfilled the task he set himself in one of his earliest lyrics: 'I will disguise the drab in mystery,/ . . . I will contrive to fill days with strange words'.

Since Klein's day a substantial contribution to the writing of poetry and fiction in Canada has been made by Jewish writers as diverse as Irving Layton, Leonard Cohen, Eli Mandel, Mordecai Richler, Miriam Waddington, Adele Wiseman, Jack Ludwig, Tom Wayman, Matt Cohen, Joe Rosenblatt, Norman Levine, and Phyllis Gotlieb. Klein, the first of this distinguished company, helped to prepare the way for the rest. When Ludwig Lewisohn wrote a foreword to Klein's first book, *Hath Not a Jew*, he called Klein not only 'the first contributor of au-thentic Jewish poetry to the English language' but added that, by not trying to disguise his Jewishness as earlier writers had done, he also became 'the first Jew to contribute authentic poetry to the literatures of English speech'.

The University of Toronto Press is currently issuing The Collected Works of A.M. Klein, making him the first Canadian writer to have his work appear in a comprehensive, multi-volume scholarly edition. So far three volumes have been published: *Beyond Sambation: Selected Essays and Editorials 1928-1955* (1982), *Short Stories* (1983), and *Literary Essays and Reviews*. A two-volume edition of the poems will follow.

Reb Levi Yitschok[1] Talks to God

Reb Levi Yitschok, crony of the Lord,
Familiar of heaven, broods these days.
His heart erupts in sighs. He will have a word
At last, with Him of the mysterious ways.

He will go to the synagogue of Berditchev[2],
And there sieve out his plaints in a dolorous sieve.

[1]Reb (or Rabbi) Levi Yitschok (d. 1809) was one of the early followers of the Baal Shem Tov, the founder of Chassidic Judaism in the eighteenth century (see note 2, p. 413). Chassidism was a populist movement that to some extent replaced the Messianic preoccupations of earlier Judaism, shifting away from an emphasis on some future deliverer to an ecstatic affirmation of the here and now achieved through a knowledge of an immanent God expressed in his visible creation. Among the Chassidic rabbis Levi Yitschok was especially noted for his intimate and direct address to God (as opposed to the traditional Judaic manner of reverential and indirect address), and for the fact that he would even call God to account and demand of him an explanation for the suffering of the Jews. G.K. Fischer (in *In Search of Jerusalem*, 1975) suggests that Klein may have been partly inspired by the traditional Yiddish folksong 'Levi Yitschok's Kaddish', which begins:

> *Good morning, Lord of the Universe!*
> *I, Levi Yitschok, son of Sarah, of Berditchev,*
> *Have come to you in a law-suit*
> *On behalf of your people Israel.*
> *What have you against your people Israel?*
> *And why do you oppress*
> *Your people Israel?*

For more information about the influence of Chassidism on the poetry of Klein, see also the essays by Phyllis Gotlieb and Fischer in *The A.M. Klein Symposium* (1975).

[2]Town in the Ukraine of which Levi Yitschok was Rabbi.

Rebono shel Olam[3]—he begins—
Who helps you count our little sins?
Whosoever it be, saving your grace,
I would declare before his face,   10
He knows no ethics,
No, nor arithmetics.

For if from punishments we judge the sins,
Thy midget Hebrews, even when they snore,
Are most malefic djinns,[4]
And wicked to the core of their heart's core;
Not so didst thou consider them,
Thy favourite sons of yore.

How long wilt thou ordain it, Lord, how long
Will Satan fill his mickle-mouth[5] with mirth,   20
Beholding him free, the knave who earned the thong,[6]
And Israel made the buttocks of the earth?

The moon grinned from the window-pane; a cat
Standing upon a gable, humped and spat;
Somewhere a loud mouse nibbled at a board,
A spider wove a niche in the House of the Lord.

Reb Levi Yitschok talking to himself,
Addressed his infant arguments to God:
Why hast thou scattered him like biblic dust,
To make a union with unhallowed sod,   30
Building him temples underneath a mound,
Compatriot of the worm in rain-soaked ground?

The lion of Judah![7] no such parable
Is on my lips; no lion, nor lion's whelp,
But a poor bag'o'bones goat[8] which seeks thy help,
A scrawny goat, its rebel horns both broken,
Its beard uncouthly plucked, its tongue so dumbly lolling
Even its melancholy ma-a- remains unspoken.

The candles flicker,
And peeping through the windows, the winds snicker.   40

---

[3]'Master of the universe' (Hebrew); a traditional ejaculation similar to 'God in Heaven!'
[4]Or 'jinn': here, evil spirits.
[5]Large mouth (archaic).
[6]Whip, lash.
[7]Judah is the ancestor of the twelve tribes of Israel; in Genesis 49:9 Jacob, his father, prophesies power for him saying: 'Judah is a lion's whelp: from the prey my son, thou art gone up . . .'
[8]Recalling the scapegoat (Leviticus 16:8); in general, that which suffers for the sins of others.

The mice digest some holy rune,
And gossip of the cheeses of the moon. . . .

Where is the trumpeted Messiah? Where
The wine long-soured into vinegar?
Have cobwebs stifled his mighty shofar?[9] Have
Chilblains weakened his ass's one good hoof?[1]

So all night long Reb Levi Yitschok talked,
Preparing words on which the Lord might brood.
How long did even angels guard a feud?
When would malign Satanas[2] be unfrocked?   50
Why were the tortured by their echoes mocked?
Who put Death in his ever-ravenous mood?
Good men groaned: Hunger; bad men belched of food;
Wherefore? And why? Reb Levi Yitschok talked . . .
Vociferous was he in his monologue.
He raged, he wept. He suddenly went mild
Begging the Lord to lead him through the fog;
Reb Levi Yitschok, an ever-querulous child,
Sitting on God's knees in the synagogue,
Unanswered even when the sunrise smiled.   60

1940

[9]A horn made of ram's horn, the shofar is sounded on ceremonial occasions; traditionally, when the Messiah finally comes he will be 'trumpeted' by a great shofar, the sounding of which will also denote the final defeat of Satan.
[1]Traditionally the Messiah will first manifest himself riding on an ass. That his ass is lame seems to be Reb Levi's own ironic jest.
[2]Satan.

Heirloom

My father bequeathed me no wide estates;
No keys and ledgers were my heritage;
Only some holy books with *yahrzeit*[1] dates
Writ mournfully upon a blank front page—

[1]'Literally anniversary. It is customary to inscribe the date of the passing of an ancestor on the flyleaf of some sacred book. Special prayers are said on that anniversary date' (Klein's note; the notes by Klein to this poem, and to 'Psalm VI' and 'Autobiographical', are from a 1945 letter to A.J.M. Smith, reprinted in *The A.M. Klein Symposium*.

Books of the Baal Shem Tov,[2] and of his wonders;
Pamphlets upon the devil and his crew;
Prayers against road demons, witches, thunders;
And sundry other tomes for a good Jew.

Beautiful: though no pictures on them,[3] save
The scorpion crawling on a printed track;   10
The Virgin floating on a scriptural wave,
Square letters twinkling in the Zodiac.

The snuff left on this page, now brown and old,
The tallow stains of midnight liturgy—
These are my coat of arms, and these unfold
My noble lineage, my proud ancestry!

And my tears, too, have stained this heirloomed ground,
When reading in these treatises some weird
Miracle, I turned a leaf and found
A white hair fallen from my father's beard.   20

1940

[2]'Literally, the Master of the Good Name—a saintly rabbi of the eighteenth century, founder of the movement known as Chassidism; he placed good works above scholarship. He was a simple good man, a St Francis of Assisi, without birds or flowers' (Klein).
[3]'Hebrew prayer books are never illustrated. The only drawings that appear in the liturgy are the signs of the Zodiac illustrating the prayers for rain and fertility' (Klein).

Psalm XXXVI: A Psalm Touching Genealogy

Not sole was I born, but entire genesis:
For to the fathers that begot me, this
Body is residence. Corpuscular,
They dwell in my veins, they eavesdrop at my ear,
They circle, as with Torahs, round my skull,
In exit and in entrance all day pull
The latches of my heart, descend, and rise—
And there look generations through my eyes.

1944

The Rocking Chair

It seconds the crickets of the province. Heard
in the clean lamplit farmhouses of Quebec,—
wooden,—it is no less a national bird;
and rivals, in its cage, the mere stuttering clock.
To its time, the evenings are rolled away;
and in its peace the pensive mother knits
contentment to be worn by her family,
grown-up, but still cradled by the chair in which she sits.

It is also the old man's pet, pair to his pipe,
the two aids of his arithmetic and plans,   10
plans rocking and puffing into market-shape;
and it is the toddler's game and dangerous dance.
Moved to the verandah, on summer Sundays, it is,
among the hanging plants, the girls, the boy-friends,
sabbatical and clumsy, like the white haloes
dangling above the blue serge suits of the young men.

It has a personality of its own;
is a character (like that old drunk Lacoste,
exhaling amber,[1] and toppling on his pins);
it is alive; individual; and no less   20
an identity than those about it. And
it is tradition. Centuries have been flicked
from its arcs, alternately flicked and pinned.
It rolls with the gait of St Malo.[2] It is act

and symbol, symbol of this static folk
which moves in segments, and returns to base,—
— a sunken pendulum; *invoke, revoke;*
loosed yon, leashed hither, motion on no space.
O, like some Anjou ballad, all refrain,[3]
which turns about its longing, and seems to move   30
to make a pleasure out of repeated pain,
its music moves, as if always back to a first love.

1948

[1]Perfume (perhaps, from having drunk bay rum or cologne).
[2]With the walk of sailors. (St Malo is a town on the coast of France.)
[3]Anjou is a former province of western France. What Klein seems to have in mind is the repetitive quality of those French-Canadian songs that had their roots in medieval France. About these, Edith Fowke quotes an early traveller in Canada: '[the song] seems endless. After each short line comes the refrain, and the story twines itself along like a slender creeping plant' (*The Penguin Book of Canadian Folk Songs*, 1973).

Political Meeting

For Camillien Houde[1]

On the school platform, draping the folding seats,
they wait the chairman's praise and glass of water.
Upon the wall the agonized Y[2] initials their faith.

Here all are laic;[3] the skirted brothers have gone.
Still, their equivocal absence is felt, like a breeze
that gives curtains the sounds of surplices.

The hall is yellow with light, and jocular;
suddenly some one lets loose upon the air
the ritual bird which the crowd in snares of singing

catches and plucks, throat, wings, and little limbs.   10
Fall the feathers of sound, like *alouette's*.[4]
The chairman, now, is charming, full of asides and wit,

building his orators, and chipping off
the heckling gargoyles popping in the hall.
(Outside, in the dark, the street is body-tall,

flowered with faces intent on the scarecrow thing
that shouts to thousands the echoing
of their own wishes.) The Orator has risen!

Worshipped and loved, their favourite visitor,
a country uncle with sunflower seeds in his pockets,   20
full of wonderful moods, tricks, imitative talk,

he is their idol: like themselves, not handsome,
not snobbish, not of the *Grande Allée! Un homme!*[5]
Intimate, informal, he makes bear's compliments

to the ladies; is gallant; and grins;
goes for the balloon, his opposition, with pins;
jokes also on himself, speaks of himself

[1](1889-1958), mayor of Montreal almost continuously from 1928 to 1954; also MPP for Quebec in the 1920s, later elected MP in 1949. During the Second World War, Houde was interned because of his stand against conscription: he advised French Canadians to resist serving in what he viewed as an English cause.
[2]The crucifix.
[3]Of the laity; not priestly.
[4]Banquets and social gatherings in Quebec traditionally opened or closed with the singing of the folk song 'Alouette'. Klein's lines here play with the fact that in the refrain ('je t'y plumerai'), the singers promise to pluck the skylark's head, beak, nose, eyes, neck, wings, feet, etc.
[5]i.e. a man of the people, not from an aristocratic neighbourhood.

in the third person, slings slang, and winks with folklore;
and knows now that he has them, kith and kin.
Calmly, therefore, he begins to speak of war,   30

praises the virtue of being *Canadien*,
of being at peace, of faith, of family,
and suddenly his other voice: *Where are your sons?*[6]

He is tearful, choking tears; but not he
would blame the clever English; in their place
he'd do the same, maybe.

Where *are* your sons?
                        The whole street wears one face,
shadowed and grim; and in the darkness rises
the body-odour of race.   40

1948

[6]A rallying cry among Québécois in their opposition to conscription.

Portrait of the Poet as Landscape

I

Not an editorial-writer, bereaved with bartlett,[1]
mourns him, the shelved Lycidas.[2]
No actress squeezes a glycerine tear for him.
The radio broadcast lets his passing pass.
And with the police, no record. Nobody, it appears,
either under his real name or his alias,
missed him enough to report.

It is possible that he is dead, and not discovered.
It is possible that he can be found some place
in a narrow closet, like the corpse in a detective story,   10
standing, his eyes staring, and ready to fall on his face.
It is also possible that he is alive
and amnesiac, or mad, or in retired disgrace,
or beyond recognition lost in love.

We are sure only that from our real society
he has disappeared; he simply does not count,
except in the pullulation[3] of vital statistics—

[1]Bartlett's *Familiar Quotations*.
[2]'Lycidas (1637) is Milton's pastoral elegy mourning the death by drowning of the young poet Edward King.
[3]Rapid breeding; teeming.

somebody's vote, perhaps, an anonymous taunt
of the Gallup poll, a dot in a government table—
but not felt, and certainly far from eminent—   20
in a shouting mob, somebody's sigh.

O, he who unrolled our culture from his scroll—
the prince's quote, the rostrum-rounding roar—
who under one name made articulate
heaven, and under another the seven-circled air,[4]
is, if he is at all, a number, an x,
a Mr Smith in a hotel register,—
incognito, lost, lacunal.[5]

II
The truth is he's not dead, but only ignored—
like the mirroring lenses forgotten on a brow   30
that shine with the guilt of their unnoticed world.
The truth is he lives among neighbours, who, though they will allow
him a passable fellow, think him eccentric, not solid,
a type that one can forgive, and for that matter, forgo.

Himself he has his moods, just like a poet.
Sometimes, depressed to nadir, he will think all lost,
will see himself as throwback, relict,[6] freak,
his mother's miscarriage, his great-grandfather's ghost,
and he will curse his quintuplet senses, and their tutors
in whom he put, as he should not have put, his trust.   40

Then he will remember his travels over that body—
the torso verb, the beautiful face of the noun,
and all those shaped and warm auxiliaries!
A first love it was, the recognition of his own.
Dear limbs adverbial, complexion of adjective,
dimple and dip of conjugation!

And then remember how this made a change in him
affecting for always the glow and growth of his being;
how suddenly was aware of the air, like shaken tinfoil,[7]
of the patents of nature, the shock of belated seeing,   50
the lonelinesses peering from the eyes of crowds;
the integers of thought; the cube-roots of feeling.

---

[4]According to early pre-Copernican versions of the universe, the earth was surrounded by seven concentric spheres (the sun, the moon, and the five known planets).
[5]i.e. of a lacuna or empty space.
[6]An organism from a previous age surviving in a changed environment.
[7]An echo of the opening lines of Gerard Manley Hopkins' 'God's Grandeur':
    The world is charged with the grandeur of God.
    It will flame out, like shining from shook foil.

Thus, zoomed to zenith, sometimes he hopes again,
and sees himself as a character, with a rehearsed role:
the Count of Monte Cristo,[8], come for his revenges;
the unsuspected heir, with papers; the risen soul;
or the chloroformed prince awaking from his flowers;
or—deflated again—the convict on parole.

III

He is alone; yet not completely alone.
Pins on a map of a colour similar to his,   60
each city has one, sometimes more than one;
here, caretakers of art, in colleges;
in offices, there, with arm-bands, and green-shaded;
and there, pounding their catalogued beats in libraries,—

everywhere menial, a shadow's shadow.
And always for their egos—their outmoded art.
Thus, having lost the bevel[9] in the ear,
they know neither up nor down, mistake the part
for the whole, curl themselves in a comma,
talk technics, make a colon their eyes. They distort—   70

such is the pain of their frustration—truth
to something convolute and cerebral.
How they do fear the slap of the flat of the platitude!
Now Pavlov's victims, their mouths water at bell,
the platter empty.
                    See they set twenty-one jewels
into their watches; the time they do not tell!

Some, patagonian[1] in their own esteem,
and longing for the multiplying word,
join party and wear pins, now have a message,   80
an ear, and the convention-hall's regard.
Upon the knees of ventriloquists, they own,
of their dandled[2] brightness, only the paint and board.

And some go mystical, and some go mad.
One stares at a mirror all day long, as if
to recognize himself; another courts

---

[8]In the novel *The Count of Monte Cristo* (1844-5), by Alexandre Dumas *père*, an innocent man, imprisoned on trumped-up charges, escapes to the Island of Monte Cristo, where he finds fabulous riches. He returns to Paris a powerful man and, under various guises, takes revenge on those responsible for his ill treatment.
[9]A tool for ascertaining angles.
[1]Gigantic (because the Patagonian Indians of South America are said to be the tallest human beings).
[2]Moved lightly up and down on the knee.

angels,—for here he does not fear rebuff;
and a third, alone, and sick with sex, and rapt,
doodles him symbols convex and concave.

O schizoid solitudes! O purities   90
curdling upon themselves! Who live for themselves,
or for each other, but for nobody else;
desire affection, private and public loves;
are friendly, and then quarrel and surmise
the secret perversions of each other's lives.

IV
He suspects that something has happened, a law
been passed, a nightmare ordered. Set apart,
he finds himself, with special haircut and dress,
as on a reservation. Introvert.
He does not understand this; sad conjecture   100
muscles and palls thrombotic on his heart.

He thinks an impostor, having studied his personal biography,
his gestures, his moods, now has come forward to pose
in the shrivering vacuums his absence leaves.
Wigged with his laurel, that other, and faked with his face,
he pats the heads of his children, pecks his wife,
and is at home, and slippered, in his house.

So he guesses at the impertinent silhouette
that talks to his phone-piece and slits open his mail.
Is it the local tycoon who for a hobby   110
plays poet, he so epical in steel?
The orator, making a pause? Or is that man
he who blows his flash of brass in the jittering hall?

Or is he cuckolded by the troubadour
rich and successful out of celluloid?
Or by the don who unrhymes atoms? Or
the chemist death built up? Pride, lost impostor's pride,
it is another, another, whoever he is,
who rides where he should ride.

V
Fame, the adrenalin: to be talked about;   120
to be a verb; to be introduced as *The:*
to smile with endorsement from slick paper; make
caprices anecdotal; to nod to the world; to see
one's name like a song upon the marquees played;

to be forgotten with embarrassment; to be—
to be.

It has its attractions, but is not the thing;
nor is it the ape mimesis[3] who speaks from the tree
ancestral; nor the merkin joy[4] . . .
Rather it is stark infelicity 130
which stirs him from his sleep, undressed, asleep
to walk upon roofs and window-sills and defy
the gape of gravity.

VI
Therefore he seeds illusions. Look, he is
the nth Adam taking a green inventory
in world but scarcely uttered, naming, praising,
the flowering fiats in the meadow, the
syllabled fur, stars aspirate, the pollen
whose sweet collision sounds eternally.
For to praise 140

the world—he, solitary man—is breath
to him. Until it has been praised, that part
has not been. Item by exciting item—
air to his lungs, and pressured blood to his heart.—
they are pulsated, and breathed, until the map,
not the world's, but his own body's chart!

And now in imagination he has climbed
another planet, the better to look
with single camera view upon this earth—
its total scope, and each afflated[5] tick, 150
its talk, its trick, its tracklessness—and this,
this he would like to write down in a book!

To find a new function for the déclassé craft
archaic like the fletcher's;[6] to make a new thing;
to say the word that will become sixth sense;
perhaps by necessity and indirection bring
new forms to life, anonymously, new creeds—
O, somehow pay back the daily larcenies of the lung!

These are not mean ambitions. It is already something
merely to entertain them. Meanwhile, he 160

[3]Imitation; perhaps in reference to the Aristotelian concept of poetry as an imitation of an action.
[4]A deceptive joy; 'merkin': a wig for the female pubic area.
[5]Breathed upon, inspired.
[6]Arrow-makers.

makes of his status as zero a rich garland,
a halo of his anonymity,
and lives alone, and in his secret shines
like phosphorus. At the bottom of the sea.

1948

Autobiographical[1]

Out of the ghetto streets where a Jewboy
Dreamed pavement into pleasant bible-land,
Out of the Yiddish slums where childhood met
The friendly beard, the loutish Sabbath-goy,[2]
Or followed, proud, the Torah-escorting band,[3]
Out of the jargoning city I regret,
Rise memories, like sparrows rising from
The gutter-scattered oats,
Like sadness sweet of synagogal hum,
Like Hebrew violins   10
Sobbing delight upon their eastern notes.

Again they ring their little bells, those doors[4]
Deemed by the tender-year'd, magnificent:
Old Ashkenazi's[5] cellar, sharp with spice;
The widows' double-parloured candy-stores
And nuggets sweet bought for one sweaty cent;
The warm fresh-smelling bakery, its pies,
Its cakes, its navel'd bellies of black bread;
The lintels candy-poled
Of barber-shop, bright-bottled, green, blue, red;   20
And fruit-stall piled, exotic,
And the big synagogue door, with letters of gold.

Again my kindergarten home is full—
Saturday night—with kin and compatriot:

[1]This poem first appeared in *The Canadian Forum* in 1943; it later became one of the 'glosses' in *The Second Scroll*.
[2]'A Gentile employed by Jews to kindle their fires on the Sabbath, such labour being prohibited on that day to the children of Israel. Goy = Gentile' (Klein).
[3]'The Torah is the scroll of the Law, written on parchment. When such a scroll is donated to a synagogue by a rich knave who seeks with his piety to atone for the wretchedness of his soul, the said scroll is customarily carried from the home of the donor through the streets leading to the synagogue, the whole to the accompaniment of music, to wit, a couple of violins and a flute' (Klein).
[4]'The impression of my childhood days is that the only people who kept groceries were widows, who always had little bells over their doors, so that they might hear the entering customer, even from the remoteness of the back kitchen, the emporium usually being located in the front double-parlor' (Klein).
[5]Jews of central-European descent, as opposed to Sephardic Jews (from Spain and Portugal).

My brothers playing Russian card-games; my
Mirroring sisters looking beautiful,
Humming the evening's imminent fox-trot;
My uncle Mayer, of blessed memory,
Still murmuring Maariv,[6] counting holy words;
And the two strangers, come   30
Fiery from Volhynia's[7] murderous hordes—
The cards and humming stop.
And I too swear revenge for that pogrom.

Occasions dear: the four-legged aleph[8] named
And angel pennies dropping on my book;[9]
The rabbi patting a coming scholar-head;
My mother, blessing candles, Sabbath-flamed,
Queenly in her Warsovian perruque;[1]
My father pickabacking me to bed
To tell tall tales about the Baal Shem Tov—[2]   40
Letting me curl his beard.
Oh memory of unsurpassing love,
Love leading a brave child
Through childhood's ogred corridors, unfear'd!

The week in the country at my brother's—(May
He own fat cattle in the fields of heaven!)
Its picking of strawberries from grassy ditch,
Its odour of dogrose and of yellowing hay—
Dusty, adventurous, sunny days, all seven!—
Still follow me, still warm me, still are rich   50
With the cow-tinkling peace of pastureland.
The meadow'd memory
Is sodded with its clover, and is spanned
By that same pillow'd sky
A boy on his back one day watched enviously.

And paved again the street: the shouting boys,
Oblivious of mothers on the stoops,
Playing the robust robbers and police,
The corn-cob battle—all high-spirited noise

---

[6]Evening prayer (Hebrew).

[7]Province in the northwest Ukraine; the site of pogroms against the Jews.

[8]'The first letter of the Hebrew alphabet, cf. Alpha. Called "running" because written with four legs . . .' (Klein).

[9]'If I knew my lesson well, my father would, unseen, drop a penny on my book, and then proclaim it the reward of angels for good study' (Klein).

[1]'Jewesses (married and pious) wear perruques. The custom has died out in America; but not for my mother' (Klein). A perruque (also spelled 'peruke') is a wig. 'Warsovian': in the style of Warsaw.

[2]See p. 313, note 2.

Competitive among the lot-drawn groups.   60
Another day, of shaken apple trees
In the rich suburbs, and a furious dog,
And guilty boys in flight;
Hazelnut games,[3] and games in the synagogue—
The burrs, the Haman rattle,[4]
The Torah-dance on Simchas-Torah night.[5]

Immortal days of the picture calendar
Dear to me always with the virgin joy
Of the first flowering of senses five,
Discovering birds, or textures, or a star,   70
Or tastes sweet, sour, acid, those that cloy;
And perfumes. Never was I more alive.
All days thereafter are a dying off,
A wandering away
From home and the familiar. The years doff
Their innocence.
No other day is ever like that day.

I am no old man fatuously intent
On memoirs, but in memory I seek
The strength and vividness of nonage days,   80
Not tranquil recollection of event.
It is a fabled city that I seek;
It stands in Space's vapours and Time's haze;
Thence comes my sadness in remembered joy
Constrictive of the throat;
Thence do I hear, as heard by a Jewboy,
The Hebrew violins,
Delighting in the sobbed Oriental note.

1951

---

[3]*Nisslach* or 'Nuts', a game played during Passover. In one version, players tossed handfuls of hazelnuts at a small hole dug in the ground, guessing in advance whether the number to drop in would be odd or even.

[4]"The Ninth of Ab (a month of the Jewish calendar) commemorates the destruction of the Temple. It is a day of mourning and fasting. It is customary on that day for youngsters to gather burrs and thistles, bring them to the synagogue, and throw them—not always with impunity—into the beards of the mourning elders—so as to give a touch of realism to their historic weeping. For the kids, this is a lot of fun' (Klein). 'Haman rattle': 'Haman is the villain of the Book of Esther. On Purim, which is the festival commemorating its events, the Book of Esther is read in the synagogue. Every time the name of Haman is uttered by the reader of the scroll, the youngsters, armed with rattles, make a furious noise, so as to drown out those unspeakable syllables' (Klein).

[5]Festival celebrating God's giving his law to Moses; it is marked by the carrying of the parchment scrolls containing the Law seven (or more) times around the synagogue in a dancing procession.

Dorothy Livesay

b. 1909

Winnipeg has been a focal point for Dorothy Livesay. There her parents, both newspaper reporters, met; there she was born; and there she still regularly returns. Livesay grew up in a household in which her mother, Florence Randal Livesay, wrote her own poetry and translated Ukrainian poems and novels, while her iconoclast father, John F.B. Livesay, pursued his interest in politics and economics. In *Beginnings: A Winnipeg Childhood* (1975), a series of stories based on her early childhood, Livesay describes this home life, against a background of the 'great war' and the Winnipeg General Strike of 1919.

When Livesay's father organized the Canadian Press and became its first manager, the family moved to Toronto. There John Livesay encouraged his daughter to read great books, especially those written by women, and also to hear speakers—including advocates of women's and worker's rights. At the same time, Florence Livesay's acquaintance with both new and established Canadian writers brought her daughter into contact not only with the Victorian sensibilities that still dominated Canada's literature but with the new movements that were developing.

In this politicized and literary atmosphere, Livesay herself began to write. When she was just thirteen her first published poem appeared in the Vancouver *Province*, and in her second year at Trinity College, University of Toronto, while still in her teens, Livesay not only won the Jardine Memorial Prize for her poem 'City Wife' but had her first book, *Green Pitcher* (1928), published. After a year of graduate work at the Sorbonne, she returned to Canada in 1932 and published her second book, *Signposts*. In these early books Livesay established herself as a member of the imagist movement in Canada. Like her fellow imagists Raymond Knister and W.W.E. Ross, she sought simplicity of form and image to express direct

and unromanticized observations about everyday life.

Livesay has divided her writing into four categories: *agit-prop, documentary, lyric,* and *confessional*. The latter two divisions include the writing both of her very early period before the Depression and of her 'second season'—work done after her middle age. 'Agit-prop' is a term that arose in the Communist party during the thirties to describe writing, usually drama, in which the political techniques of agitation (oral persuasion) and propaganda (written proselytizing) are united in simple pieces for working-class audiences. In the thirties Livesay wrote a number of agit-prop plays as part of her activities in Communist and proletarian artist groups. At the same time she earned a living as a social worker in Montreal and in Englewood, New Jersey. In *Right Hand, Left Hand* (1977) she has provided her account of this period.

Out of her experiences in the Depression, Livesay fashioned 'Day and Night', a poem that expresses the concerns of the agit-prop plays, while working primarily as a 'documentary'. In applying this term to poetry Livesay is describing what she considers a particularly Canadian genre,

in which historical or other 'found' material is incorporated into a writer's own thoughts, in order to create a dialectic between the objective facts and the subjective feeling of the poet. The effect is often ironic; it is always intensely personal. ('The Documentary Poem: A Canadian Genre' in Contexts of Canadian Criticism, *1971, edited by Eli Mandel.)*

Livesay sees most of her longer poems—those collected in *The Documentaries* (1968)—working in a tradition that descends from Crawford, Lampman, and D.C. Scott, and that includes later poets such as Pratt and Birney.

In 1936 Livesay moved west, settling in Vancouver. Remaining politically active (especially as a member of the CCF) she and her future husband, Duncan Macnair, organized a writers' group that originally served as a conduit for stories and articles for the Toronto-based *New Frontier* (1936-7). She herself became a contributor to this periodical, which stood politically between the radically Communist *Masses* (1932-4), which she had earlier helped to found, and the more moderate *Canadian Forum*. During this period she also began to teach creative writing. As a result of her suggestion that a poetry magazine be started on the west coast, Alan Crawley developed *Contemporary Verse* (1941-53). In 1975 Livesay established the Winnipeg-based journal *CV/II* (the title is a tribute to Crawley's magazine).

The poetry Livesay wrote in the forties and early fifties often lacked the assured voice that her earlier political militancy had given her. Nevertheless, it was during this period that she received two Governor General's awards—one for *Day and Night* (1944), a collection of poems actually written in the mid-thirties, and one for *Poems for People* (1947). In 1958 Livesay returned to school to prepare herself for a teaching career and, while at the University of London on a grant, she learned of her husband's death. In 1960, with her children grown, she took a job in what is now Zambia, teaching for UNESCO. The three years she spent there revitalized her poetry. After her return she published *The Unquiet Bed* (1967), which drew new attention to her work—partly because of the frank sensuality of some of the poems. Since then, six more books of new poetry have appeared (the most recent is *Feeling the Worlds*, 1984), as well as her *Collected Poems: The Two Seasons* (1972), and *The Self-Completing Tree: Selected Poems* (1986). During the sixties and seventies Livesay worked as a writer-in-residence and professor of English at many universities, including New Brunswick, Alberta, Victoria, Manitoba, and Simon Fraser. In 1974 she was awarded the Lorne Pierce Medal.

For more than sixty years, Livesay has given us poems that are confessional and often epigrammatic, while adapting form to suit her content. 'Day and Night', for example, operates on the rhythms of the factory work-song and popular music. Livesay's ability to combine form and function is a result of her desire to create a poetry that celebrates the flux of life rather than imposing upon it an external order.

Green Rain

I remember long veils of green rain
Feathered like the shawl of my grandmother—
Green from the half-green of the spring trees
Waving in the valley.

I remember the road
Like the one which leads to my grandmother's house,
A warm house, with green carpets,
Geraniums, a trilling canary
And shining horse-hair chairs;
And the silence, full of the rain's falling   10
Was like my grandmother's parlour
Alive with herself and her voice, rising and falling—
Rain and wind intermingled.

I remember on that day
I was thinking only of my love

And of my love's house.
But now I remember the day
As I remember my grandmother.
I remember the rain as the feathery fringe of her shawl.

1932

The Difference

Your way of loving is too slow for me.
For you, I think, must know a tree by heart
Four seasons through, and note each single leaf
With microscopic glance before it falls—
And after watching soberly the turn
Of autumn into winter and the slow
Awakening again, the rise of sap—
Then only will you cry: 'I love this tree!'

As if the beauty of the thing could be
Made lovelier or marred by any mood   10
Of wind, or by the sun's caprice; as if
All beauty had not sprung up with the seed—
With such slow ways you find no time to love
A falling flame, a flower's brevity.

1932

Day and Night[1]

social criticisms in poetry.
Marxism & Modernism opposed

1
Dawn, red and angry, whistles loud and sends
A geysered shaft of steam searching the air.
Scream after scream announces that the churn
Of life must move, the giant arm command.
Men in a stream, a moving human belt
Move into sockets, every one a bolt.
The fun begins, a humming, whirring drum—
Men do a dance in time to the machines.

2
One step forward
Two steps back   10

---

[1]In 1968 in her 'Commentary on "Day and Night"' Livesay wrote: 'This documentary is dominated by themes of struggle: class against class, race against race. The sound of Negro spirituals mingled in my mind with Cole Porter's "Night and Day" and Lenin's words (I quote from memory): "To go two steps forward we may have to take one step back." That phrase captured my imagination for it seemed to me that the capitalist system was putting that concept in reverse.'

Shove the lever,
Push it back

While Arnot[2] whirls
A roundabout
And Geoghan shuffles
Bolts about.

One step forward
Hear it crack
Smashing rhythm—
Two steps back

Your heart-beat pounds
Against your throat
The roaring voices
Drown your shout

Across the way
A writhing whack
Sets you spinning
Two steps back—

One step forward
Two steps back.   30

3

Day and night are rising and falling
Night and day shift gears and slip rattling
Down the runway, shot into storerooms
Where only arms and a note-book remember
The record of evil, the sum of commitments.
We move as through sleep's revolving memories
Piling up hatred, stealing the remnants,
Doors forever folding before us—
And where is the recompense, on what agenda
Will you set love down? Who knows of peace?   40

Day and night
Night and day
Light rips into ribbons
What we say.

I called to love
Deep in dream:
Be with me in the daylight
As in gloom.

Be with me in the pounding
In the knives against my back   50

2'Arnot' and 'Geoghan' are names Livesay gives to two workers.

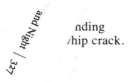

nding
/hip crack.

/ the sunlight

Day and night
Night and day
Tear up all the silence
Find the words I could not say . . .   60

4

We were stoking coal in the furnaces; red hot
They gleamed, burning our skins away, his and mine.
We were working together, night and day, and knew
Each other's stroke; and without words, exchanged
An understanding about kids at home,
The landlord's jaw, wage-cuts and overtime.
We were like buddies, see? Until they said
That nigger is too smart the way he smiles
And sauces back the foreman; he might say
Too much one day, to others changing shifts.   70
Therefore they cut him down, who flowered at night
And raised me up, day hanging over night—
So furnaces could still consume our withered skin.

Shadrach, Meshach and Abednego[3]
Turn in the furnace, whirling slow.
    Lord, I'm burnin' in the fire
    Lord, I'm steppin' on the coals
    Lord, I'm blacker than my brother
    Blow your breath down here.

    Boss, I'm smothered in the darkness   80
    Boss, I'm shrivellin' in the flames
    Boss, I'm blacker than my brother
    Blow your breath down here.
Shadrach, Meshach and Abednego
Burn in the furnace, whirling slow.

5
Up in the roller room, men swing steel
Swing it, zoom; and cut it, crash.
Up in the dark the welder's torch
Makes sparks fly like lightning reel.

---

[3]In Daniel 3, Shadrach, Meshack, and Abednego, sent by Daniel to help rule Babylon, were condemned by its king, Nebuchadnezzar, to the 'fiery furnace' for failing to worship his golden idol. These men were saved by God and emerged from the fire unharmed. The poem here echoes a popular jazz song of the period.

Now I remember storm on a field   90
The trees bow tense before the blow
Even the jittering sparrows' talk
Ripples into the still tree shield.

We are in storm that has no cease
No lull before, no after time
When green with rain the grasses grow
And air is sweet with fresh increase.

We bear the burden home to bed
The furnace glows within our hearts:
Our bodies hammered through the night   100
Are welded into bitter bread.

Bitter, yes:
But listen, friend:
We are mightier
In the end.

We have ears
Alert to seize
A weakness
In the foreman's ease

We have eyes   110
To look across
The bosses' profit
At our loss.

Are you waiting?
Wait with us
After evening
There's a hush—

Use it not
For love's slow count:
Add up hate   120
And let it mount

Until the lifeline
Of your hand
Is calloused with
A fiery brand!

Add up hunger,
Labour's ache
These are figures
That will make

The page grow crazy   130
Wheels go still,

Silence sprawling
On the till—

Add your hunger,
Brawn and bones,
Take your earnings:
Bread, not stones!

6
Into thy maw I commend my body[4]
But the soul shines without
A child's hands as a leaf are tender   140
And draw the poison out.

Green of new leaf shall deck my spirit
Laughter's roots will spread:
Though I am overalled and silent
Boss, I'm far from dead!

One step forward
Two steps back
Will soon be over:
Hear it crack!

The wheels may whirr   150
A roundabout
And neighbour's shuffle
Drown your shout

The wheel must limp
Till it hangs still
And crumpled men
Pour down the hill.

Day and night
Night and day
Till life is turned   160
The other way!

1944

---

[4]Compare Luke 23:46: 'Father, into thy hand I commit my spirit'—Jesus' final words on the cross.

Bartok[1] and the Geranium

She lifts her green umbrellas
Towards the pane
Seeking her fill of sunlight
Or of rain;
Whatever falls
She has no commentary
Accepts, extends,
Blows out her furbelows,[2]
Her bustling boughs;

And all the while he whirls   10
Explodes in space,
Never content with this small room:
Not even can he be
Confined to sky
But must speed high and higher still
From galaxy to galaxy,
Wrench from the stars their momentary notes
Steal music from the moon.

She's daylight
He is dark
She's heaven-held breath
He storms and crackles   20
Spits with hell's own spark.

Yet in this room, this moment now
These together breathe and be:
She, essence of serenity,
He in a mad intensity
Soars beyond sight
Then hurls, lost Lucifer,
From heaven's height.

And when he's done, he's out: 30
She leans a lip against the glass
And preens herself in light.

1955

---

[1]Béla Bartók (1881-1945), Hungarian composer who profoundly influenced modern music by his departure from the traditional diatonic scale; his compositions are noted for their emotional intensity.
[2]Flounces; used figuratively here to suggest that the petals are like the ornamental pleats on the hem of a gown or petticoat.

On Looking into Henry Moore[1]

1
Sun, stun me, sustain me
Turn me to stone:
Stone, goad me and gall me
Urge me to run.

When I have found
Passivity in fire
And fire in stone
Female and male
I'll rise alone
Self-extending and self-known.   10

2
The message of the tree is this:
Aloneness is the only bliss

Self-adoration is not in it
(Narcissus[2] tried, but could not win it)
Rather, to extend the root
Tombwards, be at home with death

But in the upper branches know
A green eternity of fire and snow.

3
The fire in the farthest hills
Is where I'd burn myself to bone: 20
Clad in the armour of the sun
I'd stand anew, alone

Take off this flesh, this hasty dress
Prepare my half-self for myself:
One unit, as a tree or stone
Woman in man, and man in womb.

1957

[1]English sculptor and artist (b. 1898) whose abstract portrayals of human forms attempt to unite the unconscious chaos of human nature with a sense of artistic order. Livesay sees Moore's works as androgynous, uniting male and female forces.
[2]In Greek mythology a beautiful youth who falls so in love with his own reflection that he remains entranced by it until he dies.

Ballad of Me

i
Misbegotten
born clumsy
bursting feet first
then topsy turvy
falling downstairs:
the fear of
joy of
falling.

Butterfingers
father called it   10
throwing the ball
which catch as catch can
I couldn't.

Was it the eyes' fault
seeing the tennis net
in two places?
the ball flying, falling
space-time team-up?

What happened was:
the world, chuckling sideways   20
tossed me off
left me wildly
treading air
to catch up.

ii
Everyone expected guilt
even I—
the pain was this:
to feel nothing.

1967

The Secret Doctrine of Women

The solution is always at hand:
lurking unsuspected just around
the corner; on the wave-torn shore
or vivid on a path in springing woods;
in the gnarled patience of that oak—look there!
or deep in a crowd at traffic halt
one face alight
one woman's hair

2

In a dream I heard the familiar words:
Knock, and it shall be opened unto you;   10
Seek, and ye shall find.
All day I hugged that message
close to my heart—
all month I remembered it—
all year I groped
aching for that truth, as yet unlocked
searching far and wide
and all the while you bided there
close by
offering yourself, your love.   20
As at a stroke of lightning I awoke
and found you at my side
and saw revealed
the secret doctrine we must share—
share and divide

3
A private eye, only the sun
sees us
stretched on the shore
your torso gleaming against rock
I on sand alongside   30
soaking up the whiteness of your skin
marble flow of flesh
whose veins
explore with rock
the pathway to the sea.

4
I am amazed at me
so joined
my blood racing and pounding
beside yours

my mind hooded within your head   40
the pressure of our fingers locked
as ankle is to foot
knee to thigh
heart to lung—

5
The solution
opens up like morning
seizes us   every day
with a new song:
you are the watcher in my brain
who tells me how to dream   50

6
Beside you without needing any dream
here on the boundary of land, sea, sky
I am a more living, pulsing, breathing one
than on that first blind naked thrust—
my journey into the world's light.

7
The secret doctrine of women
despair and creation

[1979]

Sheila Watson

b. 1909

Sheila Watson, née Sheila Martin Doherty, was born in New Westminster, B.C. on the Fraser River. She grew up living on the grounds of the mental hospital there (her father was the presiding physician), and she playfully alludes to this childhood and its daunting milieu in the story 'Antigone':

> My father's kingdom provides asylum in the suburbs. Near it are the convent, the churches, and the penitentiary. Above these on the hill the cemetery looks down and on the river itself.

Initially taught at home, Watson did not enter school until she was ten. After receiving a Catholic education, she enrolled at the University of British Columbia and completed a B.A. in 1931. Two years later, after taking a teaching certificate and an M.A., Watson began her career as a teacher. Until the end of the Second World War she taught in schools in small B.C. communities, including a tiny settlement in the Cariboo region, where she spent two years. In 1941 she married the poet Wilfred Watson, and after the war they taught in Ontario, British Columbia, and Alberta.

From 1949 to 1951, while an instructor at UBC, Watson wrote a series of four mythic short stories; two of them appeared in *Queen's Quarterly* (1954 and 1956) and another in the *Tamarack Review* (1959). Delicate, fascinating fables, they resemble contemporary short stories of manners and nuance except for one striking feature—their principal characters have names drawn from Greek mythology. The effect of this technique is to overlay the personal experiences at the core of these stories with the qualities of a mythic cycle. These tales were not collected in a single volume until 1979, when they were published as *Four Stories*. (This book was reissued in 1984—with the addition of a previously unpublished 'fragment' called 'And the Four Animals'—as *Five Stories*.)

In Calgary, in the early fifties, Watson completed a novel, *The Double Hook*, which grew out of her experiences in the Cariboo. (Because of its innovative style and form she had difficulty finding a publisher, and it did not appear until 1959.) After a year in Paris, Watson began graduate studies in 1957 at the University of Toronto, where she worked under Marshall McLuhan on a study of the English novelist-painter Wyndham Lewis. In 1961 she returned to Alberta and became a member of the University of Alberta's English department. She completed her Ph.D. in 1965 and continued to teach at Alberta until she retired in 1975 as full professor. She now lives in British Columbia.

Watson's active involvement in the literary community in Edmonton led her to help found, with her husband among others, the little magazine, the *White Pelican* (1970-5). Watson is a singular figure in Canadian literature. Although her fictional output—one novel, five pieces of short fiction—has been small, she has had a large influence on the contemporary Canadian novel. *The Double Hook* marked the first appearance in Canada of a work of modernist fiction in which form and idea took precedence over narrative event. This novel also broke the constraints of regionalism that had hitherto bound much Canadian fiction. Paradoxically Watson accomplished this by focusing on a definite region and—abandoning the conventions of realism—giving it a symbolic and allegorical cast, transforming it (like the landscape of her stories) into a region of the imagination.

Antigone

My father ruled a kingdom on the right bank of the river. He ruled it with a firm hand and a stout heart though he was often more troubled than Moses, who was simply trying to bring a stubborn and moody people under God's yoke. My father ruled men who thought they were gods or the instruments of gods or, at very least, god-afflicted and god-pursued. He ruled Atlas who held up the sky, and Hermes who went on endless messages, and Helen who'd been hatched from an egg, and Pan the gardener, and Kallisto the bear, and too many others to mention by name. Yet my father had no thunderbolt, no trident, no helmet of darkness. His subjects were delivered bound into his hands. He merely watched over them as the hundred-handed ones watched over the dethroned Titans so that they wouldn't bother Hellas again.

Despite the care which my father took to maintain an atmosphere of sober common sense in his whole establishment, there were occasional outbursts of self-indulgence which he could not control. For instance, I have seen Helen walking naked down the narrow cement path under the chestnut trees for no better reason, I suppose, than that the day was hot and the white flowers themselves lay naked and expectant in the sunlight. And I have seen Atlas forget the sky while he sat eating the dirt which held him up. These were things which I was not supposed to see.

If my father had been as sensible through and through as he was thought to be, he would have packed me off to boarding school when I was old enough to be disciplined by men. Instead he kept me at home with my two cousins who, except for the accident of birth, might as well have been my sisters. Today I imagine people concerned with our welfare would take such an environment into account. At the time I speak of most people thought us fortunate—especially the girls whose father's affairs had come to an unhappy issue. I don't like to revive old scandal and I wouldn't except to deny it; but it takes only a few impertinent newcomers in any community to force open cupboards which have been decently sealed by time. However, my father was so busy setting his kingdom to rights that he let weeds grow up in his own garden.

As I said, if my father had had all his wits about him he would have sent me to boarding school—and Antigone and Ismene too. I might have fallen in love with the headmaster's daughter and Antigone might have learned that no human being can be right always. She might have found out besides that from the seeds of eternal justice grow madder flowers than any which Pan grew in the gardens of my father's kingdom.

Between the kingdom which my father ruled and the wilderness flows a river. It is this river which I am crossing now. Antigone is with me.

How often can we cross the same river, Antigone asks.

Her persistence annoys me. Besides, Heraklitos made nonsense of her question years ago. He saw a river too—the Inachos, the Kephissos, the Lethaios. The name doesn't matter. He said: See how quickly the water flows. However agile a man is, however nimbly he swims, or runs, or flies, the water slips away before him. See, even as he sets down his foot the water is displaced by the stream which crowds along in the shadow of its flight.

But after all, Antigone says, one must admit that it is the same kind of water. The oolichans run in it as they ran last year and the year before. The gulls cry above the same banks. Boats drift towards the Delta and circle back against the current to gather up the catch.

At any rate, I tell her, we're standing on a new bridge. We are standing so high that the smell of mud and river weeds passes under us out to the straits. The unbroken curve of the bridge protects the eye from details of river life. The bridge is foolproof as a clinic's passport to happiness.

The old bridge still spans the river, but the cat-walk with its cracks and knot-holes, with its gap between planking and handrail has been torn down. The centre arch still grinds open to let boats up and down the river, but a child can no longer be walked on it or swung out on it beyond the water-gauge at the very centre of the flood.

I've known men who scorned any kind of bridge, Antigone says. Men have walked into the water, she says, or, impatient, have jumped from the bridge into the river below.

But these, I say, didn't really want to cross the river. They went Persephone's way, cradled in the current's arms, down the long halls under the pink feet of the gulls, under the booms and towlines, under the soft bellies of the fish.

Antigone looks at me.

There's no coming back, she says, if one goes far enough.

I know she's going to speak of her own misery and I won't listen. Only a god has the right to say: Look what I suffer. Only a god should say: What more ought I to have done for you that I have not done?

Once in winter, she says, a man walked over the river.

Taking advantage of nature, I remind her, since the river had never frozen before.

Yet he escaped from the penitentiary, she says. He escaped from the guards walking round the walls or standing with their guns in the sentry-boxes at the four corners of the enclosure. He escaped.

Not without risk, I say. He had to test the strength of the ice himself. Yet safer perhaps than if he had crossed by the old bridge where he might have slipped through a knot-hole or tumbled out through the railing.

He did escape, she persists, and lived forever on the far side of the river in the Alaska tea and bulrushes. For where, she asks, can a man go farther than to the outermost edge of the world?

The habitable world, as I've said, is on the right bank of the river. Here is the market with its market stalls—the coops of hens, the long-tongued geese, the haltered calf, the bearded goat, the shoving pigs, and the empty bodies of cows and sheep and rabbits hanging on iron hooks. My father's kingdom provides asylum in the suburbs. Near it are the convent, the churches, and the penitentiary. Above these on the hill the cemetery looks down on the people and on the river itself.

It is a world spread flat, tipped up into the sky so that men and women bend forward, walking as men walk when they board a ship at high tide. This is the world I feel with my feet. It is the world I see with my eyes.

I remember standing once with Antigone and Ismene in the square just outside the gates of my father's kingdom. Here from a bust set high on a cairn the stone eyes of Simon Fraser look from his stone face over the river that he found.

It is the head that counts, Ismene said.

It's no better than an urn, Antigone said, one of the urns we see when we climb to the cemetery above.

And all I could think was that I didn't want an urn, only a flat green grave with a chain about it.

A chain won't keep out the dogs, Antigone said.

But his soul could swing on it, Ismene said, like a bird blown on a branch in the wind.

And I remember Antigone's saying: The cat drags its belly on the ground and the rat sharpens its tooth in the ivy.

I should have loved Ismene, but I didn't. It was Antigone I loved. I should have loved Ismene because, although she walked the flat world with us, she managed somehow to see it round.

The earth is an oblate spheroid, she'd say. And I knew that she saw it there before her comprehensible and whole like a tangerine spiked through and held in place while it rotated on the axis of one of Nurse's steel sock needles. The earth was a tangerine and she saw the skin peeled off and the world parcelled out into neat segments, each segment sweet and fragrant in its own skin.

It's the head that counts, she said.

In her own head she made diagrams to live by, cut and fashioned after the eternal patterns spied out by Plato as he rummaged about in the sewing basket of the gods.

I should have loved Ismene. She would live now in some prefabricated and perfect chrysolite by some paradigm which made love round and whole. She would simply live and leave destruction in the purgatorial ditches outside her own walled paradise.

Antigone is different. She sees the world flat as I do and feels it tip beneath her feet. She has walked in the market and seen the living animals penned and the dead hanging stiff on their hooks. Yet she defies what she sees with a defiance which is almost denial. Like Atlas she tries to keep the vaulted sky from crushing the flat earth. Like Hermes she brings a message that there is life if one can escape to it in the brush and the bulrushes in some dim Hades beyond the river. It is defiance not belief and I tell her that this time we walk the bridge to a walled cave where we can deny death no longer.

Yet she asks her question still. And standing there I tell her that Heraklitos has made nonsense of her question. I should have loved Ismene for she would have taught me what Plato meant when he said in all earnest that the union of the soul with the body is in no way better than dissolution. I expect that she understood things which Antigone is too proud to see.

I turn away from her and flatten my elbows on the high wall of the bridge. I look back at my father's kingdom. I see the terraces rolling down from the red-brick buildings with their barred windows. I remember hands shaking the bars and hear fingers tearing up paper and stuffing it through the meshes. Diktynna, mother of nets and high leaping fear. O Artemis, mistress of wild beasts and wild men.

The inmates are beginning to come out on the screened verandas. They pace up and down in straight lines or stand silent like figures which appear at the same time each day from some depths inside a clock.

On the upper terrace Pan the gardener is shifting sprinklers with a hooked stick. His face is shadowed by the brim of his hat. He moves as economically as an animal between the beds of lobelia and geranium. It is high noon.

Antigone has cut out a piece of sod and has scooped out a grave. The body lies in a coffin in the shade of the magnolia tree. Antigone and I are standing. Ismene is sitting between two low angled branches of the monkey puzzle tree. Her lap is filled with daisies. She slits the stem of one daisy and pulls the stem of another through it. She is making a chain for her neck and a crown for her hair.

Antigone reaches for a branch of the magnolia. It is almost beyond her grip. The buds flame above her. She stands on a small fire of daisies which smoulder in the roots of the grass.

I see the magnolia buds. They brood above me, whiteness feathered on whiteness. I see Antigone's face turned to the light. I hear the living birds call to the sun. I speak private poetry to myself: Between four trumpeting angels at the four corners of the earth a bride stands before the altar in a gown as white as snow.

Yet I must have been speaking aloud because Antigone challenges me: You're mistaken. It's the winds the angels hold, the four winds of the earth. After the just are taken to paradise the winds will destroy the earth. It's a funeral, she says, not a wedding.

She looks towards the building.

Someone is coming down the path from the matron's house, she says.

I notice that she has pulled one of the magnolia blossoms from the branch. I take it from her. It is streaked with brown where her hands have bruised it. The sparrow which she has decided to bury lies on its back. Its feet are clenched tight against the feathers of its breast. I put the flower in the box with it.

Someone is coming down the path. She is wearing a blue cotton dress. Her cropped head is bent. She walks slowly carrying something in a napkin.

It's Kallisto the bear, I say. Let's hurry. What will my father say if he sees us talking to one of his patients?

If we live here with him, Antigone says, what can he expect? If he spends his life trying to tame people he can't complain if you behave as if they were tame. What would your father think, she says, if he saw us digging in the Institution lawn?

Pan comes closer. I glower at him. There's no use speaking to him. He's deaf and dumb.

Listen, I say to Antigone, my father's not unreasonable. Kallisto thinks she's a bear and he thinks he's a bear tamer, that's all. As for the lawn, I say quoting my father without conviction, a man must have order among his own if he is to keep order in the state.

Kallisto has come up to us. She is smiling and laughing to herself. She gives me her bundle.

Fish, she says.

I open the napkin.

Pink fish sandwiches, I say.

For the party, she says.

But it isn't a party, Antigone says. It's a funeral.

For the funeral breakfast, I say.

Ismene is twisting two chains of daisies into a rope. Pan has stopped pulling the sprinkler about. He is standing beside Ismene resting himself on his hooked stick. Kallisto squats down beside her. Ismene turns away, preoccupied, but she can't turn far because of Pan's legs.

Father said we never should
Play with madmen in the wood.

I look at Antigone.

It's my funeral, she says.

I go over to Ismene and gather up a handful of loose daisies from her lap. The sun reaches through the shadow of the magnolia tree.

It's my funeral, Antigone says. She moves possessively toward the body.

An ant is crawling into the bundle of sandwiches which I've put on the ground. A file of ants is marching on the sparrow's box.

I go over and drop daisies on the bird's stiff body. My voice speaks ritual words: Deliver me, O Lord, from everlasting death on this dreadful day. I tremble and am afraid.

The voice of a people comforts me. I look at Antigone. I look her in the eye.

It had better be a proper funeral then, I say.

Kallisto is crouched forward on her hands. Tears are running down her cheeks and she is licking them away with her tongue.

My voice rises again: I said in the midst of my days, I shall not see—

Antigone just stands there. She looks frightened, but her eyes defy me with their assertion.

It's my funeral, she says. It's my bird. I was the one who wanted to bury it.

She is looking for a reason. She will say something which sounds eternally right.

Things have to be buried, she says. They can't be left lying around anyhow for people to see.

Birds shouldn't die, I tell her. They have wings. Cats and rats haven't wings.

Stop crying, she says to Kallisto. It's only a bird.

It has a bride's flower in its hand, Kallisto says.

We shall rise again, I mutter, but we shall not all be changed.

Antigone does not seem to hear me.

Behold, I say in a voice she must hear, in a moment, in the twinkling of an eye, the trumpet shall sound.

Ismene turns to Kallisto and throws the daisy chain about her neck.

Shall a virgin forget her adorning or a bride the ornament of her breast?

Kallisto is lifting her arms towards the tree.

The bridegroom has come, she says, white as a fall of snow. He stands above me in a great ring of fire.

Antigone looks at me now.

Let's cover the bird up, she says. Your father will punish us all for making a disturbance.

He has on his garment, Kallisto says, and on his thigh is written King of Kings.

I look at the tree. If I could see with Kallisto's eyes I wouldn't be afraid of death, or punishment, or the penitentiary guards. I wouldn't be afraid of my father's belt or his honing strap or his bedroom slipper. I wouldn't be afraid of falling into the river through a knot-hole in the bridge.

But, as I look, I see the buds falling like burning lamps and I hear the sparrow twittering in its box: Woe, woe, woe because of the three trumpets which are yet to sound.

Kallisto is on her knees. She is growling like a bear. She lumbers over to the sandwiches and mauls them with her paw.

Ismene stands alone for Pan the gardener has gone.

Antigone is fitting a turf in place above the coffin. I go over and press the edge of the turf with my feet. Ismene has caught me by the hand.

Go away, Antigone says.

I see my father coming down the path. He has an attendant with him. In front of them walks Pan holding the sprinkler hook like a spear.

What are you doing here? my father asks.

Burying a bird, Antigone says.

Here? my father asks again.

Where else could I bury it? Antigone says.

My father looks at her.

This ground is public property, he says. No single person has any right to an inch of it.

I've taken six inches, Antigone says. Will you dig up the bird again?

Some of his subjects my father restrained since they were moved to throw themselves from high places or to tear one another to bits from jealousy or rage. Others who disturbed the public peace he taught to walk in the airing courts or to work in the kitchen or in the garden.

If men live at all, my father said, it is because discipline saves their life for them.

From Antigone he simply turned away.

1984

Irving Layton

b. 1912

Irving Layton has become one of Canada's best-known authors, not only because of his sizeable body of writing, which includes a number of exceptional poems, but also because of a reputation—extending well beyond his reading audience—for controversy, for obstreperous antagonism to those who fail to agree with him, and for keeping himself in the public eye. Often at the centre of bitter feuds, he has frequently added prefaces to his many books of poetry, attacking English professors, critics and reviewers, and even his fellow poets, for effete élitism, while at the same time scorning the general public for their insensitivity and lack of concern for matters of art and intellect. Al-

though sympathetic to Marxism as a young man, he later became a staunch anti-Communist who supported the U.S. involvement in Viet Nam at a time when such a stand made one a pariah in most intellectual circles. Moreover, throughout his poetry he has chronicled his sexual adventures and offered his opinions in language sufficiently frank and bawdy to offend some of his readers and lose him his first connection with a commercial press in Canada.

Layton acknowledges that he has sometimes deliberately assumed 'the role of public exhibitionist'; indeed, perhaps more than any other poet in Canada he has played the part of the artist as it was defined in the early days of the modernist movement: the gadfly and rebel, outraging the middle-class and challenging the assumptions of an anaesthetized Philistine society. He seems, at that same time, to have always been a battler by instinct. 'I would not have had it any other way,' he wrote in the Preface to *Engagements: The Prose of Irving Layton*. 'I owe them [his many conflicts] some of the most delicious moments of my life.'

Layton is more complex, however, than his public roles might suggest. For example, despite his oft-expressed scorn for academics, he holds a master's degree and has devoted almost as much of his career to teaching as to writing. As a young man he worked patiently with new immigrants to help them master English, and he also taught in a parochial school in Montreal; since then he has taught at Sir George Williams (now Concordia) University and at York University and spent a year as writer-in-residence at the University of Toronto. Similarly, despite his disparaging remarks about his rivals in poetry, he has been extremely solicitous towards beginning writers and has often taken the time to introduce both them and his creative-writing students to an understanding and appreciation of the same poets he publicly criticizes. Indeed, despite what sometimes comes across as a generalized contempt for mankind, Layton has been remarkably generous with his time and energy, answering correspondence from readers he has never met, conversing patiently after his public readings, or working with the students in his classes.

Born in Romania to Jewish parents (he later changed his family name, Lazarovitch), Irving Layton came to Montreal with his family when he was an infant. He has written of how his developmental years made him 'suspicious of both literature and reality':

Let me explain. My father was an ineffectual visionary; he saw God's footprint in a cloud and lived only for his books and meditations. A small bedroom in a slum tenement which in the torrid days steamed and blistered and sweated, he converted into a tabernacle for the Lord of Israel; and here, like the patriarch Abraham, he received his messengers. Since there was nothing angelic about me or his other children, he no more noticed us than if we had been flies on a wall. Had my mother been as otherworldly as he was, we should have starved. Luckily for us, she was not; she was tougher than nails, shrewd and indomitable. Moreover, she had a gift for cadenced vituperation; to which, doubtless, I owe my impeccable ear for rhythm. With parents so poorly matched and dissimilar, small wonder my entelechy [realization of potential] was given a terrible squint from the outset. I am not at ease in the world (what poet ever is?); but neither am I fully at ease in the world of the imagination. I require some third realm, as yet undiscovered, in which to live. My dis-ease has spurred me on to bridge the two with the stilts of poetry, or to create inside me an ironic balance of tensions. (Foreword, A Red Carpet for the Sun, 1959)

Like A.M. Klein before him and Mordecai Richler after him, Layton attended Baron Byng High School, working at a variety of jobs to earn the monthly fee of $1.50. There he first discovered his love of poetry, but—because of an argument with one of his teachers when he fell behind in payment of his fee—he was expelled in his last year. He prepared himself for his exams anyway and, after passing them, plunged into what may have been the most important phase of his education, an extended period of reading and self-instruction, supplemented by debates in the evenings at Horn's Cafeteria (a gathering place during the Depression for many of Montreal's radicals and disaffected intellectuals). Eventually he returned to school, completing a B.Sc. in agricultural science at Macdonald College in 1939. (Of this Layton has remarked, '. . . you can see the agricultural images in my poems. I worked on farms for three or four summers, something significant for an urban Jew.') After a period of wartime military service, Layton continued his education, taking an M.A. in political science at McGill in 1945. The subtitle of his thesis on British labourite Harold Laski—'The Paradoxes of a Liberal Marxist'—also testifies to Layton's 'ironic balance of tensions'.

The post-war forties was a time of intense activity for Layton, a period characterized by 'exciting personalities, living poetry twenty-four hours a day, thinking, talking, analyzing, arguing, reading and above all writing'. At McGill he met Louis Dudek (both of them published poems in the *McGill Daily*) and heard about John Sutherland's newly established mimeographed magazine *First Statement* (1942-5). Layton sent Sutherland some poems and later, with

Dudek, joined him in editing the often controversial little magazine. Together the three of them set out to establish a new poetry movement in Canada, one that would challenge the 'cosmopolitan' writers who had grouped themselves around Patrick Anderson's rival magazine *Preview* (1942-5) with a less abstract and more earthy poetry. In 'Montreal Poets of the Forties' (*Canadian Literature*, No. 14) Wynn Francis describes how the rivalry, though sometimes acrimonious, stimulated the more established poets of *Preview*, while making the younger ones at *First Statement* work harder. 'Not that we wanted to be like them,' she quotes Layton as saying, 'but we wanted to be as good as they were in our way.'

In 1945 the *First Statement* group launched a series of printed chapbooks with a collection of Layton's poems, *Here and Now*, later following this with Layton's second book, *Now is the Place* (1948). When the group around Sutherland eventually broke up, Layton and Dudek joined Raymond Souster to found Contact Press, a co-operative venture in which the editors and several younger writers funded the publication of their own books. As well as *Cerberus* (1952), an anthology of the work of all three editors, Contact Press published a number of Layton's most important books of poetry, including *The Black Huntsman* (1951), *Love the Conqueror Worm* (1952), *The Long Pea-Shooter* (1954), *The Cold Green Element* (1955), and *The Bull-Calf and Other Poems* (1956). Though these books were not much noticed in Canada, around this time Layton caught the attention of American poets and editors, and this helped to establish his reputation. Robert Creeley praised Layton's poetry in the first issue of the *Black Mountain Review* and published Layton's *In the Midst of My Fever* (1954) with his Divers Press; the American small-press editor Jonathan Williams brought out Layton's first substantial volume of selected poems, *The Improved Binoculars* (1956), and a collection of new poems, *A Laughter in the Mind* (1958). Even though the Ryerson Press reneged on its agreement to distribute *The Improved Binoculars* in Canada, this book gained Layton his first sustained readership, partly as a

result of a preface by William Carlos Williams in which, after avowing his admiration for the younger poet, Williams concluded: 'In short, I believe this poet to be capable, to be capable of anything. . . . There will, if I am not mistaken, be a battle: Layton against the rest of the world.'

Soon after this, Layton was approached by McClelland and Stewart, who agreed to publish a compilation of the poems Layton valued most from his previous books. Entitled *A Red Carpet for the Sun*, this collection won the Governor General's Award for poetry in 1959. With a commercial publisher supporting him, and an audience established in Canada at last, Layton began to publish frequently; for the next twenty years he brought out one or two works each year. He has now published more than forty books of poetry, including the 589-page *Collected Poems of Irving Layton* (1971), two collections of prose, and a memoir of his formative years, *Waiting for the Messiah* (1985).

From his first poems to his most recent ones, two aspects of Layton's personality have dominated: his exuberance and his drive to enlighten his readers. Deeply influenced by Nietzsche, Layton has declared that the 'poet has a public function as a prophet'. His poems frequently draw their vitality and express his concern over man's failures through the depiction of animals, especially animal victims: in suffering and death, these animals reflect man's own mortality while testifying to his violation of nature. But if man is often seen as a threatening predator, he finds in turn that he lives in a predatory world. 'The Cold Green Element' gives one of the fullest accounts of Layton's vision: the universe is seen here as either an indifferent sea in which we swim or drown, or else, in the image of the robin devouring the worm, as actively hostile, a consumer of life. But the poem suggests that worm-like man need not go meekly to his annihilation. Instead—recalling Isaàc Dufours in Duncan Campbell Scott's poem, 'At the Cedars'—man should acclaim his brief moment with celebration and thereby become one with 'the worm/who sang for an hour in the throat of a robin'.

Newsboy

Neither tribal nor trivial he shouts
From the city's centre where tramcars move
Like stained bacilli across the eyeballs,
Where people spore in composite buildings
From their protective gelatine of doubts,
Old ills, and incapacity to love
While he, a Joshua before their walls,[1]
Sells newspapers to the gods and geldings.

Intrusive as a collision, he is
The Zeitgeist's[2] too public interpreter,   10
A voice multiplex and democratic,
The people's voice or the monopolists';
Who with last-edition omniscience
Plays Clotho[3] to each gaping customer
With halcyon colt,[4] sex crime in an attic,
The story of a twice-jailed bigamist.

For him the mitred cardinals sweat in
Conclaves domed; the spy is shot. Empiric;[5]
An obstreperous confidant of kings,
Rude despiser of the anonymous,   20
Danubes of blood wash up his bulletins
While he domesticates disaster like
A wheat in pampas[6] of prescriptive things
With cries animal and ambiguous.

His dialectics will assault the brain,
Contrive men to voyages or murder,
Dip the periscope of their public lives
To the green levels of acidic caves;
Fever their health, or heal them with ruin,
Or with lies dangerous as a letter;   30
Finally enfold the season's cloves,
Cover a somnolent face on Sundays.

1945

[1] Joshua and his followers defeated the city of Jericho by bringing down its walls with 'a great shout' (Joshua 6:20).
[2] Spirit of the times.
[3] One of the three Fates in Greek mythology. (Clotho spins the thread of life.)
[4] i.e. one who has won a race.
[5] One who learns by observation.
[6] Argentine prairie area.

The Birth of Tragedy[1]

And me happiest when I compose poems.
     Love, power, the huzza of battle
     are something, are much;
yet a poem includes them like a pool
     water and reflection.
In me, nature's divided things—
     tree, mould on tree—
     have their fruition;
I am their core. Let them swap,
bandy, like a flame swerve   10
I am their mouth; as a mouth I serve.

And I observe how the sensual moths
     big with odour and sunshine
     dart into the perilous shrubbery;
or drop their visiting shadows
     upon the garden I one year made
of flowering stone to be a footstool
     for the perfect gods:
     who, friends to the ascending orders,
sustain all passionate meditations   20
and call down pardons
for the insurgent blood.

A quiet madman, never far from tears,
     I lie like a slain thing
     under the green air the trees
inhabit, or rest upon a chair
     towards which the inflammable air
tumbles on many robins' wings;
     noting how seasonably
     leaf and blossom uncurl   30
and living things arrange their death,
while someone from afar off
blows birthday candles for the world.

1954

---

[1] A reference to *The Birth of Tragedy out of the Spirit of Music* (1872), a work by the German philosopher Friedrich Nietzsche (1844-1900). In that book—ostensibly an attempt to explain the origins of Greek tragedy—Nietzsche discusses classical Greek culture as a union of two religious systems; the first based on the worship of the immortal gods of Olympus (such as Apollo), the second celebrating a dying god in rituals for Dionysus, the god of fertility and wine. From this observation Nietzsche generalizes two responses to the universe: 'Apollonian', which seeks the ideal world and believes in order and restraint, and 'Dionysiac', which confronts the chaos that actually underlies the appearance of order. Identifying Apollonian with 'dream' and Dionysiac with 'vision', he sees the power of Greek tragic playwrights deriving from their ability to unite Apollonian form and Dionysiac content.

The Cold Green Element

At the end of the garden walk
the wind and its satellite wait for me;
their meaning I will not know
      until I go there,
but the black-hatted undertaker

who, passing, saw my heart beating in the grass,
is also going there. Hi, I tell him,
a great squall in the Pacific blew a dead poet
      out of the water,
who now hangs from the city's gates.   10

Crowds depart daily to see it, and return
with grimaces and incomprehension;
if its limbs twitched in the air
      they would sit at its feet
peeling their oranges.

And turning over I embrace like a lover
the trunk of a tree, one of those
for whom the lightning was too much
      and grew a brilliant
hunchback with a crown of leaves.   20

The ailments escaped from the labels
of medicine bottles are all fled to the wind;
I've seen myself lately in the eyes
      of old women,
spent streams mourning my manhood,

in whose old pupils the sun became
a bloodsmear on broad catalpa[1] leaves
and hanging from ancient twigs,
      my murdered selves
sparked the air like the muted collisions   30

of fruit. A black dog howls down my blood,
a black dog with yellow eyes;
he too by someone's inadvertence
      saw the bloodsmear
on the broad catalpa leaves.

But the furies clear a path for me to the worm
who sang for an hour in the throat of a robin,
and misled by the cries of young boys
      I am again
a breathless swimmer in that cold green element.   40

1955
[1] Tree with large heart-shaped leaves.

The Fertile Muck

There are brightest apples on those trees
    but until I, fabulist, have spoken
they do not know their significance
or what other legends are hung like garlands
    on their black boughs twisting
like a rumour. The wind's noise is empty.

Nor are the winged insects better off
    though they wear my crafty eyes
wherever they alight. Stay here, my love;
you will see how delicately they deposit   10
    me on the leaves of elms
or fold me in the orient dust of summer.

And if in August joiners and bricklayers
    are thick as flies around us
building expensive bungalows for those
who do not need them, unless they release
    me roaring from their moth-proofed cupboards
their buyers will have no joy, no ease.

I could extend their rooms for them without cost
    and give them crazy sundials   20
to tell the time with, but I have noticed
how my irregular footprint horrifies them
    evenings and Sunday afternoons:
they spray for hours to erase its shadow.

How to dominate reality? Love is one way;
    imagination another. Sit here
beside me, sweet; take my hard hand in yours,
We'll mark the butterflies disappearing over the hedge
    with tiny wristwatches on their wings:
our fingers touching the earth, like two Buddhas.   30

1956

Whatever Else
Poetry Is Freedom

Whatever else poetry is freedom.
Forget the rhetoric, the trick of lying
All poets pick up sooner or later. From the river,
Rising like the thin voice of grey castratos[1]—the mist;
Poplars and pines grow straight but oaks are gnarled;
Old codgers must speak of death, boys break windows;
Women lie honestly by their men at last.

And I who gave my Kate a blackened eye
Did to its vivid changing colours
Make up an incredible musical scale;   10
And now I balance on wooden stilts and dance
And thereby sing to the loftiest casements.
See how with polish I bow from the waist.
Space for these stilts! More space or I fail!

And a crown I say for my buffoon's head.
Yet no more fool am I than King Canute,[2]
Lord of our tribe, who scanned and scorned;
Who half-deceived, believed; and, poet, missed
The first white waves come nuzzling at his feet;
Then damned the courtiers and the foolish trial   20
With a most bewildering and unkingly jest.

It was the mist. It lies inside one like a destiny.
A real Jonah it lies rotting like a lung.
And I know myself undone who am a clown
And wear a wreath of mist for a crown;
Mist with the scent of dead apples,
Mist swirling from black oily waters at evening,
Mist from the fraternal graves of cemeteries.

It shall drive me to beg my food and at last
Hurl me broken I know and prostrate on the road;   30
Like a huge toad I saw, entire but dead,
That Time mordantly had blacked; O pressed
To the moist earth it pled for entry.
I shall be I say that stiff toad for sick with mist
And crazed I smell the odour of mortality.

And Time flames like a paraffin stove
And what it burns are the minutes I live.

[1]Historically: males castrated before puberty to retain a soprano or alto singing voice into adulthood.

[2]Eleventh-century king of England who is said to have placed his throne on the shore and commanded the tide not to rise. In some versions, when the tide rolled over him anyway, he explained that he had done this to rebuke his courtiers, who thought or acted as if he had God-like powers.

At certain middays I have watched the cars
Bring me from afar their windshield suns;
What lay to my hand were blue fenders,   40
The suns extinguished, the drivers wearing sunglasses.
And it made me think I had touched a hearse.

So whatever else poetry is freedom. Let
Far off the impatient cadences reveal
A padding for my breathless stilts. Swivel,
O hero, in the fleshy groves, skin and glycerine,
And sing of lust, the sun's accompanying shadow
Like a vampire's wing, the stillness in dead feet—
Your stave[3] brings resurrection, O aggrievèd king.

1958

[3]Rod, lance; but also with the punning meaning of 'stanza'.

Keine Lazarovitch
1870-1959

When I saw my mother's head on the cold pillow,
Her white waterfalling hair in the cheeks' hollows,
I thought, quietly circling my grief, of how
She had loved God but cursed extravagantly his creatures.

For her final mouth was not water but a curse,
A small black hole, a black rent in the universe,
Which damned the green earth, stars and trees in its stillness
And the inescapable lousiness of growing old.

And I record she was comfortless, vituperative,
Ignorant, glad, and much else besides; I believe   10
She endlessly praised her black eyebrows, their thick weave,
Till plagiarizing Death leaned down and took them for his mould.

And spoiled a dignity I shall not again find,
And the fury of her stubborn limited mind;
Now none will shake her amber beads and call God blind,
Or wear them upon a breast so radiantly.

O fierce she was, mean and unaccommodating;
But I think now of the toss of her gold earrings,
Their proud carnal assertion, and her youngest sings
While all the rivers of her red veins move into the sea.   20

1961

Butterfly on Rock

The large yellow wings, black-fringed,
were motionless

They say the soul of a dead person
will settle like that on the still face

But I thought: the rock has borne this;
this butterfly is the rock's grace,
its most obstinate and secret desire
to be a thing alive made manifest

Forgot were the two shattered porcupines
I had seen die in the bleak forest.   10
Pain is unreal; death, an illusion:
There is no death in all the land,
I heard my voice cry;
And brought my hand down on the butterfly
And felt the rock move beneath my hand.

1963

A Tall Man Executes a Jig

I
So the man spread his blanket on the field
And watched the shafts of light between the tufts
And felt the sun push the grass towards him;
The noise he heard was that of whizzing flies,
The whistlings of some small imprudent birds,
And the ambiguous rumbles of cars
That made him look up at the sky, aware
Of the gnats that tilted against the wind
And in the sunlight turned to jigging motes.
Fruitflies he'd call them except there was no fruit   10
About, spoiling to hatch these glitterings,
These nervous dots for which the mind supplied
The closing sentences from Thucydides,[1]
Or from Euclid having a savage nightmare.

---

[1] The conclusion to *The Peloponnesian War* by the Greek historian Thucydides (c. 470-c. 400 B.C.) is missing. The poet here connects the gnats with the ellipses used in modern texts to indicate this incompleteness, while in the line that follows they become like the points that are the smallest defining element in Euclid's geometry.

II

Jig jig, jig jig. Like minuscule black links
Of a chain played with by some playful
Unapparent hand or the palpitant
Summer haze bored with the hour's stillness.
He felt the sting and tingle afterwards
Of those leaving their unorthodox unrest,   20
Leaving their undulant excitation
To drop upon his sleeveless arm. The grass,
Even the wildflowers became black hairs
And himself a maddened speck among them.
Still the assaults of the small flies made him
Glad at last, until he saw purest joy
In their frantic jiggings under a hair,
So changed from those in the unrestraining air.

III

He stood up and felt himself enormous.
Felt as might Donatello[2] over stone,   30
Or Plato, or as a man who has held
A loved and lovely woman in his arms
And feels his forehead touch the emptied sky
Where all antinomies[3] flood into light.
Yet jig jig jig, the haloing black jots
Meshed with the wheeling fire of the sun:
Motion without meaning, disquietude
Without sense or purpose, ephemerides[4]
That mottled the resting summer air till
Gusts swept them from his sight like wisps of smoke.   40
Yet they returned, bringing a bee who, seeing
But a tall man, left him for a marigold.

IV

He doffed his aureole of gnats and moved
Out of the field as the sun sank down,
A dying god upon the blood-red hills.
Ambition, pride, the ecstasy of sex,
And all circumstance of delight and grief,
That blood upon the mountain's side, that flood
Washed into a clear incredible pool
Below the ruddied peaks that pierced the sun.   50
He stood still and waited. If ever
The hour of revelation was come
It was now, here on the transfigured steep.
The sky darkened. Some birds chirped. Nothing else.
He thought the dying god had gone to sleep:
An Indian fakir on his mat of nails.

[2]Name taken by Donato di Niccolò (c. 1386-1466), considered to be the father of Renaissance sculpture because he was the first to portray the human figure in realistic and dynamic terms.
[3]Paradoxes, especially contradictions in law.
[4]Small insects that live only a day in their adult form (usually spelled 'ephemerids').

V

And on the summit of the asphalt road
Which stretched towards the fiery town, the man
Saw one hill raised like a hairy arm, dark
With pines and cedars against the stricken sun   60
—The arm of Moses or of Joshua.[5]
He dropped his head and let fall the halo
Of mountains, purpling and silent as time,
To see temptation coiled before his feet:
A violated grass snake that lugged
Its intestine like a small red valise.
A cold-eyed skinflint it now was, and not
The manifest of that joyful wisdom,
The mirth and arrogant green flame of life;
Or earth's vivid tongue that flicked in praise of earth.   70

VI

And the man wept because pity was useless.
'Your jig's up; the flies come like kites,' he said
And watched the grass snake crawl towards the hedge,
Convulsing and dragging into the dark
The satchel filled with curses for the earth,
For the odours of warm sedge, and the sun,
A blood-red organ in the dying sky.
Backwards it fell into a grassy ditch
Exposing its underside, white as milk,
And mocked by wisps of hay between its jaws;   80
And then it stiffened to its final length.
But though it opened its thin mouth to scream
A last silent scream that shook the black sky,
Adamant and fierce, the tall man did not curse.

VII

Beside the rigid snake the man stretched out
In fellowship of death; he lay silent
And stiff in the heavy grass with eyes shut,
Inhaling the moist odours of the night
Through which his mind tunnelled with flicking tongue
Backwards to caves, mounds, and sunken ledges   90
And desolate cliffs where come only kites,
And where of perished badgers and racoons
The claws alone remain, gripping the earth.
Meanwhile the green snake crept upon the sky,
Huge, his mailed coat glittering with stars that made
The night bright, and blowing thin wreaths of cloud
Athwart the moon; and as the weary man
Stood up, coiled above his head, transforming all.

1963

[5] A reference to Exodus 10:22: 'And Moses stretched forth his hand toward heaven; and there was a thick darkness in all the land of Egypt'; and to Joshua 10:12, in which Joshua commands the sun to stand still (glossed by later commentators as also being a command for darkness).

P.K. Page

b. 1916

Patricia Kathleen Page calls herself a traveller without a map. Certainly journeys have played an important role in her life and work. Born in England and raised in Calgary, Winnipeg, and Saint John, N.B., she moved in the 1940s to Montreal, where she worked first as a clerk and then as a scriptwriter for the National Film Board. There she met its head, W. Arthur Irwin, whom she later married; and when Irwin entered the Department of External Affairs, his diplomatic career took the two of them abroad in the early fifties to Australia, Brazil, and Mexico. It was not until 1964 that they returned to Canada and settled in Victoria, B.C.

Although P.K. Page began to write in her teens, her work did not receive public recognition until Alan Crawley published her poetry, beginning with the first issue of his *Contemporary Verse* (1941-52). Shortly after submitting her work to Crawley, Page moved to Montreal and began an association with Patrick Anderson's *Preview* (1942-5). Though she has never been a political poet, the influence of Anderson and of the social movements in Montreal in the forties is evident in her poetry of this period: her early verse expresses her concerns about the dehumanizing effect of social institutions. In 1944 Page's work appeared in *Unit of Five*, a collection of a small group of poets—including Louis Dudek, Raymond Souster, James Wreford, and its editor, Ronald Hambleton—which, like the thirties anthology, *New Provinces*, showed the artistic and philosophical positions of Canada's emerging poets. These poets were also among those included in John Sutherland's *Other Canadians* (1947), a large anthology that was published in response to the 1943 edition of A.J.M. Smith's *Book of Canadian Poetry*, which itself contained four poems by Page. During this period she also produced her own volume of poetry, *As Ten As Twenty* (1946), and shortly after she left Canada a second volume appeared, *The Metal and the Flower* (1954), which won a Governor General's Award.

Page continued to produce poetry during her three years in Australia, but after moving to Latin America she found herself unable to write; drawing and painting became her chief creative outlet. Since returning to Canada, Page has worked as both a writer and a visual artist, the latter under the name P.K. Irwin. In 1967 *Cry Ararat: Poems New and Selected* was published, followed by *The Sun and the Moon and Other Fictions* (1973), which contains short stories and a novella, *The Sun and the Moon*, written when Page was twenty-one (it was originally published in 1944 under the pseudonym 'Judith Cape'). In 1974 *Poems Selected and New* was published, followed by *Evening Dance of the Grey Flies* (1981), which contains new poems and a short story, 'Unless the eye catch fire . . .'. *The Glass Air* (1985), is a selected and new collection that also includes two essays and nine drawings. In 1987 Page brought out *Brazilian Journal*, a work based on her letters and journal entries during her stay in Brazil (1957 to 1959). This work, which demonstrates not only her abilities as a writer but also her painterly eye, contains reproductions of a number of her watercolours.

Page's poetry owes what she calls 'nourishment' to several different lyric traditions: that of the English poets of the thirties, particularly Spender, Wilfred Owen, and Auden; of certain continental writers, such as Rainer Maria Rilke and Federico García Lorca; and of Middle Eastern poets, especially those who are part of the mystical Sufi tradition. Central also to Page's use of imagery and to her philosophy are the writings of Jung and Yeats who, along with the Sufi writers, have provided the basis for her markedly Platonic poetics. She believes that poetry is an inspired creativity that calls not only for craft but also for 'a state of purity . . . a burning with some clear enough light' from which the poet receives poetic vision.

This Delphic attitude—that 'the theme chooses you' and that 'You have to be worthy of being chosen'—is central to an understanding of her poetry. Underlying her work is the image of the poet as dreamer, one who has a lifeline to the 'collective unconscious', to a 'memory of Eden or heaven'—which, as she expresses it, gives the artist the 'seed' of his work and allows him access to another dimension in which he must search for the dismembered parts of his poem before he can assemble them in the real world. Images of the individual on a spiritual quest appear in both her poems and her fiction: her characters tend to journey to a remembered garden only to find that it is not the Edenic ideal of their dreams. They exist in a fractured reality controlled by the poet's magic vision, a reality that 'makes spinach of space and time' and that often contains magical, otherworldly events:

I seem to be attempting to copy exactly something which exists in a dimension where worldly senses are inadequate. As if a thing only felt had to be extracted from invisibility and transposed into a seen thing, a heard thing. The struggle is to fit the 'made' to the 'sensed' in such a way that the whole can occupy a world larger than the one I normally inhabit. (Canadian Literature, No. 46, 1970)

Despite her preoccupation with 'invisibility', her poems are neither vague nor abstract; her highly sensual images integrate the mystical and worldly dimensions so effectively that mystery becomes a necessary part of sensory experience. Page achieves this integration chiefly by means of visual cues—references to eyes and seeing, to space and shape, and to colour—but she also makes her images dissolve into one another so as to alter the reader's concept of the nature of reality. Page's reader, along with the travellers in her poems, discovers that entrancing visual images can be distorting lenses that obscure the truth; nevertheless sensory experience remains necessary as the only pathway to revelation, the departure-point of a lifelong spiritual quest. The effect of stimulating the sensory faculties can be that described in a poem by Theodore Roszak to which Page has several times referred:

Unless the eye catch fire
  The God will not be seen
Unless the ear catch fire
  The God will not be heard
Unless the tongue catch fire
  The God will not be named
Unless the heart catch fire
  The God will not be loved
Unless the mind catch fire
  The God will not be known
(Where the Wasteland Ends,   1973)

The Stenographers

After the brief bivouac of Sunday,
their eyes, in the forced march of Monday to Saturday,
hoist the white flag, flutter in the snow-storm of paper,
haul it down and crack in the mid-sun of temper.

In the pause between the first draft and the carbon
they glimpse the smooth hours when they were children—
the ride in the ice-cart, the ice-man's name,
the end of the route and the long walk home;

remember the sea where floats at high tide
were sea marrows growing on the scatter-green vine   10
or spools of grey toffee, or wasps' nests on water;
remember the sand and the leaves of the country.

Bell rings and they go and the voice draws their pencil
like a sled across snow; when its runners are frozen

rope snaps and the voice then is pulling no burden
but runs like a dog on the winter of paper.

Their climates are winter and summer—no wind
for the kites of their hearts—no wind for a flight;
a breeze at the most, to tumble them over
and leave them like rubbish—the boy-friends of blood.   20

In the inch of the noon as they move they are stagnant.
The terrible calm of the noon is their anguish;
the lip of the counter, the shapes of the straws
like icicles breaking their tongues, are invaders.

Their beds are their oceans—salt water of weeping
the waves that they know—the tide before sleep;
and fighting to drown they assemble their sheep
in columns and watch them leap desks for their fences
and stare at them with their own mirror-worn faces.

In the felt of the morning the calico-minded,   30
sufficiently starched, insert papers, hit keys,
efficient and sure as their adding machines;
yet they weep in the vault, they are taut as net curtains
stretched upon frames. In their eyes I have seen
the pin men[1] of madness in marathon trim
race round the track of the stadium pupil.

1946

[1]'Stick figures, such as children draw' (Page).

Stories of Snow

Those in the vegetable rain retain
an area behind their sprouting eyes
held soft and rounded with the dream of snow
precious and reminiscent as those globes—
souvenir of some never-nether land—
which hold their snow-storms circular, complete,
high in a tall and teakwood cabinet.

In countries where the leaves are large as hands
where flowers protrude their fleshy chins
and call their colours,   10
an imaginary snow-storm sometimes falls
among the lilies.
And in the early morning one will waken
to think the glowing linen of his pillow

a northern drift, will find himself mistaken
and lie back weeping.
And there the story shifts from head to head,
of how in Holland, from their feather beds
hunters arise and part the flakes and go
forth to the frozen lakes in search of swans—   20
the snow-light falling white along their guns,
their breath in plumes.
While tethered in the wind like sleeping gulls
ice-boats wait the raising of their wings
to skim the electric ice at such a speed
they leap jet strips of naked water,
and how these flying, sailing hunters feel
air in their mouths as terrible as ether.
And on the story runs that even drinks
in that white landscape dare to be no colour;   30
how flasked and water clear, the liquor slips
silver against the hunters' moving hips.
And of the swan in death these dreamers tell
of its last flight and how it falls, a plummet,
pierced by the freezing bullet
and how three feathers, loosened by the shot,
descend like snow upon it.
While hunters plunge their fingers in its down
deep as a drift, and dive their hands
up to the neck of the wrist   40
in that warm metamorphosis of snow
as gentle as the sort that woodsmen know
who, lost in the white circle, fall at last
and dream their way to death.

And stories of this kind are often told
in countries where great flowers bar the roads
with reds and blues which seal the route to snow—
as if, in telling, raconteurs unlock
the colour with its complement and go
through to the area behind the eyes   50
where silent, unrefractive whiteness lies.

1946

Photos of a Salt Mine

How innocent their lives look,
how like a child's
dream of caves and winter, both combined;
the steep descent to whiteness
and the stope[1]
with its striated walls
their folds all leaning as if pointing to
the greater whiteness still,
that great white bank
with its decisive front,   10
that seam upon a slope,
salt's lovely ice.

And wonderful underfoot the snow of salt
the fine
particles a broom could sweep,
one thinks
muckers might make angels in its drifts
as children do in snow,
lovers in sheets,
lie down and leave imprinted where they lay   20
a feathered creature holier than they.

And in the outworked stopes
with lamps and ropes
up miniature matterhorns
the miners climb
probe with their lights
the ancient folds of rock—
syncline[2] and anticline—
and scoop from darkness an Aladdin's cave:
rubies and opals glitter from its walls.   30

But hoses douse the brilliance of these jewels,
melt fire to brine.
Salt's bitter water trickles thin and forms,
slow fathoms down,
a lake within a cave,
lacquered with jet—
white's opposite.
There grey on black the boating miners float
to mend the stays and struts of that old stope
and deeply underground   40
their words resound,

[1] An excavation in the form of steps made as ore is mined from vertical or steeply inclined veins.
[2] Low, troughlike fold in stratified rock, the opposite of 'anticline': fold with strata sloping downwards on both sides away from a common crest.

are multiplied by echo, swell and grow
and make a climate of a miner's voice.

So all the photographs like children's wishes
are filled with caves or winter,
innocence
has acted as a filter,
selected only beauty from the mine.
Except in the last picture,
it is shot   50
from an acute high angle. In a pit
figures the size of pins are strangely lit
and might be dancing but you know they're not.
Like Dante's vision of the nether hell[3]
men struggle with the bright cold fires of salt,
locked in the black inferno of the rock:
the filter here, not innocence but guilt.

1954

[3]Lower part of hell that contains both fire and ice.

Cry Ararat![1]

I
In the dream the mountain near
but without sound.
A dream through binoculars
seen sharp and clear:
the leaves moving, turning
in a far wind
no ear can hear.

First soft in the distance,
blue in blue air
then sharpening, quickening   10
taking on green.
Swiftly the fingers
seek accurate focus
(the bird
has vanished so often
before the sharp lens
could deliver it)
then as if from the sea

[1]Mountain range on which Noah's ark landed. As the flood-waters began to recede, Noah—believing that God would once again provide a fertile earth—sent out the dove which, on its second excursion, returned bearing an olive branch.

the mountain appears
emerging new-washed   20
growing maples and firs.
The faraway, here.

Do not reach to touch it
nor labour to hear.
Return to your hand
the sense of the hand;
return to your ear
the sense of the ear.
Remember the statue,
that space in the air   30
which with nothing to hold
what the minute is giving
is through each point
where its marble touches air.

Then will each leaf and flower
each bird and animal
become as perfect as
the thing its name evoked
when busy as a child
the world stopped at the Word   40
and Flowers more real than flowers
grew vivid and immense;
and Birds more beautiful
and Leaves more intricate
flew, blew and quilted all
the quick landscape.

So flies and blows the dream
embracing like a sea
all that in it swims
when dreaming, you desire   50
and ask for nothing more
than stillness to receive
the I-am animal,
the We-are leaf and flower,
the distant mountain near.

II
So flies and blows the dream that haunts us when we wake
to the unreality of bright day:
the far thing almost sensed by the still skin
and then the focus lost, the mountain gone.
This is the loss that haunts our daylight hours   60
leaving us parched at nightfall
blowing like last year's leaves
sibilant on blossoming trees
and thirsty for the dream of the mountain

more real than any event:
more real than strangers passing on the street
in a city's architecture white as bone
or the immediate companion.

But sometimes there is one
raw with the dream of flying: 70
'I, a bird,
landed that very instant
and complete—
as if I had drawn a circle in my flight
and filled its shape—
find air a perfect fit.
But this my grief,
that with the next tentative lift
of my indescribable wings
the ceiling looms   80
heavy as a tomb.

'Must my most exquisite and private dream
remain unleavened?
Must this flipped and spinning coin that sun
could gild and make miraculous become
so swiftly pitiful?
The vision of the flight it imitates
burns brightly in my head as if a star
rushed down to touch me where I stub against
what must forever be my underground.'   90

III
These are the dreams that haunt us,
these the fears.
Will the grey weather wake us,
toss us twice in the terrible night to tell us
the flight is cancelled
and the mountain lost?

O, then cry Ararat!

The dove believed
in her sweet wings and in the rising peak
with such a washed and easy innocence   100
that she found rest on land for the sole of her foot
and, silver, circled back,
a green twig in her beak.

The leaves that make the tree by day,
the green twig the dove saw fit
to lift across a world of water
break in a wave about our feet.
The bird in the thicket with his whistle

the crystal lizard in the grass
the star and shell   110
tassel and bell
of wild flowers blowing where we pass,
this flora-fauna flotsam, pick and touch,
requires the focus of the total I.

A single leaf can block a mountainside;
all Ararat be conjured by a leaf.

1967

Arras[1]

Consider a new habit—classical,
and trees espaliered on the wall like candelabra.
How still upon that lawn our sandalled feet.

But a peacock rattling his rattan tail and screaming
has found a point of entry. Through whose eye
did it insinuate in furled disguise
to shake its jewels and silk upon that grass?

The peaches hang like lanterns. No one joins
those figures on the arras.
                              Who am I   10
or who am I become that walking here
I am observer, other, Gemini,
starred for a green garden of cinema?

I ask, what did they deal me in this pack?
The cards, all suits, are royal when I look.
My fingers slipping on a monarch's face
twitch and grow slack.
I want a hand to clutch, a heart to crack.

No one is moving now, the stillness is
infinite. If I should make a break. . . .   20
take to my springy heels. . . . ? But nothing moves.
The spinning world is stuck upon its poles,
the stillness points a bone[2] at me. I fear
the future on this arras.
                              I confess:

It was my eye.
Voluptuous it came.

---

[1] Wall hanging, particularly a tapestry.
[2] 'Aboriginal projective magic. A prepared human or kangaroo bone is pointed by a sorcerer at an intended victim (who may be miles away) to bring about his death' (from Page's glossary of Australian terms in *Cry Ararat!*).

Its head the ferrule[3] and its lovely tail
folded so sweetly; it was strangely slim
to fit the retina. And then it shook   30
and was a peacock—living patina,
eye-bright, maculate!
Does no one care?

I thought their hands might hold me if I spoke.
I dreamed the bite of fingers in my flesh,
their poke smashed by an image, but they stand
as if within a treacle,[4] motionless,
folding slow eyes on nothing. While they stare
another line has trolled the encircling air,
another bird assumes its furled disguise   40

1967

[3]Metal cap used to reinforce or secure the end of a pole or handle—here belonging to an umbrella.
[4]Molasses or sweet syrup; used here as that which entraps the insects it attracts.

After Rain

The snails have made a garden of green lace:
broderie anglaise from the cabbages,
chantilly from the choux-fleurs, tiny veils—
I see already that I lift the blind
upon a woman's wardrobe of the mind.

Such female whimsy floats about me like
a kind of tulle, a flimsy mesh,
while feet in gum boots pace the rectangles—
garden abstracted, geometry awash—
an unknown theorem argued in green ink,   10
dropped in the bath.
Euclid in glorious chlorophyll, half drunk.

I none too sober slipping in the mud
where rigged with guys of rain
the clothes-reel gauche
as the rangey skeleton of some
gaunt delicate spidery mute
is pitched as if
listening;
while hung from one thin rib   20
a silver web—
its infant, skeletal, diminutive,

now sagged with sequins, pulled ellipsoid,
glistening.

I suffer shame in all these images.
The garden is primeval, Giovanni
in soggy denim squelches by my hub
over his ruin,
shakes a doleful head.
But he so beautiful and diademmed,   30
his long Italian hands so wrung with rain
I find his ache exists beyond my rim
and almost weep to see a broken man
made subject to my whim.

O choir him, birds, and let him come to rest
within this beauty as one rests in love,
till pears upon the bough
encrusted with
small snails as pale as pearls   40
hang golden in
a heart that knows tears are a part of love.

And choir me too to keep my heart a size
larger than seeing, unseduced by each
bright glimpse of beauty striking like a bell,
so that the whole may toll,
its meaning shine
clear of the myriad images that still—
do what I will—encumber its pure line.

1967

After Reading 'Albino Pheasants'[1]

For Pat Lane

Pale beak . . . pale eye . . . the dark imagination
flares like magnesium. Add but *pale flesh*
and I am lifted to a weightless world:
watered cerulean,[2] chrome-yellow (light)
and green, veronese[3]—if I remember—a soft wash
recalls a summer evening sky.

---

[1] A poem by Patrick Lane (see page 612). Page's poem originally appeared in 1978 as 'Sestina for Pat Lane after Reading "Albino Pheasants" '
[2] Sky blue; light, slightly greenish blue.
[3] 'Rich but light green' (Page).

At Barro de Navidad[4] we watched the sky
fade softly like a bruise. Was it imagination
that showed us Venus phosphorescent in a wash
of air and ozone?—a phosphorescence flesh   10
wears like a mantle in bright moonlight,
a natural skin-tone in that other world.

Why should I wish to escape this world?
Why should three phrases alter the colour of the sky
the clarity, texture even, of the light?
What is there about the irrepressible imagination
that the adjective *pale* modifying *beak, eye* and *flesh*
can set my sensibilities awash?

If with my thickest brush I were to lay a wash
of thinnest water-color I could make a world   20
as unlike my own dense flesh
as the high-noon midsummer sky;
but it would not catch at my imagination
or change the waves or particles of light

yet *pale* can tip the scales, make light
this heavy planet. If I were to wash
everything I own in mercury, would imagination
run rampant in that suddenly silver world—
free me from gravity, set me floating sky-
ward—thistledown—permanently disburdened of my flesh?   30

Like cygnets hatched by ducks, our minds and flesh
are imprinted[5] early—what to me is light
may be dark to one born under a sunny sky.
And however cool the water my truth won't wash
without shrinking except in its own world
which is one part matter, nine parts imagination.

I fear flesh which blocks imagination,
the light of reason which constricts the world.
Pale beak . . . pale eye . . . pale flesh . . . My sky's awash.

1981

---

[4]The west coast of Mexico, which Page describes as 'wild and unbelievable'.

[5]A young animal is said to 'imprint' on the adult animal it most often sees in the period after its birth; that is, to identify it as its parent and therefore identify itself as a member of the same species.

Deaf-mute in the Pear Tree

His clumsy body is a golden fruit
pendulous in the pear tree

Blunt fingers among the multitudinous buds

Adriatic blue the sky above and through
the forking twigs

Sun ruddying tree's trunk, his trunk
his massive head thick-nobbed with burnished curls
tight-clenched in bud

(Painting by Generalić. Primitive.)

I watch him prune with silent secateurs   10

Boots in the crotch of branches shift their weight
heavily as oxen in a stall

Hear small inarticulate mews from his locked mouth
a kitten in a box

Pear clippings fall
                  soundlessly on the ground

Spring finches sing
                  soundlessly in the leaves

A stone. A stone in ears and on his tongue

Through palm and fingertip he knows the tree's   20
quick springtime pulse

Smells in its sap the sweet incipient pears

Pale sunlight's choppy water glistens on
his mutely snipping blades

and flags and scraps of blue
above him make regatta of the day

But when he sees his wife's foreshortened shape
sudden and silent in the grass below
uptilt its face to him

then air is kisses, kisses   30

stone dissolves

his locked throat finds a little door

and through it feathered joy
flies screaming like a jay

1987

Miriam Waddington

b. 1917

Born into Winnipeg's Russian-Jewish immigrant community, Miriam Dworkin Waddington grew up in a climate of socialism and European traditions. In 1931 her parents moved to Ottawa; there, and in Montreal, she became acquainted with artists and intellectuals, many of them part of Montreal's Jewish community. During the Depression, Waddington was an undergraduate student at the University of Toronto (1936-9). After marrying, she remained in Toronto until the end of the Second World War. Although she had been writing poems since childhood, her poetry written during the war gained her public recognition. In 1943 John Sutherland offered to publish her work in his magazine, *First Statement* (1942-5); subsequently her first book, *Green World* (1945), was published by his First Statement Press. These poems, while lyrical and concerned with man's relationship to the natural world—they have been compared to those of Dylan Thomas—also reflect the social interests that led Waddington to take a diploma in social work from the University of Toronto (1942) and a Master's degree in the same field from the University of Pennsylvania (1945).

After the war Waddington moved, with her husband, to Montreal where she pursued a career in social work. While a case-worker in hospitals, prisons, and social agencies, she continued to write, publishing *The Second Silence* (1955) and *The Season's Lovers* (1958). Many poems of this period are angry responses to social conditions that Waddington observed. The strongest of these are self-reflective poems, such as 'My Lessons in the Jail'.

In 1960 Waddington, just divorced, moved back to Toronto with her young children, leaving social work to begin a new career—as a university teacher of literature, instructing evenings while she worked on a Master's in English at the University of Toronto (1968). In 1964 she accepted a full-time teaching position at York University, remaining there until her retirement as professor in 1983.

In the last twenty-five years Waddington has published five new books of poetry: *The Glass Trumpet* (1966), *Say Yes* (1969), *Driving Home: Poems New and Selected* (1972), *The Price of Gold* (1976), and *The Visitants* (1981). In 1986 her *Collected Poems* appeared. While commonplace experience has always been important to her writing, her later work has moved from a poetry emanating from social experience to a more personal, introspective one. Social inequity has been displaced as a major topic by themes of loss and mortality. While close in overall structure to the meditations on nature in *Green World*, her later poems have short lines rather than long, loose ones and a simplified, less dramatic diction.

Waddington's writing has not been limited to poetry. Her short stories have recently been collected in *Summer at Lonely Beach and Other Stories* (1982), and she has produced a body of academic and critical work. Of particular importance to her have been her studies on A.M. Klein—her Master's thesis on him was published in 1970—and John Sutherland. She has edited a collection of Klein's poems (1974), and a volume of Sutherland's prose and poetry (1972).

Both Klein and Sutherland, members of the socially active Montreal writers' movement in the forties of which Waddington was also a part, moved in their careers from a near religious faith in the efficacy of poetry for effecting social change to a profound disillusionment with their old goals. Waddington has come to share their sense of an empty and valueless world, but she has not been led to retreat from her earlier positions. While she has been greatly influenced by her European background, and her poetry has largely been determined by her being both a woman and a Jew, these aspects are overshadowed in her work by a more generalized sense of displacement. Throughout her later poems one finds accounts of a 'darkening world' in which beliefs, traditions, and relations become fragmented and are lost. Yet for Waddington the loss is always mitigated, for she retains threads of traditions that still anchor her, memories that keep her company, and an ironic sense of humour.

My Lessons in the Jail

Walk into the prison, that domed citadel
that yellow skull of stone and sutured steel,
walk under their mottoes, show your pass,
salute their Christ to whom you cannot kneel.

In the white-tiled room arrange the interview
with the man who took his daughter and learn
that every man is usual but none are equal
in the dark rivers that in them burn.

And take this man's longest bleakest year
between done act and again-done act, and take   10
his misery and need, stand against his tears
and transform them to such a truth as slakes

The very core of thirst and be sure
the thirst is his and not your own deep need
to spurt fine fountains; accept accept
his halting words—since you must learn to read

Between the lines his suffering and doubt.
Be faithful to your pity, be careworn,
though all this buffet you and beat and cruelly
test you—you chose this crown of thorns.   20

Wear it with grace and when you rise to go
thank him and don't let yourself forget
how hard it is to thank and to beholden be
one to another and spin your role out yet

For moments in the hallway, compose your face
to sale good humour, conceal your sex:
smile at the brute who runs the place
and memorized the banner *Christus Rex*.

1958

Looking for
Strawberries in June

I have to tell you
about the words I
used to know, such
words, so sheer, thin
transparent, so light
and quick, I had such
words for wind for
whatever grew
I knew a certain
leaf-language from   10
somewhere, but now

it is all used up
I have come to the
end of some line or
other like walking
on railroad ties in
the country looking
for strawberries in
June and suddenly
the ties end in the   20
middle of no-place
and I stop to look
around to take my
direction but I

don't recognize the
landscape. It is all
grey, feathery, the
voices of birds are
foreign, yet I used
to know such words   30
japanned, brushed and
papery, whitefolded
Russian flowerwords
cabbage roses, huge
holes in the head of
the universe pouring
out rosy revolutions:

and I used to know
swarthy eastern words
heavy with Hebrew, then   40
I was kidnapped by
gypsies, I knew the
up and down of their
dark-blue anger, the
leathery touch of

the fortune-telling
begging wandering
words, but what's
become of them?
I don't know, I'm   50

just standing here
on the threshold of
a different country,
everything is made
of plastic and silence;
what month is it any-
way? I'm knocking at
the door but nobody
answers. I mutter *Lenin*
Karl Marx, Walt Whitman   60
Chaucer, Hopkins, even
Archibald Lampman, but
nobody comes, I don't

know the password
I only know it has
nothing to do with
being good or true
nothing to do with
being beautiful.

1968

Icons

Suddenly
in middle age
instead of withering
into blindness
and burying myself
underground
I grow delicate
and fragile
superstitious;
I carry icons   10
I have begun
to worship
images.

I take them out
and prop them up
on bureau tops

in hotel rooms
in Spain
I study them
in locked libraries   20
in Leningrad
I untie them
from tourist packages
in Italy
they warm me
in the heatless winters
of London in the
hurry-up buses
of Picadilly.

My icons are not   30
angels or holy
babies they have
nothing to do
with saints or
madonnas, they
are mostly of
seashores summer
and love which I no
longer believe in
but I still believe   40
in the images,
I still preserve
the icons:

a Spanish factory
worker talks to me
in a street behind
the cathedral he
offers me *un poco*
amor, the scars on
his hand, his wounded   50
country and the black-
jacketed police; he
touches me on the
arm and other places,
and the alcoholic
in the blazing square
drinks brandy, confides
that fortunes can still
be made in Birmingham
but he has a bad   60
lung is hard of
hearing and owns
an apartment in Palma.

1969

The Nineteen Thirties Are Over

The nineteen thirties
are over; we survived
the depression, the Sacco-
Vanzetti[1] of childhood
saw Tom Mooney[2] smiling
at us from photographs,
put a rose on the grave
of Eugene Debs,[3] listened
to our father's stories
of the Winnipeg strike[4] and   10
joined the study groups
of the OBU[5] always keeping
one eye on the revolution.
Later we played records
with thorn needles, Josh
White's *Talking Union*[6] and
Prokofief's *Lieutenant Kije*,[7]
shuddered at the sound of
bells and all those wolves
whirling past us in snow   20
on the corner of Portage
and Main, but in my mind
summer never ended on the
shores of Gimli where we
looked across to an Icelandic
paradise we could never see
the other side of; and I
dreamed of Mexico and shining
birds who beckoned to me
from the gold-braided lianas   30
of my own wonder.

[1]Nicola Sacco (1891-1927) and Bartolomeo Vanzetti (1888-1927), Italian-born political activists living in the U.S., were tried, convicted, and executed for murder; it has been widely held that their conviction, which became emblematic of an extreme misuse of a legal system, rested more on their political activities and national origins than on evidence related to the murder.

[2]American anarchist and labour agitator, whose controversial conviction and imprisonment for a 1916 bombing in San Francisco ended with his pardon in 1939, after years of leftist activity to gain his freedom; his story was celebrated in song by folk-singer and union supporter, Woody Guthrie.

[3](1855-1926), American labour leader and five-time Socialist candidate for President of the United States (1900-20).

[4]Winnipeg General Strike, a bloody and bitter dispute (following the demobilization at the end of the First World War) that paralysed Winnipeg between 15 May and 25 June 1919.

[5]'One Big Union'; one of the many factors that played a part in the Winnipeg strike, it was based on the concept that groups of workers could achieve their goals by collectively refusing to work.

[6]Josh White (1915-1969), American folk singer and guitarist, recorded an album entitled *Talking Union*, with Pete Seeger and Woody Guthrie; 'Talking Union' is a protest song written in 1941 by Lee Hays, Mill Lampell, and Seeger.

[7]Symphonic suite for orchestra, Op. 60, from a film score of the same title (1934) by Sergei Prokofief (or Prokofiev) (1891-1953), a Soviet composer noted for his stirring and heroic compositions.

These days I step out
from the frame of my wind-
battered house into Toronto
city; somewhere I still
celebrate sunlight, touch
the rose on the grave of
Eugene Debs but I walk
carefully in this land
of sooty snow; I pass the   40
rich houses and double
garages and I am not really
this middle-aged professor
but someone from
Winnipeg whose bones ache
with the broken revolutions
of Europe, and even now
I am standing on the heaving
ploughed-up field
of my father's old war.   50

1972

Ten Years and More

When my husband
lay dying a mountain
a lake three
cities ten years
and more
lay between us:

There were our
sons my wounds
and theirs,
despair loneliness,   10
handfuls of un-
hammered nails
pictures never
hung all

The uneaten
meals and unslept
sleep; there was
retirement, and
worst of all
a green umbrella   20
he can never
take back.

I wrote him a
letter but all
I could think of
to say was: do you
remember Severn
River, the red canoe
with the sail
and lee-boards?   30

I was really saying
for the sake of our
youth and our love
I forgave him for
everything
and I was asking him
to forgive me too.

1976

Margaret Avison

b. 1918

Margaret Avison was born in Galt, Ont., and grew up there and in Alberta. She took her B.A. in English literature from Victoria College, University of Toronto, in 1940, and attended schools of creative writing at the Universities of Indiana (1955) and Chicago (1956-7)—the latter on a Guggenheim Fellowship. She returned to the University of Toronto as a graduate student in 1963. Since then Avison has worked as a librarian; as a lecturer at Scarborough College, University of Toronto; as a social worker at the Presbyterian Mission in Toronto; and as a secretary for a Southeast Asia mission. She has also been a writer-in-residence at the University of Western Ontario (1972-3) and has written book reviews, translated poems, and composed a school text on Canadian history. Meanwhile, she has worked steadily at her poetry, producing a small corpus of excellence.

Although her poems began to appear as early as the late thirties, Avison has always been diffident about collecting them for book publication. Encouraged by friends, in 1960 she finally published her first book, *Winter Sun* (which won a Governor General's Award). Two years later the American literary magazine *Origin* featured her poetry, printing thirteen poems and a letter she wrote to its editor, Cid Corman, in which she expressed her thoughts on the writing of poetry. She has since produced three more volumes, *The Dumbfounding* (1966), *sunblue* (1978), and *No Time* (1989). A volume of *Selected Poems* appeared in 1991.

Avison has written two distinct but related types of poetry. The first of these—written up to the early sixties—included poems that inquired into the nature and purpose of man, his world, and the universe. In 1963 Avison's life changed dramatically when she actively embraced Christianity and committed herself to contemplation and service; the poetry that followed reflects this commitment. The seeds of her religious concerns may, however, be seen in some of her earlier works, which depict a fallen world where spacious, open landscapes and awesome skies (like those she experienced growing up on the Prairies) are lost to a darker world of urban decay and atrophy. These poems struggle with the question of a creator who seems omnipotent but absent or unresponding. After her conversion there is a reassessment of the distance between man and God and an attempt to show the effects of a closer relationship between the two.

Avison's earlier poems—much like those of T.S. Eliot and Wallace Stevens—depend upon a wide knowledge of history and poetic tradition, of contemporary events and universal myths. A.J.M. Smith described her diction in this period as 'erudite, complex, archaic, simple, modern—an amalgam of the scientific and philosophical with the familiar and the new, a high style and low, pillaged and put to work'. This kind of poetry is dense and challenging, full of both difficulties and rewards. Witty and complex, it can juxtapose the painter's rules of vanishing-point perspective with our view of the world as we move through it; or it can turn the sonnet into a weapon against all sonnets.

Since *The Dumbfounding* Avison has progressively simplified the form of her poetry. The syntax and diction of the later poems sometimes catch the inflection of her own speech and sometimes recall the oracular voice of such visionary poets as Dickinson, Hopkins, Herbert, and Traherne. The contemplative life Avison has chosen creates a tension that replaces the intricacies of her earlier, more philosophical verse: under the text of these poems the reader senses a struggle between the natural ego of a writer and the self-effacement demanded by a religious life. She still believes, as she did in her early work, that the act of seeing is not passive, that an 'optic heart' must continue to labour intellectually and spiritually to retain its passionate Christian perspective. Her poems, especially those in *sunblue*, provide an ongoing meditation—a chronicle not only of a vision found but of the wonder and struggle it subsequently engenders.

Neverness

OR, THE ONE SHIP BEACHED
ON ONE FAR DISTANT SHORE

Old Adam, with his fist-full of plump earth,
His sunbright gaze on his eternal hill
Is not historical:
His tale is never done
For us who know a world no longer bathed
In harsh splendor of economy.
We millions hold old Adam in our thoughts
A pivot for the future-past, a core
Of the one dream that never goads to action
But stains our entrails with nostalgia   10
And wrings the sweat of death in ancient eyes.

The one-celled plant is not historical.
Leeuwenhoek[1] peered through his magic window
And in a puddle glimpsed the tiny grain
Of firmament that was before the Adam.

I'd like to pull that squinting Dutchman's sleeve
And ask what were his thoughts, lying at night,
And smelling the sad spring, and thinking out
Across the fullness of night air, smelling
The dark canal, and dusty oat-bag, cheese,   20
And wet straw-splintered wood, and rust-seamed leather
And pearly grass and silent deeps of sky
Honey-combed with its million years' of light
And prune-sweet earth
Honey-combed with the silent worms of dark.
Old Leeuwenhoek must have had ribby thoughts
To hoop the hollow pounding of his heart
Those nights of spring in 1600-odd.
It would be done if he could tell it us.

                                                          30
The tissue of our metaphysic cells
No magic window yet has dared reveal.
Our bleared world welters on
Far past the one-cell Instant. Points are spread
And privacy is unadmitted prison.

Why, now I know the lust of omnipresence!
You thousands merging lost,
        I call to you
Down the stone corridors that wall me in.

I am inside these days, snug in a job   40
In one of many varnished offices

[1] Anton van Leeuwenhoek (1632-1723), Dutch naturalist, was an important pioneer in microscopy.

Bleak with the wash of daylight
And us, the human pencils wearing blunt.
Soon I'll be out with you,
Another in the lonely unshut world
Where sun blinks hard on yellow brick and glazed,
On ads in sticky posterpaint
      And fuzzy
        At midday intersections.
The milk is washed down corded throats at noon
Along a thousand counters, and the hands   50
That count the nickel from a greasy palm
Have never felt an udder.
      The windy dark
That thrums high among towers and nightspun branches
Whirs through our temples with a dry confusion.
We sprawl abandoned into disbelief
And feel the pivot-picture of old Adam
On the first hill that ever was, alone,
And see the hard earth seeded with sharp snow
And dream that history is done.   60

        *

And if that be the dream that whortles[2] out
Into unending night
Then must the pivot Adam be denied
And the whole cycle ravelled and flung loose.
Is this the Epoch[3] when the age-old Serpent
Must writhe and loosen, slacking out
To a new pool of Time's eternal sun?
O Adam, will your single outline blur
At this long last when slow mist wells
Fuming from all the valleys of the earth?   70
Or will our unfixed vision rather blind
Through agony to the last gelid stare
And none be left to witness the blank mist?

1943

[2]Here, 'hurtles'.
[3]i.e. Armageddon, as described in Revelation; 'Serpent': Satan, see Revelation 12 ff.

The Butterfly[1]

An uproar,
a spruce-green sky, bound in iron,
the murky sea running a sulphur scum:
I saw a butterfly suddenly;
it clung between the ribs of the storm, wavering
and flung against the battering bone-wind.
I remember it, glued to the grit of that rain-strewn beach
that glowered around it, swallowed its startled design
in the larger irridescence of unstrung dark.

That wild, sour air, the miles of crouching forest, those wings,   10
when all-enveloping air is a
thinglass globe, swirling with storm,
tempt one to the abyss.

The butterfly's meaning, even though smashed.
Imprisoned in endless cycle? No. The meaning!
Can't we stab that one angle
into the curve of space that sweeps beyond
our farthest knowing, out into light's
place of invisibility?

1943, 1989

[1]'This is a revision, because I have learned that "moth" and "butterfly" are not interchangeable terms (as I had written them in ignorance in the earlier version), and because the "angle" seems indicated in Rom. 8:21 and Eph. 1:10' (Avison's note).

Perspective[1]

A sport,[2] an adventitious sprout
These eyeballs, that have somehow slipped
The mesh of generations since Mantegna?[3]

Yet I declare, your seeing is diseased
That cripples space. The fear has eaten back
Through sockets to the caverns of the brain
     And made of it a sifty habitation.

We stand beholding the one plain
And in your face I see the chastening
Of its small tapering design   10
That brings up *punkt*.[4]
     (The Infinite, you say,

[1]'This poem and the two preceding poems received their book publication in *The Book of Canadian Poetry* edited by A.J.M. Smith: 'Neverness' and 'The Butterfly' in the First Edition (1943), and 'Perspective' in the Second Edition (1948).
[2]A mutation, used later in the poem in the more familiar sense of the word.
[3]Andrea Mantegna (1431-1506), Italian painter and engraver famous for his use of perspective of great depth.
[4]Point; the vanishing point in perspective.

Is an unthinkable—and pointless too—
   Extension of that *punkt.*)

But do you miss the impact of that fierce
Raw boulder five miles off? You are not pierced
By that great spear of grass on the horizon?
   You are not smitten with the shock
      Of that great thundering sky?

Your law of optics is a quarrel   20
Of chickenfeet on paper. Does a train
Run pigeon-toed?

I took a train from here to Ottawa
On tracks that did not meet. We swelled and roared
Mile upon mightier mile, and when we clanged
Into the vasty station we were indeed
Brave company for giants.

   Keep your eyes though,
You, and not I, will travel safer back
       To Union station.   30

Your fear has me infected, and my eyes
That were my sport so long, will soon be apt
Like yours to press out dwindling vistas from
The massive flux massive Mantegna knew
And all its sturdy everlasting foregrounds.

1948

Snow

Nobody stuffs the world in at your eyes.
The optic heart must venture: a jail-break
And re-creation. Sedges and wild rice
Chase rivery pewter. The astonished cinders quake
With rhizomes.[1] All ways through the electric air
Trundle candy-bright disks; they are desolate
Toys if the soul's gates seal, and cannot bear,
Must shudder under, creation's unseen freight.
But soft, there is snow's legend: colour of mourning
Along the yellow Yangtze[2] where the wheel   10
Spins an indifferent stasis that's death's warning.
Asters of tumbled quietness reveal
Their petals. Suffering this starry blur
The rest may ring your change,[3] sad listener.

1960

[1]Rootlike stems running along or under the ground, from which roots, stalks, and leaves grow.
[2]River in China, the longest in Asia.
[3]Change ringing is the ringing of church bells in all the permutations of a given pattern; thus, to ring changes is to play with permutations.

Butterfly Bones; or Sonnet Against Sonnets

The cyanide jar seals life, as sonnets move
towards final stiffness. Cased in a white glare
these specimens stare for peering boys, to prove
strange certainties. Plane dogsled and safari
assure continuing range. The sweep-net skill,
the patience, learning, leave all living stranger.
Insect—or poem—waits for the fix, the frill
precision can effect, brilliant with danger.
What law and wonder the museum spectres
bespeak is cryptic for the shivery wings,   10
the world cut-diamond-eyed, those eyes' reflectors,
or herbal grass, sunned motes, fierce listening.
Might sheened and rigid trophies strike men blind
like Adam's lexicon locked in the mind?

1960

Tennis

Service is joy, to see or swing. Allow
All tumult to subside. Then tensest winds
Buffet, brace, viol and sweeping bow.
Courts are for love and volley. No one minds
The cruel ellipse of service and return,
Dancing white galliardes[1] at tape or net
Till point, on the wire's tip, or the long burn-
ing arc to nethercourt marks game and set.
Purpose apart, perched like an umpire, dozes,
Dreams golden balls whirring through indigo.   10
Clay blurs the whitewash but day still encloses
The albinos, bonded in their flick and flow.
Playing in musicked gravity, the pair
Score liquid Euclids[2] in foolscaps of air.

1960

---

[1] 'Galliard', a spirited dance in triple time, popular in Elizabethan England.
[2] Geometric figures; Euclid was a Greek mathematician of the third century who systematized the essentially undefined concepts of point, line, and plane.

Light (I)

The stuff of flesh and bone
is given, *datum*. Down
the stick-men, plastiscene-
people, clay-lump children, are strewn,
each casting shadow in the eye of day.

Then—listen!—I see
breath of delighting rise from
those stones the sun touches
and hear a snarl of breath
as a mouth sucks air. And with   10
shivery sighings—see: they stir
and turn and move, and power
to build, to undermine, is theirs,
is ours.

The stuff, the breath, the power to move even thumbs
and with them, things: *data*. What is
the harpsweep on the heart for?
What does the constructed power
of speculation reach for?
Each of us casts a shadow in the bewildering day,   20
               an own-shaped shadow only.

The light has looked on Light.

He from elsewhere
speaks; he breathes impasse-
crumpled hope even
in us:
that near.

1978

Light (III)

Flying Air Canada over
the foxed[1] spread snowy land,
we look where light is shed
from lucid sky on
waters that mirror light.

The magical reflectors there belie
factory   and fall-out   and run-off effluvia.

Where is the purity then,
except from so

---

[1]Marked with brown stain caused by damp (as of linen, pages, etc.); with a play on 'fox-inhabited'.

feebly far aloft? 10
Is it a longing, but to be brought to earth,
an earth so poisoned and yet precious to us?

The source of light is high
above the plane.   The window-passengers
eye those remote bright waters.

Interpreters and spoilers since the four
rivers flowed out of Eden,[2]
men have nonetheless
learned that the Pure can bless
on earth *and* from on high 20
ineradicably.

1978

[2]Genesis 2:10; the four rivers, two of which are historically known—the Tigris and the Euphrates—
and two of which are not—The Pishon ('Gusher') and the Gihon ('Bubbler')—were said to have originated from an underground ocean. They flowed out from under the Tree of Life to the four corners
of the known historical world.

Al Purdy

b. 1918

In the opening lines of 'The Country North
of Belleville' Al Purdy maps out his home
territory—a 'Bush land scrub land' near the
eastern end of Lake Ontario, a landscape
that gives a man 'some sense of what
beauty/is', yet is also 'the country of our defeat'. Although this is a region 'where the
young/leave quickly', Purdy himself has
spent most of his life in this contradictory
landscape, making it the subject of some of
his most powerful poetry. Born in Wooler, a
small town a little west of Belleville (described by Purdy as 'mythological because
the same village could not now be found'),
he attended school in nearby Trenton and
held his first jobs there and in Belleville,
where he met his wife. Although he left the
area to serve in the RCAF during the Second World War, and moved to Vancouver in
1950, since 1957 he has made his home in
Ameliasburg, a small town on Roblin Lake,

a few miles south of Belleville. Purdy has
frequently travelled away from that home
base, however, utilizing his journeys—to
Europe, the Cariboo country of British Columbia, Baffin Island, Hiroshima, South
America—to reinvigorate his poetry and to
further his reflections on the meaning of
place.

Purdy began writing poetry in his teens. In
1944 he paid to have his first book, *The Enchanted Echo*, published (only a few copies
still exist) and in the fifties he produced
three more collections of apprenticeship
work. After spending time in the later fifties
in Montreal—where, with the poet Milton
Acorn, he founded a little magazine,
Moment—Purdy began to find a sure and
distinctive voice, publishing *Poems for All
the Annettes* (1962) and *The Cariboo Horses*
(1965; winner of a Governor General's
Award). In 1968 *Poems for All the Annettes*

was reissued in an expanded edition, in which Purdy collected and revised all the poetry up to 1965 that he wished to preserve. He has published some twenty books of new poetry since then. Although he is prolific, Purdy is a stern judge of his own work; his *Collected Poems* (1986) retained only two hundred and fifty of the more than seven hundred poems he had previously published. (He estimates that he has written well over a thousand.) That book, which contains an interesting afterword by Dennis Lee, received a Governor General's Award.

An unpretentious writer who once described himself as 'a cynical Canadian nationalist, a lyrical Farley Mowat', he writes poems that are accessible, easy in diction, relaxed in tone; yet beneath their apparently simple surfaces they are often complexly affecting. Though he did not continue his formal education beyond grade ten, Purdy has always read widely and is an intense student of his craft. In his poetry he often draws upon the jobs he took during his early years, which he describes as 'a little of everything . . . Bata Shoe Factory, picking apples, six years in the R.C.A.F., store clerk in a foundry, in a Vancouver mattress factory, six months making box springs in Montreal'. A full-time writer for more than twenty-five years now, he has several times taught creative writing and been writer-in-residence at various universities. The three books Purdy has published since 1980 (*The Stone Bird*, 1981; *Piling Blood*, 1984; and *A Woman on the Shore*, 1990) contain some of his strongest work; these poems are more intense and reflective than the loosely-jointed and collo-quial poems of the sixties and seventies. He is now at work on a novel.

The most striking feature of Purdy's poetry is the sense it conveys of a mind in motion: a mind synthesizing its environment and looking for connection and meaning—even (as in 'Trees at the Arctic Circle') a mind engaged in composing the poem that we are now reading. Often the connections that the poet makes in these poems are temporal ones, for time is no less important than place to Purdy, and his poems tend to move from present to past and back again, seeking to restore lost continuities. In poems such as 'Elegy for a Grandfather' and 'Roblin Mills (2)', Purdy struggles to understand the vanished era he remembers glimpsing in his childhood. The origins of family and place even became the subject of a book-length poem, *In Search of Owen Roblin* (1974). In other poems the time span is much longer, for Purdy—like Pratt and many other modern Canadian writers—finds in the present vestiges of a more primitive era, a prehistoric past that gives meaning to 'The Cariboo Horses' and poignancy to 'Lament for the Dorsets'. For Purdy the past is a living thing, carried within us all, and a source of strength. Because we often lose sight of our past, one of Purdy's goals is to recover and respond to it. Thus 'Lament for the Dorsets' is an exemplary poem: the poet showing us the continuing life of an old work of art—'the ivory thought still warm'—while at the same time revealing how that work contains its own history, stretching back to the earliest human moments.

The Cariboo Horses

At 100 Mile House[1] the cowboys ride in rolling
stagey cigarettes with one hand reining
half-tame bronco rebels on a morning grey as stone
—so much like riding dangerous women
      with whiskey coloured eyes—
such women as once fell dead with their lovers
with fire in their heads and slippery froth on thighs
—Beaver or Carrier women maybe or
      Blackfoot squaws far past the edge of this valley
on the other side of those two toy mountain ranges   10
      from the sunfierce plains beyond

[1]Town in the British Columbia Cariboo region.

But only horses
           waiting in stables
hitched at taverns
              standing at dawn
pastured outside the town with
jeeps and fords and chevvys and
busy muttering stake trucks rushing
importantly over roads of man's devising
over the safe known roads of the ranchers   20
families and merchants of the town
            On the high prairie
are only horse and rider
             wind in dry grass
clopping in silence under the toy mountains
dropping sometimes and
            lost in the dry grass
            golden oranges of dung

Only horses
           no stopwatch memories or palace ancestors   30
not Kiangs[2] hauling undressed stone in the Nile Valley
and having stubborn Egyptian tantrums or
Onagers racing thru Hither Asia[3] and
the last Quagga[4] screaming in African highlands
           lost relatives of these
           whose hooves were thunder
the ghosts of horses battering thru the wind
whose names were the wind's common usage
whose life was the sun's
           arriving here at chilly noon   40
           in the gasoline smell of the
           dust and waiting 15 minutes
           at the grocer's

1965

[2]Species of wild Asian ass, as are onagers.
[3]The Near East.
[4]A zebra-like animal of southern Africa that became extinct in the nineteenth century.

The Country North of Belleville

Bush land scrub land—
           Cashel Township and Wollaston
Elzevir McClure and Dungannon
green lands of Weslemkoon Lake
where a man might have some
           opinion of what beauty
is and none deny him
              for miles—

Yet this is the country of defeat
where Sisyphus[1] rolls a big stone   10
year after year up the ancient hills
picnicking glaciers have left strewn
with centuries' rubble
                          backbreaking days
                          in the sun and rain
when realization seeps slow in the mind
without grandeur or self deception in
                          noble struggle
of being a fool—

A country of quiescence and still distance   20
a lean land
               not like the fat south
with inches of black soil on
               earth's round belly—
And where the farms are
               it's as if a man stuck
both thumbs in the stony earth and pulled

                          it apart
                          to make room
enough between the trees   30
for a wife
               and maybe some cows and
               room for some
of the more easily kept illusions—
And where the farms have gone back
to forest
               are only soft outlines
               shadowy differences—

Old fences drift vaguely among the trees
               a pile of moss-covered stones   40
gathered for some ghost purpose
has lost meaning under the meaningless sky
               —they are like cities under water
and the undulating green waves of time
               are laid on them—

This is the country of our defeat
               and yet
during the fall plowing a man
might stop and stand in a brown valley of the furrows
               and shade his eyes to watch for the same   50
               red patch mixed with gold
               that appears on the same

[1]As a punishment for his misdeeds, Sisyphus was condemned to Hades, where his task was to roll a large boulder to the top of a hill, at which point it rolled back down. In *Le Mythe de Sisyphe* (1942) Albert Camus depicts him as a symbol of existentialist man.

                spot in the hills
                year after year
                and grow old
        plowing and plowing a ten-acre field until
        the convolutions run parallel with his own brain—

        And this is a country where the young
                        leave quickly
        unwilling to know what their fathers know   60
        or think the words their mothers do not say—

        Herschel Monteagle and Faraday
        lakeland rockland and hill country
        a little adjacent to where the world is
        a little north of where the cities are and
        sometime
        we may go back there
                        to the country of our defeat
        Wollaston Elzevir and Dungannon
        and Weslemkoon lake land   70
        where the high townships of Cashel
                        McClure and Marmora once were—

        But it's been a long time since
        and we must enquire the way
                of strangers —

        1965, rev. 1972

Trees at the Arctic Circle

(Salix cordifolia—Ground Willow)

        They are 18 inches long
        or even less
        crawling under rocks
        grovelling among the lichens
        bending and curling to escape
        making themselves small
        finding new ways to hide
        Coward trees
        I am angry to see them
        like this   10
        not proud of what they are
        bowing to weather instead
        careful of themselves
        worried about the sky
        afraid of exposing their limbs
        like a Victorian married couple

        I call to mind great Douglas firs

I see tall maples waving green
and oaks like gods in autumn gold
the whole horizon jungle dark   20
and I crouched under that continual night
But these
even the dwarf shrubs of Ontario
mock them
Coward trees

And yet—and yet—
their seed pods glow
like delicate grey earrings
their leaves are veined and intricate
like tiny parkas   30
They have about three months
to make sure the species does not die
and that's how they spend their time
unbothered by any human opinion
just digging in here and now
sending their roots down down down
And you know it occurs to me
                about 2 feet under
those roots must touch permafrost
ice that remains ice forever   40
and they use it for their nourishment
they use death to remain alive

I see that I've been carried away
in my scorn of the dwarf trees
most foolish in my judgments
To take away the dignity
                of any living thing
even tho it cannot understand
                the scornful words
is to make life itself trivial   50
and yourself the Pontifex Maximus[1]
                of nullity
I have been stupid in a poem
I will not alter the poem
but let the stupidity remain permanent
as the trees are
in a poem
the dwarf trees of Baffin Island
                              Pangnirtung

1967

---

[1]The chief priest in ancient Rome; in later use, the Pope.

Wilderness Gothic

Across Roblin Lake, two shores away,
they are sheathing the church spire
with new metal. Someone hangs in the sky
over there from a piece of rope,
hammering and fitting God's belly-scratcher,
working his way up along the spire
until there's nothing left to nail on—
Perhaps the workman's faith reaches beyond:
touches intangibles, wrestles with Jacob,[1]
replacing rotten timber with pine thews,   10
pounds hard in the blue cave of the sky,
contends heroically with difficult problems of
gravity, sky navigation and mythopoeia,
his volunteer time and labour donated to God,
minus sick benefits of course on a non-union job—

Fields around are yellowing into harvest,
nestling and fingerling are sky and water borne,
death is yodelling quiet in green woodlots,
and bodies of three young birds have disappeared
in the sub-surface of the new county highway—   20

That picture is incomplete, part left out
that might alter the whole Dürer[2] landscape:
gothic ancestors peer from medieval sky,
dour faces trapped in photograph albums escaping
to clop down iron roads with matched greys:
work-sodden wives groping inside their flesh
for what keeps moving and changing and flashing
beyond and past the long frozen Victorian day.
A sign of fire and brimstone? A two-headed calf
born in the barn last night? A sharp female agony?   30
An age and a faith moving into transition,
the dinner cold and new-baked bread a failure,
deep woods shiver and water drops hang pendant,
double yolked eggs and the house creaks a little—
Something is about to happen. Leaves are still.
Two shores away, a man hammering in the sky.
Perhaps he will fall.

1968

---

[1] Jacob wrestled with an angel until he was given a blessing; see Genesis 32: 24-29. In this line 'with' should probably be understood in the sense of 'alongside'.
[2] Albrecht Dürer (1471-1528), painter and engraver, the greatest artist of the northern Renaissance; caught up in a period of intense change, and influential in bringing Italian Renaissance styles into Germany, Dürer also maintained some of the dominant Gothic style of earlier German art.

Lament for the Dorsets

(Eskimos extinct in the 14th century A.D.)[1]

Animal bones and some mossy tent rings
scrapers and spearheads   carved ivory swans
all that remains of the Dorset giants
who drove the Vikings back to their long ships
talked to spirits of earth and water
—a picture of terrifying old men
so large they broke the backs of bears
so small they lurk behind bone rafters
in the brain of modern hunters
among good thoughts and warm things   10
and come out at night
to spit on the stars

The big men with clever fingers
who had no dogs and hauled their sleds
over the frozen northern oceans
awkward giants
                    killers of seal
they couldn't compete with little men
who came from the west with dogs
Or else in a warm climatic cycle   20
the seals went back to cold waters
and the puzzled Dorsets scratched their heads
with hairy thumbs around 1350 A.D.
—couldn't figure it out
went around saying to each other
plaintively
          'What's wrong? What happened?
          Where are the seals gone!'
And died

Twentieth century people   30
apartment dwellers
executives of neon death
warmakers with things that explode
—they have never imagined us in their future
how could we imagine them in the past
squatting among the moving glaciers
six hundred years ago
with glowing lamps?
As remote or nearly
as the trilobites[2] and swamps   40

---

[1]The date of the mysterious disappearance of the Dorset, who were probably absorbed or expelled by the Thule Inuit, is now placed at around A.D. 1000, during a gradual warming period that began around then. To preserve good relations with the spirits of the animals they hunted, Dorset craftsmen carved finely detailed miniature replicas.

[2]Extinct arthropods from the Paleozoic period (600 million to 230 million years ago).

when coal became
or the last great reptile hissed
at a mammal the size of a mouse
that squeaked and fled

Did they ever realize at all
what was happening to them?
Some old hunter with one lame leg
a bear had chewed
sitting in a caribou-skin tent
—the last Dorset?   50
Let's say his name was Kudluk
and watch him sitting there
carving 2-inch ivory swans
for a dead grand-daughter
taking them out of his mind
the places in his mind
where pictures are
He selects a sharp stone tool
to gouge a parallel pattern of lines
on both sides of the swan   60
holding it with his left hand
bearing down and transmitting
his body's weight
from brain to arm and right hand
and one of his thoughts
turns to ivory
The carving is laid aside
in beginning darkness
at the end of hunger
and after a while wind   70
blows down the tent and snow
begins to cover him

After 600 years
the ivory thought
is still warm

1968

Roblin's Mills (2)[1]

The wheels stopped
and the murmur of voices
behind the flume's tremble
stopped
      and the wind-high ships
that sailed from Rednersville[2]
to the sunrise ports of Europe
are delayed somewhere
in a toddling breeze
The black millpond   10
turns an unreflecting eye
to look inward
like an idiot child
locked in the basement
when strangers come
whizzing past on the highway
above the dark green valley
a hundred yards below
The mill space is empty
even stones are gone   20
where hands were shaken
and walls enclosed laughter
saved up and brought here
from the hot fields
where all stories
are rolled into one
And white dust floating
above the watery mumble
and bright human sounds
to shimmer among the pollen   30
where bees dance now
Of all these things
no outline remains
no shadow on the soft air
no bent place in the heat glimmer
where the heavy walls pressed
And some of those who vanished
lost children of the time
kept after school
left alone in a graveyard   40
who may not change
or ever grow six inches
in one hot summer
or turn where the great herons

---

[1]Originally published as 'Roblin's Mills: Circa 1842'. Purdy later retitled this poem 'Roblin's Mills
(2)' to distinguish it from an earlier poem entitled 'Roblin's Mills'. Purdy also used 'Roblin's Mills
(2)' as the conclusion of his long poem *In Search of Owen Roblin* (1974).
[2]Town on the Bay of Quinte, not far from Roblin Mills.

graze the sky's low silver
—stand between the hours
in a rotting village
near the weed-grown eye
that looks into itself
deep in the black crystal   50
that holds and contains
the substance of shadows
manner and custom
            of the inarticulate
departures and morning rumours
gestures and almost touchings
announcements and arrivals
gossip of someone's marriage
when a girl or tired farm woman
whose body suddenly blushes   60
beneath a faded house dress
with white expressionless face
turns to her awkward husband
to remind him of something else
The black millpond
                  holds them
movings and reachings and fragments
the gear and tackle of living
under the water eye
all things laid aside   70
            discarded
                  forgotten
but they had their being once
and left a place to stand on

1968, rev. 1972

Man Without a Country

An eagle does not know who he is
nor yet a rat nor lice in a dog's fur
none of them know who they are
in the speechless scream and snarl of being
And yet in a dark hole in earth rat is rat
louse biting blood from flesh is louse of lice
and in the eagle's scream is the whole sum
and mystery of being one of a flying nation
of birds in darkness in blood and riding
the shining helm of the sky . . .   10

But I have heard a man say
       'This is not a country
         I am going away from here'
It was as if he had said
       'I am no man because—
         because this is not a country'
—his face twisted in contempt for himself
and he spoke of all the great things
other countries had accomplished
one country in particular he named   20
and said 'Look at them
their pride their arts and science
and above all they have not sold out
to the highest bidder
            No I will not stay
I am no man here
because this is not a country'
and the loss was his overwhelming in sadness

I can see him now in my mind
going to and fro in the world   30
hobbling around on a one-legged syllogism
crying out to himself 'I have no country!'
a warcry against himself
with nothing inside him except bitterness
and a condemnation of the place he came from
because he was not a man
because his country was not a country

Well let him be
for I have wondered who I was myself
as a youngster riding freight trains westward   40
noticing how the landscape in giant steps rose
to exceed itself in a continental hubris
of snow peaks and clouds piled skyward
with the hurtling upward roller-coaster-down sensation
that races thru blood with the alcohol of knowing
when dawn is the petals of a million flowers
with engine grit in my teeth and eyes stinging
with half the flying landscape a mince pie stuck to my face
the rest an omelet in shirt and pants and brain and under
    my fingernails   50

Call it inoculation—but not immunity
there is no immunity for place and time
and something grows inside if you feel it
and something dies if you don't

an exaltation
when I knew if anyone could ever know
what must escape telling and become feeling alone

I am a child fishing for sunfish in a river
I am learning to skate under the town bridge in Trenton
I am lost for two days in the northern forest   60
I am going to school and failing at French and Latin
I am learning what a strange lonely place is myself
reflecting the present reiterating the past
                              reconnoitring the future
These are my history
the story of myself
for I am the land
and the land has become me

Years later I think of that wandering exile
—and being an exile is beginning to understand yourself   70
as he is beginning to know that history is asleep
in all our bones the long history of becoming
He is beginning to know that the ruined grey cities
of Europe and eastern lands and ingrown culture
of the world mean nothing without a sense of place
the knowledge of here which is the centre of all things
of being a boy fishing for sunfish in a river
and always forever after knowing the direction of home
of things that resist telling the gods coded deep in memory
arriving here in total where the sun stands still at noon   80

Yes if you would like to hear his name said aloud
the name of the man without a country
for whom I feel such insulting compassion
that he would hate me for it if he knew
I can say that name but it would mean little
and perhaps he does know
and this poem of sadness and exaltation is written for him
tho poems speak names which are only words
and what words *are* there that you have not said yourself
which we must always go beyond   90
and arrive there naked
as it was in the beginning

1986

The Dead Poet

I was altered in the placenta
by the dead brother before me
who built a place in the womb
knowing I was coming:
he wrote words on the walls of flesh
painting a woman inside a woman
whispering a faint lullaby
that sings in my blind heart still

The others were lumberjacks
backwoods wrestlers and farmers   10
their women were meek and mild
nothing of them survives
but an image inside an image
of a cookstove and the kettle boiling
—how else explain myself to myself
where does the song come from?

Now on my wanderings:
at the Alhambra's lyric dazzle
where the Moors built stone poems
a wan white face peering out   20
—and the shadow in Plato's cave
remembers the small dead one
—at Samarkand in pale blue light
the words came slowly from him
—I recall the music of blood
on the Street of the Silversmiths

Sleep softly spirit of earth
as the days and nights join hands
when everything becomes one thing
wait softly brother   30
but do not expect it to happen
that great whoop announcing resurrection
expect only a small whisper
of birds nesting and green things growing
and a brief saying of them
and know where the words came from

1986

For Steve McIntyre

(1912-1984)

He said I was ignorant
and didn't mince words about it
my deficiency was GREAT BOOKS
— so I read Proust Woolf Cervantes
Dostoyevsky Joyce the works
and they were just as boring
as I'd always suspected
—but one night just before sleep
words were suddenly shining in the dark   10
like false teeth in a glass of water
like the laughter of Australopithecus
mocking other beasts surrounding his tree
like *Thalassa* for Xenophon and the Greeks
like Joshua's trumpet at Jericho
like sunlight under the bedsheets
with her arms around my neck
And I climbed down from the tree
instructed Darwin's non-evoluted
critters to get lost
delighted in the Black Sea with Xenophon   20
and the Greek Ten Thousand
and stole the wavetips' green diamonds
for my ballpoint —
All because of Steve McIntyre
a dead man who hears nothing
not *Thalassa* nor Joshua's trumpet
not Australopithecus inventing laughter
nor the tenderness I softly withdraw
from my breast in the form of   30
words that say *Goodbye*
beyond his hearing —
a man was puzzled in his mind
trying to figure it out?
— a woman half lost in a trance,
getting used to another self.

What could it have been? — not booze,
sex, mundane reward for virtue;
and maybe different for everyone,
the mystery that makes us human,   40
whatever "human" is —
then blue aftermath and depression,
ever oncoming whips of trivia
to settle ourselves in dullness.

Coming alive at the womb's doorway,
we inherited everything — sun, moon,
all: and resent knowing more than we know,
the dictatorship of the senses enough,
the stone ship we ride on enough
for now —: then the rare arrival
of something entirely beyond us,
beyond this repeated daily dying, 50
the singing moment —

1986

Mavis Gallant

b. 1922

Mavis Gallant, born Mavis de Trafford Young in Montreal, entered at the age of four a strict French-Catholic boarding school where, a Protestant child of Scots heritage, she was something of an anomaly. Her father's early death and her peripatetic education (she attended over seventeen schools in Canada and the United States) prepared her for an independent and, by choice, solitary life. After high school she worked briefly for the National Film Board and then became a reporter for the *Montreal Standard*. Gallant had begun to write fiction during these years but was disinclined to submit her work for publication. Although two of her stories— 'Good Morning and Goodbye' and 'Three Brick Walls'—were published as early as 1944 in the Montreal little magazine *Preview*

(because a friend forwarded them to its editor, Patrick Anderson), she sent out her manuscripts herself only after she had decided in 1950 to quit reporting and become a full-time writer. At twenty-eight, after a brief marriage, Gallant left Canada for Europe, settling eventually in Paris. She submitted her first story to the *New Yorker*, which returned it, saying that it was too Canadian for American readers, but asked to see more of her work. (That story, 'The Flowers of Spring', was subsequently published in *Northern Review* in 1950.) *The New Yorker* did publish her second submission in 1951; since then most of her stories—even her 'Canadian' ones—have appeared first in that magazine.

Over the years Gallant has written highly

polished, urbane short stories and novellas. They have been collected in *The Other Paris* (1956); *My Heart Is Broken* (British title: *An Unmarried Man's Summer*, 1964); *The Pegnitz Junction* (1973), linked stories about the sources of German fascism; *The End of the World and Other Stories* (1974), selected by Robert Weaver; *From the Fifteenth District* (1979); a collection of stories about Canadians, *Home Truths* (1981), which won a Governor General's Award. In the eighties Gallant published two more books of short stories, *Overhead in a Balloon: Stories of Paris* (1985), and *In Transit* (1988), which contains previously uncollected stories from the fifties and sixties. She has also written two novels, *Green Water, Green Sky* (1959) and *A Fairly Good Time* (1970), which, like her stories, are subtle yet penetrating character studies. She occasionally writes nonfiction as well, reporting and reviewing from her position as an observer of France. Many of these essays and reviews were collected in *Paris Notebooks* (1986). Her long essay in *The Affair of Gabrielle Russier* (1971), a book about a complex French legal scandal involving a teacher and her student, led to her current project: a non-fiction book about another famous episode in French law and history, the Dreyfus case.

Gallant, who has immersed herself in French culture and life for over thirty years and has been bilingual from childhood, writes only in English, believing that 'one needs a strong, complete language, fully understood to anchor one's understanding'. She has always been concerned with the individual's experience of an unfamiliar culture, and her decision to write in English while seeking out the nature and differences of other cultures is a key to understanding her work. Her stories, which capture the universal sense of alienation that has dominated modern society, are often about exiled and isolated people. To survive emotionally, her characters struggle—while hanging on to threads of their former cultures—to understand foreign environments that are alien both literally and psychologically. They are cut off not simply from their physical homeland but also from other people. Even at home they stand apart, unable to make contact, unable to join those around them. Often the psychic distance between generations is intensified by the loss of traditional codes. As in the fiction of Henry James, the truncated form of communication that prevails takes place in the twilight of an obsolescent world.

Gallant's method of portraying characters obliquely, often by focusing on specific social customs and on unconscious behaviour, recalls Proust as well as James. Little is said directly—communication is an elaborate, unspoken ritual—but what *is* said is of great importance. Consequently her dialogue is filled with nuances. Gallant's detached characters, unable to make outspoken judgments, are akin to those found in stories by Sinclair Ross, Alice Munro, Margaret Atwood, and Clark Blaise. They share a malady often portrayed in modern Canadian fiction: burdened by history yet isolated by it, they find society moving away from the familiar patterns that both bind and reassure them. Gallant, like other Canadian writers, shows her characters reacting with restraint and surviving, without comment or evaluation 'because there was no help for it'.

Although the setting of much of Gallant's writing takes place outside of the Canadian locale, she has continued many associations with Canada and has retained, along with her English language, a cultural identity with her homeland. She returned to Canada several times in the eighties; in 1983-4 she was writer-in-residence at the University of Toronto.

The Ice Wagon
Going Down the Street

Now that they are out of world affairs and back where they started, Peter Frazier's wife says, 'Everybody else did well in the international thing except us.'

'You have to be crooked,' he tells her.

'Or smart. Pity we weren't.'

It is Sunday morning. They sit in the kitchen, drinking their coffee, slowly, remembering the past. They say the names of people as if they were magic. Peter thinks, *Agnes Brusen,* but there are hundreds of other names. As a private married joke, Peter and Sheilah wear the silk dressing gowns they bought in Hong Kong. Each thinks the other a peacock, rather splendid, but they pretend the dressing gowns are silly and worn in fun.

Peter and Sheilah and their two daughters, Sandra and Jennifer, are visiting Peter's unmarried sister, Lucille. They have been Lucille's guests seventeen weeks, ever since they returned to Toronto from the Far East. Their big old steamer trunk blocks a corner of the kitchen, making a problem of the refrigerator door; but even Lucille says the trunk may as well stay where it is, for the present. The Fraziers' future is so unsettled; everything is still in the air.

Lucille has given her bedroom to her two nieces, and sleeps on a camp cot in the hall. The parents have the living-room divan. They have no privileges here; they sleep after Lucille has seen the last television show that interests her. In the hall closet their clothes are crushed by winter overcoats. They know they are being judged for the first time. Sandra and Jennifer are waiting for Sheilah and Peter to decide. They are waiting to learn where these exotic parents will fly to next. What sort of climate will Sheilah consider? What job will Peter consent to accept? When the parents are ready, the children will make a decision of their own. It is just possible that Sandra and Jennifer will choose to stay with their aunt.

The peacock parents are watched by wrens. Lucille and her nieces are much the same—sandy-colored, proudly plain. Neither of the girls has the father's insouciance or the mother's appearance—her height, her carriage, her thick hair, and sky-blue eyes. The children are more cautious than their parents; more Canadian. When they saw their aunt's apartment they had been away from Canada nine years, ever since they were two and four; and Jennifer, the elder, said, 'Well, now we're home.' Her voice is nasal and flat. Where did she learn that voice? And why should this be home? Peter's answer to anything about his mystifying children is, 'It must be in the blood.'

On Sunday morning Lucille takes her nieces to church. It seems to be the only condition she imposes on her relations: the children must be decent. The girls go willingly, with their new hats and purses and gloves and coral bracelets and strings of pearls. The parents, ramshackle, sleepy, dim in the brain because it is Sunday, sit down to their coffee and privacy and talk of the past.

'We weren't crooked,' says Peter. 'We weren't even smart.'

Sheilah's head bobs up; she is no drowner. It is wrong to say they have nothing to show for time. Sheilah has the Balenciaga.[1] It is a black afternoon dress, stiff and boned at the waist, long for the fashions of now, but neither Sheilah nor Peter would change a thread. The Balenciaga is their talisman, their treasure; and after they remember it they touch hands and think that the years are not behind them but hazy and marvelous and still to be lived.

The first place they went to was Paris. In the early 'fifties the pick of the international jobs was there. Peter had inherited the last scrap of money he knew he was ever likely to see, and it was enough to get them over: Sheilah and Peter and the babies and the steamer trunk. To their joy and astonishment they had money in the bank. They said to each other, 'It should last a year.' Peter was fastidious about the new job; he hadn't come all this distance to accept just anything. In Paris he met Hugh Taylor, who was earning enough smuggling gasoline to keep his wife in Paris and a girl in Rome. That impressed Peter, because he remembered Taylor as a sour scholarship student without the slightest talent for life. Taylor had a job, of course. He hadn't said to himself, I'll go over to Europe and smuggle gasoline. It gave Peter an idea; he saw the shape of things. First you catch your fish. Later, at an international party, he met Johnny Hertzberg, who told him Germany was the place. Hertzberg said that anyone who came out of Germany broke now was too stupid to be here, and deserved to be back home at a desk. Peter nodded, as if he had already thought of that. He began to think about Germany. Paris was fine for a holiday, but it had been picked clean. Yes, Germany. His money was running low. He thought about Germany quite a lot.

That winter was moist and delicate; so fragile that they daren't speak of it now. There seemed to be plenty of everything and plenty of time. They were living the dream of a marriage, the fabric uncut, nothing slashed or spoiled. All winter they spent their money, and went to parties, and talked about Peter's future job. It lasted four months. They spent their money, lived in the future, and were never as happy again.

After four months they were suddenly moved away from Paris, but not to Germany—to Geneva. Peter thinks it was because of the incident at the Trudeau wedding at the Ritz. Paul Trudeau was a French-Canadian Peter had known at school and in the Navy. Trudeau had turned into a snob, proud of his career and his Paris connections. He tried to make the difference felt, but Peter thought the difference was only for strangers. At the wedding reception Peter lay down on the floor and said he was dead. He held a white azalea in a brass pot on his chest, and sang, 'Oh, hear us when we cry to Thee for those in peril on the sea.' Sheilah bent over him and said, 'Peter, darling, get up. Pete, listen, every single person who can do something for you is in this room. If you love me, you'll get up.'

'I do love you,' he said, ready to engage in a serious conversation. 'She's so beautiful,' he told a second face. 'She's nearly as tall as I am. She was a model in London. I met her over in London in the war. I met her there in the war.' He lay on his back with the azalea on his chest, explaining their history. A waiter took the brass pot away, and after Peter had been hauled to his feet he knocked the waiter down. Trudeau's bride, who was freshly out of an Ursuline convent, became hysterical; and even though Paul Trudeau and Peter were old acquaint-

---

[1]A dress designed by Spanish couturier Cristobal Balenciaga. His creations were noted for their elegance.

ances, Trudeau never spoke to him again. Peter says now that French-Canadians always have that bit of spite. He says Trudeau asked the Embassy to interfere. Luckily, back home there were still a few people to whom the name 'Frazier' meant something, and it was to these people that Peter appealed. He wrote letters saying that a French-Canadian combine was preventing his getting a decent job, and could anything be done? No one answered directly, but it was clear that what they settled for was exile to Geneva: a season of meditation and remorse, as he explained to Sheilah, and it was managed tactfully, through Lucille. Lucille wrote that a friend of hers, May Fergus, now a secretary in Geneva, had heard about a job. The job was filing pictures in the information service of an international agency in the Palais des Nations. The pay was so-so, but Lucille thought Peter must be getting fed up doing nothing.

Peter often asks his sister now who put her up to it—what important person told her to write that letter suggesting Peter go to Geneva?

'Nobody,' says Lucille. 'I mean, nobody in the way *you* mean. I really did have this girl friend working there, and I knew you must be running through your money pretty fast in Paris.'

'It must have been somebody pretty high up,' Peter says. He looks at his sister admiringly, as he has often looked at his wife.

Peter's wife had loved him in Paris. Whatever she wanted in marriage she found that winter, there. In Geneva, where Peter was a file clerk and they lived in a furnished flat, she pretended they were in Paris and life was still the same. Often, when the children were at supper, she changed as though she and Peter were dining out. She wore the Balenciaga, and put candles on the card table where she and Peter ate their meal. The neckline of the dress was soiled with make-up. Peter remembers her dabbing on the make-up with a wet sponge. He remembers her in the kitchen, in the soiled Balenciaga, patting on the make-up with a filthy sponge. Behind her, at the kitchen table, Sandra and Jennifer, in buttonless pajamas and bunny slippers, ate their supper of marmalade sandwiches and milk. When the children were asleep, the parents dined solemnly, ritually, Sheilah sitting straight as a queen.

It was a mysterious period of exile, and he had to wait for signs, or signals, to know when he was free to leave. He never saw the job any other way. He forgot he had applied for it. He thought he had been sent to Geneva because of a misdemeanor and had to wait to be released. Nobody pressed him at work. His immediate boss had resigned, and he was alone for months in a room with two desks. He read the *Herald-Tribune,* and tried to discover how things were here—how the others ran their lives on the pay they were officially getting. But it was a closed conspiracy. He was not dealing with adventurers now but civil servants waiting for pension day. No one ever answered his questions. They pretended to think his questions were a form of wit. His only solace in exile was the few happy weekends he had in the late spring and early summer. He had met another old acquaintance, Mike Burleigh. Mike was a serious liberal who had married a serious heiress. The Burleighs had two guest lists. The first was composed of stuffy people they felt obliged to entertain, while the second was made up of their real friends, the friends they wanted. The real friends strove hard to become stuffy and dull and thus achieve the first guest list, but few succeeded. Peter went on the first list straight away. Possibly Mike didn't understand, at the beginning, why Peter was pretending to be a file clerk. Peter had such an air—he might have been sent by a universal inspector to see how things in Geneva were being run.

Every Friday in May and June and part of July, the Fraziers rented a sky-blue Fiat and drove forty miles east of Geneva to the Burleighs' summer house. They brought the children, a suitcase, the children's tattered picture books, and a token bottle of gin. This, in memory, is a period of water and water birds; swans, roses, and singing birds. The children were small and still belonged to them. If they remember too much, their mouths water, their stomachs hurt. Peter says, 'It was fine while it lasted.' Enough. While it lasted Sheilah and Madge Burleigh were close. They abandoned their husbands and spent long summer afternoons comparing their mothers and praising each other's skin and hair. To Madge, and not to Peter, Sheilah opened her Liverpool childhood with the words 'rat poor'. Peter heard about it later, from Mike. The women's friendship seemed to Peter a bad beginning. He trusted women but not with each other. It lasted ten weeks. One Sunday, Madge said she needed the two bedrooms the Fraziers usually occupied for a party of sociologists from Pakistan, and that was the end. In November, the Fraziers heard that the summer house had been closed, and that the Burleighs were in Geneva, in their winter flat; they gave no sign. There was no help for it, and no appeal.

Now Peter began firing letters to anyone who had ever known his late father. He was living in a mild yellow autumn. Why does he remember the streets of the city dark, and the windows everywhere black with rain? He remembers being with Sheilah and the children as if they clung together while just outside their small shelter it rained and rained. The children slept in the bedroom of the flat because the window gave on the street and they could breathe air. Peter and Sheilah had the living-room couch. Their window was not a real window but a square on a well of cement. The flat seemed damp as a cave. Peter remembers steam in the kitchen, pools under the sink, sweat on the pipes. Water streamed on him from the children's clothes, washed and dripping overhead. The trunk, upended in the children's room, was not quite unpacked. Sheilah had not signed her name to this life; she had not given in. Once Peter heard her drop her aitches. 'You kids are lucky,' she said to the girls. 'I never 'ad so much as a sit-down meal. I ate chips out of a paper or I 'ad a butty[2] out on the stairs.' He never asked her what a butty was. He thinks it means bread and cheese.

The day he heard 'You kids are lucky' he understood they were becoming in fact something they had only *appeared* to be until now—the shabby civil servant and his brood. If he had been European he would have ridden to work on a bicycle, in the uniform of his class and condition. He would have worn a tight coat, a turned collar, and a dirty tie. He wondered then if coming here had been a mistake, and if he should not, after all, still be in a place where his name meant something. Surely Peter Frazier should live where 'Frazier' counts? In Ontario even now when he says 'Frazier' an absent look comes over his hearer's face, as if its owner were consulting an interior guide. What is Frazier? What does it mean? Oil? Power? Politics? Wheat? Real estate? The creditors had the house

[2]Slang for 'sandwich', especially in Liverpool; e.g., a jam butty.

sealed when Peter's father died. His aunt collapsed with a heart attack in some-body's bachelor apartment, leaving three sons and a widower to surmise they had never known her. Her will was a disappointment. None of that generation left enough. One made it: the granite Presbyterian immigrants from Scotland. Their children, a generation of daunted women and maiden men, held still. Peter's fa-ther's crowd spent: they were not afraid of their fathers, and their grandfathers were old. Peter and his sister and his cousins lived on the remains. They were left the rinds of income, of notions, and the memories of ideas rather than ideas in-tact. If Peter can choose his reincarnation, let him be the oppressed son of a Scot-tish parson. Let Peter grow up on cuffs and iron principles. Let him make the for-tune! Let him flee the manse! When he was small his patrimony was squandered under his nose. He remembers people dancing in his father's house. He re-members seeing and nearly understanding adultery in a guest room, among a pile of wraps. He thought he had seen a murder; he never told. He remembers licking glasses wherever he found them—on window sills, on stairs, in the pantry. In his room he listened while Lucille read Beatrix Potter. The bad rabbit stole the carrot from the good rabbit without saying please, and downstairs was the noise of the party—the roar of the crouched lion. When his father died he saw the chairs up-side down and the bailiff's chalk marks. Then the doors were sealed.

He has often tried to tell Sheilah why he cannot be defeated. He remembers his father saying, 'Nothing can touch us,' and Peter believed it and still does. It has prevented his taking his troubles too seriously. 'Nothing can be as bad as this,' he will tell himself. 'It is happening to me.' Even in Geneva, where his status was file clerk, where he sank and stopped on the level of the men who never emi-grated, the men on the bicycles—even there he had a manner of strolling to work as if his office were a pastime, and his real life a secret so splendid he could share it with no one except himself.

In Geneva Peter worked for a woman—a girl. She was a Norwegian from a small town in Saskatchewan. He supposed they had been put together because they were Canadians; but they were as strange to each other as if 'Canadian' meant any number of things, or had no real meaning. Soon after Agnes Brusen came to the office she hung her framed university degree on the wall. It was one of the gritty, prideful gestures that stand for push, toil, and family sacrifice. He thought, then, that she must be one of a family of immigrants for whom educa-tion is everything. Hugh Taylor had told him that in some families the older chil-dren never marry until the youngest have finished school. Sometimes every sec-ond child is sacrificed and made to work for the education of the next born. Those who finish college spend years paying back. They are white-hot Protes-tants, and they live with a load of work and debt and obligation. Peter placed his new colleague on scraps of information. He had never been in the West.

She came to the office on a Monday morning in October. The office was over-heated and painted cream. It contained two desks, the filing cabinets, a map of the world as it had been in 1945, and the Charter of the United Nations left be-hind by Agnes Brusen's predecessor. (She took down the Charter without asking Peter if he minded, with the impudence of gesture you find in women who wouldn't say boo to a goose; and then she hung her college degree on the nail where the Charter had been.) Three people brought her in—a whole committee. One of them said, 'Agnes, this is Pete Frazier. Pete, Agnes Brusen. Pete's Canadian, too, Agnes. He knows all about the office, so ask him anything.'

Of course he knew all about the office: he knew the exact spot where the cord of the venetian blind was frayed, obliging one to give an extra tug to the right.

The girl might have been twenty-three: no more. She wore a brown tweed suit with bone buttons, and a new silk scarf and new shoes. She clutched an unscratched brown purse. She seemed dressed in going-away presents. She said, 'Oh, I never smoke,' with a convulsive movement of her hand, when Peter offered his case. He was courteous, hiding his disappointment. The people he worked with had told him a Scandinavian girl was arriving, and he had expected a stunner. Agnes was a mole: she was small and brown, and round-shouldered as if she had always carried parcels or younger children in her arms. A mole's profile was turned when she said goodbye to her committee. If she had been foreign, ill-favored though she was, he might have flirted a little, just to show that he was friendly; but their being Canadian, and suddenly left together, was a sexual damper. He sat down and lit his own cigarette. She smiled at him, questioningly, he thought, and sat as if she had never seen a chair before. He wondered if his smoking was annoying her. He wondered if she was fidgety about drafts, or allergic to anything, and whether she would want the blind up or down. His social compass was out of order because the others couldn't tell Peter and Agnes apart. There was a world of difference between them, yet it was she who had been brought in to sit at the larger of the two desks.

While he was thinking this she got up and walked around the office, almost on tiptoe, opening the doors of closets and pulling out the filing trays. She looked inside everything except the drawers of Peter's desk. (In any case, Peter's desk was locked. His desk is locked wherever he works. In Geneva he went into Personnel one morning, early, and pinched his application form. He had stated on the form that he had seven years' experience in public relations and could speak French, German, Spanish, and Italian. He has always collected anything important about himself—anything useful. But he can never get on with the final act, which is getting rid of the information. He has kept papers about for years, a constant source of worry.)

'I know this looks funny, Mr Ferris,' said the girl. 'I'm not really snooping or anything. I just can't feel easy in a new place unless I know where everything is. In a new place everything seems so hidden.'

If she had called him 'Ferris' and pretended not to know he was Frazier, it could only be because they had sent her here to spy on him and see if he had repented and was fit for a better place in life. 'You'll be all right here,' he said. 'Nothing's hidden. Most of us haven't got brains enough to have secrets. This is Rainbow Valley.' Depressed by the thought that they were having him watched now, he passed his hand over his hair and looked outside to the lawn and the parking lot and the peacocks someone gave the Palais des Nations years ago. The peacocks love no one. They wander about the parked cars looking elderly, bad-tempered, mournful, and lost.

Agnes had settled down again. She folded her silk scarf and placed it just so, with her gloves beside it. She opened her new purse and took out a notebook and a shiny gold pencil. She may have written

Duster for desk
Kleenex
Glass jar for flowers
Air-Wick because he smokes
Paper for lining drawers

because the next day she brought each of these articles to work. She also brought a large black Bible, which she unwrapped lovingly and placed on the left-hand corner of her desk. The flower vase—empty—stood in the middle, and the Kleenex made a counterpoise for the Bible on the right.

When he saw the Bible he knew she had not been sent to spy on his work. The conspiracy was deeper. She might have been dispatched by ghosts. He knew everything about her, all in a moment: he saw the ambition, the terror, the dry pride. She was the true heir of the men from Scotland; she was at the start. She had been sent to tell him, 'You can begin, but not begin again.' She never opened the Bible, but she dusted it as she dusted her desk, her chair, and any surface the cleaning staff had overlooked. And Peter, the first days, watching her timid movements, her insignificant little face, felt, as you feel the approach of a storm, the charge of moral certainty round her, the belief in work, the faith in undertakings, the bread of the Black Sunday. He recognized and tasted all of it: ashes in the mouth.

After five days their working relations were settled. Of course, there was the Bible and all that went with it, but his tongue had never held the taste of ashes long. She was an inferior girl of poor quality. She had nothing in her favor except the degree on the wall. In the real world, he would not have invited her to his house except to mind the children. That was what he said to Sheilah. He said that Agnes was a mole, and a virgin, and that her tics and mannerisms were sending him round the bend. She had an infuriating habit of covering her mouth when she talked. Even at the telephone she put up her hand as if afraid of losing anything, even a word. Her voice was nasal and flat. She had two working costumes, both dull as the wall. One was the brown suit, the other a navy-blue dress with changeable collars. She dressed for no one; she dressed for her desk, her jar of flowers, her Bible, and her box of Kleenex. One day she crossed the space between the two desks and stood over Peter, who was reading a newspaper. She could have spoken to him from her desk, but she may have felt that being on her feet gave her authority. She had plenty of courage, but authority was something else.

'I thought—I mean, they told me you were the person . . .' She got on with it bravely: 'If you don't want to do the filing or any work, all right, Mr Frazier. I'm not saying anything about that. You might have poor health or your personal reasons. But it's got to be done, so if you'll kindly show me about the filing I'll do it. I've worked in Information before, but it was a different office, and every office is different.'

'My dear girl,' said Peter. He pushed back his chair and looked at her, astonished. 'You've been sitting there fretting, worrying. How insensitive of me. How trying for you. Usually I file on the last Wednesday of the month, so you see, you just haven't been around long enough to see a last Wednesday. Not another word, please. And let us not waste another minute.' He emptied the heaped baskets of photographs so swiftly, pushing 'Iran—Smallpox Control' into 'Irish Red Cross' (close enough), that the girl looked frightened, as if she had raised a whirlwind. She said slowly, 'If you'll only show me, Mr Frazier, instead of doing it so fast, I'll gladly look after it, because you might want to be doing other things, and I feel the filing should be done every day.' But Peter was too busy to answer, and so she sat down, holding the edge of her desk.

'There,' he said, beaming. 'All done.' His smile, his sunburst, was wasted, for the girl was staring round the room as if she feared she had not inspected everything the first day after all; some drawer, some cupboard, hid a monster. That evening Peter unlocked one of the drawers of his desk and took away the application form he had stolen from Personnel. The girl had not finished her search.

'How could you *not* know?' wailed Sheilah. 'You sit looking at her every day. You must talk about *something*. She must have told you.'

'She did tell me,' said Peter, 'and I've just told you.'

It was this: Agnes Brusen was on the Burleighs' guest list. How had the Burleighs met her? What did they see in her? Peter could not reply. He knew that Agnes lived in a bed-sitting room with a Swiss family and had her meals with them. She had been in Geneva three months, but no one had ever seen her outside the office. 'You *should* know,' said Sheilah. 'She must have something, more than you can see. Is she pretty? Is she brilliant? What is it?'

'We don't really talk,' Peter said. They talked in a way: Peter teased her and she took no notice. Agnes was not a sulker. She had taken her defeat like a sport. She did her work and a good deal of his. She sat behind her Bible, her flowers, and her Kleenex, and answered when Peter spoke. That was how he learned about the Burleighs—just by teasing and being bored. It was a January afternoon. He said, '*Miss* Brusen. Talk to me. Tell me everything. Pretend we have perfect rapport. Do you like Geneva?'

'It's a nice clean town,' she said. He can see to this day the red and blue anemones in the glass jar, and her bent head, and her small untended hands.

'Are you learning beautiful French with your Swiss family?'

'They speak English.'

'Why don't you take an apartment of your own?' he said. Peter was not usually impertinent. He was bored. 'You'd be independent then.'

'I am independent,' she said. 'I earn my living. I don't think it proves anything if you live by yourself. Mrs Burleigh wants me to live alone, too. She's looking for something for me. It mustn't be dear. I send money home.'

Here was the extraordinary thing about Agnes Brusen: she refused the use of Christian names and never spoke to Peter unless he spoke first, but she would tell anything, as if to say, 'Don't waste time fishing. Here it is.'

He learned all in one minute that she sent her salary home, and that she was a friend of the Burleighs. The first he had expected; the second knocked him flat.

'She's got to come to dinner,' Sheilah said. 'We should have had her right from the beginning. If only I'd known! But *you* were the one. You said she looked like—oh, I don't even remember. A Norwegian mole.'

She came to dinner one Saturday night in January, in her navy-blue dress, to which she had pinned an organdy gardenia. She sat upright on the edge of the sofa. Sheilah had ordered the meal from a restaurant. There was lobster, good wine, and a *pièce-montée*[3] full of kirsch and cream. Agnes refused the lobster; she had never eaten anything from the sea unless it had been sterilized and tinned, and said so. She was afraid of skin poisoning. Someone in her family had skin poisoning after having eaten oysters. She touched her cheeks and neck to show where the poisoning had erupted. She sniffed her wine and put the glass down without tasting it. She could not eat the cake because of the alcohol it contained. She ate an egg, bread and butter, a sliced tomato, and drank a glass of ginger ale. She seemed unaware she was creating disaster and pain. She did not help clear away the dinner plates. She sat, adequately nourished, decently dressed, and waited to learn why she had been invited here—that was the feeling Peter had. He folded the card table on which they had dined, and opened the window to air the room.

'It's not the same cold as Canada, but you feel it more,' he said, for something to say.

'Your blood has gotten thin,' said Agnes.

Sheilah returned from the kitchen and let herself fall into an armchair. With her eyes closed she held out her hand for a cigarette. She was performing the haughty-lady act that was a family joke. She flung her head back and looked at Agnes through half-closed lids; then she suddenly brought her head forward, widening her eyes.

'Are you skiing madly?' she said.

'Well, in the first place there hasn't been any snow,' said Agnes. 'So nobody's doing any skiing so far as I know. All I hear is people complaining because there's no snow. Personally, I don't ski. There isn't much skiing in the part of Canada I come from. Besides, my family never had that kind of leisure.'

'Heavens,' said Sheilah, as if her family had every kind.

I'll bet they had, thought Peter. On the dole.

Sheilah was wasting her act. He had a suspicion that Agnes knew it was an act but did not know it was also a joke. If so, it made Sheilah seem a fool, and he loved Sheilah too much to enjoy it.

'The Burleighs have been wonderful to me,' said Agnes. She seemed to have divined why she was here, and decided to give them all the information they wanted, so that she could put on her coat and go home to bed. 'They had me out to their place on the lake every weekend until the weather got cold and they moved back to town. They've rented a chalet for the winter, and they want me to come there, too. But I don't know if I will or not. I don't ski, and, oh, I don't know—I don't drink, either, and I don't always see the point. Their friends are too rich and I'm too Canadian.'

She had delivered everything Sheilah wanted and more: Agnes was on the first guest list and didn't care. No, Peter corrected; doesn't know. Doesn't care and doesn't know.

'I thought with you Norwegians it was in the blood, skiing. And drinking,' Sheilah murmured.

'Drinking, maybe,' said Agnes. She covered her mouth and said behind her spread fingers, 'In our family we were religious. We didn't drink or smoke. My brother was in Norway in the war. He saw some cousins. Oh,' she said, unexpectedly loud, 'Harry said it was just terrible. They were so poor. They had flies in their kitchen. They gave him something to eat a fly had been on. They didn't have a real toilet, and they'd been in the same house about two hundred years. We've only recently built our own home, and we have a bathroom and two toilets. I'm from Saskatchewan,' she said. 'I'm not from any other place.'

Surely one winter here had been punishment enough? In the spring they would remember him and free him. He wrote Lucille, who said he was lucky to have a job at all. The Burleighs had sent the Fraziers a second-guest list Christmas card. It showed a Moslem refugee child weeping outside a tent. They treasured the card and left it standing long after the others had been given the children to cut up. Peter had discovered by now what had gone wrong in the friendship— Sheilah had charged a skirt at a dressmaker to Madge's account. Madge had told her she might, and then changed her mind. Poor Sheilah! She was new to this part of it—to the changing humors of independent friends. Paris was already a year in the past. At Mardi Gras, the Burleighs gave their annual party. They invited everyone, the damned and the dropped, with the prodigality of a child at prayers. The invitation said 'in costume', but the Fraziers were too happy to wear a disguise. They might not be recognized. Like many of the guests they expected to meet at the party, they had been disgraced, forgotten, and rehabilitated. They would be anxious to see one another as they were.

On the night of the party, the Fraziers rented a car they had never seen before and drove through the first snowstorm of the year. Peter had not driven since last summer's blissful trips in the Fiat. He could not find the switch for the windshield wiper in this car. He leaned over the wheel. 'Can you see on your side?' he asked. 'Can I make a left turn here? Does it look like a one-way?'

'I can't imagine why you took a car with a right-hand drive,' said Sheilah.

He had trouble finding a place to park; they crawled up and down unknown streets whose curbs were packed with snow-covered cars. When they stood at last on the pavement, safe and sound, Peter said. 'This is the first snow.'

'I can see that,' said Sheilah. 'Hurry, darling. My hair.'

'It's the first snow.'

'You're repeating yourself,' she said. 'Please hurry, darling. Think of my poor shoes. My *hair*.'

She was born in an ugly city, and so was Peter, but they have this difference: she does not know the importance of the first snow—the first clean thing in a dirty year. He would have told her then that this storm, which was wetting her feet and destroying her hair, was like the first day of the English spring, but she made a frightened gesture, trying to shield her head. The gesture told him he did not understand her beauty.

'Let me,' she said. He was fumbling with the key, trying to lock the car. She took the key without impatience and locked the door on the driver's side; and then, to show Peter she treasured him and was not afraid of wasting her life or her beauty, she took his arm and they walked in the snow down a street and around a corner to the apartment house where the Burleighs lived. They were, and are, a united couple. They were afraid of the party, and each of them knew it. When they walk together, holding arms, they give each other whatever each can spare.

Only six people had arrived in costume. Madge Burleigh was disguised as Manet's 'Lola de Valence',[4] which everyone mistook for Carmen. Mike was an Impressionist painter, with a straw hat and a glued-on beard. 'I am all of them,' he said. He would rather have dressed as a dentist, he said, welcoming the Fraziers as if he had parted from them the day before, but Madge wanted him to look as if he had created her. 'You know?' he said.

'Perfectly,' said Sheilah. Her shoes were stained and the snow had softened her lacquered hair. She was not wasted; she was the most beautiful woman here.

About an hour after their arrival, Peter found himself with no one to talk to. He had told about the Trudeau wedding in Paris and the pot of azaleas, and after he mislaid his audience he began to look round for Sheilah. She was on a window seat, partly concealed by a green velvet curtain. Facing her, so that their profiles were neat and perfect against the night, was a man. Their conversation was private and enclosed, as if they had in minutes covered leagues of time and arrived at the place where everything was implied, understood. Peter began working his way across the room, toward his wife, when he saw Agnes. He was granted the sight of her drowning face. She had dressed with comic intention, obviously with care, and now she was a ragged hobo, half tramp, half clown. Her hair was tucked up under a bowler hat. The six costumed guests who had made the same mistake—the ghost, the gypsy, the Athenian maiden, the geisha, the Martian, and the apache—were delighted to find a seventh; but Agnes was not amused; she was gasping for life. When a waiter passed with a crowded tray, she took a glass without seeing it; then a wave of the party took her away.

Sheilah's new friend was named Simpson. After Simpson said he thought perhaps he'd better circulate, Peter sat down where he had been. 'Now look, Sheilah,' he began. Their most intimate conversations have taken place at parties. Once at a party she told him she was leaving him; she didn't, of course. Smiling, blue-eyed, she gazed lovingly at Peter and said rapidly, 'Pete, shut up and listen. That man. The man you scared away. He's a big wheel in a company out in India or someplace like that. It's gorgeous out there. Pete, the *servants*. And it's warm. It never never snows. He says there's heaps of jobs. You pick them off the trees like . . . orchids. He says it's even easier now than when we owned all those places, because now the poor pets can't run anything and they'll pay *fortunes*. Pete, he says it's warm, it's heaven, and Pete, they pay.'

A few minutes later, Peter was alone again and Sheilah part of a closed, laughing group. Holding her elbow was the man from the place where jobs grew like orchids. Peter edged into the group and laughed at a story he hadn't heard. He

[4]A painting by Edouard Manet (1832-83) of the Spanish dancer whom he and Baudelaire admired as being *'un bijou rose et noir'*. 'Carmen': entrancing but heartless Spanish *femme fatale*, the heroine of Bizet's renowned opera of the same name (1875).

heard only the last line, which was, 'Here comes another tunnel.' Looking out from the tight laughing ring, he saw Agnes again, and he thought, I'd be like Agnes if I didn't have Sheilah. Agnes put her glass down on a table and lurched toward the doorway, head forward. Madge Burleigh, who never stopped moving around the room and smiling, was still smiling when she paused and said in Peter's ear, 'Go with Agnes, Pete. See that she gets home. People will notice if Mike leaves.'

'She probably just wants to walk around the block,' said Peter. 'She'll be back.'

'Oh, stop thinking about yourself, for once, and see that that poor girl gets home,' said Madge. 'You've still got your Fiat, haven't you?'

He turned away as if he had been pushed. Any command is a release, in a way. He may not want to go in that particular direction, but at least he is going somewhere. And now Sheilah, who had moved inches nearer to hear what Madge and Peter were murmuring, said, 'Yes, go, darling,' as if he were leaving the gates of Troy.[5]

Peter was to find Agnes and see that she reached home: this he repeated to himself as he stood on the landing, outside the Burleighs' flat, ringing for the elevator. Bored with waiting for it, he ran down the stairs, four flights, and saw that Agnes had stalled the lift by leaving the door open. She was crouched on the floor, propped on her fingertips. Her eyes were closed.

'Agnes,' said Peter. '*Miss* Brusen, I mean. That's no way to leave a party. Don't you know you're supposed to curtsey and say thanks? My God, Agnes, anybody going by here just now might have seen you! Come on, be a good girl. Time to go home.'

She got up without his help and, moving between invisible crevasses, shut the elevator door. Then she left the building and Peter followed, remembering he was to see that she got home. They walked along the snowy pavement, Peter a few steps behind her. When she turned right for no reason, he turned, too. He had no clear idea where they were going. Perhaps she lived close by. He had forgotten where the hired car was parked, or what it looked like; he could not remember its make or its color. In any case, Sheilah had the key. Agnes walked on steadily, as if she knew their destination, and he thought, Agnes Brusen is drunk in the street in Geneva and dressed like a tramp. He wanted to say, 'This is the best thing that ever happened to you, Agnes; it will help you understand how things are for some of the rest of us.' But she stopped and turned and, leaning over a low hedge, retched on a frozen lawn. He held her clammy forehead and rested his hand on her arched back, on muscles as tight as a fist. She straightened up and drew a breath but the cold air made her cough. 'Don't breathe too deeply,' he said. 'It's the worst thing you can do. Have you got a handkerchief?' He passed his own handkerchief over her wet weeping face, upturned like the face of one of his little girls. 'I'm out without a coat,' he said, noticing it. 'We're a pair.'

'I never drink,' said Agnes. 'I'm just not used to it.' Her voice was sweet and quiet. He had never seen her so peaceful, so composed. He thought she must

---

[5] An allusion to the flight of the Trojans during the destruction of Troy by the Greeks.

surely be all right, now, and perhaps he might leave her here. The trust in her tilted face had perplexed him. He wanted to get back to Sheilah and have her explain something. He had forgotten what it was, but Sheilah would know. 'Do you live around here?' he said. As he spoke, she let herself fall. He had wiped her face and now she trusted him to pick her up, set her on her feet, take her wherever she ought to be. He pulled her up and she stood, wordless, humble, as he brushed the snow from her tramp's clothes. Snow horizontally crossed the lamplight. The street was silent. Agnes had lost her hat. Snow, which he tasted, melted on her hands. His gesture of licking snow from her hands was formal as a handshake. He tasted snow on her hands and then they walked on.

'I never drink,' she said. They stood on the edge of a broad avenue. The wrong turning now could lead them anywhere; it was the changeable avenue at the edge of towns that loses its houses and becomes a highway. She held his arm and spoke in a gentle voice. She said, 'In our house we didn't smoke or drink. My mother was ambitious for me, more than for Harry and the others.' She said, 'I've never been alone before. When I was a kid I would get up in the summer before the others, and I'd see the ice wagon going down the street. I'm alone now. Mrs Burleigh's found me an apartment. It's only one room. She likes it because it's in the old part of town. I don't like old houses. Old houses are dirty. You don't know who was there before.'

'I should have a car somewhere,' Peter said. 'I'm not sure where we are.'

He remembers that on this avenue they climbed into a taxi, but nothing about the drive. Perhaps he fell asleep. He does remember that when he paid the driver Agnes clutched his arm, trying to stop him. She pressed extra coins into the driver's palm. The driver was paid twice.

'I'll tell you one thing about us,' said Peter. 'We pay everything twice.' This was part of a much longer theory concerning North American behavior, and it was not Peter's own. Mike Burleigh had held forth about it on summer afternoons.

Agnes pushed open a door between a stationer's shop and a grocery, and led the way up a narrow inside stair. They climbed one flight, frightening beetles. She had to search every pocket for the latchkey. She was shaking with cold. Her apartment seemed little warmer than the street. Without speaking to Peter she turned on all the lights. She looked inside the kitchen and the bathroom and then got down on her hands and knees and looked under the sofa. The room was neat and belonged to no one. She left him standing in this unclaimed room—she had forgotten him—and closed a door behind her. He looked for something to do— some useful action he could repeat to Madge. He turned on the electric radiator in the fireplace. Perhaps Agnes wouldn't thank him for it; perhaps she would rather undress in the cold. 'I'll be on my way,' he called to the bathroom door.

She had taken off the tramp's clothes and put on a dressing gown of orphanage wool. She came out of the bathroom and straight toward him. She pressed her face and rubbed her cheek on his shoulder as if hoping the contact would leave a scar. He saw her back and her profile and his own face in the mirror over the fireplace. He thought, This is how disasters happen. He saw floods of sea water moving with perfect punitive justice over reclaimed land; he saw lava covering vineyards and overtaking of dogs and stragglers. A bridge over an abyss snapped in two and the long express train, suddenly V-shaped, floated like snow. He thought amiably of every kind of disaster and thought, This is how they occur.

Her eyes were closed. She said, 'I shouldn't be over here. In my family we didn't drink or smoke. My mother wanted a lot from me, more than from Harry and the others.' But he knew all that; he had known from the day of the Bible, and because once, at the beginning, she had made him afraid. He was not afraid of her now.

She said, 'It's no use staying here, is it?'

'If you mean what I think, no.'

'It wouldn't be better anywhere.'

She let him see full on her blotched face. He was not expected to do anything. He was not required to pick her up when she fell or wipe her tears. She was poor quality, really—he remembered having thought that once. She left him and went quietly into the bathroom and locked the door. He heard taps running and supposed it was a hot bath. He was pretty certain there would be no more tears. He looked at his watch: Sheilah must be home, now, wondering what had become of him. He descended the beetles' staircase and for forty minutes crossed the city under a windless fall of snow.

The neighbor's child who had stayed with Peter's children was asleep on the living-room sofa. Peter woke her and sent her, sleepwalking, to her own door. He sat down, wet to the bone, thinking, I'll call the Burleighs. In half an hour I'll call the police. He heard a car stop and the engine running and a confusion of two voices laughing and calling goodnight. Presently Sheilah let herself in, rosy-faced, smiling. She carried his trenchcoat over her arm. She said, 'How's Agnes?'

'Where were you?' he said. 'Whose car was that?'

Sheilah had gone into the children's room. He heard her shutting their window. She returned, undoing her dress, and said, 'Was Agnes all right?'

'Agnes is all right. Sheilah, this is about the worst . . .'

She stepped out of the Balenciaga and threw it over a chair. She stopped and looked at him and said, 'Poor old Pete, are you in love with Agnes?' And then, as if the answer were of so little importance she hadn't time for it, she locked her arms around him and said, 'My love, we're going to Ceylon.'

Two days later, when Peter strolled into his office, Agnes was at her desk. She wore the blue dress, with a spotless collar. White and yellow freesias were symmetrically arranged in the glass jar. The room was hot, and the spring snow, glued for a second when it touched the window, blurred the view of parked cars.

'Quite a party,' Peter said.

She did not look up. He sighed, sat down, and thought if the snow held he would be skiing at the Burleighs' very soon. Impressed by his kindness to Agnes, Madge had invited the family for the first possible weekend.

Presently Agnes said, 'I'll never drink again or go to a house where people are drinking. And I'll never bother anyone the way I bothered you.'

'You didn't bother me,' he said. 'I took you home. You were alone and it was late. It's normal.'

'Normal for you, maybe, but I'm used to getting home by myself. Please never tell what happened.'

He stared at her. He can still remember the freesias and the Bible and the heat in the room. She looked as if the elements had no power. She felt neither heat nor cold. 'Nothing happened,' he said.

'I behaved in a silly way. I had no right to. I led you to think I might do something wrong.'

'*I* might have tried something,' he said gallantly. 'But that would be my fault and not yours.'

She put her knuckle to her mouth and he could scarcely hear. 'It was because of you. I was afraid you might be blamed, or else you'd blame yourself.'

'There's no question of any blame,' he said. 'Nothing happened. We'd both had a lot to drink. Forget about it. Nothing *happened*. You'd remember if it had.'

She put down her hand. There was an expression on her face. Now she sees me, he thought. She had never looked at him after the first day. (He has since tried to put a name to the look on her face; but how can he, now, after so many voyages, after Ceylon, and Hong Kong, and Sheilah's nearly leaving him, and all their difficulties—the money owed, the rows with hotel managers, the lost and found steamer trunk, the children throwing up the foreign food?) She sees me now, he thought. What does she see?

She said, 'I'm from a big family. I'm not used to being alone. I'm not a suicidal person, but I could have done something after that party, just not to see any more, or think or listen or expect anything. What can I think when I see these people? All my life I heard, Educated people don't do this, educated people don't do that. And now I'm here, and you're all educated people, and you're nothing but pigs. You're educated and you drink and do everything wrong and you know what you're doing, and that makes you worse than pigs. My family worked to make me an educated person, but they didn't know you. But what if I didn't see and hear and expect anything any more? It wouldn't change anything. You'd all be still the same. Only *you* might have thought it was your fault. You might have thought you were to blame. It could worry you all your life. It would have been wrong for me to worry you.'

He remembered that the rented car was still along a snowy curb somewhere in Geneva. He wondered if Sheilah had the key in her purse and if she remembered where they'd parked.

'I told you about the ice wagon,' Agnes said. 'I don't remember everything, so you're wrong about remembering. But I remember telling you that. That was the best. It's the best you can hope to have. In a big family, if you want to be alone, you have to get up before the rest of them. You get up early in the morning in the summer and it's you, you, once in your life alone in the universe. You think you know everything that can happen . . . Nothing is ever like that again.'

He looked at the smeared window and wondered if this day could end without disaster. In his mind he saw her falling in the snow wearing a tramp's costume, and he saw her coming to him in the orphanage dressing gown. He saw her drowning face at the party. He was afraid for himself. The story was still unfinished. It had to come to a climax, something threatening to him. But there was no climax. They talked that day, and afterward nothing else was said. They went on in the same office for a short time, until Peter left for Ceylon; until somebody read the right letter, passed it on for the right initials, and the Fraziers began the Oriental tour that should have made their fortune. Agnes and Peter were too tired to speak after that morning. They were like a married couple in danger, taking care.

But what were they talking about that day, so quietly, such old friends? They talked about dying, about being ambitious, about being religious, about different kinds of love. What did she see when she looked at him—taking her knuckle slowly away from her mouth, bringing her hand down to the desk, letting it rest there? They were both Canadians, so they had this much together—the knowledge of the little you dare admit. Death, near-death, the best thing, the wrong thing—God knows what they were telling each other. Anyway, nothing happened.

When, on Sunday mornings, Sheilah and Peter talk about those times, they take on the glamor of something still to come. It is then he remembers Agnes Brusen. He never says her name. Sheilah wouldn't remember Agnes. Agnes is the only secret Peter has from his wife, the only puzzle he pieces together without her help. He thinks about families in the West as they were fifteen, twenty years ago—the iron-cold ambition, and every member pushing the next one on. He thinks of his father's parties. When he thinks of his father he imagines him with Sheilah, in a crowd. Actually, Sheilah and Peter's father never met, but they might have liked each other. His father admired good-looking women. Peter wonders what they were doing over there in Geneva—not Sheilah and Peter, *Agnes* and Peter. It is almost as if they had once run away together, silly as children, irresponsible as lovers. Peter and Sheilah are back where they started. While they were out in world affairs picking up microbes and debts, always on the fringe of disaster, the fringe of a fortune, Agnes went on and did—what? They lost each other. He thinks of the ice wagon going down the street. He sees something he has never seen in his life—a Western town that belongs to Agnes. Here is Agnes—small, mole-faced, round-shouldered because she has always carried a younger child. She watches the ice wagon and the trail of ice water in a morning invented for her: hers. He sees the weak prairie trees and the shadows on the sidewalk. Nothing moves except the shadows and the ice wagon and the changing amber of the child's eyes. The child is Peter. He has seen the grain of the cement sidewalk and the grass in the cracks, and the dust, and the dandelions at the edge of the road. He is there. He has taken the morning that belongs to Agnes, he is up before the others, and he knows everything. There is nothing he doesn't know. He could keep the morning, if he wanted to, but what can Peter do with the start of a summer day? Sheilah is here, it is a true Sunday morning, with its dimness and headache and remorse and regrets, and this is life. He says, 'We have the Balenciaga.' He touches Sheilah's hand. The children have their aunt now, and he and Sheilah have each other. Everything works out, somehow or other. Let Agnes have the start of the day. Let Agnes think it was invented for her. Who wants to be alone in the universe? No, begin at the beginning: Peter lost Agnes. Agnes says to herself somewhere, Peter is lost.

1964

Eli Mandel

b. 1922

Elias Wolf Mandel grew up in the small western-Canadian town of Estevan, Sask., which, with the neighbouring towns of Hoffer and Hirsch, provided him not only with a strong sense of Russian-Jewish culture but with the *idea* of the Prairie West—both important elements in his poetry. He left Estevan to attend the University of Saskatchewan. After serving as an army medical corpsman in the Second World War he returned to the university for graduate work, completing an M.A. in 1949 and then starting Ph.D. studies at the University of Toronto. During this period Mandel began to publish poetry in John Sutherland's *Northern Review*, Raymond Souster's *Contact*, and the Montreal journal *CIV/n*. In 1954 his work—along with that of Gael Turnbull and Phyllis Webb—was featured in *Trio*, published by Souster's Contact Press. In the same year Mandel joined the staff of the Collège Militaire Royal de Saint-Jean (where he taught until the completion of his Ph.D. in 1957) and became part of the literary community in nearby Montreal.

In 1957 Mandel returned west to join the University of Alberta's English faculty. Ten years later he became a member of the Humanities and English departments at York University, Toronto, where he remained until his retirement in 1987. In 1982 Mandel became a fellow of the Royal Society of Canada.

As well as being a teacher, a poet, and a critic, Mandel has also been an important editor. His anthologies include *Poetry 62/Poésie 62* (1961, edited with Jean-Guy Pilon), *Poets of Contemporary Canada: 1960-1970* (1972), *Five Modern Canadian Poets* (1970), and *Eight More Canadian Poets* (1972). His anthology of essays, *Contexts of Canadian Criticism* (1971), provides an overview of the influences of culture and theory on the criticism of Canadian

literature. In 1986 Mandel edited another collection of essays, *A Passion for Identity*, with David Taras.

Mandel's own poetry is a further reflection of his interest in the range of Canadian literary activity. His early work, the 'Minotaur Poems' in *Trio* as well as *The Fuseli Poems* (1960), tends toward abstract, mythopoeic meditations, a type of writing associated with Canadian poets of this period who were influenced by Northrop Frye. His next collection, *Black and Secret Man* (1964), was followed by *An Idiot Joy* (1967), which won a Governor General's Award. (In 1973 Mandel included poems from these volumes in *Crusoe: Poems New and Selected*.) While continuing to reflect Mandel's belief in man's inherently dark and deceptive side, these books showed—in their increased social awareness and in their spare, more accessible, style—the influence of his earlier contact with the Montreal poets. In *Stony Plain* (1973), *Out of Place* (1977), and *Life Sentence* (1981) Mandel's poetry is concerned with observation and event, and its style is even more stripped-down—features it shares with the work of west-coast writers such as those in the *Tish* movement, and with the prairie poetry of John Newlove.

The drive to make connections—to create a poetry that draws together widely varied places, individuals, and periods, and to find meaning in their relationships—informs all of Mandel's work. Even his criticism tends to unite divergent elements of culture and literature into a personal vision. In the lectures and critical essays collected in *Criticism: The Silent-Speaking World* (1966), *Another Time* (1977), and *The Family Romance* (1986), he allows the reader to follow the development of his thought from his initial consideration of a problem, through his processes of associating seemingly unrelated elements, to a final synthesizing of these elements in his conclusion.

Mandel's best poems develop in the same associative manner, describing a pattern of response and a process of moving from perception of a single event or thing to a growing understanding of its real importance, its hidden meaning. Appropriately the title of his collected poems, *Dreaming Backwards*

(1981), is a metaphor for the general meditative nature of his poetry. For Mandel the writer is a kind of healer, a shaman, who through the trickery of words and syntax tears away the confusion and complexity of a duplicitous present to reveal a truth that lies beyond self and time.

Houdini[1]

I suspect he knew that trunks are metaphors,
could distinguish between the finest rhythms
unrolled on rope or singing in a chain
and knew the metrics of the deepest pools

I think of him listening to the words
spoken by manacles, cells, handcuffs,
chests, hampers, roll-top desks, vaults,
especially the deep words spoken by coffins

escape, escape: quaint Harry in his suit
his chains, his desk, attached to all attachments   10
how he'd sweat in that precise struggle
with those binding words, wrapped around him
like that mannered style, his formal suit

and spoken when? by whom? What thing first said
'there's no way out?'; so that he'd free himself,
leap, squirm, no matter how, to chain himself again,
once more jump out of the deep alive
with all his chains singing around his feet
like the bound crowds who sigh, who sigh.

1967

---

[1]Harry Houdini, born Ehrich Weiss (1874-1926), stage magician and escape artist; his most dramatic escapes were those from chains while inside a trunk under water and from a buried coffin.

On the 25th Anniversary of the Liberation of Auschwitz:[1]

MEMORIAL SERVICES, TORONTO, JANUARY 25, 1970
YMHA BLOOR & SPADINA

the name is hard
a German sound made out of
the gut guttural throat
y scream yell ing open
voice mouth growl
    and sweat
'the only way out of Auschwitz
is through the chimneys'[2]
    of course
that's second hand that's told   10
again Sigmund Sherwood (Sobolewski)[3]
twisting himself into that sentence
before us on the platform
    the poem

shaping itself late in the after
noon later than it would be:

Pendericki's 'Wrath of God'[4]
moaning electronic Polish theatric
the screen silent
    framed by the name   20
looking away from/pretending not there
no name no not name no

   Auschwitz
  in GOTHIC lettering [5]
    the hall
a parody a reminiscence a nasty memory

[1]The German name for Oswiecim, a southern Polish city and the location of the notorious Nazi extermination camp in which prisoners—Polish, Russian, and, beginning in 1941, Jewish—were tortured, experimented upon, and killed *en masse* in acid showers that produced cyanide gas. They were then cremated in ovens to keep the soil from being poisoned by the burial of this large number of corpses. The German commander of the camp, Rudolf Hess, admitted to the murder of over 2,500,000; Allied Forces estimated the figure to be as high as four million.

[2]Deputy Commandant Karl Fritzsch—who first tried Zyklon B, the commercial form of hydrocyanic acid preferred by the Nazis for exterminating human beings—was fond of greeting incoming prisoners with this expression.

[3]A survivor of five years' imprisonment at Auschwitz who spoke at the Toronto Memorial Service; a socialist, Sherwood (his Polish name was Sobolewski) was one of the earliest prisoners brought to Auschwitz, where few inmates survived more than several months.

[4]*Dies Irae*, for soloist, choir, and orchestra, was composed in 1967 by Krysztof Penderecki (b. 1933), Polish composer of experimental music that employs unconventional sounds, including electronic ones, along with unusual vocal articulation; his music is often freakish and eerie.

[5]Gothic letters over the entrance-way to Auschwitz spelled out the words '*Arbeit Macht Frei*' ('Work Makes One Free')—an ironic motto, because those who were not immediately destroyed in the death chambers were worked to death. Mandel has indicated that he was here also invoking other senses of the word 'gothic', including its particular association with German art and architecture as well as the word's original meaning of 'primitive' or 'barbaric'.

the Orpheum in Estevan before Buck Jones[6]
the Capitol in Regina before Tom Mix
waiting for the guns
waiting for the cowboy killers   30
one two three
            Legionnaires
Polish ex-prisoners Association
Legions
       their medals their flags

so the procession, the poem gradual
ly insistent beginning to shape itself
with the others
            walked with them
into the YMHA Bloor & Spadina   40
thinking apocalypse shame degradation
thinking bones and bodies melting
thickening thinning melting bones and bodies
thinking not mine / must speak clearly
the poet's words / Yevtyshenko[7] at Baba-Yar

there   this January   snow
heavy wet   the wind   heavy wet
the street grey white slush melted concrete
bones and bodies melting slush
               saw   50
with the others
        the prisoner
in the YMHA hall Bloor & Spadina
arms wax stiff body stiff unnatural
coloured face blank eyes
          walked
with the others toward the screen
toward the pictures
         SLIDES
       this is mother   60
       this is father
       this is
         the one who is
waving her arms like that
is the one who
        like

[6]Cowboy hero in silent movies, as was Tom Mix. Mandel is here ironically counterpointing the memory of himself as a Jewish youngster cheering for the cowboy—that is, for the 'white man' against the Indian—with the genocide that he as an adult later confronted.

[7]Russian poet Yevgeny Yevtushenko (b. 1933) wrote a poem entitled 'Babi Yar' about a ravine near Kiev in which many thousands of Jews were massacred and buried during the Second World War. Writing of the Russian pogroms against the Jews in pre-Revolutionary Russia and against anti-semitism in Europe and Russia, Yevtushenko sees all who struggle against totalitarianism as being under similar attack.

I mean running with her breasts bound
ing
    running
        with her hands here and there   70
with her here and
          there
hands
    that   that is
the poem becoming the body
becoming the faint hunger
ing body
      prowling
          through
words the words words the words   80
opening   mouths ovens
the generals smiling saluting
in their mythic uniforms god-like
generals uniforms with the black leather
with the straps and the intricate leather
the phylacteries[8] and the prayer shawl
corsets and the boots and the leather straps

and the shining faces of the generals in their boots
and their stiff wax bodies their unnatural faces
and their blank eyes and their hands their stiff hands   90
and the generals in their straps and wax and stiff
staying standing
        melting bodies and thickening
        quick flesh on flesh handling
        hands
    the poem flickers, fades
the four Yarzeit candles[9] guttering one
    each four million lights dim
my words drift
        smoke from chimneys and ovens   100
    a bad picture, the power failing
pianist clattering on and over and through
the long Saturday afternoon in the Orpheum
    while the whitehatted star spangled cowboys
      shot the dark men and shot the dark men
      and we threw popcorn balls and grabbed
      each other and cheered:
          me jewboy yelling
for the shot town and the falling men
    and the lights come on   110
      and

[8]Small leather boxes containing scriptures on parchments that are bound to the forehead and left forearm of orthodox Jews during morning worship, except on the Sabbath and on holidays.
[9]Candles burned on the anniversary of a death, usually lighted by children commemorating the death of parents or close relatives.

         with the others
standing in silence

the gothic word hangs
over us on a shroud-white screen

and we drift away
                to ourselves
                        to the late Sunday Times
                                the wet snow
                                the city   120

                        a body melting

1973

Instructions:

(ON THE NATURE OF DOUBLES AND DOUBLING)

all mirrors should be covered[1]
do not look deeply into a sink of hot water
ditto cold
wear rings on only two fingers
your eyes are doubles doubled
everything divides by two or is uneven
poetry consists in the doubling of words
doubled words are poetic words
this is the true meaning of duplicity
each poem speaks to another poem   10
the language of poetry is a secret language
these are the true doubles

false doubles are ones and threes
four is a good number

[1]After a family member's death, mirrors in a Jewish home are covered until the end of Shivah, the solemn period of mourning lasting seven days after the funeral—an ancient practice that stems in part from an old belief that the soul of the newly dead could become trapped in a reflection.

doubled names are: eli[2]   elijah
                      jesse   jesus
                      paul   saul
                      joseph pharoah
                                  etc.

in Hebrew this is common   20
no one knows the jewish name of god
indian names are secret
poetry is the naming of secret names
among these are:
                god
                spirit
                alphabets

                names in stone
                doubled names
                the psalms   30
                hoodoos
                animals
                eyes
                jewels

the place of no shadows called badlands
the place of shadows called badlands
you begin to see the difficulties

1977

[2]The high priest of Israel who, having lost the favour of God, did not hear God's voice when he spoke in the night to Samuel, Eli's young assistant (1 Samuel); in contrast, Elijah the prophet not only heard and saw God but was granted miraculous powers (1 and 2 Kings). (Mandel's first name, Elias, is a variant form of Elijah—though he is usually known as Eli.) 'Jesse': the father of David and ancestor of Jesus (1 Samuel 16; Matthew 1). 'Paul': the apostle who as Saul of Tarsus was a bitter persecutor of the early Christians before experiencing a sudden conversion when he heard the voice of God on the road to Damascus; he became the leading Christian missionary and theologian (Acts 9ff). 'Joseph': the youngest son of Jacob who, after being sold into bondage by his brothers, rose to become the prime minister of Egypt when he was the only person able to interpret the Pharaoh's prophetic dreams.

Ventriloquists

There is so much to be said—imitating
one another: the act of love,
say, speaking with tongues. Yet it was a while
before I saw we gave these words
to one another and heard our voices
elsewhere than the place they were
speaking beside oneself, throwing voices
away across the room, to other places.

Now seeing him this way I know
myself an imitation. I hear   10
his voice reading my poems written by him.
Later in darkness
on the question of love
it is more complex.

Do you love me?
The question ontological now,
She hears only his words
asking a question about me.

How do you do that?
It is a trick with my tongue   20
he says and with your ear
Look closely and you'll see
I don't move my lips.
The way the blade enters
is just as mysterious as the tongue,
perhaps not as deadly
though he has nothing more to say
not even questions now.

As for myself I remain
wondering where I have gone.   30

1981

Margaret Laurence

1926-1987

Born Jean Margaret Wemys in Neepawa, Man., Margaret Laurence tranformed this small prairie town in which she grew up into Manawaka, the backdrop for five interrelated works of fiction that begin with *The Stone Angel* (1964) and conclude with *The Diviners* (1974). Laurence's early years in Neepawa—in which she struggled to reconcile several deaths in her family (including her mother's when she was four and her father's when she was nine) with the powerful vision of a just God that was handed down from her Scots-Presbyterian grandparents—colour all her Manawaka fiction, especially the highly autobiographical Vanessa MacLeod stories, collected in *A Bird in the House* (1970). Like Vanessa, the adolescent Laurence felt herself trapped in her grandfather's house. The award in 1943 of a Manitoba scholarship that allowed her to attend United College in Winnipeg enabled her to escape and begin an independent life.

Marrying Jack Laurence in 1948, Margaret Laurence moved with her engineer husband to England in 1949 and in the following year to Africa, where they remained until 1957. In Africa Laurence began her career as a writer, first with *A Tree for Poverty* (1954), a translation and recasting of Somali poetry and tales, and then with a series of stories about the Africans she saw caught in a transitional moment between the old tribal world and the modern one. Her African stories, set in the Gold Coast (now Ghana), which began to appear in periodicals in 1954, were collected in *The Tomorrow-Tamer* (1963). Three other books grew out of Laurence's African years: *This Side Jordan* (1960), a novel that deals with Ghana's struggle for independence; *The Prophet's Camel Bell* (1963), an account of two years spent in Somaliland, prepared from the journal she kept while there; and *Long Drums and Cannons* (1968), a critical study of the English-language writers emerging in Nigeria. Although *This Side Jordan* remains an apprentice novel, Laurence's African short stories are among her best work, and her experience of the various African struggles for freedom and nationhood sharpened her sense of Canada as a new country that in its own way was still coming to terms with its colonial inheritance.

Laurence seems to have valued the perspective gained through expatriation. After five years back in Canada, she separated from her husband and moved to England, and it was there that the first three Manawaka novels—*The Stone Angel, A Jest of God* (1966), and *The Fire-Dwellers* (1969)—were written. These novels were influential in Canada in demonstrating the power and universality of regionalism and established Laurence as the foremost Canadian novelist of the decade. In 1969 Laurence began returning to Canada, spending summers at a cottage on the Otonabee River and winters in England. During this period she also served as writer-in-residence at the University of Toronto, Trent University, and the University of Western Ontario. In 1971 she was named a Companion of the Order of Canada. She moved back to Canada permanently in 1974, settling in Lakefield, Ont. From 1981 through 1983 she was Chancellor of Trent University. Throughout the eighties she also worked on behalf of conservation groups, such as Energy Probe.

In 1974 Laurence published *The Diviners*, her most ambitious work of fiction, which draws together characters and themes from the four other Manawaka novels and, by its use of reciprocal parallels with *The Stone Angel*, provides a formal close to the sequence. Like *A Jest of God*, *The Diviners* won a Governor General's Award. She later published only children's stories and short non-fiction pieces. *Heart of a Stranger* (1976) is a selection of her essays from the previous twelve years. After Laurence died in 1987, her daughter Jocelyn brought to final form a collection of Laurence's memoirs begun in 1985, *Dance on the Earth* (1989).

From her early African writing through

the later novels, and even in a children's book, such as *Jason's Quest* (1970), Laurence repeatedly chronicled a search for a life that is not only autonomous but that can be led with joy. However, powerful forces work against the individual in this search, as ninety-year-old Hagar Shipley at last realizes in the moving close to *The Stone Angel*:

This knowing comes upon me so forcefully, so shatteringly, and with such bitterness as I have never felt before. I must always, always, have wanted that—simply to rejoice. How is it I never could? . . . Every good joy I might have held, in my man or any child of mine or even the plain light of morning, of walking the earth, all were forced to a standstill by some brake of proper appearances— oh, proper to whom? When did I ever speak the heart's truth?

Pride was my wilderness, and the demon that led me there was fear. I was alone, never anything else, and never free, for I carried my chains within me, and they spread out from me and shackled all I touched.

But even though Hagar and the women of her era seem unable to experience fully either freedom or joy, the Laurence protagonists who follow Hagar come closer to grasping that ideal—and, as we discover in *The Diviners*, Hagar's struggle (her name is the same as that of Abraham's bondswoman in the Bible) has served to free Morag (whose name is the Scottish equivalent of Sarah, Abraham's wife).

The way in which Hagar's experiences eventually touch and help Morag suggests the importance of *inheritance* as a theme for Laurence. Inheritance—which becomes not only genetic makeup, but also the unobserved but profoundly shaping influences of culture, society, and environment—is a prominent theme in all her Manawaka fiction. While our inheritance is often the restraint against which we must struggle, it is also our chief source of strength, the thing that allows us to survive in a world characterized by bewildering uncertainty.

Laurence herself has left an inheritance: her fiction brings the life and landscape of Canada into the reader's imagination and gives expression to the complexity of our cultural heritage. In 1965 Northrop Frye wrote: 'There is no Canadian writer of whom we can say what we say of the world's major writers, that their readers can grow up inside their work without ever being aware of circumference.' Today the fully realized world contained in Margaret Laurence's work provides the unbounded pleasures that such a reading experience can give.

To Set Our House in Order

When the baby was almost ready to be born, something went wrong and my mother had to go into hospital two weeks before the expected time. I was wakened by her crying in the night, and then I heard my father's footsteps as he went downstairs to phone. I stood in the doorway of my room, shivering and listening, wanting to go to my mother but afraid to go lest there be some sight there more terrifying than I could bear.

'Hello—Paul?' my father said, and I knew he was talking to Dr Cates. 'It's Beth. The waters have broken, and the fetal position doesn't seem quite—well, I'm only thinking of what happened the last time, and another like that would be—I wish she were a little huskier, damn it—she's so—no, don't worry, I'm quite all right. Yes, I think that would be the best thing. Okay, make it as soon as you can, will you?'

He came back upstairs, looking bony and dishevelled in his pyjamas, and running his fingers through his sand-coloured hair. At the top of the stairs, he came face to face with Grandmother MacLeod, who was standing there in her quilted black satin dressing gown, her slight figure held straight and poised, as though she were unaware that her hair was bound grotesquely like white-feathered wings in the snare of her coarse night-time hairnet.

'What is it, Ewen?'

'It's all right, Mother. Beth's having—a little trouble. I'm going to take her into the hospital. You go back to bed.'

'I told you,' Grandmother MacLeod said in her clear voice, never loud, but distinct and ringing like the tap of a sterling teaspoon on a crystal goblet, 'I did tell you, Ewen, did I not, that you should have got a girl in to help her with the housework? She would have rested more.'

'I couldn't afford to get anyone in,' my father said. 'If you thought she should've rested more, why didn't you ever—oh God, I'm out of my mind to-night—just go back to bed, Mother, please. I must get back to Beth.'

When my father went down to the front door to let Dr Cates in, my need over-came my fear and I slipped into my parents' room. My mother's black hair, so neatly pinned up during the day, was startingly spread across the white pillow-case. I stared at her, not speaking, and then she smiled and I rushed from the doorway and buried my head upon her.

'It's all right, honey,' she said. 'Listen, Vanessa, the baby's just going to come a little early, that's all. You'll be all right. Grandmother MacLeod will be here.'

'How can she get the meals?' I wailed, fixing on the first thing that came to mind. 'She never cooks. She doesn't know how.'

'Yes, she does,' my mother said. 'She can cook as well as anyone when she has to. She's just never had to very much, that's all. Don't worry—she'll keep everything in order, and then some.'

My father and Dr Cates came in, and I had to go, without ever saying anything I had wanted to say. I went back to my own room and lay with the shadows all around me. I listened to the night murmurings that always went on in that house, sounds which never had a source, rafters and beams contracting in the dry air, perhaps, or mice in the walls, or a sparrow that had flown into the attic through the broken skylight there. After a while, although I would not have believed it possible, I slept.

The next morning I questioned my father. I believed him to be not only the best doctor in Manawaka, but also the best doctor in the whole of Manitoba, if not in the entire world, and the fact that he was not the one who was looking after my mother seemed to have something sinister about it.

'But it's always done that way, Vanessa,' he explained. 'Doctors never attend members of their own family. It's because they care so much about them, you see, and—'

'And what?' I insisted, alarmed at the way he had broken off. But my father did not reply. He stood there, and then he put on that difficult smile with which adults seek to conceal pain from children. I felt terrified, and ran to him, and he held me tightly.

'She's going to be fine,' he said. 'Honestly she is. Nessa, don't cry—'

Grandmother MacLeod appeared beside us, steel-spined despite her apparent fragility. She was wearing a purple silk dress and her ivory pendant. She looked as though she were all ready to go out for afternoon tea.

'Ewen, you're only encouraging the child to give way,' she said. 'Vanessa, big girls of ten don't make such a fuss about things. Come and get your breakfast. Now, Ewen, you're not to worry. I'll see to everything.'

Summer holidays were not quite over, but I did not feel like going out to play with any of the kids. I was very superstitious, and I had the feeling that if I left the house, even for a few hours, some disaster would overtake my mother. I did not, of course, mention this feeling to Grandmother MacLeod, for she did not believe in the existence of fear, of if she did, she never let on. I spent the morning morbidly, in seeking hidden places in the house. There were many of these—odd-shaped nooks under the stairs, small and loosely nailed-up doors at the back of clothes closets, leading to dusty tunnels and forgotten recesses in the heart of the house where the only things actually to be seen were drab oil paintings stacked upon the rafters, and trunks full of outmoded clothing and old photograph albums. But the unseen presences in these secret places I knew to be those of every person, young or old, who had ever belonged to the house and had died, including Uncle Roderick who got killed on the Somme,[1] and the baby who would have been my sister if only she had managed to come to life. Grandfather MacLeod, who had died a year after I was born, was present in the house in more tangible form. At the top of the main stairs hung the mammoth picture of a darkly uniformed man riding upon a horse whose prancing stance and dilated nostrils suggested that the battle was not yet over, that it might indeed continue until Judgment Day. The stern man was actually the Duke of Wellington, but at the time I believed him to be my grandfather MacLeod, still keeping an eye on things.

We had moved in with Grandmother MacLeod when the Depression got bad and she could no longer afford a housekeeper, but the MacLeod house never seemed like home to me. Its dark red brick was grown over at the front with Virginia creeper that turned crimson in the fall, until you could hardly tell brick from leaves. It boasted a small tower in which Grandmother MacLeod kept a weedy collection of anaemic ferns. The verandah was embellished with a profusion of wrought-iron scrolls, and the circular rose-window upstairs contained glass of many colours which permitted an outlooking eye to see the world as a place of absolute sapphire or emerald, or if one wished to look with a jaundiced eye, a hateful yellow. In Grandmother MacLeod's opinion, their features gave the house style.

Inside a multitude of doors led to rooms where my presence, if not actually forbidden, was not encouraged. One was Grandmother MacLeod's bedroom, with its stale and old-smelling air, the dim reek of medicines and lavender sachets. Here resided her monogrammed dresser silver, brush and mirror, nail-buffer and button hook and scissors, none of which must even be fingered by me now, for she meant to leave them to me in her will and intended to hand them over in the same flawless and unused condition in which they had always been kept. Here, too, were the silver-framed photographs of Uncle Roderick—as a

---

[1] One of the most costly campaigns of the First World War. The British offensive at the Somme, which began in July 1915, was joined by the 4th Canadian Division in September; despite severe losses on both sides, the results were indecisive.

child, as a boy, as a man in his Army uniform. The massive walnut spool bed had obviously been designed for queens or giants, and my tiny grandmother used to lie within it all day when she had migraine, contriving somehow to look like a giant queen.

The living room was another alien territory where I had to tread warily, for many valuable objects sat just-so on tables and mantelpiece, and dirt must not be tracked in upon the blue Chinese carpet with its birds in eternal motionless flight and its water-lily buds caught forever just before the point of opening. My mother was always nervous when I was in this room.

'Vanessa, honey,' she would say, half apologetically, 'why don't you go and play in the den, or upstairs?'

'Can't you leave her, Beth?' my father would say. 'She's not doing any harm.'

'I'm only thinking of the rug,' my mother would say, glancing at Grandmother MacLeod, 'and yesterday she nearly knocked the Dresden shepherdess off the mantel. I mean, she can't help it, Ewen, she has to run around—'

'Goddamn it, I know she can't help it,' my father would growl, glaring at the smirking face of the Dresden shepherdess.

'I see no need to blaspheme, Ewen,' Grandmother MacLeod would say quietly, and then my father would say he was sorry, and I would leave.

The day my mother went to the hospital, Grandmother MacLeod called me at lunch-time, and when I appeared, smudged with dust from the attic, she looked at me distastefully as though I had been a cockroach that had just crawled impertinently out of the woodwork.

'For mercy's sake, Vanessa, what have you been doing with yourself? Run and get washed this minute. Here, not that way—you use the back stairs, young lady. Get along now. Oh—your father phoned.'

I swung around. 'What did he say? How is she? Is the baby born?'

'Curiosity killed a cat,' Grandmother MacLeod said, frowning. 'I cannot understand Beth and Ewen telling you all these things, at your age. What sort of vulgar person you'll grow up to be, I dare not think. No, it's not born yet. Your mother's just the same. No change.'

I looked at my grandmother, not wanting to appeal to her, but unable to stop myself. 'Will she—will she be all right?'

Grandmother MacLeod straightened her already-straight back. 'If I said definitely yes, Vanessa, that would be a lie, and the MacLeods do not tell lies, as I have tried to impress upon you before. What happens is God's will. The Lord giveth, and the Lord taketh away.'

Appalled, I turned away so she would not see my face and my eyes. Surprisingly, I heard her sigh and felt her papery white and perfectly manicured hand upon my shoulder.

'When your Uncle Roderick got killed,' she said, 'I thought I would die. But I didn't die, Vanessa.'

At lunch, she chatted animatedly, and I realised she was trying to cheer me in the only way she knew.

'When I married your Grandfather MacLeod,' she related, 'he said to me, "Eleanor, don't think because we're going to the prairies that I expect you to live roughly. You're used to a proper house, and you shall have one.'' He was as good as his word. Before we'd been in Manawaka three years, he'd had this place built. He earned a good deal of money in his time, your grandfather. He soon had more patients than either of the other doctors. We ordered our dinner service and all our silver from Birks' in Toronto. We had resident help in those days, of course, and never had less than twelve guests for dinner parties. When I had a tea, it would always be twenty or thirty. Never any less than half a dozen different kinds of cake were ever served in this house. Well, no one seems to bother much these days. Too lazy, I suppose.'

'Too broke,' I suggested. 'That's what Dad says.'

'I can't bear slang,' Grandmother MacLeod said. 'If you mean hard up, why don't you say so? It's mainly a question of management, anyway. My accounts were always in good order, and so was my house. No unexpected expenses that couldn't be met, no fruit cellar running out of preserves before the winter was over. Do you know what my father used to say to me when I was a girl?'

'No,' I said. 'What?'

'God loves Order,' Grandmother MacLeod replied with emphasis. 'You remember that, Vanessa. God loves Order—he wants each one of us to set our house in order. I've never forgotten those words of my father's. I was a MacInnes before I got married. The MacInnes is a very ancient clan, the lairds of Morven and the constables of the Castle of Kinlochaline. Did you finish that book I gave you?'[2]

'Yes,' I said. Then, feeling some additional comment to be called for, 'It was a swell book, Grandmother.'

This was somewhat short of the truth. I had been hoping for her cairngorm[3] brooch on my tenth birthday, and had received instead the plaid-bound volume entitled *The Clans and Tartans of Scotland.* Most of it was too boring to read, but I had looked up the motto of my own family and those of some of my friends' families. *Be then a wall of brass. Learn to suffer. Consider the end. Go carefully.* I had not found any of these slogans reassuring. What with Mavis Duncan learning to suffer, and Laura Kennedy considering the end, and Patsy Drummond going carefully, and I spending my time in being a wall of brass, it did not seem to me that any of us were going to lead very interesting lives. I did not say this to Grandmother MacLeod.

'The MacInnes motto is *Pleasure Arises from Work*,' I said.

'Yes,' she agreed proudly. 'And an excellent motto it is, too. One to bear in mind.'

She rose from the table, rearranging on her bosom the looped ivory beads that held the pendant on which a fullblown ivory rose was stiffly carved.

'I hope Ewen will be pleased,' she said.

'What at?'

---

[2] Vanessa would have discovered in Robert Bain's *The Clans and Tartans of Scotland* (1938, and many subsequent editions; the mottoes were added later) that the MacInneses were 'a Celtic clan of ancient origin', their earliest-known territory that of Morven. Bain says that they 'remained in possession of Morven, and as late as 1645 it appears that a MacInnes was in command of the Castle of Kinlochaline when it was besieged and burnt. . . .'

[3] Also called 'Scotch topaz'; a semi-precious stone frequently worn as part of the Highland Scots costume.

'Didn't I tell you?' Grandmother MacLeod said. 'I hired a girl this morning, for the housework. She's to start tomorrow.'

When my father got home that evening, Grandmother MacLeod told him her good news. He ran one hand distractedly across his forehead.

'I'm sorry, Mother, but you'll just have to unhire her. I can't possibly pay anyone.'

'It seems distinctly odd,' Grandmother MacLeod snapped, 'that you can afford to eat chicken four times a week.'

'Those chickens,' my father said in an exasperated voice, 'are how people are paying their bills. The same with the eggs and the milk. That scrawny turkey that arrived yesterday was for Logan MacCardney's appendix, if you must know. We probably eat better than any family in Manawaka, except Niall Cameron's. People can't entirely dispense with doctors or undertakers. That doesn't mean to say I've got any cash. Look, Mother, I don't know what's happening with Beth. Paul thinks he may have to do a Caesarean. Can't we leave all this? Just leave the house alone. Don't touch it. What does it matter?'

'I have never lived in a messy house, Ewen,' Grandmother MacLeod said, 'and I don't intend to begin now.'

'Oh Lord,' my father said. 'Well, I'll phone Edna, I guess, and see if she can give us a hand, although God knows she's got enough, with the Connor house and her parents to look after.'

'I don't fancy having Edna Connor in to help,' Grandmother MacLeod objected.

'Why not?' my father shouted. 'She's Beth's sister, isn't she?'

'She speaks in such a slangy way,' Grandmother MacLeod said. 'I have never believed she was a good influence on Vanessa. And there is no need for you to raise your voice to me, Ewen, if you please.'

I could barely control my rage. I thought my father would surely rise to Aunt Edna's defence. But he did not.

'It'll be all right,' he soothed her. 'She'd only be here for part of the day, Mother. You could stay in your room.'

Aunt Edna strode in the next morning. The sight of her bobbed black hair and her grin made me feel better at once. She hauled out the carpet sweeper and the weighted polisher and got to work. I dusted while she polished and swept, and we got through the living room and front hall in next to no time.

'Where's her royal highness, kiddo?' she enquired.

'In her room,' I said. 'She's reading the catalogue from Robinson & Cleaver.'

'Good Glory, not again?' Aunt Edna cried. 'The last time she ordered three linen tea-cloths and two dozen serviettes. It came to fourteen dollars. Your mother was absolutely frantic. I guess I shouldn't be saying this.'

'I knew anyway,' I assured her. 'She was at the lace handkerchiefs section when I took up her coffee.'

'Let's hope she stays there. Heaven forbid she should get onto the banqueting cloths. Well, at least she believes the Irish are good for two things—manual labour and linen-making. She's never forgotten Father used to be a blacksmith, before he got the hardware store. Can you beat it? I wish it didn't bother Beth.'

'Does it?' I asked, and immediately realised this was a wrong move, for Aunt Edna was suddenly scrutinising me.

'We're making you grow up before your time,' she said. 'Don't pay any attention to me, Nessa. I must've got up on the wrong side of the bed this morning.'

But I was unwilling to leave the subject.

'All the same,' I said thoughtfully, 'Grandmother MacLeod's family were the lairds of Morven and the constables of the Castle of Kinlochaline. I bet you didn't know that.'

Aunt Edna snorted. 'Castle, my foot. She was born in Ontario, just like your Grandfather Connor, and her father was a horse doctor. Come on, kiddo, we'd better shut up and get down to business here.'

We worked in silence for a while.

'Aunt Edna—' I said at last, 'what about Mother? Why won't they let me go and see her?'

'Kids aren't allowed to visit maternity patients. It's tough for you, I know that. Look, Nessa, don't worry. If it doesn't start tonight, they're going to do the operation. She's getting the best of care.'

I stood there, holding the feather duster like a dead bird in my hands. I was not aware that I was going to speak until the words came out.

'I'm scared,' I said.

Aunt Edna put her arms around me, and her face looked all at once stricken and empty of defences.

'Oh, honey, I'm scared, too,' she said.

It was this way that Grandmother MacLeod found us when she came stepping lightly down into the front hall with the order in her hand for two dozen lace-bordered handkerchiefs of pure Irish linen.

I could not sleep that night, and when I went downstairs, I found my father in the den. I sat down on the hassock beside his chair, and he told me about the operation my mother was to have the next morning. He kept on saying it was not serious nowadays.

'But you're worried,' I put in, as though seeking to explain why I was.

'I should at least have been able to keep from burdening you with it,' he said in a distant voice, as though to himself. 'If only the baby hadn't got itself twisted around—'

'Will it be born dead, like the little girl?'

'I don't know,' my father said. 'I hope not.'

'She'd be disappointed, wouldn't she, if it was?' I said bleakly, wondering why I was not enough for her.

'Yes, she would,' my father replied. 'She won't be able to have any more, after this. It's partly on your account that she wants this one, Nessa. She doesn't want you to grow up without a brother or sister.'

'As far as I'm concerned, she didn't need to bother,' I retorted angrily.

My father laughed. 'Well, let's talk about something else, and then maybe you'll be able to sleep. How did you and Grandmother make out today?'

'Oh, fine, I guess. What was Grandfather MacLeod like, Dad?'

'What did she tell you about him?'

'She said he made a lot of money in his time.'

'Well, he wasn't any millionaire,' my father said, 'but I suppose he did quite well. That's not what I associate with him, though.'

He reached across to the bookshelf, took out a small leather-bound volume and opened it. On the pages were mysterious marks, like doodling, only much neater and more patterned.

'What is it?' I asked.

'Greek,' my father explained. 'This is a play called *Antigone*. See, here's the title in English. There's a whole stack of them on the shelves there. *Oepidus Rex*. *Electra*. *Medea*. They belonged to your Grandfather MacLeod. He used to read them often.'

'Why?' I enquired, unable to understand why anyone would pore over those undecipherable signs.

'He was interested in them,' my father said. 'He must have been a lonely man, although it never struck me that way at the time. Sometimes a thing only hits you a long time afterwards.'

'Why would he be lonely?' I wanted to know.

'He was the only person in Manawaka who could read these plays in the original Greek,' my father said. 'I don't suppose many people, if anyone, had even read them in English translations. Maybe he would have liked to be a classical scholar—I don't know. But his father was a doctor, so that's what he was. Maybe he would have liked to talk to somebody about these plays. They must have meant a lot to him.'

It seemed to me that my father was talking oddly. There was a sadness in his voice that I had never heard before, and I longed to say something that would make him feel better, but I could not, because I did not know what was the matter.

'Can you read this kind of writing?' I asked hesitantly.

My father shook his head. 'Nope. I was never very intellectual, I guess. Rod was always brighter than I, in school, but even he wasn't interested in learning Greek. Perhaps he would've been later, if he'd lived. As a kid, all I ever wanted to do was go into the merchant marine.'

'Why didn't you, then?'

'Oh well,' my father said offhandedly, 'a kid who'd never seen the sea wouldn't have made much of a sailor. I might have turned out to be the seasick type.'

I had lost interest now that he was speaking once more like himself.

'Grandmother MacLeod was pretty cross today about the girl,' I remarked.

'I know,' my father nodded. 'Well, we must be as nice as we can to her, Nessa, and after a while she'll be all right.'

Suddenly I did not care what I said.

'Why can't she be nice to us for a change?' I burst out. 'We're always the ones who have to be nice to her.'

My father put his hand down and slowly tilted my head until I was forced to look at him.

'Vanessa,' he said, 'she's had troubles in her life which you really don't know much about. That's why she gets migraine sometimes and has to go to bed. It's not easy for her these days, either—the house is still the same, so she thinks other things should be, too. It hurts her when she finds they aren't.'

'I don't see—' I began.

'Listen,' my father said, 'you know we were talking about what people are interested in, like Grandfather MacLeod being interested in Greek plays? Well, your grandmother was interested in being a lady, Nessa, and for a long time it seemed to her that she was one.'

I thought of the Castle of Kinlochaline, and of horse doctors in Ontario.

'I didn't know—' I stammered.

'That's usually the trouble with most of us,' my father said. 'You go on up to bed now. I'll phone tomorrow from the hospital as soon as the operation's over.'

I did sleep at last, and in my dreams I could hear the caught sparrow fluttering in the attic, and the sound of my mother crying, and the voices of the dead children.

My father did not phone until afternoon. Grandmother MacLeod said I was being silly, for you could hear the phone ringing all over the house, but nevertheless I refused to move out of the den. I had never before examined my father's books, but now, at a loss for something to do, I took them out one by one and read snatches here and there. After I had been doing this for several hours, it dawned on me that most of the books were of the same kind. I looked again at the titles.

Seven-League Boots.[4] *Arabia Deserta. The Seven Pillars of Wisdom. Travels in Tibet. Count Lucknor the Sea Devil.* And a hundred more. On a shelf by themselves were copies of the *National Geographic* magazine, which I looked at often enough, but never before with the puzzling compulsion which I felt now, as though I were on the verge of some discovery, something which I had to find out and yet did not want to know. I riffled through the picture-filled pages. Hibiscus and wild orchids grew in a soft-petalled confusion. The Himalayas stood lofty as gods, with the morning sun on their peaks of snow. Leopards snarled from the vined depths of a thousand jungles. Schooners buffeted their white sails like the wings of giant angels against the great sea winds.

'What on earth are you doing?' Grandmother MacLeod enquired waspishly, from the doorway. 'You've got everything scattered all over the place. Pick it all up this minute, Vanessa, do you hear?'

So I picked up the books and magazines, and put them all neatly away, as I had been told to do.

When the telephone finally rang, I was afraid to answer it. At last I picked it up. My father sounded faraway, and the relief in his voice made it unsteady.

'It's okay, honey. Everything's fine. The boy was born alive and kicking after all. Your mother's pretty weak, but she's going to be all right.'

I could hardly believe it. I did not want to talk to anyone. I wanted to be by myself, to assimilate the presence of my brother, towards whom, without ever having seen him yet, I felt such tenderness and such resentment.

[4]Five classic works of travel literature, published between the two world wars, by Richard Halliburton, C.M. Doughty, T.E. Lawrence, H. Harrier, and Lowell Thomas respectively.

That evening, Grandmother MacLeod approached my father, who, still dazed with the unexpected gift of neither life now being threatened, at first did not take her seriously when she asked what they planned to call the child.

'Oh, I don't know. Hank, maybe, or Joe. Fauntleroy, perhaps.'

She ignored his levity.

'Ewen,' she said, 'I wish you would call him Roderick.'

My father's face changed. 'I'd rather not.'

'I think you should,' Grandmother MacLeod insisted, very quietly, but in a voice as pointed and precise as her silver nail-scissors.

'Don't you think Beth ought to decide?' my father asked.

'Beth will agree if you do.'

My father did not bother to deny something that even I knew to be true. He did not say anything. Then Grandmother MacLeod's voice, astonishingly, faltered a little.

'It would mean a great deal to me,' she said.

I remembered what she had told me—*When your Uncle Roderick got killed, I thought I would die. But I didn't die.* All at once, her feeling for that unknown dead man became a reality for me. And yet I held it against her, as well, for I could see that it had enabled her to win now.

'All right,' my father said tiredly. 'We'll call him Roderick.'

Then, alarmingly, he threw back his head and laughed.

'Roderick Dhu!' he cried. 'That's what you'll call him, isn't it? Black Roderick. Like before. Don't you remember? As though he were a character out of Sir Walter Scott, instead of an ordinary kid who—'

He broke off, and looked at her with a kind of desolation in his face.

'God, I'm sorry, Mother,' he said. 'I had no right to say that.'

Grandmother MacLeod did not flinch, or tremble, or indicate that she felt anything at all.

'I accept your apology, Ewen,' she said.

My mother had to stay in bed for several weeks after she arrived home. The baby's cot was kept in my parents' room, and I could go in and look at the small creature who lay there with his tightly closed fists and his feathery black hair. Aunt Edna came in to help each morning, and when she had finished the housework, she would have coffee with my mother. They kept the door closed, but this did not prevent me from eavesdropping, for there was an air register in the floor of the spare room, which was linked somehow with the register in my parents' room. If you put your ear to the iron grille, it was almost like a radio.

'Did you mind very much, Beth?' Aund Edna was saying.

'Oh, it's not the name I mind,' my mother replied. 'It's just the fact that Ewen felt he had to. You know that Rod had only had the sight of one eye, didn't you?'

'Sure, I knew. So what?'

'There was only a year and a half between Ewen and Rod,' my mother said, 'so they often went around together when they were youngsters. It was Ewen's air-rifle that did it.'

'Oh Lord,' Aunt Edna said heavily. 'I suppose she always blamed him?'

'No, I don't think it was so much that, really. It was how he felt himself. I think he even used to wonder sometimes if—but people shouldn't let themselves think like that, or they'd go crazy. Accidents do happen, after all. When the war came, Ewen joined up first. Rod should never have been in the Army at all, but he couldn't wait to get in. He must have lied about his eyesight. It wasn't so very noticeable unless you looked at him closely, and I don't suppose the medicals were very thorough in those days. He got in as a gunner, and Ewen applied to have him in the same company. He thought he might be able to watch out for him, I guess, Rod being—at a disadvantage. They were both only kids. Ewen was nineteen and Rod was eighteen when they went to France. And then the Somme. I don't know, Edna, I think Ewen felt that if Rod had had proper sight, or if he hadn't been in the same outfit and had been sent somewhere else—you know how people always think these things afterwards, not that it's ever a bit of use. Ewen wasn't there when Rod got hit. They'd lost each other somehow, and Ewen was looking for him, not bothering about anything else, you know, just frantically looking. Then he stumbled across him quite by chance. Rod was still alive, but—'

'Stop it, Beth,' Aunt Edna said. 'You're only upsetting yourself.'

'Ewen never spoke of it to me,' my mother went on, 'until once his mother showed me the letter he'd written to her at the time. It was a peculiar letter, almost formal, saying how gallantly Rod had died, and all that. I guess I shouldn't have, but I told him she'd shown it to me. He was very angry that she had. And then, as though for some reason he were terribly ashamed, he said—*I had to write something to her, but men don't really die like that, Beth. It wasn't that way at all.* It was only after the war that he decided to come back and study medicine and go into practice with his father.'

'Had Rod meant to?' Aunt Edna asked.

'I don't know,' my mother said slowly. 'I never felt I should ask Ewen that.'

Aunt Edna was gathering up the coffee things, for I could hear the clash of cups and saucers being stacked on the tray.

'You know what I heard her say to Vanessa once, Beth? *The MacLeods never tell lies.* Those were her exact words. Even then, I didn't know whether to laugh or cry.'

'Please, Edna—' my mother sounded worn out now. 'Don't.'

'Oh Glory,' Aunt Edna said remorsefully, 'I've got all the delicacy of a two-ton truck. I didn't mean Ewen, for heaven's sake. That wasn't what I meant at all. Here, let me plump up your pillows for you.'

Then the baby began to cry, so I could not hear anything more of interest. I took my bike and went out beyond Manawaka, riding aimlessly along the gravel highway. It was late summer, and the wheat had changed colour, but instead of being high and bronzed in the fields, it was stunted and desiccated, for there had been no rain again this year. But in the bluff where I stopped and crawled under the barbed wire fence and lay stretched out on the grass, the plentiful poplar leaves were turning to a luminous yellow and shone like church windows in the sun. I put my head down very close to the earth and looked at what was going on there. Grasshoppers with enormous eyes ticked and twitched around me, as though the dry air were perfect for their purposes. A ladybird laboured mightily to climb a blade of grass, fell off, and started all over again, seeming to be un-aware that she possessed wings and could have flown up.

I thought of the accidents that might easily happen to a person—or, of course, might not happen, might happen to somebody else. I thought of the dead baby, my sister, who might as easily have been I. Would she, then, have been lying here in my place, the sharp grass making its small toothmarks on her brown arms, the sun warming her to the heart? I thought of the leatherbound volumes of Greek, and the six different kinds of iced cakes that used to be offered always in the MacLeod house, and the pictures of leopards and green seas. I thought of my brother, who had been born alive after all, and now had been given his life's name.

I could not really comprehend these things, but I sensed their strangeness, their disarray. I felt that whatever God might love in this world, it was certainly not order.

1970

James Reaney

b. 1926

James Reaney was born on a farm near Stratford, Ont., and attended a nearby one-room school and then Stratford Collegiate. In 1944 he enrolled in the University of Toronto and, while still an undergraduate, be-gan publishing stories and poems in *Contemporary Verse*, *Northern Review*, *Canadian Forum*, and elsewhere. He re-ceived his B.A. in English in 1948 and an M.A. in 1949. In that same year he pub-lished his first collection of poems, *The Red Heart*, which won a Governor General's Award and brought him to early prominence at twenty-three. In the fall of 1949 Reaney joined the English department in the Uni-versity of Manitoba; his years there (1949-56 and 1958-60) mark the only time he has ever lived outside Ontario. In 1958 he completed his doctoral degree at the University of To-ronto, writing a thesis about Spenser's influ-ence on Yeats. While involved in this schol-arly study, Reaney wrote a playful imitation of *The Shepheardes Calender* entitled *A Suit of Nettles* (1958), a sequence of poems that transforms Spenser's dialogues between shepherds tending their flocks in an idealized pastoral landscape into conversations among

geese on an Ontario farm. Dense and fre-quently witty, *A Suit of Nettles* won Reaney a second Governor General's Award.

Around this time Reaney also began to write pieces for performance. He composed a libretto for *Night-Blooming Cereus*, an op-era by John Beckwith (performed on the CBC in 1959 and staged the next year) and wrote *The Killdeer* and *One-Man Masque* (both produced in 1960), as well as *The Sun and the Moon* (produced in 1965). In 1962, following the publication of *The Killdeer and Other Plays* and *Twelve Letters to a Small Town*, a sequence of poems about Stratford read on CBC radio, Reaney was awarded a third Governor General's Award. These works, and the prolific dramatic output that followed, established him as the leading dra-matist of the sixties, and many of the plays—including *Colours in the Dark* (1969) and *Listen to the Wind* (1972)—were eventu-ally published. *The Killdeer* (revised and shortened), *Three Desks*, and *The Easter Egg* were collected in *Masks of Childhood* (1972).

In the late sixties Reaney immersed him-self in the exhaustive research, writing, and extensive revision that eventually led to the creation of his major theatrical achievement, *The Donnellys*, a trilogy of plays (*Sticks and Stones*, 1975; *The St Nicholas Hotel*, 1976; and *Handcuffs*, 1977) about a contumacious Irish family who lived near London, Ont., in the second half of the nineteenth century and were massacred by a suspicious and intolerant community. (When *The Donnellys* toured nationally in 1975, Reaney travelled with the NDWT company; his account of the tour was published in 1977 as *14 Barrels from Sea to Sea*.) Like all of Reaney's plays, *The Donnellys* often subverts the formal conventions of realistic theatre: it is poetic in style and frequently departs from traditional narrative exposition. Reaney has continued to collaborate with Beckwith, and they created a second opera, *The Shivaree* (1978), as well as a 'detective opera', *Crazy to Kill* (1989), which mixed live action with puppets.

In all his writing James Reaney has created a world in which the local and regional often reveal the mythic and universal. Not only are his poetry and drama grounded in his own experience (especially that of growing up in Perth County, Ont.) and in the history of his region, but he is so convinced of the need to know one's home place intimately that he sometimes teaches a course in Ontario culture and literature by beginning with a close consideration of the actualities of daily existence and a careful scrutiny of maps. At the same time Reaney has long been convinced of the importance of myth in human society. His contact with Northrop Frye when he was an undergraduate, and again when he worked on his doctoral thesis under Frye, led him to consider the theories of literature contained in Frye's *Anatomy of Criticism*, and to read Carl Jung and others who have written on the mythic dimensions of the mind. In an important essay on *Alphabet*, the literary magazine that Reaney founded and edited, Margaret Atwood points out that Reaney wrote of making a form that would be 'Documentary on one side and myth on the other: Life and Art'; she suggests that this tension betwen myth and documentary (which for her is parallel to 'the exchange between the observing and the observed' is both central to Reaney's poetic vision and peculiarly Canadian ('Eleven Years of "Alphabet" ', *Canadian Literature*, No. 49, 1971).

The extent of Reaney's interest in the creative dimension and power of the human mind is conveyed by the full title of his literary magazine: *Alphabet: A Semi-Annual Devoted to the Iconography of the Imagination* (1960-71). Begun the year Reaney moved from Manitoba to the University of Western Ontario, *Alphabet* was a significant influence on the Canadian literary scene. Not only did it help redirect the attention of contemporary writers to myth, but it suggested—by the often arbitrary juxtaposition of its diverse contents to the mythic figure announced for each issue—that the presence of myth in a work is derived as much from the mind's quest for meaning as from anything inherent in individual stories and poems. At the same time, title and subtitle when taken together set up an opposition between the universalizing tendency of myth and the particulars out of which language grows, the very letters themselves. (Before beginning to publish his magazine Reaney trained as a typesetter and for a time typeset each issue.) Among the many emerging writers of the decade published in *Alphabet* was bp Nichol, whose concrete poetry literally attempted to create art out of the alphabet by treating letters as things in themselves— an act that influenced Reaney in his later work.

Even while he was teaching, editing, and writing plays, Reaney never stopped working on his poetry. The sequence 'A Message to Winnipeg' (broadcast 1960) grew out of Reaney's decision to learn to read his new western landscape in a way that made it as meaningful to him as his native Ontario. It was followed by *The Dance of Death at London, Ontario* (1963), a satiric sequence of poems about his new home town. *Poems* (1972), edited and with an introduction by Germaine Warkentin, is a large selection of Reaney's poetry, including poems from his plays. In that same year Reaney wrote an introduction to a new reprint of *The Collected Poems* of Isabella Valancy Crawford, a poet whose early mythologizing of nature and its opposing forces had long interested him.

Because Reaney is less interested in objective reality than in the imaginative structures into which the mind orders that reality—that is, not in what happens but in what we make of what happens—the rural community provides him not so much with events as with examples of the power of words to transform reality into stories, songs, folktales, nursery rhymes, and individual flights of fancy. Indeed, in 'The Alphabet' and 'Starling with a Split-Tongue' language itself is a source of magic. In Reaney's poetry, and in his plays, we sense a mind seeking to make the world comprehensible. But since both mind and world oscillate between innocence and experience, and between dreaming and waking— in ways that make it hard to say which is which—comprehension remains elusive. The figure of the child, which recurs throughout Reaney's work, holds the secret truths that we as adults yearn for, and it is to this child in all of us that Reaney, in his constant playfulness, is ultimately speaking.

The School Globe

Sometimes when I hold
Our faded old globe
That we used at school
To see where oceans were
And the five continents,
The lines of latitude and longitude,
The North Pole, the Equator and the South Pole—
Sometimes when I hold this
Wrecked blue cardboard pumpkin
I think: here in my hands   10
Rest the fair fields and lands
Of my childhood
Where still lie or still wander
Old games, tops and pets;
A house where I was little
And afraid to swear
Because God might hear and
Send a bear
To eat me up;
Rooms where I was as old   20
As I was high;
Where I loved the pink clenches,
The white, red and pink fists
Of roses; where I watched the rain
That Heaven's clouds threw down
In puddles and rutfuls
And irregular mirrors
Of soft brown glass upon the ground.
This school globe is a parcel of my past,
A basket of pluperfect[1] things.   30
And here I stand with it
Sometime in the summertime
All alone in an empty schoolroom
Where about me hang
Old maps, an abacus, pictures,
Blackboards, empty desks.
If I raise my hand

[1]More than perfect; in grammar the tense that denotes completed action (expressed in English by the auxiliary *had*).

No tall teacher will demand
What I want.
But if someone in authority   40
Were here, I'd say
Give me this old world back
Whose husk I clasp
And I'll give you in exchange
The great sad real one
That's filled
Not with a child's remembered and pleasant skies
But with blood, pus, horror, death, stepmothers, and lies.

1949

The Alphabet

Where are the fields of dew?
I cannot keep them.
They quip and pun
The rising sun
Who plucks them out of view:
But lay down fire-veined jasper!

For out of my cloudy head
Come Ay Ee I Oh and U,
Five thunders shouted;
Drive in sardonyx!   10

And Ull Mm Nn Rr and hisSsings
Proclaim huge wings;
Pour in sea blue sapphires!

Through my bristling hair
Blows Wuh and Yuh
Puh, Buh, Phuh and Vuh,
The humorous air:
Lift up skies of chalcedony!

Huh, Cuh, Guh and Chuh
Grunt like pigs in my acorn mind: 20
Arrange these emeralds in a meadow!

Come down Tuh, Duh and Thuh!
Consonantly rain
On the windowpane
Of the shrunken house of the heart;
Lift up blood red sardius!

Lift up golden chrysolite!
Juh, Quuh, Zuh and X

Scribble heavens with light,
Steeples take fright.   30

In my mouth like bread
Stands the shape of this glory;
Consonants and vowels
Repeat the story:
And sea-green beryl is carried up!

The candle tongue in my dark mouth
Is anguished with its sloth
And stung with self-scoff
As my eyes behold this treasure.
Let them bring up topaz now!   40

Dazzling chrysoprase!
Dewdrops tempt dark wick to sparkle.
Growl Spark! you whelp and cur,
Leap out of tongue kennel
And candle sepulchre.

I faint in the hyacinthine quarries!
My words pursue
Through the forest of time
The fading antlers of this dew.

A B C D E F G H I J K L M   50
Take captive the sun
Slay the dew quarry
Adam's Eve is morning rib
Bride and bridegroom marry
Still coffin is rocking crib
Tower and well are one
The stone is the wind, the wind is the stone
New Jerusalem[1]
N O P Q R S T U V W X Y Z!

1960, 1972

---

[1]The final paradise after Armageddon according to Revelation; see Revelation 21-2, which is the source of the imagery of the poem.

The Lost Child

Long have I looked for my lost child.
I hear him shake his rattle
Slyly in the winter wind
In the ditch that's filled with snow.

He pinched and shrieked and ran away
At the edge of the November forest.
The hungry old burdock stood
By the dead dry ferns.

Hear him thud that ball!
The acorns fall by the fence.   10
See him loll in the St. Lucy sun,[1]
The abandoned sheaf in the wire.

Oh Life in Death! my bonny nursling
Merry drummer in the nut brown coffin,
With vast wings outspread I float
Looking and looking over the empty sea

And there! in the—on the rolling death
Rattling a dried out gourd
Floated the mysterious cradle
Filled with a source.

I push the shore and kingdom to you,
Oh winter walk with seedpod ditch:
I touch them to the floating child
And lo! Cities and gardens, shepherds and smiths.

1962[2]

[1]St Lucy's Day, 13 December, was traditionally thought of as the shortest day of the year and the
beginning of the winter solstice.
[2]Originally the final poem in *One-man Masque*.

Starling with a Split Tongue[1]

Some boys caught me
In the yard
And with a jackknife they
Split my tongue into speech
So in a phrenological[2] cage
Here in the garage I stay
And say

[1]Folk belief holds that splitting the tongues of crows, ravens, and starlings makes it possible to teach
them how to speak.
[2]i.e. 'skull-like'; phrenology (literally the study of the mental faculties) is the pseudo-scientific
theory that the shape of the skull gives evidence of personality and mental ability.

The cracklewords passersby taught.
I say I know not what
Though I pray I do not pray   10
Though I curse I do not curse
Though I talk I do not talk

'I thought that made it kinda nice'
I heard her say as she began slipping on the ice

The the I am	An a am I
I and am are the & a	Who is are? Who saw war?
I rock a little pronoun	It does instead of me
I rose as I	Nooned as you
Lay down as he or she	Begat we, you & they

My eggs are covered with commas   20

    'Yuh remember when she fell down in a fit?'
Reveries Jake from the bottom of the pit.

Before beforeday	after St After's Massacre
While the while is on	Since since is since
Let's wait till till	Or until if you like
I come from from	to Whither Bay
Down Whence Road	but not To-day

As still as infinitives were the	Stones
Filled with adjectives were the	Trees
And with adverbs the	Pond 30

This all is a recorded announcement
        This all is a recorded announcement
'I thought that made it kinda nice'
'Yuh remember . . . . in a fit?'
              Darkness deep
Now fills the garage and its town
            With wordless sleep.

Who split their tongues? I ask.
Of Giant Jackknife in the sky.
Who split their tongues into lie mask   40
And lie face; split their hand
Into this way, that way, up and down,
Divided their love into restless hemispheres,
Split into two—one seeing left, one right
Their once one Aldebaran[3] all-seeing eye?
In the larger garage of the endless starlight
        Do they not croak as I?

1964, 1972

---

[3]One of the brightest stars in the sky (actually a double star).

Phyllis Webb

b. 1927

Phyllis Webb was born in Victoria, B.C., and grew up there and in Vancouver. In 1949 she received a B.A. in English and philosophy from the University of British Columbia. After an unsuccessful campaign as a CCF candidate, Webb moved to Montreal, where she worked as a secretary and attended graduate school at McGill for one year. In 1960 she returned to Vancouver and taught at UBC for four years. She then accepted a job with the CBC in Toronto as a program organizer and broadcaster (she had been freelancing for the CBC since 1955). From 1966 to 1969 she was executive producer of the radio program 'Ideas', which she had brought into being. Aided largely by government bursaries and awards, Webb was able to spend extended periods during the fifties and sixties in London, Paris, and San Francisco. Since 1969, when she left full-time radio work and returned to British Columbia, she has lived on Salt Spring Island and has taught at the Universities of British Columbia, Victoria, and Alberta.

Webb's first book, *Trio* (1954), was a showcase for her work and that of two other new writers, Gael Turnbull and Eli Mandel. In the next eleven years she produced three poetry collections: *Even Your Right Eye* (1956), *The Sea Is Also a Garden* (1962), and *Naked Poems* (1965). There followed a period of virtual silence—*Selected Poems 1954-1965* was published in 1971—until *Wilson's Bowl* appeared in 1980. Since then three more works have been published: *Talking: Selected Radio Talks and Other Essays* (1981); *Selected Poems: The Vision Tree* (1982), a Governor General's Award winner that includes some new work; and *Water and Light: ghazals and anti-ghazals* (1984).

Though Webb's poetry tends to be pessimistic, it is rarely morbid because it is always leavened with wit. Her concern with despair, suicide, and death is linked to a conscious existentialism (unusual in Canadian poetry), which is similar to that of Kierkegaard and Gide. While investigating what she sees as a sterile, even meaningless, world she presents her readers with strategies for survival. The topics of break-up and break-down—of major importance since the Second World War to writers as diverse as John Berryman, Doris Lessing, Adrienne Rich, and Margaret Atwood—have led her to suggest in her poetry that the individual must seek protective isolation and silence. In her own life she has found these in the silence of her native region: the beaches, water, and gardens of the Gulf Islands.

Webb's poetry, however, is not entirely introspective. Many of her poems allude to a wide range of interests in the world around her. The body of her work has been influenced on the one hand by the intricacies of metaphysical poetry techniques (as in 'Marvell's Garden' and 'The Glass Castle') and on the other by the stylistic simplicity of the Black Mountain and San Francisco poetry movements. The complex structuring of much of her poetry resembles the work of contemporary scientists building new chromosomes and atoms: she tries to obey what she calls

the physics of the poem. Energy/Mass.
Waxy splendour, the massive quiet of the
fallen tulip petals. So much depends upon:
the wit of the syntax, the rhythm and speed of
the fall, the drop, the assumption of a specific
light, curved. (Talking)

Lear[1] on the Beach at Break of Day

Down on the beach at break of day
observe Lear calmly observing the sea:
he tosses the buttons of his sanity
like aged pebbles into the bay;

cold, as his sexless daughters were,
the pebbles are round by a joyless war,
worn down on a troubled, courtly ground,
they drop in the sea without a sound;

and the sea repeats their logical sin,
shedding ring after ring of watery thin   10
wheels of misfortune of crises shorn
which spin to no end—and never turn.

And there Lear stands, alone.
The sun is rising and the cliffs aspire,
and there Lear stands, with dark small stones
in his crazed old hands. But farther and higher

he hurls them now, as if to free
himself with them. But only stones drop
sullenly, a hardened crop,
into the soft, irrational sea.   20

1954

[1] In *King Lear*, Lear, having given over his throne to his daughters Goneril and Regan in exchange for
their looking after him, is driven mad by their cruel and unfeeling treatment as they struggle against
one another for complete power.

Marvell's Garden[1]

Marvell's garden, that place of solitude,[2]
is not where I'd choose to live
yet is the fixed sundial[3]
that turns me round
unwillingly
in a hot glade
as closer, closer I come to contradiction

[1] This poem contains many responses and allusions to 'The Garden' by the British poet Andrew Marvell (1621-78).
[2] Marvell chooses to be solitary in the garden, declaring: 'Society is all but rude/To this delicious solitude'.
[3] The sundial in Marvell's poem is equated with the garden itself; in the seventeenth century the sundial was often a symbol of a stable point against which to measure the illusions of experience.

to the shade green within the green shade.[4]

The garden where Marvell scorned love's solicitude[5]—
that dream—and played instead an arcane solitaire,   10
shuffling his thoughts like shadowy chance
across the shrubs of ecstasy,
and cast the myths away to flowering hours
as yes, his mind, that sea, caught at green
thoughts shadowing a green infinity.

And yet Marvell's garden was not Plato's
garden[6]—and yet—he *did* care more for the form
of things than for the thing itself—
ideas and visions,
resemblances and echoes,   20
things seeming and being
not quite what they were.

That was his garden, a kind of attitude
struck out of an earth too carefully attended,
wanting to be left alone.
And I don't blame him for that.
God knows, too many fences fence us out
and his garden closed in on Paradise.[7]

On Paradise! When I think of his hymning
Puritans in the Bermudas,[8] the bright oranges   30
lighting up that night! When I recall
his rustling tinsel hopes
beneath the cold decree of steel.[9]
Oh, I have wept for some new convulsion
to tear together this world and his.

---

[4]In this stanza and the next, Webb refers to lines in Marvell's poem:
> The mind, that ocean where each kind
> Does straight its own resemblance find;
> Yet it creates, transcending these,
> Far other worlds, and other seas;
> Annihilating all that's made
> To a green thought in a green shade.

[5]Marvell rejects physical love, approving of the mythical stories in which young women escape seduction when they are transformed into flora.

[6]Marvell, while affirming the Platonic concept of ideal forms, departed from most of his contemporary Neo-Platonists in his belief that man's mind (equated in 'The Garden' with the ocean, which was said to contain a parallel to every external thing) was superior to nature, and thus to the ideal reality, because it not only had a pre-existent knowledge of all the 'forms' of reality but also could imaginatively create new 'forms' that have never before existed. In this stanza Webb plays with the contradictory meanings suggested by the word 'form'.

[7]Marvell equates his garden to Eden before the creation of Eve and the fall of man.

[8]In the poem 'Bermudas', Marvell depicts religious dissenters rowing ashore to the Bermudas (long celebrated as a kind of earthly paradise), singing a hymn of praise to God that includes the lines: 'He hangs in shades the orange bright,/Like golden lamps in a green night.'

[9]Marvell himself was twice exiled to the Bermudas as a result of ecclesiastical persecution. Throughout his life he sought a middle ground in the political strife of England, which was being torn by civil war.

But then I saw his luminous plumèd Wings[1]
prepared for flight,
and then I heard him singing glory
in a green tree,
and then I caught the vest he'd laid aside   40
all blest with fire.

And I have gone walking slowly in
his garden of necessity
leaving brothers, lovers, Christ
outside my walls
where they have wept without
and I within.

1956

[1]In 'The Garden' the poet undergoes a spiritual transformation:
>*Casting the body's vest aside,*
>*My soul into the boughs does glide:*
>*There like a bird it sits, and sings,*
>*Then whets and combs its silver wings.*

The Glass Castle

The glass castle is my image for the mind
that if outmoded has its public beauty.
It can contain both talisman and leaf,
and private action, homely disbelief.
And I have lived there as you must
and scratched with diamond and gathered diamond dust,
have signed the castle's tense and fragile glass
and heard the antique whores and stoned Cassandras[1]
call me, and I answered in the one voice I knew,
'I am here. I do not know . . .'   10
but moved the symbols and polished up the view.
For who can refrain from action—
there is always a princely kiss for the Sleeping Beauty—
when even to put out the light takes a steady hand,
for the reward of darkness in a glass castle
is starry and full of glory.

I do not mean I shall not crack the pane.
I merely make a statement, judicious and polite,
that in this poise of crystal space
I balance and I claim the five gods of reality[2]   20
to bless and keep me sane.

1962

[1]Cassandra was a Trojan soothsayer whose curse it was to have her prophecies ignored.
[2]That is, the five senses.

To Friends Who Have Also Considered Suicide

It's still a good idea.
Its exercise is discipline:
to remember to cross the street without looking,
to remember not to jump when the cars side-swipe,
to remember not to bother to have clothes cleaned,
to remember not to eat or want to eat,
to consider the numerous methods of killing oneself,
that is surely the finest exercise of the imagination:
death by drowning, sleeping pills, slashed wrists,
kitchen fumes, bullets through the brain or through   10
the stomach, hanging by the neck in attic or basement,
a clean frozen death—the ways are endless.
And consider the drama! It's better than a whole season
at Stratford when you think of the emotion of your
family on hearing the news and when you imagine
how embarrassed some will be when the body is found.
One could furnish a whole chorus in a Greek play
with expletives and feel sneaky and omniscient
at the same time. But there's no shame
in this concept of suicide.   20
It has concerned our best philosophers
and inspired some of the most popular
of our politicians and financiers.
Some people swim lakes, others climb flagpoles,
some join monasteries, but we, my friends,
who have considered suicide take our daily walk
with death and are not lonely.
In the end it brings more honesty and care
than all the democratic parliaments of tricks.
It is the 'sickness unto death';[1] it is death;   30
it is not death; it is the sand from the beaches
of a hundred civilizations, the sand in the teeth
of death and barnacles our singing tongue:
and this is 'life' and we owe at least this much
contemplation to our western fact: to Rise,
Decline, Fall, to futility and larks,
to the bright crustaceans of the oversky.

1962

---

[1]Phrase taken from *The Sickness Unto Death* (1849) by Danish philosopher and theologian Sören Kierkegaard (1813-55); for Kierkegaard, the 'sickness unto death' is despair.

For Fyodor[1]

I am a beetle in the cabbage soup they serve up for geniuses
in the House of the Dead.[2]

I am a black beetle and loll seductively at the bottom of the
warm slop.

Someday, Fyodor, by mistake you'll swallow me down and I'll become
a part of your valuable gutworks.

In the next incarnation I hope to imitate that idiot and saint,
Prince Myshkin,[3] drop off my wings for his moronic glory.

Or, if I miss out on the Prince, Sonya or Dunya might do.

I'm not joking. I am not the result of bad sanitation in the
kitchen, as you think.

Up here in Omsk in Siberia beetles are not accidents but destinies.

I'm drowning fast, but even in this condition I realize your bad
tempered haughtiness is part of your strategy.

You are about to turn this freezing hell into an ecstatic emblem.   10
A ferocious shrine.

Ah, what delicious revenge. But take care! A fit is coming![4]
Now, now I'll leap into your foaming mouth and jump your tongue.
Now I stamp on this not quite famous tongue

shouting: Remember Fyodor, you may hate men but it's here in
Omsk you came to love mankind.

But you don't hear, do you: there you are writhing in epileptic visions.

Hold your tongue! You can't speak yet. You are mine, Dostoevsky.

I am to slip down your gullet and improve myself.

---

[1]Fyodor Dostoevski (1821-81), Russian novelist. This 'portrait' poem is part of Webb's unfinished sequence 'The Kropotkin Poems', which examines the ramifications of the Russian Revolution upon modern society. Webb has commented: 'In "For Fyodor" the beetle is aggressive, enraged, monologuing dramatically along the extended line. Poor Fyodor, foaming at the mouth, harangued by this Trickster . . . Big-mouthed, proletarian, revolting beetle. The balance of power unbalanced . . . Notes from the Insect Underground. Spider Webb' (Talking).
[2]The prison in Omsk, Siberia, that is the setting for Dostoevski's 1862 novel, The House of the Dead; this novel is based on his experiences while serving four years' hard labour in this prison.
[3]Central character of The Idiot (1868); Sonya and Dunya are two characters from Crime and Punishment (1866).
[4]Dostoevski suffered from epilepsy.

I can almost hear what you'll say: 20

> Crime and Punishment
> Suffering and Grace

and of the dying

> pass by and forgive
> us our happiness

1980

Eschatology[1] of Spring

Death, Judgement, Heaven, Hell,
and Spring. The Five Last Things,
the least of which I am, being in
the azaleas and dog-toothed violets
of the South of Canada. Do not tell me
this is a cold country. I am also in
the camellias and camas of early, of
abrupt birth.
We are shooting up for the bloody
judgement of the six o'clock news.   10
Quick, cut us out from the deadlines
of rotting newspapers, quick, for the
tiny skeletons and bulbs will tell you
how death grows and grows in Chile and
Chad. Quick, for the small bones pinch
me and insects divulge occult excrement
in the service of my hyacinth, my trailing
begonia. And if you catch me resting
beside the stream, sighing against
the headlines of this pastoral, take   20
up your gun, the flowers blossoming
from its barrel, and join this grief, this
grief: that there are lambs, elegant black-
footed lambs in this island's eschatology,
Beloved.

1981

[1]The branch of theology that is concerned with the ultimate or last things. Webb has added Spring to the traditional Four Last Things.

Robert Kroetsch

b. 1927

Growing up in Heisler, Alta., Robert Kroetsch saw first-hand the hardships that drought and depression brought to the Prairies in the thirties. Despite that sombre background, he is best known as a comic novelist whose fiction often recalls the wild and bawdy tall tales of the western beer hall. More than simply tall tales, his novels move towards the retelling of some of the great myths. But while drawing on classical mythology and North American Indian tales, Kroetsch provides his reader with parodies as much as with parallels, creating a blend of comedy and fantasy that marked a new departure in Canadian fiction.

After earning an undergraduate degree at the University of Alberta in 1948, Kroetsch, a would-be writer in search of experience, journeyed north to the Slave River. He spent some time as a labourer on the Fort Smith Portage, two seasons sailing on Mackenzie riverboats, and several years in Labrador. He then travelled east to study at McGill University under Hugh MacLennan. During his summers he attended the Bread Loaf School of English at Middlebury College, Vermont, where he completed an M.A. In 1965 he entered the Writers' Workshop program at the University of Iowa, earning his Ph.D. in 1961 with the draft of a novel (an early version of *The Studhorse Man*). He remained in the U.S. for the next fourteen years, teaching at the State University of New York at Binghamton, before returning to Canada in 1975. He has taught at the Universities of Lethbridge and Calgary and is now Professor of English at the University of Manitoba.

In 1965 Kroetsch published *But We Are Exiles*, a novel about the crew of a riverboat on the Mackenzie. In the fiction that followed he undertook what he felt to be the chief task of the western-Canadian novelist: to write his environment into existence and to discover the myths appropriate to the

place. In a conversation with Margaret Laurence recorded in *Creation* (1970), Kroetsch remarked: 'In a sense we haven't got an identity until somebody tells our story. The fiction makes us real.' Kroetsch's most extended attempt to tell that story is in his Out West trilogy (he calls it a 'triptych') of novels: *The Words of My Roaring* (1966), *The Studhorse Man* (1969), for which he won a Governor General's Award, and *Gone Indian* (1973). These books, forming an extended investigation of an imagined Alberta landscape through four decades, playfully consider the political movements of the Depression thirties, the social dislocations following the Second World War, and the naive pastoralism of the sixties and early seventies. (Kroetsch's travel book, *Alberta*, 1968, by providing a more personal and objective response to his native province, serves as an interesting counterpoint to his triptych.) In 1975 Kroetsch published his fifth novel, *Badlands*, a surreal work about river-rafting through the Alberta Badlands in search of dinosaur bones. The densely layered composition of Kroetsch's fiction is made apparent in *The Crow Journals* (1980), a history of the construction of his next novel, *What the Crow Said* (1978). In *Alibi* (1983), Kroetsch began what he describes as the start of a second trilogy.

During the seventies he turned much of his creative energy to poetry, collecting in *The Stone Hammer Poems* (1975) the short poems he had written in the previous decade. The title poem movingly documents the writer's struggle to elicit meaning from the objects of the past. Very interested in questions about form and structure in the modern long poem, Kroetsch also published in 1975 *The Ledger*, a long poem that was the beginning of what Kroetsch then envisioned as a life-long poetic work-in-progress; it was continued with *Seed Catalogue* in 1977. In 1981 Kroetsch brought together in *Field*

Notes the parts of the poem he had so far published. In a preface to that book, Eli Mandel wrote:

We have not had such an endeavour before, at least not in this country; for this is the long poem, not just the narrative, of which Northrop Frye has written, not the documentary, of which Dorothy Livesay has much to say, but something big enough to hold the world and time, a space for the vast geography, a time for hidden history.

Kroetsch subsequently published several more parts of this poem. In 1989 he drew the loosely unified sequence together in a single volume entitled *Completed Field Notes: The Long Poems of Robert Kroetsch* and declared the project finished. He maintains that this book marks his farewell to poetry.

Through his teaching, lecturing, and critical essays, and as co-founder in 1972 of the American critical journal *Boundary 2: A Journal of Post-Modern Literature*, Kroetsch has worked both to locate Canadian literature in an international context and to make the Canadian academic and literary communities more aware of recent international developments in literary theory. Many of the ideas associated with postmodernism—for example, the use of parody as a way of responding to inherited form and tradition; the resistance to closure and to overriding unity in literary works; and a self-reflexivity in writing that brings questions of textuality and process into the foreground of the work, while undermining the authority of both writer and reader—have influenced Kroetsch's criticism (as well as his poetry and fiction), and through him they have become more generally available to Canadian writers.

The critical and theoretical depths that emerge when Kroetsch discusses his own writing are particularly evident in *Labyrinths of Voice* (1981), a book of conversations with Shirley Neuman and Robert Wilson. Among his many critical essays—collected in *The Lovely Treachery of Words: Essays Selected and New* (1989)—'Unhiding the Hidden' has had special impact. An essay about the way Canadian writers are burdened by their cultural inheritance, it expresses Kroetsch's belief that writers must 'un-name' themselves and their environment. This act is dramatized in Kroetsch's vision of Grove's creating an identity after 'exfoliating' back to blankness in 'F.P. Grove: The Finding'. For Canadian writers, and for prairie writers in particular, such 'uncreating' can enable them to perceive the essential elements of their 'home place'—which might otherwise be concealed by inherited concepts. The poet's meditations on something as familiar as a seed catalogue can remind us that the catalogue mailed to farm families was a symbolic object because it brought each year the promise of a new spring to come—and, along with that promise, certain less visible, unexamined values. *Seed Catalogue* not only brings some of that hidden ideology to the surface, it playfully calls into question even our assumptions about spring itself: in the Canadian prairies perhaps all one can assert is, 'winter was ending'.

F. P. Grove: The Finding[1]

I

Dreaming the well-born   hobo of yourself
against the bourgeois father[2]   dreaming Europe
if only to find   a place to be from

the hobo tragedian   pitching bundles
riding a freight   to the impossible city
the fallen archangel   of Brandon or Winnipeg

in all your harvesting   real
or imagined   did you really find
four aged stallions[3]   neigh

in your cold undertaking   on those trails north   10
in all the (dreamed) nights   in stooks
in haystacks   dreaming the purified dreamer

who lured you   to a new man (back
to the fatal earth)   inventing (beyond
America) a new world   did you find

did you dream   the French priest who hauled you
out of your *fleurs du mal*[4]   and headlong
into a hundred drafts   real

or imagined   of the sought form
(there are no models)   and always   20
(there are only models)   alone

2

alone in the cutter   in the blizzard[5]
two horses   hauling you into the snow
that buries the road   burying the forest

---

[1]This poem is constructed around references to three of Grove's books. *Over Prairie Trails* (1922), *A Search for America* (1927), and *In Search of Myself* (1946). See pp. 186-7.

[2]In *In Search of Myself*, Grove describes his father as a wealthy Swedish landowner. In *A Search for America*, he recounts twenty years of wandering across North America as a tramp and a hobo. Both books were long thought of as autobiographical accounts but later discovered to be highly dramatized fictions.

[3]In Chapter Five of *In Search of Myself*, Grove says, 'I was hired as a teamster, and I owed the job to one single fact, namely, that of not being afraid of handling any kind of horse, not even the team I was offered which consisted of four aged stallions.'

[4]According to Chapter Six of *In Search of Myself* Grove was persuaded to begin his teaching career by a chance encounter with a French priest who saw him reading Baudelaire's *Fleurs du mal* in a North Dakota train station.

[5]From here to the conclusion, the poem is based on the sketch 'Snow' from *Over Prairie Trails* (reprinted on pp. 187-204), which describes a particularly harrowing winter journey.

the layered mind   exfoliating[6]
back to the barren sea   (Greek to us,
Grove)   back to the blank sun

and musing snow to yourself   new
to the old rite of burial   the snow
lifting the taught man   into the coyote self   30

the silence of sight   'as if I were not myself
who yet am I'   riding the drifted snow
to your own plummeting   alone and alone

the *wirklichkeit*[7]   of the word itself
the name under the name   the sought
and calamitous edge   of the white earth

the horses   pawing the empty fall
the hot breath on the zero day   the man
seeing the new man so vainly   alone

we say with your waiting wife   (but she   40
was the world   before you invented it
old liar)   'You had a hard trip?'

1975

[6]Grove says that the snow-drifts he was crossing 'showed that curious appearance that we also find in the glaciated surfaces of granite rock and which, in them, geologists call exfoliation' (192).
Later Grove writes that as he looked at 'the infertile waste' around him: 'Unaccountably two Greek words formed on my lips: Homer's Pontos atrygetos—the barren sea' (195).
[7]Reality; actual fact (German).

Seed Catalogue

I.

No. 176—*Copenhagen Market Cabbage:* 'This *new introduction, strictly speaking,* is in every respect a *thoroughbred,* a *cabbage* of *highest pedigree,* and is *creating considerable flurry* among *professional gardeners* all *over the world.*'

We took the storm windows/off
the south side of the house
and put them on the hotbed.
Then it was spring. Or, no:
then winter was ending.

      'I wish to say we had lovely success
      this summer with the seed purchased   10
      of you. We had the finest Sweet

Corn in the country, and Cabbage
were dandy.'
—W.W. Lyon, South Junction, Man.

My mother said:
Did you wash your ears?
You could grow cabbages
in those ears.

Winter was ending.
This is what happened: 20
we were harrowing the garden.
You've got to understand this:
I was sitting on the horse.
The horse was standing still.
I fell off.

The hired man laughed: how
in hell did you manage to
fall off a horse that was
standing still?

Bring me the radish seeds,   30
my mother whispered.

Into the dark of January
the seed catalogue bloomed

a winter proposition, if
spring should come, then,

with illustrations:

No. 25—*McKenzie's Improved Golden Wax Bean:* 'THE MOST PRIZED OF ALL BEANS.
Virtue is its own reward. We have had *many expressions* from *keen discriminating
gardeners extolling our seed* and *this variety.*'

Beans, beans,   40
the musical fruit;
the more you eat,
the more you virtue.

My mother was marking the first row
with a piece of binder twine, stretched
between two pegs.

The hired man laughed: just
about planted the little bugger.
Cover him up and see what grows.

My father didn't laugh. He was puzzled   50
by any garden that was smaller than a
quarter-section of wheat and summerfallow.

the home place: N.E. 17-42-16-w4th Meridian.

the home place: one and a half miles west of Heisler, Alberta,
          on the correction line road
          and three miles south.

No trees
around the house.
Only the wind.
Only the January snow.   60
Only the summer sun.
The home place:
a terrible symmetry.

How do you grow a gardener?

        Telephone Peas
        Garden Gem Carrots
        Early Snowcap Cauliflower
        Perfection Globe Onions
        Hubbard Squash
        Early Ohio Potatoes   70

This is what happened—at my mother's wake. This
is a fact—the World Series was in progress. The
Cincinnati Reds were playing the Detroit Tigers.
It was raining. The road to the graveyard was barely
passable. The horse was standing still. Bring me
the radish seeds, my mother whispered.

2.
My father was mad at the badger: the badger was digging holes in the potato patch,
threatening man and beast with broken limbs (I quote). My father took the double-
barrelled shotgun out into the potato patch and waited.

Every time the badger stood up, it looked like a little man, come out of the ground. 80
Why, my father asked himself—Why would so fine a fellow live under the ground?
Just for the cool of roots? The solace of dark tunnels? The blood of gophers?

My father couldn't shoot the badger. He uncocked the shotgun, came back to the
house in time for breakfast. The badger dug another hole. My father got mad again.
They carried on like that all summer.

                    Love is an amplification
                    by doing/over and over.
                    by doing/over and over.

                    Love is a standing up
                    to the loaded gun.

                    Love is a burrowing. 90

One morning my father actually shot at the badger. He killed a magpie that was

cking away at a horse turd about fifty feet beyond and to the right of the spot
ere the badger had been standing.

week later my father told the story again. In that version he intended to hit the
gpie. Magpies, he explained, are a nuisance. They eat robins' eggs. They're
rder to kill than snakes, jumping around the way they do, nothing but feathers.

st call me sure-shot,
father added.

. 1248—*Hubbard Squash:* 'As *mankind* seems to have a *particular fondness* for
ash, *Nature* appears to have *especially* provided this *matchless* variety of   100
erlative flavour.'

> *Love is a leaping up*
> *and down.*
>
> *Love*
> *is a break in the warm flesh.*

a cooker, it heads the list for warted squash. The
es are of strong running growth; the fruits are large,
e shaped, of a rich deep green colour, the rind is
ooth . . .'

t how do you grow a lover?   110

s is the God's own truth:
ying dirty is a mortal sin
priest told us, you'll go to hell
burn forever (with illustrations)—

as our second day of cathechism
Germaine and I went home that
rnoon   if it's that bad, we
to each other   we realized
better quit   we realized

s do it just one last time   120
quit.

s is the God's own truth:
chism, they called it,
boys had to sit in the pews
the right, the girls on the left.
ls were like underwear that you
e inside. If boys and girls sat
ether—

m and Eve got caught
ying dirty.   130

This is the truth.
We climbed up into a granary
full of wheat   to the gunny sacks
the binder twine was shipped in—

we spread the paper from the sacks
smooth sheets   on the soft wheat
Germaine and I   were we were like/one

we had discovered, don't ask me
how, where—but when the priest said
playing dirty we knew—well—   140

he had named it   he had named
our world   out of existence
(the horse   was standing still)

—This is my first confession. Bless me father I played
dirty so long, just the other day, up in the granary
there by the car shed—up there on the Brantford Binder
Twine gunny sacks and the sheets of paper—Germaine
with her dress up and her bloomers down—

—Son. For penance, keep your peter in your pants
for the next thirteen years.   150

But how—

      Adam and Eve and Pinch-Me
      went down to the river to swim—
      Adam and Eve got drownded.

But how do you grow a lover?

      We decided we could do it
      just one last time.

4.
It arrived in winter, the seed catalogue, on a January
day. It came into town on the afternoon train.

Mary Hauck, when she came west from Bruce County, Ontario,   160
arrived in town on a January day. She brought along
her hope chest.

She was cooking in the Heisler Hotel. The Heisler Hotel
burned down on the night of June 21, 1919. Everything
in between: lost. Everything: an absence

of satin sheets
of embroidered pillowcases
of tea-towels and English china
of silver serving spoons.

How do you grow a prairie town?   170

> The gopher was the model.
> Stand up straight:
> telephone poles
> grain elevators
> church steeples.
> Vanish, suddenly: the
> gopher was the model.

How do you grow a past/
to live in

the absence of silkworms   180
the absence of clay and wattles (whatever the hell
            they are)
the absence of Lord Nelson
the absence of kings and queens
the absence of a bottle opener, and me with a vicious
            attack of the 26-ounce flu
the absence of both Sartre and Heidegger
the absence of pyramids
the absence of lions
the absence of lutes, violas and xylophones   190
the absence of a condom dispenser in the Lethbridge Hotel and
            me about to screw an old Blood whore. I was
            in love.
the absence of the Parthenon, not to mention the Cathédrale de
            Chartres
the absence of psychiatrists
the absence of sailing ships
the absence of books, journals, daily newspapers and everything
            else but the *Free Press Prairie Farmer* and *The
            Western Producer*   200
the absence of gallows (with apologies to Louis Riel)
the absence of goldsmiths
the absence of the girl who said that if the Edmonton Eskimos
            won the Grey Cup she'd let me kiss her
            nipples in the foyer of the Palliser Hotel. I
            don't know where she got to.
the absence of Heraclitus
the absence of the Seine, the Rhine, the Danube, the Tiber and
            the Thames. Shit, the Battle River ran dry
            one fall. The Strauss boy could piss across it.   210
            He could piss higher on a barn wall than any
            of us. He could piss right clean over the
            principal's new car.
the absence of ballet and opera
the absence of Aeneas

How do you grow a prairie town?

Rebuild the hotel when it burns down. Bigger. Fill it
full of a lot of A-I Hard Northern Bullshitters.

—You ever hear the one about the woman who buried
    her husband with his ass sticking out of the ground   220
    so that every time she happened to walk by she could
    give it a swift kick?

—Yeh, I heard it.

5.
I planted some melons, just to see what would
happen. Gophers ate everything.

            I applied to the Government.
            I wanted to become a postman,
            to deliver real words
            to real people.

            There was no one to receive   230
            my application

I don't give a damn if I do die do die do die do die do die
do die do die do die do die do die do die do die do die do
die do die do die do die do die do die do die do die do die
do

6.
No. 339—*McKenzie's Pedigreed Early Snowcap Cauliflower:* 'Of the many *varieties*
of *vegetables* in *existence*, *Cauliflower* is *unquestionably* one of the *greatest*
inheritances of the *present generation, particularly Western Canadians.* There is *no*
place in the *world* where *better cauliflowers* can be *grown* than right here in the *West.*
The *finest specimens* we have *ever seen*, larger and of *better quality*, are *annually* 2
grown here on our *prairies.* Being *particularly* a *high altitude plant* it *thrives* to a
point of *perfection* here, *seldom seen* in *warmer climes.*'

But how do you grow a poet?

Start: with an invocation
invoke—

His muse is
his muse/if
memory is

and you have
no memory then   250
no meditation

no song (shit
we're up against it)

　　　　　　　　　　how about that girl
　　　　　　　　　　you felt up in the
　　　　　　　　　　school barn or that
　　　　　　　　　　girl you necked with
　　　　　　　　　　out by Hastings' slough
　　　　　　　　　　and ran out of gas with
　　　　　　　　　　and nearly froze to
　　　　　　　　　　death with/or that　　　260
　　　　　　　　　　girl in the skating
　　　　　　　　　　rink shack who had on
　　　　　　　　　　so much underwear you
　　　　　　　　　　didn't have enough
　　　　　　　　　　prick to get past her/
　　　　　　　　　　CCM skates

Once upon a time in the village of Heisler—

—Hey, wait a minute.
　　That's a story.

How do you grow a poet?　　　　　　　　　270

　　　　　　　　　　For appetite: cod-liver
　　　　　　　　　　oil.
　　　　　　　　　　For bronchitis: mustard
　　　　　　　　　　plasters.
　　　　　　　　　　For pallor and failure to fill
　　　　　　　　　　the woodbox: sulphur
　　　　　　　　　　& molasses.
　　　　　　　　　　For self-abuse: ten Our
　　　　　　　　　　Fathers & ten Hail Marys.
　　　　　　　　　　For regular bowels: Sunny Boy　　　280
　　　　　　　　　　Cereal.

How do you grow a poet?

'It's a pleasure to advise that I
won the First Prize at the Calgary
Horticultural Show . . . This is my
first attempt. I used your seeds.'

　　　　　　　　　　Son, this is a crowbar.
　　　　　　　　　　This is a willow fencepost.
　　　　　　　　　　This is a sledge.
　　　　　　　　　　This is a roll of barbed wire.　　　290
　　　　　　　　　　This is a bag of staples.
　　　　　　　　　　This is a claw hammer.

We give form to this land by running
a series of posts and three strands
of barbed wire around a quarter-section.

> First off I want to take that
> crowbar and drive 1,156 holes
> in that gumbo.
> And the next time you want to
> write a poem   300
> we'll start the haying.

How do you grow a poet?

> This is a prairie road.
> This road is the shortest distance
> between nowhere and nowhere.
> This road is a poem.

> Just two miles up the road
> you'll find a porcupine
> dead in the ditch. It was
> trying to cross the road.   310

As for the poet himself
we can find no record
of his having traversed
the land/in either direction

no trace of his coming
or going/only a scarred
page, a spoor of wording
a reduction to mere black

and white/a pile of rabbit   320
turds that tells us
all spring long
where the track was

poet . . . say uncle.

How?

Rudy Wiebe: 'You must lay great black steel lines of
fiction, break up that space with huge design and, like
the fiction of the Russian steppes, build a giant
artifact. No song can do that . . .'

February 14, 1976. Rudy, you
took us there: to the Oldman River   330
Lorna & Byrna, Ralph & Steve and me
you showed us where
the Bloods surprised the Crees

the next coulee/ surprise.
em to death. And after
u showed us Rilke's word
ebensgliedes.

udy: Nature thou art.

rome Grass (Bromus Inermis): 'No amount of cold will kill it. It *withstands* the
mmer suns. Water may stand on it for several weeks without apparent injury. The   340
ots push through the soil, throwing up new plants continually. It *starts quicker*
an other grasses in the spring. *Remains green* longer in the fall. *Flourishes under
solute neglect.'*

e end of winter:
eding/time.

*ow do you grow
oet?*

)
was drinking with Al Purdy. We went round and round
the restaurant on top of the Chateau Lacombe. We
ere the turning centre in the still world, the winter   350
Edmonton was hardly enough to cool our out-sights.

e waitress asked us to leave. She was rather insistent;
e were bad for business, shouting poems at the paying
stomers. Twice, Purdy galloped a Cariboo horse
ght straight through the dining area.

ow that's what I call
piss-up.

                                                    'No song can do that.'

)
o. 2362—*Imperialis Morning
ory:* 'This is the wonderful *Jap-*   360
ese Morning Glory, celebrated the
orld over for its *wondrous beauty*
both flowers and foliage.'

nday, January 12, 1975. This evening after
reading *The Double Hook:* looking at Japanese prints.
ot at actors. Not at courtesans. Rather: Hiroshige's
ries, *Fifty-Three Stations on the Tokaido.*

om the *Tokaido* series: 'Shono-Haku-u.' The
re-assed travellers, caught in a sudden shower.
en and trees, bending. How it is in a rain shower/   370

that you didn't see coming. And couldn't have avoided/
even if you had.

                    The double hook:
                    the home place.

                    The stations of the way:
                    the other garden

                    Flourishes.
                    Under absolute neglect.

(c)
Jim Bacque said (I was waiting for a plane,
after a reading; Terminal 2, Toronto)—he said,   380
You've got to deliver the pain to some woman,
don't you?

—Hey, Lady.
    You at the end of the bar.
    I wanna tell you something.

—Yuh?

—Pete Knight—of Crossfield,
    Alberta. Bronc-Busting Champion
    of the World. You ever hear of
    Pete Knight, the King of All   390
    Cowboys, Bronc-Busting Champion
    of the World?

—Huh-uh.

—You know what I mean? King
    of *All* Cowboys . . . Got
    killed—by a horse.
    He fell off.

—You some kind of nut
    or something?

8.

                                        We silence words   40
                                        by writing them down.

THIS IS THE LAST WILL AND TESTAMENT
OF ME, HENRY L. KROETSCH:

(a) [yes, his first bequest]

To my son Frederick my carpenter tools.

It was his first bequest. First,
a man must build.

hose horse-barns around Heisler—
ose perfectly designed barns
ith the rounded roofs—only Freddie   410
ew how to build them. He mapped
e parklands with perfect horse-barns.

        I remember my Uncle Freddie.
        (The farmers no longer
        use horses.)

        Back in the 30s, I remember
        he didn't have enough money
        to buy a pound of coffee.

        Every morning at breakfast
        he drank a cup of hot water   420
        with cream and sugar in it.

        Why, I asked him one morning—
        I wasn't all that old—why
        do you do that? I asked him.

        Jesus Christ, he said. He was
        a gentle man, really. Don't you
        understand *anything?*

he danger of merely living.

shell/exploding
the black sky: a   430
range planting

bomb/exploding
the earth: a
range

an/falling
n the city.
illed him dead.

was a strange
lanting.

e absence of my cousin who was shot down while bombing   440
e city that was his maternal great-grandmother's
rthplace. He was the navigator. He guided himself
that fatal occasion:

            —a city he had
              forgotten
            —a woman he had
              forgotten

He intended merely to release a cargo of bombs on a
target and depart. The exploding shell was:

a) an intrusion on a design that was not his, or   450

b) an occurrence which he had in fact, unintentionally,
   himself designed, or

c) it is essential that we understand this matter
   because:

He was the first descendant of that family to return
to the Old Country. He took with him: a cargo of bombs.

> Anna Weller: *Geboren* Köln, 1849.
> Kenneth MacDonald: Died Cologne, 1943.

> A terrible symmetry.

A strange muse: forgetfulness. Feeding her far children   460
to ancestral guns, blasting them out of the sky, smack/
into the earth. Oh, she was the mothering sort. Blood/
on her green thumb.

10.

After the bomb/blossoms   *Poet, teach us*
After the city/falls   *to love our dying.*
After the rider/falls
(the horse   *West is a winter place.*
standing still)   *The palimpsest of prairie*

                             under the quick erasure
                             of snow, invites a flight.   470

How/do you grow a garden?

                   No. 3060—*Spencer Sweet Pea:*
                   Pkt $.10; oz $.25;
                   quarter lb $.75; half lb $1.25.

Your sweet peas
climbing the staked
chicken wire,
climbing the stretched
binder twine by
the front porch   480

taught me the smell
of morning, the grace
of your tired
hands, the strength
of a noon sun, the
colour of prairie grass

taught me the smell
of my sweating armpits.

(b)

How do you a garden grow?
How do you grow a garden?   490

'*Dear Sir,*
    The longest brome grass I remember seeing was one night in Brooks. We were on
our way up to the Calgary Stampede, and reached Brooks about 11 P.M., perhaps
earlier because there was still a movie on the drive-in screen. We unloaded Cindy, and
I remember tying her up to the truck box and the brome grass was up to her hips. We
laid down in the back of the truck—on some grass I pulled by hand—and slept for
about three hours, then drove into Calgary.

Amie'

(c)

No trees
around the house,   500
only the wind.
Only the January snow.
Only the summer sun.

Adam and Eve got drownded—
Who was left?

1977

Timothy Findley

b. 1930

Born in Toronto, Timothy Irving Frederick Findley left high school before graduating and then pursued an acting career. He appeared in local plays and in a television series based on Stephen Leacock's *Sunshine Sketches of a Little Town*, and eventually joined the Stratford Shakespearean Company for the Festival's first season (1953), before travelling to England to study at London's Central School. While playing in *The Matchmaker* in London, Findley began to write fiction. Although his first story was published in *Tamarack Review* in 1956, he did not become a full-time writer until 1962, after his return to Canada.

Findley has written everything from ads for a country-and-western radio station and arts reports for CBC radio, to articles, stories, reviews, novels, and screenplays (*Don't Let The Angels Fall*, 1969, and *The Wars*, 1983). He has also written scripts and plays for radio and television (several for *Whiteoaks of Jalna*, 1971-2) as well as those written in collaboration with William Whitehead, with whom he lives in Cannington, Ontario (among others they include *The National Dream*, 1974, *Dieppe*, 1979, and *Other People's Children*, 1980). Findley was playwright-in-residence at the National Arts Centre in Ottawa (1974-5), Chairman of the Writers' Union of Canada (1977-8), and writer-in-residence at the University of Toronto (1978-9). He was made an Officer of the Order of Canada in 1986.

Although Findley's novels are marked by appalling acts of violence—fires, killings, wars—the fiercest struggles are waged internally by lonely characters (like Ben's father in 'Stones') against their world and themselves, to retain their sanity. Findley locates the source of these breakdowns in the modern myth of perfection. He challenges the notion of the perfect family in *The Last of the Crazy People* (1967), that of the perfect America in *The Butterfly Plague* (1969), and questions war-time heroism in his Governor General's Award-winning novel, *The Wars* (1977), and honour in *Famous Last Words* (1981). Although these last two novels deal with the First and Second World Wars, a topic that has often claimed Findley's attention, their elaborate narrative frames call attention to their existence as fictions as well as to their factual or historical nature. In *The Wars*, Robert Ross's story of his World War I experiences is narrated and pieced together by an unnamed biographer-historian; in *Famous Last Words* the story of the period between the wars is told by Hugh Selwyn Mauberley, the titular hero of Ezra Pound's thirteen-part poem (1920). Findley has written two other novels (*Not Wanted on the Voyage*, 1984, and *The Telling of Lies a Mystery*, 1986), and two plays, *Can You See Me Yet?* (1977) and *John A.—Himself!* (produced in 1979).

Findley has published two collections of short fiction, *Dinner Along the Amazon* (1984), which gathered stories written over the previous thirty years, and *Stones* (1988). The later book deals with the power of memories, even those that are lost or repressed. It opens with the act of sprinkling ashes over stones, a ritual that is repeated in the final story, 'Stones'. Like other stories in the collection, 'Stones' describes a relationship that is disrupted, in this case by the overwhelming horror of a wartime memory that haunts David Max and his family—just as the tragedy of Dieppe has haunted Findley and so many other Canadians of his generation.

Stones

We lived on the outskirts of Rosedale, over on the wrong side of Yonge Street. This was the impression we had, at any rate. Crossing the streetcar tracks put you in another world.

One September, my sister, Rita, asked a girl from Rosedale over to our house after school. Her name was Allison Pritchard and she lived on Cluny Drive. When my mother telephoned to see if Allison Pritchard could stay for supper, Mrs Pritchard said she didn't think it would be appropriate. That was the way they talked in Rosedale: very polite; oblique and cruel.

Over on our side—the west side—of Yonge Street, there were merchants—and this, apparently, made the difference to those whose houses were in Rosedale. People of class were not meant to live in the midst of commerce.

Our house was on Gibson Avenue, a cul-de-sac with a park across the road. My bedroom window faced a hockey rink in winter and a football field in summer. Cy, my brother, was a star in either venue. I was not. My forte, then, was the tricycle.

Up at the corner, there was an antique store on one side and a variety shop on the other. In the variety shop, you could spend your allowance on penny candy, Eskimo pies and an orange drink I favoured then called *Stubby*. *Stubby* came in short, fat bottles and aside from everything else—the thick orange flavour and the ginger in the bubbles—there was something wonderfully satisfying in the fact that it took both hands to hold it up to your lips and tip it down your throat.

Turning up Yonge Street, beyond the antique store, you came to The Women's Bakery, Adam's Grocery, Oskar Schickel, the butcher and Max's Flowers. We were Max's Flowers. My mother and my father wore green aprons when they stood behind the counter or went back into the cold room where they made up wreaths for funerals, bouquets for weddings and corsages for dances at the King Edward Hotel. Colonel Matheson, retired, would come in every morning on his way downtown and pick out a boutonnière from the jar of carnations my mother kept on the counter near the register. Once, when I was four, I caused my parents untold embarrassment by pointing out that Colonel Matheson had a large red growth on the end of his nose. The 'growth' was nothing of the sort, of course, but merely the result of Colonel Matheson's predilection for gin.

Of the pre-war years, my overall memory is one of perfect winters, heavy with snow and the smell of coal- and wood-smoke mingling with the smell of bread and cookies rising from The Women's Bakery. The coal-smoke came from our furnaces and the wood-smoke—mostly birch and maple—came to us from the chimneys of Rosedale, where it seemed that every house must have a fireplace in every room.

Summers all smelled of grass being cut in the park and burning tar from the road crews endlessly patching the potholes in Yonge Street. The heat of these summers was heroic and the cause of many legends. Mister Schickel, the butcher, I recall once cooked an egg on the sidewalk outside his store. My father, who was fond of Mister Schickel, made him a bet of roses it could not be done. I think Mister Schickel's part of the bet was pork chops trimmed of excess fat. When the egg began to sizzle, my father slapped his thigh and whistled and he sent my sister, Rita, in to get the flowers. Mister Schickel, however, was a graceful man and when he placed his winnings in the window of his butcher shop, he also placed a card that read: *Thanks to Max's Flowers one dozen roses.*

The Great Depression held us all in thrall, but its effects on those of us who were used to relative poverty—living on the west side on Yonge Street—were not so debilitating as they were on the far side in Rosedale. The people living there regarded money as something you had—as opposed to something you went out and got—and they were slower to adjust to what, for them, was the unique experience of deprivation.

I remember, too, that there always seemed to be a tramp at the door: itinerants asking if—for the price of a meal, or the meal itself—they could carry out the ashes, sweep the walks or pile the baskets and pails in which my father brought his flowers from the market and the greenhouse.

Our lives continued in this way until about the time I was five—in August of 1939. Everyone's life, I suppose, has its demarcation lines—its latitudes and longitudes passing through time. Some of these lines define events that everyone shares—others are confined to personal—even to secret lives. But the end of summer 1939 is a line drawn through the memory of everyone who was then alive. We were all about to be pitched together into a melting pot of violence from which a few of us would emerge intact and the rest of us would perish.

My father joined the army even before the war had started. He went downtown one day and didn't come back till after suppertime. I noticed that he hadn't taken the truck but had ridden off on the streetcar. I asked my mother why he had worn his suit on a weekday and she replied *because today is special*. But that was all she said.

At the table, eating soufflé and salad, my brother, Cy—who was nine years old that summer—talked about the World's Fair in New York City and pictures he'd seen of the future in magazines. The Great World's Fair was a subject that had caught all our imaginations with its demonstrations of new appliances, aeroplanes and motor cars. Everything was 'streamlined' in 1939; everything designed with swept-back lines as if we were all preparing to shoot off into space. Earlier that summer, the King and Queen of England had come to Canada, riding on a streamlined train whose blue-painted engine was sleek and slim as something in a silver glove. In fact, the King and Queen had arrived in Toronto just up Yonge Street from where we lived. We got permission from the Darrow family, who lived over Max's Flowers, to stand on the roof and watch the parade with its Mounties in scarlet and its Black Watch Band and the King and Queen, all blue and white and smiling, sitting in an open Buick called a *McLaughlin—built*, according to Cy, *right here in Canada*! For one brief moment while all these symbols of who we were went marching past, the two communities—one on either side of Yonge Street—were united in a surge of cheering and applause. But after the King and Queen were gone, the ribbon of Yonge Street divided us again. It rained.

Now, Cy and Rita were arguing over the remnants in the soufflé dish. Cy held the classic belief that what was in the dish was his by virtue of his being the eldest child. He also held the classic belief that girls were meant to be second in everything. Rita, who was always hungry but never seemed to gain an ounce, held none of these beliefs and was capable of fighting Cy for hours on end when our parents weren't present. With Mother at the table, however, the argument was silenced by her announcement that the soufflé dish and all the delicious bits of cheese and egg that clung to its sides would be set aside for our father.

Then—or shortly thereafter—our father did indeed arrive, but he said he wasn't hungry and he wanted to be left alone with Mother.

In half an hour the children were called from the kitchen where we had been do-ing the dishes and scooping up the remains of the meal. I—the child my mother called *The Rabbit*—had been emptying the salad bowl, stuffing my mouth with let-tuce, tomatoes and onion shards and nearly choking in the process. We all went into the sitting-room with food on our lips and tea towels in our hands: Father's three lit-tle Maxes—Cy and Rita and Ben. He looked at us then, as he always did, with a measure of pride he could never hide and a false composure that kept his lips from smiling, but not his eyes. I look back now on that moment with some alarm when I realize my father was only twenty-seven years old—an age I have long survived and doubled.

'Children, I have joined the army,' he said—in his formal way, as if we were his customers. 'I am going to be a soldier.'

Our mother had been weeping before we entered the room, but she had dried her eyes because she never allowed us to witness her tears. Now, she was smiling and si-lent. After a moment, she left the room and went out through the kitchen into the garden where, in the twilight, she found her favourite place and sat in a deck-chair amidst the flowers.

Cy, for his part, crowed with delight and yelled with excitement. He wanted to know if the war would last until he was a man and could join our father at the front.

Father, I remember, told him the war had not yet begun and the reason for his en-listment was precisely so that Cy and I could not be soldiers. 'There will be no need for that,' he said.

Cy was immensely disappointed. He begged our father to make the war go on till 1948, when he would be eighteen.

Our father only laughed at that.

'The war,' he said, 'will be over in 1940.'

I went out then and found our mother in the garden.

'What will happen to us while he's away?' I asked.

'Nothing,' she said. And then she said: 'come here.'

I went and leaned against her thigh and she put her arm around my shoulder and I could smell the roses somewhere behind us. It was getting dark.

'Look up there,' she said. 'The stars are coming out. Why don't you count them?'

This was her way of distracting me whenever my questions got out of hand. Either she told me to count the stars or go outside and dig for China. *There's a shovel in the shed*, she would tell me. *You get started and I will join you.* Just as if we would be in China and back by suppertime.

But that night in August, 1939, I wasn't prepared to bite. I didn't want to dig for China and I didn't want to count the stars. I'd dug for China so many times and had so many holes in the yard that I knew I would never arrive; it was much too far and, somehow, she was making a fool of me. As for the stars: 'I counted them last night,' I told her. 'And the night before.'

'Oh?' she said—and I felt her body tense, though she went on trying to inject a sense of ease when she spoke. 'So tell me,' she said. 'How many are there?'

'Twelve,' I said.

'Ah,' she said. And sighed. 'Just twelve. I thought there might be more than twelve.'

'I mean twelve zillion,' I said with great authority.

'Oh,' she said. 'I see. And you counted them all?'

'Unh-hunh.'

For a moment she was quiet. And then she said: 'what about that one there?'

One week later, the war began. But my father had already gone.

On the 14th of February, 1943, my father was returned. He came back home from the war. He did this on a Sunday and I recall the hush that fell upon our house, as indeed it seemed to have fallen over all the city. Only the sparrows out in the trees made sound.

We had gone downtown to the Exhibition Grounds to meet him. The journey on the streetcar took us over an hour, but Mother had splurged and hired a car and driver to take us all home. The car, I remember, embarrassed me. I was afraid some friend would see me being driven—sitting up behind a chauffeur.

A notice had come that told us the families of all returning soldiers would be permitted to witness their arrival. I suspect the building they used for this was the one now used to house the Royal Winter Fair and other equestrian events. I don't remember what it was called and I'm not inclined to inquire. It was enough that I was there that once—and once remains enough.

We sat in the bleachers, Cy and Rita and Mother and me, and there was a railing holding us back. There must have been over a thousand people waiting to catch a glimpse of someone they loved—all of them parents, children or wives of the men returning. I was eight years old that February—almost nine and feeling I would never get there. Time was like a field of clay and all the other children I knew appeared to have cleared it in a single bound while I was stuck in the mud and barely able to lift my feet. I hated being eight and dreaded being nine. I wanted to be ten—the only dignified age a child could be, it seemed to me. Cy, at ten, had found a kind of silence I admired to the point of worship. Rita, who in fact was ten that year and soon to be eleven, had also found a world of silence in which she kept herself secreted—often behind closed doors. Silence was a sign of valour.

The occasion was barely one for public rejoicing. The men who were coming home were mostly casualties whose wounds, we had been warned, could be distressing and whose spirit, we had equally been warned, had been damaged in long months of painful recuperation. Plainly, it was our job to lift their spirits and to deny the severity of their wounds. Above all else, they must not be allowed to feel they could not rejoin society at large. A man with no face must not be stared at.

Our father's wounds were greater by far than we had been told. There was not a mark on his body, but—far inside—he had been destroyed. His mind had been severely damaged and his spirit had been broken. No one had told me what this might have made of him. No one had said *he may never be kind again.* No one had said *he will never sleep again without the aid of alcohol.* No one had said *he will try to kill your mother.* No one had said *you will not be sure it's him when you see him.* Yet all these things were true.

I had never seen a military parade without a band. The effect was eerie and upsetting. Two or three officers came forward into the centre of the oval. Somebody started shouting commands and a sergeant-major, who could not yet be seen, was heard outside the building counting off the steps.

I wanted drums. I wanted bugles. Surely this ghostly, implacable sound of marching feet in the deadening sand was just a prelude to everyone's standing up and cheering and the music blaring forth. But, no. We all stood up, it is true, the minute the first of the columns rounded the wooden corner of the bleachers and came into sight. But no one uttered a sound. One or two people threw their hands up over their mouths—as if to stifle cries—but most of us simply stood there—staring in disbelief.

Nurses came with some of the men, supporting them. Everyone was pale in the awful light—and the colours of their wounds and bruises were garish and quite unreal. There was a predominance of yellow flesh and dark maroon scars and of purple welts and blackened scabs. Some men wore bandages—some wore casts and slings. Others used canes and crutches to support themselves. A few had been the victims of fire, and these wore tight, blue skull-caps and collarless shirts and their faces and other areas of uncovered skin were bright with shining ointments and dressings.

It took a very great while for all these men and women—perhaps as many as two hundred of them—to arrive inside the building and make their way into the oval. They were being lined up in order of columns—several long lines, and each line punctuated here and there with attendant nurses. The voices of the sergeant-major and of the adjutant who was taking the parade were swallowed up in the dead acoustics, and—far above us—pigeons and sparrows moved among the girders and beams that supported the roof. I still had not seen Father.

At last, because my panic was spreading out of control, I tugged my mother's elbow and whispered that I couldn't see him. Had there been a mistake and he wasn't coming at all?

'No,' she told me—looking down at me sideways and turning my head with her ungloved fingers. 'There he is, there,' she said. 'But don't say anything, yet. He may not know we're here.'

My father's figure could only be told because of his remarkable height. He was six feet four and had always been, to me, a giant. But now his height seemed barely greater than the height of half a dozen other men who were gathered out in the sand. His head was bowed, though once or twice he lifted his chin when he heard the commands. His shoulders, no longer squared, were rounded forward and dipping towards his centre. His neck was so thin I thought that someone or something must have cut over half of it away. I studied him solemnly and then looked up at my mother.

She had closed her eyes against him because she could not bear to look.

Later on that night, when everyone had gone to bed but none of us had gone to sleep, I said to Cy: 'what is it?'

'What?'

'That's happened to Dad. . . .'

Cy didn't answer for a moment and then he said: 'Dieppe.'

I didn't understand. I thought it was a new disease.

We were told the next day not to mention at school that our father had come back home. Nothing was said about why it must be kept a secret. That was a bitter disappointment. Other children whose fathers had returned from overseas were always the centre of attention. Teachers, beaming smiles and patting heads, would congratulate them just as if they had won a prize. Classmates pestered them with questions: *what does he look like? Have you seen his wounds? How many Germans did he kill?*

But we had none of this. All we got was: *what did you do on the weekend?*
Nothing.

All day Monday, Father remained upstairs. Our parents' bedroom was on the second floor directly over the sitting-room. Also, directly underneath the bedroom occupied by Cy and me. We had heard our mother's voice long into the night, apparently soothing him, telling him over and over again that everything was going to be all right.

We could not make out her words, but the tone of her voice was familiar. Over time, she had sat with each of us, deploying her comforts in all the same cadences and phrases, assuring us that pains and aches and sicknesses would pass.

Because we could not afford to lose the sale of even one flower, neither the single rose bought once a week by Edna Holmes to cheer her ailing sister, nor the daily boutonnière of Colonel Matheson—our mother had persuaded Mrs Adams, the grocer's wife, to tend the store while she 'nipped home' once every hour to see to Father's needs. It was only later that we children realized what those needs entailed. He was drinking more or less constantly in every waking hour, and our mother's purpose was first to tempt him with food—which he refused—and then to make certain that his matches and cigarettes did not set fire to the house.

On the Wednesday, Father emerged from his shell around two o'clock in the afternoon. We were all at school, of course, and I have only the account of what follows from my mother. When she returned at two, Mother found that Father had come down into the hallway, fully dressed in civilian clothes. He had already donned his greatcoat when she arrived. She told me that, at first, he had seemed to be remarkably sober. He told her he wanted to go outside and walk in the street. He wanted to go and see the store, he said.

'But you can't wear your greatcoat, David,' she told him.

'Why?'

'Because you're in civilian dress. You know that's not allowed. A man was arrested just last week.'

'I wasn't here last week,' said my father.

'Nevertheless,' my mother told him, 'this man was arrested because it is not allowed.'

'But I'm a soldier!' my father yelled.

My mother had to play this scene with all the care and cunning she could muster. The man who had been arrested had been a deserter. All that winter, desertions had been increasing and there had been demonstrations of overt disloyalty. People had shouted *down with the King!* and had booed the Union Jack. There were street gangs of youths who called themselves *Zombies* and they hung around the Masonic Temple on Yonge Street and the Palais Royale at Sunnyside. Some of these young men were in uniform, members of the Home Guard: reserves who had been promised, on joining up, they would not be sent overseas. They may have disapproved of the war, but they did not disapprove of fighting. They waited outside the dancehalls, excessively defensive of their manhood, challenging the servicemen who were dancing inside to *come out fighting and show us your guts!* Men had been killed in such encounters and the encounters had been increasing. The government was absolutely determined to stamp these incidents out before they spread across the country. These were the darkest hours of the war and morale, both in and out of the Forces, was at its lowest ebb. If my father had appeared on the street with his military greatcoat worn over his civilian clothes, it would have been assumed he was a *Zombie* or a deserter and he would have been arrested instantly. Our neighbours would have turned him in, no matter who he was. Our patriotism had come to that.

'I don't have a civilian overcoat,' my father said. 'And don't suggest that I put on my uniform, because I won't. My uniform stinks of sweat and I hate it.'

'Well, you aren't going out like that,' my mother said. 'That's all there is to it. Why not come to the kitchen and I'll fix you a sandwich. . . .'

'I don't want a goddamned sandwich,' my father yelled at her. 'I want to see the store!'

At this point, he tore off his greatcoat and flung it onto the stairs. And then, before my mother could prevent him, he was out the door and running down the steps.

My mother—dressed in her green shop apron and nothing but a scarf to warm her—raced out after him.

What would the neighbours think? What would the neighbours say? How could she possibly explain?

By the time she had reached the sidewalk, my father had almost reached the corner. But, when she got to Yonge Street, her fears were somewhat allayed. My father had not gone into Max's Flowers but was standing one door shy of it, staring into the butcher's window.

'What's going on here?' he said, as my mother came abreast of him.

Mother did not know what he meant.

'Where is Mister Schickel, Lily?' he asked her.

She had forgotten that, as well.

'Mister Schickel has left,' she told him—trying to be calm—trying to steer my father wide of the butcher's window and in towards their own front stoop.

'Left?' my father shouted. 'He's only just managed to pay off his mortgage! And who the hell is this impostor, Reilly?'

'Reilly?'

'Arthur Reilly the bloody butcher!' My father pointed at and read the sign that had replaced *Oskar Schickel, Butcher* in the window.

'Mister Reilly has been there most of the winter, David. Didn't I write and tell you that?' She knew very well she hadn't.

My father blinked at the meagre cuts of rationed meat displayed beyond the glass and said: 'what happened to Oskar, Lily? Tell me.'

And so, she had to tell him, like it or not.

Mister Schickel's name was disagreeable—stuck up there on Yonge Street across from Rosedale—and someone from Park Road had thrown a stone through the window.

There. It was said.

'But Oskar wasn't a German,' my father whispered. 'He was a Canadian.'

'But his name was German, David.'

My father put his fingers against the glass and did not appear to respond to what my mother had said.

At last, my mother pulled at his arm. 'Why not come back home,' she said. 'You can come and see the shop tomorrow.'

My father, while my mother watched him, concentrated very hard and moved his finger over the dusty glass of Oskar Schickel's store.

'What are you doing, David?'

'Nothing,' said my father. 'Setting things right, that's all.'

Then he stepped back and said to her: 'now—we'll go home.'

What he had written was:

Oskar Schickel: Proprietor in absentia.

Mother said that Mrs Reilly rushed outside as soon as they had reached the corner and she washed the window clean.

This was the only remaining decent thing my father did until the day he died.

The rest was all a nightmare.

I had never seen Dieppe. I had seen its face in photographs. I had read all the books and heard all the stories. The battle, of which my father had been a victim, had taken place in August of 1942—roughly six months before he was returned to us. Long since then, in my adult years, I have seen that battle, or seen its parts, through the medium of documentary film. It was only after Cy and Rita had vetted these films that I was able to watch. Till then, I had been afraid I would catch my father's image unawares—fearful that somehow our eyes would meet in that worst of moments. I couldn't bear the thought of seeing him destroyed. So, I had seen all this—the photographs, the books, the films—but I had never seen the town of Dieppe itself until that day in May of 1987 when I took my father's ashes there to scatter them.

Before I can begin this ending, I have to make it clear that the last thing I want to provoke is the sentimental image of a wind-blown stretch of rocky beach with a rainbow of ashes arching over the stones and blowing out to sea. If you want that image, let me tell you that had been the way it was when Cy, my brother, and Rita, my sister, and I went walking, wading into the ocean south of Lunenburg, Nova Scotia—where our mother had been born—to cast her ashes into the air above the Atlantic. Then there was almost music and we rejoiced because our mother had finally gained her freedom from a life that had become intolerable. But in Dieppe, when I shook my father's ashes out of their envelope, there was no rejoicing. None.

I felt, in fact, as if I had brought the body of an infidel into a holy place and laid it down amongst the true believers. Still, this was what my father had wanted—and how could I refuse him? Neither Cy nor Rita would do it for him. *Gone*, they had said. *Good riddance.*

And so it fell to me.

I was always the least informed. I was always the most inquisitive. During my childhood, nobody told me—aside from the single word *Dieppe*—what it was that had happened to my father. And yet, perhaps because I knew the least and because I was the youngest and seemed the most naïve and willing, it was more than often me he focused on.

His tirades would begin in silence—the silence we had been warned of when he first returned. He would sit at the head of the table, eating a piece of fish and drinking from a glass of beer. The beer was always dark in colour. Gold.

Our dining-room had a window facing west. Consequently, winter sunsets in particular got in his eyes.

Curtain, he would say at his plate—and jab his fork at me.

If I didn't understand because his mouth was full, my mother would reach my sleeve and pull it with her fingers. *The curtain, Ben*, she would say. *Your father's eyes.*

Yes, ma'am. Down I'd get and pull the curtain.

Then, no sooner would I be reseated than my father—still addressing his plate—would mumble *lights.* And I would rise and turn on the lights. Then, when I was back at last in my chair, he would look at me and say, without apparent rancour, *why don't you tell me to shove the goddamn curtain up my ass?*

You will understand my silence in response to this if you understand that—before he went away—the worst my father had ever said in our presence had been *damn* and *hell.* The ultimate worst had been *Christ!* when he'd nearly sliced his finger off with a knife. Then, however, he hadn't known that anyone was listening. And so, when he started to talk this way—and perhaps especially at table—it paralyzed me.

Cy or Mother would sometimes attempt to intervene, but he always cut them off with something worse than he'd said to me. Then he would turn his attention back in my direction and continue. He urged me to refuse his order, then to upbraid him, finally to openly defy him—call him the worst of the words he could put in my mouth and hit him. Of course, I never did any of these things, but the urging, the cajoling and ultimately the begging never ceased.

One night, he came into the bedroom where I slept in the bunk-bed over Cy and he shouted at me *why don't you fight back?* Then he dragged my covers off and threw me onto the floor against the bureau. All this was done in the dark, and after my mother had driven me down in the truck to the Emergency Ward of Wellesley Hospital, the doctors told her that my collar-bone was broken. I heard my mother saying *yes, he fell out of bed.*

Everyone—even I—conspired to protect him. The trouble was, my father had no wish to protect himself. At least, it seemed that way until a fellow veteran of Dieppe turned up one day in the shop and my father turned on him with a pair of garden shears and tried to drive him back onto Yonge Street. Far from being afraid of my father, the other man took off his jacket and threw it in my father's face and all the while he stood there, the man was yelling at my father: *Coward! Coward! Yellow Bastard!*

Then, he turned around and walked away. The victor.

Thinking for sure the police would come, my mother drew the blind and closed the shop for the rest of the day.

But that was not the end of it. She gathered us together out on the porch and Cy was told to open a can of pork and beans and to make what our mother called a *passel of toast.* He and Rita and I were to eat this meal in the kitchen, after which Cy, who'd been handed a dollar bill my mother had lifted from the till, was to take us down to the Uptown Theatre where an Abbott and Costello film was playing. All these ordinary things we did. Nonetheless, we knew that our father had gone mad.

It was summer then and when the movie was over, I remember Cy and Rita and I stood on the street and the sidewalks gave off heat and the air around us smelled of peanuts and popcorn and Cy said: 'I don't think it's safe to go home just yet.' For almost an hour, we wandered on Yonge Street, debating what we should do and, at last, we decided we would test the waters by going and looking at the house and listening to see if there was any yelling.

Gibson Avenue only has about twenty houses, most of them semi-detached—and all of them facing south and the park. The porches and the stoops that night were filled with our neighbours drinking beer from coffee cups and fanning themselves with paper plates and folded bits of the *Daily Star.* They were drinking out of cups—you could smell the beer—because the law back then forbade the public consumption, under any circumstance, of alcohol. Whatever you can hide does not exist.

Passing, we watched our neighbours watching us—the Matlocks and the Wheelers and the Conrads and the Bolts—and we knew they were thinking *there go the Max kids and David Max, their father, tried to kill a man today in his store with gardening shears. . . .*

'Hello, Cy.'

'Hello.'

'Ben. Rita.'

'Hi.'

'Good-night. . .'

We went and stood together on the sidewalk out in front of our house.

Inside, everything seemed to be calm and normal. The lights were turned on in their usual distribution—most of them downstairs. The radio was playing. Someone was singing *Praise the Lord and Pass the Ammunition.*

Cy went up the steps and turned the handle. He was brave—but I'd always known that. Rita and I were told to wait on the porch.

Two minutes passed—or five—or ten—and finally Cy returned. He was very white and his voice was dry, but he wasn't shaking and all he said was: 'you'd best come in. I'm calling the police.'

Our father had tried to kill our mother with a hammer. She was lying on the sofa and her hands were broken because she had used them trying to fend off the blows.

Father had disappeared. The next day, he turned himself in because, as he told the doctors, he had come to his senses. He was kept for a year and a half—almost until the war was over—at the Asylum for the Insane on Queen Street. None of us children was allowed to visit him there—but our mother went to see him six months after he had been committed. She told me they sat in a long, grey room with bars on all the windows. My father wore a dressing gown and hadn't shaved. Mother said he couldn't look her in the eyes. She told him that she forgave him for what he had done. But my father never forgave himself. My mother said she never saw his eyes again.

Two weeks after our father had tried to kill our mother, a brick was thrown through the window of Max's Flowers. On the brick, a single word was printed in yellow chalk.

Murderer.

Mother said: 'there's no way around this, now. I'm going to have to explain.'

That was how we discovered what had gone wrong with our father at Dieppe.

Our mother had known this all along, and I still have strong suspicions Cy had found it out and maybe Rita before our mother went through the formal procedure of sitting us down and telling us all together. Maybe they had thought I was just too young to understand. Maybe Cy and maybe Rita hadn't known. Maybe they had only guessed. At any rate, I had a very strong sense that I was the only one who received our mother's news in a state of shock.

Father had risen, since his enlistment in 1939, all the way up from an NCO to the rank of captain. Everyone had adored him in the army. He was what they called a natural leader. His men were particularly fond of him and they would, as the saying goes, have followed him anywhere. Then came Dieppe. All but a handful of those who went into battle there were Canadians. This was our Waterloo. Our Gettysburg.

There isn't a single history book you can read—there isn't a single man who was there who won't tell you—there isn't a single scrap of evidence in any archive to suggest that the battle of Dieppe was anything but a total and appalling disaster. Most have called it a slaughter.

Dieppe is a port and market town on the coast of Normandy in northern France. In 1942, the British High Command had chosen it to be the object of a practice raid in preparation for the invasion of Europe. The Allies on every front were faltering, then. A gesture was needed, and even the smallest of victories would do.

And so, on the 19th of August, 1942, the raid on Dieppe had taken place—and the consequent carnage had cost the lives of over a thousand Canadians. Over two thousand were wounded or taken prisoner. Five thousand set out; just over one thousand came back.

My father never left his landing craft.

He was to have led his men ashore in the second wave of troops to follow the tanks—but, seeing the tanks immobilized, unable to move because the beaches were made of stone and the stones had jammed the tank tracks—and seeing the evident massacre of the first wave of troops whose attempt at storming the shore had been repulsed by machine-gun fire from the cliffs above the town—my father froze in his place and could not move. His men—it is all too apparent—did not know what to do. They had received no order to advance and yet, if they stayed, they were sitting ducks.

In the end, though a handful escaped by rushing forward into the water, the rest were blown to pieces when their landing craft was shelled. In the meantime, my father had recovered enough of his wits to crawl back over the end of the landing craft, strip off his uniform and swim out to sea where he was taken on board a British destroyer sitting offshore.

The destroyer, H.M.S. *Berkley*, was ultimately hit and everyone on board, including my father—no one knowing who he was—was transferred to another ship before the *Berkley* was scuttled where she sat. My father made it all the way back to England, where his burns and wounds were dressed and where he debated taking advantage of the chaos to disappear, hoping that, in the long run, he would be counted among the dead.

His problem was, his conscience had survived. He stayed and, as a consequence, he was confronted by survivors who knew his story. He was dishonourably discharged and sent home to us. Children don't understand such things. The only cowards they recognize are figures cut from comic books or seen on movie screens.

Fathers cannot be cowards.

It is impossible.

*

His torment and his grief were to lead my father all the way to the grave. He left our mother, in the long run, though she would not have wished him to do so and he lived out his days in little bars and back-street beer parlours, seeking whatever solace he could find with whores and derelicts whose stories might have matched his own. The phone would ring and we would dread it. Either it was him or news of him—either his drunken harangue or the name of his most recent jail.

He died in the Wellesley Hospital, the place where I was born—and when he was dying he asked to see his children. Cy and Rita 'could not be reached,' but I was found—where he'd always found me—sitting within yelling distance. Perhaps this sounds familiar to other children—of whatever age—whose parents, whether one of them or both of them, have made the mistake of losing faith too soon in their children's need to love.

I would have loved a stone.

If only he had known.

He sensed it, maybe, in the end. He told me he was sorry for everything—and meant it. He told me the names of all his men and he said he had walked with them all through hell, long since their deaths, to do them honour. He hoped they would understand him, now.

I said they might.

He asked if his ashes could be put with theirs.

Why not, I thought. *A stone among stones.*

The beaches at Dieppe can throw you off balance. The angle at which they slope into the water is both steep and dangerous. At high tide you can slide into the waves and lose your footing before you've remembered how to swim. The stones are treacherous. But they are also beautiful.

My father's ashes were contraband. You can't just walk about with someone's remains, in whatever form, in your suitcase. Stepping off the *Sealink* ferry, I carried my father in an envelope addressed to myself in Canada. This was only in case I was challenged. There was hardly more than a handful of him there. I had thrown the rest of him into the English Channel as the coast of Normandy was coming into view. It had been somewhat more than disconcerting to see the interest his ashes caused amongst the gulls and other sea birds. I had hoped to dispose of him in a private way, unnoticed. But a woman with two small children came and stood beside me at the railing and I heard her explain that *this nice gentleman is taking care of our feathered friends*. I hoped that, if my father was watching, he could laugh. I had to look away.

The ferry arrived in the early afternoon and—once I had booked myself into La Présidence Hotel—I went for a walk along the promenade above the sea-wall. It being May, the offshore breeze was warm and filled with the faintest scent of apple trees in bloom.

I didn't want to relive the battle. I hadn't come to conjure ghosts. But the ghosts and the battle are palpable around you there, no matter what your wishes are. The sound of the tide rolling back across the stones is all the cue you need to be reminded of that summer day in 1942. I stood that evening, resting my arms along the wall and thinking *at last, my father has come ashore.*

In the morning, before the town awoke, I got up in the dark and was on the beach when the sun rose inland beyond the cliffs. I wore a thick woollen sweater, walking shorts and a pair of running shoes. The envelope was in my pocket.

The concierge must have thought I was just another crazy North American off on my morning run. He grunted as I passed and I pretended not to know that he was there. Out on the beach, I clambered over retaining walls and petrified driftwood until I felt I was safely beyond the range of prying eyes.

The stones at Dieppe are mostly flint—and their colours range from white through yellow to red. The red stones look as if they have been washed in blood and the sight of them takes your breath away. I hunkered down above them, holding all that remained of my father in my fist. He felt like a powdered stone—pummelled and broken.

I let him down between my fingers, feeling him turn to paste—watching him divide and disappear.

He is dead and he is gone.

Weekends, our parents used to take us walking under the trees on Crescent Road. This was on the Rosedale side of Yonge Street. My brother Cy and I were always dressed in dark blue suits whose rough wool shorts would chafe against our thighs. Our knee socks—also blue—were turned down over thick elastic garters. Everything itched and smelled of Sunday. Cy had cleats on his shoes because he walked in such a way as to wear his heels *to the bone*, as my mother said—and causing much expense. The cleats made a wondrous clicking noise and you could always hear him coming. I wanted cleats, but I was refused because, no matter how I tried, I couldn't walk like that.

The houses sat up neat as pins beyond their lawns—blank-eyed windows, steaming chimneys—havens of wealth and all the mysteries of wealth.

Father often walked behind us. I don't know why. Mother walked in front with Rita. Rita always wore a dress that was either red or blue beneath her princess coat and in the wintertime she wore a sort of woollen cloche that was tied with a knitted string beneath her chin. Her Mary Jane shoes were just like Shirley Temple's shoes—which, for a while, was pleasing to Rita; then it was not. Rita always had an overpowering sense of image.

After the advent of our father's return, she said from the corner of her mouth one Sunday as we walked on Crescent Road that she and Cy and I had been named as if we were manufactured products: *Cy Max Office Equipment; Rita Max Household Appliances* and *Ben Max Watches.* This, she concluded, was why our father had always walked behind us. Proudly, he was measuring our performance. Now, he had ceased to walk behind us and our mother led us forward dressed in black.

Tick. Tick. Tick. That's me. The Ben Max Watch.

I have told our story. But I think it best—and I like it best—to end with all of us moving there beneath the trees in the years before the war. Mister and Mrs David Max out walking with their children any Sunday afternoon in any kind of weather but the rain.

Colonel Matheson, striding down his walk, is caught and forced to grunt acknowledgement that we are there. He cannot ignore us, after all. We have seen him every weekday morning, choosing his boutonnière and buying it from us.

1988

Jay Macpherson

b. 1931

Born in England, Jay Macpherson moved with her mother and brother to Newfoundland in 1940, and in 1944 to Ottawa, where she later attended Carleton College (now Carleton University), receiving her B.A. in 1951. After a year in London and a subsequent year in Montreal (completing library school at McGill University), Macpherson entered graduate school at the University of Toronto (M.A., 1955; Ph.D., 1964). She has remained at Toronto where she has been a member of the English department of Victoria College since 1954.

Macpherson's poems first appeared at the end of the forties in Alan Crawley's magazine, *Contemporary Verse*. She produced two chapbooks, *Nineteen Poems* (1952), published on the occasion of her twenty-first birthday by Robert Graves' Seizin Press, and *O Earth Return* (1954), printed by her own small press. From 1954 to 1963 Macpherson's Emblem Books published poets such as Daryl Hine, Dorothy Livesay, Alden Nowlan, and Al Purdy. In 1957 Oxford University Press published *The Boatman*, her best-known book and winner of a Governor General's Award, which incorporated new poems and much of her earlier poetry into a complex, unified work. For the next decade Macpherson wrote little new poetry, although she published a textbook for young readers on Greek mythology, *Four Ages of Man* (1962), and added sixteen new poems to be included with her earlier book when it was republished as *The Boatman and Other Poems* (1968). In 1974 she completed and published privately a new sequence of poems, *Welcoming Disaster*, which is simpler and more colloquial in style than *The Boatman*. *Poems Twice Told* (1981) reprints *The Boatman and Other Poems* and *Welcoming Disaster* in one volume. In 1982 she published a scholarly work, *The Spirit of Solitude: Conventions and Continuities in Late Romance*.

Macpherson, who has been strongly influenced by Northrop Frye, is one of several poets of the fifties who began an extensive exploration of myth. Her poetry is central to that of the 'mythopoeic school', which includes the writing of James Reaney and the early work of Irving Layton and Eli Mandel. Like the poems of Yeats and of A.J.M. Smith, it exists at the pole of modernism opposite to that in which realism, documentation, and repertorial accuracy are valued. *The Boatman* in particular represents the antithesis of the experiential poetics exemplified by Raymond Souster and Louis Dudek. In James Reaney's words, 'The situations, the beings, the speakers are all gloriously artificial like the themes of Bach, which no "real" bird, no "real" train whistle could imitate or has ever imitated. Artifice is a theme as well as a feature of Macpherson's poetry' (*Canadian Literature*, 3, 1960). *The Boatman* is constructed around the myth of Noah and his ark: Noah, builder and preserver, is an allegorical representation of the artist (the creative aspect of man) and the ark is his work of art. Art is presented as not simply an imitation of the world but a reflection of the ideal as well as the real, epitomizing an eternity that contains both Eden and Sodom, the serpent and the seraph. In *The Boatman*, Macpherson is making both a philosophical and theological statement: man, by creating a microcosm within himself, can hold the macrocosm of the universe.

The sequence of poems in *Welcoming Disaster* concerns a narrator who, psychologically paralyzed, makes use of images garnered from horror films to guide her on a descent (the welcomed 'disaster') into the unconscious, so that she can free the psyche into action. As the poet narrator is forced to examine her own nature, she comes to recognize familiar things and situations that have been rearranged and dislocated as they are in horror stories and dreams: they have been transformed by the individual subconscious into a personal symbolism that encompasses all aspects of self. The reader sees in the sequence a mythology of personality in which creativity gives—as it did in *The Boatman*—substance to life's emptiness.

Although these two books are complex, the individual poems of which they are composed are simple in form and diction. At the same time the poems contain resonant echoes—recalling a line or the style of a writer (such as Milton, Blake, Yeats, or Eliot) or suggesting a source (such as myth, the Bible, or nursery rhymes)—that give them great richness. The effect, as Northrop Frye observes, is that 'one has a sense of re-reading as well as reading, of meeting new poems with a recognition that is integrally and specifically linked with the rest of one's poetic experience.' (*The Bush Garden*, 1971).

From *The Boatman*[1]

The Thread

Each night I do retrace
My heavy steps and am compelled to pass
To earlier places, but take up again
The journey's turning skein.[2]

The thread Night's daughters[3] spin
Runs from birth's dark to death's, a shining line.
The snipping Fate attends its end and mine,
Ends what the two begin.

My mother gave to lead
My blind steps through the maze a daedal thread[4]   10
Who slept, who wept on Naxos now star-crowned
Reigns she whom I disowned.

The ceaseless to and from
Hushes the cry of the insatiate womb
That I wind up the journey I have come
And follow it back home.

---

[1]The sequence of seventy-nine poems that makes up *The Boatman* is divided into six parts (I. Poor Child, II. O Earth Return, III. The Plowman in Darkness, IV. The Sleepers, V. The Boatman, VI. The Fisherman). 'The Thread' is from Part I; 'The Boatman' and 'The Anagogic Man' from Part V; and 'The Fisherman'—which concludes the sequence—from Part VI.

[2]Although the principal myth used in this poem is that of Theseus, who followed a magic ball of thread into the labyrinth to kill the Minotaur and retraced his steps with the thread as a guide to escape from the maze, this stanza is also reminiscent of another escape: Aeneas's from Hades after he entered the underworld via the cave next to the lake, Avernus. In relating the Theseus myth in *Four Ages of Man*, Macpherson translates from Virgil:

  The descent to Avernus is easy: but to retrace your way and escape to the upper world, that is the difficulty. (Aeneid, *VI, 126*)

[3]The Fates—Clotho, Lachesis, and Atropos; the thread of life is spun on Clotho's spindle, measured on Lachesis' rod, and snipped by Atropos' shears.

[4]Theseus was given the magic ball of thread by Ariadne, who had received it from Daedalus. Ariadne, the daughter of King Minos and half-sister of the Minotaur, goes against her family when she helps Theseus in exchange for his pledge of marriage. Theseus, however, escapes from Crete with Ariadne, only to abandon her on the island of Naxos where she is found weeping by Dionysus, who marries her and gives her a crown that becomes the constellation Corona Borealis.

The Boatman

You might suppose it easy
For a maker not too lazy
To convert the gentle reader to an Ark:
But it takes a willing pupil
To admit both gnat and camel
—Quite an eyeful, all the crew that must embark.

After me when comes the deluge
And you're looking round for refuge
From God's anger pouring down in gush and spout,
Then you take the tender creature   10
—You remember, that's the reader—
And you pull him through his navel inside out.

That's to get his beasts outside him,
For they've got to come aboard him,
As the best directions have it, two by two.
When you've taken all their tickets
And you've marched them through his sockets,
Let the tempest bust Creation: heed not you.

For you're riding high and mighty
In a gale that's pushing ninety   20
With a solid bottom under you—that's his.
Fellow flesh affords a rampart,
And you've got along for comfort
All the world there ever shall be, was, and is.[1]

[1]A recasting of the second line of the response *Gloria Patri:*
   Glory be to the Father, and to the Son: and to the Holy Ghost.
   As it was in the beginning, is now, and ever shall be world without end. Amen.

The Anagogic[1] Man

Noah walks with head bent down;
For between his nape and crown
He carries, balancing with care,
A golden bubble round and rare.

Its gently shimmering sides surround
All us and our worlds, and bound
Art and life, and wit and sense,
Innocence and experience.

Forbear to startle him, lest some
Poor soul to its destruction come,   10
Slipped out of mind and past recall
As if it never was at all.

[1]Literally spiritual or uplifted; in *Anatomy of Criticism* (1957) Frye writes 'On the anagogic level,
man is the container of nature . . . Nature is now inside the mind of an infinite man . . .'; in the interpretation of allegory, the universal level.

O you that pass, if still he seems
One absent-minded or in dreams,
Consider that your senses keep
A death far deeper than his sleep.

Angel, declare: what sways when Noah nods?
The sun, the stars, the figures of the gods.

The Fisherman

The world was first a private park
Until the angel,[1] after dark,
Scattered afar to wests and easts
The lovers and the friendly beasts.

And later still a home-made boat
Contained Creation set afloat,
No rift nor leak that might betray
The creatures to a hostile day.

But now beside the midnight lake
One single fisher[2] sits awake   10
And casts and fights and hauls to land
A myriad forms upon the sand.

Old Adam on the naming-day
Blessed each and let it slip away:
The fisher of the fallen mind
Sees no occasion to be kind,

But on his catch proceeds to sup;
Then bends, and at one slurp sucks up
The lake and all that therein is
To slake that hungry gut of his,   20

Then whistling makes for home and bed
As the last morning breaks in red;
But God the Lord with patient grin
Lets down his hook and hoicks[3] him in.

1957

[1]Traditionally it is believed that the archangel Michael drove Adam and Eve from the Garden of Eden.
[2]See Matthew 4:18-20 and Mark 1:16-17 for Christ's description of the apostles as fishers of men. The fisherman in Macpherson's poetry is also associated with the Fisher King, the sacred mythic ruler who fishes to sustain the life of his kingdom. Usually the fish provide wisdom as well as sustenance. The myth's most familiar manifestation is in the Grail legend contained in the King Arthur narratives. For further information, see Jessie L. Weston's *From Ritual to Romance* (1920).
[3]Yanks up.

A Lost Soul

Some are plain lucky—we ourselves among them:
Houses with books, with gardens, all we wanted,
Work we enjoy, with colleagues we feel close to—
    Love we have, even:

True love and candid, faithful, strong as gospel,
Patient, untiring, fond when we are fretful.
Having so much, how is it that we ache for
    Those darker others?

Some days for them we could let slip the whole damn
Soft bed we've made ourselves, our friends in Heaven   10
Let slip away, buy back with blood our ancient
    Vampires and demons.

First loves and oldest, what names shall I call you?
Older to me than language, old as breathing,
Born with me, in this flesh: by now I know you're
    Greed, pride and envy.

Too long I've shut you out, denied acquaintance,
Favoured less barefaced vices, hoped to pass for
Reasonable, rate with those who are more inclined to
    Self-hurt than murder.   20

You were my soul: in arrogance I banned you.
Now I recant—return, possess me, take my
Hands, bind my eyes, infallibly restore my
    Share in perdition.

1974

Alice Munro

b. 1931

Alice Munro has divided her life between two regions of Canada. Born Alice Laidlaw, she grew up in Wingham, Ont., and at nineteen moved to nearby London to attend the University of Western Ontario. After two years there she married Bill Munro and with him settled in British Columbia. She lived in Vancouver and Victoria for more than twenty years, writing, helping her husband manage a bookstore, and raising three daughters. In 1972 she returned to western Ontario; she now lives in Clinton, not far from Wingham, with her second husband.

Munro began writing early—her first published work appeared in UWO's undergraduate literary magazine in 1950—but it was only in 1961, when she wrote 'The Red Dress, 1946', that she found her real voice. A slow and meticulous craftsman, she did not publish her first collection of stories, *Dance of the Happy Shades*, until 1968. This book signalled the advent of a major new short-story writer and won her a Governor General's Award for fiction. (She received a second in 1978.) As well as four more collections of short fiction, *Something I've Been Meaning to Tell You* (1974), *The Moons of Jupiter* (1982), *The Progress of Love* (1986), and *Friend of My Youth* (1990), Munro has published two linked story-sequences sometimes described as novels: *Lives of Girls and Women* (1971) and *Who Do You Think You Are?* (1978). Most of Munro's new stories—like those of Mavis Gallant—appear first in *The New Yorker*.

Munro's narrative structures are frequently developed through the use of oppositions, which may take the form of contrasting characters (such as Et and Char in 'Something I've Been Meaning to Tell You'), the balancing of the 'female' world against the 'male', or the playing off of *then* against *now*. This last opposition, one of the most prominent features of Munro's writing, gives her stories a complex movement back and forth across time that reproduces the movement of the mind in its act of recovering and reassessing the past. Indeed, Munro sees fiction as something to move around in,

even to live in. She says that her conception of the story can be explained by how she reads stories written by other people:

I can start reading anywhere; from beginning to end, from end to beginning, from any point in between in either direction. So obviously I don't take up a story and follow it as if it were a road, taking me somewhere, with views and neat diversions along the way. I go into it, and move back and forth and settle here and there, and stay in it for a while. It's more like a house. (Making It New: Contemporary Canadian Stories, *edited by John Metcalf, 1982*)

Munro furnishes her fictional 'houses' meticulously. A regionalist, she usually sets her stories in small-town Ontario, working with material she knows personally and evoking fully realized milieus. At the same time, beneath the ordinariness of the world she creates, disaster often lurks (or is longed for) and many secrets are glimpsed but remain untold. Munro once remarked in an interview with Jill Gardiner:

. . . the whole act of writing is more an attempt at recognition than of understanding, because I don't understand many things. I feel a kind of satisfaction in just approaching something that is mysterious and important. . . . I believe that we don't solve these things—in fact our explanations take us further away. (M.A. thesis, University of New Brunswick).

Munro's stories often emphasize uncertainty. For example, in 'Something I've Been Meaning to Tell You', Et—the character through whose consciousness the events are filtered—seems both compelled to tell her story and yet unable or unwilling to tell it all. ('She could not tell . . .' begins the second sentence, suggesting a limitation both in her understanding and in her articulation.) In a Munro story what is unsaid or omitted is often as important as what we are told; these narratives resist giving up their mysteries and challenge the reader to look carefully beneath their surfaces.

Something I've Been Meaning To Tell You

'Anyway he knows how to fascinate the women,' said Et to Char. She could not tell if Char went paler, hearing this, because Char was pale in the first place as anybody could get. She was like a ghost now, with her hair gone white. But still beautiful, she couldn't lose it.

'No matter to him the age or the size,' Et pressed on. 'It's natural to him as breathing, I guess. I only hope the poor things aren't taken in by it.'

'I wouldn't worry,' Char said.

The day before, Et had taken Blaikie Noble up on his invitation to go along on one of his tours and listen to his spiel. Char was asked too, but of course she didn't go. Blaikie Noble ran a bus. The bottom part of it was painted red and the top part was striped, to give the effect of an awning. On the side was painted: LAKESHORE TOURS, INDIAN GRAVES, LIMESTONE GARDENS, MILLIONAIRE'S MANSION, BLAIKIE NOBLE, DRIVER, GUIDE. Blaikie had a room at the hotel, and he also worked on the grounds, with one helper, cutting grass and clipping hedges and digging the borders. What a comedown, Et had said at the beginning of the summer when they first found out he was back. She and Char had known him in the old days.

So Et found herself squeezed into his bus with a lot of strangers, though before the afternoon was over she had made friends with a number of them and had a couple of promises of jackets needing letting out, as if she didn't have enough to do already. That was beside the point, the thing on her mind was watching Blaikie.

And what did he have to show? A few mounds with grass growing on them, covering dead Indians, a plot full of odd-shaped, grayish-white, dismal-looking limestone things—far-fetched imitations of plants (there could be the cemetery, if that was what you wanted)—and an old monstrosity of a house built with liquor money. He made the most of it. A historical discourse on the Indians, then a scientific discourse on the Limestone. Et had no way of knowing how much of it was true. Arthur would know. But Arthur wasn't there; there was nobody there but silly women, hoping to walk beside Blaikie to and from the sights, chat with him over their tea in the Limestone Pavilion, looking forward to having his strong hand under their elbows, the other hand brushing somewhere around the waist, when he helped them down off the bus ('I'm not a tourist,' Et whispered sharply when he tried it on her).

He told them the house was haunted. The first Et had ever heard of it, living ten miles away all her life. A woman had killed her husband, the son of the millionaire, at least it was believed she had killed him.

'How?' cried some lady, thrilled out of her wits.

'Ah, the ladies are always anxious to know the means,' said Blaikie, in a voice like cream, scornful and loving. 'It was a slow—poison. Or that's what they said. This is all hearsay, all local gossip.' (*Local my foot,* said Et to herself.) 'She didn't appreciate his lady friends. The wife didn't. No.'

He told them the ghost walked up and down in the garden, between two rows of blue spruce. It was not the murdered man who walked, but the wife, regretting. Blaikie smiled ruefully at the busload. At first Et had thought his attentions were all false, an ordinary commercial flirtation, to give them their money's worth. But gradually she was getting a different notion. He bent to each woman he talked to—it didn't matter how fat or scrawny or silly she was—as if there was one thing in her he would like to find. He had a gentle and laughing but ultimately serious, narrowing look (was that the look men finally had when they made love, that Et would never see?) that made him seem to want to be a deep-sea diver diving down, down through all the emptiness and cold and wreckage to discover the one thing he had set his heart on, something small and precious, hard to locate, as a ruby maybe on the ocean floor. That was a look she would like to have described to Char. No doubt Char had seen it. But did she know how freely it was being distributed?

Char and Arthur had been planning a trip that summer to see Yellowstone Park and the Grand Canyon, but they did not go. Arthur suffered a series of dizzy spells just at the end of school, and the doctor put him to bed. Several things were the matter with him. He was anemic, he had an irregular heartbeat, there was trouble with his kidneys. Et worried about leukemia. She woke at night, worrying.

'Don't be silly,' said Char serenely, 'He's overtired.'

Arthur got up in the evenings and sat in his dressing gown. Blaikie Noble came to visit. He said his room at the hotel was a hole above the kitchen, they were trying to steam-cook him. It made him appreciate the cool of the porch. They played the games that Arthur loved, schoolteacher's games. They played a geography game, and they tried to see who could make the most words out of the name Beethoven. Arthur won. He got thirty-four. He was immensely delighted.

'You'd think you'd found the Holy Grail,' Char said.

They played 'Who Am I?' Each of them had to choose somebody to be—real or imaginary, living or dead, human or animal—and the others had to try to guess it in twenty questions. Et got who Arthur was on the thirteenth question. Sir Galahad.

'I never thought you'd get it so soon.'

'I thought back to Char saying about the Holy Grail.'

'*My strength is as the strength of ten,*' said Blaikie Noble, '*Because my heart is pure.*[1] I didn't know I remembered that.'

'You should have been King Arthur,' Et said. 'King Arthur is your namesake.'

'I should have. King Arthur was married to the most beautiful woman in the world.'

'Ha,' said Et. 'We all know the end of that story.'

Char went into the living room and played the piano in the dark.

> *The flowers that bloom in the spring, tra-la,*
> *Have nothing to do with the case. . . .*[2]

---

[1] Tennyson, 'Sir Galahad'. The whole poem is about Galahad's being faithful to the quest for the Grail rather than seeking the favour of ladies. Galahad's behaviour contrasts with that of Sir Lancelot, the knight who betrays King Arthur by committing adultery with Queen Guinevere—'the end of that story' to which Et refers.

[2] From a song in Gilbert and Sullivan's *The Mikado*. The lines quoted refer to the 'case' of Nanki-Poo who, in love with Yum-Yum, is forced into an engagement with Katisha, 'a most unattractive old thing, tra-la, with a caricature of a face'.

When Et arrived, out of breath, that past June, and said, 'Guess who I saw downtown on the street?' Char, who was on her knees picking strawberries, said, 'Blaikie Noble.'

'You've seen him.'

'No,' said Char. 'I just knew. I think I knew by your voice.'

A name that had not been mentioned between them for thirty years. Et was too amazed then to think of the explanation that came to her later. Why did it need to be a surprise to Char? There was a postal service in this country, there had been all along.

'I asked him about his wife,' she said. 'The one with the dolls.' (As if Char wouldn't remember.) 'He says she died a long time ago. Not only that. He married another one and she's dead. Neither could have been rich. And where is all the Nobles' money, from the hotel?'

'We'll never know,' said Char, and ate a strawberry.

The hotel had just recently been opened up again. The Nobles had given it up in the twenties and the town had operated it for a while as a hospital. Now some people from Toronto had bought it, renovated the dining room, put in a cocktail lounge, reclaimed the lawns and garden, though the tennis court seemed to be beyond repair. There was a croquet set put out again. People came to stay in the summers, but they were not the sort of people who used to come. Retired couples. Many widows and single ladies. Nobody would have walked a block to see them get off the boat, Et thought. Not that there was a boat any more.

That first time she met Blaikie Noble on the street she had made a point of not being taken aback. He was wearing a creamy suit and his hair, that had always been bleached by the sun, was bleached for good now, white.

'Blaikie. I knew either it was you or a vanilla ice-cream cone. I bet you don't know who I am.'

'You're Et Desmond and the only thing different about you is you cut off your braids.' He kissed her forehead, nervy as always.

'So you're back visiting old haunts,' said Et, wondering who had seen that.

'Not visiting. Haunting.' He told her then how he had got wind of the hotel opening up again, and how he had been doing this sort of thing, driving tour buses, in various places, in Florida and Banff. And when she asked he told her about his two wives. He never asked was she married, taking for granted she wasn't. He never asked if Char was, till she told him.

Et remembered the first time she understood that Char was beautiful. She was looking at a picture taken of them, of Char and herself and their brother who was drowned. Et was ten in the picture, Char fourteen and Sandy seven, just a couple of weeks short of all he would ever be. Et was sitting in an armless chair and Char was behind her, arms folded on the chair-back, with Sandy in his sailor suit cross-legged on the floor—or marble terrace, you would think, with the effect made by what had been nothing but a dusty, yellowing screen, but came out in the picture a pillar and draped curtain, a scene of receding poplars and fountains. Char had pinned her front hair up for the picture and was wearing a bright blue, ankle-length silk dress—of course the color did not show—with complicated black velvet piping. She was smiling slightly, with great composure. She could have been eighteen, she could have been twenty-two. Her beauty was not of the fleshy timid sort most often featured on calendars and cigar boxes of the period, but was sharp and delicate, intolerant, challenging.

Et took a long look at this picture and then went and looked at Char, who was in the kitchen. It was washday. The woman who came to help was pulling clothes through the wringer, and their mother was sitting down resting and staring through the screen door (she never got over Sandy, nobody expected her to). Char was starching their father's collars. He had a tobacco and candy store on the Square and wore a fresh collar every day. Et was prepared to find that some metamorphosis had taken place, as in the background, but it was not so. Char, bending over the starch basin, silent and bad-humored (she hated washday, the heat and steam and flapping sheets and chugging commotion of the machine—in fact, she was not fond of any kind of housework), showed in her real face the same almost disdainful harmony as in the photograph. This made Et understand, in some not entirely welcome way, that the qualities of legend were real, that they surfaced where and when you least expected. She had almost thought beautiful women were a fictional invention. She and Char would go down to watch the people get off the excursion boat, on Sundays, walking up to the Hotel. So much white it hurt your eyes, the ladies' dresses and parasols and the men's summer suits and Panama hats, not to speak of the sun dazzling on the water and the band playing. But looking closely at those ladies, Et found fault. Coarse skin or fat behind or chicken necks or dull nests of hair, probably ratted. Et did not let anything get by her, young as she was. At school she was respected for her self-possession and her sharp tongue. She was the one to tell you if you had been at the blackboard with a hole in your stocking or a ripped hem. She was the one who imitated (but in a safe corner of the schoolyard, out of earshot, always) the teacher reading 'The Burial of Sir John Moore.'[3]

All the same it would have suited her better to have found one of those ladies beautiful, not Char. It would have been more appropriate. More suitable than Char in her wet apron with her cross expression, bent over the starch basin. Et was a person who didn't like contradictions, didn't like things out of place, didn't like mysteries or extremes.

She didn't like the bleak notoriety of having Sandy's drowning attached to her, didn't like the memory people kept of her father carrying the body up from the beach. She could be seen at twilight, in her gym bloomers, turning cartwheels on the lawn of the stricken house. She made a wry mouth, which nobody saw, one day in the park when Char said, 'That was my little brother who was drowned.'

The park overlooked the beach. They were standing there with Blaikie Noble, the hotel owner's son, who said, 'Those waves can be dangerous. Three or four years ago there was a kid drowned.'

And Char said—to give her credit, she didn't say it tragically, but almost with

---

[3]'The Burial of Sir John Moore at Corunna', written in 1816 by Charles Wolfe on an English general who died fighting the French.

amusement, that he should know so little about Mock Hill people—'That was my little brother who was drowned.'

Blaikie Noble was not any older than Char—if he had been, he would have been fighting in France—but he had not had to live all his life in Mock Hill. He did not know the real people there as well as he knew the regular guests at his father's hotel. Every winter he went with his parents to California, on the train. He had seen the Pacific surf. He had pledged allegiance to their flag. His manners were democratic, his skin was tanned. This was at a time when people were not usually tanned as a result of leisure, only work. His hair was bleached by the sun. His good looks were almost as notable as Char's but his were corrupted by charm, as hers were not.

It was the heyday of Mock Hill and all the other towns around the lakes, of all the hotels which in later years would become Sunshine Camps for city children, T.B. sanatoriums, barracks for R.A.F. training pilots in World War II. The white paint on the hotel was renewed every spring, hollowed-out logs filled with flowers were set on the railings, pots of flowers swung on chains above them. Croquet sets and wooden swings were set out on the lawns, the tennis court rolled. People who could not afford the hotel, young workingmen, shop clerks and factory girls from the city, stayed in a row of tiny cottages, joined by latticework that hid their garbage pails and communal outhouses, stretching far up the beach. Girls from Mock Hill, if they had mothers to tell them what to do, were told not to walk out there. Nobody told Char what to do, so she walked along the boardwalk in front of them in the glaring afternoon, taking Et with her for company. The cottages had no glass in their windows, they had only propped-up wooden shutters that were closed at night. From the dark holes came one or two indistinct, sad or drunk invitations, that was all. Char's looks and style did not attract men, perhaps intimidated them. All through high school in Mock Hill she had not one boy friend. Blaikie Noble was her first, if that was what he was.

What did this affair of Char's and Blaikie Noble's amount to in the summer of 1918? Et was never sure. He did not call at the house, at least not more than once or twice. He was kept busy, working at the hotel. Every afternoon he drove an open excursion wagon, with an awning on top of it, up the lakeshore road, taking people to look at the Indian graves and the limestone garden and to glimpse through the trees the Gothic stone mansion, built by a Toronto distiller and known locally as Grog Castle. He was also in charge of the variety show the hotel put on once a week, with a mixture of local talent, recruited guests, and singers and comedians brought in especially for the performance.

Late mornings seemed to be the time he and Char had. 'Come on,' Char would say, 'I have to go downtown,' and she would in fact pick up the mail and walk part way round the Square before veering off into the park. Soon Blaikie Noble would appear from the side door of the hotel and come bounding up the steep path. Sometimes he would not even bother with the path but jump over the back fence, to amaze them. None of this, the bounding or jumping, was done the way some boy from Mock Hill High School might have done it, awkwardly yet naturally. Blaikie Noble behaved like a man imitating a boy; he mocked himself but was graceful, like an actor.

'Isn't he stuck on himself?' said Et to Char, watching. The position she had taken up right away on Blaikie was that she didn't like him.

'Of course he is,' said Char.

She told Blaikie. 'Et says you're stuck on yourself.'

'What did you say?'

'I told her you had to be, nobody else is.'

Blaikie didn't mind. He had taken the position that he liked Et. He would with a quick tug loosen and destroy the arrangement of looped-up braids she wore. He told them things about the concert artists. He told them the Scottish ballad singer was a drunk and wore corsets, that the female impersonator even in his hotel room donned a blue nightgown with feathers, that the lady ventriloquist talked to her dolls—they were named Alphonse and Alicia—as if they were real people, and had them sitting up in bed one on each side of her.

'How would you know that?' Char said.

'I took her up her breakfast.'

'I thought you had maids to do that.'

'The morning after the show I do it. That's when I hand them their pay envelope and give them their walking papers. Some of them would stay all week if you didn't inform them. She sits up in bed trying to feed them bits of bacon and talking to them and doing them answering back, you'd have a fit if you could see.'

'She's cracked I guess,' Char said peacefully.

One night that summer Et woke up and remembered she had left her pink organdy dress on the line, after handwashing it. She thought she heard rain, just the first few drops. She didn't, it was just leaves rustling, but she was confused, waking up like that. She thought it was far on in the night, too, but thinking about it later she decided it might have been only around midnight. She got up and went downstairs, turned on the back kitchen light, and let herself out the back door, and standing on the stoop pulled the clothesline towards her. Then almost under her feet, from the grass right beside the stoop, where there was a big lilac bush that had grown and spread, untended, to the size of a tree, two figures lifted themselves, didn't stand or even sit up, just roused their heads as if from bed, still tangled together some way. The back kitchen light didn't shine directly out but lit the yard enough for her to see their faces. Blaikie and Char.

She never did get a look at what state their clothes were in, to see how far they had gone or were going. She wouldn't have wanted to. To see their faces was enough for her. Their mouths were big and swollen, their cheeks flattened, coarsened, their eyes holes. Et left her dress, she fled into the house and into her bed where she surprised herself by falling asleep. Char never said a word about it to her next day. All she said was, 'I brought your dress in, Et. I thought it might rain.' As if she had never seen Et out there pulling on the clothesline. Et wondered. She knew if she said, 'You saw me,' Char would probably tell her it had been a dream. She let Char think she had been fooled into believing that, if that was what Char was thinking. That way, Et was left knowing more; she was left knowing what Char looked like when she lost her powers, abdicated. Sandy drowned, with green stuff clogging his nostrils, couldn't look more lost than that.

Before Christmas the news came to Mock Hill that Blaikie Noble was married. He had married the lady ventriloquist, the one with Alphonse and Alicia. Those dolls, who wore evening dress and had sleek hairdos in the style of Vernon and Irene Castle,[4] were more clearly remembered than the lady herself. The only thing people recalled for sure about her was that she could not have been under forty. A nineteen-year-old boy. It was because he had not been brought up like other boys, had been allowed the run of the hotel, taken to California, let mix with all sorts of people. The result was depravity, and could have been predicted.

Char swallowed poison. Or what she thought was poison. It was laundry blueing. The first thing she could reach down from the shelf in the back kitchen. Et came home after school—she had heard the news at noon, from Char herself in fact, who had laughed and said, 'Wouldn't that kill you?'—and she found Char vomiting into the toilet. 'Go get the Medical Book,' Char said to her. A terrible involuntary groan came out of her. 'Read what it says about poison.' Et went instead to phone the doctor. Char came staggering out of the bathroom holding the bottle of bleach they kept behind the tub. 'If you don't put up the phone I'll drink the whole bottle,' she said in a harsh whisper. Their mother was presumably asleep behind her closed door.

Et had to hang up the phone and look in the ugly old book where she had read long ago about childbirth and signs of death, and had learned about holding a mirror to the mouth. She was under the mistaken impression that Char had been drinking from the bleach bottle already, so she read all about that. Then she found it was the blueing. Blueing was not in the book, but it seemed the best thing to do would be to induce vomiting, as the book advised for most poisons— Char was at it already, didn't need to have it induced—and then drink a quart of milk. When Char got the milk down she was sick again.

'I didn't do this on account of Blaikie Noble,' she said between spasms. 'Don't you ever think that. I wouldn't be such a fool. A pervert like him. I did it because I'm sick of living.'

'What are you sick of about living?' said Et sensibly when Char had wiped her face.

'I'm sick of this town and all the stupid people in it and Mother and her dropsy and keeping house and washing sheets every day. I don't think I'm going to vomit any more. I think I could drink some coffee. It says coffee.'

Et made a pot and Char got out two of the best cups. They began to giggle as they drank.

'I'm sick of Latin,' Et said. 'I'm sick of Algebra. I think I'll take blueing.'

'Life is a burden,' Char said. 'O Life, where is thy sting?'

'O Death. O Death, where is thy sting?'[5]

'Did I say Life? I meant Death. O Death, where is thy sting? Pardon me.'

One afternoon Et was staying with Arthur while Char shopped and changed books at the Library. She wanted to make him an eggnog, and she went searching in Char's cupboard for the nutmeg. In with the vanilla and the almond extract

[4]An American ballroom dance team, popular in 1912-17.
[5]I Corinthians 5:55: 'O death, where is thy sting? O grave, where is thy victory?'

and the artificial rum she found a small bottle of a strange liquid. *Zinc phosphide*. She read the label and turned it around in her hands. A rodenticide. Rat poison, that must mean. She had not known Char and Arthur were troubled with rats. They kept a cat, old Tom, asleep now around Arthur's feet. She unscrewed the top and sniffed at it, to know what it smelled like. Like nothing. Of course. It must taste like nothing too, or it wouldn't fool the rats.

She put it back where she had found it. She made Arthur his eggnog and took it in and watched him drink it. A slow poison. She remembered that from Blaikie's foolish story. Arthur drank with an eager noise, like a child, more to please her, she thought, than because he was so pleased himself. He would drink anything you handed him. Naturally.

'How are you these days, Arthur?'

'Oh, Et. Some days a bit stronger, and then I seem to slip back. It takes time.'

But there was none gone, the bottle seemed full. What awful nonsense. Like something you read about, Agatha Christie. She would mention it to Char and Char would tell her the reason.

'Do you want me to read to you?' she asked Arthur, and he said yes. She sat by the bed and read to him from a book about the Duke of Wellington. He had been reading it by himself but his arms got tired holding it. All those battles, and wars, and terrible things, what did Arthur know about such affairs, why was he so interested? He knew nothing. He did not know why things happened, why people could not behave sensibly. He was too good. He knew about history but not about what went on, in front of his eyes, in his house, anywhere. Et differed from Arthur in knowing that something went on, even if she could not understand why; she differed from him in knowing there were those you could not trust.

She did not say anything to Char after all. Every time she was in the house she tried to make some excuse to be alone in the kitchen, so that she could open the cupboard and stand on tiptoe and look in, to see it over the tops of the other bottles, to see that the level had not gone down. She did think maybe she was going a little strange, as old maids did; this fear of hers was like the absurd and harmless fears young girls sometimes have, that they will jump out a window, or strangle a baby, sitting in its buggy. Though it was not her own acts she was frightened of.

Et looked at Char and Blaikie and Arthur, sitting on the porch, trying to decide if they wanted to go in and put the light on and play cards. She wanted to convince herself of her silliness. Char's hair, and Blaikie's too, shone in the dark. Arthur was almost bald now and Et's own hair was thin and dark. Char and Blaikie seemed to her the same kind of animal—tall, light, powerful, with a dangerous luxuriance. They sat apart but shone out together. *Lovers*. Not a soft word, as people thought, but cruel and tearing. There was Arthur in the rocker with a quilt over his knees, foolish as something that hasn't grown its final, most necessary, skin. Yet in a way the people like Arthur were the most trouble-making of all.

'I love my love with an R, because he is ruthless. His name is Rex, and he lives in a—restaurant.'

'I love my love with an A, because he is absent-minded. His name is Arthur, and he lives in an ashcan.'

'Why Et,' Arthur said. 'I never suspected. But I don't know if I like about the ashcan.'

'You would think we were all twelve years old,' said Char.

After the blueing episode Char became popular. She became involved in the productions of the Amateur Dramatic Society and the Oratorio Society, although she was never much of an actress or a singer. She was always the cold and beautiful heroine in the plays, or the brittle exquisite young society woman. She learned to smoke, because of having to do it onstage. In one play Et never forgot, she was a statue. Or rather, she played a girl who had to pretend to be a statue, so that a young man fell in love with her and later discovered, to his confusion and perhaps disappointment, that she was only human. Char had to stand for eight minutes perfectly still on stage, draped in white crepe and showing the audience her fine indifferent profile. Everybody marvelled at how she did it.

The moving spirit behind the Amateur Dramatic Society and the Oratorio Society was a high school teacher new to Mock Hill, Arthur Comber. He taught Et history in her last year. Everybody said he gave her A's because he was in love with her sister, but Et knew it was because she worked harder than she ever had before; she learned the History of North America as she had never learned anything in her life. Missouri Compromise. Mackenzie to the Pacific, 1793. She never forgot.

Arthur Comber was thirty or so, with a high bald forehead, a red face in spite of not drinking (that later paled) and a clumsy, excited manner. He knocked a bottle of ink off his desk and permanently stained the History Room floor. 'Oh dear, oh dear,' he said, crouching down to the spreading ink, flapping at it with his handkerchief. Et imitated that. 'Oh dear, oh dear!' 'Oh good heavens!' All his flustery exclamations and miscalculated gestures. Then, when he took her essay at the door, his red face shining with eagerness, giving her work and herself such a welcome, she felt sorry. That was why she worked so hard, she thought, to make up for mocking him.

He had a black scholar's gown he wore over his suit, to teach in. Even when he wasn't wearing it, Et could see it on him. Hurrying along the street to one of his innumerable, joyfully undertaken obligations, flapping away at the Oratorio singers, jumping on stage—so the whole floor trembled—to demonstrate something to the actors in a play, he seemed to her to have those long ridiculous crow's wings flapping after him, to be as different from other men, as absurd yet intriguing, as the priest from Holy Cross. Char made him give up the gown altogether, after they were married. She had heard that he tripped in it, running up the steps of the school. He had gone sprawling. That finished it, she ripped it up.

'I was afraid one of these days you'd really get hurt.'

But Arthur said, 'Ah. You thought I looked like a fool.'

Char didn't deny it, though his eyes on her, his wide smile, were begging her to. Her mouth twitched at the corners, in spite of herself. Contempt. Fury. Et saw, they both saw, a great wave of that go over her before she could smile at him and say, 'Don't be silly.' Then her smile and her eyes were trying to hold on to him, trying to clutch onto his goodness (which she saw, as much as anybody else did, but which finally only enraged her, Et believed, like everything else about him, like his sweaty forehead and his galloping optimism), before that boiling wave could come back again, altogether carry her away.

Char had a miscarriage during the first year of her marriage and was sick for a long time afterwards. She was never pregnant again. Et by this time was not living in the house; she had her own place on the Square, but she was there one time on washday, helping Char haul the sheets off the line. Their parents were both dead by that time—their mother had died before and their father after the wedding—but it looked to Et like sheets for two beds.

'It gives you plenty of wash.'

'What does?'

'Changing sheets like you do.'

Et was often there in the evening, playing rummy with Arthur while Char, in the other room, picked at the piano in the dark. Or talking and reading library books with Char, while Arthur marked his papers. Arthur walked her home. 'Why do you have to go off and live by yourself anyway?' he scolded her. 'You ought to come back and live with us.'

'Three's a crowd.'

'It wouldn't be for long. Some man is going to come along some day and fall hard.'

'If he was such a fool as to do that I'd never fall for him, so we'd be back where we started.'

'I was a fool that fell for Char, and she ended up having me.'

Just the way he said her name indicated that Char was above, outside, all ordinary considerations—a marvel, a mystery. No one could hope to solve her, they were lucky just being allowed to contemplate her. Et was on the verge of saying, 'She swallowed blueing once over a man that wouldn't have her,' but she thought what would be the good of it, Char would only seem more splendid to him, like a heroine out of Shakespeare. He squeezed Et's waist as if to stress their companionable puzzlement, involuntary obeisance, before her sister. She felt afterwards the bumpy pressure of his fingers as if they had left dents just above where her skirt fastened. It had felt like somebody absent-mindedly trying out the keys of a piano.

Et had set up in the dressmaking business. She had a long narrow room on the Square, once a shop, where she did all her fitting, sewing, cutting, pressing and, behind a curtain, her sleeping and cooking. She could lie in bed and look at the squares of pressed tin on her ceiling, their flower pattern, all her own. Arthur had not liked her taking up dressmaking because he thought she was too smart for it. All the hard work she had done in History had given him an exaggerated idea of her brains. 'Besides,' she told him, 'it takes more brains to cut and fit, if you do it right, than to teach people about the War of 1812. Because, once you learn that, it's learned and isn't going to change you. Whereas every article of clothing you make is an entirely new proposition.'

'Still it's a surprise,' said Arthur, 'to see the way you settle down.'

It surprised everybody, but not Et herself. She made the change easily, from a girl turning cartwheels to a town fixture. She drove the other dressmakers out of business. They had been meek, unimportant creatures anyway, going around to people's houses, sewing in back rooms and being grateful for meals. Only one serious rival appeared in all Et's years, and that was a Finnish woman who called herself a designer. Some people gave her a try, because people are never satisfied, but it soon came out she was all style and no fit. Et never mentioned her, she let people find out for themselves; but afterwards, when this woman had left town and gone to Toronto—where, from what Et had seen on the streets, nobody knew a good fit from a bad—Et did not restrain herself. She would say to a customer she was fitting, 'I see you're still wearing that herringbone my foreigner friend tacked together for you. I saw you on the street.'

'Oh, I know,' the woman would say. 'But I do have to wear it out.'

'You can't see yourself from behind anyway, what's the difference.'

Customers took this kind of thing from Et, came to expect it, even. She's a terror, they said about her, Et's a terror. She had them at a disadvantage, she had them in their slips and corsets. Ladies who looked quite firm and powerful, outside, were here immobilized, apologetic, exposing such trembly, meek-looking thighs squeezed together by corsets, such long sad breast creases, bellies blown up and torn by children and operations.

Et always closed her front curtains tight, pinning the crack.

'That's to keep the men from peeking.'

Ladies laughed nervously.

'That's to keep Jimmy Saunders from stumping over to get an eyeful.'

Jimmy Saunders was a World War I veteran who had a little shop next to Et's, harness and leather goods.

'Oh, Et. Jimmy Saunders has a wooden leg.'

'He hasn't got wooden eyes. Or anything else that I know of.'

'Et you're terrible.'

Et kept Char beautifully dressed. The two steadiest criticisms of Char, in Mock Hill, were that she dressed too elegantly, and that she smoked. It was because she was a teacher's wife that she should have refrained from doing either of these things, but Arthur of course let her do anything she liked, even buying her a cigarette holder so she could look like a lady in a magazine. She smoked at a high school dance, and wore a backless satin evening dress, and danced with a boy who had got a high school girl pregnant, and it was all the same to Arthur. He did not get to be Principal. Twice the school board passed him over and brought in somebody from outside, and when they finally gave him the job, in 1942, it was only temporarily and because so many teachers were away at war.

Char fought hard all these years to keep her figure. Nobody but Et and Arthur knew what effort that cost her. Nobody but Et knew it all. Both of their parents had been heavy, and Char had inherited the tendency, though Et was always as thin as a stick. Char did exercises and drank a glass of warm water before every meal. But sometimes she went on eating binges. Et had known her to eat a dozen cream puffs one after the other, a pound of peanut brittle, or a whole lemon meringue pie. Then pale and horrified she took down Epsom salts, three or four or five times the prescribed amount. For two or three days she would be sick, de-hydrated, purging her sins, as Et said. During these periods she could not look at food. Et would have to come and cook Arthur's supper. Arthur did not know about the pie or the peanut brittle or whatever it was, or about the Epsom salts. He thought she had gained a pound or two and was going through a fanatical phase of dieting. He worried about her.

'What is the difference, what does it matter?' he would say to Et. 'She would still be beautiful.'

'She won't do herself any harm,' said Et, enjoying her food, and glad to see that worry hadn't put him off his. She always made him good suppers.

It was the week before the Labor Day weekend. Blaikie had gone to Toronto, for a day or two he said.

'It's quiet without him,' said Arthur.

'I never noticed he was such a conversationalist,' Et said.

'I only mean in the way that you get used to somebody.'

'Maybe we ought to get unused to him,' said Et.

Arthur was unhappy. He was not going back to the school; he had obtained a leave of absence until after Christmas. Nobody believed he would go back then.

'I suppose he has his own plans for the winter,' he said.

'He may have his own plans for right now. You know I have my customers from the hotel. I have my friends. Ever since I went on that excursion, I hear things.'

She never knew where she got the inspiration to say what she said, where it came from. She had not planned it at all, yet it came so easily, believably.

'I hear he's taken up with a well-to-do woman down at the hotel.'

Arthur was the one to take an interest, not Char.

'A widow?'

'Twice, I believe. The same as he is. And she has the money from both. It's been suspected for some time and she was talking about it openly. He never said anything, though. He never said anything to you, did he, Char?'

'No,' said Char.

'I heard this afternoon that now he's gone, and she's gone. It wouldn't be the first time he pulled something like this. Char and I remember.'

Then Arthur wanted to know what she meant and she told him the story of the lady ventriloquist, remembering even the names of the dolls, though of course she left out all about Char. Char sat through this, even contributing a bit.

'They might come back but my guess is they'd be embarrassed. He'd be em-barrassed. He'd be embarrassed to come here, anyway.'

'Why?' said Arthur, who had cheered up a little through the ventriloquist story. 'We never set down any rule against a man getting married.'

Char got up and went into the house. After a while they heard the sound of the piano.

The question often crossed Et's mind in later years—what did she mean to do about this story when Blaikie got back? For she had no reason to believe he would not come back. The answer was that she had not made any plans at all. She had not planned anything. She supposed she might have wanted to make trouble between him and Char—make Char pick a fight with him, her suspicions roused even if rumors had not been borne out, make Char read what he might do again in the light of what he had done before. She did not know what she wanted. Only to throw things into confusion, for she believed then that somebody had to, before it was too late.

Arthur made as good a recovery as could be expected at his age, he went back to teaching history to the senior classes, working half-days until it was time for him to retire. Et kept up her own place on the Square and tried to get up and do some cooking and cleaning for Arthur, as well. Finally, after he retired, she moved back into the house, keeping the other place only for business purposes. 'Let people jaw all they like,' she said. 'At our age.'

Arthur lived on and on, though he was frail and slow. He walked down to the Square once a day, dropped in on Et, went and sat in the park. The hotel closed down and was sold again. There was a story that it was going to be opened up and used as a rehabilitation center for drug addicts, but the town got up a petition and that fell through. Eventually it was torn down.

Et's eyesight was not as good as it used to be, she had to slow down. She had to turn people away. Still she worked, every day. In the evenings Arthur watched television or read, but she sat out on the porch, in the warm weather, or in the dining room in winter, rocking and resting her eyes. She came and watched the news with him, and made him his hot drink, cocoa or tea.

There was no trace of the bottle. Et went and looked in the cupboard as soon as she could—having run to the house in response to Arthur's early morning call, and found the doctor, old McClain, coming in at the same time. She ran out and looked in the garbage, but she never found it. Could Char have found the time to bury it? She was lying on the bed, fully and nicely dressed, her hair piled up. There was no fuss about the cause of death as there is in stories. She had complained of weakness to Arthur the night before, after Et had gone, she had said she thought she was getting the flu. So the old doctor said heart, and let it go. Nor could Et ever know. Would what was in that bottle leave a body undisfigured, as Char's was? Perhaps what was in the bottle was not what it said. She was not even sure that it had been there that last evening, she had been too carried away with what she was saying to go and look, as she usually did. Perhaps it had been thrown out earlier and Char had taken something else, pills maybe. Perhaps it really was her heart. All that purging would have weakened anybody's heart.

Her funeral was on Labor Day and Blaikie Noble came, cutting out his bus tour. Arthur in his grief had forgotten about Et's story, was not surprised to see Blaikie there. He had come back to Mock Hill on the day Char was found. A few hours too late, like some story. Et in her natural confusion could not remember what it was. Romeo and Juliet, she thought later. But Blaikie of course did not do away with himself afterwards, he went back to Toronto. For a year or two he sent

Christmas cards, then was not heard of any more. Et would not be surprised if her story of his marrying had not come true in the end. Only her timing was mistaken.

Sometimes Et had it on the tip of her tongue to say to Arthur, 'There's something I've been meaning to tell you.' She didn't believe she was going to let him die without knowing. He shouldn't be allowed. He kept a picture of Char on his bureau. It was the one taken of her in her costume for that play, where she played the statue-girl. But Et let it go, day to day. She and Arthur still played rummy and kept up a bit of garden, along with raspberry canes. If they had been married, people would have said they were very happy.

1974

Mordecai Richler

b. 1931

Mordecai Richler was born in Montreal at the beginning of the Depression. His experience of growing up in the working-class neighbourhood around St Urbain Street, and of attending Baron Byng, the predominantly Jewish high school nearby, is recorded in both his fiction and in sketches such as 'The Summer My Grandmother Was Supposed to Die'. Richler's childhood and adolescence were dominated by the conflicts provoked by Fascism—the Spanish Civil War and the Second World War—and in his writing he has often expressed regret that his generation was too young to take part in those heroic events. As a student at Sir George Williams College (now part of Concordia University), Richler made friends with the veterans returned from Europe; after they graduated he dropped out and, using savings from a life-insurance policy, left Canada. He spent the next two years in Europe, chiefly in Paris—of which he has said, '. . . it was, in the truest sense, my university. St Germain des Prés was my campus, Montparnasse my frat house'—and became part of a group of young and aspiring expatriate writers who would gather in the cafés to try out their wit and irony on each other.

Returning to Canada in 1952, Richler worked briefly for the CBC. In 1954 *The Acrobats*—about Spain after the Civil War and written while Richler was in Europe—was published in England. This first novel, which shows its author beginning his career under the influence of Hemingway, Sartre, and Malraux, seems seriously marred by its disjointed construction and occasionally overblown writing; however, it was surprisingly successful and was reprinted in an American paperback edition and translated into Danish, Norse, and German.

Convinced that he had to return to Europe to fulfil his literary ambitions, Richler moved to England soon after *The Acrobats* appeared. The novel he published the following year, *Son of a Smaller Hero* (1955), gives an account of a young Jew's struggle to free himself from the restrictions of family, ghetto, and North American society in general, and ends with a similar decision to leave Canada. His treatment of Montreal Jewry in that novel, and his later ironic portrayal of the London expatriate writers and film-makers who had taken refuge from American McCarthyism (in *A Choice of Enemies*, 1957), revealed Richler's willingness to expose for critical examination those communities of which he was a member.

Although he did not return to Montreal until 1972, Richler continued to write about his Montreal past, and in 1959 he published the novel that established his reputation, *The Apprenticeship of Duddy Kravitz*, a morally complex story of a bumptious young hustler who will go to any lengths to achieve his goals. In this novel, and in *Saint Urbain's Horseman* (1971), in which Duddy briefly reappears, as well as in *Joshua Then and Now* (1980), Richler shows the particular qualities that have most attracted his readers: an impressive ability to create fully developed characters and to locate them in authentic and densely textured milieus. The two novels that Richler published in the sixties—*The Incomparable Atuk* (1963) and *Cocksure* (1968)—are works of a very different sort: mordant and surreal fables that marked him as the most vitriolic satirist of his generation. The savage and frequently bawdy humour of *Cocksure* (one of Richler's own favourites) made it an object of controversy when it was chosen for a Governor General's Award. Richler won a second award for *Saint Urbain's Horseman*, which portrays a rootless expatriate who, all but overwhelmed by the 'competing mythologies' of the modern world, creates a new mythic figure to suit his own needs. His most recent novel is *Solomon Gursky Was Here* (1989), a sprawling narrative that deals with four generations and spans over one hundred and thirty-eight years of Canadian history.

Richler has helped to finance his career as a novelist, and filled the time between novels, by working as a script-writer for radio, television, and films (including *Life at the Top*, 1965; *The Apprenticeship of Duddy Kravitz*, 1973; and *Fun with Dick and Jane*, 1977) and as a freelance journalist. Some of his journalism has been collected in *Hunting Tigers under Glass* (1968); *Shovelling Trouble* (1972); *The Great Comic Book Heroes and Other Essays* (1978, a selection from the two earlier volumes); and *Home Sweet Home: My Canadian Album* (1981). In 1969 his various autobiographical sketches about his youth were collected in *The Street*. Richler is also the author of two successful children's books, *Jacob Two-Two Meets the Hooded Fang* (1975) and *Jacob Two-Two and the Dinosaur* (1987), and of the text of a travel book, *Images of Spain* (1977). He is the editor of two anthologies: *Canadian Writing Today* (1970) and *The Best of Modern Humour* (1983).

The Summer My Grandmother Was Supposed to Die

Dr Katzman discovered the gangrene on one of his monthly visits. 'She won't last a month,' he said.

He said the same the second month, the third and the fourth, and now she lay dying in the heat of the back bedroom.

'God in heaven,' my mother said, 'what's she holding on for?'

The summer my grandmother was supposed to die we did not chip in with the Greenbaums to take a cottage in the Laurentians. My grandmother, already bedridden for seven years, could not be moved again. The doctor came twice a week. The only thing was to stay in the city and wait for her to die or, as my mother said, pass away. It was a hot summer, her bedroom was just behind the kitchen, and when we sat down to eat we could smell her. The dressings on my grandmother's left leg had to be changed several times a day and, according to Dr Katzman, any day might be her last in this world. 'It's in the hands of the Almighty,' he said.

'It won't be long now,' my father said, 'and she'll be better off, if you know what I mean?'

A nurse came every day from the Royal Victorian Order. She arrived punctually at noon and at five to twelve I'd join the rest of the boys under the outside staircase to peek up her dress as she climbed our second-storey flat. Miss Bailey favoured absolutely beguiling pink panties, edged with lace, and that was better than waiting under the stairs for Cousin Bessie, for instance, who wore enormous cotton bloomers, rain or shine.

I was sent out to play as often as possible, because my mother felt it was not good for me to see somebody dying. Usually, I would just roam the scorched streets. There was Duddy, Gas sometimes, Hershey, Stan, Arty and me.

'Before your grandmaw kicks off,' Duddy said, 'she's going to roll her eyes and gurgle. That's what they call the death-rattle.'

'Aw, you know everything. *Putz.*'

'I read it, you jerk,' Duddy said, whacking me one, 'in Perry Mason.'

Home again I would usually find my mother sour and spent. Sometimes she wept.

'She's dying by inches,' she said to my father one stifling night, 'and none of them ever come to see her. Oh, such children,' she added, going on to curse them vehemently in Yiddish.

'They're not behaving right. It's certainly not according to Hoyle,' my father said.

Dr Katzman continued to be astonished. 'It must be will-power alone that keeps her going,' he said. 'That, and your excellent care.'

'It's not my mother any more in the back room, Doctor. It's an animal. I want her to die.'

'Hush. You don't mean it. You're tired.' Dr Katzman dug into his black bag and produced pills for her to take. 'Your wife's a remarkable woman,' he told my father.

'You don't so say,' my father replied, embarrassed.

'A born nurse.'

My sister and I used to lie awake talking about our grandmother. 'After she dies,' I said, 'her hair will go on growing for another twenty-four hours.'

'Says who?'

'Duddy Kravitz. Do you think Uncle Lou will come from New York for the funeral?'

'I suppose so.'

'Boy, that means another fiver for me. Even more for you.'

'You shouldn't say things like that or her ghost will come back to haunt you.'

'Well, I'll be able to go to her funeral anyway. I'm not too young any more.'

I was only six years old when my grandfather died, and so I wasn't allowed to go to his funeral.

I have one imperishable memory of my grandfather. Once he called me into his study, set me down on his lap, and made a drawing of a horse for me. On the horse he drew a rider. While I watched and giggled he gave the rider a beard and the fur-trimmed round hat of a rabbi, a *straimel*, just like he wore.

My grandfather had been a Zaddik,[1] one of the Righteous, and I've been assured that to study Talmud with him had been an illuminating experience. I wasn't allowed to go to his funeral, but years later I was shown the telegrams of condolence that had come from Eire and Poland and even Japan. My grandfather

[1] Holy man (Hebrew); the Talmud is an extensive set of commentaries on the Torah (the first five books of the Bible).

had written many books: a translation of the Book of Splendour (the Zohar)[2] into modern Hebrew, some twenty years' work, and lots of slender volumes of sermons, hasidic tales, and rabbinical commentaries. His books had been published in Warsaw and later in New York.

'At the funeral,' my mother said, 'they had to have six motorcycle policemen to control the crowds. It was such a heat that twelve women fainted—and I'm *not* counting Mrs Waxman from upstairs. With her, you know, *anything* to fall into a man's arms. Even Pinsky's. And did I tell you that there was even a French Canadian priest there?'

'Aw, you're kidding me.'

'The priest was some *knacker*.[3] A bishop maybe. He used to study with the *zeyda*. The *zeyda* was a real personality, you know. Spiritual and worldly-wise at the same time. Such personalities they don't make any more. Today rabbis and peanuts come in the same size.'

But, according to my father, the *zeyda* (his father-in-law) hadn't been as celebrated as all that. 'There are things I could say,' he told me. 'There was another side to him.'

My grandfather had sprung from generations and generations of rabbis, his youngest son was a rabbi, but none of his grandchildren would be one. My Cousin Jerry was already a militant socialist. I once heard him say, 'When the men at the kosher bakeries went out on strike the *zeyda* spoke up against them on the streets and in the *shuls*.[4] It was of no consequence to him that the men were grossly underpaid. His superstitious followers had to have bread. Grandpappy,' Jerry said, 'was a prize reactionary.'

A week after my grandfather died my grandmother suffered a stroke. Her right side was completely paralysed. She couldn't speak. At first it's true, she could manage a coherent word or two and move her right hand enough to write her name in Hebrew. Her name was Malka. But her condition soon began to deteriorate.

My grandmother had six children and seven step-children, for my grandfather had been married before. His first wife had died in the old country. Two years later he had married my grandmother, the only daughter of the most affluent man in the *shtetl*,[5] and their marriage had been a singularly happy one. My grandmother had been a beautiful girl. She had also been a shrewd, resourceful and patient wife. Qualities, I fear, indispensible to life with a Zaddik. For the synagogue paid my grandfather no stipulated salary and much of the money he picked up here and there he had habitually distributed among rabbinical students, needy immigrants and widows. A vice, for such it was to his impecunious family, which made him as unreliable a provider as a drinker. To carry the analogy fur-

---

[2]The most influential work of the cabalistic or mystical tradition of Judaism and therefore of especial importance to Chassidic (or Hasidic) Jews; the Zohar is an eclectic mixture of tales, secret wisdom, folklore, dream interpretation, numerology, spiritual commentary, and mysticism dating from the thirteenth century. Because of the amount of superstitious lore it contained, the laity were sometimes warned against studying it.

[3]Big shot (Yiddish; the initial 'k' is sounded); '*zeyda*': grandfather (Yiddish).

[4]Synagogues (Yiddish).

[5]Literally 'village' (Yiddish): any of the ghettos to which Jews were once confined in Eastern Europe.

ther, my grandmother had to make hurried, surreptitious trips to the pawnbroker with her jewellery. Not all of it to be redeemed, either. But her children had been looked after. The youngest, her favourite, was a rabbi in Boston, the oldest was the actor-manager of a Yiddish theatre in New York, and another was a lawyer. One daughter lived in Montreal, two in Toronto. My mother was the youngest daughter and when my grandmother had her stroke there was a family conclave and it was decided that my mother would take care of her. This was my father's fault. All the other husbands spoke up—they protested hotly that their wives had too much work—they could never manage it—but my father detested quarrels and so he was silent. And my grandmother came to stay with us.

Her bedroom, the back bedroom, had actually been promised to me for my seventh birthday, but now I had to go on sharing a room with my sister. So naturally I was resentful when each morning before I left for school my mother insisted that I go in and kiss my grandmother goodbye.

'Bouyo-bouyo,' was the only sound my grandmother could make.

During those first hopeful months—'Twenty years ago who would have thought there'd be a cure for diabetes?' my father asked. 'Where there's life, you know.'—my grandmother would smile and try to speak, her eyes charged with effort; and I wondered if she knew that I was waiting for her room.

Even later there were times when she pressed my hand urgently to her bosom with her surprisingly strong left arm. But as her illness dragged on and on she became a condition in the house, something beyond hope or reproach, like the leaky ice-box, there was less recognition and more ritual in those kisses. I came to dread her room. A clutter of sticky medicine bottles and the cracked toilet chair beside the bed; glazed but imploring eyes and a feeble smile, the wet smack of her crooked lips against my cheeks. I flinched from her touch. And after two years, I protested to my mother, 'What's the use of telling her I'm going here or I'm going there? She doesn't even recognize me any more.'

'Don't be fresh. She's your grandmother.'

My uncle who was in the theatre in New York sent money regularly to help support my grandmother and, for the first few months, so did the other children. But once the initial and sustaining excitement had passed the children seldom came to our house any more. Anxious weekly visits—'And how is she today, poor lamb?'—quickly dwindled to a dutiful monthly looking in, and then a semi-annual visit, and these always on the way to somewhere.

When the children did come my mother was severe with them. 'I have to lift her on that chair three times a day maybe. And what makes you think I always catch her in time? Sometimes I have to change her linen twice a day. That's a job I'd like to see your wife do,' she said to my uncle, the rabbi.

'We could send her to the Old People's Home.'

'Now there's an idea,' my father said.

'Not so long as I'm alive.' My mother shot my father a scalding look, 'Say something, Sam.'

'Quarreling will get us nowhere. It only creates bad feelings.'

Meanwhile, Dr Katzman came once a month. 'It's astonishing,' he would say each time. 'She's as strong as a horse.'

'Some life for a person,' my father said. 'She can't speak—she doesn't recognize anybody—what is there for her?'

The doctor was a cultivated man; he spoke often for women's clubs, sometimes on Yiddish literature and other times, his rubicund face hot with menace, the voice taking on a doomsday tone, on the cancer threat. 'Who are we to judge?' he asked.

Every evening, during the first few months of my grandmother's illness, my mother would read her a story by Sholem Aleichem.[6] 'Tonight she smiled,' my mother would report defiantly. 'She understood. I can tell.'

Bright afternoons my mother would lift the old lady into a wheelchair and put her out in the sun and once a week she gave her a manicure. Somebody always had to stay in the house in case my grandmother called. Often, during the night, she would begin to wail unaccountably and my mother would get up and rock her mother in her arms for hours. But in the fourth year of my grandmother's illness the strain began to tell. Besides looking after my grandmother, my mother had to keep house for a husband and two children. She became scornful of my father and began to find fault with my sister and me. My father started to spend his evenings playing pinochle at Tansky's Cigar & Soda. Weekends he took me to visit his brothers and sisters. Wherever my father went people had little snippets of advice for him.

'Sam, you might as well be a bachelor. One of the other children should take the old lady for a while. You're just going to have to put your foot down for once.'

'Yeah, in your face maybe.'

My Cousin Libby, who was at McGill, said, 'This could have a very damaging effect on the development of your children. These are their formative years, Uncle Samuel, and the omnipresence of death in the house . . .'

'What you need is a boy friend,' my father said. '*And how.*'

After supper my mother took to falling asleep in her chair, even in the middle of Lux Radio Theatre. One minute she would be sewing a patch on my breeches or making a list of girls to call for a bingo party, proceeds for the Talmud Torah,[7] and the next she would be snoring. Then, inevitably, there came the morning she just couldn't get out of bed and Dr Katzman had to come round a week before his regular visit. 'Well, well, this won't do, will it?'

Dr Katzman led my father into the kitchen. 'Your wife's got a gallstone condition,' he said.

My grandmother's children met again, this time without my mother, and decided to put the old lady in the Jewish Old People's Home on Esplanade Street. While my mother slept an ambulance came to take my grandmother away.

'It's for the best,' Dr Katzman said, but my father was in the back room when my grandmother held on tenaciously to the bedpost, not wanting to be moved by the two men in white.

'Easy does it, granny,' the younger man said.

Afterwards my father did not go to see my mother. He went out for a walk.

---

[6]The pen-name of Sholom Rabinowitz (1859-1916), a Russian-born American Jewish writer famous for his folktale-like comic stories written in Yiddish.
[7]Hebrew school.

When my mother got out of bed two weeks later her cheeks had regained their normal pinkish hue; for the first time in months, she actually joked with me. She became increasingly curious about how I was doing in school and whether or not I shined my shoes regularly. She began to cook special dishes for my father again and resumed old friendships with the girls on the parochial school board. Not only did my father's temper improve, but he stopped going to Tansky's every night and began to come home early from work. But my grandmother's name was seldom mentioned. Until one evening, after I'd had a fight with my sister, I said, 'Why can't I move into the back bedroom now?'

My father glared at me. 'Big-mouth.'

'It's empty, isn't it?'

The next afternoon my mother put on her best dress and coat and new spring hat.

'Don't go looking for trouble,' my father said.

'It's been a month. Maybe they're not treating her right.'

'They're experts.'

'Did you think I was never going to visit her? I'm not inhuman, you know.'

'Alright, go.' But after she had gone my father stood by the window and said, 'I was born lucky, and that's it.'

I sat on the outside stoop watching the cars go by. My father waited on the balcony above, cracking peanuts. It was six o'clock, maybe later, when the ambulance slowed down and rocked to a stop right in front of our house. 'I knew it,' my father said. 'I was born with all the luck.'

My mother got out first, her eyes red and swollen, and hurried upstairs to make my grandmother's bed.

'You'll get sick again,' my father said.

'I'm sorry, Sam, but what could I do? From the moment she saw me she cried and cried. It was terrible.'

'They're recognized experts there. They know how to take care of her better than you do.'

'Experts? Expert murderers you mean. She's got bedsores, Sam. Those dirty little Irish nurses they don't change her linen often enough, they hate her. She must have lost twenty pounds in there.'

'Another month and you'll be flat on your back again. I'll write you a guarantee, if you want.'

My father became a regular at Tansky's again and, once more, I had to go in and kiss my grandmother in the morning. Amazingly, she had begun to look like a man. Little hairs had sprouted on her chin, she had grown a spiky grey moustache, and she was practically bald.

Yet again my uncles and aunts sent five dollar bills, though erratically, to help pay for my grandmother's support. Elderly people, former followers of my grandfather, came to inquire about the old lady's health. They sat in the back bedroom with her, leaning on their canes, talking to themselves and rocking to and fro. 'The Holy Shakers,' my father called them. I avoided the seamed, shrunken old men because they always wanted to pinch my cheeks or trick me with a dash of snuff and laugh when I sneezed. When the visit with my grandmother was over the old people would unfailingly sit in the kitchen with my mother for another hour, watching her make *lokshen*,[8] slurping lemon tea out of a saucer. They would recall the sayings and books and charitable deeds of the late Zaddik.

'At the funeral,' my mother never wearied of telling them, 'they had to have six motorcycle policemen to control the crowds.'

In the next two years there was no significant change in my grandmother's condition, though fatigue, ill-temper, and even morbidity enveloped my mother again. She fought with her brothers and sisters and once, after a particularly bitter quarrel, I found her sitting with her head in her hands. 'If, God forbid, I had a stroke,' she said, 'would you send me to the Old People's Home?'

'Of course not.'

'I hope that never in my life do I have to count on my children for anything.'

The seventh summer of my grandmother's illness she was supposed to die and we did not know from day to day when it would happen. I was often sent out to eat at an aunt's or at my other grandmother's house. I was hardly ever at home. In those days they let boys into the left-field bleachers of Delormier Downs free during the week and Duddy, Gas sometimes, Hershey, Stan, Arty and me spent many an afternoon at the ball park. The Montreal Royals, kingpin of the Dodger farm system, had a marvellous club at the time. There was Jackie Robinson, Roy Campanella, Lou Ortiz, Red Durrett, Honest John Gabbard, and Kermit Kitman. Kitman was our hero. It used to give us a charge to watch the crafty little Jew, one of ours, running around out there with all those tall dumb southern crackers. 'Hey, Kitman,' we would yell, 'Hey, shmo-head, if your father knew you played ball on *shabus*—'[9] Kitman, alas, was all field and no hit. He never made the majors. 'There goes Kermit Kitman,' we would holler, after he had gone down swinging again, 'the first Jewish strike-out king of the International League.' This we promptly followed up by bellowing choice imprecations in Yiddish.

It was after one of these games, on a Friday afternoon, that I came home to find a crowd gathered in front of our house.

'That's the grandson,' somebody said.

A knot of old people stood staring at our front door from across the street. A taxi pulled up and my aunt hurried out, hiding her face in her hands.

'After so many years,' a woman said.

'And probably next year they'll discover a cure. Isn't that always the case?'

The flat was clotted. Uncles and aunts from my father's side of the family, strangers, Dr Katzman, neighbours, were all milling around and talking in hushed voices. My father was in the kitchen, getting out the apricot brandy. 'Your grandmother's dead,' he said.

'Where's Maw?'

'In the bedroom with . . . You'd better not go in.'

'I want to see her.'

My mother wore a black shawl and glared down at a knot of handkerchief clutched in a fist that had been cracked by washing soda. 'Don't come in here,' she said.

---

[8]Noodles (Yiddish).
[9]The Sabbath (Yiddish).

Several bearded round-shouldered men in shiny black coats surrounded the bed. I couldn't see my grandmother.

'Your grandmother's dead.'

'Daddy told me.'

'Go wash your face and comb your hair.'

'Yes.'

'You'll have to get your own supper.'

'Sure.'

'One minute. The *baba*[1] left some jewellery. The necklace is for Rifka and the ring is for your wife.'

'Who's getting married?'

'Better go and wash your face. Remember behind the ears, please.'

Telegrams were sent, the obligatory long distance calls were made, and all through the evening relatives and neighbours and old followers of the Zaddik poured into the house. Finally, the man from the funeral parlour arrived.

'There goes the only Jewish businessman in town,' Segal said, 'who wishes all his customers were German.'

'This is no time for jokes.'

'Listen, life goes on.'

My Cousin Jerry had begun to affect a cigarette holder. 'Soon the religious mumbo-jumbo starts,' he said to me.

'Wha'?'

'Everybody is going to be sickeningly sentimental.'

The next day was the sabbath and so, according to law, my grandmother couldn't be buried until Sunday. She would have to lie on the floor all night. Two grizzly women in white came to move and wash the body and a professional mourner arrived to sit up and pray for her. 'I don't trust his face,' my mother said. 'He'll fall asleep.'

'He won't fall asleep.'

'You watch him, Sam.'

'A fat lot of good prayers will do her now. Alright! Okay! I'll watch him.'

My father was in a fury with Segal.

'The way he goes after the apricot brandy you'd think he never saw a bottle in his life before.'

Rifka and I were sent to bed, but we couldn't sleep. My aunt was sobbing over the body in the living room; there was the old man praying, coughing and spitting into his handkerchief whenever he woke; and the hushed voices and whimpering from the kitchen, where my father and mother sat. Rifka allowed me a few drags off her cigarette.

'Well, *pisherke*,[2] this is our last night together. Tomorrow you can take over the back room.'

'Are you crazy?'

'You always wanted it for yourself, didn't you?'

'She died in there, but.'

'So?'

[1] Old woman; grandmother (Russian/Yiddish).
[2] A mild Yiddish vulgarity; idiomatically 'a little squirt', a nobody.

'I couldn't sleep in there now.'

'Good night and happy dreams.'

'Hey, let's talk some more.'

'Did you know,' Rifka said, 'that when they hang a man the last thing that happens is that he has an orgasm?'

'A wha'?'

'Skip it. I forgot you were still in kindergarten.'

'Kiss my Royal Canadian—'

'At the funeral, they're going to open the coffin and throw dirt in her face. It's supposed to be earth from Eretz.³ They open it and you're going to have to look.'

'Says you.'

A little while after the lights had been turned out Rifka approached my bed, her head covered with a sheet and her arms raised high. 'Bouyo-bouyo. Who's that sleeping in my bed? Woo-woo.'

My uncle who was in the theatre and my aunt from Toronto came to the funeral. My uncle, the rabbi, was there too.

'As long as she was alive,' my mother said, 'he couldn't even send her five dollars a month. I don't want him in the house, Sam. I can't bear the sight of him.'

'You're upset,' Dr Katzman said, 'and you don't know what you're saying.'

'Maybe you'd better give her a sedative,' the rabbi said.

'Sam will you speak up for once, please.'

Flushed, eyes heated, my father stepped up to the rabbi. 'I'll tell you this straight to your face, Israel,' he said. 'You've gone down in my estimation.'

The rabbi smiled a little.

'Year by year,' my father continued, his face burning a brighter red, 'your stock has gone down with me.'

My mother began to weep and she was led unwillingly to a bed. While my father tried his utmost to comfort her, as he muttered consoling things, Dr Katzman plunged a needle into her arm. 'There we are,' he said.

I went to sit on the stoop outside with Duddy. My uncle, the rabbi, and Dr Katzman stepped into the sun to light cigarettes.

'I know exactly how you feel,' Dr Katzman said. 'There's been a death in the family and the world seems indifferent to your loss. Your heart is broken and yet it's a splendid summer day . . . a day made for love and laughter . . . and that must seem very cruel to you.'

The rabbi nodded; he sighed.

'Actually,' Dr Katzman said, 'it's remarkable that she held out for so long.'

'Remarkable?' the rabbi said. 'It's written that if a man has been married twice he will spend as much time with his first wife in heaven as he did on earth. My father, may he rest in peace, was married to his first wife for seven years and my mother, may she rest in peace, has managed to keep alive for seven years. Today in heaven she will be able to join my father, may he rest in peace.'

Dr Katzman shook his head. 'It's amazing,' he said. He told my uncle that he

³The land (of Jerusalem); the Promised Land.

was writing a book based on his experiences as a healer. 'The mysteries of the human heart.'

'Yes.'

'Astonishing.'

My father hurried outside. 'Dr Katzman, please. It's my wife. Maybe the injection wasn't strong enough. She just doesn't stop crying. It's like a tap. Can you come in, please?'

'Excuse me,' Dr Katzman said to my uncle.

'Of course.' My uncle turned to Duddy and me. 'Well, boys,' he said, 'what would you like to be when you grow up?'

1969

Alden Nowlan

1933-1983

The sympathy for victims of emotional and economic poverty that is often expressed in the writing of Alden Nowlan derives in part from personal experience. Nowlan grew up near Nova Scotia's Annapolis Valley, in a small 'thin-soil' settlement that he describes as little touched by the Depression because it was already impoverished. Although he quit school in grade five, eventually going to work in nearby lumber mills and on farms, he continued his education by reading whatever he could find. At nineteen he took a position on the Hartland *Observer* in New Brunswick. During his ten years as a journalist and editor at the *Observer*, and later at the Saint John *Telegraph-Journal*, he developed a simple, direct style that may be seen in the poetry and short fiction he began writing in the mid-1950s. In 1957 he met Maritime poet and educator Fred Cogswell, whose encouragement led to the publication of Nowlan's first collection of poems, *The Rose and the Puritan* (1958). Since then Nowlan has published eleven more volumes of poetry, including *Bread, Wine and Salt* (1967), which won a Governor General's Award; *The Mysterious Naked Man* (1969); *Playing the Jesus Game: Selected Poems* (1970); *Smoked Glass* (1977); and *I Might Not Tell Everybody This* (1982). He has also

written short stories—collected in *Miracle at Indian River* (1968)—that deal with the brutal cultural trap in which his fellow Maritimers are caught. *Double Exposure*, a collection of his journalistic pieces, was published in 1978. Nowlan's novel, *Various Persons Named Kevin O'Brien* (1973), is an essentially autobiographical account of his difficult boyhood. Another novel, *The Wanton Troopers* (1988), which was found in Nowlan's papers, also deals with the autobiographical character Kevin O'Brien. Three more books were published posthumously: *Early Poems* (1983); *Will Ye Let the Mummers In?* (1984), a book of short stories; and *An Exchange of Gifts: Poems New and Selected* (1985).

From 1969 on, Nowlan was associated with the University of New Brunswick, while working as a writer and freelance journalist. In the 1970s he collaborated with Walter Learning in writing plays; two of them focus on popular figures—Frankenstein (in *Frankenstein: The Man Who Became God*, 1974), and Sherlock Holmes (in *The Incredible Murder of Cardinal Tosca*, 1978).

In his poetry, as in his stories, Nowlan is a chronicler—he called himself a 'witness'—of a rural Maritime way of life that has remained virtually unchanged for centuries.

510 | Alden Nowlan

He has observed that when he moved to small-town New Brunswick, he also moved from the eighteenth century into the twentieth, leaving behind a boyhood home that had 'no furnace, no plumbing, no electricity, no refrigerator, no telephone . . . [a home, where] we used kerosene lamps and on the coldest winter nights water froze in the bucket in the kitchen'. Nowlan pictures a Maritimes landscape (as in 'On the Barrens' and 'Canadian January Night') that seems primitive in comparison with those seen in such famous nineteenth-century poems as Roberts' 'Tantramar Revisited' and Carman's 'Low Tide on Grand Pré'. The perspective of Nowlan's poems is notably different from that of his predecessors: he captures not the picturesque but the commonplace. Unlike Roberts or Carman, Nowlan is not a detached observer telling his audience about a region but is a part of his milieu and its reporter—a dual role that he often found uncomfortable. A harsh, uncompromising realism in his poetry prevents it from becoming mundane or naive. The sentimentality implicit in focusing on the crippling effects of the guilt and repression that Nowlan saw as his cultural heritage ('I am a product of a culture that fears any display of emotion and attempts to repress any true communication') is regularly undercut by an ironic humour that suggests imagination is man's only real escape from adversity and deprivation.

Temptation

The boy is
badgering the man
to lower him down the
face of the cliff
to a narrow shelf
about eight feet
below:
'Your hands are strong,
and I'm not afraid.
The ledge is wide enough,   10
I won't hurt myself
even if you let go.'

'Don't be a fool.
You'd break every bone
in your body.
Where in God's name
do you get such ideas?
It's time we went home.'

But there is no
conviction in the   20
man's voice and
the boy persists;
nagging his wrists,
dragging him nearer.
Their summer shirts
balloon in the wind.

While devils whisper
what god-like sport
it would be

to cling to the   30
edge of the world
and gamble
one's only son
against the wind
and rocks
and sea.

1967

The First Stirring of the Beasts

The first stirring of the beasts
is heard at two or three or four
in the morning, depending on the season.

You lie, warm and drowsy, listening,
wondering how there is so much difference
between the sounds
cattle and horses make,
moving in their stanchions[1] or halters,
so much difference that you can't explain,
so that if someone asked you   10
which of them is moving now?
you couldn't answer
but lying there, not quite awake,
you know, although it doesn't matter,
and then a rooster crows
and it sounds, or maybe you imagine this,
unsure and a little afraid,
                          and after a little
there are only the sounds of night
that we call silence.   20

The second stirring of the beasts
is the one everybody understands.
You hear it at dawn
and if you belong here
you get up.
Anyway, there is no mystery
in it, it is the other stirring,
the first brief restlessness
which seems to come for no reason
that makes you ask yourself   30
what are they awake for?

1969

[1]Two vertical posts between which a cow's head is placed to keep the animal in its stall.

Country Full of Christmas

Country full of Christmas,
the stripped, suspicious elms
groping for the dun sky—
what can I give my love?

The remembrance—mouse hawks
scudding on the dykes, above
the wild roses; horses and cattle
separate in the same field.
It is not for my love.

Do you know that foxes   10
believe in nothing
but themselves—everything
is a fox disguised: men, dogs and rabbits.

1969

Canadian January Night

Ice storm: the hill
a pyramid of black crystal
down which the cars
slide like phosphorescent beetles
while I, walking backwards in obedience
to the wind, am possessed
of the fearful knowledge
my compatriots share
but almost never utter:
this is a country   10
where a man can die
                    simply from being
caught outside.

1971

On the Barrens

'Once when we were hunting cattle
    on the barrens,'
so began many of the stories they told,
gathered in the kitchen, a fire still
    the focus of life then,
the teapot on the stove as long as
    anyone was awake,
mittens and socks left to thaw on
    the open oven door,
chunks of pine and birch piled   10
    halfway to the ceiling,
and always a faint smell of smoke
    like spice in the air,
the lamps making their peace with
    the darkness,
the world not entirely answerable
    to man.

They took turns talking, the listeners
    puffed their pipes,
he whose turn it was to speak used his   20
    as an instrument,
took his leather pouch from a pocket
    of his overalls,
gracefully, rubbed tobacco between
    his rough palms
as he set the mood, tamped it into
    the bowl
at a moment carefully chosen, scratched
    a match when it was necessary
to prolong the suspense. If his pipe   30
    went out it was no accident,
if he spat in the stove it was done
    for a purpose.
When he finished he might lean back
    in his chair so that it stood
on two legs; there'd be a short silence.

The barrens were flat clay fields,
    twenty miles from the sea
and separated from it by dense woods
    and farmlands.   40
They smelled of salt and the wind
    blew there
constantly as it does on the shore
    of the North Atlantic.

There had been a time, the older men
    said, when someone had owned

the barrens but something had happened
long ago and now anyone who wanted to
    could pasture there.
The cattle ran wild all summer,   50
sinewy little beasts, ginger-coloured
    with off-white patches,
grazed there on the windswept barrens
    and never saw a human
until fall when the men came to round
    them up,
sinewy men in rubber boots and tweed caps
    with their dogs beside them.

Some of the cattle would by now have
    forgotten   60
there'd been a time before they'd
    lived on the barrens.
They'd be truly wild, dangerous, the
    men would loose the dogs on them,
mongrel collies, barn dogs with the
    dispositions of convicts
who are set over their fellows,
    the dogs would go for the nose,
sink their teeth in the tender flesh,
    toss the cow on its side,   70
bleating, hooves flying, but shortly
    tractable.
There were a few escaped,
    it was said, and in a little while
they were like no other cattle—
    the dogs feared them,
they roared at night and the men
    lying by their camp-fires
heard them and moaned in their sleep,
    the next day tracking them   80
found where they'd pawed the moss,
    where their horns had scraped
bark from the trees—all the stories
    agreed
in this: now there was nothing to do
    but kill them.

1977

Leonard Cohen

b. 1934

Born and raised in Montreal, Leonard Norman Cohen graduated from McGill (B.A., 1955) and briefly attended graduate school at Columbia University before returning to Montreal and becoming a professional writer. Over the next twenty years he not only began to publish the poetry he had been writing since his teens, but saw two novels through the press by the time he was thirty-two and expanded his career to become a successful songwriter and singer. Cohen left Canada in 1963, spending ten years as an expatriate, largely on the Greek island of Hydra and in a California Zen monastery. Since the early seventies he has divided his time between Montreal and abroad.

Cohen's first book of poetry, *Let Us Compare Mythologies* (1956), shows what Sandra Djwa calls his 'Black Romantic' viewpoint. It was influenced by the American Beat movement, which rejected the structures of society for the ideal of personal freedom and embraced, in romantic fascination with self-destruction, a bohemian way of life largely associated with drugs, sexual permissiveness, and other forms of social experimentation. In *Let Us Compare Mythologies* Cohen not only assumed the Beat position of social outsider, but also took on the role of myth-maker. Finding that the myths and legends he grew up with were no longer adequate, he began a search for a new myth that could provide meaning, a synthesis of different, often hostile, traditions—particularly those of his Jewish, Westmount childhood and the working-class Catholic values that he experienced in French Montreal. Out of Cohen's mythmaking came a central theme: the necessity of achieving sainthood, which received its fullest expression in his second novel, *Beautiful Losers* (1966). (His most idealized figure of the modern secular saint appears in the poem 'Suzanne Takes You Down'.) Although other Canadian writers, such as Robertson Davies, have also been concerned with sainthood, few share the notion that occupied Cohen in this period of his work: that the individual must actively seek his own martyrdom at the hands of an inherently hostile society.

In Cohen's second collection, *The Spice-Box of Earth* (1961), a preoccupation with eroticism emerged that has continued to be central to his later work. While the poems in *Spice-Box* are often read for their sensual surfaces, they are rarely valentines. In Cohen's writing, erotic experience is linked to death and violence and is thus not so much a union between two people as a means of saintly purification. *Flowers for Hitler* (1964) gives further prominence to death, violence, and eroticism and employs rhetoric that allies it with the protest poetry of the mid-sixties; the first of Cohen's books intended to alienate the reader, it is also his most explicit piece of social criticism. The perversely dark visions of these and later poems, however, are frequently countered by Cohen's use of traditional styles and conventions that recall the work of Renaissance poets and of Yeats and Eliot, or else by the excessively lush surfaces that Cohen—much like the nineteenth-century Decadents—sometimes gives to his writing.

In the sixties, his most prolific period, Cohen wrote his two novels, *The Favorite Game* (1963) and *Beautiful Losers*. While the earlier novel is the more conventional in form, both books are not so much narrative works as exercises in introspection and perspective. *The Favorite Game*, indebted to Joyce's *Portrait of the Artist as a Young Man* as well as to the tradition of the American-Jewish novel and to contemporary film, gives the reader Cohen's first important treatment of madness, a topic extensively developed in *Beautiful Losers*. More than any other work *Beautiful Losers* ties together all the important elements in Cohen's writing. A pornographic, self-indulgent book, it is nevertheless a dazzling tour-de-force, the novel as stylistic exhibition: myths and images embellish one another as Cohen builds what he calls 'a model of sainthood'—

516 | Leonard Cohen

the achievement of a self-destructive Dionysiac madness.

In the late sixties, as a result of his success as a songwriter and performer, Cohen became a media personality—the artist-hero who was his own creation, playing out the role of sacrificial victim. Like Norman Mailer and Allen Ginsberg, Cohen was given to grand gestures (such as refusing a Governor General's Award in 1969), and assumed the pose of ageless, wandering rebel whose public and personal identities are one and whose task is to exhibit his own martyrdom. In this he continued his project of presenting, as Michael Ondaatje has observed, 'Cohen's dreamworlds, Cohen and death, Cohen and love, the legend of Cohen—no matter what the topic is, Cohen is at the centre of the story' (*Leonard Cohen*, 1967). Cohen toured North America and Europe and produced seven records. His songs not only gained him international fame ('Suzanne' became one of the most recorded popular songs of the decade) but they also contain some of his best writing.

As early as 1966, however, there were signs of Cohen's having reached a point of stasis as a poet. The collection *Parasites of Heaven* (1966) seemed to be largely culled from the rejects of his earlier books. The small group of new poems in *Selected Poems: 1956-1968* (1968) were more closely related to his songs, in their simplicity and subdued style, than to his other poetry; and even the writing of new songs almost ceased in the early seventies. In 1972 he published *The Energy of Slaves*, a nihilistic and grim collection based on the themes of suicide and artistic burnout. He produced no new books until *Death of a Lady's Man* (1978), a mixture of poetry, prose-poems, and prose that is presented in the form of excerpts from a longer work, 'My Life in Art', accompanied by running commentaries and extensive quotations from notebook sources. The conflict in *Death of a Lady's Man* between redemption and desire becomes more explicit in the poetic meditations of *Book of Mercy* (1984) and in the songs of Cohen's later albums. His religious vision has been revitalized (as has his interest in political structures). While Cohen's writing continues to present a world largely without faith in the divine—indeed, without faith in any secular authority or even in the individual self—his recent work suggests a spiritual reality in which eroded belief can be restored and the soul regained. Suffering may be necessary to salvation, but martyrdom is no longer an end in itself.

You Have the Lovers

You have the lovers,
they are nameless, their histories only for each other,
and you have the room, the bed and the windows.
Pretend it is a ritual.
Unfurl the bed, bury the lovers, blacken the windows,
let them live in that house for a generation or two.
No one dares disturb them.
Visitors in the corridor tip-toe past the long closed door,
they listen for sounds, for a moan, for a song:
nothing is heard, not even breathing.   10
You know they are not dead,
you can feel the presence of their intense love.
Your children grow up, they leave you,
they have become soldiers and riders.
Your mate dies after a life of service.
Who knows you? Who remembers you?
But in your house a ritual is in progress:
it is not finished: it needs more people.

One day the door is opened to the lover's chamber.
The room has become a dense garden,   20
full of colours, smells, sounds you have never known.
The bed is smooth as a wafer of sunlight,
in the midst of the garden it stands alone.
In the bed the lovers, slowly and deliberately and silently,
perform the act of love.
Their eyes are closed,
as tightly as if heavy coins of flesh lay on them.
Their lips are bruised with new and old bruises.
Her hair and his beard are hopelessly tangled.
When he puts his mouth against her shoulder   30
she is uncertain whether her shoulder
has given or received the kiss.
All her flesh is like a mouth.
He carries his fingers along her waist
and feels his own waist caressed.
She holds him closer and his own arms tighten around her.
She kisses the hand beside her mouth.
It is his hand or her hand, it hardly matters,
there are so many more kisses.
You stand beside the bed, weeping with happiness,   40
you carefully peel away the sheets
from the slow-moving bodies.
Your eyes are filled with tears, you barely make out the lovers.
As you undress you sing out, and your voice is magnificent
because now you believe it is the first human voice
heard in that room.
The garments you let fall grow into vines.
You climb into bed and recover the flesh.
You close your eyes and allow them to be sewn shut.
You create an embrace and fall into it.   50
There is only one moment of pain or doubt
as you wonder how many multitudes are lying beside your body,
but a mouth kisses and a hand soothes the moment away.

1961

A Kite Is a Victim

A kite is a victim you are sure of.
You love it because it pulls
gentle enough to call you master,
strong enough to call you fool;
because it lives
like a desperate trained falcon
in the high sweet air,
and you can always haul it down
to tame it in your drawer.

A kite is a fish you have already caught   10
in a pool where no fish come,
so you play him carefully and long,
and hope he won't give up,
or the wind die down.

A kite is the last poem you've written,
so you give it to the wind,
but you don't let it go
until someone finds you
something else to do.

A kite is a contract of glory   20
that must be made with the sun,
so you make friends with the field
the river and the wind,
then you pray the whole cold night before,
under the travelling cordless moon,
to make you worthy and lyric and pure.

1961

Suzanne Takes You Down

Suzanne takes you down
to her place near the river,
you can hear the boats go by
you can stay the night beside her.
And you know that she's half crazy
but that's why you want to be there
and she feeds you tea and oranges
that come all the way from China.
Just when you mean to tell her
that you have no gifts to give her,   10
she gets you on her wave-length
and she lets the river answer
that you've always been her lover.
        And you want to travel with her,
        you want to travel blind
        and you know that she can trust you
        because you've touched her perfect body
        with your mind.

Jesus was a sailor
when he walked upon the water[1]   20
and he spent a long time watching
from a lonely wooden tower
and when he knew for certain

[1]The account of Jesus' walking on the wave-tossed sea to his disciples on a ship can be found in Matthew 14:22-33. Peter tried to emulate him, but lost faith and began to sink.

only drowning men could see him
he said All men will be sailors then
until the sea shall free them,
but he himself was broken
long before the sky would open,
forsaken, almost human,
he sank beneath your wisdom like a stone.   30
    And you want to travel with him,
    you want to travel blind
    and you think maybe you'll trust him
    because he touched your perfect body
    with his mind.

Suzanne takes your hand
and she leads you to the river,
she is wearing rags and feathers
from Salvation Army counters.
The sun pours down like honey   40
on our lady of the harbour
as she shows you where to look
among the garbage and the flowers,
there are heroes in the seaweed
there are children in the morning,
they are leaning out for love
they will lean that way forever
while Suzanne she holds the mirror.
    And you want to travel with her
    and you want to travel blind   50
    and you're sure that she can find you
    because she's touched her perfect body
    with her mind.

1966

Two Went to Sleep

Two went to sleep
almost every night
one dreamed of mud
one dreamed of Asia
visiting a zeppelin
visiting Nijinsky
Two went to sleep
one dreamed of ribs
one dreamed of senators
Two went to sleep   10
two travellers
The long marriage
in the dark
The sleep was old
the travellers were old
one dreamed of oranges
one dreamed of Carthage
Two friends asleep
years locked in travel
Good night my darling   20
as the dreams waved goodbye
one travelled lightly
one walked through water
visiting a chess game
visiting a booth
always returning
to wait out the day
One carried matches
one climbed a beehive
one sold an earphone   30
one shot a German

Two went to sleep
every sleep went together
wandering away
from an operating table
one dreamed of grass
one dreamed of spokes
one bargained nicely
one was a snowman
one counted medicine   40
one tasted pencils
one was a child
one was a traitor
visiting heavy industry
visiting the family
Two went to sleep
none could foretell
one went with baskets
one took a ledger
one night happy   50
one night in terror
Love could not bind them
Fear could not either
they went unconnected
they never knew where
always returning
to wait out the day
parting with kissing
parting with yawns
visiting Death till   60
they wore out their welcome
visiting Death till
the right disguise worked

1966

Book of Mercy

49

unto you, and all my glory soiled unto you. Do not let the spark of my soul go out in the even sadness. Let me raise the brokenness to you, to the world where the breaking is for love. Do not let the words be mine, but change them into truth. With these lips instruct my heart, and let fall into the world what is broken in the world. Lift me up to the wrestling of faith. Do not leave me where the sparks go out, and the jokes are told in the dark, and new things are called forth and appraised in the scale of the terror. Face me to the rays of love, O source of light, or face me to the majesty of your darkness, but not here, do not leave me here, where death is forgotten, and the new thing grins.

50   I LOST MY WAY, I FORGOT

to call on your name. The raw heart beat against the world, and the tears were for my lost victory. But you are here. You have always been here. The world is all forgetting, and the heart is a rage of directions, but your name unifies the heart, and the world is lifted into its place. Blessed is the one who waits in the traveller's heart for his turning.

1984

Everybody Knows[1]

Everybody knows that the dice are loaded. Everybody rolls with their fingers crossed. Everybody knows the war is over. Everybody knows the good guys lost. Everybody knows the fight was fixed: the poor stay poor, the rich get rich. That's how it goes. Everybody knows.

Everybody knows that the boat is leaking. Everybody knows the captain lied. Everybody got this broken feeling like their father or their dog just died. Everybody talking to their pockets. Everybody wants a box of chocolates and a long stem rose. Everybody knows.

Everybody knows that you love me, baby. Everybody knows that you really do. Everybody knows that you've been faithful, give or take a night or two. Everybody knows you've been discreet, but there were so many people you just had to meet without your clothes. And everybody knows.

And everybody knows that it's now or never. Everybody knows that it's me or you. And everybody knows that you live forever when you've done a line or two. Everybody knows the deal is rotten: Old Black Joe's still pickin' cotton for your ribbons and bows. And everybody knows.

Everybody knows that the Plague is coming. Everybody knows that it's moving fast. Everybody knows that the naked man and woman—just a shining artifact of the past. Everybody knows the scene is dead, but there's gonna be a meter on your bed that will disclose what everybody knows.

And everybody knows that you're in trouble. Everybody knows what you've been through, from the bloody cross on top of Calvary to the beach at Malibu. Everybody knows it's coming apart: take one last look at this Sacred Heart before it blows. And everybody knows.

[1988]

[1]Lyrics taken from Cohen's album *I am Your Man.*

Leon Rooke

b. 1934

Leon Rooke immigrated to Canada in 1969 and settled in Victoria, B.C., where he remained until 1988, when he moved to Eden Mills, Ont. Born and educated in North Carolina, he began writing short stories in high school—though his initial recognition came as a dramatist while attending Mars Hill College (1953-5). He continued to write both stories and plays as a student at the University of North Carolina (B.A. 1957). From 1957 to 1964 he travelled extensively in the United States, picking up temporary jobs and serving eighteen months in the army. He was writer-in-residence at UNC in 1965 and then remained in the area as a journalist on a weekly Durham newspaper. He is now a full-time writer who occasionally teaches creative writing.

Rooke has had several plays produced, including *Ms. America*, *Sword/Play*, and *Of Ice and Men* (a play about hockey); three of his plays have been published: *Krokodile* (1973), *Sword/Play* (1974), and *Cakewalk* (1980). In the late fifties his fiction began to appear in journals, and his first collection of short stories, *Last One Home Sleeps in the Yellow Bed*, was published in 1968. A prolific writer, Rooke has published eight collections of short fiction since 1977. The most recent, *How I Saved The Province* (1989), contains three stories and a novella about 'Wacky' Bennett. He has also published four short novels: *Vault* (1973), *Fat Woman* (1980), *The Magician in Love* (1981), and *Shakespeare's Dog* (1983), which received a Governor General's Award for fiction. In 1989 his first full-length novel, *A Good Baby*, appeared. A moral fable about a man drawn into the entanglements of family despite himself, it—like 'A Bolt of White Cloth'—is not bound by the conventions of traditional realism.

Because for Rooke life takes place as much in the mind as outside it, his fiction focuses on the validity of imaginative and emotional experience. The most striking feature of Rooke's work, which is mainly told from the viewpoint of first-person narrators, is its use of dramatic voices that present the reader not so much with plots as with the inner workings of the mind. His stories therefore often take the form of monologues—recastings of the narrators' experience, illusions, and fantasies—that are most effective when read aloud. (Rooke himself is well known for his flamboyant public readings of his work.) These narrators speak in the present, about a past whose locale and time are relatively unimportant. Close to drama, especially the absurdist plays of Ionesco, these stories have dramatic immediacy: they seem to occur as we read them. Unlike many contemporary writers, Rooke does not seek to alienate or disconnect his readers from the text, but rather emphasizes their dependence on the voice of the speaker as the only stable point of reference in his fiction. Because of the relative unimportance of plot in his fiction, and because he so often abandons the conventions of realism, Rooke has been seen as one of the influential postmodernists in Canada in the last decade. Not entirely comfortable with that categorization, he distanced himself, in a recent essay, from 'fictive forms which process the invention of fiction inventing itself inventing fiction' and affirmed instead that:

Fiction is for the unknown, the unadmitted, the strangers ever at humanity's door, it is about the dead who could not speak for themselves, and the living who have not the opportunity . . . (Brick, No. *33, 1988*)

A Bolt of White Cloth

A man came by our road carrying an enormous bolt of white cloth on his back. Said he was from the East. Said whoever partook of this cloth would come to know true happiness. Innocence without heartbreak, he said, if that person proved worthy. My wife fingered his cloth, having in mind something for new curtains. It was good quality, she said. Beautifully woven, of a fine, light texture, and you certainly couldn't argue with the colour.

'How much is it?' she asked.

'Before I tell you that,' the man said, 'you must tell me truthfully if you've ever suffered.'

'Oh, I've suffered,' she said. 'I've known suffering of some description every day of my natural life.'

I was standing over by the toolshed, with a big smile. My wife is a real joker, who likes nothing better than pulling a person's leg. She's known hardships, this and that upheaval, but nothing I would call down-and-out suffering. Mind you, I don't speak for her. I wouldn't pretend to speak for another person.

This man with the bolt of cloth, however, he clearly had no sense of my wife's brand of humour. She didn't get an itch of a smile out of him. He kept the cloth neatly balanced on his shoulder, wincing a little from the weight and from however far he'd had to carry it, staring hard and straight at my wife the whole time she fooled with him, as if he hoped to peer clear through to her soul. His eyes were dark and brooding and hollowed out some. He was like no person either my wife or me had ever seen before.

'Yes,' he said, 'but suffering of what kind?'

'Worse than I hope forever to carry, I'll tell you that,' my wife said. 'But why are you asking me these questions? I like your cloth and if the price is right I mean to buy it.'

'You can only buy my cloth with love,' he said.

We began right then to understand that he was some kind of oddity. He was not like anybody we'd ever seen and he didn't come from around here. He'd come from a place we'd never heard of, and if that was the East, or wherever, then he was welcome to it.

'Love?' she said. 'Love? There's *love* and there's *love*, mister. What kind are you talking about?' She hitched a head my way, rolling her eyes, as if to indicate that if it was *passionate* love he was talking about then he'd first have to do something with me. He'd have to get me off my simmer and onto full boil. That's what she was telling him, with this mischief in her eyes.

I put down my pitchfork about here, and strolled nearer. I liked seeing my wife dealing with difficult situations. I didn't want to miss anything. My life with that woman has been packed with the unusual. Unusual circumstances, she calls them. Any time she's ever gone out anywhere without me, whether for a day or an hour or for five minutes, she's come back with whopping good stories about what she's seen and heard and what's happened to her. She's come back with reports on these unusual circumstances, these little adventures in which so many people have done so many extraordinary things or behaved in such fabulous or foolish ways. So what was rare this time, I thought, was that it had come visiting. She hadn't had to go out and find it.

'Hold these,' my wife told me. And she put the washtub of clothes in my hands, and went back to hanging wet pieces on the line, which is what she'd been doing when this man with the bolt of cloth ventured up into our yard.

'Love,' she told him. 'You tell me what kind I need, if I'm to buy that cloth. I got good ears and I'm listening.'

The man watched her stick clothespins in her mouth, slap out a good wide sheet, and string it up. He watched her hang two of these, plus a mess of towels, and get her mouth full again before he spoke. He looked about the unhappiest I've ever seen any man look. He didn't have any joy in him. I wondered why he didn't put down that heavy bolt of cloth, and why he didn't step around into a spot of shade. The sun was lick-killing bright in that yard. I was worried he'd faint.

'The ordinary kind,' he said. 'Your ordinary kind of love will buy this cloth.'

My wife flapped her wash and laughed. He was really tickling her. She was having herself a wonderful time.

'What's ordinary?' she said. 'I've never known no *ordinary* love.'

He jumped right in. He got excited just for a second.

'The kind such as might exist between the closest friends,' he said. 'The kind such as might exist between a man and his wife or between parents and children or for that matter the love a boy might have for his dog. That kind of love.'

'I've got that,' she said. 'I've had all three. Last year this time I had me a fourth, but it got run over. Up on the road there, by the tall trees, by a man in a car who didn't even stop.'

'That would have been your cat,' he said. 'I don't know much about cats.'

I put down the washtub. My wife let her arms drop. We looked at him, wondering how he knew about that cat. Then I laughed, for I figured someone down the road must have told him of my wife's mourning over that cat. She'd dug it a grave under the grapevine and said sweet words over it. She sorely missed that cat.

'What's wrong with loving cats?' she asked him. 'Or beasts of the fields? I'm surprised at you.'

The man shifted his burden and worked one shoe into the ground. He stared off at the horizon. He looked like he knew he'd said something he shouldn't.

She pushed me out of the way. She wanted to get nearer to him. She had something more to say.

'Now listen to me,' she said. 'I've loved lots of things in my life. Lots and lots. *Him!* she said (pointing at me), '*it*' (pointing to our house), '*them!*' (pointing to the flower beds), '*that*' (pointing to the sky), '*those*' (pointing to the woods), '*this*' (pointing to the ground)—'practically *everything!* There isn't any of it I've hated, and not much I've been indifferent to. Including cats. So put that in your pipe and smoke it.'

Then swooping up her arms and laughing hard, making it plain she bore no grudge but wasn't just fooling.

Funny thing was, hearing her say it, I felt the same way. *It, them, that, those*—they were all beautiful. I couldn't deny it was love I was feeling.

The man with the cloth had turned each way she'd pointed. He'd staggered a time or two but he'd kept up. In fact, it struck me that he'd got a little ahead of her. That he knew where her arm was next going. Some trickle of pleasure was showing in his face. And something else was happening, something I'd never seen. He had his face lifted up to this burning sun. It was big and orange, that sun, and scorching-hot, but he was staring smack into it. He wasn't blinking or squinting. His eyes were wide open.

Madness or miracle, I couldn't tell which.

He strode over to a parcel of good grass.

'I believe you mean it,' he said. 'How much could you use?'

He placed the bolt of white cloth down on the grass and pulled out shiny scissors from his back pocket.

'I bet he's blind,' I whispered to my wife. 'I bet he's got false eyes.'

My wife shushed me. She wasn't listening. She had her excitement hat on; her *unusual circumstances* look. He was offering free cloth for love, ordinary love, and she figured she'd go along with the gag.

'How much?'

'Oh,' she said, 'maybe eight yards. Maybe ten. It depends on how many windows I end up doing, plus what hang I want, plus the pleating I'm after.'

'You mean to make these curtains yourself?' he asked. He was already down on his knees, smoothing the bolt. Getting set to roll it out.

'Why, sure,' she said. 'I don't know who else would do it for me. I don't know who else I would ask.'

He nodded soberly, not thinking about it. 'That's so,' he said casually. 'Mend your own fences first.' He was perspiring in the sun, and dishevelled, as though he'd been on the road a long time. His shoes had big holes in them and you could see the blistered soles of his feet, but he had an air of exhilaration now. His hair fell down over his eyes and he shoved the dark locks back. I got the impression that some days he went a long time between customers; that he didn't find cause to give away this cloth every day.

He got a fair bit unrolled. It certainly did look like prime goods, once you saw it spread out on the grass in that long expanse.

'It's so pretty!' My wife said. 'Heaven help me, but I think it is *prettier* than grass!'

'It's pretty, all right,' he said. 'It's a wing-dinger. Just tell me when to stop,' he said. 'Just shout yoo-hoo.'

'Hold up a minute,' she said. 'I don't want to get greedy. I don't want you rolling off more than we can afford.'

'You can afford it,' he said.

He kept unrolling. He was up past the well house by now, whipping it off fast, though the bolt didn't appear to be getting any smaller. My wife had both hands up over her mouth. Half of her wanted to run into the house and get her purse so she could pay; the other half wanted to stay and watch this man unfurl his beautiful cloth. She whipped around to me, all agitated.

'I believe he means it,' she said. 'He means us to have this cloth. What do I do?'

I shook my head. This was her territory. It was the kind of adventure constant to her nature and necessary to her well-being.

'Honey,' I said, 'you deal with it.'

The sun was bright over everything. It was whipping-hot. There wasn't much wind but I could hear the clothes flapping on the line. A woodpecker had himself a pole somewhere and I could hear him pecking. The sky was wavy blue. The trees seemed to be swaying.

He was up by the front porch now, still unrolling. It surprised us both that he could move so fast.

'Yoo-hoo,' my wife said. It was no more than a peep, the sound you make if a butterfly lands on your hand.

'Wait,' he said. 'One thing. One question I meant to ask. All this talk of love, your *it*, your *those* and *them*, it slipped my mind.'

'Let's hear it,' my wife said. 'Ask away.' It seemed to me that she spoke out of a trance. That she was as dazzled as I was.

'You two got no children,' he said. 'Why is that? You're out here on this nice farm, and no children to your name. Why is that?'

We hadn't expected this query from him. It did something to the light in the yard and how we saw it. It was as if some giant dark bird had fluttered between us and the sun. Without knowing it, we sidled closer to each other. We fumbled for the other's hand. We stared off every which way. No one on our road had asked that question in a long, long time; they hadn't asked it in some years.

'We're not able,' we said. Both of us spoke at the same time. It seemed to me that it was my wife's voice which carried; mine was some place down in my chest, and dropping, as if it meant to crawl on the ground.

'We're not able,' we said. That time it came out pure, without any grief to bind it. It came out the way we long ago learned how to say it.

'Oh,' he said. 'I see.' He mumbled something else. He kicked the ground and took a little walk back and forth. He seemed angry, though not at us. 'Wouldn't you know it?' he said. 'Wouldn't you know it?'

He swore a time or two. He kicked the ground. He surely didn't like it.

'We're over that now,' my wife said. 'We're past that caring.'

'I bet you are,' he said. 'You're past that little misfortune.'

He took to unrolling his bolt again, working with his back to the sun. Down on his knees, scrambling, smoothing the material. Sweating and huffing. He was past the front porch now, and still going, getting on toward that edge where the high weeds grew.

'About here, do you think?' he asked.

He'd rolled off about fifty yards.

My wife and I slowly shook our heads, not knowing what to think.

'Say the word,' he told us. 'I can give you more if more is what you want.'

'I'd say you were giving us too much,' my wife said. 'I'd say we don't need nearly that much.'

'Never mind that,' he said. 'I'm feeling generous today.'

He nudged the cloth with his fingers and rolled off a few yards more. He would have gone on unwinding his cloth had the weeds not stopped him. He stood and looked back over the great length he had unwound.

'Looks like a long white road, don't it?' he said. 'You could walk that road and your feet never get dirty.'

My wife clenched my hand; it was what we'd both been thinking.

SnipSnipSnip. He began snipping. His scissors raced over the material. *SnipSnipSnip.* The cloth was sheared clear and clean of his bolt, yet it seemed to me the size of the bolt hadn't lessened any. My wife saw it too.

'He's got cloth for all eternity,' she said. 'He could unroll that cloth till dooms-day.'

The man laughed. We were whispering this, but way up by the weeds he heard us. 'There's doom and there's doom,' he said. '*Which* doomsday?'

I had the notion he'd gone through more than one. That he knew the picture from both sides.

'It *is* smart as grass,' he said. 'Smarter. It never needs watering.' He chuckled at that, spinning both arms. Dancing a little. 'You could make *nighties* out of this,' he said. 'New bedsheets. Transform your whole bedroom.'

My wife made a face. She wasn't too pleased, talking *nighties* with another man.

Innocence without heartbreak, I thought. That's what we're coming to.

He nicely rolled up the cloth he'd sheared off and presented it to my wife. 'I hope you like it,' he said. 'No complaints yet. Maybe you can make yourself a nice dress as well. Maybe two or three. Make him some shirts. I think you'll find there's plenty here.'

'Goodness, it's light,' she said.

'Not if you've been carrying it long as I have,' he said. He pulled a blue bandanna from his pocket and wiped his face and neck. He ran his hand through his hair and slicked it back. He looked up at the sky. His dark eyes seemed to have cleared up some. They looked less broody now. 'Gets hot,' he said, 'working in this sun. But a nice day. I'm glad I found you folks home.'

'Oh, we're most always home,' my wife said.

I had to laugh at that. My wife almost never *is* home. She's forever gallivanting over the countryside, checking up on this person and that, taking them her soups and jams and breads.

'We're homebodies, us two.'

She kept fingering the cloth and sighing over it. She held it up against her cheek and with her eyes closed rested herself on it. The man hoisted his own bolt back on his shoulder; he seemed ready to be going. I looked at my wife's closed lids, at the soft look she had.

I got trembly, fearful of what might happen if that cloth didn't work out.

'Now look,' I said to him, 'what's wrong with this cloth? Is it going to rot inside a week? Tomorrow is some *other* stranger going to knock on our door saying we owe him a hundred or five hundred dollars for this cloth? Mister, I don't understand you,' I said.

He hadn't bothered with me before; now he looked me dead in the eye. 'I can't help being a stranger,' he said. 'If you never set eyes on me before, I guess that's what I would have to be. Don't you like strangers? Don't you trust them?'

My wife jumped in. Her face was fiery, like she thought I had wounded him. 'We like strangers just fine,' she said. 'We've helped out many a-one. No, I can't say our door has ever been closed to whoever it is comes by. Strangers can sit in our kitchen just the same as our friends.'

He smiled at her but kept his stern look for me. 'As to your questions,' he said, 'You're worried about the golden goose, I can see that. Fair enough. No, your cloth will not rot. It will not shred, fade, or tear. Nor will it ever need cleaning, either. This cloth requires no upkeep whatsoever. Though a sound heart helps. A sweet disposition, too. Innocence without heartbreak, as I told you. And your wife, if it's her making the curtains or making herself a dress, she will find it to be an amazingly easy cloth to work with. It will practically do the job itself. No, I don't believe you will ever find you have any reason to complain of the quality of that cloth.'

My wife had it up to her face again. She had her face sunk in it.

'Goodness,' she said, 'it's *soft*! It smells so fresh. It's like someone singing a song to me.'

The man laughed. 'It *is* soft,' he said. 'But it can't sing a note, or has never been known to.'

It was my wife singing. She had this little hum under the breath.

'This is the most wonderful cloth in the world,' she said.

He nodded. 'I can't argue with you on that score,' he said. Then he turned again to me. 'I believe your wife is satisfied,' he said. 'But if you have any doubts, if you're worried someone is going to knock on your door tomorrow asking you for a hundred or five hundred dollars, I suppose I could write you up a guarantee. I could give you a PAID IN FULL.'

He was making me feel ashamed of myself. They both were. 'No, no,' I said, 'if she's satisfied then I am. And I can see she's tickled pink. No, I beg your pardon. I meant no offense.'

'No offense taken,' he said.

But his eyes clouded a token. He gazed off at our road and up along the stand of trees and his eyes kept roaming until they snagged the sun. He kept his eyes there, unblinking, open, staring at the sun. I could see the red orbs reflected in his eyes.

'There is one thing,' he said.

I caught my breath and felt my wife catch hers. The hitch? A hitch, after all? Coming so late?

We waited.

He shuffled his feet. He brought out his bandanna and wiped his face again. He stared at the ground.

'Should you ever stop loving,' he said, 'you shall lose this cloth and all else. You shall wake up one morning and it and all else will no longer be where you left it. It will all be gone and you will not know where you are. You will not know what to do with yourself. You will wish you'd never been born.'

My wife's eyes went saucer-size.

He had us in some kind of spell.

Hocus-pocus, I thought. He is telling us some kind of hocus-pocus. Yet I felt my skin shudder; I felt the goose bumps rise.

'That's it?' my wife said. 'That's the only catch?'

He shrugged. 'That's it,' he said. 'Not much, is it? Not a whisper of menace for a pair such as yourselves.'

My wife's eyes were gauzed over; there was a wetness in them.

'Hold on,' she said. 'Don't you be leaving yet. Hold this, honey.'

She put the cloth in my arms. Then she hastened over to the well, pitched the bucket down, and drew it up running over with fresh water.

'Here,' she said, coming back with a good dipperful. 'Here's a nice drink of cool water. You need it on a day like this.'

The man drank. He held the dipper in both hands, with the tips of his fingers, and drained the dipper dry, then wiped his chin with the back of a hand.

'I did indeed,' he said. 'That's very tasty water. I thank you.'

'That's good water,' she said. 'That well has been here lo a hundred years. You could stay on for supper,' she said. 'It's getting on toward that time and I have a fine stew on the stove, with plenty to spare.'

'That's kind of you,' he said back, 'and I'm grateful. But I'd best pass on up your road while there's still daylight left, and see who else might have need of this cloth.'

My wife is not normally a demonstrative woman, not in public. Certainly not with strangers. You could have knocked me over with a feather when she up and kissed him full on the mouth, with a nice hug to boot.

'There's payment,' she said, 'if our money's no good.'

He blushed, trying to hide his pleasure. It seemed to me she had him wrapped around her little finger . . . or the other way around.

'You kiss like a woman,' he said. 'Like one who knows what kissing is for, and can't hardly stop herself.'

It was my wife's turn to blush.

I took hold of her hand and held her down to grass, because it seemed to me another kiss or two and she'd fly right away with him.

He walked across the yard and up by the well house, leaving by the same route he had come. Heading for the road. At the turn, he spun around and waved.

'You could try the Hopkins place!' my wife called. 'There's a fat woman down that road got a sea of troubles. She could surely use some of that cloth.'

He smiled and again waved. Then we saw his head and his bolt of white cloth bobbing along the weeds as he took the dips and rises in the road. Then he went on out of sight.

'There's that man with some horses down that road!' my wife called. 'You be careful of him!'

It seemed we heard some sound come back, but whether it was his we couldn't say.

My wife and I stood a long time in the yard, me holding the dipper and watching her, while she held her own bolt of cloth in her arms, staring off to where he'd last been.

Then she sighed dreamily and went inside.

I went on down to the barn and looked after the animals. Getting my feeding done. I talked a spell to them. Talking to animals is soothing to me, and they like it too. They pretend to stare at the walls or the floor as they're munching their feed down, but I know they listen to me. We had us an *unusual circumstances* chat. 'That man with the cloth,' I said. 'Maybe you can tell me what you make of him.'

Thirty minutes later I heard my wife excitedly calling me. She was standing out on the back doorstep, with this incredulous look.

'I've finished,' she said. 'I've finished the windows. *Nine* windows. It beats me how.'

I started up to the house. Her voice was all shaky. Her face flushed, flinging her arms about. Then she got this new look on.

'Wait!' she said. 'Stay there! Give me ten minutes!'

And she flung herself back inside, banging the door. I laughed. It always gave me a kick how she ordered me around.

I got the milk pail down under the cow. Before I'd touched and drained all four teats she was calling again.

'Come look, come look, oh come look!'

She was standing in the open doorway, with the kitchen to her back. Behind her, through the windows, I could see the streak of a red sunset and how it lit up the swing of trees. But I wasn't looking there. I was looking at her. Looking and swallowing hard and trying to remember how a body produced human speech. I had never thought of white as a color she could wear. White, it pales her some. It leaves her undefined and washes out what parts I like best. But she looked beautiful now. In her new dress she struck me down to my bootstraps. She made my chest break.

'Do you like it?' she said.

I went running up to her. I was up against her, hugging her and lifting her before she'd even had a chance to get set. I'd never held on so tightly or been so tightly held back.

Truth is, it was the strangest thing. Like we were both so innocent we hadn't yet shot up out of new ground.

'Come see the curtains,' she whispered. 'Come see the new sheets. Come see what else I've made. You'll see it all. You'll see how our home has been transformed.'

I crept inside. There was something holy about it. About it and about us and about those rooms and the whole wide world. Something radiant. Like you had to put your foot down easy and hold it down or you'd float on up.

'That's it,' she said. 'That's how I feel too.'

That night in bed, trying to figure it out, we wondered how Ella Mae down the road had done. How the people all along our road had made out.

'No worry,' my wife said. 'He'll have found a bonanza around here. There's heaps of decent people in this neck of the woods.'

'Wonder where he is now?' we said.

'Wonder where he goes next?'

'Where he gets that cloth?'

'Who he *is*?'

We couldn't get to sleep, wondering about that.

1984

Rudy Wiebe

b. 1934

Born in a Mennonite farming community in northern Saskatchewan, near Fairholm, Rudy Wiebe grew up in a polyglot environment in which the Low German dialect was the language of everyday life, English that of school, and High German that of religion. After receiving his primary and secondary education in Saskatchewan and Alberta, where his family moved in 1947, Wiebe graduated from the University of Alberta in 1966. He then continued his studies at the University of Tübingen, West Germany, and completed his M.A. back at the University of Alberta. (His thesis was the manuscript of his first novel.) After earning a teaching certificate at the University of Manitoba and a Bachelor of Theology from the Mennonite Brethren Bible College, Wiebe worked for a year and a half for the *Mennonite Brethren Herald*, a weekly church publication. He resigned following a controversy over the details about Mennonite life revealed in *Peace Shall Destroy Many* (1962), a novel about the crisis a young man faces when he must choose between Mennonite pacifism and aligning himself with the general social atmosphere of Canada during the Second World War. He took a job teaching English at a Mennonite liberal arts college in Indiana, where he remained until 1967, when he accepted his present position in the English department of the University of Alberta.

Wiebe's second novel, *First and Vital Candle* (1966), describes a crisis of faith for a young man who, displaced from modern society, cannot find a satisfactory alternative among the native peoples in the North. Wiebe's next three books—*The Blue Mountains of China* (1970), a complex, panoramic history of the Mennonites; *The Temptations of Big Bear* (1973, Governor General's Award), an account of the disintegration of Indian culture that resulted from the growth of the Canadian nation; and *The Scorched-Wood People* (1977), the related story of Louis Riel's struggle to establish recognition for the Métis—are all epic stories of minority peoples who fight to maintain the integrity of their communities. *The Mad Trapper* (1980) chronicles the struggle between an isolated individual who has turned to violence and self-destruction, and the members of the northern community who must hunt him. In 1983 Wiebe published *My Lovely Enemy*, a love story set against an account of a historian's struggle to make sense of the past and of his own relationship to history. Wiebe's short fiction was collected in *Where is the Voice Coming From?* (1974); he later provided stories for *Alberta / A Celebration* (1979). Stories selected from both books were republished in *The Angel of the Tar Sands and Other Stories* (1982). Wiebe has also written a play, *Far as the Eye Can See* (1977), and edited a number of anthologies, some focusing on the western-Canadian short story, and others, such as *The Storymakers* (1970), placing the Canadian short story in an international context. In 1989 *Playing Dead: A Contemplation Concerning the Arctic*, a collection of Wiebe's essays about the North, was published.

The single most important feature of Wiebe's writing is the moral vision that derives from his religious background. Central to Mennonite belief is the rejection of wordly loyalties and values, particularly those associated with the state, in favour of commitment to a Christian community. (Revolutionary pacifists, Mennonites fled Germany and the Netherlands in the eighteenth and nineteenth centuries, going to Russia and the Americas, as much in an effort to preserve their community as to avoid the persecution and violence they had frequently encountered.) Wiebe believes that today this close, nonconformist community is no longer functioning as it should: he sees the Mennonites in North America as having accepted middle-class values and goals and become part of the modern, urban culture. Still, even though much of the original vitality of the community has been replaced by a reverence for heritage—which offers no free choices for the individual—and the once revolutionary new ways have become rituals, Wiebe considers these eroded communities better than none at all. Wiebe addresses these concens and his own role as an artist in his essays and interviews in *A Voice in the Land* (1981).

Wiebe does not see the loss of community and the alienation of the individual as unique to the Mennonites, and his fiction confronts these problems in other and larger contexts as well. In his three major novels he outlines what he sees as the obligatory human action: remaining true to one's beliefs while attempting to build, maintain, or re-establish a community—a spiritual collective that gains its identity from the antagonism of the outside world and from the martyrdom its leaders freely seek. The spiritual ideals that Wiebe's heroes seek to maintain are those that are reinforced by a historical consciousness—an ongoing involvement with, and devotion to, the past.

While Wiebe's interest in uniting present with historical events is not uncommon in Canadian writing, his faith in the redemptive value of revitalized history is. His method of reclaiming the forgotten past by adding imagined details of daily life and individual perceptions to material available in documents is an attempt to provide his readers with the texture of a spiritual community that is missing from their own experience. In a way that is parallel to his belief that communities must be almost inaccessible to those outside them, Wiebe makes entry into his fictional worlds difficult, through the use of unfamiliar dialects, a sometimes opaque style, complex time shifts, and meticulous detail. It is as if he writes his novels for an audience that shares his views, or is at least willing to be converted or tested. 'Where is the Voice Coming From?'—one of Wiebe's best-known stories—dramatizes his interest in the complex relationship of document, history, and fiction. In it Wiebe gives powerful expression to a sense of paradox that he shares with many of his contemporaries: while the act of turning events into stories may be falsifying, it is also our only way of knowing the past.

Where Is the Voice Coming From?

The problem is to make the story.

One difficulty of this making may have been excellently stated by Teilhard de Chardin: 'We are continually inclined to isolate ourselves from the things and events which surround us . . . as though we were spectators, not elements, in what goes on.' Arnold Toynbee does venture, 'For all that we know, Reality is the undifferentiated unity of the mystical experience,' but that need not here be considered. This story ended long ago; it is one of finite acts, of orders, of elemental feelings and reactions, of obvious legal restrictions and requirements.

Presumably all the parts of the story are themselves available. A difficulty is that they are, as always, available only in bits and pieces. Though the acts themselves seem quite clear, some written reports of the acts contradict each other. As if these acts were, at one time, too well known; as if the original nodule of each particular fact had from somewhere received non-factual accretions; or even more, as if, since the basic facts were so clear perhaps there were a larger number of facts than any one reporter, or several, or even any reporter had ever attempted to record. About facts that are still simply told by this mouth to that ear, of course, even less can be expected.

An affair seventy-five years old should acquire some of the shiny transparency of an old man's skin. It should.

Sometimes it would seem that it would be enough—perhaps more than enough—to hear the names only. The grandfather One Arrow; the mother Spotted Calf; the father Sounding Sky; the wife (wives rather, but only one of them seems to have a name, though their fathers are Napaise, Kapahoo, Old Dust, The Rump)—the one wife named, of all things, Pale Face; the cousin Going-Up-To-Sky; the brother-in-law (again, of all things) Dublin. The names of the police sound very much alike; they all begin with Constable or Corporal or Sergeant, but here and there an Inspector, then a Superintendent and eventually all the resonance of an Assistant Commissioner echoes down. More. Herself: Victoria, by the Grace of God etc., etc., QUEEN, defender of the Faith, etc., etc.; and witness 'Our Right Trusty and Right Well-beloved Cousin and Councillor the Right Honorable Sir John Campbell Hamilton-Gordon, Earl of Aberdeen; Viscount Formartine, Baron Haddo, Methlic, Tarves and Kellie, in the Peerage of Scotland; Viscount Gordon of Aberdeen, County of Aberdeen, in the Peerage of the United Kingdom; Baronet of Nova Scotia, Knight Grand Cross of Our Most Distinguished Order of Saint Michael and Saint George, etc., Governor General of Canada'. And of course himself: in the award proclamation named 'Jean-Baptiste' but otherwise known only as Almighty Voice.

But hearing cannot be enough; not even hearing all the thunder of A Proclamation: 'Now Hear Ye that a reward of FIVE HUNDRED DOLLARS will be paid to any person or persons who will give such information as will lead . . . (etc., etc.) this Twentieth day of April, in the year of Our Lord one thousand eight hundred and ninety-six, and the Fifty-ninth year of Our Reign . . .' etc. and etc.

Such hearing cannot be enough. The first item to be seen is the piece of white bone. It is almost triangular, slightly convex—concave actually as it is positioned at this moment with its corners slightly raised—graduating from perhaps a strong eighth to a weak quarter of an inch in thickness, its scattered pore structure varying between larger and smaller on its perhaps polished, certainly shiny surface. Precision is difficult since the glass showcase is at least thirteen inches deep and therefore an eye cannot be brought as close as the minute inspection of such a small, though certainly quite adequate, sample of skull would normally require. Also, because of the position it cannot be determined whether the several hairs, well over a foot long, are still in some manner attached or not.

The seven-pounder cannon can be seen standing almost shyly between the showcase and the interior wall. Officially it is known as a gun, not a cannon, and clearly its bore is not large enough to admit a large man's fist. Even if it can be believed that this gun was used in the 1885 Rebellion and that on the evening of Saturday, May 29, 1897 (while the nine-pounder, now unidentified, was in the process of arriving with the police on the special train from Regina), seven shells (all that were available in Prince Albert at that time) from it were sent shrieking into the poplar bluffs as night fell, clearly such shelling could not and would not disembowel the whole earth. Its carriage is now nicely lacquered, the perhaps oak spokes of its petite wheels (little higher than a knee) have been recently scraped, puttied and varnished; the brilliant burnish of its brass breeching testifies with what meticulous care charmen and women have used nationally-advertised cleaners and restorers.

Though it can also be seen, even a careless glance reveals that the same concern has not been expended on the one (of two) .44 calibre 1866 model Winchesters apparently found at the last in the pit with Almighty Voice. It also is preserved in a glass case; the number 1536735 is still, though barely, distinguishable on the brass cartridge section just below the brass saddle ring. However, perhaps because the case was imperfectly sealed at one time (though sealed enough not to warrant disturbance now), or because of simple neglect, the rifle is obviously spotted here and there with blotches of rust and the brass itself reveals discolorations almost like mildew. The rifle bore, the three long strands of hair themselves, actually bristle with clots of dust. It may be that this museum cannot afford to be as concerned as the other; conversely, the disfiguration may be something inherent in the items themselves.

The small building which was the police guardroom at Duck Lake, Saskatchewan Territory, in 1895 may also be seen. It had subsequently been moved from its original place and used to house small animals, chickens perhaps, or pigs—such as a woman might be expected to have under her responsibility. It is, of course, now perfectly empty, and clean so that the public may enter with no more discomfort than a bend under the doorway and a heavy encounter with disinfectant. The door-jamb has obviously been replaced; the bar network at one window is, however, said to be original; smooth still, very smooth. The logs inside have been smeared again and again with whitewash, perhaps paint, to an insistent point of identity-defying characterlessness. Within the small rectangular box of these logs not a sound can be heard from the streets of the, probably dead, town.

> *Hey Injun you'll get hung for stealing that steer*
> *Hey Injun for killing that government cow you'll get three*
> *weeks on the woodpile Hey Injun*

The place named Kinistino seems to have disappeared from the map but the Minnechinass Hills have not. Whether they have ever been on a map is doubtful but they will, of course, not disappear from the landscape as long as the grass grows and the rivers run. Contrary to general report and belief, the Canadian prairies are rarely, if ever, flat and the Minnechinass (spelled five different ways and translated sometimes as 'The Outside Hill', sometimes as 'Beautiful Bare Hills') are dissimilar from any other of the numberless hills that everywhere block out the prairie horizon. They are bare; poplars lie tattered along their tops, almost black against the straw-pale grass and sharp green against the grey soil of the plowing laid in half-mile rectangular blocks upon their western slopes. Poles holding various wires stick out of the fields, back down the bend of the valley; what was once a farmhouse is weathering into the cultivated earth. The poplar bluff where Almighty Voice made his stand has, of course, disappeared.

The policemen he shot and killed (not the ones he wounded, of course) are easily located. Six miles east, thirty-nine miles north in Prince Albert, the English Cemetery. Sergeant Colin Campbell Colebrook, North West Mounted Police Registration Number 605, lies presumably under a gravestone there. His name is seventeenth in a very long 'list of non-commissioned officers and men who have died in the service since the inception of the force.' The date is October 29, 1895, and the cause of death is anonymous: 'Shot by escaping Indian prisoner near Prince Albert.' At the foot of this grave are two others: Constable John R. Kerr, No. 3040, and Corporal C. H. S. Hockin. No. 3106. Their cause of death on May 28, 1897 is even more anonymous, but the place is relatively precise: 'Shot by Indians at Min-etch-inass Hills, Prince Albert District.'

The gravestone, if he has one, of the fourth man Almighty Voice killed is more difficult to locate. Mr Ernest Grundy, postmaster at Duck Lake in 1897, apparently shut his window the afternoon of Friday, May 28, armed himself, rode east twenty miles, participated in the second charge into the bluff at about 6:30 p.m., and on the third sweep of that charge was shot dead at the edge of the pit. It would seem that he thereby contributed substantially not only to the Indians' bullet supply, but his clothing warmed them as well.

The burial place of Dublin and Going-Up-To-Sky is unknown, as is the grave of Almighty Voice. It is said that a Métis named Henry Smith lifted the latter's body from the pit in the bluff and gave it to Spotted Calf. The place of burial is not, of course, of ultimate significance. A gravestone is always less evidence than a triangular piece of skull, provided it is large enough.

Whatever further evidence there is to be gathered may rest on pictures. There are, presumably, almost numberless pictures of the policemen in the case, but the only one with direct bearing is one of Sergeant Colebrook who apparently insisted on advancing to complete an arrest after being warned three times that if he took another step he would be shot. The picture must have been taken before he joined the force; it reveals him a large-eared young man, hair brush-cut and ascot tie, his eyelids slightly drooping, almost hooded under thick brows. Unfortunately a picture of Constable R. C. Dickson, into whose charge Almighty Voice was apparently committed in that guardroom and who after Colebrook's death was convicted of negligence, sentenced to two months hard labour and discharged, does not seem to be available.

There are no pictures to be found of either Dublin (killed early by rifle fire) or Going-Up-To-Sky (killed in the pit), the two teenage boys who gave their ultimate fealty to Almighty Voice. There is, however, one said to be of Almighty Voice, Junior. He may have been born to Pale Face during the year, two hundred and twenty-one days that his father was a fugitive. In the picture he is kneeling before what could be a tent, he wears striped denim overalls and displays twin babies whose sex cannot be determined from the double-laced dark bonnets they wear. In the supposed picture of Spotted Calf and Sounding Sky, Sounding Sky stands slightly before his wife; he wears a white shirt and a striped blanket folded over his left shoulder in such a manner that the arm in which he cradles a long rifle cannot be seen. His head is thrown back; the rim of his hat appears as a black half-moon above eyes that are pressed shut in, as it were, profound concentration; above a mouth clenched thin in a downward curve. Spotted Calf wears a long dress, a sweater which could also be a man's dress coat, and a large fringed and embroidered shawl which would appear distinctly Doukhobor in origin if the scroll patterns on it were more irregular. Her head is small and turned slightly towards her husband so as to reveal her right ear. There is what can only be called a quizzical expression on her crumpled face; it may be she does not understand what is happening and that she would have asked a question, perhaps of her husband, perhaps of the photographers, perhaps even of anyone, anywhere in the world if such questioning were possible for an Indian lady.

There is one final picture. That is one of Almighty Voice himself. At least it is purported to be of Almighty Voice himself. In the Royal Canadian Mounted Police Museum on the Barracks Grounds just off Dewdney Avenue in Regina, Saskatchewan, it lies in the same showcase, as a matter of fact immediately beside, that triangular piece of skull. Both are unequivocally labelled, and it must be assumed that a police force with a world-wide reputation would not label *such* evidence incorrectly. But here emerges an ultimate problem in making the story.

There are two official descriptions of Almighty Voice. The first reads: 'Height about five feet, ten inches, slight build, rather good looking, a sharp hooked nose with a remarkably flat point. Has a bullet scar on the left side of his face about 1½ inches long running from near corner of mouth towards ear. The scar cannot be noticed when his face is painted but otherwise is plain. Skin fair for an Indian.' The second description is on the Award Proclamation: 'About twenty-two years old, five feet ten inches in height, weight about eleven stone, slightly erect, neat small feet and hands; complexion inclined to be fair, wavy dark hair to shoulders, large dark eyes, broad forehead, sharp features and parrot nose with flat tip, scar on left cheek running from mouth towards ear, feminine appearance.'

So run the descriptions that were, presumably, to identify a well-known fugitive in so precise a manner that an informant could collect five hundred dollars—a considerable sum when a police constable earned between one and two dollars a day. The nexus of the problems appears when these supposed official descriptions are compared to the supposed official picture. The man in the picture is standing on a small rug. The fingers of his left hand touch a curved Victorian settee, behind him a photographer's backdrop of scrolled patterns merges to vaguely paradisiacal trees and perhaps a sky. The moccasins he wears makes it impossible to deduce whether his feet are 'neat small'. He may be five feet, ten inches tall, may weigh eleven stone, he certainly is 'rather good looking' and, though it is a frontal view, it may be that the point of his long and flaring nose could be 'remarkably flat'. The photograph is slightly over-illuminated and so the unpainted complexion could be 'inclined to be fair'; however, nothing can be seen of a scar, the hair is not wavy and shoulder-length but hangs almost to the waist in two thick straight braids worked through with beads, fur, ribbons and cords. The right hand that holds the corner of the blanket-like coat in position is large and, even in the high illumination, heavily veined. The neck is concealed under coiled beads and the forehead seems more low than 'broad'.

Perhaps, somehow, these picture details could be reconciled with the official description if the face as a whole were not so devastating.

On a cloth-backed sheet two feet by two and one-half feet in size, under the Great Seal of the Lion and the Unicorn, dignified by the names of the Deputy of the Minister of Justice, the Secretary of State, the Queen herself and all the heaped detail of her 'Right Trusty and Right Well Beloved Cousin', this description concludes: 'feminine appearance'. But the pictures: any face of history, any believed face that the world acknowledges as *man*—Socrates, Jesus, Attila, Genghis Khan, Mahatma Gandhi, Joseph Stalin—no believed face is more *man* than this face. The mouth, the nose, the clenched brows, the eyes—the eyes are large, yes, and dark, but even in this watered-down reproduction of unending reproductions of that original, a steady look into those eyes cannot be endured. It is a face like an ax.

It is now evident that the de Chardin statement quoted at the beginning has relevance only as it proves itself inadequate to explain what has happened. At the same time, the inadequacy of Aristotle's much more famous statement becomes evident: 'The true difference [between the historian and the poet] is that one relates what *has* happened, the other what *may* happen.' These statements cannot explain the storyteller's activity since, despite the most rigid application of impersonal investigation, the elements of the story have now run me aground. If ever I could, I can no longer pretend to objective, omnipotent disinterestedness. I am no longer *spectator* of what *has* happened or what *may* happen: I am become *element* in what is happening at this very moment.

For it is, of course, I myself who cannot endure the shadows on that paper which are those eyes. It is I who stand beside this broken veranda post where two corner shingles have been torn away, where barbed wire tangles the dead weeds on the edge of this field. The bluff that sheltered Almighty Voice and his two friends has not disappeared from the slope of the Minnechinass, no more than the sound of Constable Dickson's voice in that guardhouse is silent. The sound of his speaking is there even if it has never been recorded in an official report:

> *hey injun you'll get*
> *hung*
> *for stealing that steer*
> *hey injun for killing that government*
> *cow you'll get three*
> *weeks on the woodpile hey injun*

The unknown contradictory words about an unprovable act that move a boy to defiance, an implacable Cree warrior long after the three-hundred-and-fifty-year war is ended, a war already lost the day the Cree watch Cartier hoist his gun ashore at Hochelaga and they begin the long retreat west; these words of incomprehension, of threatened incomprehensible law are there to be heard just as the unmoving tableau of the three-day siege is there to be seen on the slopes of the Minnechinass. Sounding Sky is somewhere not there, under arrest, but Spotted Calf stands on a shoulder of the Hills a little to the left, her arms upraised to the setting sun. Her mouth is open. A horse rears, riderless, above the scrub willow at the edge of the bluff, smoke puffs, screams tangle in rifle barrage, there are wounds, somewhere. The bluff is so green this spring, it will not burn and the ragged line of seven police and two civilians is staggering through, faces twisted in rage, terror, and rifles sputter. Nothing moves. There is no sound of frogs in the night; twenty-seven policemen and five civilians stand in cordon at thirty-yard intervals and a body also lies in the shelter of a gully. Only a voice rises from the bluff:

> *We have fought well*
> *You have died like braves*
> *I have worked hard and am hungry*
> *Give me food*

but nothing moves. The bluff lies, a bright green island on the grassy slope surrounded by men hunched forward rigid over their long rifles, men clumped out of rifle-range, thirty-five men dressed as for fall hunting on a sharp spring day, a small gun positioned on a ridge above. A crow is falling out of the sky into the bluff, its feathers sprayed as by an explosion. The first gun and the second gun are in position, the beginning and end of the bristling surround of thirty-five Prince Albert Volunteers, thirteen civilians and fifty-six policemen in position relative to the bluff and relative to the unnumbered whites astride their horses, standing up in their carts, staring and pointing across the valley, in position relative to the bluff and the unnumbered Indians squatting silent along the higher ridges of the Hills, motionless mounds, faceless against the Sunday morning sunlight edging between and over them down along the tree tips, down into the shadows of the bluff. Nothing moves. Beside the second gun the red-coated officer has flung a handful of grass into the motionless air, almost to the rim of the red sun.

And there is a voice. It is an incredible voice that rises from among the young poplars ripped of their spring bark, from among the dead somewhere lying there, out of the arm-deep pit shorter than a man; a voice rises over the exploding smoke and thunder of guns that reel back in their positions, worked over, serviced by the grimed motionless men in bright coats and glinting buttons, a voice so high and clear, so unbelievably high and strong in its unending wordless cry.

The voice of 'Gitchie-Manitou Wayo'—interpreted as 'voice of the Great Spirit' —that is, The Almighty Voice. His death chant no less incredible in its beauty than in its incomprehensible happiness.

I say 'wordless cry' because that is the way it sounds to me. I could be more accurate if I had a reliable interpreter who would make a reliable interpretation. For I do not, of course, understand the Cree myself.

1982

George Bowering

b. 1935

A playful sense of humour has led George Bowering to add to the substantial body of work under his own name so many poems and reviews under various pseudonyms that his bibliographers may never straighten out all the questions of authorship. He has similarly confused his biographers by giving at least three different towns as his birthplace: Osoyoos, Penticton, and Oliver. ('A very slow birth in a fast-moving car' is the way he once explained this.) In any case, these towns are all near one another in the Okanagan Valley of British Columbia where he grew up. He left to become an aerial photographer for the RCAF (1954-7) and then enrolled at the University of British Columbia, where he eanred a B.A. in history (1960) and an M.A. in English (1963).

At UBC Bowering studied creative writing under Earle Birney and visiting professor Robert Creeley (who was Bowering's M.A. thesis adviser). Along with Frank Davey, Fred Wah, Daphne Buckle (Daphne Marlatt), and Lionel Kearns, he became part of a group of aspiring poets whose writing evinced an affinity with contemporary American movements. In particular, UBC professor Warren Tallman put these students in touch with the aesthetic theories and poetic practices current on the American west coast, especially those derived from William Carlos Williams and the Black Mountain movement (a school of poetry begun at Black Mountain College in North Carolina by Charles Olson, Robert Duncan, and Creeley), and from other *avant-garde* writers including Jack Spicer and Beat poet Allen Ginsberg. Following a 1961 visit to Vancouver by Duncan—who discussed Black Mountain theories and also talked about the importance of 'little magazines' in new poetry movements—these young B.C. poets decided to launch their own literary periodical. The anagramatically-named *Tish* became a monthly poetry 'newsletter' that patterned itself in part after such magazines as *Origin* in the U.S. and Louis Dudek's *Delta* in Canada.

The writers associated with the magazine, who came to be called the '*Tish* group', were greatly influenced by the Black Mountain movement's spare style (derived from the imagist tradition), its use of a loose poetic line based on the rhythms and pauses of colloquial speech, its emphasis on local and regional aspects of experience, and its belief in the communal nature of writing. Especially interested in the long poem (in the tradition of Williams's *Paterson*) and in the serial poem (as developed by Spicer), they rejected the lyric mode associated with what they decried as the 'humanism' and 'romanticism' of poetry from eastern Canada and the eastern U.S. Following Olson, they called for a poetry of essentials, accurate and objective, written by poets who, as Bowering later said, 'turned their attention upon the factual things that make up the world, men included among them' (*Tish*, No. 20, 1963).

Although *Tish* lasted for eight years (forty-five issues), its founders left after issue No. 19 to pursue other interests. Bowering accepted a teaching position at the University of Calgary, and went from there to the University of Western Ontario for further graduate studies before becoming writer-in-residence, and subsequently professor, at Sir George Williams University (now part of Concordia). In 1971 he returned to British Columbia to teach English and creative writing at Simon Fraser University. After leaving *Tish*, Bowering remained committed to little-magazine publishing in Canada, first founding and editing *Imago* (1964-74) and then becoming contributing editor for Frank Davey's influential literary journal, *Open Letter* (1965-).

The most prolific of the *Tish* group, Bowering has published some twenty-eight books of poetry, most of them with small presses. His first book, *Sticks & Stones* (with a preface by Creeley), appeared in 1963 as a Tish-book. Bowering received a Governor General's Award in 1969 for two of his books of poetry: *Rocky Mountain Foot* and *The Gangs of Kosmos*. In 1971 *Touch: Selected Poems 1960-70* was published, in 1980 *Selected Poems: Particular Accidents*, and in 1985 *Seventy-one Poems for People*. Since 1970 Bowering's most important poetry has taken the form of loosely unified long poems; several of these are reprinted in *The Catch* (1976) and in *West Window* (1982). The book-length poem, *Kerrisdale Elegies* (1985), a meditative sequence, has been recognized as Bowering's finest work. In this book, Bowering, like other poets of the *Tish*-group, avoids rhetorical devices as well as myth and metaphor, preferring a language and style close to common speech. (Indeed, two of his long works—*Autobiology*, 1972, and *A Short Sad Book*, 1977—seem to straddle the borderline between prose and poetry.) His poetry is saved from prosiness, however, by a subtle musical quality in the diction and rhythms, and from slackness by its sharply etched observations.

Bowering has also written a number of prose works. His fiction includes both short stories (collected in *Flycatcher & Other Stories*, 1974; *Protective Footwear: Stories and Fables*, 1978; and *A Place to Die*, 1983);

and novels: *A Mirror on the Floor* (1967); *Burning Water* (1980), which won Bowering his second Governor General's Award; and *Caprice* (1987). Although he has written critical pieces since his association with *Tish*, in the eighties he returned to criticism with new intensity, publishing four collections of earlier and new essays: *A Way with Words* (1982); *The Mask in Place: Essays on Fiction in North America* (1983); *Craft Slices* (1985); and *Imaginary Hand* (1988).

All of Bowering's writing—like that of other members of the *Tish* group—strives to communicate a sense of *process*, a sense of the writer contained in his writing and of the work as a part of his life. Such writing is post-modern in its rejection of the modernist doctrine of the artist as a detached maker of impersonal and permanent artifacts. It is through Bowering's personal awareness of his own loss that we are brought to his larger subject in *Kerrisdale Elegies*—the loss of culture and identity. Elegy as a form is not only appropriate to the subject, but it situates this sequence in a long Canadian tradition; a lament for lost ideals is a recurrent feature of both prose and poetry in Canada. In elegiac works the writer, by mourning and expressing a particular bereavement, assumes a sacrifical role. His isolation and loneliness serve to relieve readers of their own.

From *Kerrisdale Elegies*

ELEGY TWO

Dead poets' voices I have heard in my head
are not terrifying.
         They tell me like lovers
we are worth speaking to,
            I am a branch
a singing bird will stand on for a moment.

Like a singing branch I call out in return. How
do otherwise?
         Rather that than couple
with a swan on 41st Avenue.
              When Hilda
appeared in my dream, she did not visit, she
walked by, into the other room,
              and I didn't fall

10

in fear, but in love.

Inside.

Out there was the fortunate fall, mountains
glistening with creation,
                    a glacier between them,
flowing bright out of the working god's fingers,   20
first orchards rising from the melt, light
shaped on crest and cut,
                    the roll of storms
shaking new trees, flattening the grass,
                                        quick lakes
a scatter of mirrors, clouds in them, all
favour, all breathing side to side, all
being outside,
            all blossom.

As for us, we dissolve into hungers,   30
                                our breath
disappears every minute,
                    our skin flakes off
and lies unseen on the pavement.
                                She says
I've got you under my skin, yes, she says
you walk with me wherever I go,
                            you are
the weather.

            I reply with a call for help,   40
I'm disappearing,
                there's a change in the weather.

In love we have a secret language we dont remember.
We catch a word or two,
                    as the wind passes,
we turn an ear to the cool,
                    it's gone. The trees
shake their leaves to say look,
                        we're alive.
The house you've sat in for years remains   50
against all odds,
            a part of the earth.

We are the wisps,
            we flit invisible
around all that wood.
                They dont even hear us,

they may be waiting for us to say something important.

Late night on 37th Avenue I see lovers
on each other in a lamplit Chevrolet.

Do their hands know for certain that's skin   60
they glide over?
            I have rubbed my neck in exhaustion,
and almost believe I've touched something.

Is that a reason to look forward to next year?
Still, being dead
is no bed of roses.

Half the beautiful ones I have known are gone,
what's the hurry?
            On this street the school girls
grow up and disappear into kitchens,   70
                        a breeze
shakes the blossoms from my cherry tree,
there's cat hair all over the rug.
                    What happened
to that smile that was on your face
a minute ago?
            God, there goes another breath,
and I go with it,
            I was further from my grave
two stanzas back, I'm human.   80
                    Will the universe
notice my unattached molecules drifting thru?

Will the dead poets notice our lines appearing among them,
or are their ears filled with their own music?

Will their faces look as blank as these I pass
on 41st Avenue?
            I'm not talking about
making that great anthology,
                    I am recalling that god
who said excuse me, I wasnt listening, sorry.   90

Yet if they see the morning,
                    safe from their first
rough sea,
            if they smooth each other's hair,
talk about their weekend shopping—are they
what they were?
                    Are they as far from time?

Do they kiss, and try to kiss again, and say
inside, yes I remember this?
$\qquad\qquad$ Does a mask $\qquad\qquad\qquad$ 100
feel the touch of a mask;
$\qquad\qquad\qquad$ does the face
beneath the mask feel the mask?

Did you see ancient Fred and whitened Ginger
in the morning paper,
$\qquad\qquad$ June 25, 1982? Now
each time we see them glide by each other's
garments in black & white youth, we stand
amazed.
$\qquad\qquad$ How light that touch, how quick, $\qquad\qquad$ 110
how foreign to the dull surge of our own passion,
we thought.
$\qquad\qquad\qquad$ They generated enormous energy, yet
met like eyelashes.
$\qquad\qquad\qquad$ They were exactly like us.
God, if he choose,
$\qquad\qquad$ can press us into
sausage patties,
$\qquad\qquad$ he can flatten a car,
furl up a street, $\qquad\qquad\qquad\qquad$ 120
$\qquad\qquad$ tuck us into our own shoes.

But the moony flesh in the sedan
turns like the firmament,
$\qquad\qquad\qquad$ he is entangled
in legs and gearshift,
$\qquad\qquad\qquad$ she likely says yes
and grows to meet his growth,
$\qquad\qquad\qquad$ dumb imitation
of the burgeoning garden in the nearby yard.

I grow more frail as they fill the car, $\qquad\qquad$ 130
already disappearing,
$\qquad\qquad\qquad$ should I ask them
whether I exist?

Si me soubmectz, leur serviteur
En tout ce que puis faire et dire,
A les honnorer de bon cuer

I know they put their hands there and there
because their early fancy now arrives,
$\qquad\qquad\qquad$ an island

risen from a placid sea.   140
                An actual breast, a leg
that does not disappear below conflicting pictures.

But the ones who have touched me have
disintegrated into seraphs and books.

These half-undressed in the front seat
have nearly slipped from time,
                elastic hours
making Pleiades of the street.

We step out of cars, finally,
                movies come to an end,   150
we need a place at last that will fit us,
we need a cabin, a creek, a few trees,
maybe a typewriter and a sink.
                We are evaporating
as our heroes did.
            We cannot pursue our fragments
as they separate into earth and stars.

ELEGY FIVE

The white ball acts upon them as a stone in a pool.
They run, they bend, they leap, they fall
to the patchy green carpet,
walled away from the factory city.

The eye up high for a moment catches
a soft human Diamond,
           a star
twinkt in a moment by the hurl, the ex-
stacy of the thing among them.

                The giant at first   10
leaps then tumbles,
           his feet quick to return
to artificial earth.
           What holds him there
is not anywhere.

The crowd opens,
           rises like a row of poppies,
and subsides,
           scattering peanut shells like petals.

They surround the never-dying game,   20
a stem that feeds their seeming boredom,
the late innings,
                    the mom at home
basting a roast.
                    Children stray thru the stands,
faces away from the centre.

A thin fine play in the eighth
draws a flutter of hands.

The wrinkled neck of the third base coach
mocks his uniform,   30
                    or vice versa.
He wears no spikes,
                    but shoes like slippers.
His stomach falls over his double-knit belt.

His statistics lie like the skeleton of another man
in yearbooks out of print.

He never stands in the coach's box, as if
afraid it might be a grave.

*

Beauty is the first prod of fear,
                    the young   40
shortstop knows it but does not say it.
                              Tobacco
bulges his cheek,
                    his movement speaks
of his parentage,
                    a swan and a gangster.

He is simple for three hours.

He knows the ground between his feet.

You play thru your injuries,
                    you play   50
hurt,
        you knew it was waiting for you,
you remember your first bad arm,
it said your pension would be full of pain.

You hit the ground every day,
knocked over in the middle of your grace,
a green apple hitting every branch

on the way to the sun-beaten orchard floor;

your team-mates' play called it into being,

$\qquad$ your fall $\qquad$ 60

seen a hundred times on the screen,
a way down, and out.

$\qquad$ You bounce up

without a smile,

$\qquad$ but the crowd says 'ahh,'

and you look quick at your manager,

$\qquad$ dad,

were you watching me.

$\qquad$ He is looking in his book,

but your sore body grins $\qquad$ 70
all the way back to the dugout,
unaware of your steps over the grave.

Already the stands are noisy
with the call for some hitting,

$\qquad$ the home half

cuts the pain from your knees,

$\qquad$ your heart

hides in the shade,

$\qquad$ hoping the pitcher

will serve unwritten fate,

$\qquad$ your wooden friend $\qquad$ 80

will find a fatness,

$\qquad$ you will run

to throw yourself to earth again,

$\qquad$ let me in.

$*$

Baseball angel,

$\qquad$ it's early summer,

$\qquad$ accept him,

lighten the air,

$\qquad$ open the infield,

$\qquad$ give him $\qquad$ 90

one white rainbow today,

$\qquad$ set him on second,

the lovely red dirt all over his flannel.

Extra
basis.

$\qquad$ And shine bright shadows on the tan skin

of that sweetheart with the odd designation:
ball girl.

      I watch her blossom these years,
call her Debbie though I dont know her;   100

she sits in a simple folding chair next to the stands,
glove on her hand,
           blonde hair spilling from her cap,
long tan thighs,
        tall white sox.

She is not baseball at all,
but a harmless grace here,
         a tiny joy
glimpsed one time each inning,
             when she bends   110
and, oh God give us extra innings,
picks up the ball.

      We applaud, and nature
is good.

Les humains savent tant de jeux l'amour la mourre
L'amour jeu des nombrils ou jeu de la grande oie
La mourre jeu de nombre illusoire des doigts
Seigneur faites Deigneur qu'on jour je m'enamoure

Watching the game of work,
          I wonder at the big owe   120
how dark in my heart is the place where we all
could not make the play,
        fell to earth crooked,
swung a bat too late,
        threw far over the fielder's head,
cringed in fear of the hardness,
or the coach who scorned our fear.

Here is the fancied green of our wishes,
here where I still think the ballplayers are older than I,
this is where they are unreasonably adept,   130
where our failure is turned inside out,
by quick hands and an always white ball.

I sit in section nine and sometimes wonder why,
but know I am at ground zero
where art is made,
        where there is no profit,
no loss,

        The planet lies perfect in its orbit.
Diamonds,
        this green diamond at Little Mountain,   140
where these younger than we leap and run and fall
like our older brothers,
            where we shout inanities
from our high wall,
        our wit echoes loudly
from the right-field fence.

          This is not
poetry,
     neither is it play;
          it is life   150
whether you like it or not,
         money
changes hands,
      the sun goes purple and gold
behind the trees,
       the lights come on bright,
the ball is white,
      and someone
has to pay for it.

Dear spooks:
      if there were a domed stadium between the stars
upon whose astroturf athletic lovers
made plays beyond the hearts of these heroes,
daring ozone catches in deepest centre,
           stolen base
in a cloud of crystal,
       delightful silent hand-shakes
at home plate—

     and if they could arouse the crowd
of long-ghosted millions to a standing ovation,   170
a thunder-clap around the park,

        would that throng
cast blossoms of immortality over nine heads,
bring at last a satisfied smile to the face
between these shoulders here on earth,
         on the road,
in last place?

1984

Joy Kogawa

b. 1935

Born in Vancouver, Joy Kogawa found that the 1941 attack on Pearl Harbour—which generally changed the lives of Japanese-Canadians living on the West Coast—radically altered her own childhood. Separated by the Canadian government from home and possessions, Kogawa and her family were evacuated to a 'shack' in Slocan, B.C., and then to 'a smaller shack' in Coaldale, Alta. Deeply affected by the unjust treatment of Japanese-Canadians during the Second World War (many of whom were interned for the duration), Kogawa has written about these events in her poetry and in the short story 'Obasan', which grew into the novel *Obasan* (1981) as well as into *Naomi's Road* (a 1986 children's book that has become a school text in Japan). Kogawa has also worked as a political activist, seeking legal reparations for Japanese-Canadians adversely affected by government policies during the Second World War.

The daughter of an Anglican clergyman, Kogawa studied theology in Toronto, as well as music at the Royal Conservatory. She subsequently lived in Vancouver, Grand Forks, Moose Jaw, Saskatoon, and Ottawa, before settling permanently in Toronto in 1979. She worked as an elementary school teacher and a writer in the Prime Minister's office (1974-6), and has served as writer-in-residence at the University of Ottawa (1978).

Kogawa has published four collections of poems: *The Splintered Moon* (1967), *A Choice of Dreams* (1974), *Jericho Road* (1977), and *Woman in the Woods* (1985). In a poetry that is often epigrammatic, she uses specific events and sharply defined images to evoke larger philosophical issues. Gently shifting her poems towards allegory, she works in a way that might be compared to that of the Japanese craftsman (Naomi's grandfather) mentioned in 'Obasan', who uses a plane requiring a *pulling* motion rather than a *pushing* one ('a fundamental difference in workmanship')—she avoids didacticism by striving to elicit the reader's feelings rather than imposing her conclusions. Even in her longer poems about the internment (such as 'What do I Remember of the Evacuation' and 'Road Building by Pick Axe'), significance lies not so much in their collection of facts, figures, and personal memories, as in the implications that the reader finds in this data.

In *Obasan* the family's silence about the forced evacuation of the Japanese compels Naomi to gather information for herself from documents that have been responsible for changing her life. The novel itself becomes another document, one that exposes the inadequacies of 'historical truth' by challenging the accounts of 'the Japanese threat' with a different version—Naomi's—of the internment. Naomi learns that her family's story is constructed not only from events and versions of reality, but also from the silence that surrounds the experience. In the story 'Obasan' we see the compassion that Naomi gains from her search: behind easy judgements and the discovery that society's injustice is the sum of lesser evils, she finds the love and understanding that account for the survival during the war of the family's honour and values. This discovery is echoed by Kogawa in the poem 'What do I Remember of the Evacuation':

I remember how careful my parents were
Not to bruise us with bitterness.

Obasan

She is sitting at the kitchen table when I come in. She is so deaf now that my knocking does not rouse her and when she sees me she is startled.

'O,' she says, and the sound is short and dry as if there is no energy left to put any inflection into her voice. She begins to rise but falters and her hands, outstretched in greeting, fall to the table. She says my name as a question.

I put my shoulder bag down, remove the mud-caked boots and stand before her.

'Obasan,' I say loudly and take her hands. My aunt is not one for hugs and kisses. She peers into my face. 'O,' she says again.

I nod in reply. We stand for a long time in silence. I open my mouth to ask, 'Did he suffer very much?' but the question feels pornographic.

'Everyone dies some day,' she says eventually. She tilts her head to the side as if it's all too heavy inside.

I hang my jacket on a coat peg and sit beside her.

The house is familiar but has shrunk over the years and is even more cluttered than I remember. The wooden table is covered with a plastic table cloth over a blue and white cloth. Along one edge are African violets in profuse bloom, salt and pepper shakers, a soya sauce bottle, an old radio, a non-automatic toaster, a small bottle full of toothpicks. She goes to the stove and turns on the gas flame under the kettle.

'Everyone dies some day,' she says again and looks in my direction, her eyes unclear and sticky with a gum-like mucus. She pours the tea. Tiny twigs and bits of popcorn circle in the cup.

When I last saw her nine years ago, she told me her tear ducts were clogged. I have never seen her cry. Her mouth is filled with a gummy saliva as well. She drinks warm water often because her tongue sticks to the roof of her false plate.

'Thank you,' I say, taking the cup in both hands.

Uncle was disoriented for weeks, my cousin's letter told me. Towards the end he got dizzier and dizzier and couldn't move without clutching things. By the time they got him to the hospital, his eyes were rolling.

'I think he was beginning to see everything upside down again,' she wrote, 'the way we see when we are born.' Perhaps for Uncle, everything had started reversing and he was growing top to bottom, his mind rooted in an upstairs attic of humus and memory, groping backwards through cracks and walls to a moist cellar. Down to water. Down to the underground sea.

Back to the fishing boat, the ocean, the skiff moored off Vancouver Island where he was born. Like Moses, he was an infant of the waves, rocked to sleep by the lap lap and '*Nen, nen, korori*', his mother's voice singing the ancient Japanese lullaby. His father, Japanese craftsman, was also a son of the sea which had tossed and coddled his boatbuilding ancestors for centuries. And though he had crossed the ocean from one island as a stranger coming to an island of strangers, it was the sea who was his constant landlord. His fellow tenants, the Songhee Indians of Esquimalt, and the fishermen, came from up and down the B.C. coast to his workshop in Victoria, to watch, to barter and to buy.

In the framed family photograph hanging above the sideboard, Grandfather sits on a chair with his short legs not quite square on the floor. A long black cape hangs from his shoulders. His left hand clutches a pair of gloves and the top of a cane. On a pedestal beside him is a top hat, open end up. Uncle stands slightly to his right, and behind, with his hand like Napoleon's in his vest. Sitting to their left is Grandmother in a lace and velvet suit with my mother in her arms. They all look in different directions, carved and rigid with their expressionless Japanese faces and their bodies pasted over with Rule Britannia. There's not a ripple out of place.

And then there is the picture, not framed, not on display, showing Uncle as a young man smiling and proud in front of an exquisitely detailed craft. Not a fishing boat, not an ordinary yacht—a creation of many years and many winter evenings—a work of art. Uncle stands, happy enough for the attention of the camera, eager to pass on the message that all is well. That forever and ever all is well.

But many things happen. There is the voice of the RCMP officer saying 'I'll keep that one,' and laughing as he cuts through the water. 'Don't worry, I'll make good use of her.' The other boats are towed away and left to rot. Hundreds of Grandfather's boats belonging to hundreds of fishermen.

The memories are drowned in a whirlpool of protective silence. 'For the sake of the children,' it is whispered over and over. '*Kodomo no tame.*'

And several years later, sitting in a shack on the edge of a sugar beet field in southern Alberta, Obasan is watching her two young daughters with their school books doing homework in the light of a coal oil lamp. Her words are the same, '*Kodomo no tame.*' For their sakes, they will survive the dust and the wind, the gumbo, the summer oven sun. For their sakes, they will work in the fields, hoeing, thinning acres of sugar beets, irrigating, topping, harvesting.

'We must go back,' Uncle would say on winter evenings, the ice thick on the windows. But later, he became more silent.

'*Nen nen.*' Rest, my dead uncle. The sea is severed from your veins. You have been cut loose.

They were feeding him intravenously for two days, the tubes sticking into him like grafting on a tree. But Death won against the medical artistry.

'Obasan, will you be all right?' I ask.

She clears her throat and wipes dry skin off her lips but does not speak. She rolls a bit of dried up jam off the table cloth. She isn't going to answer.

The language of grief is silence. She knows it well, its idioms, its nuances. She's had some of the best tutors available. Grief inside her body is fat and powerful. An almighty tapeworm.

Over the years, Grief has roamed like a highwayman down the channels of her body with its dynamite and its weapons blowing up every moment of relief that tried to make its way down the road. It grew rich off the unburied corpses inside her body.

Grief acted in mysterious ways, its melancholy wonders to perform. When it had claimed her kingdom fully, it admitted no enemies and no vengeance. Enemies belonged in a corridor of experience with sense and meaning, with justice and reason. Her Grief knew nothing of these and whipped her body to resignation until the kingdom was secure. But inside the fortress, Obasan's silence was that of a child bewildered.

'What will you do now?' I ask.

What choices does she have? Her daughters, unable to rescue her or bear the silent rebuke of her suffering have long since fled to the ends of the earth. Each has lived a life in perpetual flight from the density of her inner retreat—from the rays of her inverted sun sucking in their lives with the voracious appetite of a dwarf star. Approaching her, they become balls of liquid metal—mercurial—unpredictable in their moods and sudden departures. Especially for the younger daughter, departure is as necessary as breath. What metallic spider is it in her night that hammers a constant transformation, lacing open doors and windows with iron bars.

'What will you do?' I repeat.

She folds her hands together. I pour her some more tea and she bows her thanks. I take her hands in mine, feeling the silky wax texture.

'Will you come and stay with us?' Are there any other words to say? Her hands move under mine and I release them. Her face is motionless. 'We could leave in a few days and come back next month.'

'The plants. . . .'

'Neighbours can water them.'

'There is trouble with the house,' she says. 'This is an old house. If I leave. . . .'

'Obasan,' I say nodding, 'it is your house.'

She is an old woman. Every homemade piece of furniture, each pot holder and child's paper doily, is a link in her lifeline. She has preserved in shelves and in cupboards, under layers of clothing in closets—a daughter's rubber ball, colouring books, old hats, children's dresses. The items are endless. Every short stub pencil, every cornflake box stuffed with paper bags and old letters is of her ordering. They rest in the corners of the house like parts of her body, hair cells, skin tissue, food particles, tiny specks of memory. This house is now her blood and bones.

She is all old women in every hamlet in the world. You see her on a street corner in a village in southern France, in her black dress and her black stockings. She is squatting on stone steps in a Mexican mountain village. Everywhere she stands as the true and rightful owner of the earth, the bearer of love's keys to unknown doorways, to a network of astonishing tunnels, the possessor of life's infinite personal details.

'I am old,' she says.

These are the words my grandmother spoke that last night in the house in Victoria. Grandmother was too old then to understand political expediency, race riots, the yellow peril. I was too young.

She stands up slowly. 'Something in the attic for you,' she says.

We climb the narrow stairs one step at a time carrying a flashlight with us. Its dull beam reveals mounds of cardboard boxes, newspapers, magazines, a trunk. A dead sparrow lies in the nearest corner by the eaves.

She attempts to lift the lid of the trunk. Black fly corpses fall to the floor. Between the wooden planks, more flies fill the cracks. Old spider webs hang like blood clots, thick and black from the rough angled ceiling.

Our past is as clotted as old webs hung in dark attics, still sticky and hovering, waiting for us to adhere and submit or depart. Or like a spider with its skinny hairy legs, the past skitters out of the dark, spinning and netting the air, ready to snap us up and ensnare our thoughts in old and complex perceptions. And when its feasting is complete, it leaves its victims locked up forever, dangling like hollowed out insect skins, a fearful calligraphy, dry reminders that once there was life flitting about in the weather.

But occasionally a memory that refuses to be hollowed out, to be categorized, to be identified, to be explained away, comes thudding into the web like a giant moth. And in the daylight, what's left hanging there, ragged and shredded is a demolished fly trap, and beside it a bewildered eight-legged spinning animal.

My dead refuse to bury themselves. Each story from the past is changed and distorted, altered as much by the present as the present is shaped by the past. But potent and pervasive as a prairie dust storm, memory and dream seep and mingle through cracks, settling on furniture, into upholstery. The attic and the living room encroach onto each other, deep into their invisible places.

I sneeze and dust specks pummel across the flashlight beam. Will we all be dust in the end—a jumble of faces and lives compressed and powdered into a few lines of statistics—fading photographs in family albums, the faces no longer familiar, the clothing quaint, the anecdotes lost?

I use the flashlight to break off a web and lift the lid of the trunk. A strong whiff of mothballs assaults us. The odour of preservation. Inside, there are bits of lace and fur, a 1920s nightgown, a shoe box, red and white striped socks. She sifts through the contents, one by one.

'That's strange,' she says several times.

'What are you looking for?' I ask.

'Not here. It isn't here.'

She turns to face me in the darkness. 'That's strange,' she says and leaves her questions enclosed in silence.

I pry open the folds of a cardboard box. The thick dust slides off like chocolate icing sugar—antique pollen. Grandfather's boat building tools are wrapped in heavy cloth. These are all he brought when he came to this country wearing a western suit, western shoes, a round black hat. Here is the plane with a wooden handle which he worked by pulling it towards him. A fundamental difference in workmanship—to pull rather than push. Chisels, hammer, a mallet, a thin pointed saw, the handle extending from the blade like that of a kitchen knife.

'What will you do with these?' I ask.

'The junk in the attic,' my cousin's letter said, 'should be burned. When I come there this summer, I'll have a big bonfire. It's a fire trap. I've taken the only things that are worth keeping.'

Beneath the box of tools is a pile of *Life* magazines dated in the 1950s. A subscription maintained while the two daughters were home. Beside the pile is another box containing shoe boxes, a metal box with a disintegrating elastic band, several chocolate boxes. Inside the metal box are pictures, duplicates of some I have seen in our family albums. Obasan's wedding photo—her mid-calf dress hanging straight down from her shoulders, her smile glued on. In the next picture, Uncle is a child wearing a sailor suit.

The shoe box is full of documents.

Royal Canadian Mounted Police, Vancouver, B.C., March 4, 1942. A folded mimeographed paper authorizes Uncle as the holder of a numbered Registration Card to leave a Registered Area by truck for Vernon where he is required to report to the local Registrar of Enemy Aliens, not later than the following day. It is signed by the RCMP superintendant.

Uncle's face, young and unsmiling looks up at me from the bottom right hand corner of a wallet size ID card. 'The bearer whose photograph and specimen of signature appear hereon, has been duly registered in compliance with the provisions of Order-in-Council PC 117.' A purple stamp underneath states 'Canadian Born'. His thumb print appears on the back with marks of identification specified—scar on back of right hand.

There is a letter from the Department of the Secretary of State. Office of the Custodian. Japanese Evacuation Section. 506 Royal Bank Bldg. Hastings and Granville. Vancouver, B.C.

Dear Sir.

Dear Uncle. With whom were you corresponding and for what did you hope? That the enmity would cease? That you could return to your boats? I have grown tired, Uncle, of seeking the face of the enemy hiding in the thick forests of the past. You were not the enemy. The police who came to your door were not the enemy. The men who rioted against you were not the enemy. The Vancouver alderman who said 'Keep B.C. White' was not the enemy. The men who drafted the Order-in-Council were not the enemy. He does not wear a uniform or sit at a long meeting table. The man who read your timid letter, read your polite request, skimmed over your impossible plea, was not your enemy. He had an urgent report to complete. His wife was ill. The phone rang all the time. The senior staff was meeting in two hours. The secretary was spending too much time over coffee breaks. There were a billion problems to attend to. Injustice was the only constant in a world of flux. There were moments when expedience demanded decisions which would later be judged unjust. Uncle, he did not always know what he was doing. You too did not have an all compassionate imagination. He was just doing his job. I am just doing my work, Uncle. We are all just doing our jobs.

My dear dead Uncle. Am I come to unearth our bitterness that our buried love too may revive?

'Obasan, what shall we do with these?'

She has been waiting at the top of the stairs, holding the railing with both hands. I close the shoe box and replace the four interlocking flaps of the cardboard box. With one hand I shine the flashlight and with the other, guide her as I precede her slowly down the stairs. Near the bottom she stumbles and I hold her small body upright.

'Thank you, thank you,' she says. This is the first time my arms have held her. We walk slowly through the living room and back to the kitchen. Her lips are trembling as she sits on the wooden stool.

Outside, the sky of the prairie spring is painfully blue. The trees are shooting out their leaves in the fierce wind, the new branches elastic as whips. The sharp-edged clarity is insistent as trumpets.

But inside, the rooms are muted. Our inner trees, our veins, are involuted, cocooned, webbed. The blood cells in the trunks of our bodies, like tiny specks of light, move in a sluggish river. It is more a potential than an actual river—an electric liquid—the current flowing in and between us, between our generations. Not circular, as in a whirlpool, or climactic and tidal as in fountains or spray—but brooding. Bubbling. You expect to hear barely audible pip-pip electronic tones, a pre-concert tuning up behind the curtains in the darkness. Towards the ends of our branches and fingertips, tiny human-shaped flames or leaves break off and leap towards the shadows. My arms are suffused with a suppressed urge to hold.

At the edges of our flesh is a hint of a spiritual osmosis, an eagerness within matter, waiting to brighten our dormant neurons, to entrust our stagnant cells with movement and dance.

    Obasan drinks her tea and makes a shallow scratching sound in her throat. She shuffles to the door and squats beside the boot tray. With a putty knife, she begins to scrape off the thick clay like mud that sticks to my boots.

[1978], 1984

Where There's a Wall

Where there's a wall
there's a way through a
gate or door. There's even
a ladder perhaps and a
sentinel who sometimes sleeps.
There are secret passwords you
can overhear. There are methods
of torture for extracting clues
to maps of underground passages.
There are zeppelins, helicopters,   10
rockets, bombs, battering rams,
armies with trumpets whose
all at once blast shatters
the foundations.

Where there's a wall there are
words to whisper by loose bricks,
wailing prayers to utter, birds
to carry messages taped to their feet.
There are letters to be written—
poems even.   20

Faint as in a dream
is the voice that calls
from the belly
of the wall.

1985

Road Building by Pick Axe

The Highway

Driving down the
highway from Revelstoke –
the road built by
forced labour – all the
Nisei[1] having no
choice etcetera etcetera
and mentioning this in
passing to this Englishman
who says when he
came to Canada from   10
England he wanted to
go to Vancouver too but
the quota for professors
was full so he was
forced to go to Toronto.

Found Poem

Uazusu Shoji
who was twice wounded
while fighting with the Princess Pats
in World War I
had purchased nineteen acres of land
under the Soldiers Settlement Act
and established a chicken farm.

His nineteen acres
a two-storied house
four chicken houses   10
and electric incubator
and 2,500 fowl
were sold for $1,492.59.

After certain deductions
for taxes and sundries were made
Mr Shoji received a cheque
for $39.32.

The Day After

The day after Sato-sensei[2]
received the Order of Canada

[1] Pronounced 'knee-say', a name for second-generation Japanese-Canadians. 'Issei' means first generation, 'Sansei' third generation.

[2] 'Sensei': teacher.

he told some of us Nisei
the honour he received
was our honour, our glory
our achievement.

And one Nisei remembered
the time Sensei went to Japan
met the emperor
and was given a rice cake   10
how Sensei brought it back to Vancouver
took the cake to a baker and
had it crushed into powder
so that each pupil might
receive a tiny bit.

And someone suggested
he take the Order of Canada medal
and grind it to bits
to share with us.

Memento

Trapped in
a clear plastic
hockey-puck
paperweight
is a black ink sketch
of a jaunty outhouse.

Slocan Reunion—
August 31, 1974
Toronto.

May 3, 1981

I'm watching the flapping
green ferry flag on the
way to Victoria—
the white dogwood flower
centred by a yellow dot.

A small yellow dot
in a B.C. ferry boat—

In the Vancouver Daily Province
a headline today reads   10
'Western Canada Hatred
Due to Racism.'

Ah my British
British Columbia, my
first brief home.

For Issei in Nursing Homes

Beneath the waiting
in the garden in
late autumn—how
the fruit falls without
a thud, the white
hoary hair falls and
falls and strangers
tread the grey walk ways
of the concrete garden.

How without vegetation how
without touch the old ones
lie in their slow days.

With pick axe then
or dynamite

that in their last breaths, a
green leaf, yes, and
grandchild bringing gifts.

1985

Minerals from Stone

For many years
androgynous with truth
I molded fact and fantasy
and where they met
made the crossroads home.

Here the house built
by lunatic limbs
fashioning what is not
into what might be—

a palace cave   10
for savage saints with
hunting knife still moist.

Bring me no longer
your spoils.
I have a house in the
shadows now and have
learned to eat minerals
straight from stone.

1985

Audrey Thomas

b. 1935

Born in Binghamton, New York, Audrey
Grace Callahan was educated at Smith College, with a year abroad at St Andrews University, Scotland. After completing her B.A.
at Smith in 1955, she returned to Britain,
taking employment as a teacher in Birmingham. There she married Ian Thomas, and
immigrated with him to British Columbia in
1959. She completetd an M.A. at the University of British Columbia in 1963, writing a
thesis on Henry James, and—after spending
two years in Ghana—returned to UBC for
further graduate studies. In 1972, following a
divorce, she and her three daughters settled
on Galiano Island off the B.C. coast.

Thomas published her first short story, 'If
One Green Bottle', in the *Atlantic Monthly*
in 1965; two years later it and nine other stories were collected in *Ten Green Bottles*. She
has since published *Ladies and Escorts*
(1977); *Real Mothers* (1981); *Two in the
Bush and Other Stories* (1981), which draws
from her first two collections; and *Goodbye
Harold, Good Luck* (1986). In addition to
her short fiction, Thomas has written several
longer works, beginning with the novel *Mrs.
Blood* (1970) and the paired novellas published as *Munchmeyer and Prospero on the
Island* (1971). In *Songs My Mother Taught
Me* (1973) she provides a fictional account of
her childhood and adolescence. *Blown
Figures* (1975), an experimental novel based
on her African experience, was followed by
Latakia (1979), a short novel about a failed
love affair and the failures of language.

Intertidal Life (1984) is Thomas's most ambitious exploration of sexual identity and of
the way the books we read, the metaphors
we use, and even the names we give things
influence our lives.

This fiction is usually about a
woman—often called Isobel in the early
work—whose life resembles the author's.
(Like Thomas, she had an unhappy childhood and a traumatic miscarriage in Ghana.)
However, Thomas does not simply recreate
her own experience, for although she breaks
down the barrier that divides fiction from
life, she does so without attempting either
documentary narrative or confessional writing. Her stories are not so much about what
occurred as about what *seemed* to have happened. For Thomas event is less important
than perception.

Thomas calls herself a woman's writer
who, in dealing with the questions women
confront in today's society, usually focuses
on conflict between men and women. Her
stories are of two types: those that treat the
physical aspect—and its effects on women's
bodies—of relationships between the sexes,
and those that deal with intellectual dynam-
ics, especially when the protagonist is an artist. The central female character in her
fiction is often fragmented, either because
she verges on schizophrenia or because she
and the external narrator of the story share
one consciousness. Such divisions—which
not only allow Thomas to dramatize the individual's capacity for a variety of responses to

a single event but call attention to the split between Thomas's own life and the fiction she makes of it—have led her to make intricate use of complementary perspectives. For example, the paired novellas *Munchmeyer and Prospero on the Island* take the form of the diary of a woman writing (on an island resembling Galiano) a novel called 'Munchmeyer', which takes the form of a male writer's diary. In such fiction male and female are shown to be as much aspects of one another as they are separate forces. Such doubling and mirroring appears elsewhere in Thomas's fiction, as in *Latakia*, where the protagonist—in love with another writer—finds herself competing with the man's wife in a way that suggests that neither the conventional nor independent roles available to contemporary women proves satisfactory.

Thomas's work can profitably be viewed in the context of postmodern writing. Her interest in the psychological breakdown of the individual has implications for her narrative structures. They often seem destabilized in ways that call into question our assumptions about the nature of fiction, suggesting that conventions need to be 'deconstructed' if writing is to reflect the flux of contemporary experience. In 'The Man with Clam Eyes', for example, Thomas changes the reader's sense of the 'reality' of the story as she shifts its modes of presentation: it opens with a paragraph that chronicles the 'facts' about a woman's retreat from society after a failed romance, but it ends as a fantastic fable. By playing with the rules of storytelling—for example, inserting bracketed information about setting and the narrator's incidental actions, as in a play or film-script—Thomas forces the reader to become aware of fiction as a text, rather than as a substitute reality. When she breaks with realistic or linear plot development in the story's conclusion—showing the narrator looking back on herself as a separate character still living in the cottage she has left behind—Thomas reminds us that stories are arbitrary, unreal, and partial. Such willingness to disorient the reader's sense of where 'reality' resides in fiction is one of the characteristics that distinguish postmodernism from modernism: readers must experience disorientation at first-hand, instead of being allowed to perceive alienation vicariously, through the dramatized experience of the characters.

The Man With Clam Eyes

I came to the sea because my heart was broken. I rented a cabin from an old professor who stammered when he talked. He wanted to go far away and look at something. In the cabin there is a table, a chair, a bed, a woodstove, an aladdin lamp. Outside there is a well, a privy, rocks, trees and the sea.

(The lapping of waves, the scream of gulls.)

I came to this house because my heart was broken. I brought wine in green bottles and meaty soup bones. I set an iron pot on the back of the stove to simmer. I lit the lamp. It was no longer summer and the wind grieved around the door. Spiders and mice disapproved of my arrival. I could hear them clucking their tongues in corners.

(The sound of the waves and the wind.)

This house is spotless, shipshape. Except for the spiders. Except for the mice in corners, behind the walls. There are no clues. I have brought with me wine in green bottles, an eiderdown quilt, my brand-new *Bartlett's Familiar Quotations*. On the inside of the front jacket it says, 'Who said: 1. In wildness is the preservation of the world. 2. All hell broke loose. 3. You are the sunshine of my life.'

I want to add another. I want to add two more. Who said, 'There is no nice way of saying this?' Who said, 'Let's not go over it again?'   The wind grieves around the door. I stuff the cracks with rags torn from the bottom of my skirt. I am sad. Shall I leave here then? Shall I go and lie outside his door calling whoo—whoo—whoo like the wind?

(The sound of the waves and the wind.)

I drink all of the wine in one green bottle. I am like a glove. Not so much shapeless as empty, waiting to be filled up. I set my lamp in the window. I sleep to the sound of the wind's grieving.

(Quiet breathing, the wind still there, but soft,
then gradually fading out. The passage of
time, then seagulls, and then waves.)

How can I have slept when my heart is broken? I dreamt of a banquet table under green trees. I was a child and ate ripe figs with my fingers. Now I open the door—

(West-coast birds, the towhee with its strange
cry, and the waves.)

The sea below is rumpled and wrinkled and the sun is shining. I can see islands and then more islands, as though my island had spawned islands in the night. The sun is shining. I have never felt so lonely in my life. I go back in. I want to write a message and throw it out to sea. I rinse my wine bottle from last night and set it above the stove to dry. I sit at the small table thinking. My message must be clear and yet compelling, like a lamp lit in a window on a dark night. There is a blue bowl on the table and a rough spoon carved from some sweet-smelling wood. I eat porridge with raisins while I think. The soup simmers on the back of the stove. The seagulls outside are riding the wind and crying ME ME ME. If this were a fairy tale, there would be someone here to help me, give me a ring, a cloak, a magic word. I bang on the table in my frustration. A small drawer pops open.

(Sound of the wind, the waves lapping.)

Portents and signs mean something, point to something, otherwise—too cruel. The only thing in the drawer is part of a manuscript, perhaps some secret hobby of the far-off professor. It is a story about a man on a train from Genoa to Rome. He has a gun in his pocket and is going to Rome to kill his wife. After the conductor comes through, he goes along to the lavatory, locks the door, takes out the gun, then stares at himself in the mirror. He is pleased to note that his eyes are clear and clam.   *Clam?* Pleased to note that his eyes are clear and clam?   I am not quick this morning. It takes me a while before I see what has happened. And then I laugh. How can I laugh when my heart is cracked like a dropped plate? But I laugh at the man on the train to Rome, staring at himself in the mirror—the man with clam eyes. I push aside the porridge and open my *Bartlett's Familiar Quotations*. I imagine Matthew Arnold—'The sea is clam tonight . . .' or Wordsworth—'it is a beauteous evening, clam and free . . .' I know what to say in my message.

The bottle is dry. I take the piece of paper and push it in. Then the cork, which I seal with wax from a yellow candle. I will wait just before dark.

(The waves, the lapping sea. The gulls, loud
and then gradually fading out. Time passes.)

Men came by in a boat with a pirate flag. They were diving for sea urchins and
when they saw me sitting on the rocks they gave me one. They tell me to crack it
open and eat the inside, here, they will show me how. I cry No and No, I want to
watch it for a while. They shrug and swim away.   All afternoon I watched it in
pleasant idleness. I had corrected the typo of course—I am that sort of person—but
the image of the man with clam eyes wouldn't leave me and I went down on the
rocks to think. That's when I saw the divers with their pirate flag; that's when I was
given the gift of the beautiful maroon sea urchin. The rocks were as grey and wrinkled as elephants, but warm, with enormous pores and pools licked out by the wind
and the sea. The sea urchin is a dark maroon, like the lips of certain black men I
have known. It moves constantly back/forth, back/forth with all its spines turning. I
take it up to the cabin. I let it skate slowly back and forth across the table. I keep it
wet with water from my bucket. The soup smells good. This morning I add carrots,
onions, potatoes, bay leaves and thyme. How can I be hungry when my heart is broken? I cut bread wiith a long, sharp knife, holding the loaf against my breast. Before
supper I put the urchin back into the sea.

(Sound of the wind and the waves.)

My bottle is ready and there is a moon. I have eaten soup and drunk wine and nibbled at my bread. I have read a lot of un-familiar quotations. I have trimmed the
wick and lit the lamp and set it in the window. The sea is still tonight and the moon
has left a long trail of silver stretching almost to the rocks.

(Night sounds. A screech owl. No wind, but
the waves lapping.)

I go down to the sea as far as I can go. I hold the corked bottle in my right hand
and fling it towards the stars. For a moment I think that a hand has reached up and
caught it as it fell back towards the sea. I stand there. The moon and the stars light
up my loneliness. How will I fall asleep when my heart is broken?

(Waves, then fading out. The sound of the
wild birds calling.)

I awoke with the first bird. I lay under my eiderdown and watched my breath in
the cold room. I wondered if the birds could understand one another, if a chickadee
could talk with a junco, for example. I wondered whether, given the change in seasons and birds, there was always the same first bird. I got up and lit the fire and put a
kettle on for washing.

(The iron stove is opened and wood lit.
It catches, snaps and crackles.
Water is poured into a large kettle.)

When I went outside to fling away the water, he was there, down on the rocks below me, half-man, half-fish. His green scales glittered like sequins in the winter sunlight. He raised his arm and beckoned to me.

(Sound of the distant gulls.)

We have been swimming. The water is cold, cold, cold. Now I sit on the rocks, combing out my hair. He tells me stories. My heart darts here and there like a frightened fish. The tracks of his fingers run silver along my leg. He told me that he is a drowned sailor, that he went overboard in a storm at sea. He speaks with a strong Spanish accent.

He has been with the traders who bought for a pittance the sea-otters' pelts which trimmed the robes of Chinese mandarins. A dozen glass beads would be bartered with the Indians for six of the finest skins.

With Cook he observed the transit of Venus in the cloudless skies of Tahiti.

With Drake he had sailed on 'The Golden Hind' for the Pacific Coast. They landed in a bay off California. His fingers leave silver tracks on my bare legs. I like to hear him say it—Cal-ee fórn-ya. The Indians there were friendly. The men were naked but the women wore petticoats of bulrushes.

Oh how I like it when he does that.

He was blown around the Cape of Good Hope with Diaz. Only they called it the Cape of Storms. The King did not like the name and altered it.   Oh.

His cool tongue laps me. My breasts bloom in the moonlight. We dive—and rise out of the sea, gleaming. He decorates my hair with clamshells and stars, my body with sea-lettuce. I do not feel the cold. I laugh. He gives me a rope of giant kelp and I skip for him in the moonlight. He breaks open the shells of mussels and pulls out their sweet flesh with his long fingers. We tip the liquid into our throats; it tastes like tears. He touches me with his explorer's hands.

(Waves, the sea—loud—louder. Fading out.)

I ask him to come with me, up to the professor's cabin. 'It is impóss-ee-ble,' he says. He asks me to go with him. 'It is impóss-ee-ble,' I say. 'Not at all.'

I cannot breathe in the water. I will drown. I have no helpful sisters. I do not know a witch.

(Sea, waves, grow louder, fade,
fading but not gone.)

He lifts me like a wave and carries me towards the water. I can feel the roll of the world. My legs dissolve at his touch and flow together. He shines like a green fish in the moonlight. 'Is easy,' he says, as my mouth fills up with tears. 'Is nothing.' The last portions of myself begin to shift and change.

I dive beneath the waves! He clasps me to him. We are going to swim to the edges of the world, he says, and I believe him.

I take one glance backwards and wave to the woman in the window. She has lit the lamp. She is eating soup and drinking wine. Her heart is broken. She is thinking about a man on a train who is going to kill his wife. The lamp lights up her loneliness. I wish her well.

1986

Alistair MacLeod

b. 1936

Born in North Battleford, Sask., Alistair MacLeod grew up in various small prairie settlements in Saskatchewan and Alberta until 1946, when his parents moved back to the family farm in Cape Breton. He graduated from high school there and worked to support himself in a variety of jobs (salesman, editor, logger, truck driver, public-relations man, miner, and teacher), put himself through Nova Scotia Teachers' College, and during the sixties earned degrees at St Francis Xavier University (B.A., B.Ed.), the University of New Brunswick (M.A.), and the University of Notre Dame (Ph.D., 1968). He taught at the University of Indiana for three years before taking his present position at the University of Windsor in 1969. He teaches English and creative writing and is fiction editor for the *University of Windsor Review*.

MacLeod's fiction began to appear in journals in Canada and the United States while he was still a graduate student. Although his output is small—MacLeod has published only two collections of short stories, *The Lost Salt Gift of Blood* (1976) and *As Birds Bring Forth the Sun* (1986)—he has received international recognition. In these stories Maritime life—although it is austere and even dangerous—provides a sense of stability and tradition that is threatened or lacking elsewhere. The world they depict is rich in memory and filled with narratives that, however old, retain their pertinence and dramatic immediacy. For MacLeod, as for many contemporary Canadian writers, fiction is often a meeting-place for realism and fable or folk-tale, where the everyday world takes on the power of myth.

As Birds Bring Forth the Sun

Once there was a family with a Highland name who lived beside the sea. And the man had a dog of which he was very fond. She was large and grey, a sort of staghound from another time. And if she jumped up to lick his face, which she loved to do, her paws would jolt against his shoulders with such force that she would come close to knocking him down and he would be forced to take two or three backward steps before he could regain his balance. And he himself was not a small man, being slightly over six feet and perhaps one hundred and eighty pounds.

She had been left, when a pup, at the family's gate in a small handmade box and no one knew where she had come from or that she would eventually grow to such a size. Once, while still a small pup, she had been run over by the steel wheel of a horse-drawn cart which was hauling kelp from the shore to be used as fertilizer. It was in October and the rain had been falling for some weeks and the ground was soft. When the wheel of the cart passed over her, it sunk her body into the wet earth as well as crushing some of her ribs; and apparently the silhouette of her small crushed body was visible in the earth after the man lifted her to his chest while she yelped and screamed. He ran his fingers along her broken bones, ignoring the blood and urine which fell upon his shirt, trying to soothe her bulging eyes and her scrabbling front paws and her desperately licking tongue.

The more practical members of his family, who had seen run-over dogs before, suggested that her neck be broken by his strong hands or that he grasp her by the hind legs and swing her head against a rock, thus putting an end to her misery. But he would not do it.

Instead, he fashioned a small box and lined it with woollen remnants from a sheep's fleece and one of his old and frayed shirts. He placed her within the box and placed the box behind the stove and then he warmed some milk in a small saucepan and sweetened it with sugar. And he held open her small and trembling jaws with his left hand while spooning in the sweetened milk with his right, ignoring the needle-like sharpness of her small teeth. She lay in the box most of the remaining fall and into the early winter, watching everything with her large brown eyes.

Although some members of the family complained about her presence and the odour from the box and the waste of time she involved, they gradually adjusted to her; and as the weeks passed by, it became evident that her ribs were knitting together in some form or other and that she was recovering with the resilience of the young. It also became evident that she would grow to a tremendous size, as she outgrew one box and then another and the grey hair began to feather from her huge front paws. In the spring she was outside almost all of the time and followed the man everywhere; and when she came inside during the following months, she had grown so large that she would no longer fit into her accustomed place behind the stove and was forced to lie beside it. She was never given a name but was referred to in Gaelic as *cù mòr glas*, the big grey dog.

By the time she came into her first heat, she had grown to a tremendous height, and although her signs and her odour attracted many panting and highly aroused suitors, none was big enough to mount her and the frenzy of their disappointment and the longing of her unfulfilment were more than the man could stand. He went, so the story goes, to a place where he knew there was a big dog. A dog not as big as she was, but still a big dog, and he brought him home with him. And at the proper time he took the *cù mòr glas* and the big dog down to the sea where he knew there was a hollow in the rock which appeared only at low tide. He took some sacking to provide footing for the male dog and he placed the *cù mòr glas* in the hollow of the rock and knelt beside her and steadied her with his left arm under her throat and helped position the male dog above her and guided his blood-engorged penis. He was a man used to working with the breeding of animals, with the guiding of rams and bulls and stallions and often with the funky smell of animal semen heavy on his large and gentle hands.

The winter that followed was a cold one and ice formed on the sea and frequent squalls and blizzards obliterated the offshore islands and caused the people to stay near their fires much of the time, mending clothes and nets and harness and waiting for the change in season. The *cù mòr glas* grew heavier and even more large until there was hardly room for her around the stove or even under the table. And then one morning, when it seemed that spring was about to break, she was gone.

The man and even his family, who had become more involved than they cared to admit, waited for her but she did not come. And as the frenzy of spring wore on, they busied themselves with readying their land and their fishing gear and all of the things that so desperately required their attention. And then they were into summer and fall and winter and another spring which saw the birth of the man and his wife's twelfth child. And then it was summer again.

That summer the man and two of his teenaged sons were pulling their herring nets about two miles offshore when the wind began to blow off the land and the water began to roughen. They became afraid that they could not make it safely back to shore, so they pulled in behind one of the offshore islands, knowing that they would be sheltered there and planning to outwait the storm. As the prow of their boat approached the gravelly shore, they heard a sound above them, and looking up they saw the *cù mòr glas* silhouetted on the brow of the hill which was the small island's highest point.

'*M'eudal cù mòr glas*' shouted the man in his happiness—*m'eudal* meaning something like dear or darling; and as he shouted, he jumped over the side of his boat into the waist-deep water, struggling for footing on the rolling gravel as he waded eagerly and awkwardly towards her and the shore. At the same time, the *cù mòr glas* came hurtling down towards him in a shower of small rocks dislodged by her feet; and just as he was emerging from the water, she met him as she used to, rearing up on her hind legs and placing her huge front paws on his shoulders while extending her eager tongue.

The weight and speed of her momentum met him as he tried to hold his balance on the sloping angle and the water rolling gravel beneath his feet, and he staggered backwards and lost his footing and fell beneath her force. And in that instant again, as the story goes, there appeared over the brow of the hill six more huge grey dogs hurtling down towards the gravelled strand. They had never seen him before; and seeing him stretched prone beneath their mother, they misunderstood, like so many armies, the intention of their leader.

They fell upon him in a fury, slashing his face and tearing aside his lower jaw and ripping out his throat, crazed with blood-lust or duty or perhaps starvation. The *cù mòr glas* turned on them in her own savagery, slashing and snarling and, it seemed, crazed by their mistake; driving them bloodied and yelping before her, back over the brow of the hill where they vanished from sight but could still be heard screaming in the distance. It all took perhaps little more than a minute.

The man's two sons, who were still in the boat and had witnessed it all, ran sobbing through the salt water to where their mauled and mangled father lay; but there was little they could do other than hold his warm and bloodied hands for a few brief moments. Although his eyes 'lived' for a small fraction of time, he could not speak to them because his face and throat had been torn away, and of course there was nothing they could do except to hold and be held tightly until that too slipped away and his eyes glazed over and they could no longer feel his hands holding theirs. The storm increased and they could not get home and so they were forced to spend the night huddled beside their father's body. They were afraid to try to carry the body to the rocking boat because he was so heavy and they were afraid that they might lose even what little of him remained and they were afraid also, huddled on the rocks, that the dogs might return. But they did not return at all and there was no sound from them, no sound at all, only the moaning of the wind and the washing of the water on the rocks.

In the morning they debated whether they should try to take his body with them or whether they should leave it and return in the company of older and wiser men. But they were afraid to leave it unattended and felt that the time needed to cover it with protective rocks would be better spent in trying to get across to their home shore. For a while they debated as to whether one should go in the boat and the other remain on the island, but each was afraid to be alone and so in the end they managed to drag and carry and almost float him towards the bobbing boat. They lay him facedown and covered him with what clothes there were and set off across the still-rolling sea. Those who waited on the shore missed the large presence of the man within the boat and some of them waded into the water and others rowed out in skiffs, attempting to hear the tearful message called out across the rolling waves.

The *cù mòr glas* and her six young dogs were never seen again, or perhaps I should say they were never seen again in the same way. After some weeks, a group of men circled the island tentatively in their boats but they saw no sign. They went again and again but found nothing. A year later, and grown much braver, they beached their boats and walked the island carefully, looking into the small sea caves and the hollows at the base of the wind-ripped trees, thinking perhaps that if they did not find the dogs, they might at least find their whitened bones; but again they discovered nothing.

The *cù mòr glas*, though, was supposed to be sighted here and there for a number of years. Seen on a hill in one region or silhouetted on a ridge in another or loping across the valleys or glens in the early morning or the shadowy evening. Always in the area of the half perceived. For a while she became rather like the Loch Ness Monster or the Sasquatch on a smaller scale. Seen but not recorded. Seen when there were no cameras. Seen but never taken.

The mystery of where she went became entangled with the mystery of whence she came. There was increased speculation about the handmade box in which she had been found and much theorizing as to the individual or individuals who might have left it. People went to look for the box but could not find it. It was felt she might have been part of a *buidseachd* or evil spell cast on the man by some mysterious enemy. But no one could go much farther than that. All of his caring for her was recounted over and over again and nobody missed any of the ironies.

What seemed literally known was that she had crossed the winter ice to have her pups and had been unable to get back. No one could remember ever seeing her swim; and in the early months at least, she could not have taken her young pups with her.

The large and gentle man with the smell of animal semen often heavy on his hands was my great-great-great-grandfather, and it may be argued that he died because he was too good at breeding animals or that he cared too much about their fulfilment and well-being. He was no longer there for his own child of the spring who, in turn, became my great-great-grandfather, and he was perhaps too much there in the memory of his older sons who saw him fall beneath the ambiguous force of the *cù mòr glas*. The youngest boy in the boat was haunted and tormented by the awfulness of what he had seen. He would wake at night screaming that he had seen the *cù mòr glas a'bhàis*, the big grey dog of death, and his screams filled the house and the ears and minds of the listeners, bringing home again and again the consequences of their loss. One morning, after a night in which he saw the *cù mòr glas a'bhàis* so vividly that his sheets were drenched with sweat, he walked to the high cliff which faced the island and there he cut his throat with a fish knife and fell into the sea.

The other brother lived to be forty, but, again so the story goes, he found himself in a Glasgow pub one night, perhaps looking for answers, deep and sodden with the whiskey which had become his anaesthetic. In the half darkness he saw a large, grey-haired man sitting by himself against the wall and mumbled something to him. Some say he saw the *cù mòr glas a'bhàis* or uttered the name. And perhaps the man heard the phrase through ears equally affected by drink and felt he was being called a dog or a son of a bitch or something of that nature. They rose to meet one another and struggled outside into the cobblestoned passageway behind the pub where, most improbably, there were supposed to be six other large, grey-haired men who beat him to death on the cobblestones, smashing his bloodied head into the stone again and again before vanishing and leaving him to die with his face turned to the sky. The *cù mòr glas a'bhàis* had come again, said his family, as they tried to piece the tale together.

This is how the *cù mòr glas a'bhàis* came into our lives, and it is obvious that all of this happened a long, long time ago. Yet with succeeding generations it seemed the spectre had somehow come to stay and that it had become *ours*—not in the manner of an unwanted skeleton in the closet from a family's ancient past but more in the manner of something close to a genetic possibility. In the deaths of each generation, the grey dog was seen by some—by women who were to die in childbirth; by soldiers who went forth to the many wars but did not return; by those who went forth to feuds or dangerous love affairs; by those who answered mysterious midnight messages; by those who swerved on the highway to avoid the real or imagined grey dog and ended in masses of crumpled steel. And by one professional athlete who, in addition to his ritualized athletic superstitions, carried another fear or belief as well. Many of the man's descendants moved like careful hemophiliacs, fearing that they carried unwanted possibilities deep within them. And others, while they laughed, were like members of families in which there is a recurrence over the generations of repeated cancer or the diabetes which comes to those beyond middle age. The feeling of those who may say little to others but who may say often and quietly to themselves, 'It has not happened to me,' while adding always the cautionary '*yet.*'

I am thinking all of this now as the October rain falls on the city of Toronto and the pleasant, white-clad nurses pad confidently in and out of my father's room. He lies quietly amidst the whiteness, his head and shoulders elevated so that he is in that hospital position of being neither quite prone nor yet sitting. His hair is white upon his pillow and he breathes softly and sometimes unevenly, although it is difficult ever to be sure.

My five grey-haired brothers and I take turns beside his bedside, holding his heavy hands in ours and feeling their response, hoping ambiguously that he will speak to us, although we know that it may tire him. And trying to read his life and ours into his eyes when they are open. He has been with us for a long time, well into our middle age. Unlike those boys in that boat of so long ago, we did not see him taken from us in our youth. And unlike their youngest brother who, in turn, became our great-great-grandfather, we did not grow into a world in which there was no father's touch. We have been lucky to have this large and gentle man so deep into our lives.

No one in this hospital has mentioned the *cù mòr glas a'bhàis*. Yet as my mother said ten years ago, before slipping into her own death as quietly as a grownup child who leaves or enters her parents' house in the early hours, 'It is hard to *not* know what you do know.'

Even those who are most skeptical, like my oldest brother who has driven here from Montreal, betray themselves by their nervous actions. 'I avoided the Greyhound bus stations in both Montreal and Toronto,' he smiled upon his arrival, and then added, 'Just in case.'

He did not realize how ill our father was and has smiled little since then. I watch him turning the diamond ring upon his finger, knowing that he hopes he will not hear the Gaelic phrase he knows too well. Not having the luxury, as he once said, of some who live in Montreal and are able to pretend they do not understand the 'other' language. You cannot *not* know what you do know.

Sitting here, taking turns holding the hands of the man who gave us life, we are afraid for him and for ourselves. We are afraid of what he may see and we are afraid to hear the phrase born of the vision. We are aware that it may become confused with what the doctors call 'the will to live' and we are aware that some beliefs are what others would dismiss as 'garbage.' We are aware that there are men who believe the earth is flat and that the birds bring forth the sun.

Bound here in our own peculiar mortality, we do not wish to see or see others see that which signifies life's demise. We do not want to hear the voice of our father, as did those other sons, calling down his own particular death upon him.

We would shut our eyes and plug our ears, even as we know such actions to be of no avail. Open still and fearful to the grey hair rising on our necks if and when we hear the scrabble of the paws and the scratching at the door.

1986

John Newlove

b. 1938

On the move since childhood, John Herbert Newlove grew up in a number of farming communities in his native Saskatchewan before leaving the Prairies in 1960. Since then he has lived in California, British Columbia, Ontario, Quebec, and the Maritimes. He returned to the West in 1979, living first in Regina (his birthplace), and then in Nelson, B.C., before moving to Ottawa in 1986. A poet since his late teens, he has supported himself primarily as an editor and writer. Since the appearance of his first book, *Grave Sirs* (1962), he has published ten collections, among which are *Moving in Alone* (1965);

Black Night Window (1968); *The Cave* (1970); *Lies* (1972), winner of a Governor General's Award; and *The Fat Man: Selected Poems 1962-1972* (1977).

Early in his career Newlove developed the distinctive prairie voice—spare, and free of complex imagery and metaphor—later heard in the poetry of other western writers (including Robert Kroetsch and Eli Mandel). This voice is particularly well suited to Newlove's harsh vision of the world. His clipped syntax and austere diction give an ironic tone to his natural lyricism and create a dissonant style that expresses the psychic dissonance resulting from the combination of his wonder at the prairie landscape and the restless malaise that denies him complete union with his environment. In Newlove's work mankind, lacking control over its fate, searches fruitlessly for some pattern to give meaning to life but repeatedly fails to recognize such order as exists. The dominant tone of Newlove's writing is therefore pessimistic, sometimes even nihilistic. The personal poetry of his early books, in which his youthful *esprit* leavened his natural cynicism, gives way in later works to depictions of a joyless death amid universal alienation. In this work only occasional figures from the past—Riel, Hearne, and the nomadic Indians that peopled the West—achieve a necessary, if harrowing, integration with the landscape. In contrast to these heroic types are the many defeated personae who dwell in a world marred by man's corrupt nature. Although Newlove's 1981 book *The Green Plain* offers some retreat from this dark view, his 1986 collection, *The Night the Dog Smiled*, which contains both new poems and revisions of earlier unpublished work, returns to a bleak vision of man as a corrupted inhabitant of an indifferent universe.

Four Small Scars

This scar beneath my lip
is symbol of a friend's rough love
though some would call it anger,
mistakenly. This scar

crescent on my wrist
is symbol of a woman's delicate anger
though some would call it love,
mistakenly. My belly's scar

is symbol of a surgical precision:
no anger, no love. The small   10
fading mark on my hand

is token of my imprecision,
of my own carving, my anger and my love.

1965

The Double-Headed Snake

Not to lose the feel of the mountains
while still retaining the prairies
is a difficult thing. What's lovely
is whatever makes the adrenalin run;
therefore I count terror and fear among
the greatest beauty. The greatest
beauty is to be alive, forgetting nothing,
although remembrance hurts
like a foolish act, is a foolish act.

Beauty's whatever   10
makes the adrenalin run. Fear
in the mountains at night-time's
not tenuous, it is not the cold
that makes me shiver, civilized man,
white, I remember
the stories of the Indians,
Sis-i-utl, the double-headed snake.[1]

Beauty's what makes
the adrenalin run. Fear at night
on the level plains, with no horizon   20
and the stars too bright, wind bitter
even in June, in winter
the snow harsh and blowing,
is what makes me
shiver, not the cold air alone.

And one beauty cancels another. The plains
seem secure and comfortable
at Crow's Nest Pass;[2] in Saskatchewan
the mountains are comforting
to think of; among   30
the eastwardly diminishing hills
both the flatland and the ridge
seem easy to endure.

As one beauty
cancels another, remembrance
is a foolish act, a double-headed snake
striking in both directions, but I
remember plains and mountains, places
I come from, places I adhere and live in.

1968

[1] According to Newlove, a figure from west-coast Indian tales; the sight of either end of the snake
turns one to stone.
[2] Pass in the Rocky Mountains between Alberta and British Columbia through which a branch CPR
line was built in 1898.

Samuel Hearne[1] in Wintertime

I

In this cold room
I remember the smell of manure
on men's heavy clothes as good,
the smell of horses.

It is a romantic world
to readers of journeys
to the Northern Ocean—

especially if their houses are heated
to some degree, Samuel.

Hearne, your camp must have smelled
like hell whenever you settled down
for a few days of rest and journal-work:

hell smeared with human manure,
hell half-full of raw hides,
hell of sweat, Indians, stale fat,
meat-hell, fear-hell, hell of cold.

2

One child is back from the doctor's while
the other one wanders about in dirty pants
and I think of Samuel Hearne and the land—

puffy children coughing as I think,
crying, sick-faced,
vomit stirring in grey blankets
from room to room.

It is Christmastime—
the cold flesh shines.
No praise in merely enduring.

3

Samuel Hearne did more
in the land (like all the rest

full of rocks and hilly country,
many very extensive tracts of land,

[1](1745-92), early Canadian explorer and author of a classic travel narrative, *A Journey from Prince of Wales's Fort in Hudson's Bay to the Northern Ocean* (1795), about his explorations in the North (see pp. 18-26). The conclusion of Newlove's poem alludes to a famous passage in that book recounting Hearne's accompanying a band of Indians in their massacre of an Eskimo village; in it Hearne describes the death of an eighteen-year-old girl who, when struck by a spear, twisted herself about his legs and—as Hearne pleaded for mercy for her—was dispatched by two more Indians, her body 'twining round their spears like an eel!' (The full account is reprinted on pp. 23-6.)

tittimeg, pike and barble,[2]

and the islands:
the islands, many
of them abound

as well as the main
land does
with dwarf woods,

chiefly pine
in some parts intermixed
with larch and birch) than endure.   40

The Indians killed twelve deer.
It was impossible to describe
the intenseness of the cold.

4
And, Samuel Hearne,
I have almost begun to talk

as if you wanted to be
gallant, as if you went
through that land for a book—

as if you were not SAM, wanting
to know, to do a job.   50

5
There was that Eskimo girl
at Bloody Falls, at your feet,

Samuel Hearne, with two spears in her,
you helpless before your helpers,

and she twisted about them like
an eel, dying, never to know.

1968

---

[2]Three types of fish that Hearne found in the north.

Ride Off Any Horizon

Ride off any horizon
and let the measure fall
where it may—

on the hot wheat,
on the dark yellow fields
of wild mustard, the fields

of bad farmers, on the river,
on the dirty river full
of boys and on the throbbing

powerhouse and the low dam   10
of cheap cement and rocks
boiling with white water,

and on the cows and their powerful
bulls, the heavy tracks
filling with liquid at the edge

of the narrow prairie
river running steadily away.

*

Ride off any horizon
and let the measure fall
where it may—   20

among the piles of bones
that dot the prairie

in vision and history
(the buffalo and deer,

dead indians, dead settlers
the frames of lost houses

left behind in the dust
of the depression,

dry and profound, that
will come again in the land   30

and in the spirit, the land
shifting and the minds

blown dry and empty—
I have not seen it! except

in pictures and talk—
but there is the fence

covered with dust, laden,
the wrecked house stupidly empty)—

here is a picture for your wallet,
of the beaten farmer and his wife   40
leaning toward each other—

sadly smiling, and emptied of desire.

*

Ride off any horizon
and let the measure fall
where it may—

off the edge
of the black prairie

as you thought you could fall,
a boy at sunset

not watching the sun   50
set but watching the black earth,

never-ending they said in school,
round: but you saw it ending,

finished, definite, precise—
visible only miles away.

*

Ride off any horizon
and let the measure fall
where it may—

on a hot night the town
is in the streets—   60

the boys and girls
are practising against

each other, the men
talk and eye the girls—

the women talk and
eye each other, the indians
play pool: eye on the ball.

*

Ride off any horizon
and let the measure fall
where it may—   70

and damn the troops, the horsemen
are wheeling in the sunshine,
the cree, practising

for their deaths: mr poundmaker,
gentle sweet mr bigbear,
it is not unfortunately

quite enough to be innocent,
it is not enough merely
not to offend—

at times to be born   80
is enough, to be
in the way is too much—

some colonel otter[1], some
major-general middleton will
get you, you—

indian. It is no good to say,
I would rather die
at once than be in that place—

though you love that land more,
you will go where they take you.   90

*

Ride off any horizon
and let the measure fall!—

where it may;
it doesn't have to be

the prairie. It could be
the cold soul of the cities

blown empty by commerce
and desiring commerce
to fill up emptiness.

[1] Sir William Dillon Otter (1843-1929), Canadian colonel in command to the militia that relieved the settlers under attack at Fort Battleford and who was defeated by Poundmaker at Cut Knife Hill. 'Major-General Middleton': Sir Frederick Dobson Middleton (1825-98), British commander of the Canadian militia during the suppression of the North West Rebellion.

The streets are full of people.   100

It is night, the lights
are on; the wind

blows as far as it may. The streets
are dark and full of people.

Their eyes are fixed as far as
they can see beyond each other—

to the concrete horizon, definite,
tall against the mountains,
stopping vision visibly.

1968

Jack Hodgins

b. 1938

Jack Hodgins has published two books of short stories, *Spit Delaney's Island* (1977) and *The Barclay Family Theatre* (1981), and three novels: *The Invention of the World* (1977), *The Resurrection of Joseph Bourne* (1979), and *The Honorary Patron* (1987). Hodgins' narratives centre on the community life of northern Vancouver Island, where he was born and has spent much of his adult life. Raised in the small farming and logging town of Merville, B.C.—in which, according to Hodgins, everyone was either a relative or a friend—he attended the University of British Columbia, receiving a B.Ed. in 1961. He then took a job teaching high-school English in Nanaimo, where he remained until 1979. After a period as writer-in-residence and professor at the University of Ottawa, and a visit to Australia as a result of winning the Canada-Australia Literary Prize, he returned to Vancouver Island to teach at the University of Victoria.

Hodgins' storytelling often combines the anecdotal feeling of the back-country yarn with the magic quality of myth. His novels are flamboyant epics with a sense of the marvellous that recalls the fiction of such Latin American writers as Jorge-Luis Borges and Gabriel García Márquez. The fantastic elements that appear in much of Hodgins' writing seems to arise naturally from the innocently corrupt island communities that are his settings. Unlike the planned settlements of the mainland, these Edens gone to seed have evolved haphazardly—founded by a madman in *The Invention of the World*, restored by a dead man in *The Resurrection of Joseph Bourne*, confronted by a homecomer in *The Honorary Patron*—and in their ingrown state, normality and eccentricity exist in comfortable symbiosis. In such a world Hodgins does not need to create new mythologies; he selects from those abundantly available to him.

While Hodgins' extravagant vision is characteristically western, it differs from that of many western novelists. It develops from a Vancouver Island environment that—in contrast to the empty prairie landscapes of Sinclair Ross, W.O. Mitchell, and even Robert Kroetsch—seems plentiful and almost idyllic. However, this environment is also constricted and often (as in the story below) becomes ironic as a result of disappointed expectations.

By the River

But listen, she thinks, it's nearly time.

And flutters, leaf-like, at the thought. The train will rumble down the valley, stop at the little shack to discharge Styan, and move on. This will happen in half an hour and she has a mile still to walk.

Crystal Styan walking through the woods, through bush, is not pretty. She knows that she is not even a little pretty, though her face is small enough, and pale, and her eyes are not too narrow. She wears a yellow wool sweater and a long cotton skirt and boots. Her hair, tied back so the branches will not catch in it, hangs straight and almost colourless down her back. Some day, she expects, there will be a baby to play with her hair and hide in it like someone behind a waterfall.

She has left the log cabin, which sits on the edge of the river in a stand of birch, and now she follows the river bank upstream. A mile ahead, far around the bend out of sight, the railroad tracks pass along the rim of their land and a small station is built there just for them, for her and Jim Styan. It is their only way in to town, which is ten miles away and not much of a town anyway when you get there. A few stores, a tilted old hotel, a movie theatre.

Likely, Styan would have been to a movie last night. He would have stayed the night in the hotel, but first (after he had seen the lawyer and bought the few things she'd asked him for) he would pay his money and sit in the back row of the theatre and laugh loudly all the way through the movie. He always laughs at everything, even if it isn't funny, because those figures on the screen make him think of people he has known; and the thought of them exposed like this for just anyone to see embarrasses him a little and makes him want to create a lot of noise so people will know he isn't a bit like that himself.

She smiles. The first time they went to a movie together she slouched as far down in the seat as she could so no one could see she was there or had anything to do with Jim Styan.

The river flows past her almost silently. It has moved only a hundred miles from its source and has another thousand miles to go before it reaches the ocean, but already it is wide enough and fast. Right here she has more than once seen a moose wade out and then swim across to the other side and disappear into the cedar swamps. She knows something, has heard somewhere that farther downstream, miles and miles behind her, an Indian band once thought this river a hungry monster that liked to gobble up their people. They say that Coyote their god-hero dived in and subdued the monster and made it promise never to swallow people again. She once thought she'd like to study that kind of thing at a university or somewhere, if Jim Styan hadn't told her grade ten was good enough for anyone and a life on the road was more exciting.

What road? she wonders. There isn't a road within ten miles. They sold the rickety old blue pickup the same day they moved onto this place. The railroad was going to be all they'd need. There wasn't any place they cared to go that the train, even this old-fashioned milk-run outfit, couldn't take them easily and cheaply enough.

But listen, she thinks, it's nearly time.

The trail she is following swings inland to clim a small bluff and for a while she is engulfed by trees. Cedar and fir are dark and thick and damp. The green new growth on the scrub bushes has nearly filled in the narrow trail. She holds her skirt up a little so it won't be caught or ripped, then runs and nearly slides down the hill again to the river's bank. She can see in every direction for miles and there isn't a thing in sight which has anything to do with man.

'Who needs them?' Styan said, long ago.

It was with that kind of question—questions that implied an answer so obvious only a fool would think to doubt—that he talked her first out of the classroom and then right off the island of her birth and finally up here in the mountains with the river and the moose and the railroad. It was as if he had transported her in this falling-apart pickup not only across the province about as far as it was possible to go, but also backwards in time, perhaps as far as her grandmother's youth or even farther. She washes their coarse clothing in the river and depends on the whims of the seasons for her food.

'Look!' he shouted when they stood first in the clearing above the cabin. 'It's as if we're the very first ones. You and me.'

They swam in the cold river that day and even then she thought of Coyote and the monster, but he took her inside the cabin and they made love on the fir-bough bed that was to be theirs for the next five years. 'We don't need any of them,' he sang. He flopped over on his back and shouted up into the rafters. 'We'll farm it! We'll make it go. We'll make our own world!' Naked, he was as thin and pale as a celery stalk.

When they moved in he let his moustache grow long and droopy like someone in an old, brown photograph. He wore overalls which were far too big for him and started walking around as if there were a movie camera somewhere in the trees and he was being paid to act like a hillbilly instead of the city-bred boy he really was. He stuck a limp felt hat on the top of his head like someone's uncle Hiram and bought chickens.

'It's a start,' he said.

'Six chickens?' She counted again to be sure. 'We don't even have a shed for them.'

He stood with his feet wide apart and looked at her as if she were stupid. 'They'll lay their eggs in the grass.'

'That should be fun,' she said. 'A hundred and sixty acres is a good-size pen.'

'It's a start. Next spring we'll buy a cow. Who needs more?'

Yes who? They survived their first winter here, though the chickens weren't so lucky. The hens got lice and started pecking at each other. By the time Styan got around to riding in to town for something to kill the lice a few had pecked right through the skin and exposed the innards. When he came back from town they had all frozen to death in the yard.

At home, back on her father's farm in the blue mountains of the island, nothing had ever frozen to death. Her father had cared for things. She had never seen anything go so wrong there, or anyone have to suffer.

She walks carefully now, for the trail is on the very edge of the river bank and is spongy and broken away in places. The water, clear and shallow here, back-eddies into little bays where cattail and bracken grow and where water-skeeters walk on their own reflection. A beer bottle glitters where someone, perhaps a guide on the river, has thrown it—wedged between stones as if it has been there as long as they have. She keeps her face turned to the river, away from the acres and acres of forest which are theirs.

Listen, it's nearly time, she thinks. And knows that soon, from far up the river valley, she will be able to hear the throbbing of the train, coming near.

She imagines his face at the window. He is the only passenger in the coach and sits backwards, watching the land slip by, grinning in expectation or memory or both. He tells a joke to old Bill Cobb the conductor but even in his laughter does not turn his eyes from outside the train. One spot on his forehead is white where it presses against the glass. His fingers run over and over the long drooping ends of his moustache. He is wearing his hat.

Hurry, hurry, she thinks. To the train, to her feet, to him.

She wants to tell him about the skunk she spotted yesterday. She wants to tell him about the stove, which smokes too much and needs some kind of clean-out. She wants to tell him about her dream; how she dreamed he was trying to go into the river and how she pulled and hauled on his feet but he wouldn't come out. He will laugh and laugh at her when she tells him, and his laughter will make it all right and not so frightening, so that maybe she will be able to laught at it too.

She has rounded the curve in the river and glances back, way back, at the cabin. It is dark and solid, not far from the bank. Behind the poplars the cleared fields are yellowing with the coming of fall but now in all that place there isn't a thing alive, unless she wants to count trees and insects. No people. No animals. It is scarcely different from her very first look at it. In five years their dream of livestock has been shelved again and again.

Once there was a cow. A sway-backed old Jersey.

'This time I've done it right,' he said. 'Just look at this prize.'

And stepped down off the train to show off this cow, a wide-eyed beauty that looked at her through a window of the passenger coach.

'Maybe so, but you'll need a miracle, too, to get that thing down out of there.'

A minor detail to him, who scooped her up and swung her around and kissed her hard, all in front of the old conductor and the engineer who didn't even bother to turn away. 'Farmers at last!' he shouted. 'You can't have a farm without a cow. You can't have a baby without a cow.'

She put her head inside the coach, looked square into the big brown eyes, glanced at the sawed-off horns. 'Found you somewhere, I guess,' she said to the cow. 'Turned out of someone's herd for being too old or senile or dried up.'

'An auction sale,' he said, and slapped one hand on the window glass. 'I was the only one there who was desperate. But I punched her bag and pulled her tits; she'll do. There may even be a calf or two left in her sway-backed old soul.'

'Come on, bossy,' she said. 'This is no place for you.'

But the cow had other ideas. It backed into a corner of the coach and shook its lowered head. Its eyes, steady and dull, never left Crystal Styan.

'You're home,' Styan said. 'Sorry there's no crowd here or a band playing music, but step down anyway and let's get started.'

'She's not impressed,' she said. 'She don't see any barn waiting out there either, not to mention hay or feed of any kind. She's smart enough to know a train coach is at least a roof over her head.'

The four of them climbed over the seats to get behind her and pushed her all the way down the aisle. Then, when they had shoved her down the steps, she fell on her knees on the gravel and let out a long unhappy bellow. She looked around, bellowed again, then stood up and high-tailed it down the tracks. Before Styan even thought to go after her she swung right and headed into bush.

Styan disappeared into the bush, too, hollering, and after a while the train moved on to keep its schedule. She went back down the trail and waited in the cabin until nearly dark. When she went outside again she found him on the river bank, his feet in the water, his head resting against a birch trunk.

'What the hell,' he said, and shook his head and didn't look at her.

'Maybe she'll come back,' she said.

'A bear'll get her before then, or a cougar. There's no hope of that.'

She put a hand on his shoulder but he shook it off. He'd dragged her from place to place right up this river from its mouth, looking and looking for his dream, never satisfied until he saw this piece of land. For that dream and for him she had suffered.

She smiles, though, at the memory. Because even then he was able to bounce back, resume the dream, start building new plans. She smiles, too, because she knows there will be a surprise today; there has always been a surprise. When it wasn't a cow it was a bouquet of flowers or something else. She goes through a long list in her mind of what it may be, but knows it will be none of them. Not once in her life has anything been exactly the way she imagined it. Just so much as foreseeing something was a guarantee it wouldn't happen, at least not in the exact same way.

'Hey you, Styan!' she suddenly calls out. 'Hey you, Jim Styan. Where are you?' And laughs, because the noise she makes can't possibly make any difference to the world, except for a few wild animals that might be alarmed.

She laughs again, and slaps one hand against her thigh, and shakes her head. Just give her—how many minutes now?—and she won't be alone. These woods will shudder with his laughter, his shouting, his joy. That train, that kinky little train will drop her husband off and then pass on like a stay-stitch thread pulled from a seam.

'Hey you, Styan! What you brought this time? A gold brooch? An old nanny goat?'

The river runs past silently and she imagines that it is only shoulders she is seeing, that monster heads have ducked down to glide by but are watching her from eyes grey as stone. She wants to scream out 'Hide, you crummy cheat, my Coyote's coming home!' but is afraid to tempt even something that she does not believe in. And anyway she senses—far off—the beat of the little train coming down the valley from the town.

And when it comes into sight she is there, on the platform in front of the little sagging shed, watching. She stands tilted far out over the tracks to see, but never dares—even when it is so far away—to step down onto the ties for a better look.

The boards beneath her feet are rotting and broken. Long stems of grass have grown up through the cracks and brush against her legs. A squirrel runs down the slope of the shed's roof and yatters at her until she turns and lifts her hand to frighten it into silence.

She talks to herself, sings almost to the engine's beat—'Here he comes, here he comes'—and has her smile already as wide as it can be. She smiles into the side of the locomotive sliding past and the freight car sliding past and keeps on smiling even after the coach has stopped in front of her and it is obvious that Jim Styan is not on board.

Unless of course he is hiding under one of the seats, ready to leap up, one more surprise.

But old Bill Cobb the conductor backs down the steps, dragging a gunny sack out after him. 'H'lo there, Crystal,' he says. 'He ain't aboard today either, I'm afraid.' He works the gunny sack out onto the middle of the platform. 'Herbie Stark sent this, it's potatoes mostly, and cabbages he was going to throw out of his store.'

She takes the tiniest peek inside the sack and yes, there are potatoes there and some cabbages with soft brown leaves.

The engineer steps down out of his locomotive and comes along the side of the train rolling a cigarette. 'Nice day again,' he says with barely a glance at the sky. 'You makin' out all right?'

'Hold it,' the conductor says, as if he expects the train to move off by itself. 'There's more.' He climbs back into the passenger car and drags out a cardboard box heaped with groceries. 'The church ladies said to drop this off,' he says. 'They told me make sure you get every piece of it, but I don't know how you'll ever get it down to the house through all that bush.'

'She'll manage,' the engineer says. He holds a lighted match under the ragged end of his cigarette until the loose tobacco blazes up. 'She's been doing it—how long now?—must be six months.'

The conductor pushes the cardboard box over against the sack of potatoes and stands back to wipe the sweat off his face. He glances at the engineer and they both smile a little and turn away. 'Well,' the engineeer says, and heads back down the tracks and up into his locomotive.

The conductor tips his hat, says 'Sorry,' and climbs back into the empty passenger car. The train releases a long hiss and then moves slowly past her and down the tracks into the deep bush. She stands on the platform and looks after it a long while, as if a giant hand is pulling, slowly, a stay-stitching thread out of a fuzzy green cloth.

1976

Margaret Atwood

b. 1939

Since winning a Governor General's Award at twenty-seven (for *The Circle Game*, her first full-length book), Margaret Atwood has created a substantial body of writing—poetry, fiction, and criticism—which has gained her an international reputation. She has also been active in the publishing and writing community—she was an editor for the House of Anansi and a member of its board in the early seventies, the president of the Writers' Union in 1982-3, and the editor of *The New Oxford Book of Canadian Verse* in 1982 and (with Robert Weaver) *The Oxford Book of Canadian Short Stories* in 1986 —and has lectured and read from her work in Canada, the U.S., Europe, Russia, and Australia.

Born in Ottawa, Atwood grew up there, in Sault Ste Marie, and in Toronto. As a result of her father's entomological research she spent extended periods of her childhood with her family in the northern Ontario and Quebec bush, and did not attend a full year of formal school until grade eight. In 1957 she entered Victoria College, University of Toronto (where her teachers included Northrop Frye), completing her B.A. in 1961 and publishing a slim book of poems, *Double Persephone*, the same year. She then enrolled in graduate studies at Harvard, taking a master's degree (1962) and beginning a doctoral thesis on 'the English metaphysical romances' of George MacDonald and H. Rider Haggard. She worked briefly as a market researcher; then between 1964 and 1973 she taught English or was writer-in-residence at various Canadian universities. Since that time she has been a full-time writer, living first on a farm near Alliston, Ont. and then (since 1980) in Toronto—but she continues to travel widely, and has accepted residencies as a writer that have carried her for extended periods to Germany, the U.S., and Australia.

Atwood's writing can be separated into two main periods. The poems collected in *The Circle Game* (1966), *The Animals in*

That Country (1968), *Procedures for Underground* (1970), and *You Are Happy* (1974)—as well as those in the book-length sequences *The Journals of Susanna Moodie* (1970) and *Power Politics* (1973)—share the tone and themes of the novels of this period: *The Edible Woman* (1969), *Surfacing* (1972), and *Lady Oracle* (1976). Utilizing a stark and unemotional style, this writing can startle readers out of conventional expectations and into new ways of perceiving—as in the short poem that opens *Power Politics*:

> You fit into me
> like a hook into an eye
>
> a fish hook
> an open eye.

Frequently written from the point of view of alienated individuals (sometimes on the verge of breakdown), this poetry and fiction express a distrust of the everyday world, finding it a place of deceptive appearances and emotional shallowness. To this world Atwood opposes the claims made on us by dreams, hallucinations, and visions, showing her readers that it is only through descents into the psyche and the rediscovery of the primitive and mythic dimensions of both mind and world that one can experience wholeness.

For Atwood the problem of inauthenticity —a central theme for many contemporary writers—is especially associated with women (in *Power Politics* and *The Edible Woman*) and with Canadians (in *Surfacing* and *The Journals of Susanna Moodie*). She has written on the dangers of a colonial mentality, and the consequent lack of Canadian identity, not only in her poetry and fiction, but also in *Survival: A Thematic Guide to Canadian Literature* (1972). In this popular work of literary criticism—which came out of and fuelled the cultural nationalism of its time—she builds on Northrop Frye's 'garrison' thesis, arguing that Canadians are not only alienated from their environment but, having existed in a colonial relationship first to England and then to America, are obsessed with a sense of themselves as victims. Although her reading of the literature has been criticized as one-sided and subjective, this study revealed to many a previously unrecognized coherence in Canadian culture and stimulated valuable debate about Canadian literature and criticism. *Survival* also sheds light on Atwoood's own work: her fiction and poetry develop out of the tradition she describes and are intended as a corrective to it. ('This above all, to refuse to be a victim' is the final lesson learned by the protagonist of *Surfacing*.) In 1982 Atwood published *Second Words*, a large selection of reviews, lectures, and essays, some of which complement or comment on *Survival*.

In moving towards the post-colonial society that Atwood desires, the writer has a special function—that of helping to claim a psychic space. In 'Northrop Frye Observed' she writes:

Frye's push towards naming, towards an interconnected system, seems to me a Canadian reaction to a Canadian situation. Stranded in the midst of a vast space which nobody has made sense out of for you, you settle down to map-making, charting the territory, the discovery of where things are in relation to each other, the extraction of meaning. (Second Words, *1982*)

Although Atwood's ideas are often visible in her writing, one should not overlook her craftsmanship. For example, in an interview with Joyce Carol Oates on the occasion of the American publication of her *Selected Poems*, Atwood emphasized the way 'a texture of sound . . . is at least as important to me as the "argument" ', explaining:

My poems usually begin with words or phrases which appeal more because of their sound than their meaning, and the movement and phrasing of a poem are very important to me. But like many modern poets I tend to conceal rhymes by placing them in the middle of lines, and to avoid immediate alliteration and assonance in favour of echoes placed later in the poems. (The New York Times Book Review, *21 May 1978*)

The publication in 1976 and 1977 of two compilations of earlier work, *Selected Poems* and *Dancing Girls* (a collection of short stories), marked the end of a phase in Atwood's writing career. In her work of the late seventies and the eighties—the poetry of *Two-Headed Poems* (1978), *True Stories*

(1981), and *Interlunar* (1984); the stories in *Bluebeard's Egg* (1983); and the novels *Life Before Man* (1979), *Bodily Harm* (1981), *The Handmaid's Tale* (1985), and *Cat's Eye* (1988)—Atwood does not abandon the concerns of her earlier writing, but she does employ a greater range of style and topics. She is by turns more lyrical and personal, and more satirical and political. She treats domestic subjects in some of her poems, and even gives the reader glimpses of members of her own family. The characters in her novels are more fully drawn and more varied (in *Life Before Man* she uses a male viewpoint for the first time), while in a poem such as 'Variation on the Word *Sleep*' she can write without irony of a woman's love for a man. At the same time politics assumes a new importance. *Two-Headed Poems* takes its title from a sequence of poems about Canada's division between two cultures. (The title also suggests a preoccupation with doubleness and duality that has always been present in Atwood's work.) Elsewhere in that book, as well as the sequence in *True Stories* called 'Notes Towards a Poem That Cannot Be Written', protesting against torture as an instrument of political repression, Atwood adopts a global perspective reflecting her association with Amnesty International. The sense that Canada must now look beyond its own borders is also evident in *Bodily Harm*, a tale of a Canadian travel-writer's naïve involvement in a political coup in the Caribbean, and in *The Handmaid's Tale*, a futuristic dystopian fable about a repressive American society governed by right-wing religious fundamentalists.

In 1986 Atwood published *Selected Poems II*, a volume that drew together poems from the previous ten years and new work. About an eighth of that book is prose poetry ('Marrying the Hangman' below is an example)—an indication of Atwood's interest in this form, which abandons the poetic line while maintaining many other qualities of the lyric poem. An earlier collection, *Murder in the Dark* (1983), made up entirely of short prose pieces, was identified by its subtitle as 'short fictions and prose poems'. (Atwood's use of such 'short fictions' can be associated with contemporary 'minimalist' writing, which seeks to reduce narrative to a few essentials. In all her work—whether fiction, non-fiction, or poetry—Atwood takes very seriously both the power of the written word and the writer's duty to society. As a passage in *Murder in the Dark* suggests, writing is an act of great consequence, and so, therefore, is reading:

. . . *Beneath the page is a story. Beneath the page is everything that has ever happened, most of which you would rather not hear about.*

Touch the page at your peril: it is you who are blank and innocent, not the page. Nevertheless you want to know, nothing will stop you. You touch the page, it's as if you've drawn a knife across it, the page has been hurt now, a sinuous wound opens, a thin incision. Darkness wells through. ('The Page')

This is a Photograph of Me

It was taken some time ago.
At first it seems to be
a smeared
print: blurred lines and grey flecks
blended with the paper;

then, as you scan
it, you see in the left-hand corner
a thing that is like a branch: part of a tree
(balsam or spruce) emerging
and, to the right, halfway up   10
what ought to be a gentle
slope, a small frame house.

In the background there is a lake,
and beyond that, some low hills.

(The photograph was taken
the day after I drowned.

I am in the lake, in the center
of the picture, just under the surface.

It is difficult to say where
precisely, or to say   20
how large or small I am:
the effect of water
on light is a distortion

but if you look long enough,
eventually
you will be able to see me.)

1966

Progressive Insanities
of a Pioneer

i

He stood, a point
on a sheet of green paper
proclaiming himself the centre,

with no walls, no borders
anywhere; the sky no height
above him, totally un-
enclosed
and shouted:

Let me out!

ii

He dug the soil in rows,   10
imposed himself with shovels.
He asserted
into the furrows, I
am not random.

The ground
replied with aphorisms:

a tree-sprout, a nameless
weed, words
he couldn't understand.

iii

The house pitched   20
the plot staked
in the middle of nowhere

At night the mind
inside, in the middle
of nowhere.

The idea of an animal
patters across the roof.

In the darkness the fields
defend themselves with fences
in vain: 30
            everything
            is getting in.

iv

By daylight he resisted.
He said, disgusted
with the swamp's clamourings and the outbursts
of rocks.

> This is not order
> but the absence
> of order

He was wrong, the unanswering   40
forest implied:

> It was
> an ordered absence

v

For many years
he fished for a great vision,
dangling the hooks of sown
roots under the surface
of the shallow earth.

It was like
enticing whales with a bent   50
pin. Besides he thought

in that country
only the worms were biting.

vi

If he had known unstructured
space is a deluge
and stocked his log house-
boat with all the animals

even the wolves,

he might have floated.

But obstinate he   60
stated, The land is solid
and stamped,

watching his foot sink
down through stone
up to the knee.

vii

Things
refused to name themselves; refused
to let him name them.

The wolves hunted
outside.   70

On his beaches, his clearings,
by the surf of under-
growth breaking
at his feet, he foresaw
disintegration
                    and in the end
through eyes
made ragged by his
effort, the tension
between subject and object,   80

the green
vision, the unnamed
whale invaded.

1968

From *The Journals of Susanna Moodie*[1]

From JOURNAL I, 1832-1840

Further Arrivals

After we had crossed the long illness
that was the ocean, we sailed up-river

On the first island
the immigrants threw off their clothes
and danced like sandflies[2]

---

[1]In this book Atwood uses the historical Susanna Moodie (1803-85) as the speaker in poems inspired by her two narratives of settlement, *Roughing It in the Bush* (1852) and *Life in the Clearings* (1853). Many of the people and events alluded to in the poems reprinted here may be found in the selections from *Roughing It in the Bush* on pp. 71-97.

[2]In the first chapter of *Roughing It* the Moodies visited Grosse Isle for an afternoon while their ship stood off shore following an inspection by health officers (Quebec was then experiencing a cholera epidemic): 'Never shall I forget the extraordinary spectacle that met our sight . . . A crowd of many hundred Irish emigrants had been landed . . . and all this motley crew—men, women, and children . . . —were employed in washing clothes. . . . The men and boys were *in* the water, while the women, with their scanty garments tucked above their knees, were tramping their bedding in tubs or in holes in the rocks. Those [not washing] were running to and fro, screaming and scolding in no measured terms . . . all accompanying their vociferations with violent and extraordinary gestures, quite incomprehensible to the uninitiated.'

We left behind one by one
the cities rotting with cholera,
one by one our civilized
distinctions

and entered a large darkness.   10

It was our own
ignorance we entered.

I have not come out yet

My brain gropes nervous
tentacles in the night, sends out

fears hairy as bears,
demands lamps; or waiting

for my shadowy husband, hears
malice in the trees' whispers.

I need wolf's eyes to see   20
the truth.

I refuse to look in a mirror.

Whether the wilderness is
real or not
depends on who lives there.

The Planters

They move between the jagged edge
of the forest and the jagged river
on a stumpy patch of cleared land

my husband, a neighbour, another man
weeding the few rows
of string beans and dusty potatoes.

They bend, straighten; the sun
lights up their faces and hands, candles
flickering in the wind against the

unbright earth. I see them; I know   10
none of them believe they are here.
They deny the ground they stand on,

pretend this dirt is the future.
And they are right. If they let go
of that illusion solid to them as a shovel,

open their eyes even for a moment
to these trees, to this particular sun
they would be surrounded, stormed, broken

in upon by branches, roots, tendrils, the dark
side of light   20
as I am.

The Wereman

My husband walks in the frosted field
an X, a concept
defined against a blank;
he swerves, enters the forest
and is blotted out.

Unheld by my sight
what does he change into
what other shape
blends with the under-
growth, wavers across the pools   10
is camouflaged from the listening
swamp animals

At noon he will
return; or it may be
only my idea of him
I will find returning
with him hiding behind it.

He may change me also
with the fox eye, the owl
eye, the eightfold   20
eye of the spider

I can't think
what he will see
when he opens the door

Departure from the Bush

I, who had been erased
by fire, was crept in
upon by green
                (how
lucid a season)

In time the animals
arrived to inhabit me,

first one
  by one, stealthily
(their habitual traces   10
burnt); then
having marked new boundaries
returning, more
confident, year
by year, two
by two

but restless: I was not ready
altogether to be moved into

They could tell I was
too heavy: I might   20
capsize;

I was frightened
by their eyes (green or
amber) glowing out from inside me

I was not completed; at night
I could not see without lanterns.

He wrote, We are leaving. I said
I have no clothes
left I can wear

The snow came. The sleigh was a relief;[1]   30
its track lengthened behind,
pushing me towards the city

and rounding the first hill, I was
(instantaneous)
unlived in: they had gone.

There was something they almost taught me
I came away not having learned.

---

[1]In the final chapter of *Roughing It* ('Adieu to the Woods') Moodie describes how, after her husband
had been appointed Sheriff of Victoria District, she passed 'the last night I ever spent in the bush—in
the dear forest home which I had loved in spite of all hardships', and then departed for Belleville,
with her household, by sleigh.

From JOURNAL II, 1840-1871

Death of a Young Son by Drowning

He, who navigated with success
the dangerous river of his own birth
once more set forth

on a voyage of discovery
into the land I floated on
but could not touch to claim.

His feet slid on the bank,
the currents took him;
he swirled with ice and trees in the swollen water

and plunged into distant regions,   10
his head a bathysphere;
through his eyes' thin glass bubbles

he looked out, reckless adventurer
on a landscape stranger than Uranus
we have all been to and some remember.

There was an accident; the air locked,
he was hung in the river like a heart.
They retrieved the swamped body,

cairn of my plans and future charts,
with poles and hooks   20
from among the nudging logs.

It was spring, the sun kept shining, the new grass
lept to solidity;
my hands glistened with details.

After the long trip I was tired of waves.
My foot hit rock. The dreamed sails
collapsed, ragged.

        I planted him in this country
        like a flag.

Dream 2: Brian the Still-Hunter[1]

The man I saw in the forest
used to come to our house
every morning, never said anything;
I learned from the neighbours later
he once tried to cut his throat.

I found him at the end of the path
sitting on a fallen tree
cleaning his gun.

There was no wind;
around us the leaves rustled.   10

He said to me:
I kill because I have to

but every time I aim, I feel
my skin grow fur
my head heavy with antlers
and during the stretched instant
the bullet glides on its thread of speed
my soul runs innocent as hooves.

Is God just to his creatures?

I die more often than many.   20

He looked up and I saw
the white scar made by the hunting knife
around his neck.

When I woke
I remembered: he has been gone
twenty years and not heard from.

---

[1]A 'still-hunter' is one who hunts stealthily on foot. In Chapter 10 of *Roughing It* Moodie describes
her friendship with Brian, a man once subject to such fits of depression that he had tried to commit
suicide. Brian tells her a vivid story of watching a 'noble deer' pulled down by a pack of wolves, concluding:

　'*At that moment he seemed more unfortunate even than myself, for I could not see in what manner
he had deserved his fate. All his speed and energy, his courage and fortitude, had been exerted in
vain. I had tried to destroy myself; but he, with every effort vigorously made for self-preservation,
was doomed to meet the fate he dreaded! Is God just to his creatures?*'

Moodie ends the chapter by saying:

*We parted with the hunter as an old friend; and we never met again. His fate was a sad one. After we
left that part of the country, he fell into a moping melancholy, which ended in self-destruction.*

From JOURNAL III, 1871-1969

Thoughts from Underground[1]

When I first reached this country
I hated it
and I hated it more each year:

in summer the light a
violent blur, the heat
thick as a swamp,
the green things fiercely
shoving themselves upwards, the
eyelids bitten by insects

In winter our teeth were brittle   10
with cold. We fed on squirrels.
At night the house cracked.
In the mornings, we thawed
the bad bread over the stove.

Then we were made successful
and I felt I ought to love
this country.
          I said I loved it
and my mind saw double.

I began to forget myself   20
in the middle
of sentences. Events
were split apart

I fought. I constructed
desperate paragraphs of praise, everyone
ought to love it because

and set them up at intervals

          due to natural resources, native industry, superior
          penitentiaries
          we will all be rich and powerful   30

flat as highway billboards

          who can doubt it, look how
          fast Belleville is growing

(though it is still no place for an english gentleman)

1970

---

[1] This poem is spoken by Moodie after her death.

Tricks with Mirrors

i

It's no coincidence
this is a used
furniture warehouse.

I enter with you
and become a mirror.

Mirrors
are the perfect lovers,

that's it, carry me up the stairs
by the edges, don't drop me,

that would be bad luck,   10
throw me on the bed

reflecting side up,
fall into me,

it will be your own
mouth you hit, firm and glassy,

your own eyes you find you
are up against   closed   closed

ii

There is more to a mirror
than you looking at

your full-length body   20
flawless but reversed,

there is more than this dead blue
oblong eye turned outwards to you.

Think about the frame.
The frame is carved, it is important,

it exists, it does not reflect you,
it does not recede and recede, it has limits

and reflections of its own.
There's a nail in the back

to hang it with; there are several nails,   30
think about the nails,

pay attention to the nail

marks in the wood,

they are important too.

iii
Don't assume it is passive
or easy, this clarity

with which I give you yourself.
Consider what restraint it

takes: breath withheld, no anger
or joy disturbing the surface   40

of the ice.
You are suspended in me

beautiful and frozen, I
preserve you, in me you are safe.

It is not a trick either,
it is a craft:

mirrors are crafty.

iv
I wanted to stop this,
this life flattened against the wall,

mute and devoid of colour,   50
built of pure light,

this life of vision only, split
and remote, a lucid impasse.

I confess: this is not a mirror,
it is a door

I am trapped behind.
I wanted you to see me here,

say the releasing word, whatever
that may be, open the wall.

Instead you stand in front of me   60
combing your hair.

v
You don't like these metaphors.
All right:

Perhaps I am not a mirror.
Perhaps I am a pool.

Think about pools.

1974

Marrying the Hangman[1]

She has been condemned to death by hanging. A man may
escape this death by becoming the hangman, a woman by
marrying the hangman. But at the present time there is no
hangman; thus there is no escape. There is only a death,
indefinitely postponed. This is not fantasy, it is history.

*

To live in prison is to live without mirrors. To live without
mirrors is to live without the self. She is living selflessly, she
finds a hole in the stone wall and on the other side of the wall, a
voice. The voice comes through darknesss and has no face. This
voice becomes her mirror.

*

In order to avoid her death, her particular death, with wrung
neck and swollen tongue, she must marry the hangman. But
there is no hangman, first she must create him, she must
persuade this man at the end of the voice, this voice she has
never seen and which has never seen her, this darkness, she
must persuade him to renounce his face, exchange it for the
impersonal mask of death, of official death which has eyes but
no mouth, this mask of a dark leper. She must transform his
hands so they will be willing to twist the rope around throats that
have been singled out as hers was, throats other than hers. She
must marry the hangman or no one, but that is not so bad. Who
else is there to marry?

*

[1]"Jean Corolère, a drummer in the colonial troops at Québec, was imprisoned for duelling in 1751. In
the cell next to his was Françoise Laurent, who had been sentenced to hang for stealing. Except for
letters of pardon, the only way at the time for someone under sentence of death to escape hanging
was, for a man, to become a hangman, or, for a woman, to marry one. Françoise persuaded Corolère
to apply for the vacant (and undesirable) post of executioner, and also to marry her.—Condensed
from the *Dictionary of Canadian Biography*, Volume III, 1741-1770' (Atwood's note).

You wonder about her crime. She was condemned to death for stealing clothes from her employer, from the wife of her employer. She wished to make herself more beautiful. This desire in servants was not legal.

*

She uses her voice like a hand, her voice reaches through the wall, stroking and touching. What could she possibly have said that would have convinced him? He was not condemned to death, freedom awaited him. What was the temptation, the one that worked? Perhaps he wanted to live with a woman whose life he had saved, who had seen down into the earth but had nevertheless followed him back up to life. It was his only chance to be a hero, to one person at least, for if he became the hangman the others would despise him. He was in prison for wounding another man, on one finger of the right hand, with a sword. This too is history.

*

My friends, who are both women, tell me their stories, which cannot be believed and which are true. They are horror stories and they have not happened to me, they have not yet happened to me, they have happened to me but we are detached, we watch our unbelief with horror. Such things cannot happen to us, it is afternoon and these things do not happen in the afternoon. The trouble was, she said, I didn't have time to put my glasses on and without them I'm blind as a bat, I couldn't even see who it was. These things happen and we sit at a table and tell stories about them so we can finally believe. This is not fantasy, it is history, there is more than one hangman and because of this some of them are unemployed.

*

He said: the end of walls, the end of ropes, the opening of doors, a field, the wind, a house, the sun, a table, an apple.

She said: nipple, arms, lips, wine, belly, hair, bread, thighs, eyes, eyes.

They both kept their promises.

*

The hangman is not such a bad fellow. Afterwards he goes to the refrigerator and cleans up the leftovers, though he does not wipe up what he accidentally spills. He wants only the simple things: a chair, someone to pull off his shoes, someone to watch him while he talks, with admiration and fear, gratitude if possible, someone in whom to plunge himself for rest and renewal. These things can best be had by marrying a woman who has been condemned to death by other men for wishing to be beautiful. There is a wide choice.

*

Everyone said he was a fool.
Everyone said she was a clever woman.
They used the word *ensnare*.

*

What did they say the first time they were alone together in the same room? What did he say when she had removed her veil and he could see that she was not a voice but a body and therefore finite? What did she say when she discovered that she had left one locked room for another? They talked of love, naturally, though that did not keep them busy forever.

*

The fact is there are no stories I can tell my friends that will make them feel better. History cannot be erased, although we can soothe ourselves by speculating about it. At that time there were no female hangmen. Perhaps there have never been any, and thus no man could save his life by marriage. Though a woman could, according to the law.

*

He said: foot, boot, order, city, fist, roads, time, knife.

She said: water, night, willow, rope hair, earth belly, cave, meat, shroud, open, blood.

They both kept their promises.

1978

Variation on the Word *Sleep*

I would like to watch you sleeping,
which may not happen.
I would like to watch you,
sleeping. I would like to sleep
with you, to enter
your sleep as its smooth dark wave
slides over my head

and walk with you through that lucent
wavering forest of bluegreen leaves
with its watery sun & three moons   10
towards the cave where you must descend,
towards your worst fear

I would like to give you the silver
branch, the small white flower, the one
word that will protect you
from the grief at the center
of your dream, from the grief
at the center. I would like to follow
you up the long stairway
again & become   20
the boat that would row you back
carefully, a flame
in two cupped hands
to where your body lies
beside me, and you enter
it as easily as breathing in

I would like to be the air
that inhabits you for a moment
only. I would like to be that unnoticed
& that necessary.   30

1981

Another Elegy

Strawberries, pears, fingers, the eyes
of snails: the other shapes water
takes. Even leaves are liquid
arrested. To die
is to dry, lose juice,
the sweet pulp sucked out. To enter
the time of rind and stone.

Your clothes hang shrivelling

in the closet, your other body once
filled with your breath.   10
When I say *body*, what
is that a word for?
Why should the word *you*
remain attached to that suffering?
Wave upon wave, as we say.

I think of your hair burning
first, a scant minute
of halo; later, an afterglow
of bone, red slash of sunset.
The body a cinder or luminescent   20
saint, or Turner seascape.

Fine words, but why do I want
to tart up death?
Which needs no decoration,
which is only a boat,
plain and wooden
and ordinary, without eyes
painted on it,
sightless and hidden
in fog and going somewhere   30
else. Away from the shore.

My dear, my voyager, my scant handful
of ashes: I'd scatter you
if I could, this way, on the river.
A wave is neither form
nor energy. Both. Neither.

1986

The Resplendent Quetzal

Sarah was sitting near the edge of the sacrificial well. She had imagined something smaller, more like a wishing well, but this was huge, and the water at the bottom wasn't clear at all. It was mud-brown; a few clumps of reeds were growing over to one side, and the trees at the top dangled their roots, or were they vines, down the limestone walls into the water. Sarah thought there might be some point to being a sacrificial victim if the well were nicer, but you would never get her to jump into a muddy hole like that. They were probably pushed, or knocked on the head and thrown in. According to the guidebook the water was deep but it looked more like a swamp to her.

Beside her a group of tourists was being rounded up by the guide, who obviously wanted to get the whole thing over with so he could cram them back onto their pink and purple striped *turismo* bus and relax. These were Mexican tourists, and Sarah found it reassuring that other people besides Canadians and Americans wore big hats and sunglasses and took pictures of everything. She wished she and Edward could make these excursions at a less crowded time of year, if they had to make them at all, but because of Edward's teaching job they were limited to school holidays. Christmas was the worst. It would be the same even if he had a different job and they had children, though; but they didn't have any.

The guide shooed his charges back along the gravel path as if they were chickens, which was what they sounded like. He himself lingered beside Sarah, finishing his cigarette, one foot on a stone block, like a conquistador. He was a small dark man with several gold teeth, which glinted when he smiled. He was smiling at Sarah now, sideways, and she smiled back serenely. She liked it when these men smiled at her or even when they made those juicy sucking noises with their mouths as they walked behind her on the street; so long as they didn't touch. Edward pretended not to hear them. Perhaps they did it so much because she was blonde: blondes were rare here. She didn't think of herself as beautiful, exactly; the word she had chosen for herself some time ago was 'comely'. Comely to look upon. You would never use that word for a thin woman.

The guide tossed his cigarette butt into the sacrificial well and turned to follow his flock. Sarah forgot about him immediately. She'd felt something crawling up her leg, but when she looked nothing was there. She tucked the full skirt of her cotton dress in under her thighs and clamped it between her knees. This was the kind of place you could get flea bites, places with dirt on the ground, where people sat. Parks and bus terminals. But she didn't care, her feet were tired and the sun was hot. She would rather sit in the shade and get bitten than rush around trying to see everything, which was what Edward wanted to do. Luckily the bites didn't swell up on her the way they did on Edward.

Edward was back along the path, out of sight among the bushes, peering around with his new Leitz binoculars. He didn't like sitting down, it made him restless. On these trips it was difficult for Sarah to sit by herself and just think. Her own binoculars, which were Edward's old ones, dangled around her neck; they weighed a ton. She took them off and put them into her purse.

His passion for birds had been one of the first things Edward had confided to her. Shyly, as if it had been some precious gift, he'd shown her the lined notebook he'd started keeping when he was nine, with its awkward, boyish printing—*Robin, Bluejay, Kingfisher*—and the day and the year recorded beside each name. She'd pretended to be touched and interested, and in fact she had been. She herself didn't have compulsions of this kind; whereas Edward plunged totally into things, as if they were oceans. For a while it was stamps; then he took up playing the flute and nearly drove her crazy with the practising. Now it was pre-Columbian ruins, and he was determined to climb up every heap of old stones he could get his hands on. A capacity for dedication, she guessed you would call it. At first Edward's obsessions had fascinated her, since she didn't understand them, but now they merely made her tired. Sooner or later he'd dropped them all anyway, just as he began to get really good or really knowledgeable; all but the birds. That had remained constant. She herself, she thought, had once been one of his obsessions.

It wouldn't be so bad if he didn't insist on dragging her into everything. Or rather, he had once insisted; he no longer did. And she had encouraged him, she'd let him think she shared or at least indulged his interests. She was becoming less indulgent as she grew older. The waste of energy bothered her, because it was a waste, he never stuck with anything, and what use was his encyclopaedic knowledge of birds? It would be different if they had enough money, but they were always running short. If only he would take all that energy and do something productive with it, in his job for instance. He could be a principal if he wanted to, she kept telling him that. But he wasn't interested, he was content to poke along doing the same thing year after year. His Grade Six children adored him, the boys especially. Perhaps it was because they sensed he was a lot like them.

He'd started asking her to go birding, as he called it, shortly after they'd met, and of course she had gone. It would have been an error to refuse. She hadn't complained, then, about her sore feet or standing in the rain under the dripping bushes trying to keep track of some nondescript sparrow, while Edward thumbed through his *Peterson's Field Guide* as if it were the Bible or the bird was the Holy Grail. She'd even become quite good at it. Edward was nearsighted, and she was quicker at spotting movement than he was. With his usual generosity he acknowledged this, and she'd fallen into the habit of using it when she wanted to get rid of him for a while. Just now, for instance.

'There's something over there.' She'd pointed across the well to the tangle of greenery on the other side.

'Where?' Edward had squinted eagerly and raised his binoculars. He looked a little like a bird himself, she thought, with his long nose and stilt legs.

'That thing there, sitting in that thing, the one with the tufts. The sort of bean tree. It's got orange on it.'

Edward focused. 'An oriole?'

'I can't tell from here. . . . Oh, it just flew.' She pointed over their heads while Edward swept the sky in vain.

'I think it lit back there, behind us.'

That was enough to send him off. She had to do this with enough real birds to keep him believing, however.

Edward sat down on the root of a tree and lit a cigarette. He had gone down the first side-path he'd come to; it smelled of piss, and he could see by the decomposing Kleenexes further along that this was one of the places people went when they couldn't make it back to the washroom behind the ticket counter.

He took off his glasses, then his hat, and wiped the sweat off his forehead. His face was red, he could feel it. Blushing, Sarah called it. She persisted in attributing it to shyness and boyish embarrassment; she hadn't yet deduced that it was simple rage. For someone so devious she was often incredibly stupid.

She didn't know, for instance, that he'd found out about her little trick with the birds at least three years ago. She'd pointed to a dead tree and said she saw a bird in it, but he himself had inspected that same tree only seconds earlier and there was nothing in it at all. And she was very careless: she described oriole-coloured birds behaving like kingbirds, woodpeckers where there would never be any woodpeckers, mute jays, neckless herons. She must have decided he was a total idiot and any slipshod invention would do.

But why not, since he appeared to fall for it every time. And why did he do it, why did he chase off after her imaginary birds, pretending he believed her? It was partly that although he knew what she was doing to him, he had no idea why. It couldn't be simple malice, she had enough outlets for that. He didn't want to know the real reason, which loomed in his mind as something formless, threatening and final. Her lie about the birds was one of the many lies that propped things up. He was afraid to confront her, that would be the end, all the pretences would come crashing down and they would be left standing in the rubble, staring at each other. There would be nothing left to say and Edward wasn't ready for that.

She would deny everything anyway. 'What do you mean? Of course I saw it. It flew right over there. Why would I make up such a thing?' With her level gaze, blonde and stolid and immovable as a rock.

Edward had a sudden image of himself, crashing out of the undergrowth like King Kong, picking Sarah up and hurling her over the edge, down into the sacrificial well. Anything to shatter that imperturbable expression, bland and pale and plump and smug, like a Flemish Madonna's. Self-righteous, that's what it was. Nothing was ever her fault. She hadn't been like that when he'd met her. But it wouldn't work: as she fell she would glance at him, not with fear but with maternal irritation, as if he'd spilled chocolate milk on a white tablecloth. And she'd pull her skirt down. She was concerned for appearances, always.

Though there would be something inappropriate about throwing Sarah into the sacrificial well, just as she was, with all her clothes on. He remembered snatches from the several books he'd read before they came down. (And that was another thing: Sarah didn't believe in reading up on places beforehand. 'Don't you want to understand what you're looking at?' he'd asked her. 'I'll see the same thing in any case, won't I?' she said. 'I mean, knowing all those facts doesn't change the actual statue or whatever.' Edward found this attitude infuriating; and now that they were here, she resisted his attempts to explain things to her by her usual passive method of pretending not to hear.

'That's a Chac-Mool,[1] see that? That round thing on the stomach held the bowl where they put the hearts, and the butterfly on the head means the soul flying up to the sun.'

'Could you get out the suntan lotion, Edward. I think it's in the tote bag, in the left-hand pocket.'

And he would hand her the suntan lotion, defeated once again.)

No, she wouldn't be a fit sacrifice, with or without lotion. They only threw people in—or perhaps they jumped in, of their own free will—for the water god, to make it rain and ensure fertility. The drowned were messengers, sent to carry requests to the god. Sarah would have to be purified first, in the stone sweathouse beside the well. Then, naked, she would kneel before him, one arm across

---

[1] A statute of Toltec origin, a reclining figure with a shallow dish for offerings on its stomach. The various details of the setting suggest that the story takes place at Chichén-Itzá in Yucatan.

her breast in the attitude of submission. He added some ornaments: a gold necklace with a jade medallion, a gold circlet adorned with feathers. Her hair, which she usually wore in a braid coiled at the back of her head, would be hanging down. He thought of her body, which he made slimmer and more taut, with an abstract desire which was as unrelated as he could make it to Sarah herself. This was the only kind of desire he could feel for her any more: he had to dress her up before he could make love to her at all. He thought about their earlier days, before they'd married. It was almost as if he'd had an affair with another woman, she had been so different. He'd treated her body then as something holy, a white and gold chalice, to be touched with care and tenderness. And she had liked this; even though she was two years older than he was and much more experienced she hadn't minded his awkwardness and reverence, she hadn't laughed at him. Why had she changed?

Sometimes he thought it was the baby, which had died at birth. At the time he'd urged her to have another right away, and she'd said yes, but nothing had happened. It wasn't something they talked about. 'Well, that's that,' she said in the hospital afterwards. A perfect child, the doctor said; a freak accident, one of those things that happen. She'd never gone back to university either and she wouldn't get a job. She sat at home, tidying the apartment, looking over his shoulder, towards the door, out the window, as if she was waiting for something.

Sarah bowed her head before him. He, in the feathered costume and long-nosed, toothed mask of the high priest, sprinkled her with blood drawn with thorns from his own tongue and penis. Now he was supposed to give her the message to take to the god. But he couldn't think of anything he wanted to ask for.

And at the same time he thought: what a terrific idea for a Grade Six special project! He'd have them build scale models of the temples, he'd show the slides he'd taken, he'd bring in canned tortillas and tamales for a Mexican lunch, he'd have them make little Chac-Mools out of papier-mâché . . . and the ball game where the captain of the losing team had his head cut off, that would appeal to them, they were blood-thirsty at that age. He could see himself up there in front of them, pouring out his own enthusiasm, gesturing, posturing, acting it out for them, and their response. . . . Yet afterwards he knew he would be depressed. What were his special projects anyway but a substitute for television, something to keep them entertained? They liked him because he danced for them, a funny puppet, inexhaustible and a little absurd. No wonder Sarah despised him.

Edward stepped on the remains of his cigarette. He put his hat back on, a wide-brimmed white hat Sarah had bought for him at the market. He had wanted one with a narrower brim, so he could look up through his binoculars without the hat getting in his way; but she'd told him he would look like an American golfer. It was always there, that gentle, patronizing mockery.

He would wait long enough to be plausible; then he would go back.

Sarah was speculating about how she would be doing this whole trip if Edward had conveniently died. It wasn't that she wished him dead, but she couldn't imagine any other way for him to disappear. He was omnipresent, he pervaded her life like a kind of smell; it was hard for her to think or act except in reference to him. So she found it harmless and pleasant to walk herself through the same itinerary they were following now, but with Edward removed, cut neatly out of the picture. Not that she would be here at all if it wasn't for him. She would prefer to lie in a deck chair in, say, Acapulco, and drink cooling drinks. She threw in a few dark young men in bathing suits, but took them out: that would be too complicated and not relaxing. She had often thought about cheating on Edward—somehow it would serve him right, though she wasn't sure what for—but she had never actually done it. She didn't know anyone suitable, any more.

Suppose she was here, then, with no Edward. She would stay at a better hotel, for one thing. One that had a plug in the sink; they had not yet stayed in a hotel with a plug. Of course that would cost more money, but she thought of herself as having more money if Edward were dead: she would have all of his salary instead of just part of it. She knew there wouldn't be any salary if he really were dead, but it spoiled the fantasy to remember this. And she would travel on planes, if possible, or first-class buses, instead of the noisy, crowded second-class ones he insisted on taking. He said you saw more of the local colour that way and there was no point going to another country if you spent all your time with other tourists. In theory she agreed with this, but the buses gave her headaches and she could do without the closeup tour of squalor, the miserable thatched or tin-roofed huts, the turkeys and tethered pigs.

He applied the same logic to restaurants. There was a perfectly nice one in the village where they were staying, she'd seen it from the bus and it didn't look that expensive; but no, they had to eat in a seedy linoleum-tiled hutch, with plastic-covered tablecloths. They were the only customers in the place. Behind them four adolescent boys were playing dominoes and drinking beer, with a lot of annoying laughter, and some smaller children watched television, a program that Sarah realized was a re-run of *The Cisco Kid*,[2] with dubbed voices.

On the bar beside the television set there was a crèche, with three painted plaster Wise Men, one on an elephant, the others on camels. The first Wise Man was missing his head. Inside the stable a stunted Joseph and Mary adored an enormous Christ Child which was more than half as big as the elephant. Sarah wondered how the Mary could possibly have squeezed out this colossus; it made her uncomfortable to think about it. Beside the crèche was a Santa Claus haloed with flashing lights, and beside that a radio in the shape of Fred Flintstone, which was playing American popular songs, all of them ancient.

'*Oh someone help me, help me, plee-ee-ee-eeze* . . .'

'Isn't that Paul Anka?' Sarah asked.

But this wasn't the sort of thing Edward could be expected to know. He launched into a defence of the food, the best he'd had in Mexico, he said. Sarah refused to give him the consolation of her agreement. She found the restaurant even more depressing than it should have been, especially the crèche. It was painful, like a cripple trying to walk, one of the last spastic gestures of a religion no one, surely, could believe in much longer.

Another group of tourists was coming up the path behind her, Americans by

[2] An American western TV series (1951-6) that had the unusual feature of a cowboy hero and his companion who were Mexican-Americans, albeit stereotypes.

the sound of them. The guide was Mexican, though. He scrambled up onto the altar, preparing to give his spiel.

'Don't go too near the edge, now.'

'Who me, I'm afraid of heights. What d'you see down there?'

'Water, what am I supposed to see?'

The guide clapped his hands for attention. Sarah only half-listened: she didn't really want to know anything more about it.

'Before, people said they threw nothing but virgins in here,' the guide began. 'How they could tell that, I do not know. It is always hard to tell.' He waited for the expected laughter, which came. 'But this is not true. Soon, I will tell you how we have found this out. Here we have the altar to the rain god Tlaloc . . .'

Two women sat down near Sarah. They were both wearing cotton slacks, high-heeled sandals and wide-brimmed straw hats.

'You go up the big one?'

'Not on your life. I made Alf go up, I took a picture of him at the top.'

'What beats me is why they built all those things in the first place.'

'It was their religion, that's what he said.'

'Well, at least it would keep people busy.'

'Solve the unemployment problem.' They both laughed.

'How many more of these ruins is he gonna make us walk around?'

'Beats me. I'm about ruined out. I'd rather go back and sit on the bus.'

'I'd rather go shopping. Not that there's much to buy.'

Sarah, listening, suddenly felt indignant. Did they have no respect? The sentiments weren't that far from her own of a moment ago, but to hear them from these women, one of whom had a handbag decorated with tasteless straw flowers, made her want to defend the well.

'Nature is very definitely calling,' said the woman with the handbag. 'I couldn't get in before, there was such a lineup.'

'Take a Kleenex,' the other woman said. 'There's no paper. Not only that, you just about have to wade in. There's water all over the floor.'

'Maybe I'll just duck into the bushes,' the first woman said.

Edward stood up and massaged his left leg, which had gone to sleep. It was time to go back. If he stayed away too long, Sarah would be querulous, despite the fact that it was she herself who had sent him off on this fool's expedition.

He started to walk back along the path. But then there was a flash of orange, at the corner of his eye. Edward swivelled and raised his binoculars. They were there when you least expected it. It was an oriole, partly hidden behind the leaves; he could see the breast, bright orange, and the dark barred wing. He wanted it to be a Hooded Oriole, he had not yet seen one. He talked to it silently, begging it to come out into the open. It was strange the way birds were completely magic for him the first time only, when he had never seen them before. But there were hundreds of kinds he would never see; no matter how many he saw there would always be one more. Perhaps this was why he kept looking. The bird was hopping further away from him, into the foliage. *Come back,* he called to it wordlessly, but it was gone.

Edward was suddenly happy. Maybe Sarah hadn't been lying to him after all, maybe she had really seen this bird. Even if she hadn't, it had come anyway, in answer to his need for it. Edward felt he was allowed to see birds only when they wanted him to, as if they had something to tell him, a secret, a message. The Aztecs thought hummingbirds were the souls of dead warriors, but why not all birds, why just warriors? Or perhaps they were the souls of the unborn, as some believed. 'A jewel, a precious feather,' they called an unborn baby, according to *The Daily Life of the Aztecs. Quetzal,* that was *feather.*

'This is the bird I want to see,' Sarah said when they were looking through *The Birds of Mexico* before coming down.

'The Resplendent Quetzal,' Edward said. It was a green and red bird with spectacular iridescent blue tail plumes. He explained to her that Quetzal Bird meant Feather Bird. 'I don't think we're likely to see it,' he said. He looked up the habitat. ' *"Cloud forests."* I don't think we'll be in any cloud forests.'

'Well, that's the one I want,' Sarah said. 'That's the only one I want.'

Sarah was always very determined about what she wanted and what she didn't want. If there wasn't anything on a restaurant menu that appealed to her, she would refuse to order anything; or she would permit him to order for her and then pick around the edges, as she had last night. It was no use telling her that this was the best meal they'd had since coming. She never lost her temper or her self-possession, but she was stubborn. Who but Sarah for instance would have insisted on bringing a collapsible umbrella to Mexico in the dry season? He'd argued and argued, pointing out its uselessness and the extra weight, but she'd brought it anyway. And then yesterday afternoon it had rained, a real cloudburst. Everyone else had run for shelter, huddling against walls and inside the temple doorways, but Sarah had put up her umbrella and stood under it, smugly. This had infuriated him. Even when she was wrong, she always managed, somehow, to be right. If only just once she would admit . . . what? That she could make mistakes. This was what really disturbed him: her assumption of infallibility.

And he knew that when the baby had died she had blamed it on him. He still didn't know why. Perhaps it was because he'd gone out for cigarettes, not expecting it to be born so soon. He wasn't there when she was told; she'd had to take the news alone.

'It was nobody's fault,' he told her repeatedly. 'Not the doctor's, not yours. The cord was twisted.'

'I know,' she said, and she had never accused him; nevertheless he could feel the reproach, hanging around her like a fog. As if there was anything he could have done.

'I wanted it as much as you did,' he told her. And this was true. He hadn't thought of marrying Sarah at all, he'd never mentioned it because it had never occurred to him she would agree, until she told him she was pregnant. Up until that time, she had been the one in control; he was sure he was just an amusement for her. But the marriage hadn't been her suggestion, it had been his. He'd dropped out of Theology, he'd taken his public-school teaching certificate that summer in order to support them. Every evening he had massaged her belly, feeling the child move, touching it through her skin. To him it was a sacred thing, and he included her in his worship. In the sixth month, when she had taken to lying on her back, she had begun to snore, and he would lie awake at night listening to these gentle snores, white and silver they seemed to him, almost songs, mysterious talismans. . . . Unfortunately Sarah had retained this habit, but he no longer felt the same way about it.

When the child had died, he was the one who had cried, not Sarah. She had never cried. She got up and walked around almost immediately, she wanted to get out of the hospital as quickly as possible. The baby clothes she'd been buying disappeared from the apartment; he never found out what she'd done with them, he'd been afraid to ask.

Since that time he'd come to wonder why they were still married. It was illogical. If they'd married because of the child and there was no child, and there continued to be no child, why didn't they separate? But he wasn't sure he wanted this. Maybe he was still hoping something would happen, there would be another child. But there was no use demanding it. They came when they wanted to, not when you wanted them to. They came when you least expected it. A jewel, a precious feather.

'Now I will tell you,' said the guide. 'The archaeologists have dived down into the well. They have dredged up more than fifty skeletons, and they have found that some of them were not virgins at all but men. Also, most of them were children. So as you can see, that is the end of the popular legend.' He made an odd little movement from the top of the altar, almost like a bow, but there was no applause. 'They do not do these things to be cruel,' he continued. 'They believe these people will take a message to the rain god, and live forever in his paradise at the bottom of the well.'

The woman with the handbag got up. 'Some paradise,' she said to her friend. 'I'm starting back. You coming?'

In fact the whole group was moving off now, in the scattered way they had. Sarah waited until they had gone. Then she opened her purse and took out the plaster Christ Child she had stolen from the crèche the night before. It was inconceivable to her that she had done such a thing, but there it was, she really had.

She hadn't planned it beforehand. She'd been standing beside the crèche while Edward was paying the bill, he'd had to go into the kitchen to do it as they were very slow about bringing it to the table. No one was watching her: the domino-playing boys were absorbed in their game and the children were riveted to the television. She'd just suddenly reached out her hand, past the Wise Men and through the door of the stable, picked the child up and put it into her purse.

She turned it over in her hands. Separated from the dwarfish Virgin and Joseph, it didn't look quite so absurd. Its diaper was cast as part of it, more like a tunic, it had glass eyes and a sort of page-boy haircut, quite long for a newborn. A perfect child, except for the chip out of the back, luckily where it would not be noticed. Someone must have dropped it on the floor.

You could never be too careful. All the time she was pregnant, she'd taken meticulous care of herself, counting out the vitamin pills prescribed by the doctor and eating only what the books recommended. She had drunk four glass of milk a day, even though she hated milk. She had done the exercises and gone to the classes. No one would be able to say she had not done the right things. Yet she had been disturbed by the thought that the child would be born with something wrong, it would be a mongoloid or a cripple, or a hydrocephalic with a huge liquid head like the ones she'd seen taking the sun in their wheelchairs on the lawn of the hospital one day. But the child had been perfect.

She would never take that risk, go through all that work again. Let Edward strain his pelvis till he was blue in the face; 'trying again,' he called it. She took the pill every day, without telling him. She wasn't going to try again. It was too much for anyone to expect of her.

What had she done wrong? She hadn't done anything wrong, that was the trouble. There was nothing and no one to blame, except, obscurely, Edward; and he couldn't be blamed for the child's death, just for not being there. Increasingly since that time he had simply absented himself. When she no longer had the child inside her he had lost interest, he had deserted her. This, she realized, was what she resented most about him. He had left her alone with the corpse, a corpse for which there was no explanation.

'Lost' people called it. They spoke of her as having lost the child, as though it was wandering around looking for her, crying plaintively, as though she had neglected it or misplaced it somewhere. But where? What limbo had it gone to, what watery paradise? Sometimes she felt as if there had been some mistake, the child had not been born yet. She could still feel it moving, ever so slightly, holding on to her from the inside.

Sarah placed the baby on the rock beside her. She stood up, smoothing out the wrinkles in her skirt. She was sure there would be more flea bites when she got back to the hotel. She picked up the child and walked slowly towards the well, until she was standing at the very brink.

Edward, coming back up the path, saw Sarah at the well's edge, her arms raised above her head. *My God,* he thought, *she's going to jump.* He wanted to shout to her, tell her to stop, but he was afraid to startle her. He could run up behind her, grab her . . . but she would hear him. So he waited, paralyzed, while Sarah stood immobile. He expected her to hurtle downwards, and then what would he do? But she merely drew back her right arm and threw something into the well. Then she turned, half stumbling, towards the rock where he had left her and crouched down.

'Sarah,' he said. She had her hands over her face; she didn't lift them. He kneeled so he was level with her. 'What is it? Are you sick?'

She shook her head. She seemed to be crying, behind her hands, soundlessly and without moving. Edward was dismayed. The ordinary Sarah, with all her perversity, was something he could cope with, he'd invented ways of coping. But he was unprepared for this. She had always been the one in control.

'Come on,' he said, trying to disguise his desperation, 'you need some lunch, you'll feel better.' He realized as he said this how fatuous it must sound, but for once there was no patronizing smile, no indulgent answer.

'This isn't like you,' Edward said, pleading, as if that was a final argument which would snap her out of it, bring back the old calm Sarah.

Sarah took her hands away from her face, and as she did so Edward felt cold fear. Surely what he would see would be the face of someone else, someone entirely different, a woman he had never seen before in his life. Or there would be no face at all. But (and this was almost worse) it was only Sarah, looking much as she always did.

She took a Kleenex out of her purse and wiped her nose. *It is like me,* she thought. She stood up and smoothed her skirt once more, then collected her purse and her collapsible umbrella.

'I'd like an orange,' she said. 'They have them, across from the ticket office. I saw them when we came in. Did you find your bird?'

1977

Patrick Lane

b. 1939

Born in Nelson, B.C., Pat Lane grew up in the British Columbia interior, near Vernon, and has remained a resident of western Canada most of his life. After high school he began to travel extensively through North and South America, working at such manual jobs as logger and miner. (His time in Latin America provided him with material for many of his poems.) He began to write poetry in his early twenties, around the time of the death of his brother, the *Tish* poet Red Lane (whose collected work he later edited). In 1966 he helped found, with poets bill bissett and Seymour Mayne, Very Stone House, a small press that was later called Very Stone House in Transit (1971-80), an allusion to Lane's moving from place to place. This press brought out his first book, *Letters From the Savage Mind* (1966). Since then he has written a number of broadsheets, pamphlets, and books of poetry, among which are *Beware the Months of Fire* (1974); *Unborn Things* (1975); *Albino Pheasants* (1977); *Poems New and Selected* (1978), which won a Governor General's Award; *No Longer Two People* (1979), written with Lorna Uher (Lorna Crozier); *The Measure* (1980); *Old Mother* (1982); *A Linen Crow, a Caftan Magpie* (1984); *Selected Poems* (1987), which contains a section of new work; and *Winter Poems* (1990). Since 1976 he has taught creative writing, or been a writer-in-residence, at the University of

Notre Dame at Nelson, Concordia University, and the Universities of Manitoba, Ottawa, Alberta, and Toronto. Since 1986 Lorna Crozier and he have shared an appointment in the English department at the University of Saskatchewan with the fiction writer David Carpenter.

Much of Pat Lane's poetry is anecdotal narrative, usually depicting the incidents in the life of the poor and the working class. Extremes of violence, Lane suggests, characterize man's behaviour as much as that of the lower animals, and animals in his poetry—whether predators or prey—are frequently emblematic of man. Birds, in particular, appear as objects of man's mindless aggression, as victims of a predatory universe, or as symbols of human vulnerability. Lane's is a vision of a capricious universe in which life and death are ceaselessly transformed into one another, and no one can long remain with hands unbloodied.

This view of linked creation and destruction (which recalls the Indian trickster *mythos* investigated by other western writers such as Robert Kroetsch and Sheila Watson) is developed by a violently beautiful lyricism, balanced precariously between the sensual and the sensational, that shocks the reader out of complacency. Lane, like the existentialists before him, sees the individual as living intensely only in the face of danger and death. Because of this his poetry is often an affirmation of destruction: by bringing such moments of intensity to his readers, he forces them to confront their own values and ways of life.

Poetry for Lane provides catharsis not only for the reader but for the poet himself, whom he sees as an outlaw, escaping the restraints of society for the bondage of art:

He is the outlaw surging beyond the only free-dom he knows, beauty in bondage, and so spins towards the margins of his experience like a rotting apple at the end of a string being swung in the hands of a satyr, and the locus of that spinning is the word *surrounded and permeated with desire and feeling*. ('To the Outlaw', New: American and Canadian Poetry, *no. 15, 1971*).

Because I Never Learned

For John

Because I never learned how
to be gentle and the country
I lived in was hard with dead
animals and men I didn't question
my father when he told me
to step on the kitten's head
after the bus had run over
its hind quarters.

Now, twenty years later,
I remember only: 10
the silence of the dying
when the fragile skull collapsed
under my hard bare heel,
the curved tongue in the dust
that would never cry again
and the small of my father's back
as he walked tall away.

1974

Albino Pheasants

At the bottom of the field
where thistles throw their seeds
and poplars grow from cotton[1] into trees
in a single season I stand among the weeds.
Fenceposts hold each other up with sagging wire.
Here no man walks except in wasted time.
Men circle me with cattle, cars and wheat.
Machines rot on my margins.
They say the land is wasted when it's wild

[1] i.e. the downy poplar seeds.

and offer plows and apple trees to tame   10
but in the fall when I have driven them away
with their guns and dogs and dreams
I walk alone. While those who'd kill
lie sleeping in soft beds
huddled against the bodies of their wives
I go with speargrass and hooked burrs
and wait upon the ice alone.

Delicate across the mesh of snow
I watch the pale birds come
with beaks the colour of discarded flesh.   20
White, their feathers are white,
as if they had been born in caves
and only now have risen to the earth
to watch with pink and darting eyes
the slowly moving shadows of the moon.
There is no way to tell men what we do . . .
the dance they make in sleep
withholds its meaning from their dreams.
That which has been nursed in bone
rests easy upon frozen stone   30
and what is wild is lost behind closed eyes:
albino birds, pale sisters, succubi.[2]

1977

[2]Female demons who descend upon and have sexual intercourse with men while they sleep.

Stigmata[1]

For Irving Layton[2]

What if there wasn't a metaphor
and the bodies were only bodies
bones pushed out in awkward fingers?
Waves come to the seawall, fall away,
children bounce mouths against the stones
that man has carved to keep the sea at bay
and women walk with empty wombs
proclaiming freedom to the night.
Through barroom windows rotten with light
eyes of men open and close like fists.   10

I bend beside a tidal pool and take a crab from the sea.
His small green life twists helpless in my hand

[1]Marks corresponding to the crucifixion wounds of Christ.
[2]See pp. 342-53; compare particularly 'Butterfly on Rock' (where the poet crushes the butterfly under his hand) with the conclusion to this poem.

the living bars of bone and flesh
a cage made by the animal I am.
This thing, the beat, the beat of life
now captured in the darkness of my flesh
struggling with claws as if it could tear its way
through my body back to the sea.
What do I know of the inexorable beauty,
the unrelenting turning of the wheel I am inside me?   20
Stigmata. I hold a web of blood.

I dream of the scrimshawed[3] teeth of endless whales,
the oceans it took to carve them. Drifting ships
echo in fog the wounds of Leviathan[4]
great grey voices giving cadence to their loss.
The men are gone
who scratched upon white bones their destiny.
Who will speak of the albatross in the shroud of the man,
the sailor who sinks forever in the Mindanao Deep?[5]
I open my hand. The life leaps out.   30

1977

[3]Intricately carved; scrimshaw is usually made from whale ivory, bone, or shells.
[4]Biblical sea monster; a whale.
[5]Deepest point in the oceans.

The Witnesses

To know as the word is known, to know little
or less than little, nothing, to contemplate
the setting sun and sit for hours, the world
turning you into the sun as day begins again

To remember words, to remember nothing
but words and make out of nothing the past,
to remember my father, the McLeod Kid
carrying the beat, riding against time

On the rodeo circuit of fifty years ago
the prairie, stretched wet hide   10
scraped by a knife, disappearing everywhere
to know the McLeod Kid was defeated

To know these things
to climb into the confusions
which are only words, to climb into desire
to ride in the sun, to ride against time

The McLeod Kid raking his spurs on the mare
the cheers from the wagon-backs
where the people sit to watch the local
boy ride against the riders from Calgary   20

To spit melon seeds into the dust
to roll cigarettes, to leave them hanging
from the lip, to tip your hat back and grin
to laugh or not laugh, to climb into darkness

Below the stands and touch Erla's breast
to eat corn or melons, to roll cigarettes
to drink beer, bottles hidden in paper bags
to grin at the RCMP, horseless, dust on their boots

To watch or not watch, to surround the spectacle
horses asleep in their harness, tails switching   30
bees swarming on melon rinds, flys buzzing
and what if my words are their voices

What if I try to capture an ecstasy that is not
mine, what if these are only words saying
this was or this was not, a story told to me
until I now no longer believe it was told to me

The witnesses dead, what if I create a past
that never was, make out of nothing
a history of my people whether in pain
or ecstasy, my father riding in the McLeod Rodeo   40

The hours before dawn when in the last of darkness
I make out of nothing a man riding against time
and thus my agony, the mare twisted sideways
muscles bunched in knots beneath her hide

Her mane, black hair feathered in the wind
that I believe I see, caked mud in her eyes
the breath broken from her body and the McLeod Kid
in the air, falling, the clock stopped.

1978

The Long Coyote Line

For Andy Suknaski

The long coyote line crosses the pure
white and the prairie is divided
again by hunger. The snowshoe hare
thin as January creates a running
circle encompassing a moon of snow
as the lean lope of the coyote
cuts in a curving radius
bringing escape down to a single terror.
It is the long line, coyote, and the man
who stands in your small disturbance   10
counting the crystals of blood and bone:
three by three, coyote, hare and the howl
where the true prairie begins.

1980

Monarch I

Half-pet, half-wildness, Monarch leads
his thirteen hens in an endless search
for food. Range birds, they return
to the pen only for sleep. He guides them
through the day, one eye upon the sky
for the falling hawk, the other on the earth.
He hates their wandering.
His beak drives them from the brush
where they've gone to lay, their clucks
his torment. They fly from their beds   10
in squawking clusters. Only the brooding
ones are left alone. He knows the mother's
eye. It is his only fear.

When they are lost he scratches at the dirt
and calls out food. They run from everywhere,
push him away and peck at the nothing there.
During the sun he mounts them one by one,
his hard black beak holding their heads
as his spurs rake their sides. The soft
flesh tears. The hens brace stiff wings   20
against the ground and hold him there.
When he is done, some wounded, some surprised,
they flip the tangle of their tails,
rub beaks to stone and cluck contentedly.

Then darkness moves among the trees
and shadows stretch like necks into the grass.
He drives them from their graves of dust
to the safety of the pen. Drinking and scratching
they search for parasites among their feathers.
The preening over, they rise on ruffled wings,   30
settle above his head. In the bramble thickets
three brooding hens are left. Theirs is
a single eye. He does not go to them.
Their warning chirr keeps him far away.

He counts the rest and gives one final crow,
then satisfied and finally tired,
lifts to his isolate perch among them.
Claws locked, the hens pull night
into their breasts. They sleep a flying dream.
Monarch's red eyes close, they open, search   40
the gathered dark for weasel sound or fox,
then close like wounds upon a restless sleep.

1982

Weasel

Thin as death,
the dark brown weasel slides
like smoke through night's hard silence.
The worlds of the small are still. He glides
beneath the chicken house. Bird life
above him sleeps in feathers as he creeps
among the stones, small nose testing every board
for opening, a hole small as an eye, a fallen knot,
a crack where time has broken through.
His sharp teeth chatter.   10
Again and again he quests the darkness
below the sleeping birds. A mouse freezes,
small mouth caught by silence in the wood.
His life is quick. He slips into his hole.
Thin as death, the dark brown weasel slides
like smoke. His needles worry wood.
The night is long.
Above him bird blood beats.

1982

There Is a Time

For Robert Kroetsch

There is a time when the world is hard,
the winters cold and a woman
sits before a door, watching through wood
for the arrival of a man. Perhaps a child is ill
and it is not winter after all. Perhaps
the dust settles in a child's breath,
a breath so fragile it barely exists.
Tuberculosis or pneumonia. Perhaps
these words place her there, these words
naming the disease and still not curing it.   10

Maybe it is not the man she waits for.
We want it to be someone. We want
someone to relieve this hour. On the next farm
the nearest woman to the woman is also sitting
in dust or cold and watching a door. She is no help.
So let it be the man. He is in the barn
watching the breathing of his horses.
They are slow and beautiful,
their breath almost freezing in perfect clouds.
Their harness hanging down from the stalls   20
gleams, although old and worn. He is old and worn.
The woman is waiting behind the door
but he is afraid to go there because of her eyes
and the child who is dying.

There is a time when it is like this,
when the hours are this cold, when the hours
are no longer than a bit of dust in an eye,
a frozen cloud of breath, a single splinter in a door
large enough to be a life it is so small and perfect.
Perhaps there are soldiers coming from far away,   30
their buttons dull with dust or bright with cold,
though we cannot imagine why they would come here,
or a storm rolling down from the north
like a millwheel into their lives.

Perhaps it is winter.
There is snow. Or it could be dust.
Maybe there is no child, no man, no woman
and the words we imagined have not been invented
to name the disease there is no child to catch.
Maybe the names were there in a time before them   40
and they have been forgotten. For now let them die

as we think of them and after they are dead
we will imagine them alive again,
the barn, the breath, the woman, the door.

1982

Dennis Lee

b. 1939

Dennis Beynon Lee has been shaped by Toronto: born in that city, raised in suburban Etobicoke, educated at the University of Toronto Schools and at Victoria College, University of Toronto (B.A., 1962; M.A., 1965), he continues to make it his home. In 1967, with Dave Godfrey, Lee founded the House of Anansi Press, which became the nucleus of a group of young writers, including Margaret Atwood, Matt Cohen, Graeme Gibson, and Michael Ondaatje. Lee is an influential editor who, after leaving the directorship of Anansi in 1972, continued to work with Canadian publishers, first Macmillan and then McClelland and Stewart. A teacher as well as an editor, Lee has been an instructor at Victoria College, Rochdale College (a short-lived educational collective that Lee helped found), and York University. He has also been writer-in-residence at Trent University, the University of Toronto, and, on a special exchange fellowship, at the University of Edinburgh.

Since Lee's rather conventional first collection, *Kingdom of Absence* (1967), his poetry has developed in two apparently divergent directions: on the one hand he has written complex, often difficult meditations and social commentaries; and on the other he has become a popular author of children's verse. His second book, *Civil Elegies* (1968), is a sequence of poems that reflects his intense feelings about the public responsibilities of the individual; it was revised for *Civil Elegies and Other Poems* (1972), which won a Governor General's Award. In this poetry Lee begins an exploration of the multiple voices, public and private, that an individual assumes in life. He continues to experiment with a complex blend of authorial and narra-

tive voices in his next three long poems: *Not Abstract Harmonies But* (1974), *The Death of Harold Ladoo* (1976), and *The Gods* (1978). In 1979 these poems (substantially revised) were published in a single volume entitled *The Gods*. 'Riffs', his most recently published long poem (it appeared in *Tasks of Passion*, 1982, a book of essays by and about Lee) represents an experiment with poetic voice, one that attempts to produce a literary equivalent to jazz varations. A new long poem, 'Nightwatch', that grows out of this play of poetic voice and musical phrasing will appear as part of a forthcoming volume that will draw together his new and selected poems.

Believing that Canadian children needed an indigenous and living poetry, Lee also undertook the writing of 'kids' stuff' in the mid-sixties. His whimsical and zany children's verse has grown steadily in popularity since the appearance of *Wiggle to the Laundromat* (1970) and *Alligator Pie* (1974). They were followed by *Nicholas Knock and Other People* (1974), *Garbage Delight* (1977), *The Ordinary Bath* (1979), *Jelly Belly* (1983), and *Lizzy's Lion* (1984). From 1983 to 1986 he wrote song lyrics (with Phil Balsam) for Jim Henson's television show *Fraggle Rock*. (That association also led him to work on scripts for the Henson films *The Dark Crystal*, 1983, and *Labyrinth*, 1986.) Lee also wrote the songs for the musical dramas based on Mordecai Richler's two children's books. In 1987 he published *The Difficulty of Living on Other Planets*, rhymed comic poems he describes as 'kid's stuff for adults'.

At the centre of Lee's work—as a poet, children's writer, lyricist, essayist, educator, and editor—is a struggle with modernism.

Lee is concerned not just with the modernist literary movement but with cultural modernism in general: the philosophical and technological developments that have radically altered twentieth-century living. He sees the shift from an unselfconscious way of life (in which ethics and belief were indivisible, and one always had a sense of belonging) to our contemporary, compartmentalized existence (in which complete relativity is the only absolute) as resulting in an erosion of faith in oneself and in what one perceives to be reality. The individual can find himself in a kind of double bind. He can either erroneously accept his milieu as 'real', or attempt to define what makes it inauthentic—but to do the latter is also to acquiesce to the modernist environment, since for Lee defining falsifies a thing by restricting it to a limited idea.

For Lee the individual's dilemma is also that of Canada. In *Civil Elegies*—as well as in his seminal essay 'Cadence, Country, Silence' and his critical and philosophical book *Savage Fields* (1977)—he delineates the factors that fill contemporary Canadians with a sense of self-alienation and irrevocable loss. Viewing Canada as disenfranchised by modernity and by its colonial history, Lee searches in this poem for a way to reclaim a local existence and to define a national one. He seeks to restore both literature and life to a mystical experience in which separate concepts such as form and content, or writer and reader, are replaced by an emerging, intuitive wholeness.

It follows that Lee's work cannot be easily analysed. In addition to being shaped by his continuing struggle with modernism, it is enriched by his interest in meditation and music; the influence of German philosophy and poetry; and the struggle to evolve a civil and personal *self* within his writing. Because Lee is a writer of process (he compulsively revises all his work, even long after its original publication), his poetry and essays do not form a stable corpus of discrete units but become a single work in progress, one that is always subject to further revision, always in development, always aspiring to a philosophy of life that lies beyond the written page. Deep within his work is a religious impulse that manifests itself as an urge to create cosmologically, to edit the messy stuff of life into a vision that is whole *and* all-inclusive because it contains comprehensively the very nature of *being*.

Civil Elegies

I

Often I sit in the sun and brooding over the city, always
in airbone shapes among the pollution I hear them, returning;
pouring across the square
in fetid descent, they darken the towers
and the wind-swept place of meeting and whenever
the thick air clogs my breathing it teems with their presence.
Many were born in Canada, and living unlived lives they died
of course but died truncated, stunted, never at
home in native space and not yet
citizens of a human body of kind. And it is Canada   10
that specialized in this deprivation. Therefore the spectres arrive,
      congregating in bitter droves, thick in the April sunlight,
accusing us and we are no different, though you would not expect
the furies assembled in hogtown and ring me round, invisible, demanding
what time of our lives we wait for till we shall start to be.
Until they come the wide square stretches out
serene and singly by moments it takes us in, each one for now

a passionate civil man, until it
sends us back to the acres of gutted intentions,
back to the concrete debris, to parking scars and the four-square tiers 20
of squat and righteous lives. And here
once more, I watch the homing furies' arrival.

I sat one morning by the Moore, off to the west
ten yards and saw though diffident my city nailed against the sky
in ordinary glory.
It is not much to ask. A place, a making,
two towers, a teeming, a genesis, a city.
And the men and women moved in their own space,
performing their daily lives, and their presence occurred
in time as it occurred, patricians in   30
muddy York and made their compact together against the gangs of the new.
And as that crumpled before the shambling onset, again the
lives we had not lived in phalanx invisibly staining
the square and vistas, casting back I saw
regeneration twirl its blood and the rebels riding
riderless down Yonge Street, plain men much
goaded by privilege—our other origin, and cried
'Mackenzie knows a word, Mackenzie
knows a meaning!' but it was not true. Eight hundred-odd steely Canadians
turned tail at the cabbage patch when a couple of bullets fizzed   40
and the loyalists, scared skinny by the sound of their own gunfire,
gawked and bolted south to the fort like rabbits,
the rebels for their part bolting north to the pub: the first
spontaneous mutual retreat in the history of warfare.
Canadians, in flight.

Buildings oppress me, and the sky-concealing wires
bunch zigzag through the air. I know
the dead persist in
buildings, by-laws, porticos—the city I live in
is clogged with their presence; they   50
dawdle about in our lives and form a destiny, still
incomplete, still dead weight, still
demanding whether Canada will be.

But the mad bomber, Chartier of Major Street, Chartier
said it: that if a country has no past,
neither is it a country and promptly
blew himself to bits in the parliament john, leaving as civil testament
assorted chunks of prophet, twitching and
bobbing to rest in the flush.
And what can anyone do in this country, baffled and   60
making our penance for ancestors, what did they leave us? Indian-swindlers,

stewards of unclaimed earth and rootless what does it matter if they, our
forebears' flesh and bone were often
good men, good men do not matter to history.
And what can we do here now, for at last we have no notion
of what we might have come to be in America, alternative, and how make public
a presence which is not sold out utterly to the modern? utterly? to the
savage inflictions of what is for real, it pays off, it is only
accidentally less than human?

In the city I long for, green trees still   70
asphyxiate. The crowds emerge at five from jobs
that rankle and lag. Heavy developers
pay off aldermen still; the craft of neighbourhood,
its whichway streets and generations
anger the planners, they go on jamming their maps
with asphalt panaceas; single men
still eke out evenings courting, in parks, alone.
A man could spend a lifetime looking for
peace in that city. And the lives give way around him—marriages
founder, the neighbourhoods sag—until   80
the emptiness comes down on him to stay.
But in the city I long for men complete
their origins. Among the tangle of
hydro, hydrants, second mortgages, amid
the itch for new debentures, greater expressways,
in sober alarm they jam their works of progress, asking where in truth
they come from and to whom they must belong.
And thus they clear a space in which
the full desires of those that begot them, great animating desires
that shrank and grew hectic as the land pre-empted their lives   90
might still take root, which eddy now and
drift in the square, being neither alive nor dead.
And the people accept a flawed inheritance
and they give it a place in their midst, forfeiting progress, forfeiting
dollars, forfeiting yankee visions of cities that in time it might grow
whole at last in their lives, they might
belong once more to their forebears, becoming their own men.

To be our own men! in dread to live
the land, our own harsh country, beloved, the prairie, the foothills—
and for me it is lake by rapids by stream-fed lake, threading   100
north through the terminal vistas of black spruce, in a
bitter, cherished land it is farm after
farm in the waste of the continental outcrop—
for me it is Shield but wherever terrain informs our lives and claims us;
and then, no longer haunted by
unlived presence, to live the cities:

to furnish, out of the traffic and smog and the shambles of dead precursors,
a civil habitation that is
human, and our own.

The spectres drift across the square in rows.   110
How empire permeates! And we sit down
in Nathan Phillips Square, among the sun,
as if our lives were real.
Lacunae. Parking lots. Regenerations.
Newsstand euphorics and Revell's sign, that not
one countryman has learned, that
men and women live that
they may make that
life worth dying. Living. Hey,
the dead ones! Gentlemen, generations of   120
acquiescent spectres gawk at the chrome
on American cars on Queen Streeet, gawk and slump and retreat.
And over the square where I sit, congregating above the Archer
they crowd in a dense baffled throng and the sun does not shine through.

2

Master and Lord, where
are you?
A man moves back and forth
between what must be done to save the world
and what will save his soul,
and neither is real. For many years
I could not speak your name, nor now but
even stilled at times by openings like
joy my whole life
aches, the streets I walk along to work declare   10
your absence, the headlines
declare it, the nation, and
over and over the harried lives I
watch and live with, holding my breath and
sometimes a thing rings true—
they all give way and declare your real absence.

Master and Lord,
let be. I can say
nothing about you that does not
vanish like tapwater.   20
I know
the world is not enough; a woman straightens
and turns from the sink and asks her life the
question, why should she

fake it? and after a moment she
shrugs, and returns to the sink. A man's
adrenalin takes hold, at a meeting he makes
his point, and pushes and sees that
things will happen now . . . and then in the pause he knows
there are endless things in the world and this is not for real.   30

Whatever is lovely, whatever deserves
contempt, whatever dies—
over and over, in every thing we meet
we meet that emptiness.

It is a homecoming, as men once knew
their lives took place in you.
And we cannot get on, no matter how we
rearrange our lives and we cannot let go for
then there is nothing at all.

Master and Lord, there was a   40
measure once.
There was a time when men could say
my life, my job, my home
and still feel clean.
The poets spoke of earth and heaven. There were no symbols.

9

Here, as I sit and watch, the rusty leaves hang taut with departure.
The last few tourists pose by the Moore and snap their proof that they
    were also alive.
And what if there is no regenerative absence?
What if the void that compels us is only
a mood gone absolute?
We would have to live in the world.
What if the dreary high-rise is nothing but
banks of dreary high-rise, it does not
release the spirit by fraying its attachment,
for the excellent reason that there is no place else to go?   10
We would have to live in it, making our lives on earth.
Or else a man might go on day by day
in love with emptiness, dismayed each time he meets
good friends, fine buildings and grass in the acres of concrete, feeling the
city's erotic tug begin once more, perpetually
splayed alive by the play of his bungled desires,
though some do not salute the death of the body
before they have tested its life, but crippled they summon together
the fury from within, they tilt at

empire, empire, lethal adversary;   20
but I am one who came to
idolatry, as in a season of God,
taking my right to be from nothingness.

Across the square the crisp leaves blow in gusts, tracing
the wind's indignant lift in corners,
filling the empty pool.
People plod past through the raw air, lost in their overcoats.
I hunch down close to my chest and eat smoke.

But when the void became void I did
let go, though derelict for months   30
and I was easy, no longer held by its negative presence
as I was earlier disabused of many things in the world
including Canada, and came to know I still had access to them,
and I promised to honour each one of my country's failures of nerve and its sellouts.

To rail and flail at a dying civilisation,
to rage in imperial space, condemning
soviet bombers, american bombers—to go on saying
no to history is good.
And yet a man does well to leave that game behind, and go and find
some saner version of integrity,   40
although he will not reach it where he longs to, in the
vacant spaces of his mind—they are so
occupied. Better however to try.

But we are not allowed to enter God's heaven, where it is all a
drowsy beatitude, nor is God, the realm above our heads but
must grow up on earth.
Nor do we have recourse to void.
For void is not a place, nor
negation of a place.
Void is not the high cessation of the lone self's burden,   50
crowned with the early nostalgias;
nor is it rampant around the corner, endlessly possible.
We enter void when void no longer exists.

And best of all is finding a place to be
in the early years of a better civilisation.
For we are a conquered nation: sea to sea we bartered
eveything that counts, till we have
nothing to lose but our forebears' will to lose.
Beautiful riddance!
And some will make their choice and eat imperial meat.   60
But many will come to themselves, for there is

no third way at last and these will
spend their lives at war, though not with
guns, not yet—with motherwit and guts, sustained
by bloody-minded reverence among the things which are,
and the long will to be in Canada.

The leaves, although they cling against the
wind do not resist their time of dying.
And I must learn to live it all again, depart again—
the storm-wracked crossing, the nervous descent, the barren wintry land,   70
and clearing a life in the place where I belong, re-entry
to bare familiar streets, first sight of coffee mugs,
reconnaissance of trees, of jobs done well or badly,
flashes of workday people abusing their power,
abusing their lives, hung up, sold out and
feeling their lives wrenched out of whack
by the steady brunt of the continental breakdown;
finding a place among the ones who live
on earth somehow, sustained in fits and starts
by the deep ache and presence and sometimes the joy of what is.   80

Freely out of its dignity the void must
supplant itself. Like God like the soul it must
surrender its ownness, like eternity it must
re-instil itself in the texture of our being here.
And though we have seen our most precious words
withdraw, like smudges of wind from a widening water-calm,
though they will not be charged with presence again in our lifetime that is
well, for now we have access to new nouns—
as water, copout, tower, body, land.

Earth, you nearest, allow me.   90
Green of the earth and civil grey:
within me, without me and moment by
moment allow me for to
be here is enough and earth you
strangest, you nearest, be home.

1972

Fred Wah

b. 1939

Born in Swift Current, Sask., of Chinese and Scandinavian parents, Fred Wah moved with his family to Trail, B.C., when he was four, and grew up there and in nearby Nelson. As a teenager he played trumpet in a band called the Kampus Kings (Lionel Kearns was the saxophonist). He left the Kootenay region in 1959 to study music at the University of British Columbia; there he became involved with the *Tish* group of west-coast writers that included Daphne Marlatt and George Bowering. Interested in the poetics of the Black Mountain school (particularly in its emphasis on simple syntax, concreteness, and a desire for organic rather than inherited literary forms), Wah studied with Robert Creeley at Albuquerque, New Mexico and later, as a graduate student, in Buffalo at the State University of New York, where he also worked with Charles Olson, the founder and major theorist of Black Mountain poetics. He returned to the Kootenays in 1967, and worked as a teacher at Selkirk College in Castlegar, B.C., and as head of the creative writing program at David Thompson University Centre in Nelson. He now lives in South Slocan, between Nelson and Castlegar.

Since 1961, when he was one of the founding editors of *Tish*, Wah has been active as an editor of literary magazines. In New Mexico he founded and edited *Sum* (1964-5); in Buffalo he worked on the editorial staff of *Niagara Frontier Review* and *The Magazine of Further Studies*; in Castlegar he edited *Scree*, as well as an anthology of West Kootenay writing and photographs. Since its inception in 1965, Wah has been a contributing editor to *Open Letter*, which has served as a forum for discussions of contemporary writing and poetics in Canada; he was also a co-editor of its sister electronic literary magazine, *Swift Current*.

Wah has published several books of poetry: *Lardeau: Selected First Poems* (1965), *Mountain* (1967), *Tree* (1972), *Among* (which includes work from his first three books; 1972), *Earth* (1974), *Pictograms from the Interior of B.C.* (1975), *Selected Poems:* *Loki is Buried at Smoky Creek* (1980), *Breathin' my name with a sigh* (1981), *Owner's Manual* (1982), and *Waiting for Saskatchewan* (1985), for which he received a Governor General's Award.

Always interested in the poet's connections with place—a general concern of the *Tish* group—Wah has rejected traditional prose forms as a way of articulating those connections. His poetry, which records his explorations into the world of sight and sound around him, is sometimes difficult and demands to be read aloud. It expresses place through the experience of sound, in such early poems as 'Song' ('What a wonderful way/ To come into the city/ All over the bridge/ O/ver/the bridge'); through explorations of the relationship between visual and verbal representations, in *Pictograms from the Interior of B.C.*; and through an investigation of the relationship with particulars of place and with parents, in *Waiting for Saskatchewan*. In this last collection, Wah grapples largely with the influence of his father. The 'Elite' sequence of prose poems, which takes its name from the family café in Swift Current, deals with the poet's return to the prairies and his desire to understand his father, a figure who dominates the collection. 'Relation Speaks' is a poem about returns of a different kind. Here Wah tells us that knowledge must be collected, though the links and connections sometimes become clear only afterwards. Wah feels the importance of Saskatchewan, for instance, long after he leaves it; and the significance of his father emerges only after his father's death, which is being mourned in this collection of poetry.

'I lie here and wait for life again' is taken from *Breathin' My Name With a Sigh*, which George Bowering, in his introduction to *Selected Poems*, calls Wah's 'book of air, poems of the breath'. ('Wah' is equated with the sound of breathing out with a sigh.) The speaker in this poem tries to catch his breath, gasping for answers as he gasps for air.

I lie here and wait for life again[1]

I lie here and wait for life again
no one told me this happens
not death but a consequence of it
the physical isn't a world
at least it wasn't this morning
when I ran up the road out of breath
yet that is what I most desire.
Information. What leads up to death,
is only information.

1981

[1] 'I lie here and wait for life again' first appeared in a manuscript edition (Coach House Press, 1978), and was later published in *Selected Poems* (1980). That version differs substantially from the one printed above, which is taken from *Breathin' my name with a sigh* (1981).

Waiting for Saskatchewan

Waiting for saskatchewan
and the origins grandparents countries places converged
europe asia railroads carpenters nailed grain elevators
Swift Current my grandmother in her house
he built on the street
and him his cafes namely the 'Elite' on Center
looked straight ahead Saskatchewan points to it
Erickson Wah Trimble houses train station tracks
arrowed into downtown fine clay dirt prairies wind waiting
for Saskatchewan to appear for me again over the edge   10
horses led to the huge sky the weight and colour of it
over the mountains as if the mass owed me such appearance
against the hard edge of it sits on my forehead
as the most political place I know these places these strips
laid beyond horizon for eyesight the city so I won't have to go
near it as origin town flatness appears later in my stomach why
why on earth would they land in such a place
mass of pleistocene
sediment plate wedge
arrow sky beak horizon still waiting for that   20
I want it back, wait in this snowblown winter night
for that latitude of itself its own largeness
my body to get complete
it still owes me, it does

1985

Relation speaks

Relation speaks. Tree talks hierarchy loop subject returns.
Knowledge a bag of things to be changed later to
knowledge. Statement of instructions horoscope Wah
language reads reading out of order in order to speak to
itself feed picked up lists family and complete branches/
worlds end there.

1985

Elite 3[1]

I'm on the prairies this winter. I haven't been here in the winter since I was four years old. It's not Swift Current, or Speedy Creek as some here call it, but there are certain flavours which are unmistakeably part of us. The ethnicity here feels so direct. I mean the Chinese are still connected to China, the Ukrainians so Ukrainian, in the bar the Icelanders tell stories about Iceland, the Swede still has an accent, the French speak French. Here you're either a Wiebe or a Friesen, or not. What is a Metis, anyway? I know when you came back from China you must have felt more Chinese than anything else. But I remember you saying later that the Chinese didn't trust you and the English didn't trust you. You were a half-breed, Eurasian. I remember feeling the possibility of that word 'Eurasian' for myself when I first read it in my own troubled adolescence. I don't think you ever felt the relief of that exotic identity though. In North America white is still the standard and you were never white enough. But you weren't pure enough for the Chinese either. You never knew the full comradeship of an ethnic community. So you felt single, outside, though you played the game as we all must. To be a mix here on the prairies is still noticed. I remember going into Macleods in Swift Current a few years ago and sensing that most of the women in the store were just like Granny Erickson. I don't think you felt there was anyone else in the world like you.

1985

[1]Pronounced 'ee-light' [Wah's note].

Clark Blaise

b. 1940

Clark Blaise is a border-crosser. Born in North Dakota of an English-Canadian mother and a French-Canadian father, he moved frequently in his youth as his father failed in one business enterprise after another. Rarely completing a grade in any single school, Blaise lived in Florida, Georgia, New Jersey, Ohio, Kentucky, and Manitoba (where his mother still lives). He took a B.A. from Denison University in 1961 and then attended Harvard University (studying with Bernard Malamud) and the University of Iowa's Writers' Workshop, where he earned an M.F.A. in 1964. He taught English at the University of Wisconsin after that. Then in 1966 he moved to Canada and took a teaching post at Sir George Williams (now Concordia University) in Montreal. In 1978 he moved to Toronto, where he taught at York University and co-edited, with John Metcalf, the annual anthology *Best Canadian Stories*. Since 1980 he has held various teaching appointments and residencies, mostly in the U.S. In 1986-7 he returned to Concordia as writer-in-residence.

Having grown up in the United States thinking of himself as a Canadian, Blaise has come to see himself as a permanent outsider, displaced in French- and English-Canada as well as in the U.S. He thinks of himself as a 'resident alien' and has given that title to one of his books. In it he writes:

Sociologically, I am an American. Psychologically, a Canadian. Sentimentally, a Québécois. By marriage, part of the Third World. My passport says Canadian, but I was born in America; my legal status says immigrant. Resident Alien. Everywhere I see dualities. His work has dealt extensively with this estrangement, transforming autobiographical incidents into parables of alienation. Confessional in tone, his narratives tend to reveal the innermost self of his narrators—a shadow self that embodies feelings of repressed guilt arising from displacement. Blaise's first collection of short stories, *North American Education* (1973), traces the

lives of three characters (all resembling the author) who lack a home country and are unable to become a part of any environment. *Tribal Justice* (1974), expands on this theme: the stories in this collection not only look at the alienation of such outsiders, but also at the way membership in any group—whether ethnic, racial, geographical, or religious—leads to some degree of social exclusion. Blaise's travel narrative, *Days and Nights in Calcutta* (1977), written with his wife, the novelist Bharati Mukherjee, continues this attempt to explore the experience of the outsider; the observations of Blaise, clearly an alien in India, are paired with those of Mukherjee who, through her marriage and the language in which she writes, has chosen alienation. Blaise and Mukherjee also collaborated on a book about the 1985 Air India flight that was brought down by a bomb after its departure from Toronto: *The Sorrow and the Terror: The Haunting Legacy of the Air India Tragedy* (1987).

Blaise's first novel, *Lunar Attractions* (1979), also makes use of autobiography, and reflects on the traumatic childhood portrayed in several of the earlier stories. His second novel, *Lusts* (1983), explores a topic outside of his personal experience (the life and death of a fictional poet who resembles Sylvia Plath), but even that book—conveyed in an exchange of letters between her husband and her biographer—becomes a meditation on autobiography and its implications. More recently, in *Resident Alien* (1986), Blaise places personal accounts of his own life alongside short stories made from that life-experience—to show the complicated relationship between life and fiction. In introducing his own stories in *New Canadian Writing 1968* (his first book appearance), he described his typical story in a way that still characterizes most of his later writing: 'an adult voice of unspecified age and circumstance describes a test that he failed years earlier, and the deeper chaos that has resulted. . . . The failure stems not from a lack of nerve or ambition or courage or even intelligence . . . but rather from a sudden contact with infinity'. This notion of a failed struggle for enlightenment—which Blaise associates with the philosopher Pascal and with the Jansenist Catholicism Blaise inherited from his father—is a feature of all his fiction. Unlike James Joyce's short fictions that offer sudden insights as small epiphanies, a Blaise story ends with an 'anti-epiphany'—a discovery, not of the unifying factor that will suddenly make sense of the chaos of life but of a subterranean void that throws the innocent world of childhood into confusion and despair.

The structures of Blaise's stories are determined by this moment of Jansenist realization that one's will is corrupt and one's environment depraved. He builds his narratives around parallels and echoes—using images (such as 'eyes') that draw together the apparently unrelated elements of the story. At moments of horrific discovery in these narratives such a central image is transformed into an emblem of chaos, and the other images that have been associated with it become repugnant by association. Thus Blaise's stories do not follow the classic short-story structure of a single line of action. They are composed of disparate narrative threads that join not in a climax of event—little action takes place in a Blaise story—but in a climax of apprehension: the uncovering of a hidden 'unfathomable complexity, the insolent infinity that defeats our humanity' *(New Canadian Writing 1968)*.

Eyes

You jump into this business of a new country cautiously. First you choose a place where English is spoken, with doctors and bus lines at hand, and a supermarket in a *centre d'achats* not too far away. You ease yourself into the city, approaching by car or bus down a single artery, aiming yourself along the boulevard that begins small and tree-lined in your suburb but broadens into the canyoned aorta of the city five miles beyond. And by that first winter when you know the routes and bridges, the standard congestions reported from the helicopter on your favorite radio station, you start to think of moving. What's the good of a place like this when two of your neighbors have come from Texas and the French paper you've dutifully subscribed to arrives by mail two days late? These French are all around you, behind the counters at the shopping center, in a house or two on your block; why isn't your little boy learning French at least? Where's the nearest *maternelle?* Four miles away.

In the spring you move. You find an apartment on a small side street where dogs outnumber children and the row houses resemble London's, divided equally between the rundown and remodeled. Your neighbors are the young personalities of French television who live on delivered chicken, or the old pensioners who shuffle down the summer sidewalks in pajamas and slippers in a state of endless recuperation. Your neighbors pay sixty a month for rent, or three hundred; you pay two-fifty for a two-bedroom flat where the walls have been replastered and new fixtures hung. The bugs *d'antan*[1] remain, as well as the hulks of cars abandoned in the fire alley behind, where downtown drunks sleep in the summer night.

Then comes the night in early October when your child is coughing badly, and you sit with him in the darkened nursery, calm in the bubbling of a cold-steam

[1] Of yesteryear.

vaporizer while your wife mends a dress in the room next door. And from the dark, silently, as you peer into the ill-lit fire alley, he comes. You cannot believe it at first, that a rheumy, pasty-faced Irishman in slate-gray jacket and rubber-soled shoes has come purposely to *your* small parking space, that he has been here before and he is not drunk (not now, at least, but you know him as a pan-handler on the main boulevard a block away), that he brings with him a crate that he sets on end under your bedroom window and raises himself to your window ledge and hangs there nose-high at a pencil of light from the ill-fitting blinds. And there you are, straining with him from the uncurtained nursery, watching the man watching your wife, praying silently that she is sleeping under the blanket. The man is almost smiling, a leprechaun's face that sees what you cannot. You are about to lift the window and shout, but your wheezing child lies just under you; and what of your wife in the room next door? You could, perhaps, throw open the window and leap to the ground, tackle the man before he runs and smash his face into the bricks, beat him senseless then call the cops . . . Or bet-ter, find the camera, afix the flash, rap once at the window and shoot when he turns. Do nothing and let him suffer. *He is at your mercy,* no one will ever again be so helpless—but what can you do? You know, somehow, he'll escape. If you hurt him, he can hurt you worse, later, viciously. He's been a regular at your window, he's watched the two of you when you prided yourself on being young and alone and masters of the city. He knows your child and the park he plays in, your wife and where she shops. He's a native of the place, a man who knows the city and maybe a dozen such windows, who knows the fire escapes and alleys and roofs, knows the habits of the city's heedless young.

And briefly you remember yourself, an adolescent in another country slither-ing through the mosquito-ridden grassy fields behind a housing development, peering into those houses where newlyweds had not yet put up drapes, how you could spend five hours in a motionless crouch for a myopic glimpse of a slender arm reaching from the dark to douse a light. Then you hear what the man cannot; the creaking of your bed in the far bedroom, the steps of your wife on her way to the bathroom, and you see her as you never have before: blond and tall and rangily built, a north-Europe princess from a constitutional monarchy, sensuous mouth and prominent teeth, pale, tennis-ball breasts cupped in her hands as she stands in the bathroom's light.

'How's Kit?' she asks. 'I'd give him a kiss except that there's no blind in there,' and she dashes back to bed, nude, and the man bounces twice on the win-dow ledge.

'You coming?'

You find yourself creeping from the nursery, turning left at the hall and then running to the kitchen telephone; you dial the police, then hang up. How will you prepare your wife, not for what is happening, but for what has already taken place?

'It's stuffy in here,' you shout back, 'I think I'll open the window a bit.' You take your time, you stand before the blind blocking his view if he's still looking, then bravely you part the curtains. He is gone, the crate remains upright. 'Do we have any masking tape?' you ask, lifting the window a crack.

And now you know the city a little better. A place where millions come each summer to take pictures and walk around must have its voyeurs too. And that place in all great cities where rich and poor co-exist is especially hard on the people in-between. It's health you've been seeking, not just beauty; a tough urban health that will save you money in the bargain, and when you hear of a place twice as large at half the rent, in a part of town free of Texans, English, and French, free of young actors and stewardesses who deposit their garbage in pizza boxes, you move again.

It is, for you, a city of Greeks. In the summer you move you attend a movie at the corner cinema. The posters advertise a war movie, in Greek, but the uniforms are unfamiliar. Both sides wear mustaches, both sides handle machine guns, both leave older women behind dressed in black. From the posters outside there is a promise of sex; blond women in slips, dark-eyed peasant girls. There will be rubble, executions against a wall. You can follow the story from the stills alone: mustached boy goes to war, embraces dark-eyed village girl. Black-draped mother and admiring young brother stand behind. Young soldier, mustache fuller, embraces blond prostitute on a tangled bed. Enter soldiers, boy hides under sheets. Final shot, back in village. Mother in black; dark-eyed village girl in black. Young brother marching to the front.

You go in, pay your ninety cents, pay a nickel in the lobby for a wedge of *halvah*-like sweets. You understand nothing, you resent their laughter and you even resent the picture they're running. Now you know the Greek for 'Coming Attractions', for this is a gangster movie at least thirty years old. The eternal Mediterranean gangster movie set in Athens instead of Naples or Marseilles, with smaller cars and narrower roads, uglier women and more sinister killers. After an hour the movie flatters you. No one knows you're not a Greek, that you don't belong in this theatre, or even this city. That, like the Greeks, you're hanging on.

Outside the theatre the evening is warm and the wide sidewalks are clogged with Greeks who nod as you come out. Like the Ramblas in Barcelona,[2] with children out past midnight and families walking back and forth for a long city block, the men filling the coffeehouses, the women left outside, chatting. Not a blond head on the sidewalk, not a blond head for miles. Greek music pours from the coffeehouses, flies stumble on the pastry, whole families munch their *torsades molles*[3] as they walk. Dry goods are sold at midnight from the sidewalk, like New York fifty years ago. You're wandering happily, glad that you moved, you've rediscovered the innocence of starting over.

Then you come upon a scene directly from Spain. A slim blond girl in a floral top and white pleated skirt, tinted glasses, smoking, with bad skin, ignores a persistent young Greek in a shiny Salonika[4] suit. 'Whatsamatta?' he demands, slapping a ten-dollar bill on his open palm. And without looking back at him she drifts closer to the curb and a car makes a sudden squealing turn and lurches to a stop on the cross street. Three men are inside, the back door opens and not a word is exchanged as she steps inside. How? What refinement of gesture did we

[2]La Ramblas is the main street in Barcelona.
[3]Pastry twists.
[4]Seaport in northeastern Greece.

immigrants miss? You turn to the Greek boy in sympathy, you know just how he feels, but he's already heading across the street, shouting something to his friends outside a barbecue stand. You have a pocketful of bills and a Mediterranean soul, and money this evening means a woman, and blond means whore and you would spend it all on another blond with open pores; all this a block from your wife and tenement. And you hurry home.

Months later you know the place. You trust the Greeks in their stores, you fear their tempers at home. Eight bathrooms adjoin a central shaft, you hear the beatings of your son's friends, the thud of fist on bone after the slaps. Your child knows no French, but he plays cricket with Greeks and Jamaicans out in the alley behind Pascal's hardware. He brings home the oily tires from the Esso station, plays in the boxes behind the appliance store. You watch from a greasy back window, at last satisfied. None of his friends is like him, like you. He is becoming Greek, becoming Jamaican, becoming a part of this strange new land. His hair is nearly white; you can spot him a block away.

On Wednesdays the butcher quarters his meat. Calves arrive by refrigerator truck, still intact but for their split-open bellies and sawed-off hooves. The older of the three brothers skins the carcass with a small thin knife that seems all blade. A knife he could shave with. The hide rolls back in a continuous flap, the knife never pops the membrane over the fat.

Another brother serves. Like yours, his French is adequate. *'Twa lif d'hamburger'*, you request, still watching the operation on the rickety sawhorse. Who could resist? It's a Levantine treat, the calf's stumpy legs high in the air, the hide draped over the edge and now in the sawdust, growing longer by the second.

The store is filling. The ladies shop on Wednesday, especially the old widows in black overcoats and scarves, shoes and stockings. Yellow, mangled fingernails. Wednesdays attract them with boxes in the window, and they call to the butcher as they enter, the brother answers, and the women dip their fingers in the boxes. The radio is loud overhead, music from the Greek station.

'Une et soixante, m'sieur. Du bacon, jambon?'

And you think, taking a few lamb chops but not their saltless bacon, how pleased you are to manage so well. It is a Byzantine moment with blood and widows and sides of dripping beef, contentment in a snowy slum at five below.

The older brother, having finished the skinning, straightens, curses, and puts away the tiny knife. A brother comes forward to pull the hide away, a perfect beginning for a gameroom rug. Then, bending low at the rear of the glistening carcass, the legs spread high and stubby, the butcher digs in his hands, ripping hard where the scrotum is, and pulls on what seems to be a strand of rubber, until it snaps. He puts a single glistening prize in his mouth, pulls again and offers the other to his brother, and they suck.

The butcher is singing now, drying his lips and wiping his chin, and still he's chewing. The old black-draped widows with the parchment faces are also chewing. On leaving, you check the boxes in the window. Staring out are the heads of pigs and lambs, some with the eyes lifted out and a red socket exposed. A few are loose and the box is slowly dissolving from the blood, and the ice beneath.

The women have gathered around the body; little pieces are offered to them from the head and entrails. The pigs' heads are pink, perhaps they've been boiled, and hairless. The eyes are strangely blue. You remove your gloves and touch the skin, you brush against the grainy ear. How the eye attracts you! How you would like to lift one out, press its smoothness against your tongue, then crush it in your mouth. And you cannot. Already your finger is numb and the head, it seems, has shifted under you. And the eye, in panic, grows white as your finger approaches. You would take that last half inch but for the certainty, in this world you have made for yourself, that the eye would blink and your neighbors would turn upon you.

1973

Gwendolyn MacEwen

1941-1987

Born in Toronto and raised there and in Winnipeg, Gwendolyn MacEwen published her first poem at seventeen in the *Canadian Forum* and left school a year later to become a writer. By the time she was twenty she had published privately two chapbooks, *Sela* (1961) and *The Drunken Clock* (1961), and two years later had her first commercial publication with *The Rising Fire*. She subsequently produced eight poetry collections: *A Breakfast for Barbarians* (1966); *The Shadow-Maker* (1969); *The Armies of the Moon* (1972); *The Fire Eaters* (1976); *The T.E. Lawrence Poems* (1982); and *Afterworlds* (1987), which—like *The Shadow-Maker*—received a Governor General's Award. Her two volumes of selected poetry are *Magic Animals* (1975), which also contains a few new poems, and *Earthlight* (1982).

As well as writing poetry she worked with a number of other literary forms. She wrote two novels, *Julian the Magician* (1963) and *King of Egypt, King of Dreams* (1971), which reflected her interest in the richness of myth and history from a variety of periods and cultures. (The Mediterranean and the Middle East were of particular interest to her, and she travelled extensively in those areas; *Mermaids and Ikons: A Greek Summer*, 1978, is a memoir of one journey.) Her collection of short stories, *Noman* (1972), although set in 'Kanada', also exhib-

its this predisposition for the foreign and the fantastic. She also wrote plays and dramatic documentaries for CBC radio; one of these, 'Terror and Erebus' (a poetic drama about the Franklin expedition), is reprinted in *Afterworlds*. She created a new version of Euripides' 'The Trojan Women' and with Nikos Tsingos, translated two long poems by Greek poet Yannis Ritsos (the play and translations appear in *Trojan Women*, 1981).

Beneath the fluid and rich surfaces of MacEwen's work is an unusual personal mythology constructed from sources as diverse as commonplace Canadian experience ('The Portage'), the bizarre romance of war *(The T.E. Lawrence Poems)*, and the mystery of the ancient past *(King of Egypt, King of Dreams)*. Out of the bits and pieces of various myths and legends, MacEwen creates paired oppositions, such as spirit and flesh, the magical and the mundane, male and female. These contraries are the basis of her world view, in which the occult and the everyday world exist together in harmonious simultaneity, and one must learn to move between them with ease.

Existing in all these realms is a recurrent figure that Margaret Atwood identified as MacEwen's male muse or animus ('MacEwen's Muse' in *Second Words*, 1982). Sometimes a god incarnate, sometimes man in divine transmutation, this figure can ascend to universal levels or fall into the commonplace specifics of life and death. He appears as Icarus, Manzini, Julian, Noman, Akhenaton (the Egyptian pharaoh), and T.E. Lawrence.

MacEwen often used these figures as oracular I-narrators, and through a humorous blend of incantatory diction and cadences from the casual language of speech, she both affirmed their vitality and undercut their heroic attempts to exist simultaneously in the mythic and phenomenal worlds. As the poet-critic D.G. Jones observed, MacEwen is a poet who can 'say then what most will not, that we are ambiguous, that our exorbitant hungers and satisfactions are both erotic and holy, that their incestuous relations may spawn a bestial phantasmagoria or project an angelic visitation . . .' (Introduction to *Earthlight*).

Icarus[1]

Feather and wax, the artful wings
bridge a blue gulf between
the stiff stone tower
and its languid god, fat sky.

The boy, bent to the whim of wind,
the blue, and the snarling sun
form a brief triumvirate
—flesh, feather, light—
locked in the jaws of the noon
they rule with fleeting liberty.   10

    These are the wings, then,
    a legacy of hollow light—
    feathers, a quill to write
    white poetry across the sky.

Through the mouth of the air, the boy
sees his far father, whose muscled flight
is somehow severed from his own.
Two blinking worlds, and Daedalus'
unbound self is a thing apart.

    You, bound for that other area   20
    know that this legacy of mindflight
    is all you have to leave me.

The boy, Icarus, twists the threads of his throat
and his eyes argue with the sun
on a flimsy parallel, and
the mouth of the sun eager, eager,
smuggles a hot word to the boy's ear.

    But flying, locked in dark dream,

---

[1]Character from Greek mythology who escaped with his father Daedalus (the master craftsman and inventor) by means of wings made of wax and feathers. Forgetful of Daedalus's warning not to fly too close to the sun, which might melt the wax, or to the sea, which might get his feathers wet, Icarus soared too high and fell to his death.

I see Queen Dream, Queen Flight,
the last station of the poet   30
years above my brow, and

Something, something in the air,
in the light's flight, in the vaguely
voluptuous arc of the wings
drives a foreign rhythm into his arms,
his arms which are lean, white willows.

Icarus feels his blood race to his wrist
in a marathon of red light. Swifter,
swift, he tears away the slow veil
from his tendons; the playful biceps   40
sing; they wish new power to the beautiful
false wings
and the boy loops up into tall cobalt.
His hair is a swirl of drunken light,
his arms are wet blades; wings wed with arms.

        You knew
        I would get drunk on beauty.
        The famous phantom quill
        would write me, pull me
        through the eye   50
        of needle noon.

Crete is a huge hump of a black whore beneath him.
Her breasts, two wretched mountains
tremble under his eye.
All is black, except the sun in slow explosion;
a great war strangles his vision
and knots his flying nerve.
Black, and fire, and the boy.

        You and your legacy!
        You knew I would try to   60
        slay the sunlight.

Look, Icarus has kissed the sun
and it sucks the wax,
feathers and wax.
The wings are melting!

The boy Icarus is lean and beautiful.
His body grows limp and falls.
It is cruel poetry set
to the tempo of lightning; it is too swift,
this thin descent.   70

On the lips of the Aegean:

globules of wax,
strands of wet light,

> the lean poem's flesh
> tattered and torn
> by a hook
> of vengeful fire . . .

Combustion of brief feathers

1961

Manzini:[1] Escape Artist

now there are no bonds except the flesh; listen—
there was this boy, Manzini, stubborn with
gut stood with black tights and a turquoise
leaf across his sex

and smirking while the big
brute tied his neck arms legs, Manzini
naked waist up and white with sweat

struggled. Silent, delinquent, he
was suddenly all teeth and knee, straining slack
and excellent with sweat, inwardly   10

wondering if Houdini would take as long
as he; fighting time and the drenched
muscular ropes, as though his tendons were worn
on the outside—

as though his own guts were the ropes
encircling him; it was beautiful; it was thursday; listen—
there was this boy, Manzini

finally free, slid as snake from
his own sweet agonized skin, to throw his entrails
white upon the floor   20
with a cry of victory—

now there are no bonds except the flesh,
but listen, it was thursday, there was this boy,
Manzini—

1966

[1]Manzini was an American magician whom MacEwen met in the mid-sixties; regarding Houdini (mentioned below), see p. 416, n. 1.

The Portage

We have travelled far with ourselves
and our names have lengthened;
    we have carried ourselves
on our backs, like canoes
in a strange portage, over trails,
insinuating leaves
and trees dethroned like kings,
    from water-route to
    water-route
seeking the edge, the end,   10
the coastlines of this land.

On earlier journeys we
were master ocean-goers
going out, and evening always found us
spooning the ocean from our boat,
    and gulls, undiplomatic
    couriers brought us
cryptic messages from shore
till finally we sealords vowed
we'd sail no more.   20

Now under a numb sky, sombre
cumuli weigh us down;
the trees are combed for winter
and bears' tongues have melted
all the honey;
    there is a lourd[1]
suggestion of thunder;
subtle drums under
the candid hands of Indians
are trying to tell us   30
why we have come.

But now we fear movement
and now we dread stillness;
we suspect it was the land
that always moved, not our ships;
we are in sympathy with the fallen
trees; we cannot relate
    the causes of our grief.
We can no more carry
our boats our selves   40
over these insinuating trails.

1969

[1]Sluggish, dull.

Dark Pines under Water

This land like a mirror turns you inward
And you become a forest in a furtive lake;
The dark pines of your mind reach downward,
You dream in the green of your time,
Your memory is a row of sinking pines.

Explorer, you tell yourself this is not what you came for
Although it is good here, and green;
You had meant to move with a kind of largeness,
You had planned a heavy grace, an anguished dream.

But the dark pines of your mind dip deeper   10
And you are sinking, sinking, sleeper
In an elementary world;
There is something down there and you want it told.

1969

From *The T.E. Lawrence Poems*

The Real Enemies[1]

In that land where the soul aged long before the body,
My nameless men, my glamorous bodyguards,
                                        died for me.
My deadly friends with their rouged lips and pretty eyes
            died for me; *my bed of tulips* I called them,
            who wore every color but the white
            that was mine alone to wear.

But they could not guard me against the real enemies—
Omnipotence, and the Infinite—
                        those beasts the soul invents   10
            and then bows down before.
The real enemies were not the men of Fakhri Pasha,[2] nor
Were they even of this world.
                        One could never conquer them,
Never. Hope was another of them. Hope, most brutal of all.

For those who thought clearly, failure was the only goal.

---

[1]The narrative voice of this poem, 'The Void', and the other poems in *The T.E. Lawrence Poems*, is that of Thomas Edward Lawrence (1888-1935), known as Lawrence of Arabia. Author, archaeologist, and soldier, Lawrence led a successful rebellion of the Arabs against the Turks during the First World War and became a near-legendary figure. He subsequently assumed the name T.E. Shaw and retired to self-imposed obscurity to write *The Seven Pillars of Wisdom* (1926), his account of his Arabian adventure.
[2]The leader of the Turkish forces.

Only failure could redeem you, there where the soul aged
      long before the body.
You failed at last, you fell into the delicious light
      and were free.   20

And there was much honor in this;
          it was a worthy defeat.
Islam is surrender—the passionate surrender of the self,
      the puny self, to God.
We declared a Holy War upon Him and were victors as He won.

The Void

The last truly foolish thing I did was some years ago
When I flew the Hejaz[1] flag from the pinnacle of All Souls;
I knew then that I was becoming an aging schoolboy,
      a master-prig with an ego as big
      as an ostrich egg. A pity,
      for I was still young.

Now I'm gray-haired, half-blind, and shaking at the knees;
There's something almost obscene about the few gold teeth
      I got in nineteen-thirty. What
      have I done, what am I doing, what   10
      am I going to do?
Days seem to dawn, suns to shine, evenings to follow.
I have burned all my bridges behind me; this is high, dry
      land.

I'm going around shooting the same camel in the head[2]
Over and over; I'm a pilgrim forever circling the Kaaba,[3]
      which has none of its sides or angles equal,
      for whatever that's worth.
Have you ever been a leaf, and fallen from your tree
      in Autumn? It's like that.   20

Poets put things like shirt-sleeves or oysters
Into their poems, to prevent you from laughing at them
      before they have laughed at themselves.
      I have put an ostrich egg in this one
      to amuse you. I have already laughed.

[1]District of Arabia (its capital is Mecca) from which the Arab revolt against Turkey began in 1916.
'All Souls': one of the colleges at Oxford University; Lawrence's family lived in Oxford and he graduated from Jesus College.
[2]In 'The Virgin Warrior', an earlier poem in the sequence, MacEwen alludes to Lawrence's first outing as a soldier during which, in excited confusion, he shot his own camel in the head.
[3]The most sacred Moslem shrine; located in Mecca, it is towards this shrine that Moslems face when praying and to which they must make at least one pilgrimage.

Where are my noble brothers, my bodyguards, my friends,
Those slender camelmen who rode with me to the ends
           of the desert? When does the great dream end?
           With my right wrist recently broken,
           I write this sad, left-handed poem.   30

1982

The Death of the Loch Ness Monster

Consider that the thing has died before we proved it ever lived
           and that it died of loneliness, dark lord of the loch,
fathomless Worm, great Orm, this last of our mysteries—
           haifend ane meikill fin on ilk syde
           with ane taill and ane terribill heid—
and that it had no tales to tell us, only that it lived there,
           lake-locked, lost in its own coils,
waiting to be found; in the black light of midnight
           surfacing, its whole elastic length unwound,
and the sound it made as it broke the water   10
           was the single plucked string of a harp—
this newt or salamander, graceful as a swan,
           this water-snake, this water-horse, this water-dancer.

Consider him tired of pondering the possible existence of man
           whom he thinks he has sighted sometimes on the shore,
and rearing up from the purple churning water,
           weird little worm head swaying from side to side,
he denies the vision before his eyes;
           his long neck, swan of Hell, a silhouette against the moon,
his green heart beating its last,   20
           his noble, sordid soul in ruins.

Now the mist is a blanket of doom, and we pluck from the depths
           a prize of primordial slime—
the beast who was born from some terrible ancient kiss,
           lovechild of unspeakable histories,
this ugly slug, half blind no doubt, and very cold,
           his head which is horror to behold
no bigger than our own;
           whom we loathe, for his kind ruled the earth before us,
who died of loneliness in a small lake in Scotland,
           and in his mind's dark land,
where he dreamed up his luminous myths, the last of which was man.

1987

Polaris

OR, GULAG NIGHTSCAPES

At midnight in this foreign country
in the vivid snow as cold as vodka
you stand watching constellations which are ever
       so slowly turning
and the great bear of Russia is ever so slowly turning
round and round in the forest behind you.

You ask yourself are you
       the fixed centre of this scene
and you will stand here forever witnessing
the movement of stars, politics of the northern sky,   10
kinesis of snow?

You begin with freedom as a word,
freedom in its bleakest, purest form
and proceed through crazy stations of the compass
to this kingdom of snow where
       freedom is a prison; it is
Russia or America or the republic of your mind
where governments and constellations are endlessly rotating
and everything is a lie; there is no governing body,
there is nothing to direct you   20
       on your course, there
is no right course, there is no guiding star.

Yet

Everything points to Polaris—
endlessly still star, endlessly unturning,
Alpha in Ursa Minor,
first letter in the alphabet of midnight, and
       America like a giant crystal
is ever so slowly turning, deflecting starlight,
the real and imagined missiles of real and imagined enemies.   30

If you consult the polestar for the truth
of your present position, you will learn that you have no
       position, position is illusion (consider this
endlessly still self, endlessly turning);
this prison is actually your freedom, and
       it is you, it is you, you
are the only thing in this frozen night which is really moving.

1987

Daphne Marlatt

b. 1942

Born Daphne Buckle in Melbourne, Australia, Daphne Marlatt spent her early childhood in Penang, a northern Malayasian island, before coming to Vancouver in 1951. She entered the University of British Columbia in 1960, and studied there with Warren Tallman, Robert Creeley, and Earle Birney. She also became closely involved with the *Tish* group (which included George Bowering and Fred Wah). Interested in writing about their specific locality, these western writers gained inspiration from the 1963 Vancouver Poetry Conference, which was attended by Charles Olson, Robert Duncan, Robert Creeley, Allen Ginsberg, Denise Levertov, Margaret Avison, and Philip Whalen. In 1964 Marlatt moved to Bloomington, Indiana, where she met D. Alexander, who not only introduced her to the new kinds of poetry he was publishing in *Odda Tala*, but encouraged her to find in speech patterns a source and structure for her own writing. In 1971 Marlatt moved back to the West Coast with her son, Kit. As well as teaching (at Capilano College, Kootenay Lake School of the Arts in Nelson, and the University of British Columbia), she has been involved in editing several periodicals: the *Capilano Review* (1973-6), the experimental prose magazine *periodics* (1977-81), and the poetry journal *Island* (1981-4). More recently her work has been informed by contemporary French feminist theory. She is a founding member of the Canadian feminist editorial collective *tessera* (which publishes a journal dealing with feminist literary theory), a member of West Coast Women and Words (which grew out of the 1983 conference 'Les femmes et les mots' and publishes *West Word*), and was the Ruth Wynn Woodward Professor in Women's Studies at Simon Fraser University (1989-90). Since May 1989 Marlatt has lived on Saltspring Island.

Marlatt's interest in the patterns of speech and thought have led her to explore a range of forms in her poetry and prose. She has published several collections of poetry: *leaf/leafs* (1969); *Vancouver Poems* (1972); *Steveston* (1974), a long poem about the Japanese fishing village in the mouth of the Fraser River (she continues to work on this poem in various forms); *here and there* (1981); *mauve* and *character* (1985; 1986 in translation with Nicole Brossard); and *Double Negative* (with Betsy Warland; 1988). She has also published several poetic narratives: *Frames of a Story* (1968), *Rings* (1971), *Our Lives* (1975), *The Story, She Said* (1977), *What Matters, Writing 1968-70* (1980), *How Hug a Stone* (a record of her journey to England with her son, Kit; 1983), and *Touch to my Tongue* (a series of love poems addressed to Betsy Warland; 1984). Marlatt is the author of two prose works, *Zócalo* (1977) and the novel *Ana Historic* (1988).

The subject of Marlatt's writing is language—the thrill and play of its sounds and rhythms, its potential for the creation of meaning, and its inevitable limitations. 'Coming Home', for example, is a narrative drawn from her personal experience of living in Indiana and Wisconsin before returning to Vancouver in 1971; it is less concerned with Marlatt, driving with her son to Vancouver, than with Marlatt feeling her way through the pathways of language to the 'wet/ground' that is home in this poem. She observes that she grounds her experience in the body of language itself.

Marlatt explains that by 1971 she had 'abandoned the textbook notion of sentence as the container for a completed thought'. Writing open-form poetry had taught her that 'the line was no box for a certain measure of words, but a moving step in the process of thought' (*Open Letter* 1982). The first few lines of 'Imagine: a town', from *Steveston*, illustrate this principle: each line adds to the preceding one, questioning, qualifying, or commenting upon it, but never actually completing it.

The punctuation in 'Imagine: a town' and in 'At Birch Bay' functions like the line-breaks in poetry, forcing readers to pause and reflect. In 'At Birch Bay' especially, Marlatt's readers must follow the rise and fall of the poem, its sweeps and turns. This poem is an excellent example of what Charles Olson called 'proprioceptive' writing, which, as Fred Wah explains in his introduction to Marlatt's *Selected Writing: Net* *Work* (1980), aims to 'accurately reflect the condition of the writer at the moment of the writing'. Marlatt invites her readers to participate in the creation of meaning: as she says in 'The Measure of the Sentence' (*Open Letter* 1982), more than thinking about the poem, readers must hear and feel the poem's 'movement toward, and against, conclusion'.

From *Steveston*

Imagine: a town

Imagine a town running
                 (smoothly?
a town running before a fire
canneries burning
             (do you see the shadow of charred stilts
on cool water? do you see enigmatic chance standing
just under the beam?

            He said they were playing cards in the
Chinese mess hall, he said it was dark (a hall? a shack.
they were all, crowded together on top of each other.   10
He said somebody accidentally knocked the oil lamp over, off
the edge

      where stilts are standing, Over the edge of the
dyke a river pours, uncalled for, unending:

                 where chance lurks
fishlike, shadows the underside of pilings, calling up his hall
the bodies of men & fish corpse piled on top of each other (residue
time is, the delta) rot, an endless waste the trucks of production
grind to juice, driving through

                smears, blood smears in the dark   20
dirt) this marshland silt no graveyard can exist in but water swills,
endlessly out of itself to the mouth

             ringed with residue, where
chance flicks his tail & swims, through.

1974

Coming Home

if it's to
get lost, lose
way as a wave
breaks

        'goodbye'

i am not speaking of
a path, the 'right'
road, no such
wonderlust

weigh all steps   10
shift weight
to left or right to

a place where one
steps thru all erratic
wanderings down to
touch:

i am here, feel
my weight on the wet
ground

1980

At Birch Bay
             for Roy
        (thanks to Charles Olson)[1]

black, crow, leap up   fall, flap nervous wings against a steep
invisible. bank,   against wind flutters, settle,   has none of the
sweep & glide these gulls have   open to this incessant
oncoming tide   waves & foam   wind
                              Crow, rise &
(drop something   rise & (drop,   flutter,   in to his own stress
landing against this wind, over & over.   Cracking shells, having
learned this from the gulls?
                         thru time, in the rising
wind last night I dreamt, & see, now, like the crow what it is I   10
learn from you
            walking
                  walking the night as moon, moves out of

---

[1](1910-70), founder and chief theorist of the Black Mountain poetry movement, from which the *Tish* group took much of its initial impetus. The quotations in the conclusion of the poem are drawn from Olson's essay 'The Animate versus the Mechanical, and Thought' (*Additional Prose*, 1974).

cancer, out of sea & moon pre-eminent, walking the long. tiderow-
beach. alone: white shells, white backs of gulls on the further
strand, lift, onto the air, clapping wings at their
re-entry into the element, birds, know wind changes
fast as the moon, how tide makes sand disappear, no place to be
except the turbulent face of sea itself incessant. . .

                                  It was you who   20
entered my dream, entered me, in the rising wind last night, in love
in the wash of opening seas we come together in : something about a
newborn you saw (rise & drop, rise &) drop a long life line down
thru all these threshing seas, these birds, like refugees, are resting in
cloud earth sky sensorium outside my dream, outside our dream—'ends &
boundaries,' or ' ''space-activities'' in Creation.' Within which, this
marvellous 'Animate' you teach me, along with the sweep & glide these
gulls possess this (shell) their & our one & only world.

1980

Sandra Birdsell

b. 1942

Much of Sandra Birdsell's fiction is set in the imaginary Manitoban community of Agassiz (named after Lake Agassiz, which once covered much of present-day Manitoba) and the valley that surrounds it. Agassiz is the fictional counterpart of Morris, Manitoba, where Birdsell, the fifth of ten children, was born and raised by her Métis father and Russian-Mennonite mother. Birdsell left home temporarily at fifteen and worked as a waitress in southern Manitoba, before moving permanently to Winnipeg in 1967. She describes this period as one in which she raised three daughters at home, while working at 'many, many full-and part-time jobs' (*Books in Canada*, May, 1986). Encouraged by Robert Kroetsch and Rudy Wiebe (who shares her Mennonite background), she successfully applied for an arts grant, which allowed her to write full-time.

Birdsell worked as a scriptwriter, playwright, and film-maker, and wrote more than thirty stories and a novel before she began her explorations of the fictional world of Agassiz. Two collections of linked short stories, *Night Travellers* (1982) and *Ladies of the House* (1984), were subsequently

brought together in *Agassiz Stories* (1987). These, together with her novel, *The Missing Child* (1989), deal with four generations of the Lafreniere family, especially the Métis father (Maurice, the town barber), the Mennonite mother of seven (Mika), and their three daughters (Betty, Truda, and Lureen). Each of these stories describing specific episodes in the lives of the family members can stand alone, but they are closely linked by the repetition of characters, events, and themes. For example, flooding is central to both the stories and to Birdsell's novel: just as Agassiz is threatened by water (*Night Travellers* begins and *The Missing Child* ends during a time of flood), its inhabitants are often overcome by the flood of memories and emotions. In 'The Wednesday Circle', for example, Betty's fear of being alone with Mr Joy unleashes the floodwaters.

Birdsell's fiction recalls that of other writers, such as Gabrielle Roy and Margaret Laurence, whose realist works describe the diversity of Manitoban communities. But it also resembles the fiction of Alice Munro, whose linked stories focus on female characters in rural communities. Like Munro, Birdsell writes against the realist tradition as much as she writes within it; her fascination with an imaginary world that lies behind and beyond the restrictions of everyday causality is particularly apparent in the magic realism of her novel, *The Missing Child*. Although the conventions of realist plausibility are not violated in Birdsell's short stories, the world of the imagination is brought to life through personal and communal memory, through stories shared between people and generations.

The Wednesday Circle

Betty crosses the double planks that span the ditch in front of Joys' yard. Most people have only one plank. But Mrs Joy needs two. Mrs Joy is a possible candidate for the circus. Like sleeping with an elephant, Betty's father says often. But Mr and Mrs Joy, the egg people, don't sleep together. Betty knows this even though she's never gone further than inside their stale smelling kitchen.

The highway is a smeltering strip of gunmetal grey at her back. It leads to another town like the one she lives in. If you kept on going south, you would get to a place called Pembina in the States and a small dark tavern where a woman will serve under-age kids beer. Laurence, Betty's friend, knows about this. But if you turn from the highway and go west, there are dozens of villages and then the Pembina Hills which Betty has seen on one occasion, a school trip to the man-made lake at Morden. Home of the rich and the godly, Betty's father calls these villages. Wish the godly would stay home. Can't get a seat in the parlour on Friday nights.

Beyond her lies a field in summer fallow and a dirt road rising to a slight incline and then falling as it meets the highway. Before her is the Joys' crumbling yellow cottage, flanked on all sides by greying bales of straw which have swollen and broken free from their bindings and are scattered about the yard. Behind the cottage is the machine shed. Behind the machine shed and bumping up against the prairie is the chicken coop.

Because Mika, Betty's mother, sends her for the eggs instead of having them delivered by Mr Joy, she gets them cheaper.

Betty balances the egg cartons beneath her chin and pushes open the gate. It shrieks on its rusty hinges. The noise doesn't affect her as it usually does. Usually, the noise is like a door opening into a dark room and she is filled with dread. Today, she is prepared for it. Today is the day for the Wednesday Circle. The church ladies are meeting at her home. Even now, they're there in the dining room, sitting in a circle with their Bibles in their laps. It's like women and children in the centre. And arrows flying. Wagons are going up in flames and smoke. The goodness and matronly wisdom of the Wednesday Circle is a newly discovered thing. She belongs with them now. They can reach out to protect her even here, by just being what they are. And although she wants nothing to happen today, she is prepared for the worst.

'Come on in,' Mrs Joy calls from the kitchen.

Betty sets the egg cartons down on the steps and enters the house. Mrs Joy's kitchen resembles a Woolworth store. There are porcelain dogs and cats in every corner on knick-knack shelves. Once upon a time, she used to love looking at those figurines but now she thinks they're ugly.

The woman sits in her specially made chair which is two chairs wired together. Her legs are stretched out in front resting up on another chair. Out of habit, Betty's heart constricts because she knows the signs. Mrs Joy is not up to walking back to the chicken coop with her. And that's how it all began.

'Lo, I am with you always even unto the end of the world,' her mind recites.

These verses rise unbidden. She has memorized one hundred of them and won a trip to a summer Bible camp at Lake Winnipeg. She has for the first time seen the ocean on the prairie and tried to walk on water. The waves have lifted and pulled her out where her feet couldn't touch the sandy bottom and she has been swept beneath that mighty sea and heard the roaring of the waves in her head and felt the sting of fish water in her nostrils. Like a bubble of froth she is swept beneath the water, back and forth by the motion of the waves. She is drowning. What happens is just as she's heard. Her whole life flashes by. Her head becomes a movie screen playing back every lie and swearing, malicious and unkind deeds, thoughts, words. There is not one thing that makes her look justified for having done or said them. And then her foot touches a rock and she pushes herself forward in desperation, hoping it's the right direction.

Miraculously, it is. She bounces forward from the depths to where she can tiptoe to safety, keeping her nose above the waves. She runs panting with fear to her cabin. She pulls the blankets over her. She tells no one. But that evening in the chapel during devotions, the rustling wind in the poplars against the screen causes her to think of God. When they all sing, 'Love Lifted Me,' the sunset parts the clouds above the water so there is a crack of gold where angels hover, watching. So she goes forward to the altar with several others and has her name written in the Book of Life. They tell her the angels are clapping and she thinks she can hear them there at that crack of gold which is the door to heaven. She confesses every sin she's been shown in the water except for one. For some reason, it wasn't there in the movie. And they are such gentle, smiling nice people who have never done what she's done. So she can't bring herself to tell them that Mr Joy puts his hands in her pants.

'Rainin' today, ain't it child?' Mrs Joy asks.

'No, not yet,' Betty says. 'It's very muggy.'

'Don't I know it,' she says.

'Are your legs sore?' Betty asks.

'Oh Lord, yes, how they ache,' Mrs Joy says and rolls her eyes back into her head. Her jersey dress is a tent stretched across her knees. She cradles a cookie tin in her lap.

'That's too bad,' Betty says.

A chuckle comes from deep inside her mammoth chest. 'You sound just like your mother,' she says. 'And you're looking more and more like her each time I see you. You're just like an opal, always changing.'

God's precious jewels, Mrs Joy calls them when she visits Mika. She lines them up verbally, Betty and her sisters and brothers, comparing chins, noses. This one here, she says about Betty, she's an opal. You oughta keep a watch over that one. Always changing. But it just goes to show, His mysteries does He perform. Not one of them the same.

'Thank you,' Betty says, but she hates being told she looks like her mother. Mika has hazel eyes and brown hair. She is blonde and blue-eyed like her Aunt Elizabeth.

'Well, you know where the egg pail is,' Mrs Joy says, dismissing her with a flutter of her pudgy hand.

'Aren't you coming?' Betty asks.

'Not today, girl. It aches me so to walk. You collect the eggs and then you jest find Mr Joy and you pay him. He gets it in the end anyhow.'

Betty looks around the kitchen. His jacket is missing from its hook on the wall. She goes over to the corner by the window and feigns interest in the porcelain figures. She picks one up, sets it down. His truck is not in the yard.

'Where is he?'

'Went to town for something,' Mrs Joy says. 'But I thought he'd be back by now. Doesn't matter though, jest leave the money in the back porch.'

The egg pail thumps against her leg as she crosses the yard to the chicken coop. She walks towards the cluttered wire enclosure, past the machine shed. The doors are open wide. The hens scratch and dip their heads in her direction as she approaches. Hope rises like an erratic kite as she passes the shed and there are no sounds coming from it. She stamps her feet and the hens scatter before her, then circle around and approach her from behind, silently. She quickly gathers three dozen of the warm, straw-flecked eggs, and then steps free of the stifling smelly coop out into the fresh moist air. She is almost home-free. She won't have to face anything today. It has begun to rain. Large spatters spot her white blouse, feel cool on her back. She sets the pail down on the ground beside the egg cartons and begins to transfer the eggs.

'Here, you don't have to do that outside.' His sudden voice, as she fills the egg cartons, brings blood to her face, threatens to pitch her forward over the pail.

He strides across the yard from the shed. 'Haven't got enough sense to come in out of the rain,' he says. 'Don't you know you'll melt? Be nothing left of you but a puddle.'

He carries the pail, she carries the cartons. He has told her: Mrs Joy is fat and lazy, you are my sunshine, my only sunshine. I would like six little ones running around my place too, but Mrs Joy is fat and lazy. His thin hand has gone from patting her on the head with affection, to playfully slapping her on the behind, graduated then to tickling her armpits and ribs and twice now, his hands have been inside her underpants.

'Be not afraid,' a verse leaps into her head. 'For I am with you.' She will put her plan into action. The Wednesday Circle women are strong and mighty. She knows them all, they're her mother's friends. She'll just go to them and say, Mr Joy feels me up, and that will be the end of it.

She walks behind him, her heart pounding. He has an oil rag hanging from his back pocket and his boots are caked with clay, adding inches to his height.

'I'm waiting for my parts,' he says over his shoulder. 'Can't do anything until I get that truck fixed.' Sometimes he talks to her as though she were an adult. Sometimes as though she were ten again and just coming for the eggs for the first time. How old are you, he'd asked the last time and was surprised when she said, fourteen. My sunshine has grown up.

They enter the machine shed and he slides the doors closed behind them, first one and then the other, leaving a sliver of daylight beaming through where the doors join. A single light bulb dangles from a wire, shedding a circle of weak yellow light above the truck, not enough to clear the darkness from the corners.

'Okay-dokey,' he says and puts the pail of eggs on the workbench. 'You can work here. I've got things to do.' He goes over to the truck, disappears beneath its raised hood.

Then he's back at the workbench, searching through his tool-box. 'Seen you with your boyfriend the other day,' he says. 'That Anderson boy.'

'He's not my boyfriend,' she says.

'I saw you,' he says. His usual bantering tone is missing. 'The two of you were in the coulee.' Then his breath is warm on the side of her face as he reaches across her. His arm knocks against her breast, sending pain shooting through her chest. I need a bra, she has told Mika. Whatever for? Wear an undershirt if you think you really need to.

'Do you think it's a good idea to hang around in the coulee with your boyfriend?'

'He's not my boyfriend,' she says. 'I told you.'

He sees her flushed cheeks, senses her discomfort. 'Aha,' he says. 'So he is. You can't fool me.'

She moves away from him. Begins to stack the cartons up against her chest, protection against his nudgings. Why is it that everyone but her own mother notices that she has breasts now?

'Don't rush off,' he says. 'Wait until the rain passes.' The sound of it on the tin roof is like small pebbles being dropped one by one.

He takes the cartons from her and sets them back on the workbench. He smiles and she can see that perfect decayed circle between his front teeth. His hair is completely grey even though he's not as old as her father. He starts to walk past her, back towards the truck and then suddenly he grasps her about the waist and begins to tickle her ribs. She is slammed up against him and gasping for breath. His whiskers prickle against her neck. She tastes the bitterness of his flannel shirt.

She pushes away. 'Stop.'

He holds her tighter. 'You're so pretty,' he says. 'No wonder the boys are chasing you. When I'm working in here, know what I'm thinking all the time?'

'Let me go.' She continues to push against his bony arms.

'I'm thinking about all the things I could do to you.'

Against her will, she has been curious to know. She feels desire rising when he speaks of what he would like to do. He has drawn vivid word-pictures that she likes to reconstruct until her face burns. Only it isn't Mr Joy in the pictures, it's Laurence. It's what made her pull aside her underpants so he could fumble inside her moist crevice with his grease-stained fingers.

'Show me your tits,' he whispers into her neck. 'I'll give you a dollar if you do.'

She knows the only way out of this is to tell. When the whole thing is laid out before the Wednesday Circle, she will become whiter than snow. 'No,' she says.

'What do you mean, no,' he says, jabbing her in the ribs once again.

'I'm going to tell,' she says. 'You can't make me do anything anymore because I'm going to tell on you.' She feels as though a rock has been taken from her stomach. He is ugly. He is like a salamander dropping from the sky after a rainstorm into a mincemeat pail. She doesn't know how she could ever have liked him.

'Make you?' he says. 'Make you? Listen here, girlie, I've only done what you wanted me to do.'

She knows this to be true and not true. She isn't certain how she has come to accept and even expect his fondling. It has happened over a course of four years, gradually, like growing.

She walks to the double doors where the light shines through. 'Open them, please,' she says.

'Open them yourself,' he says. She can feel the presence of the Wednesday Circle. The promise of their womanly strength is like a lamp unto her feet. They will surround her and protect her. Freedom from his word-pictures will make her a new person.

'You say anything,' he says. 'You say one thing and I'll have some pretty stories to tell about you. You betcha.'

'That woman,' Mika is saying to the Wednesday Circle as Betty enters the dining room. 'That woman. She has absolutely no knowledge of the scriptures. She takes everything out of context.' Mika is standing at the buffet with a china teacup in her hand. Betty steps into the circle of chairs and sits down in Mika's empty one. Mika stops talking, throws her a look of surprise and question. The other women greet her with smiles, nods.

'Did you get the eggs?' Mika asks.

Betty feels her mouth stretching, moving of its own accord into a silly smile. She knows the smile irritates Mika but she can't help it. At times like these, her face moves on its own. She can hear her own heartbeat in her ears, like the ocean, roaring.

'What now?' Mika asks, worried.

'What do you mean, she takes everything out of context?' Mrs Brawn asks, ignoring Betty. It's her circle. She started it off, arranging for the church women to meet in each others' homes twice a month to read scripture and sew things which they send to a place in the city where they are distributed to the poor. The women are like the smell of coffee to Betty and at the same time, they are like the cool opaque squares of Mika's lemon slice which is arranged on bread and butter plates on the table. They are also like the sturdy varnished chairs they sit on. To be with them now is the same as when she was a child and thought that if you could always be near an adult when you were ill, you wouldn't die.

'My, my,' Mika mimics someone to demonstrate to Mrs Brawn what she means. She places her free hand against her chest in a dramatic gesture. 'They are different, ain't they? God's precious jewels. Just goes to show, His mysteries does He perform.'

Betty realizes with a sudden shock that her mother is imitating Mrs Joy.

Mrs Brawn takes in Mika's pose with a stern expression and immediately Mika looks guilty, drops her hand from her breast and begins to fill cups with coffee.

'I suppose that we really can't expect much from Mrs Joy,' Mika says with her back to them. Betty hears the slight mocking tone in her voice that passes them by.

Heads bent over needlework nod their understanding. The women's stitches form thumbs, forest-green fingers; except for the woman who sits beside Betty. With a hook she shapes intricate spidery patterns to lay across varnished surfaces, the backs of chairs. What the poor would want with those, I'll never know, Mika has said privately. But they include the doilies in their parcels anyway because they have an understanding. They whisper that this white-haired woman has known suffering.

She works swiftly. It seems to Betty as though the threads come from the ends of her fingers, white strings with a spot of red every few inches. It looks as though she's cut her finger and secretly bleeds the colour into the lacy scallops. The women all unravel and knit and check closely for evenness of tension.

Mika enters the circle of chairs then, carrying the tray of coffee, and begins to make her way around it. She continues to speak of Mrs Joy.

'Are you looking forward to school?' the white-haired woman asks Betty. Her voice is almost a whisper, a knife peeling skin from a taut apple. Betty senses that it has been difficult for her to speak, feels privileged that she has.

'Yes, I miss school.'

The woman blinks as she examines a knot in her yarn. She scrapes at it with her large square thumbnail which is flecked oddly with white fish-hook-shaped marks. 'Your mother tells us you were at camp,' she says. 'What did you do there?'

Mika approaches them with the tray of coffee. 'I just wish she hadn't picked me out, that's all,' Mika says. 'She insists on coming over here in the morning and it's impossible to work with her here. And Mr Joy is just as bad. I send Betty for the eggs now because he used to keep me at the door talking.'

Mr Joy is just as bad. Mr Joy makes me ashamed of myself and I let him do it. The woman shakes loose the doily; it unfolds into the shape of a star as she holds it up.

'You like it?' the white-haired woman asks Betty.

'It's pretty.'

'Maybe I give it to you.'

'Ah, Mika,' a woman across the circle says, 'she just knows where she can find the best baking in town.'

Then they all laugh; even the quiet woman beside Betty has a dry chuckle over the comment, only Mrs Brawn doesn't smile. She stirs her coffee with more force than necessary and sets the spoon alongside it with a clang.

'Obesity is no laughing matter,' she says. 'Mrs Joy is a glutton and that's to be pitied. We don't laugh at sin, the wages of sin is death.'

'But the gift of God is eternal life through Jesus Christ our Lord,' the woman says so softly, the words are nail filings dropping into her lap. If Betty hadn't seen her lips moving, she wouldn't have heard it. 'God forgives,' the woman says then, louder. She is an odd combination of young and old. Her voice and breasts are young but her hair is white.

Mika stands before them with the tray of coffee. 'Not always,' Mika says. 'There's the unpardonable sin, don't forget about that.' She seems pleased to have remembered this.

'Which is?' the woman asks.

'Well, suicide,' Mika says. 'It has to be, because when you think of it, it's something you can't repent of once the deed is done.' Mika smiles around the circle as if to say to them, see, I'm being patient with this woman who has known suffering.

'Perhaps there is no need to repent,' the woman says.

'Pardon?'

'In Russia,' the woman begins and then stops to set her thread down into her lap. She folds her hands one on top of the other and closes her eyes. The others, sensing a story, fall silent.

'During the revolution in Russia, there was once a young girl who was caught by nine soldiers and was their prisoner for two weeks. She was only thirteen. These men had their way with her many times, each one taking their turn, every single night. In the end, she shot herself. What about her?'

'I've never heard of such a case,' Mika says. She sounds as though she resents hearing of it now.

'There are always such cases,' the woman says. 'If God knows the falling of a single sparrow, He is also merciful. He knows we're only human.'

Mrs Brawn sets her knitting down on the floor in front of her chair, leans forward slightly. 'Oh, He knows,' she says. 'But he never gives us more than we can bear. When temptation arises, He gives us the strength to resist.' She closes her statement with her hands, like a conductor pinching closed the last sound.

Betty watches as the white-haired woman twists and untwists her yarn into a tight ring around her finger. 'I don't believe for one moment,' she says finally, 'that God would condemn such a person to hell. Jesus walked the earth and so He knows.'

'No, no,' Mika says from the buffet. 'He doesn't condemn us, don't you see? That's where you're wrong. We condemn ourselves. We make that choice.'

'And what choice did that young girl have?' the woman asks. 'It was her means of escape. God provided the gun.'

Mika holds the tray of lemon squares up before her as though she were offering them to the sun. She looks stricken. Deep lines cut a sharp V above her nose. 'You don't mean that,' she says. 'Suicide is unpardonable. I'm sure of it. Knowing that keeps me going. Otherwise, I would have done it myself long ago.'

There is shocked silence and a rapid exchange of glances around the circle, at Betty, to see if she's heard.

'You shouldn't say such things,' Mrs Brawn says quietly. 'For shame. You have no reason to say that.'

The white-haired woman speaks with a gaunt smile. 'Occasionally,' she says, 'in this room, someone dares to speak the truth.'

'What do you mean?' asks Mrs Brawn.

'Look at us,' the woman says. 'We're like filthy rags to Him in our self-righteousness. We obey because we fear punishment, not because we love.'

Betty sees the grease spot on her blouse where his arm has brushed against her breast. Her whole body is covered in handprints. The stone is back in her stomach. She feels betrayed. For a moment the women are lost inside their own thoughts and they don't notice as she rises from her chair and sidles over to the door. Then, as if on some signal, their conversation resumes its usual level, each one waiting impatiently for the other to be finished so they can speak their words. Their laughter and goodwill have a feeling of urgency, of desperation. Betty stands at the door; a backward glance and she sees the white-haired woman bending over her work once again, eyes blinking rapidly, her fingers moving swiftly and the doily, its flecked pattern spreading like a web across her lap.

1982

Michael Ondaatje

b. 1943

Philip Michael Ondaatje grew up in Ceylon (now Sri Lanka), speaking both English and Singhalese. At ten he joined his mother in England, where he received his secondary schooling and then, in 1962, he moved to Canada, which became his permanent home. As an undergraduate he attended Bishop's University and the University of Toronto, from which he earned a B.A. in 1965. After taking an M.A. at Queen's (1967), he taught English at the University of Western Ontario (1967-70) until he joined the faculty of Glendon College, York University, where he has remained.

Ondaatje began writing seriously at twenty, the year after he came to Canada; his first book of poems, *The Dainty Monsters* (1967), appeared some four years later. In 1969 he published a long poem, *The Man with Seven Toes*, a unified sequence of poems suggested by the experience of a woman who was shipwrecked off the Queensland coast of Australia. In the following year he combined poetry and prose in *The Collected Works of Billy the Kid: Left Handed Poems*, which won a Governor General's Award. Since then he has produced another book of short poems, *Rat Jelly* (1973), and the collection *There's a Trick with a Knife I'm Learning to Do: Poems 1963-1978* (1979), which is made up of selections from *The Dainty Monsters* and *Rat Jelly* plus nineteen new poems. It won him a second Governor General's Award. His most recent book of poems, *Secular Love* (1984), is an autobiographical sequence. Some of these poems first appeared in *Running in the Family* (1982), a work of prose and poetry in which Ondaatje constructs a narrative from his family history.

Both Ondaatje's prose and poetry—even the short poems—evince his strong interest in narrative and narrative form. *The Man with Seven Toes* and *The Collected Works of Billy the Kid* are full-length narratives, assembled from discrete pieces. The latter book, chronicling Billy's career and Pat Gar-

rett's pursuit of him, joins Ondaatje's own prose and poetry to quotations, an interview with Billy, and historical photographs. In 1976 Ondaatje published a novel, *Coming Through Slaughter*, about American jazz musician Buddy Bolden; like *Billy the Kid*, it is a portrait of an outsider driven to violence and self-destruction both by society and by himself. His most recent work of fiction is the novel *In the Skin of a Lion* (1987), which captures the heroism of the workers who constructed the edifices of modernism. In dramatizing the building of twentieth-century Toronto, Ondaatje uses 'magic realist' techniques—in which the narrative seems both realistic and surreal at the same time—to make the ordinary become fantastic.

Ondaatje has also worked in other forms. He adapted *The Man With Seven Toes*, *Billy the Kid*, and *Coming Through Slaughter* for the stage, and in the early seventies he made three films, including one on bp Nichol (*The Sons of Captain Poetry*, 1970) and another on Theatre Passe Muraille's 'The Farm Show'. As well he has written a short critical study, *Leonard Cohen* (1970), and has edited three anthologies, including *Personal Fictions* (1977), a collection of short stories by Blaise, Munro, Thomas, and Wiebe; and the *Long Poem Anthology* (1979), a collection of several contemporary Canadian experiments with the long poem. He is also associated as an adviser and editor with Coach House Press.

The passage from Italo Calvino that Ondaatje chose as an epigraph to the new poetry in *There's a Trick with a Knife* suggests the difficulties of communication inevitably experienced by a person who crosses cultural boundaries: 'Newly arrived and totally ignorant of the levantine languages, Marco Polo could express himself only with gestures, leaps, cries of wonder and horror, animal barkings or hootings, or with objects he took from his knapsacks—ostrich plumes, peashooters, quartzes—which he arranged in front of him. . . .' Ondaatje's own sense of otherness often results in a poetry of vivid gestures (such as his wife's running her hands through her hair at the end of 'Billboards', or—the gesture turned violent—the brandishing of the penknife in 'The Time around Scars'), and through carefully realized physical objects or documentation. The contrast between the psychic distance from his environment that is communicated in a reticent, at times coldly objective, voice, and the warmth and familiarity that arise out of his sharply etched depictions of everyday, domestic events, gives his work a dramatic emotional intensity. Just as Polo chose which objects to carry with him and which ones to take out of his knapsack, Ondaatje brings us a selected reality in the events and people he depicts. He pictures a rich but dangerous world in which vitality always carries with it the risk of being scarred—a world of violent beauty, like that of the Henri Rousseau paintings he admires. In Ondaatje's writing, destruction is as commonplace as creation and hate as available as love; his is a vision of lives lived in extremes. As he writes of family, friends, historical figures, or himself, he both weaves a gothic web of interrelations and juxtapositions and lays open these complexities through a butally sensory language. The surgical precision of this writing holds both author and reader at a great distance from the subject; his characters are watched but not joined. There is everywhere in this work a buried internal conflict, the union of personal violence and tenderness simultaneously felt and carefully held in check.

The Time Around Scars

A girl whom I've not spoken to
or shared coffee with for several years
writes of an old scar.
On her wrist it sleeps, smooth and white,
the size of a leech.
I gave it to her
brandishing a new Italian penknife.
Look, I said turning,
and blood spat onto her shirt.

My wife has scars like spread raindrops   10
on knees and ankles,
she talks of broken greenhouse panes
and yet, apart from imagining red feet,
(a nymph out of Chagall[1])
I bring little to that scene.
We remember the time around scars,
they freeze irrelevant emotions
and divide us from present friends.
I remember this girl's face,
the widening rise of surprise.   20

And would she
moving with lover or husband
conceal or flaunt it,
or keep it at her wrist
a mysterious watch.

[1]Marc Chagall (b. 1887), Russian-born French artist whose paintings often have a quality of fairytale fantasy.

And this scar I then remember
is medallion of no emotion.

30

I would meet you now
and I would wish this scar
to have been given with
all the love
that never occurred between us.

1967

Billboards

'Even his jokes were exceedingly drastic.' [1]

My wife's problems with husbands, houses,
her children that I meet
at stations in Kingston, in Toronto, in London Ontario
—they come down the grey steps
bright as actors after their drugged four hour ride
of spilled orange juice and comics
(when will they produce a gun and shoot me
at Union Station by Gate 4?)
Reunions for Easter egg hunts
kite flying, Christmases.   10
They descend on my shoulders every holiday.
All this, I was about to say,
invades my virgin past.

When she lay beginning
this anthology of kids
I moved—blind but senses
jutting faux pas, terrible humour,
shifted with a sea of persons,
breaking when necessary
into smaller self sufficient bits of mercury.   20
My mind a carefully empty diary
till I hit the barrier reef
that was my wife—
                    there
the right bright fish
among the coral.

With her came the locusts of history—
innuendoes she had missed
varied attempts at seduction (even rape)
dogs who had been bred   30

<hr>

[1]Willa Cather's comment on Stephen Crane (from 'When I Knew Stephen Crane', originally published in *Library*, 23, June 1900, and reprinted in *The Prairie Schooner*, 1949).

and killed by taxis or brain disease.
Numerous problems I was unequal to.
Here was I trying to live
with a neutrality so great
I'd have nothing to think of,
just to sense
and kill it in the mind.
Nowadays I somehow get the feeling
I'm in a complex situation,
one of several billboard posters   40
blending in the rain.

I am writing this with a pen my wife has used
to write a letter to her first husband.
On it is the smell of her hair.
She must have placed it down between sentences
and thought, and driven her fingers round her skull
gathered the slightest smell of her head
and brought it back to the pen.

1973

Letters & Other Worlds

'for there was no more darkness for him and, no doubt
like Adam before the fall, he could see in the dark' [1]

> My father's body was a globe of fear
> His body was a town we never knew
> He hid that he had been where we were going
> His letters were a room he seldom lived in
> In them the logic of his love could grow
>
> My father's body was a town of fear
> He was the only witness to its fear dance
> He hid where he had been that we might lose him
> His letters were a room his body scared

He came to death with his mind drowning.   10
On the last day he enclosed himself
in a room with two bottles of gin, later
fell the length of his body
so that brain blood moved
to new compartments
that never knew the wash of fluid
and he died in minutes of a new equilibrium.

[1] Translation from Alfred Jarry's *La Dragonne* (1943), cited in *The Banquet Years* by Roger Shattuck (1955).

His early life was a terrifying comedy
and my mother divorced him again and again.
He would rush into tunnels magnetized   20
by the white eye of trains
and once, gaining instant fame,
managed to stop a Perahara[2] in Ceylon
—the whole procession of elephants dancers
local dignitaries—by falling
dead drunk onto the street.

As a semi-official, and semi-white at that,
the act was seen as a crucial
turning point in the Home Rule Movement
and led to Ceylon's independence in 1948.   30

(My mother had done her share too—
her driving so bad
she was stoned by villagers
whenever her car was recognized)

For 14 years of marriage
each of them claimed he or she
was the injured party.
Once on the Colombo docks
saying goodbye to a recently married couple
my father, jealous   40
at my mother's articulate emotion,
dove into the waters of the harbour
and swam after the ship waving farewell.
My mother pretending no affiliation
mingled with the crowd back to the hotel.

Once again he made the papers
though this time my mother
with a note to the editor
corrected the report—saying he was drunk
rather than broken hearted at the parting of friends.   50
The married couple received both editions
of *The Ceylon Times* when their ship reached Aden.[3]

And then in his last years
he was the silent drinker,
the man who once a week
disappeared into his room with bottles
and stayed there until he was drunk
and until he was sober.

There speeches, head dreams, apologies,
the gentle letters, were composed.   60

[2]Religious ceremony celebrated by a parade.
[3]Capital of the British colony of the same name (Aden is now the capital of Southern Yemen).

With the clarity of architects
he would write of the row of blue flowers
his new wife had planted,
the plans for electricity in the house,
how my half-sister fell near a snake
and it had awakened and not touched her.
Letters in a clear hand of the most complete empathy
his heart widening and widening and widening
to all manner of change in his children and friends
while he himself edged   70
into the terrible acute hatred
of his own privacy
till he balanced and fell
the length of his body
the blood screaming in
the empty reservoir of bones
the blood searching in his head without metaphor

1973

Pig Glass

Bonjour.   This is pig glass
a piece of cloudy sea

nosed out of the earth by swine
and smoothed into pebble
run it across your cheek
it will not cut you

and this is my hand   a language
which was buried for years   touch it
against your stomach

                          The pig glass   10
I thought
was the buried eye of Portland Township
slow faded history
waiting to be grunted up
There is no past until you breathe
on such green glass
                rub it
over your stomach and cheek

The Meeks family used this section
years ago to bury tin   20
crockery forks dog tags
and each morning
pigs ease up that ocean
redeeming it again
into the possibilities of rust

one morning I found a whole axle
another day a hand crank

but this is pig glass
tested with narrow teeth
and let lie. The morning's green present   30
Portland Township jewelry.

There is the band from the ankle of a pigeon
a weathered bill from the Bellrock Cheese Factory
letters in 1925 to a dead mother I
disturbed in the room above the tractor shed.
Journals of family love
servitude to farm weather
a work glove in a cardboard box
creased flat and hard like a flower.

A bottle thrown   40
by loggers out of a wagon
past midnight
explodes against rock.
This green fragment has behind it
the *booomm* when glass
tears free of its smoothness

now once more smooth as knuckle
a tooth on my tongue.
Comfort that bites through skin
hides in the dark afternoon of my pocket.   50
Snake shade.
Determined histories of glass.

1979

Light

For Doris Gratiaen

Midnight storm. Trees walking off across the fields in fury
naked in the spark of lightning.
I sit on the white porch on the brown hanging cane chair
coffee in my hand midnight storm midsummer night.
The past, friends and family, drift into the rain shower.
Those relatives in my favourite slides
re-shot from old minute photographs so they now stand
complex ambiguous grainy on my wall.

This is my Uncle who turned up to his marriage
on an elephant. He was a chaplain.   10

This shy looking man in the light jacket and tie was infamous,
when he went drinking he took the long blonde beautiful hair
of his wife and put one end in the cupboard and locked it
leaving her tethered in an armchair.
He was terrified of her possible adultery
and this way died peaceful happy to the end.
My Grandmother, who went to a dance in a muslin dress
with fireflies captured and embedded in the cloth, shining
and witty. This calm beautiful face
organised wild acts in the tropics.
She hid the mailman in her house
after he had committed murder and at the trial
was thrown out of the court for making jokes at the judge.
Her son became a Q.C.
This is my brother at 6. With his cousin and his sister
and Pam de Voss who fell on a pen-knife and lost her eye.
My Aunt Christie. She knew Harold Macmillan[1] was a spy
communicating with her through pictures in the newspapers.
Every picture she believed asked her to forgive him,
his hound eyes pleading.
Her husband Uncle Fitzroy a doctor in Ceylon had a memory
sharp as scalpels into his 80's
though I never bothered to ask him about anything
—interested then more in the latest recordings of Bobby Darin.[2]

And this is my Mother with her brother Noel in fancy dress.
They are 7 and 8 years old, a hand-coloured photograph,
it is the earliest picture I have. The one I love most.
A picture of my kids at Halloween
has the same contact and laughter.
My Uncle dying at 68, and my Mother a year later dying at 68.
She told me about his death and the day he died
his eyes clearing out of illness as if seeing
right through the room the hospital and she said
he saw something so clear and good his whole body
for a moment became youthful and she remembered
when she sewed badges on his trackshirts.
Her voice joyous in telling me this, her face light and clear.
(My firefly Grandmother also dying at 68).

These are the fragments I have of them, tonight
in this storm, the dogs restless on the porch.
They were all laughing, crazy, and vivid in their prime.
At a party my drunk Father
tried to explain a complex operation on chickens
and managed to kill them all in the process, the guests
having dinner an hour later while my Father slept
and the kids watched the servants clean up the litter
of beaks and feathers on the lawn.

20

30

40

50

[1](b. 1894), prime minister of the United Kingdom from 1957 to 1963.
[2]American pop singer of the fifties.

These are their fragments, all I remember,
wanting more knowledge of them. In the mirror and in my kids
I see them in my flesh. Wherever we are   60
they parade in my brain and the expanding stories
connect to the grey grainy pictures on the wall,
as they hold their drinks or 20 years later
hold grandchildren, pose with favourite dogs,
coming through the light, the electricity, which the storm
destroyed an hour ago, a tree going down by the highway
so that now inside the kids play dominoes by candlelight
and out here the thick rain static the spark of my match to a cigarette
and the trees across the fields leaving me, distinct
lonely in their own knife scars and cow-chewed bark   70
frozen in the jagged light as if snapped in their run
the branch arms waving to what was a second ago the dark sky
when in truth like me they haven't moved.
Haven't moved an inch from me.

1979

From *Running in the Family*
The Cinnamon Peeler

If I were a cinnamon peeler[1]
I would ride your bed
and leave the yellow bark dust
on your pillow.

Your breasts and shoulders would reek
you could never walk through markets
without the profession of my fingers
floating over you. The blind would
stumble certain of whom they approached
though you might bathe   10
under rain gutters, monsoon.

Here on the upper thigh
at this smooth pasture
neighbour to your hair
or the crease
that cuts your back. This ankle.
You will be known among strangers
as the cinnamon peeler's wife.

I could hardly glance at you
before marriage   20
never touch you

---

[1]One who peels the cinnamon bark, the source of the spice, from the trees.

—your keen nosed mother, your rough brothers.
I buried my hands
in saffron, disguised them
over smoking tar,
helped the honey gatherers . . .

                    *

When we swam once
I touched you in water
and our bodies remained free,
you could hold me and be blind of smell.   30
You climbed on the bank and said
                    this is how you touch other women
the grass cutter's wife, the lime burner's daughter.
And you searched your arms
for the missing perfume
                    and knew

                    what good is it
to be the lime burner's daughter
left with no trace
as if not spoken to in the act of love   40
as if wounded without the pleasure of a scar.

You touched
your belly to my hands
in the dry air and said
I am the cinnamon
peeler's wife. Smell me.

1982

'The space in which we have dissolved—does it taste of us?'

Summer night came out of the water
climbed into my car and drove home
got out of the car still wet towel round me
opened the gate and walked to the house

Disintegration of the spirit
no stars
leaf being eaten by moonlight

The small creatures who are blind
who travel with the aid
of petite white horns   10
take over the world

Sound of a moth

The screen door in its suspicion
allows nothing in, as I allow nothing in.
The raspberries my son gave me
wild, cold out of the fridge, a few I put
in my mouth, some in my shirt pocket
and forgot

I sit here   20
in a half dark kitchen
the stain at my heart
caused by this gift

1984

To a Sad Daughter

All night long the hockey pictures
gaze down at you
sleeping in your tracksuit.
Belligerent goalies are your ideal.
Threats of being traded
cuts and wounds
—all this pleases you.
O my god! you say at breakfast
reading the sports page over the Alpen
as another player breaks his ankle   10
or assaults the coach.

When I thought of daughters
I wasn't expecting this
but I like this more.
I like all your faults
even your purple moods
when you retreat from everyone
to sit in bed under a quilt.
And when I say 'like'
I mean of course 'love'   20
but that embarrasses you.
You who feel superior to black and white movies
(coaxed for hours to see *Casablanca*)
though you were moved
by *Creature from the Black Lagoon*.

One day I'll come swimming
beside your ship or someone will

and if you hear the siren
listen to it. For if you close your ears
only nothing happens. You will never change.   30

I don't care if you risk
your life to angry goalies
creatures with webbed feet.
You can enter their caves and castles
their glass laboratories. Just
don't be fooled by anyone but yourself.

This is the first lecture I've given you.
You're 'sweet sixteen' you said.
I'd rather be your closest friend
than your father. I'm not good at advice   40
you know that, but ride
the ceremonies
until they grow dark.

Sometimes you are so busy
discovering your friends
I ache with a loss
—but that is greed.
And sometimes I've gone
into *my* purple world
and lost you.   50

One afternoon I stepped
into your room. You were sitting
at the desk where I now write this.
Forsythia outside the window
and sun spilled over you
like a thick yellow miracle
as if another planet
was coaxing you out of the house
—all those possible worlds!—
and you, meanwhile, busy with mathematics.   60

I cannot look at forsythia now
without loss, or joy for you.
You step delicately
into the wild world
and your real prize will be
the frantic search.
Want everything. If you break
break going out not in.
How you live your life I don't care

but I'll sell my arms for you,   70
hold your secrets forever.

If I speak of death
which you fear now, greatly,
it is without answers,
except that each
one we know is
in our blood.
Don't recall graves.
Memory is permanent.
Remember the afternoon's   80
yellow suburban annunciation.
Your goalie
in his frightening mask
dreams perhaps
of gentleness.

1984

Paulette Jiles

b. 1943

Born in the Missouri Ozarks, Paulette Jiles moved with her family to Kansas City when she was fifteen. She attended the University of Missouri (B.A. 1968), and studied Spanish Literature at the Universidad de Autonoma in Mexico, before coming to Canada in 1969. Jiles, who has travelled extensively in Europe and North America, has worked for CBC radio in Public Affairs, and, from 1973 to 1983, she lived in the Canadian Arctic and subarctic, working mostly in native communications. From 1983 until its closing, she taught creative writing at David Thompson University Centre in Nelson, B.C., where she now lives.

Narrative is a driving force in Jiles's poetry. In the early poems of *Mindscapes* (a 1971 anthology that also includes work by Susan Musgrave, Tom Wayman, and Dale Zieroth), as well as in *Waterloo Express* (1973) and *Celestial Navigations* (a collection of new and selected poems; 1984), stories press against the confines of stanzas, lines, and metaphors. Jiles has spoken of her frustration at being encouraged to emulate the Modernist poets, such as T.S. Eliot—to 'write in that droopy kind of diffident, laid-back, cynical, disengaged tone'. Instead, she wanted to explore 'a completely different tradition in which one was engaged, passionately, with the story and your audience' (*Toronto Star*, 16 Dec. 1989). In *The Jesse James Poems* (1988), a series of linked poems that is part folktale, part commonplace book, Jiles uses an alternative oral tradition to explore the way stories handed down in her own family intersect with one of the myths of her native region. Jiles has also written several works of fiction, often poetic in tone: *Sitting in the Club Car Drinking Rum and Karma-Kola, A Manual of Etiquette for Ladies Crossing Canada by Train* (1986, a love story and detective-fiction spoof made up of short prose passages), *The Late Great Human Road Show* (1986, a science-fiction novel about nuclear disaster in Toronto), and *Song to the Rising Sun* (1989, a collection of radio plays). *Blackwater*

(1988) draws together poems and prose from her first four books.

Jiles's fondness for strong metaphors adds resonance to the narrative pull of her poetry and prose. As the titles of her books—and of poems such as 'Rock Climbing' and 'Night Flight to Attiwapiskat'—suggest, the journey is one of her most important metaphors.

The travelling metaphor also describes the way her poems work: Jiles attempts to give readers of her poems the sense of beginning a journey. By creating a serial effect, a pathway of linked images, Jiles takes her readers somewhere new—not so much to a conclusion as to a point of departure.

Rock Climbing

I

If I could hang on the Niagara Escarpment forever
then I would be a pendulum,
a hanged man or a barometer, emerging in time
to the weather and the hours.
I would be a sign to people; useful as a spoon,
an instrument of calculation: the failed climber.

In my blue rock-helmet and orange harness
I wouldn't spook children, like the dead pilot
in *Lord of the Flies*;[1] I would be orderly and dry,
shucked of thoughts like the moulting falcon in the zoo.   10
I wouldn't have fallen out of a war, but just stupidity,

being on the wrong step at the worst time. My feet
would have shot out and debris come down after me
perhaps for twenty feet. And when I stopped it would be
with a jolt on the end of the rope like a card at last
in the right slot. I would swing suspended

from my old faithful piton, growing to love it more
with the years. My rope would always invite ascent;
I would ignore it, occupied with circulation and
birches, regarding it as I would a drying umbilical cord,   20
a telephone wire gone dead.

2

But it is the rope itself
full of lunatic assertions
that electrifies the hanger-on with the insistence
of a heart attack;
there is always the hope this world
might be less normal than it appeared;

---

[1] A novel by William Golding in which a group of young boys stranded on an island encounters the horrors of life—those around them (symbolized by a dead pilot's decaying body—the 'Lord of the Flies' of the title) and those within them.

these slow considerations have
changed my heavy head.
Hand over hand I am   30
getting you on the end of the line.
Hello, you fast talker.
Guess who this is.

1984

Horror Stories

Women talk about people dying. We do this compulsively.
I have heard us everywhere, in Spanish Morocco,
Mexico, in Egremont Township, and the far
North. I have sampled all these strange tales.
People die in the most odd and terrible ways.
The only other people who talk like this are
policemen. Only they are more serious and
the stories are not second hand.

My mother reads a book about the San
Francisco earthquake and perforce she must   10
describe it to me: the fires, the bodies,
the collapsing walls which shoot out bricks
like cannonballs, beheading folks.
I have a collection of tales myself. There
are a couple I do not tell.

All women believe they are Scheherazade.[1] They believe
they too will or are about to die
in burning buildings. By telling these tales they
divert. It was other people all along.
Now maybe with the story of the   20
train wreck you will leave
me alone. Did I say alone,
let me restate that, let me
begin again.

1984

---

[1]Scheherazade is 'the teller of a thousand tales' in the 'Arabian Nights'. Her skill and resourcefulness
as a storyteller enable her to escape death at the hands of her husband, the king.

Night Flight to Attiwapiskat

We are flying directly into darkness, the
dim polestar rides on the starboard wing, Orion
and his blue gems freeze in the southwest.

Our rare and singular lives are in the hands of the
pilot; after him the radar and one engine. There were
two engines when we started out but the other one
died. We watch

the starboard propeller feather in slow, coarse
revolutions. The pilot says we will make Attiwapiskat or   10
some place.
            Icarus,[1] our pilot and our downfall.

Two thousand feet below dim lakes pour past as if
on their way to a laundromat. How could we have
sunk so low?
At times like this I consider life after death
as if it were a binary system, there are
no half-lives. We track cautiously down
the Milky Way, home of nebulae and Cygnus.[2]

We are footloose in the corridors of the aurora.   20

The long stream of my life is flying out behind
this airplane like skywriting on the subarctic
night, fluttering, whipped with urgency. Each
episode was always cut off from the last, I used
to find myself a series of hostile strangers, startled
in doorways. Now they

gather themselves up, the wives, daughters, friends,
victims, perpetrators, the one with the pen and the
other carrying a blank mask, another at present
at the cleaners.   30

They catch up and slam together like
a deck of cards, packed into the present
moment. Is there a soul in there, a queen?
I draw one out; it's the ace of airplanes.
The radar repeats a fixed,

[1]See note page 636
[2]A prominent constellation.

green idea. The pilot feels for the radio touch
of Thunder Bay.

At a thousand feet we make quick decisions
about our loyalties, the other engine might fail,
the suitcases of our hearts might be opened with
all that contraband, the jewels and screams, we
might have things to declare;
      the observable universe is my native country
      poetry is my mother tongue
      the ideas I have purchased on this side of the
border don't amount to more than a hundred dollars.
What comes after this?

What do you mean, what comes after this?
This is it.
Attiwapiskat approaches, a Cree village
on a cold salt coast, flying patchwork quilts in
several more colours than are found in nature,
shining with blue-white runway lights.

We will sleep in the guesthouse tonight, that
refuge of displaced persons. The pilot will
go down and repair the valve and say nothing happened.
(We flew into darkness at the rim of the world,
where distant lights broke through and something
failed us. Then at the edge when we were stamped
and ready to go through we were turned back.) We
can unload and forget it. But I will remember
and then go back and forget again.
This is Attiwapiskat, everything is as it should be.
We slide down to the airstrip through salt fogs
from Hudson Bay that slip through the night like
airborne bedsheets.
We get off, still life with sleeping bags.
Approaching us is an earthman,
speaking Cree.

1984

North Shore
of Lake Superior: The Truth

The nature of absolute truth is that it is too boring to endure without a frontal lobotomy, and there is for most of us no virtue in it; and the universe is not putting out any daily editions anyhow that we can understand, and here's the Regina *Leader-Post* among all the magazines and dailies in the lounge car—a blue little prairie gazette, but what can you do? With its subtle Saskatchewan heart.

Truth is an absolute concept thought up after the invention of protracted and deliberate lying, which came shortly after the invention, not of speech, but of grammar. She reads the newspapers from Canada's major cities back in the lounge car. She considers taking up white-collar crime to take care of her debts, white-collar crime being the single lifetime adventure of accountants—double entries are their way of shooting rapids and smoking Camels—but she decides against it. She'd have to get a white-collar job first, and having an affair on a train isn't the way to go about that. Should she be an *adventuress*? She shakes out the Thunder Bay *Times-News* and discovers that a bush plane has disappeared in the subarctic somewhere to the north of them. *I bet you wish you'd taken a train*, she thought, but of course being an American she doesn't know that there are no trains up there. *Adventuress*, she thinks, remembering Paulette Goddard[1] playing some exotic Métis character named Yvette with a knife in her teeth, who was rescued by a Mountie, the Mountie dressed in vast tentlike furs with tails of things hanging off all over him. *Adventuress, I love that word.* She looks out the lounge car window; the train is racing south. *It goes with my hat.* The train thinks up more steam to say to the world like a smartass comment, speeding around the solid granite mountains of the North Shore, full of backchat and passengers. Oooooooooooooeeeeeeee, you can imagine it saying. Do your own sound track for this one. Do yourself a Doppler[2] and imagine it, steam and all.

1986

---

[1]American actress of the thirties and forties. Jiles is referring to her 1940 film, *Northwest Mounted Police.*
[2]The Doppler effect (named after the nineteenth-century mathematician C.J. Doppler) is the apparent change in sound and light waves produced by movement; it causes the characteristic rising and falling sound of a train whistle heard by a stationary observer when a train passes.

bp Nichol

1944-1988

Born in Vancouver, Barrie Phillip Nichol was raised there and in Winnipeg and Port Arthur (now part of Thunder Bay). He began writing poetry in the early sixties while attending the University of British Columbia, where he became acquainted with the work of Earle Birney, bill bissett, and the poets of the *Tish* movement. Unhappy with the lyrics he was then writing, Nichol found himself attracted to the visual experiments of Birney and bissett. After teaching grade four in Port Coquitlam, B.C. for part of a year, he left British Columbia to settle in Toronto. While employed at the University of Toronto library, he began to create 'concrete' or visual poetry. In 1964 Nichol and David Aylward started *Ganglia* magazine and Ganglia press; during the magazine's two-year existence it served as an outlet for west-coast writers who did not have Toronto publishers. In 1967 Nichol began *grOnk*, a newsletter devoted to visual poetry. Having met lay-analyst Lea Hindley-Smith in 1963, Nichol joined her therapy-learning group and in 1967 became part of Therafields, a therapeutic community, where he lived and worked as a lay-therapist. Throughout the eighties Nichol continued his work as an editor (for Coach House Press, Underwhich Editions, and Frank Davey's *Open Letter* magazine), while teaching creative writing at York University.

Nichol published a large array of broadsides, pamphlets, chapbooks, and full-length books; his first 'book' of poems was *Journeying & the returns* (1967; also entitled *bp*), a cardboad package that contains a record, a lyrical sequence, an envelope of visual poems, and a flip book or animated poem. In 1970 Nichol won a Governor General's Award for four publications: *Still Water*; *The Cosmic Chef*, an anthology of concrete poetry; and two booklets, *Beach Head*, a sequence of lyrics, and *The True Eventual Story of Billy the Kid*, a prose piece. In 1972 Nichol and Steve McCaffery formed the 'Toronto Research Group'

(TRG), which regularly issued theoretical statements in *Open Letter* about the nature of experimental poetry. *Selected Writing: As Elected*, a volume that includes some previously unpublished work, appeared in 1980. *Zygal: A Book of Mysteries and Translations* (1985) provides a good indication of Nichol's breadth: it contains poems that range from the traditional, such as 'Lament', to experimental work in what he and Steve McCaffery called ' "Pataphysics'—which Nichol defined as 'the science of imaginary solutions'. Nichol also experimented with a wide range of unconventional prose narratives, including *Two Novels* (1969) and *Craft Dinner* (1978).

Although Nichol's interests varied widely, he is best known for his work in concrete poetry (such as *ABC: The Aleph Beth Book*, 1971 and *LOVE; A Book of Remembrances*, 1974); his multi-volumed poem *The Martyrology* (the first books of which appeared in 1972); and his involvement in the sound poetry movement. By experimenting with visual and sound poetry, while maintaining an interest in traditional forms in which syntax continues to function as a carrier of meaning, Nichol sought to synthesize new modes of poetry and prose. For his first visual poems he employed typed arrangements of words and letters to produce concrete poetry (letters, phonemes, words, and graphic figures arranged on a page pictorially rather than verbally or syntactically); later he introduced graphic designs— drawings combined with letters or words (such as 'Allegory No. 6'). After the mid-seventies Nichol's visual poetry moved more and more towards pure graphics, particularly the cartoon.

Nichol was also committed to experiments with sound poetry, which—in contrast to visual poetry, with its concern for graphic form—seeks to recover the emotional possibilities of speech and human sound that were originally part of the oral tradition. Through the use of homonyms, unusual cadences and emphases, and (in group performances) the overlay of one utterance upon another, sound poems free the rich oral qualities of poetry from the silence of the page. Although he gave some solo performances, Nichol was most often seen and recorded as a member of The Four Horsemen, a performance poetry group that he helped to found and that has continued since his death. (Its other members are Steve McCaffery, Paul Dutton, and Rafael Barreto-Rivera.) The Horsemen perform improvised 'readings' that range from pieces made entirely of nonverbal sounds to complex contrapuntal verbal sequences. Michael Ondaatje, in his film *The Sons of Captain Poetry* (1970), caught Nichol's dynamic presence as a performer.

The Martyrology, Nichol's most ambitious and important work, unites the visual and oral aspects of his writing with the narrative and personal ones. In its opening volumes, *The Martyrology* builds up a mythology that accounts for the structure of the universe through the existence of 'saints' created from broken up or 'deconstructed' words ('storm' becomes 'St Orm'). As the focus in later books turned from the saints' stories to a more general examination of language itself, Nichol's interest in deconstructing language gave way to playful recombinations. For instance, in Book 5, Chain 8, 'eyear' combines 'eye' and 'ear', while functioning also as the sound equivalent of 'a year'. Thus words become the means of examining sound, and ideas cause new words to be formed. (*The Martyrology*, in particular, shows Nichol's relationship to postmodernist and poststructuralist interests, for in these volumes he not only deconstructs literary forms and language and uses parody both to criticize and to affirm, but also works at several levels of intertextuality in a way that invites many different readings of this work.)

By reordering and restricting language, visual image, sound, and form, Nichol invites questions about the boundaries of art, about the point at which the poem ceases to be a literary form and becomes mere sound or mere visual effect. He compels readers to reconsider distinctions between content and form. In this way Nichol's work resembles that of the Dadaists, the early twentieth-century artists who defied conventional expectations with their anti-art, thus calling into question the definition of art itself.

The Martyrology

From BOOK 3, Section VIII.

* * *

last take

late february 73   2070

dave & i look out towards the lion's gate[1]

years mass
                    events
we made it out between the lion's paws
rear shocks gone
swerving to avoid the bumps
spell of spelling cast around us
tiny ripples in the blood stream the brain stem's rooted in
a body place &
                    time   2080
the lion's month before us the lamb's born in
the door
          you are not permitted to open again
enter thru the lion's mouth the man's root gets planted in
not to be consumed
                    as tho the use of lips weren't speech
a doorway into the woman's soul intelligence comes out of
SCREAMING
          a complete thot
born from the dialogue between you   2090

or what comes forth from my mouth
born from the woman in me
handed down thru my grandma ma & lea
is what marks me most a man
that i am finally this we
this one & simple thing
my father Leo
my mother Cancer
                    she births herself
the twin mouths of women   3000
                    w's omen
it turns over & reverses itself
the mirrors cannot trick us

---

[1]The Lions Gate Bridge—connecting Vancouver with North and West Vancouver—is a mile-long
suspension bridge that is flanked by two stone lions at either end.

our words are spun within the signs our fathers left
the sibilance of s
              the cross of t
there are finally no words for you father
too many letters multiply the signs
you are the one
              the unifying   3010
no signifier when we cannot grasp the signified[2]
saints in between
                  the world of men
women
          the sign complete
the w & the circle   turning
add the E
          the three levels
linked by line
            or the two fold vision   3020
H to I
        the saints returned to this plane

the emblems were there when i began
seven years to understand
the first letter/level of
                martyrdom

CODA: Mid-Initial Sequence

faint edge of sleep
a literal fuzzing in the mind
as tho the edge of
what was held clearly   2030
became less defined
the penalty paid &
your father recognized
for what he is

for W

       HA!

the is

[2]Structuralists divide the 'signs' we use to communicate—the most prominent of which are words—
into 'signifiers' (the arbitrary conveyors of meaning, such as the combinations of letters or sounds)
and 'signified' (the underlying sense, the meaning intended).

orange

the vague light
closing the eye   2040

's lid

      home plate

the late P
      . destroyed
leaving only b
& n

beginning again

b n a

all history there

t here   2050

opposed against the suffering
we have yet to bear

last note

no t
no e

l as no

l body
l where
l w here

no w   2060
for w's sake

no is
        e
against the silent sleep

bushes

dawn

the r rises
brushes drawn
the whole scene

the w hole   2070
into which the world
disappears

d is a p
pear shaped

dear H
a p edges
into the sea

sun

the unenviable s

there is no desire for speech   2080

there is no desire to spell

each gesture
against the chaos
must be made well

there is stillness in the heart of the power
as there is stillness in the heart of the storm

between the w & the d
the in side of
the mind ╱
             ╱ 's a quiet place   2090
from which the power unwinds

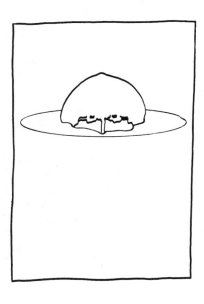

in vocation
i am
a singer

every letter
invokes a spell
ing is
the power
letters have
over me   2100

word shaping

addition of the l

within the difference
if exists

tensions a
polarity

who is moved or moves
a distinction a disparity

a.d.   a.d.
history's spoken in   2110
the first four letters

all e to z
outside the head's
measure of our kind

man's time

1976

From BOOK 5, CHAIN 8

out of the west the best rises
out of the east the beast
Leviathan[1]
       Utnapishtim's potential nemesis
a cloud of dust &
cliché in its sashay with the day-to-day
conversea in ation minor
variation
      recapitulation of
a to z themes   10

t hem e
    or e a
thrd yrs
     a vow the e makes with the l or a
capitulation
riddle read for writers: cap it!
what?
    —ulation—
    ululation of its wake

roused from depths the deep   20
double e threads our speech
full power of the beast noise
voice
we cling to   silence

Thunder Bay   roar & crash the storms made
echoed off the cliffs
so loud you thot the giant'd wake[2]
slept over the lake
millenia
     trees had covered him   30
earth filled his pores
my mother'd hide in dread
took me to bed with her
protector from the storm

[1]A mythical sea-monster, sometimes identified with Satan (Isaiah 27:1). 'Utnapishtim': in Assyro-Babylonian mythology, the Noah-like figure (prominent in the Epic of Gilgamesh, c. 2000 B.C.) who, as the only human to know of the impending world-wide deluge, built a boat to house his family and the earth's animal life. After the flood, Utnapishtim and his wife became immortal.
[2]The Sleeping Giant, a rock formation in Thunder Bay harbour, is identified in Ojibwa legend with Nanabozho, the famous trickster; he is expected to wake in the future and come to the aid of his people.

St Orm we've not forgotten you
you speak with voice of wind
power to bend the limbs of trees & man
blow down anything stands in the way of your word's truth
spoke with force
against the coarse lie we call our 'civilization'   40

so i sing
stupefied by speech
brought under the spell eyear can bring
    ought   e   e   ing
thought   she sleeps   thing
emerges from the deep
the faceless dream
dreamt dreamer ter or
entered world of shifting imagery
we try to freeze   50
make shiftless
because we feel less than
stored imagery's full weight

torn apart too often
that divisiveness
an isolation to protect the feared for work
valued as self is valued
defended as you would your life
'he laid it down for art'
does art thank us?   60

Noel Coward[3] in the 1950's
'why must the show go on?'
the 'noble soul in torment' one does grow bored with
recognizing the romanticization
self-aggrandisement of one's own pain
we all fall prey to

you address the problems as they rise
prize what is most human as
worth the struggle
                    the will to better   70
your self & others
hate that poverty of spirit ignorance breeds

---

[3](1899-1973); English dramatist, actor, and composer. Noted for his sophisticated songs and plays that were wittily critical of society, Coward was less popular in the fifties when the theatre was dominated by realistic drama; during this period he became a commercially successful cabaret performer.

Hannah Arendt[4] speaking of Eichmann
'the face of evil is ordinary'

we build it up
look for it in cops & robbers morality plays
ignore its presence in the day-to-day
out of our own naivete

the distortion or ignoring of what is obvious
(that structural scale must remain human)   80
leads to monumentalization
whatever the political belief
the ordinary man or woman is forgotten
because they are not known
sentimentalized or swept aside
noone takes the time to talk to them

noone t   t   t   t t   t t
seven crosses for our lack of humanity
        (akes)
seven crosses for our arrogance & pride   90
            (he ime)
seven crosses for our lack of humility
            (o alk o)
seven crosses for the people swept aside
                (hem
'd in then

am id St Noise
the voices
ignorance
such lack of knowing   100
starts there

a beginning only
a tentative law or
exception
lets the self reveal itself
we claim despite our fear

                    *   *   *

1982

---

[4](1906-75), German-Jewish philosopher and political theorist who escaped the Nazis and settled in the United States; in *Eichmann in Jerusalem: A Report on the Banality of Evil* (1961) Arendt argues that Adolf Eichmann (1906-62), the Nazi leader who was in charge of the execution of the Jews, represents the modern figure of evil: the rational, pragmatic bureaucrat who accepts immoral commands as part of life's banal routine.

landscape: 1

for thomas a. clark

alongthehorizongrewanunbrokenlineoftrees

1986

lament

cruelty   the land was
harsh   as is told you
a barren island marguerite de roberval was marooned on
in the mouth of the saint lawrence river
by her uncle
viceroy of canada
for having fallen in love with
a poor man
        he escaped the ship &
swam to join her   10

this is the first european family we know of
one child is born to them
there on the isle of demons
so called because the wind howled over the rocks
drowned in sound the three of them

later she is rescued
returned to france
her husband & her child dead of famine
rode out the storm her mind broken
by such cruelty as should never come again   20
out of this land to haunt us

●

innocence
        in a sense
begins on   the outcrop

that we had it & lost it (maybe)
that we never had it (closer to the truth)
that we could all be to this day
marguerite de roberval's fantasy of company
alone on the isle of demons
dreaming of a country full of people   30
a land you could grow food in
starving to death
human howling in the elemental grief

1986

Bronwen Wallace

1945-1989

In her writing Bronwen Wallace explores connections between people and places, and between the immediacies of her own life in Kingston, Ont. (the area where her family has lived for the past 200 years), and the larger issues of the post-war generation. Born in Kingston, and educated at Queen's University (B.A. 1967, M.A. 1969), she was a committed political activist, and in 1970 she moved to Windsor, where she became associated with groups dealing with working-class and women's issues; she also worked with local unionists on an oral history of the UAW (Union of Auto Workers) in Windsor. In 1977 Wallace returned permanently to Kingston; there she worked at Interval House, a shelter for abused women and children, taught at St Lawrence College and Queen's, and wrote a weekly column for the Kingston *Whig-Standard*. In 1988 she was writer-in-residence at the University of Western Ontario.

Wallace's first book of poetry, *Marrying into the Family* (1980; published in a single volume with Mary di Michele's *Bread and Chocolate*), establishes her preoccupation with the relationship between the individual and the community. This subject is explored further in subsequent poetry collections, *Signs of the Former Tenant* (1983), *Common Magic* (1985), *The Stubborn Particulars of Grace* (1987); in films made with her partner, Chris Whynot, *All You Have To Do* (1982), about the death from cancer of a friend (an experience that also gave rise to her sequence, 'The Cancer Poems'), and *That's Why I'm Talking* (1984), about fellow poets Mary di Michele, Pier Giorgio di Cicco, Carolyn Smart, and Robert Priest; and in a short-story collection, *People You'd Trust Your Life To* (1990).

Wallace, whose poems are strongly narrative in style and content, turned naturally to short-story writing in the last year of her life. Her long poetic line, not unlike Al Purdy's, captures the colloquial nature of oral speech and encourages readers to feel that they are being addressed directly by the narrators of her poems. For Wallace, stories are the currency of human exchange. 'My stories are my wealth', says a woman in 'Testimonies', 'all I have to give/ my children'. Memories, anecdotes, and inherited tales all crowd together in poems that examine the complex roles women play or the difficulty of understanding human frailties. She draws no easy conclusions, but the connections we are invited to make in poems such as 'The Watermelon Incident' affirm what Wallace called the 'grace' of everyday existence. She depicts private, yet common, features of human experience: fears of death and failure, needs for love and belonging. In 'The Woman in This Poem', for example, the woman paralysed in 'the middle of her spotless kitchen' expresses familiar anxieties: 'we stop in the middle/ of an ordinary day and/ like the woman in this poem/ begin to feel/ our own deaths/ rising slowly within us.' In contrast, poems such as 'Joseph MacLoed Daffodils' convey the heroism of living, loving, and accepting not only those around us but ourselves. To those who knew her, Wallace exemplified this heroism, the 'stubborn grace' she found in the individual members of her family and her community.

The Woman in this Poem

The woman in this poem
lives in the suburbs
with her husband and two children
each day she waits for the mail and
once a week receives
a letter from her lover
who lives in another city
writes of roses   warm patches
of sunlight on his bed
Come to me he pleads   10
I need you and the woman
reaches for the phone
to dial the airport
she will leave this afternoon
her suitcase packed
with a few light clothes

But as she is dialing
the woman in this poem
remembers the pot-roast
and the fact that it is Thursday   20
she thinks of how her husband's face
will look when he reads her note
his body curling sadly toward
the empty side of the bed

She stops dialing and begins
to chop onions for the pot-roast
but behind her back the phone
shapes itself insistently

the number for airline reservations
chants in her head   30
in an hour her children will be
home from school and after that
her husband will arrive
to kiss the back of her neck
while she thickens the gravy
and she knows that
all through dinner
her mouth will laugh and chatter
while she walks with her lover
on a beach somewhere   40

She puts the onions in the pot
and turns toward the phone
but even as she reaches
she is thinking of
her daughter's piano lessons
her son's dental appointment

Her arms fall to her side
and as she stands there
in the middle of her spotless kitchen
we can see her growing   50
old like this
and wish for something   anything
to happen   we could have her go
mad perhaps and lock herself
in the closet   crouch there
for days her dresses withering
around her like cast-off skins
or maybe she could take
to cruising the streets at night
in her husband's car   60
picking up teenage boys
and fucking them in the back seat
we can even imagine
finding her body
dumped in a ditch somewhere
on the edge of town

The woman in this poem offends us
with her useless phone and the persistent
smell of onions   we regard her as we do
the poorly calculated overdose   70
who lies in a bed somewhere
not knowing how her life drips

through her drop by measured drop
we want to think of death
as something sudden
stroke or the leap
that carries us over the railing
of the bridge in one determined arc
the pistol aimed precisely
at the right part of the brain   80
we want to hate this woman

but mostly we hate knowing
that for us too it is
moments like this
our thoughts   stiff fingers
tear at again and again
when we stop in the middle
of an ordinary day and
like the woman in this poem
begin to feel   90
our own deaths
rising slow within us

1987

Joseph Macleod Daffodils

for Isabel Huggan

'I'm planting perennials this year,' you tell me,
'because I'm scared and it's the only way I know
to tell myself I'm going to be here,
years from now, watching them come up.'
Maybe it's a phase we're going through,
since I'm at it too; lily of the valley,
under the back hedge, thinking *when Jeremy
is old enough to drive, I'll have to divide these,
put some under the cedars there; by the time
he leaves home, they'll be thick as grass*,   10
and at the same time saying
'God, we're parodies of ourselves,
sixties children, still counting on flowers,
for chrissake, to get us through.'
Knowing you'll see it that way too,
your snort of laughter
the index of my love and the wisdom

of George Eliot's[1] observation that
'a difference of taste in jokes
is a great strain on the affections.'
(Another thing we share, our delight
in quotations like that, exactly what you'd expect
from girls who grew up wearing glasses
into women who read everything;
your bathroom so much like mine,
a huge bin of books by the toilet
and on the shelves, all the bottles
turned label side out.
'The contents of somebody's bathroom,'
Diane Arbus[2] said, 'is like reading their biography.')

This doesn't help much, does it?
You're laughing, but your hands stay
clenched in your lap, still forcing
the tight, dumb bulbs into the ground
as if you could force your life
to a pattern as serene as theirs,
a calm that flourishes in darkness
to the pull of the sun.
Still, I keep on talking.
It's the only wisdom that I've got.
How about this one: you know those
big, yellow daffodils—they're called
Joseph MacLeods—well, the way they got their name
was that the man who developed them
always kept a radio on in the greenhouse
and the day the first one bloomed, in 1942,
was the day he got the news
of the Allied victory, against Rommel,
at El Alamein, and the announcer who read the news
was Joseph MacLeod. Which shows a sense of history
I can appreciate; no *El Alamein Glorias* or
Allied Victory Blooms for this guy, you can be sure.
It's like the story my mother always tells
about joining the crowds on V-E day,[3] swollen with me,
but dancing all night, thinking *now*
she can be born any time.

What I love
is how these stories try to explain

20

30

40

50

---

[1]Pseudonym of Mary Ann Evans (1819-80), a British novelist known for her depiction of provincial life.
[2]American photographer (1923-1971) known for her striking and bizarre pictures of people.
[3]8 May 1945, the date of Germany's surrender to the Allied forces, which ended the Second World War. ('V-E' stands for 'victory in Europe'.)

the fit of things, though I can see
your mood's for something more sinister.   60
Like the reason Diane Arbus gave
for photographing freaks, maybe?
'Aristocrats,' she called them,
'they've already passed their test in life.'
Being born with their trauma, that is,
while the rest of us must sit around, dreading it.
Meaning you and me. *Normal.* Look at us,
practically wizened with worry, hunched
over coffee cups, whispering of cancer and divorce,
something happening to one of the kids, our lives   70
spread between us like those articles you read
about Mid-Life Crisis or Identity Anxiety,
Conflict of Role Expectations in Modern Marriages,
the kind that tell you you can fix all that
with less red meat and more exercise,
the ones that talk as if the future's
something you decide about,
though what it all comes down to, every time,
is making do. You can call it a choice
if you want, but that doesn't change   80
what we learn to rely on,
the smaller stratagems. Whatever works.
The socks in their neat balls, tucked on the right
side of the drawer, the iris coming up each summer
in the south bed. 'Be sincere and don't fuss.'
'Noble deeds and hot baths
are the best cures for depression.'

It's what I love in you, Isabel.
How you can stand here saying
'Brave and kind. I want to get through this   90
being brave and kind,' squaring your shoulders
like a heroine in those movies our mothers watched
where people knew their problems
didn't amount to a hill of beans
in this crazy world and let it go at that,
fitting themselves to the shape
a life makes for itself without meaning to.
I love your grin from the end of my sidewalk
as you head for home, posed like a photograph.
'Perfectly Ordinary Woman on Suburban Street.'   100
'A secret about a secret,' Arbus called this kind,
'the more it tells you,
the less you know.'

1987

Testimonies

for Julie Cruickshank

As the cadence in an old woman's voice
becomes the line that will lead others
into the territory her people saw,
you make me see
the importance of your work, the long hours
taping these languages which only a few
of the elders speak now. 'My stories are my wealth,'
one woman tells you, 'all I have to give
my children,' and you help create the alphabet
that takes them there. Linguistic anthropology,   10
the science of making language
into maps. The crazy detours
it can take you on, that story
of the parrot up in Carcross, N.W.T.,
a bird someone brought over the pass
during the gold-rush and left at the Caribou Hotel
where it lived for another sixty years
entertaining customers by singing
nineteenth-century bar-room ballads
in a cockney accent. The voice of a dead miner   20
kept on in a brain the size of an acorn,
all the countries of his lifetime, contracted
to its bright, improbable presence
amid men who figure they've seen
just about everything now,
so that their sitting there, listening like that
becomes part of the story too,
just as I am added when I tell it,
as anyone will be, each version
a journey that carries us all along,   30
as the shards of pottery, carefully labelled
and carried up through layered villages
flesh out more hands
than the two that made them.

How can any of us know
what will speak for us or who
will be heard? We who are never
satisfied, eager for the evidence
no matter how it comes, slowing the car down
as we pass the accident, to see   40
what's pulled from the wreckage, crowding
the ones who were at the scene, the cop
or the ambulance driver, the survivors

stepping forward for their moment, blessed
by our terrible need to know everything.
Even those women we dread
sitting next to on buses or trains,
their bodies swelling with messy secrets,
the odour of complaint on their breath,
may be prophets. Whether we listen or not   50
won't stop them from telling
our story in their own.

Not far from where I live, a man ploughs
someone's skull up in his cornfield
and the next spring, four more, a family maybe
though no one knows even that,
their being there at all,
and longer, the only claim that's offered.
Like the farms themselves, their few rich fields
the chance deposits of a glacier.   60
Even the ones that I keep looking for,
wading through goldenrod to a house
where just inside the door, the trunk of old clothes
or the chair that didn't make it
to the load on back of the truck
bears witness to those smaller choices
we all have to make
about the future
and what can be wisely carried into it.

What your work brings you to, I see now,   70
not the past. Each site, a threshold
into this slow discovery,
the random testimony gathered
as best we can, each of us down
to essentials, as the failed are
and the dead, who bear us forward
in their fine, accurate arms.

1987

The Watermelon Incident

It was during this same summer,
in the back seat of another
speeding car, that I nearly
cut my finger off, slicing watermelon
with a jack-knife. We were all laughing
when the knife went in
to the bone, when it sucked out
one of those silences through which
blood spurted over my hand and onto the
watermelon, onto my other hand, my   10
knees, staining my new black and white
checked pedal-pushers which my mother said
were too tight anyway, made me look
cheap, like the peroxide streaks
Lorraine and I put in our hair when she
was babysitting at the Neilsons', onto
the grey plush seat and down to my
ankle socks, to my white sandals, onto
the floor, until Lorraine said 'Jesus
H. Christ,' and the car pulled over   20
rolled to a stop where we all got out
and stared. Two miles away,
the city bristled with hospitals,
antiseptic, doctors, cat-gut,
parents and tetanus shots, but we
were Beyond All That. Immortal.
And it's because I mean this
literally
that the bleeding stopped
that the end of my finger hung,   30
by a strand, from the rest of it
that Lorraine found some bandaids
she'd stuffed in her purse in case
her new shoes gave her blisters
that they held
that my mother was cooking dinner
when I got home
that my brother poked me in the ribs
and chewed with his mouth full
that nobody asked   40
that it was after the sun went down
(and in that sudden way a sunburn
will) that the pain surfaced.

Through my sleep, my hand
the size of a boxing glove
as if all the blood still in my body
pushed to that spot
where the bandaids held me together
and on whatever cool square   50
of sheet or pillow
I could find for it
kept it up: *pound-pound, pound-pound*
pound-pound, pound-pound,
until I knew for sure
it'd wake my parents
sleeping in the next room.

I'm one of those people
who believe that we remember
everything, though we may not know it.
Just the other day, in fact, I read   60
that even though we forget what we learn
when we're drunk, it'll all come back
sometime, when we're drunk again.
And that made me think
of the guy who lived in the apartment next
to the place I had before my son was born,
one of those buildings where so much
has passed from one room to another
that the walls thin out,
like those spots in an old shirt   70
where grease or sweat's been scrubbed at
so that the skin shines through,
so that every Friday night, when this guy
got drunk, I could hear the bottles
dropping, empty, to the table top
and by the tenth, maybe, the twelfth,
he'd be on to his mother, how he'd
disappointed her, he'd start wailing
and pounding the walls. Most of the time
I hated him, this old fart, sobbing   80
in his beer for Mama. I'd turn
the TV up or go for a walk,
but other nights, I guess, he must have
got in with my own sounds, somehow,
like those bits of dreams you never
quite let go, until this thing
I read on drunkenness and memory
opens the door for him and he sings there,

fiercely, in the midst of all the other stuff
about the watermelon and the knife   90
missing it, the blood and Lorraine's face,
the pain pounding out from my finger
to my wrist to my chest to my throat, my teeth
clenched over it, my parents
sleeping, soundly, on.

1983

Robert Bringhurst

b. 1946

Born to Canadian parents living in California, Robert Bringhurst was raised in Alberta, Utah, Montana, Wyoming, and British Columbia. He studied physics and linguistics at the Massachusetts Institute of Technology (1963-4; 1970-1), comparative literature at Indiana University (B.A. 1973), and received an M.F.A. in creative writing at the University of British Columbia in 1975. He became a lecturer at UBC (1975-80) and subsequently at Simon Fraser University (1983-4). Bringhurst, who has travelled and lived in the Middle East, Europe, and Latin America, reads and translates from half a dozen ancient and modern languages, and has studied the indigenous languages and cultures of North America. He was the poet-in-residence at the School of Fine Arts at The Banff Centre in 1983, and the writer-in-residence for the Writers' Federation of Nova Scotia in 1984.

Bringhurst has published several books of poetry: *The Shipwright's Log* (1972), *Cadastre* (1973), *Bergschrund* (1975), *Tzuhalem's Mountain* (1982), *The Beauty of the Weapons: Selected Poems, 1972-82* (1982), *Ocean/Paper/Stone* (1984), and *Pieces of Map, Pieces of Music* (1986). These books contain certain long poems that have been published as chapbooks: *Deuteronomy*

(1974), *Eight Objects* (1975), *Jacob Singing* (1977), *The Stonecutter's Horses* (1979). Bringhurst has also co-edited (with Geoffrey James, Russell Keziere, and Doris Shadbolt) a study of Canadian postwar art, *Visions: Contemporary Art in Canada* (1983), and, together with the Haida artist Bill Reid, has worked on a collection of Haida stories, *The Raven Steals the Light* (1984).

Bringhurst is never sentimental or confessional; rather, he provides records of an encounter with the body of knowledge the twentieth century has inherited. His highly dramatic poetry draws on a variety of cultural sources—Japanese Zen, the Bible, and North American Indian legend—and often, as in 'Deuteronomy', spoken by Moses, makes use of the dramatic monologue. The poems also indulge—readily and unfashionably—in high rhetoric, as, for example, in 'These Poems She Said'. At the same time, in poems such as 'Deuteronomy' and 'Essay on Adam', Bringhurst recalls events from our mythic past, prompting readers to see them again and reconsider them. He says that one use of poetry is 'to sing thought back into being, to personify it, state it, locate it, to clear the haze' ('Interview' in *Pieces of Map*).

Deuteronomy[1]

The bush. Yes. It burned like they say it did,
lit up like an oak in October—except
that there is no October in Egypt. Voices
came at me and told me to take off my shoes
and I did that. That desert is full of men's shoes.
And the flame screamed *I am what I am.*
I am whatever it is that is me,
and nothing can but something needs to be
done about it. If anyone
asks, all you can say is, I sent me.   10

I went, but I brought my brother to do
the talking, and I did the tricks—the Nile
full of fishguts and frogs, the air opaque
and tight as a scab, the white-hot hail,
and boils, and bugs, and when nothing had worked right
we killed them and ran. We robbed them of every
goddamned thing we could get at and carry
and took off, and got through the marsh at low tide
with the wind right, and into the desert. The animals
died, of course, but we kept moving.   20

Abraham[2] came up easy. We took
the unknown road and ate hoarfrost and used
a volcano for a compass. I had no plan.
We went toward the mountains. I wanted, always,
to die in the mountains, not in that delta.
And not in a boat, at night, in swollen water.
We travelled over dead rock and drank dead water,
and the hoarfrost wasn't exactly hoarfrost.
They claimed it tasted like coriander,
but no two men are agreed on the taste   30
of coriander. Anyway,
we ate it, and from time to time we caught quail.

Men and half-men and women, we marched
and plodded into those hills, and they exploded
into labyrinths of slag. The air licked us
like a hot tongue, twisting and flapping and gurgling
through the smoke like men suffocating or drowning, saying
An eye for an eye, and on certain occasions
two eyes for one eye. Either way, you model me
in thin air or unwritten words, not in wood,   40
not in metal. I am gone from the metal when the metal

---

[1]This poem is inspired by the biblical book of Deuteronomy, in which Moses makes farewell
addresses to his people on the eve of their entry into the promised land. The full account of the events
alluded to in the poem may be found in Exodus.

[2]Father of the Israelite nation who also led his followers to Israel (Genesis: 12-15); Moses here suggests that Abraham's journey was easier than his own.

hits the mold. You will not get me into any image
which will not move when I move, and move
with my fluency. Moses! Come up!

I went, but I wore my shoes and took a waterskin.
I climbed all day, with the dust eating holes
in my coat, and choking me, and the rock cooking me.
What I found was a couple of flat stones
marked up as if the mountain had written all over them.
I was up there a week, working to cool them, 50
hungry and sweating and unable to make sense of them,
and I fell coming down and broke both of them.
Topping it all, I found everybody down there drooling
over Aaron's cheap figurines, and Aaron chortling.

I went up again to get new stones
and the voices took after me that time and threw me
up between the rocks and said I could see them.
They were right. I could see them. I was standing right
    behind them
and I saw them. I saw the mask's insides,
and what I saw is what I have always seen. 60
I saw the fire and it flowed and it was moving away
and not up into me. I saw nothing
and it was widening all the way around me.
I collected two flat stones and I cut them
so they said what it seemed to me two stones
should say, and I brought them down without dropping them.

The blisters must have doubled my size, and Aaron said
I almost glowed in the dark when I got down.
Even so, it seemed I was pulling my stunts
more often then than in Egypt. I had to, 70
to hold them. They had to be led to new land,
and all of them full of crackpot proverbs and cockeyed
ideas about directions. Aaron and I
outbellowed them day after day and in spite of it
they died. Some of weakness, certainly, but so many of them
died of being strong. The children stood up to it
best, out of knowing no different—but with no
idea what to do with a ploughshare, no
idea what a river is. What could they do
if they got there? What can they even know how to wish for? 80
I promised them pasture, apple trees, cedar,
waterfalls, snow in the hills, sweetwater
wells instead of these arroyos, wild grapes. . . .

Words. And whatever way I say them, words only.
I no longer know why I say them, even though
the children like hearing them. They come when I call them
and their eyes are bright, but the light in them is empty.

It is too clear. It contains . . . the clarity only.
But they come when I call to them. Once I used to sing them
a song about an eagle and a stone,[3] and each time   90
I sang it, somehow the song seemed changed
and the words drifted into the sunlight. I do not
remember the song now, but I remember
that I sang it, and the song was the law and the law
was the song. The law is a song, I am certain. . . .
And I climbed to the head of this canyon. They said
I could look down at the new land
if I sat here,[4] and I think it is so, but my eyes
are no longer strong, and I am tired now of looking.

1974

[3]The eagle and the stone (or rock) are both symbols of God. For Moses' song, see Deuteronomy 32: 1-32, particularly 11-13.
[4]Pisgah; because Moses called upon God on behalf of his people when they lost faith in the Desert of Zin, he is not allowed to enter the promised land. (Numbers 20: 1-13; Deuteronomy 32: 51-2.)

Essay on Adam

There are five possibilities. One: Adam fell.
Two: he was pushed. Three: he jumped. Four:
he only looked over the edge, and one look silenced him.
Five: nothing worth mentioning happened to Adam.

The first, that he fell, is too simple. The fourth,
fear, we have tried and found useless. The fifth,
nothing happened, is dull. The choice is between:
he jumped or was pushed. And the difference between these

is only an issue of whether the demons
work from the inside out or from the outside   10
in: the one
theological question.

1975

These Poems, She Said

These poems, these poems,
these poems, she said, are poems
with no love in them. These are the poems of a man
who would leave his wife and child because
they made noise in his study. These are the poems
of a man who would murder his mother to claim
the inheritance. These are the poems of a man

like Plato, she said, meaning something I did not
comprehend but which nevertheless
offended me. These are the poems of a man   10
who would rather sleep with himself than with women,
she said. These are the poems of a man
with eyes like a drawknife,[1] with hands like a pickpocket's
hands, woven of water and logic
and hunger, with no strand of love in them. These
poems are as heartless as birdsong, as unmeant
as elm leaves, which if they love love only
the wide blue sky and the air and the idea
of elm leaves. Self-love is an ending, she said,
and not a beginning. Love means love   20
of the thing sung and not of the song or the singing.
These poems, she said. . . .
                         You are, he said,
beautiful.
          That is not love, she said rightly.

1982

[1]Woodworker's tool with a handle at each end of the blade, used to shave off surfaces.

The Reader

. . . der da mit seinem Schatten / getränktes liest
—Rainer Maria Rilke

Who reads her while she reads? Her eyes slide
under the paper, into another world
while all we hear of it
or see is the slow surf of turning pages.

Her mother might not recognize her,
soaked to the skin as she is in her own shadow.
How could you then? You with your watch and tongue
still running, tell me: how much does she lose

when she looks up? When she lifts
the ladles of her eyes, how much   10
flows back into the book, and how much
spills down the walls of the overflowing world?

Children, playing alone, will sometimes
come back suddenly, seeing what it is
to be here, and their eyes are altered. Hers too. Words
she's never said reshape her lips forever.

1986

Lorna Crozier

b. 1948

Lorna Crozier was born and raised in Swift Current. She earned her B.A. at the University of Saskatchewan and taught high-school English for ten years before taking an M.A. at the University of Alberta (1980). She has taught creative writing at several western schools, including the Saskatchewan Summer School of the Arts and the Banff School of Fine Arts, and now teaches at the University of Saskatchewan. Her published work includes seven collections of poetry (the first three under her married name, Lorna Uher): *Inside the Sky* (1976), *Crow's Black Joy* (1979), *Humans and Other Beasts* (1980), *The Weather* (1983), *The Garden Going On Without Us* (a volume of new and selected work; 1985), and *Angels of Flesh, Angels of Silence* (1988). In 1981 she co-authored *No Longer Two People* with Patrick Lane, with whom she has lived since 1979.

Crozier blends inherited myths and stories with the dailiness of prairie life in poems that employ precise, direct language, but a complex play with attitudes and perspectives. Her work, characterized by a wide range of tone and subject matter—by turns serious, witty and humourous, even bawdy— addresses the abuses of power in the contemporary world on several levels, the personal, the domestic, the literary, and the political.

Poem about Nothing

Zero is the one we didn't understand
at school. Multiplied by anything
it remains nothing.

When I ask my friend
the mathematician who studies rhetoric
if zero is a number, he says *yes*
and I feel great relief.

If it were a landscape
it would be a desert.
If it had anything to do
with anatomy, it would be
a mouth, a missing limb,
a lost organ.

  ø

Zero worms its way
     between one and one
and changes everything.
It slips inside the alphabet.

10

It is the vowel on a mute tongue,
the pupil in a blind man's eye,
the image
       of the face
he holds on his fingertips.

   ø

When you look up
from the bottom of a dry well
zero is what you see,
the terrible blue of it.

It is the rope
you knot around your throat
when your heels itch for wings.

Icarus understood zero
as he caught the smell
of burning feathers
and fell into the sea.

   ø

If you roll zero down a hill
it will grow,
swallow the towns, the farms,
the people at their tables
playing tic-tac-toe.

   ø

When the Cree chiefs
signed the treaties on the plains
they wrote *X*
beside their names.

In English, X equals zero.

   ø

I ask my friend
the rhetorician who studies mathematics
What does zero mean and keep it simple.

He says *Zip.*

20

30

40

ø

Zero is the pornographer's number.
He orders it through the mail
under a false name. It is the number
of the last man on death row,
the number of the girl who jumps
three stories to abort.

Zero starts and ends
at the same place. Some compare it
to driving across the Prairies all day
and feeling you've gone nowhere.

ø ø ø

In the beginning God made zero.

1985

Forms of Innocence

The girl can tell you exactly
where and when her innocence
took flight,
how it soared from the window
beating its wings
high above the stubble field.

A strange shape for innocence
when you think of Leda
but this girl insists
it was a swan, black
not white as you might expect.
From its head no bigger than her fist
a beak blossomed red as if wings
pumped blood up the long neck
to where the bird split the sky.

She watched this through the windshield,
lying on her back, the boy's breath
breaking above her in waves, the swan's
dark flight across the snow so beautiful
she groaned and the boy groaned with her,
not understanding the sound she made.

When she tells this story now, she says
though it was winter, she knows the swan
made it all the way to Stanley Park,
a place she's never been, just seen
in the room where no one
ever touches anything
in the book her mother keeps
open on the coffee table,
one black swan swimming   30
endless circles among the white.

1985

Fathers, Uncles, Old Friends
of the Family

Uncle Peter always told me
to wash my hands before breakfast
because I didn't know where they'd been
in the night   what they'd touched

                    and his hands
lifted me from the paddling pool,
young seal   all wet and giggly,
his farmer's hands
soft in the towel,
my mother's   10
youngest brother
                    pulling aside
my swimsuit.

Then there's the father
                    of my friend
who did it to her
till she ran away from home.
On his seventieth birthday
she visits with the grandchild
he's never seen   20
and before she can pour their tea,
he reaches out,
            grabs her breast,
then cries   says he can't help himself
and she cries too,
what's there to say to him now?

One is always
the best friend of the family.
He makes her a fishing rod
from a bamboo pole   30
and with hooks   with bait,
rows her to the middle of the lake.
Shh, shh, I won't hurt you
                              shhhh.

Years later
                your flesh crawling,
you try not to turn away
when someone you love lays a hand on you.

Where did he touch you?

                Here   and here,   40
those places no one ever named.

1988

Afterwords

A man is nothing.
A snake even less.
They put a hollow tube
like a drinking straw
between his lips.
In this, they force a snake,
stuff the opening with cloth
soaked in gasoline,
set the cloth on fire.
The snake explodes   10
down the man's windpipe.
It goes crazy in his lungs,
the man goes crazy.

A snake is not a life,
a woman even less.
Inside a woman
they sew a rat.

You ask me about Chile.
This is why it's so hard
to tell you.   20

There are sounds
we don't want to know
the meaning of   animals
that live inside us.

I must learn their language—
words to calm a snake
churning in my lungs,
words to make a rat
lie still.

1988

Mary di Michele

b. 1949

Born in Luciano, Italy, Mary di Michele immigrated to Canada with her family in 1955. Since earning a B.A. (University of Toronto, 1972) and an M.A. in English and Creative Writing (University of Windsor, 1974), she has been writer-in-residence at the Metro Toronto Reference Library (1987), the University of Regina (1987-8), the Etobicoke Libraries (1989), and Concordia University (1990). She has published six collections of poetry: *Tree of August* (1978), *Bread and Chocolate* (published together with Bronwen Wallace's *Marrying into the Family*; 1980), *Mimosa and Other Poems* (1981), *Necessary Sugar* (1983), *Immune to Gravity* (1986), and *Luminous Emergencies* (1990).

In poetry that is often deeply personal and visceral, di Michele depicts her experience as a first-generation Italian immigrant, and explores such topics as the writer's struggle with her language and art. She has influenced and been influenced by the work of Italian-Canadian poet Pier Giorgio Di Cicco and by that of the group of women writers whose poetry she anthologized in *Anything is Possible* (1984), especially Bronwen Wallace (who first drew her attention to the photographer Diane Arbus). The transition from Italy to Canada is pivotal in di Michele's work, often described as a shift in language and outlook. She compares the protean nature of memory and the fixed nature of visual images in 'Luminous Emergency', a poem about the flashes of insight that occur when one looks at things in a new light.

Luminous Emergency

*

How is it that we love
> *for the sake of what we loved*
when what we loved
> *we would not go back to loving?*

1
They say that landscape and language,
the ampersand[1], are imprinted in our minds
in the same way geese
fix on the first moving sign as Mother,
the way some love takes root
like crabgrass in the strawberries,   10
much deeper, much hardier
than the plant which fruits.

I remember Italia of the *praetutti*[2],
of Ovid, of D'Annunzio, of Silone,
of Hemingway's soldier boy self
in *A farewell to Arms*.
> And what I knew from the start.
Original.

2
From the back of grandmother's house
from her garden of pomegranate,   20
sunflower and grape,
I can see it all and rising to a greater height,
the snow-capped mountain, *Maella*[3], white *sow*
brilliant as the naked shoulder of a god in moonlight
brilliant as the cascading light at the back
as he ceremoniously turns revealing
wings.   All Da Vinci designed.

But what is moonlight to him?
or to us for that matter

---

[1]The sign '&'.

[2]'Italia of the *praetutti*': 'before everyone else', a phrase used to identify the Italy of the aboriginal Italians, especially those from the Abruzzi, the region where di Michele was born. The three writers whose names follow are associated with 'Italia of the *praetutti*' because they were forced to leave Italy: the Roman poet Ovid (43 BC-AD 18) was exiled by Augustus in AD 8; the Italian poet Gabriel D'Annunzio (1863-1938) left in 1910 to escape creditors, returned to become a nationalist leader during the First World War, later abdicating his authority in 1920; and the writer Ignazio Silone (Secondo Tranquilli, b. 1900) left the communist party in 1930 (he was one of its founders) while in exile in Switzerland.

[3]*maella*: female pig or sow.

after even the briefest   30
pause by the Sea of Tranquillity?[4]

3
We've been told that the angel doesn't distinguish
the living from the dead
or earthlight from moonlight.
The angel doesn't need
the sun like a coalminer's cap
to tunnel through the darkness
to reach us, because angelic
light is always within
as lightning bug or firefly   40
hold their blazing inside
or we could call it outside if
for the angel there were a difference
but such presence drifts
through our atmosphere as if composed
of only a slightly heavier element
the way, above the churning and dashing
of dark waves against rocks,
a fine spray flings itself across the sea

no longer one with water
yet also alien to air   50

4
This view from the hills opens
the landscape like surgery.

    In my fingers the grapes are rubbed
                    to glowing, the light
in their skins, as from dark rooms
    or the candle's flame
                    ripening with midnight.

    Such is memory
it darkens what it seems   60
to illuminate in time
whatever is preserved
            must also alter.

Like love loving us not
                    For what we are.
For what we hide.

---

[4]A crater on the moon.

5
& the bell that used to stand to the side
of the church I played
in its inverted cup

                        doppelganger[5]   70

for the clapper.

Then my left handed music was unsung
before they changed me

                        with a pencil

before they changed me

                        with a stick.

& the bell that used to stand to the side
is enclosed in a new tower.
When the Angelus rings out birds
scatter: 80

                            uccelli

                                   uccellini[6]

my own daughter's first words,
Italian bird already having something
of the sky, *cielo*, in it

& singing sweetly singing as if
to me and I find myself happy
whether this is true

                            or not

6
In the field *farfalla*[7]   90
as even in some living poet's journals
going from flower to flower
not for clover but for red poppy,
their wings silkscreened and colour
their music of interval.

The bee is a golden earring,
a stinger in the jewellery,
it's *la vespa*[8] for a country
no longer mine,
                        but the stranger's   100
in me.

---

[5]doppelganger: double, especially a supernatural double.
[6]Bird/birds.
[7]Butterfly.
[8]wasp.

7

For fauna in the mountains find
she-wolf, bear, and angel
to be seen as the wind's seen
making the trees more visible.

& if the planet were a bald husk,
& if the planet were shucked like corn & all its green
silk consumed by lightning and moth,
logged and strip-mined to the nth   110
degree and if the planet were left naked or nuked,
how would wind or angel know themselves
how would they know themselves without us
to scribble or turn up our faces

                                        in reverence?

How would wind or angel deliver
their speaking in silence?

8

Before the operation, just to hear themselves,
quack as a child, *paperino*,

                        paperino[9],

who would refuse anesthetic   120
as the neurologist probes one part
then another of the brain?
Then it's one day then another
and you are speaking in tongues
as your life rewinds to a whirring
snap

                        when faces surge to the surface
brilliantly lit as if by darkness
from which the figure in Rembrandt
emerges.   130
                        Luminous.

9

Look how I'm with her on the bench in the *Villa delle Rose*[1]
by the fountain and the amputee
statuary from Graeco-Roman times.

Nonna hasn't lost weight,
                        her soul

[9]Donald Duck.
[1]*Villa delle Rose*: 'estate of roses', a public garden.

must also be

consoled by carbohydrate,

while in the *mean*time like balloons
my own lungs have blown!   140
Now they hold twice the oxygen
although my heart is still only this

(big)

heart of hare, heart of hen,
heart of human smaller
than what remembers

(me)

10
That my tongue has been un-
Mothered. That my tongue has thickened
with English consonants and dipthongs,   150
mustard and horseradish. That burning.
That burdened.

While on my lips Italian feels
almost free, like wind in the trees
when the window's sealed shut
and you're inside trapped
into a solitary game of Scrabble.

No-   English is not so cosy!
It's hypothermic. It's haunted   160
by ghost letters & gnomic,

for it is true

*

that we love

to forget we forget
to love

1990

Snapshot

for Bronwen Wallace

If Diane Arbus hadn't been born a woman
she would have had an operation

because a woman understands the body best
as surrender to spectacle:
the super beautiful, the bearded lady,
the tycoon, the tattooed man
stretching his skin for canvas,

because nothing came between her
and her cameras,
because she wore them like jeans
shrunk to fit in a bathtub

(it makes walking difficult),

because she was swamped in equipment,
clumsy as a child playing dress-up,
because she waited, balanced in ballet shoes,
for the right moment,

that was her skill,

because she wintered in black leather skirts,
because she tried to make love
survive sex orgies,

because she is forgotten as a photographer
of children, because she worked in fashion,
because negative space plays hard to get,

you thought she was just snapping
freaks –

she caught what you wouldn't see:
your averted eyes, your face behind the box –

because knowing how to frame anything alive
makes it art,

because she felt lost but couldn't remember
how it happened.
Setting the Leica on self-timer
then rushing into her subject's clothes.

1986

David Adams Richards

b. 1950

David Adams Richards was born and raised in Newcastle, N.B. where his father owned and operated the Newcastle Opera House and, later, the two local cinemas. Richards attended St Thomas University in Fredericton, and since 1973 he has been a full-time writer, living in Fredericton until 1989. He was the writer-in-residence at the University of New Brunswick from 1983 to 1987. He now lives in Saint John and has a cottage in the Mirimachi Valley, which is the setting of his fiction.

Richards has published a book of poetry, *Small Heroics* (1972), but he is best known for his fiction, set mostly in a New Brunswick mill town on the banks of the Miramichi River. Although his novels—*The Coming of Winter* (1974; translated into Russian in 1980), *Blood Ties* (1976), *Lives of Short Duration* (1981), *Road to the Stilt House* (1985), and *Nights Below Station Street* (1988)—are written in the realist tradition, Richards is concerned less with providing 'social commentary about poverty in the Maritimes' than with dramatizing characters who have 'a sense of an inexorable spiritual duty'. He sees himself, like Thomas Hardy, as writing 'rural novels in which traditional family values, or the loss of them, is central' (*Macleans*, 13 March 1989). These novels focus on members of the community who have spiritual needs (of which they are often hardly aware) beyond the responsibilities and restrictions of their daily life in the Maritimes. Their search for elusive meaning and tranquillity is symbolized by their journeys to the river or to the nearby woods, two constants in their lives and in Richards' fiction. But, like Jane in 'A Rural Place'—the opening narrative of Richards' short-story collection *Dancers at Night* (1978)—Richards' characters discover that the price of tranquillity is high. Those who decide to pay that price become the everyday heroes of his fiction.

A Rural Place

'Maybe so,' said the man, 'I didn't say she weren't here an hour ago, I didn't say nothin, all I said is she's gone now, look ya see her in 'er room, ya see her in 'er bed?'

'No,' the woman said.

'Well she's gone.'

'She's 96 years old,' said the woman. 'She didn't just walk out onto the street and disappear—she has to be somewhere.'

'I don't care she's gone, I'm not talkin ta ya, botherin standin here arguin about it—I ain't gonna argue about it while she goes drowns herself and you stand here and argue about it!'

'I'm not arguing about it,' said the woman.

'Ya are arguin ya are,' said the man under his breath, but by this time the woman had moved along the hallway to see the administrator, and the man stood there alone in the sun that came through the high window.

'She's gone?' said the administrator.

'Yes.'

'Where to?'

'I don't know where to, we've looked just about everyplace—think we should call the police?'

'Did you look in her closet?'

'In her closet?' said the woman.

'I bet anything she's locked herself in a closet.'

'Maybe,' said the woman slowly.

'No maybe about it—I'll bet anything.'

'She's in nobody's closet around here,' said the man.

'Have you looked in them all—I mean on the third floor?'

'I looked in them all, I ain't seen her in no closet, she's in nobody's closet.'

The woman said nothing.

'How the hell would she get up on the third floor anyways?' said the man.

'I don't know.'

'Well I don't have the foggiest what's goin on round here anyways,' said the man. 'Why would she wanta hide in a closet, tell me that?'

But by this time the woman had turned and started down the hallway again.

'Just tell me that,' said the man.

'Well,' the administrator said, flicking his pencil back and forth on the desk.

'I think we should look for her,' said the woman.

'Yes perhaps—where, you mean downtown?'

'Yes perhaps,' said the woman, 'Think we should phone the police?'

'Yes perhaps.'

'Now that's just what I been standin here an sayin for over an hour,' said the man.

'Do you know what she was wearing?'

'Clothes is all—I never looked at her.'

'Probably the brown dress,' the woman said. 'She won't let anyone dress her.'

'Could possibly be,' the man said, snapping a match with his finger to light a cigarette and shaking his head.

'Yes.'

'I don't have the foggiest what's goin on round here at all,' said the man.

Janie Bell crossed the railway tracks and stood at the wharf. It was a bright September day and a wind came off the water. *The first time I crossed this river was me and my mother we came on the paddle boat to this side a the river I member we comin ta sell raspberries in the summer.* Though there were whitecaps and spray the water looked gently warm and in the fresh September heat was the taste of salt and boards and leaves changing colour. And children passed her as she waited driving their bicycles over the boarded sidewalk.

The children laughed and yelled at one another and the sound of their voices echoed along the bank and down across the water. She leaned against the timbers.

When the ferry docked there were three cars to go on and she waited until the last one started across the ramp because the man in the hat had watched her ever since the ferry entered. She walked slowly down the sidewalk onto the ferry, her black boots scraping and shuffling down its stained cement floor.

'Hello,' the man said coming out of his narrow box and standing in front of her. He stared at her small greying face where her eyes protruded, and her brown hat was pinched against her head with pins. She stood silently.

'Where ya going Mam?'

'Across the river.'

The man looked about, and under him she could hear the steady rumble of the engine and smell grease and car heat. There was sweat dribbling from the man's face when he looked about, and his fingers were smudged and dirty.

'You're from the Senior Citizens Home are you?'

'I'm 100 years old right now—I got a message from the government.'

'Oh,' the man said. He stepped back a little and rubbed his left shoulder against the small narrow box. 'You're not from the Home are you?'

'A message from the government,' she said. Her eyes protruded and as she spoke her lips moved without her mouth opening. 'I live by meself.'

'Oh,' he said. He stepped into the box and sat on the stool still watching her.

She sat on a bench at the stern as they crossed the river. For a moment everything was cold and distant. The children with the bicycles sat across from her laughing and yelling. Then the man came to them and said:

'This is yer last trip today boys.'

'It's free,' one of them said. 'We don't havta pay nothin—ya can't kick us off for not payin.'

'I'm not kickin ya off for not payin—I'm tellin ya ta stay off the ferry, ya been back and forth all day.'

'It's a free country,' one of the boys said. 'Ya don't own the ferry.'

'Ya, you don't own the ferry—what d'ya think you own the ferry?'

'Try ta get on again and you'll see who owns it.'

'Ah go sit down,' the first boy said. He was smoking a cigarette and looked around nervously when the others laughed. The man turned red and scratched his arms and below her she could hear the waves churning and see gulls climbing in the air.

'Just anyaya try ta get on 'er again and you'll see who owns the ferry—ya should be in school.' He turned and started back, nodding to her quickly.

'We're smarter than you,' the boy yelled. 'Go ta school yerself and see who owns the ferry.'

'Ya,' another boy laughed. 'Try ta figure out who owns the ferry.'

The first boy spit and butted his cigarette. 'Old fucker,' he said.

I member we'd all our raspberries in boxes and what a time gettin them boxes and then we all wanted ta go with er every one a us and she said 'Janie get yer coat on' and Isabel started cryin but when I went over ta town I diden like it anyway we hadda stand round all day waitin in the heat—it weren't no fun and when we came back Isabel said 'How's it like?' and I just said ta Isabel 'You wait until you havta start sellin raspberries' and then I handed her seven peppermints I member there was seven.

The ferry docked and she waited until the cars left and the boys screaming and yelling to each other went down the boardwalk on their bicycles. The man came out of his office and took her arm.

'You must remember the old paddleboats they had here,' he said to her.

'Yes, I member them,' she said.

'I member them,' she mumbled as he helped her along, she feeling the strength of his hand under her arm and smelling him, and the tar on the tying poles. She crooked her neck to look at him and he was smiling at her, as if she was his grandmother or some old lady he'd known for a long time. She didn't like that.

'Are you visiting relatives over here Mam?'

'Yes—*Isabel's* daughter—I'm visitin *Isabel's* daughter.'

'Are they here to meet you?'

They were at the front again, and she scraped along on the cement with her black boots while the man still held her steady and smiled. She could smell warm tar off the tying poles in the air and could see swarms of dirt in the water, and cardboard boxes looking like rags floating. The water was black in the shadows of the timbers. People watched her as he helped her across the boardwalk. His arm stiffened when he saw people watching and he no longer looked at her. Again for a moment it was distant and cold.

'Are they here to meet you Mam?'

He let go of her arm and she kept walking small and hunched as people watched her. She went to a pole and leaned against it for a moment not turning to look in case he was still there. The sun was warm again and everything sounded quiet in the September heat. The boys were at the top of the lane running their bicycles against one another and as the cars passed dust rose from their tires. She moved over the pebbles on the side of the lane, watching her feet and a car had to stop behind her when she moved onto the lane.

'Can we give you a lift somewhere?' a woman asked.

'Can we take you somewhere?' the man said. They'd pulled alongside her in their car.

'Isabel's daughter's,' she said.

'What?' the man said.

'Isabel's daughter's—Deborah's place.'

The man looked at the woman and smiled and she nudged him in the ribs with her arm, her arm looking purple in the darkness of the car.

'Well, we can take ya there I suppose,' the man said. He got out of the car and opened the back door for her and helped her into the back seat.

'Warm today ain't it,' she said.

'Yes,' he said.

'I'm goin for a visit—I'm 100 years old right now—I got a message from the government.'

'Really,' the woman said.

'The Queen sent me flowers.'

'Don't call me stupid,' the man from the ferry said.

'Ya are I can't help it if ya are.'

'I called ya didn't I soon as I got back ta town I called ya.'

'Don't matter ta me ya musta known where she was from ya musta known that, we havin everyone in the world out lookin for her—and it bein on the radio about a million times.'

'Jesus,' the man from the ferry said.

'And she isn't 100 either she's only 96.'

'Well she told me she was—she told me she had a phone call from the Prime Minister about it.'

'Well she didn't.'

'She told me.'

'And her relatives are all dead—she doesn't have a relative in the world to visit.'

'Well where in hell is she off to?'

'If we knew that we'd catch her. So she got in a car—did they know her?'

The man from the ferry shrugged and bit his lower lip, breathed deeply between his closed teeth.

'Do you know them?'

'They cross for groceries bout once a week but I don't know them.'

'Fine mess now—fine mess now.'

'Ya'd think ta Christ it was my fault—who the hell let her escape in the first place?'

'Not me.'

'Bet anything it was.'

'Run yer ferry.'

'Run yer old age place.'

The man from the Home shook his head and spit. A breeze came off the water and dried the sweat on his forehead.

'We'll haveta get the police down here,' he said.

'She couldn't be goin ta no relatives?'

'Not unless she wanted ta hitchhike ta Toronto—she's got someone there.'

The man from the ferry laughed.

The man from the Home walked back along the main street as dust rose in the noon hour September air and children dressed pale and bright came running from the schools. Everything was smelling fresh and quiet and the ferry whistle sounded, its rounded bulk moving slowly on the waves. He crossed the street and went into the corner store.

'Nice day for a change.'

'Very best of a day—pack a Players there will ya?'

'I hear on the radio ya let one out.'

'Sometime this morning I think,' he said opening the package immediately. He looked at the man behind the counter, who was grinning at him, and shrugged. 'Ya'd think the people downtown'd be a little bit smarter than that.'

'Than what?'

'Than letten an old woman like she is wander about without catchin her—like the guy in the ferry there letten her slip right through his fingers like that.'

'Call the police is what'cha gotta do.'

'We did we did,' he said, leaving the store.

'Ya should get yerself a wife an stop worrying about the old ones,' the other man yelled. Then he laughed.

He walked along the sidewalk close to the water and saw in the alley two men sitting on dried, broken bait barrels drinking wine. He lit his cigarette and felt the breeze again, gentle and sweet smelling. Above him, on the opposite street, he could hear a hammer ringing dully under the blue sky. 'I wish they'd leave me the hell alone bout gettin married,' he thought. 'It's none of their business about me gettin married.'

'How much farther is it?' the man asked. She didn't answer so he turned to look at her. 'I think she's asleep.'

'Poor old soul,' the woman said.

'I'm not cartin her all over, I wanta get back home and finish those cabinets.'

'Tcch,' the woman said moving her tongue against her teeth.

'Look ya been after me for days to do them, I couldn't breathe and you'd be yellin at me so now I wanta do them!'

'Well, I can't help it—we can't put her out in the middle of the road.'

'Christ.'

'Stop swearing.'

'I'm not swearing.'

'If you live to be 100 you'd like people to treat you kind.'

'What in hell am I doin to her?'

'What's that?' the old woman said suddenly, opening her eyes and raising her head. 'What's that?'

'You must have fell asleep,' the woman said. 'We were just wondering where you wanted to go—is it close to here?'

Janie Bell looked out one window and then the other. On her right the fields sloped to the river and cows lazed in them, and on her left the woods started again where spruce and alders and maples tangled together. She rested her head on her hand once more.

'Deborah's place,' she said.

'Yes, but where is Deborah's place?'

'Along aways—ya haven't reached it yet.'

'Down further?'

'Yes—and then back where I was brought up.'

'Back where?'

'Just hang on.'

'Okay,' the man said laughing, scratching the side of his face and shifting the gears suddenly.

'Watch yourself how you drive,' his wife said.

They drove down another five miles and the man cursed under his breath. He saw clouds forming over the bay water and he'd wanted to bring the cabinets outside to finish them. And every house he came to he'd slow down and say:

'This it?'

'No it ain't.'

Until they were down another five miles and the old woman told him to turn up a side road.

'So it's back here then?'

'Yes,' she said.

The paved road ended and a dirt road began. He geared the car down, and started up the long hill thinking 'This'll be the end of it,' but when they came to the top of the hill and he saw the road on the other side, defaced with ruts and boulders his stomach became knotted and sick.

'No-one in the world can live back here anymore,' he said looking at his wife for some explanation. 'No-one coulda lived here for at least 100 or 200 years.'

'Now Ralph, take her down the hill.'

'I'm not takin my car down that hill.'

'Now Ralph.'

'Never mind it then I'll walk,' Janie Bell said.

'No you won't walk,' the woman said, 'How much further is it?'

'Not too much further dear just down the hill where the bridge is.'

'What bridge?' Ralph said. His face looked white and sick. They could smell fall in the trees and the leaves tinged and golden were bathed in light. The boulders themselves were rich brown and far below the small river rounded a bend, its water green. 'They're tearin that old bridge down!' he said.

'How do you know?' his wife said.

'Because I know,' he yelled.

'Stop yelling with a stranger in the car.'

'Never mind I'll walk,' the old woman said. 'That's where I get out.'

'That's where yer gettin out?' the man asked clutching the steering wheel. 'What are you getting out there for—you can't get out there—no-one lives there—no-one lives down there.' He looked around at her and tried to smile, 'Look now, ya can't go gettin out there.'

'Yes,' she said.

'Now Ralph she must know more about it than you.'

'I don't care,' he said. 'No-one in the world lives back here in a thousand years.'

'Maybe ya should come back to town,' the woman said.

'No, now I'm goin for a visit,' Janie Bell said.

'That's the bridge they were talking about tearin apart,' he said, still trying to smile, 'I betcha they're workin on it right now.'

'Ralph,' she said, nudging him, 'Ralph.'

'Across the ferry,' said the administrator. 'Why would she do that—why didn't they stop her either?'

'I don't know—I suppose they just didn't think to,' said the woman.

'Who's running the ferry, a bunch of morons?' he said.

'I don't know,' said the woman, 'But surely to heavens they'll catch on and bring her back.'

'I'd better phone the police.'

'I've already done that,' said the woman.

'Well, I can't have a thing like this happening, it's bad enough as it is with all the trouble around here.'

'Yes,' she said.

'I'd love to know how she got out of the yard in the first place without you checking.'

'I was at lunch,' said the woman.

'I'd just love to know what's going on around here—a bunch of morons.'

'Yes.'

'What are the police doing—sleeping I suppose?'

'They've two cars out, and volunteers.'

'A bunch of morons.'

She sat by a tree above the bridge and all day men came and went, passing her with hooks and pevies, and all day she watched them going without a sound sitting on the fallen leaves. And now and then the grass stirred in the afternoon wind and clouds blocked the light so that the river changed from green to dusk colour, and the men's shouts sounded faint and far off.

Her hat was crooked on her head, the pins bothered her scalp and her eyes watered when the wind blew. She moved constantly in trying to be comfortable, but then her eyes stopped watering, became dry and sore, and she closed them.

'Do ya know who the hell she is?'

'Who who is?'

'That women over there, she must be 80.'

'Where?'

'Over there.'

'Where?'

'There—there look.'

'She looks like a scarecrow don't she?'

'Should talk to her see what she's doin?'

'Fuck you.'

'Should take her home and use her for a scarecrow.'

The men's shouts sounded faint and far off, the timbers cracked and split on the underbelly of the bridge. The men on the bridge roof danced in the afternoon light jumping from timber to timber as the sills groaned under weight and commotion—and laughter. Always laughter.

'Try 'er.'

'The hell with you I'm not that steady on me Jesus feet.'

'She's only 40 feet down whatcha worried about?'

'Ha.'

'She's a mere 40 feet.'

'Jump 'er.'

And she thought: *This is a nice place when Isabel was goin courtin with Bennie I came down the first time and sat here and all of a sudden Bennie comes struttin across big as life balancin himself, the bridge werent a quarter finished: 'Ya'll fall fer sure.' 'Betcha I won't.' 'What'll Isabel say now if you fall?' He hopped on one foot and then the other, his cork boots hoppin: 'Who cares what Isabel says anyway,' he laughed. 'I know who cares.' 'No sirree.' 'Ha.' 'No sirree!'*

'Go over and talk ta her Simon.'

'No.'

'Go on and see what she's doin.'

'No, you go.'

'Yer not doin any work here anyway—ya mays well go over, ya little bastard.'

'Go ta hell I work as much as you.'

'Jerkin off.'

'I work as much as you.'

'Go on over Simon see what she's fuckin doin.'

'No.'

'Hey maybe she come ta blow us.'

Simon said nothing.

'Boy what a filthy mind eh Simon?'

Simon said nothing.

'Ha.'

He came over and sat with me right here though it was different from this—there were dark pools in the water and the trees on the other side were crooked and smelt like a magic forest, their dirt and roots. Off the path to the left from me was the old mill. 'Goin ta see Isabel?' 'Nope.' 'Why not?' 'Don't want to.' I could feel him breathin moving my hair back on my neck. 'What's Isabel gonna say ta you?' 'We go ta that mill I'll show ya around.' 'What's Isabel gonna say ta that?' 'Stop mentionin her will ya?' 'Why?' 'Just will ya stop mentionin Isabel.'

Shoved by the men the timbers cracked, the braces split where they were pressed and the men yelled and hollered as the wood splashed and echoed in the river. And then the men like goats shoved and laughed at one another.

'Watch 'er,' Simon said, 'Someone'll kill themselves doin that.'

'Sookie—go see what she's doin.'

'You go see.'

'Yer no help ta us anyway—we mays well have someone on er that knows what he's doin.'

'I work as hard as you.'

'Jerkin off.'

'Go ta hell.'

'We shoulda got Orville MacDurmot for this job—he's half there anyways.'

'Go ta hell.'

'He's half there anyways.'

Simon said nothing, and the men laughing challenged one another against the open face of the bridge and the woman sat under the tree, as much to them as the black wood that acted as scarecrows in the fields. The water changed from green to brown when the clouds covered the sun, and a wind came badgering the limbs of pine and maples so that she could smell from the wind the darkening screen of autumn.

She knew the young boy on the bridge, who'd gone down to the stream for water and brought a bucket up to the men, watched her though she kept her eyes closed because of the soreness. The pins on her hat pressed into her scalp and the dress was filled with the smell of leaves.

And then after I went home that night I was scared cause poor Isabel was thinkin it was alright with Bennie, he havin a job buildin the bridge so that they'd get married. I watched her pickin raspberries in the field and I thought 'poor Isabel, poor little Isabel' but didn't care I felt so good. And then I said ta Bennie the next day. 'Ya know I'm older than you by five years.' 'Stop talkin about it,' he said. 'About what?' 'About last night—I don't wanta talk about last night—about—' 'About what Bennie, about what?' 'Nothin,' he said. He walked on the limbed sills that spanned the river. The air was close to us that day and my head was sweatin, and I felt weak as anything in my legs and head. He went down under the bridge and I knew he was drinkin. 'Ya wanta trout,' he said. 'No.' 'I'll getcha a trout,' he said. 'I don't want no friggin trout,' I said. 'What—swearin are ya; what'll yer old man say you swearin?' 'I don't want no friggin trout,' I said again. 'Whatdya mean ya don't wanta talk about last night.' He didn't answer. I said it again and he wouldn't answer. Then he came up from the pool, his eyes glassy from drinkin and on the baited pin the trout was jiggling. 'Here ya go,' he said. 'You leave me alone,' I said and then he patted me. I knew my face was ready for cryin and yet he stood there pattin me all over. I didn't do nothin. 'Here ya go,' he said, 'here ya go,' the trout still jigglin on the baited pin.

The boy came off the last timbers that spanned the river, and as the men stood working with their pevies he walked up the hillside to where she was sitting. They had said to the boy:

'Ya'd better get off now or ya'll get hurt.'

'I won't get hurt anymore than you,' he said.

'What'll yer old man say you gettin killed on the bridge.'

'My old man's got nothin ta do with it,' he said.

'No, then who got ya on the fuckin bridge in the first place, just tell me that?'

Simon said nothing.

'Just tell me that—yer useless as tits on a bull.'

'Go ta hell.'

'Didja ever use yer hands?'

Simon said nothing.

'Jerkin off maybe,' one of them said.

'Shoulda get Orville MacDurmot for this here job.'

'Go ta hell.'

So the boy stood beside the old woman and watched her breathing, her sunken chest heaving in the September air—the air that smelt clean with the bright trout running from the pools, going to the sea.

'Whatcha doin?' he asked suddenly, so that his own voice sounded strange.

'Restin,' she said, and smiled. It was an almost frightened smile. Simon watched her chest and when just a moment ago he'd thought it was heaving now it seemed it wasn't moving at all. When she put her eyes on him he turned and looked toward the bridge. The men stood, silhouetted against the embattled framework, and he could see them taking water from the bucket he'd lugged up the hill, even though the water striders still skimmed the surface of the dark water and clung against the sides of the aluminum bucket.

'What in hell da ya think she's doin?'

'Ol Simon'll find out.'

'Betcha he's already tryin ta rip off a piece.'

'A piece a what is the question.'

'Ha.'

'A piece a what is the question.'

'I wonder where in hell she come from—there a house round here?'

'Not unless ya wanta walk through to the Settlement—four mile.'

'She didn't come no four mile.'

'I didn't say she did ya fucker.'

'She got outta a car awhile ago.'

There were rocks below the bridge that suggested at one time there was a mountain, and they clung in the earth so that even the roots of trees emerged and buckled against them, and the strands of roots almost touched the water where at one time salmon lay submerged at the bottom. Simon turned back to the woman. She had sat up now to face him and was straightening the pins in her hat and smoothing her dress. A wind badgered the limbs of spruce above her.

'Whatcha doin—I mean are ya sick?' he said.

'Oh no,' she said, and smiled, 'I'm just restin—I just live over there—in Deborah's place.'

'Oh,' he said, 'Over where?'

But the woman said nothing more, and again Simon could hear the men laughing and cursing so that it embarrassed him to be standing beside the woman and listening to them, yet his face betrayed nothing. In the back of his mind was acceptance of what they'd said to him, what he imagined they were saying—and he felt that he didn't hate what they said or them for saying it; that it was nothing more than a game. And when he watched them ply the timbers on the bridge, he was ashamed for hating. Actually he was laughing with them, he thought. And now he couldn't imagine that a moment ago when they were shoving and jostling one another, he'd wanted them to fall.

The boy turned and went back down the path, over the slanting flint and shale and onto the framework again. The river was gorged and shallow in the afternoon. The woman watched as the boy moved onto the bridge, amidst the yells and hollering of the others, becoming finally indistinguishable.

Yes, Janie Bell thought, that's where 'e was standin puttin sheetin on. It was what, only about two weeks after their marriage and I come down to him and called him over, the men laughin and goin on. When he came up the path I said: 'I'm pregnant.' He didn't answer and I said it again. I said: 'I'm pregnant ta you.' 'No ya are not,' he said. 'I am.' 'Well, ya can't be.' His voice was weak and scared, and he rubbed the top of his head with his hand. I turned and walked away from him and I could almost hear him shakin. Then I went home and Isabel said: 'When ya gonna find yerself someone Janie—yer gettin on,' she laughed.

When it came time ta tell them—goin on my fourth month I couldn't hide it no longer—everyone one was at me to tell them who done it, so that they'd make him marry'd ta me. The bridge was finished and Bennie was just getting ready ta go into the woods. I didn't say nothin, except stare at him—and he'd never stay in a room with me more than a second.

'I guess Bennie'n I'll bring up the child for ya,' Isabel said one day, 'Unless yer gonna tell us who it was.' 'Yes,' Bennie said looking to my father who was sittin by the wood stove near the box, and wasn't speakin ta me at all saying 'I thought I brought them up better'n that and look what happens.' He was fixin his bucksaw and Mom always saying, 'Can'tcha take that outta the house ta do?' 'Yes,' Bennie said still lookin at Papa, his eyes almost closed: 'Isabel and I decided we'd take the kid off yer hands—I mean a single woman bringin it up and everythin—I don't mind at all; it'll be just like me own. But I wish ya'd tell everybody who did it.' He still didn't look at me but I and no-one else could see his face turnin white. I just shook my head the same as always. Then he said, 'If I ever got holda the bugger who did it I'd break his neck—to

an innocent girl.' 'I don't wantcha swearin in this house,' Papa said. 'Well, it makes me so mad,' Bennie said, his voice as loud as anything.

Simon received the first drops of rain with indifference and strode across the braced timbers, except that the men still laughed at his clumsiness. And as soon as they laughed he became aware of himself again, and of those watching him. The air had turned thick and muggy, polluted with the scent of drizzle and wood. Below them a crow called and along the riverbank the exposed roots of trees turned grey. There was the hollow thumping of a woodpecker when the men stopped working.

'How'd ya liked ta have taken this road inta town?'

'Take ya a time wouldn't it?'

'The old horse and buggy, Jesus—wouldn't a wanted ta come through in the spring.'

'Ask Simon what she's doin?'

'You.'

'Ask Simon what she's doin?'

'Waitin for us ta hop her.'

'Ha.'

Simon scooped some water from the bucket and putting a sugar cube in his mouth sucked on it as he drank. He wanted the woman to go away, so that he wouldn't *feel* her presence yet he couldn't understand why he felt that. The rain fell on the shallow water below with widening circles, there was no longer any wind and the birds were quiet. The men worked solemnly now, laughter gone the rain pressed them into grey shapes on the slanting structure as the sound of mallets hitting wood reverberated dull and lonely. He picked up his pevie and went to join them jabbing it into the sill before him to keep his balance. When he reached them the youngest one said:

'Here ya want me ta show ya how ta do it?'

'I can do it,' Simon said, 'as well as you.' He rammed his pevie against the rotted sheeting, cracking and splitting the wood yet each time he thrust forward he thought he'd lose his balance and jerked back desperately.

'I'm just tryin ta give ya a hand.'

Simon didn't answer.

'Suit yerself—I'm just tryin ta help ya out—if yer gonna be goddamn pigheaded about it it's yer fault.'

'Ha.'

'Here then,' Simon said, reddening, 'show me how ta do it.'

Simon handed his pevie to the other boy who stood just above him on one of the half-rotted braces, his left boot dangling over the edge. When Simon handed him the pevie he held it for a moment as if inspecting it and then yelling hurled it into the air. 'That's how ya use a pevie.'

'Ha.'

'That's how ya use a fuckin pevie—right boys?'

'S'pose.'

'S'pose.'

'Ha.'

It hit the water below them, and was gone.

There were sounds all that night of the wind blowing snow through the cracks in the porch and each little while Papa'd come to the door an say: 'Is he born yet?' 'No,' ol

Mrs Dunstan'd say. 'Well, I thought I heard somethin like a baby or something like that,' Papa'd say from behind the door that looked far away and pink though it was always white as long as I could remember. 'No,' she'd say again, everytime and I member me tellin her to stop sayin 'No,' and then Momma tellin Isabel ta leave the room cause she was nothin but a fuss. 'I wanta stay,' Isabel said. 'Go on wait in the kitchen, it'll be your turn someday.' 'I'll make sure the doctor gets here for sure for me,' she said. 'Yes, yes,' Momma said. 'Yes I will,' Isabel said. 'Yer nothin but a fuss,' Momma said. 'Damn,' I said, 'leave me alone everyone a ya—damn.' 'She's swearin,' Isabel said, 'she's swearin.'

Deborah was an ugly baby, I never liked her because of Bennie until I felt somethin for her when they started making her call Isabel Momma, *then I got mad, and after Momma died Papa got callin her Isabel's too; there's nothin like takin someone away from ya ta make ya start lovin them. All the men around guessin who it was that made me pregnant, even saying it was Dwight Everett who was bout ten at the time. I know it wasn't ta hurt me, but ta hurt Papa who figured he had it all hid. He'd go out to the shed and saw wood all day alone.*

When Simon went off the bridge to look for his pevie the rain was coming so hard he felt that it didn't matter if he waded the river. But he couldn't find it, and now and then the men would shout at him, giving him directions. He paid no attention to them, the one who'd thrown it yelling and shouting louder than the rest, as if he must be heard. Then he thought that it didn't matter if he found it—it wouldn't be his fault if he didn't, and he left the river again.

'I'll just tell Pete is all,' he yelled.

'Ho, ho,' the boy yelled back, 'What're ya still in school squealin to the teacher?'

He didn't answer.

'Still in school squealin to the teacher—yer old man tellin everyone not ta pick on ya.'

'Go to hell.'

He'd not go on the bridge again, he thought, and so he remained below them on the side of the shale banking for a long while staring at the vague cross-sections above him. The men, it seemed, had forgotten him already and rain beat the water in thousands of tiny shots. He shivered, turned and climbed the shale banking where myriads of streams flowed in the reddish clay saturating and being absorbed all at once. He was wet from the waist down with river water and the sweet cold rain that drove against his face and laced his coat with smudges and streaks of red mud.

He reached the top of the bank after a long while, and in the stillness (for a rain like this in the middle of the woods brought a stillness to the ground and trees standing in the ground) his heart thumped so that he could hear it in his ears—a warm wet driving sound, almost he thought, as if something mysterious inside the heart (life itself he thought) was trying to break forward into the trees and mud along the shale banking. What the men had said to him had faded again—all except for their laughter. He tried not to think of one of them falling into the water.

'My it's gettin cold now, ain't it?' the woman said to him.

'Yes,' he said. 'You should go home now.' He looked at the brown laced frills at the neck of her dress and at the coarse wrinkled folds of skin, 'I'll take you home.'

The woman's dress was soaking and beginning to smell. He took off his coat and put it over her, clumsily trying to adjust it, though he felt she didn't really know or care what he did, suddenly looking about him for assistance.

'You know I'm 100 years old right now,' Janie Bell said.

'Oh,' he said.

'The Queen sent me flowers.'

The men had decided to quit for the day. The boy who'd thrown the pevie balanced himself on struts and then came down from the bridge, while the men followed him. And the boy said.

'What in Jesus is she doin over there is what I wanta know.'

'How much she's chargin for it is what I wanta know meself.'

'Ha.'

'Maybe she needs some help,' the boy said.

'Ol Simon'll find out; why, you goin over?'

'I think she probably don't even know where she is,' the boy said, his face pensive and streaked with rain.

The men lit cigarettes and said nothing, each of them spitting now and then, and now and then looking toward the old woman and Simon who was standing beside her.

So Bennie come inta me, with Isabel right behind him—and Papa not even cold and Bennie the big man now that Papa's gone all mouth on him says: 'I don't wantcha saying yer her mother, it ain't natural for a little girl like that ta have ta know those things.' 'Know what things?' I said. 'Bennie's right,' Isabel said. 'Know what things Bennie?' I said. He looked away, and walked across the room. I started laughin hysterical and screaming and picked up my commode and threw it against the walls. 'Yer not right in the head,' Isabel said. 'First havin a baby like ya did and then makin life miserable for the people tryin ta help ya—yer not right in the head; yer not fit ta live here either, and me and Bennie bearin the brunt of all the talk about ya.' 'What talk eh Bennie—what talk?' I couldn't stop laughing. 'I never though I'd hate me own sister, flesh and blood—Dad brought us up better'n that there but I hate you,' she said. 'Yes I hate you,' Deborah said, running up to kick me. And then Isabel sat down on the chair and cried. Bennie said nothing else. I just stared and stared. 'And ya ain't coming ta church with us no more either,' Isabel said, cryin and shakin, her nose red. So after that whenever they had someone around, I sat in me room. I wouldn't bother them at all, even at Christmas cept ta take a bit of food at the table. And ya could tell Deborah thought I was crazy livin in the room off of her parents—especially as she got older, so I hated her again. And then I got pains in me head and never felt good and couldn't talk ta no-one. I could hear them in their bedroom at night too, don'tcha think I couldn't.

'Here,' the boy said, 'Ya think she needs my coat too?'

'I don't know,' Simon said.

The boy placed his coat over her also and stood beside Simon, and one by one the men came back to the truck parked in the overgrown road that led to the mill, carrying mallets and axes and pevies.

'How are you?' one of the men said. 'Where do you live?'

She didn't answer.

'I think she's crazier than a loon,' another said.

'Betcha she ain't even there—betcha she's a ghost or something.'

'Ha.'

'Shutup now.'

'Yes, shutup,' Simon said. 'Someone should phone the police.'

'I'll run out and phone the police,' the boy said, 'I think she's dyin or somethin right here.'

'She can't have too much left in 'er—she must be 80 anyways.'

'I ain't standin round here all day so hurry up.'

'Go home if ya want to—I'm not stoppin ya,' the boy said.

'Don't yap at me.'

'Well, go home if ya want to—we don't need a ton a people here.'

'Don't yap at me flap mouth—I ain't Simon.'

Simon said nothing.

'I ain't Simon for fuck's sake,' he said again.

'Everyone just shutup,' another man said.

Isabel couldn't stomach ta nurse Bennie when he was sick—so I did it, not because I wanted to, but because I had to. It was hate, not love or kindness that made me wash and scrub him, and clean the mess from the bed each and every day, with Isabel so much of a fuss she couldn't go inta the room at all. Yet even when I saw that he knew in his eyes he was dyin—would he talk? Would he speak out once and tell them, and let me rest, carrying his bucket a mess out each and every day—with Isabel and Deborah as useless and whiny as could be. And every time I'd clean him and change him about I'd look and see he couldn't say nothin—that he'd lied to himself all his life anyways. Yet I still could member him dancin with his cork boots on.

Keepin a garden till I was 88 each and every season and then my granddaughter—my own granddaughter comin ta tell me they were puttin me over there cause George had a job in Toronto and they couldn't bring me. 'I'll keep me own self,' I said. 'No now you'll be better over there Aunt Janie; it'd be like a new home with new friends.' 'I'll keep me own self,' I said again, gettin scared and lookin about the room, first the latch on the door and then the flowers I had and my commode where I glued it together. I didn't want to go. 'I keep a garden right here now,' I said. 'Aunt Janie,' she said, 'Aunt Janie.' 'I ain't yer aunt,' I said, 'at all.' 'Why, of course you're my aunt,' she said smiling, 'my great aunt,' as if I was again a child or already dead. Already dead when I kept me own garden was more than her mother or her could ever once do. I couldn't say nothing. She smiled at me. I didn't want to go.

The men swung into the box of the truck and it creaked and groaned over the washed-out road the men silent and wet, the air above them filled with the smoke of cigarettes.

'Where'd they say she's from?'

'The old folks home across the river.'

'I knew she was some sorta old just lookin at her—what was she doin over here anyway?'

'How the hell should I know?'

'Crazy old fucker probably lookin for us ta hop on her.'

'Filthy mind, eh Simon?'

Simon said nothing.

'Boy, what a filthy mind eh Simon?'

'I betcha Simon was on and off her.'

'Ha.'

'So that's whatcha were doin.'

'Go ta hell,' Simon said.

'Ha.'

'Just go to hell.'

The man walked along the wet and littered streets just before dark, in the quiet alleys rain still dripped across the tin barrels making an inconsistent drumming sound. Now and then there were the shouts and cries of children playing, the almost squalid noise of a dog barking. He crossed to the smaller street and went into the tavern where he ordered a beer and sat at an end table.

'I hear ya lost one,' the waiter said.

'We found her again,' he said. 'She probably won't make 'er though.'

'How's that?'

''Cause there's a bunch a morons around who let her get unconscious—at her age an everything.'

'Oh,' the waiter said smiling, 'You should get married anyway, and stop worrying about the old ones.'

'Shit,' he said. He stood up and left the tavern, went onto the street again. Across the water the ferry sounded in the darkness. 'I wish everyone'd just mind their own business about me getting married,' he thought. 'It's my own business if I'm gonna get married.'

1978

Rohinton Mistry

b. 1952

Born in Bombay, India, Rohinton Mistry studied mathematics and economics at the University of Bombay before immigrating to Toronto in 1975. He supported himself by working in a bank, while taking night courses in English and philosophy at the University of Toronto. When the university instituted an annual short-story contest in 1983, he entered and won. After winning the contest again the following year, as well as a *Canadian Fiction* contributor's prize, he began writing full time. His stories were collected in *Tales from Firozsha Baag* (1987). Mistry now lives with his wife in Brampton, Ontario.

Tales from Firozsha Baag is a collection of linked short stories about Parsi life in Bombay. They are connected by setting (they all take place in one apartment complex), character (the same people move between the stories as freely as they do between apartments), and theme (the trade-off between the hardships of life at home and the unknown possibilities of life in a foreign country). For example, the story 'Squatter', about a character who has returned to the complex, concerns the difficult passage from one culture to another, and the way apparently trivial changes in custom leave the individual feeling alienated. On another level, the collection is unified by tales that are repeated in different stories, related by, and about, various members of the Parsi community. The anecdote of Sarosh's return from Toronto, for instance, which is told by Nariman in 'Squatter', is remembered—differently—by Sarosh's aunt, Minocher Mirza, in 'Condolence Visit'. Another linking technique Mistry uses is Kersi Boyce's story, which frames the others; while living in a Toronto apartment building, where he encounters characters who seem at once foreign and familiar to him, as a former resident of Firozsha Baag, Boyce writes a collection of stories that resembles Mistry's own book. In 'Swimming Lessons', the last story of the collection, Kersi's parents read their son's tales of Firozsha Baag and comment on their detail, and on their inevitable inability as stories to reveal the whole truth. A similar patterning occurs in 'Squatter', when Jehangir comments on the storyteller's technique, on his careful choice of word and tone, and the pleasure he gives his audience. Thus the readers within these stories provide insights into the stories themselves.

Squatter

Whenever Nariman Hansotia returned in the evening from the Cawasji Framji Memorial Library in a good mood the signs were plainly evident.

First, he parked his 1932 Mercedes-Benz (he called it the apple of his eye) outside A Block, directly in front of his ground-floor veranda window, and beeped the horn three long times. It annoyed Rustomji who also had a ground-floor flat in A Block. Ever since he had defied Nariman in the matter of painting the exterior of the building, Rustomji was convinced that nothing the old coot did was untainted by the thought of vengeance and harassment, his retirement pastime.

But the beeping was merely Nariman's signal to let Hirabai inside know that though he was back he would not step indoors for a while. Then he raised the hood, whistling 'Rose Marie,' and leaned his tall frame over the engine. He checked the oil, wiped here and there with a rag, tightened the radiator cap, and lowered the hood. Finally, he polished the Mercedes star and let the whistling modulate into the march from *The Bridge On The River Kwai*. The boys playing in the compound knew that Nariman was ready now to tell a story. They started to gather round.

'*Sahibji*, Nariman Uncle,' someone said tentatively and Nariman nodded, careful not to lose his whistle, his bulbous nose flaring slightly. The pursed lips had temporarily raised and reshaped his Clark Gable moustache. More boys walked up. One called out, 'How about a story, Nariman Uncle?' at which point Nariman's eyes began to twinkle, and he imparted increased energy to the polishing. The cry was taken up by others, 'Yes, yes, Nariman Uncle, a story!' He swung into a final verse of the march. Then the lips relinquished the whistle, the Clark Gable moustache descended. The rag was put away, and he began.

'You boys know the great cricketers: Contractor, Polly Umrigar, and recently, the young chap, Farokh Engineer. Cricket *aficionados*, that's what you all are.' Nariman liked to use new words, especially big ones, in the stories he told, believing it was his duty to expose young minds to as shimmering and varied a vocabulary as possible; if they could not spend their days at the Cawasji Framji Memorial Library then he, at least, could carry bits of the library out to them.

The boys nodded; the names of the cricketers were familiar.

'But does any one know about Savukshaw, the greatest of them all?' They shook their heads in unison.

'This, then, is the story about Savukshaw, how he saved the Indian team from a humiliating defeat when they were touring in England.' Nariman sat on the steps of A Block. The few diehards who had continued with their games could not resist any longer when they saw the gathering circle, and ran up to listen. They asked their neighbours in whispers what the story was about, and were told: Savukshaw the greatest cricketer. The whispering died down and Nariman began.

'The Indian team was to play the indomitable MCC as part of its tour of England. Contractor was our captain. Now the MCC being the strongest team they had to face, Contractor was almost certain of defeat. To add to Contractor's troubles, one of his star batsmen, Nadkarni, had caught influenza early in the tour, and would definitely not be well enough to play against the MCC. By the way, does anyone know what those letters stand for? You, Kersi, you wanted to be a cricketer once.'

Kersi shook his head. None of the boys knew, even though they had heard the MCC mentioned in radio commentaries, because the full name was hardly ever used.

Then Jehangir Bulsara spoke up, or Bulsara Bookworm, as the boys called him. The name given by Pesi *paadmaroo* had stuck even though it was now more than four years since Pesi had been sent away to boarding-school, and over two years since the death of Dr Mody. Jehangir was still unliked by the boys in the Baag, though they had come to accept his aloofness and respect his knowledge and intellect. They were not surprised that he knew the answer to Nariman's question: 'Marylebone Cricket Club.'

'Absolutely correct,' said Nariman, and continued with the story: 'The MCC won the toss and elected to bat. They scored four hundred and ninety-seven runs in the first inning before our spinners could get them out. Early in the second day's play our team was dismissed for one hundred and nine runs, and the extra who had taken Nadkarni's place was injured by a vicious bumper that opened a gash on his forehead.' Nariman indicated the spot and the length of the gash on his furrowed brow. 'Contractor's worst fears were coming true. The MCC waived their own second inning and gave the Indian team a follow-on, wanting to inflict an inning's defeat. And this time he had to use the second extra. The second extra was a certain Savukshaw.'

The younger boys listened attentively; some of them, like the two sons of the chartered accountant in B Block, had only recently been deemed old enough by their parents to come out and play in the compound, and had not received any exposure to Nariman's stories. But the others like Jehangir, Kersi, and Viraf were familiar with Nariman's technique.

Once, Jehangir had overhead them discussing Nariman's stories, and he could not help expressing his opinion: that unpredictability was the brush he used to paint his tales with, and ambiguity the palette he mixed his colours in. The others looked at him with admiration. Then Viraf asked what exactly he meant by that. Jehangir said that Nariman sometimes told a funny incident in a very serious way, or expressed a significant matter in a light and playful manner. And these were only two rough divisions, in between were lots of subtle gradations of tone and texture. Which, then, was the funny story and which the serious? Their opinions were divided, but ultimately, said Jehangir, it was up to the listener to decide.

'So,' continued Nariman, 'Contractor first sent out his two regular openers, convinced that it was all hopeless. But after five wickets were lost for just another thirty-eight runs, out came Savukshaw the extra. Nothing mattered any more.'

The street lights outside the compound came on, illuminating the iron gate where the watchman stood. It was a load off the watchman's mind when Nariman told a story. It meant an early end to the hectic vigil during which he had to ensure that none of the children ran out on the main road, or tried to jump over the wall. For although keeping out riff-raff was his duty, keeping in the boys was as important if he wanted to retain the job.

'The first ball Savukshaw faced was wide outside the off stump. He just lifted his bat and ignored it. But with what style! What panache! As if to say, come on, you blighters, play some polished cricket. The next ball was also wide, but not as much as the first. It missed the off stump narrowly. Again Savukshaw lifted his bat, boredom written all over him. Everyone was now watching closely. The bowler was annoyed by Savukshaw's arrogance, and the third delivery was a vicious fast pitch, right down on the middle stump.

'Savukshaw was ready, quick as lightning. No one even saw the stroke of his bat, but the ball went like a bullet towards square leg.

'Fielding at square leg was a giant of a fellow, about six feet seven, weighing two hundred and fifty pounds, a veritable Brobdingnagian, with arms like branches and hands like a pair of huge *sapaat*, the kind that Dr Mody used to wear, you remember what big feet Dr Mody had.' Jehangir was the only one who did; he nodded. 'Just to see him standing there was scary. Not one ball had got past him, and he had taken some great catches. Savukshaw purposely aimed his shot right at him. But he was as quick as Savukshaw, and stuck out his huge *sapaat* of a hand to stop the ball. What do you think happened then, boys?'

The older boys knew what Nariman wanted to hear at this point. They asked, 'What happened, Nariman Uncle, what happened?' Satisfied, Nariman continued.

'A howl is what happened. A howl from the giant fielder, a howl that rang through the entire stadium, that soared like the cry of a banshee right up to the cheapest seats in the furthest, highest corners, a howl that echoed from the scoreboard and into the pavilion, into the kitchen, startling the chap inside who was preparing tea and scones for after the match, who spilled boiling water all over himself and was severely hurt. But not nearly as bad as the giant fielder at square leg. Never at any English stadium was a howl heard like that one, not in the whole history of cricket. And why do you think he was howling, boys?'

The chorus asked, 'Why, Nariman Uncle, why?'

'Because of Savukshaw's bullet-like shot, of course. The hand he had reached out to stop it, he now held up for all to see, and *dhur-dhur, dhur-dhur* the blood was gushing like a fountain in an Italian piazza, like a burst water-main from the Vihar-Powai reservoir, dripping onto his shirt and his white pants, and sprinkling the green grass, and only because he was such a giant of a fellow could he suffer so much blood loss and not faint. But even he could not last forever; eventually, he felt dizzy, and was helped off the field. And where do you think the ball was, boys, that Savukshaw had smacked so hard?'

And the chorus rang out again on the now dark steps of A Block: 'Where, Nariman Uncle, where?'

'Past the boundary line, of course. Lying near the fence. Rent asunder. Into two perfect leather hemispheres. All the stitches had ripped, and some of the insides had spilled out. So the umpires sent for a new one, and the game resumed. Now none of the fielders dared to touch any ball that Savukshaw hit. Every shot went to the boundary, all the way for four runs. Single-handedly, Savukshaw wiped out the deficit, and had it not been for loss of time due to rain, he would have taken the Indian team to a thumping victory against the MCC. As it was, the match ended in a draw.'

Nariman was pleased with the awed faces of the youngest ones around him. Kersi and Viraf were grinning away and whispering something. From one of the flats the smell of frying fish swam out to explore the night air, and tickled Nariman's nostrils. He sniffed appreciatively, aware that it was in his good wife Hirabai's pan that the frying was taking place. This morning, he had seen the pomfret she had purchased at the door, waiting to be cleaned, its mouth open and eyes wide, like the eyes of some of these youngsters. It was time to wind up the story.

'The MCC will not forget the number of new balls they had to produce that day because of Savukshaw's deadly strokes. Their annual ball budget was thrown badly out of balance. Any other bat would have cracked under the strain, but Savukshaw's was seasoned with a special combination of oils, a secret formula given to him by a *sadhu* who had seen him one day playing cricket when he was a small boy. But Savukshaw used to say his real secret was practice, lots of practice, that was the advice he gave to any young lad who wanted to play cricket.'

The story was now clearly finished, but none of the boys showed any sign of dispersing. 'Tell us about more matches that Savukshaw played in,' they said.

'More nothing. This was his greatest match. Anyway, he did not play cricket for long because soon after the match against the MCC he became a champion bicyclist, the fastest human on two wheels. And later, a pole-vaulter—when he glided over on his pole, so graceful, it was like watching a bird in flight. But he gave that up, too, and became a hunter, the mightiest hunter ever known, absolutely fearless, and so skilful, with a gun he could have, from the third floor of A Block, shaved the whisker of a cat in the backyard of C Block.'

'Tell us about that,' they said, 'about Savukshaw the hunter!'

The fat ayah, Jaakaylee, arrived to take the chartered accountant's two children home. But they refused to go without hearing about Savukshaw the hunter. When she scolded them and things became a little hysterical, some other boys tried to resurrect the ghost she had once seen: 'Ayah *bhoot*! Ayah *bhoot*!' Nariman raised a finger in warning—that subject was still taboo in Firozsha Baag; none of the adults was in a hurry to relive the wild and rampageous days that Pesi *paadmaroo* had ushered in, once upon a time, with the *bhoot* games.

Jaakaylee sat down, unwilling to return without the children, and whispered to Nariman to make it short. The smell of frying fish which had tickled Nariman's nostrils ventured into and awakened his stomach. But the story of Savukshaw the hunter was one he had wanted to tell for a long time.

'Savukshaw always went hunting alone, he preferred it that way. There are many incidents in the life of Savukshaw the hunter, but the one I am telling you about involves a terrifying situation. Terrifying for us, of course; Savukshaw was never terrified of anything. What happened was, one night he set up camp, started a fire and warmed up his bowl of chicken-*dhansaak*.'

The frying fish had precipitated famishment upon Nariman, and the subject of chicken-*dhansaak* suited him well. His own mouth watering, he elaborated: 'Mrs Savukshaw was as famous for her *dhansaak* as Mr was for hunting. She used to put in tamarind and brinjal, coriander and cumin, cloves and cinnamon, and dozens of other spices no one knows about. Women used to come from miles around to stand outside her window while she cooked it, to enjoy the fragrance and try to penetrate her secret, hoping to identify the ingredients as the aroma floated out, layer by layer, growing more complex and delicious. But always, the delectable fragrance enveloped the women and they just surrendered to the ecstacy, forgetting what they had come for. Mrs Savukshaw's secret was safe.'

Jaakaylee motioned to Nariman to hurry up, it was past the children's dinnertime. He continued: 'The aroma of savoury spices soon filled the night air in the jungle, and when the *dhansaak* was piping hot he started to eat, his rifle beside him. But as soon as he lifted the first morsel to his lips, a tiger's eyes flashed in the bushes! Not twelve feet from him! He emerged licking his chops! What do you think happened then, boys?'

'What, what, Nariman Uncle?'

Before he could tell them, the door of his flat opened. Hirabai put her head out and said, '*Chaalo ni*, Nariman, it's time. Then if it gets cold you won't like it.'

That decided the matter. To let Hirabai's fried fish, crisp on the outside, yet tender and juicy inside, marinated in turmeric and cayenne—to let that get cold would be something that *Khoedaiji* above would not easily forgive. 'Sorry boys, have to go. Next time about Savukshaw and the tiger.'

There were some groans of disappointment. They hoped Nariman's good spirits would extend into the morrow when he returned from the Memorial Library, or the story would get cold.

But a whole week elapsed before Nariman again parked the apple of his eye outside his ground-floor flat and beeped the horn three times. When he had raised the hood, checked the oil, polished the star and swung into the 'Colonel Boogie March,' the boys began drifting towards A Block.

Some of them recalled the incomplete story of Savukshaw and the tiger, but they knew better than to remind him. It was never wise to prompt Nariman until he had dropped the first hint himself, or things would turn out badly.

Nariman inspected the faces: the two who stood at the back, always looking superior and wise, were missing. So was the quiet Bulsara boy, the intelligent one. 'Call Kersi, Viraf, and Jehangir,' he said, 'I want them to listen to today's story.'

Jehangir was sitting alone on the stone steps of C Block. The others were chatting by the compound gate with the watchman. Someone went to fetch them.

'Sorry to disturb your conference, boys, and your meditation, Jehangir,' Nariman said facetiously, 'but I thought you would like to hear this story. Especially since some of you are planning to go abroad.'

This was not strictly accurate, but Kersi and Viraf did talk a lot about America and Canada. Kersi had started writing to universities there since his final high-school year, and had also sent letters of inquiry to the Canadian High Commission in New Delhi and to the U.S. Consulate at Breach Candy. But so far he had not made any progress. He and Viraf replied with as much sarcasm as their unripe years allowed, 'Oh yes, next week, just have to pack our bags.'

'Riiiight,' drawled Nariman. Although he spoke perfect English, this was the one word with which he allowed himself sometimes to take liberties, indulging in a broadness of vowel more American than anything else. 'But before we go on with today's story, what did you learn about Savukshaw, from last week's story?'

'That he was a very talented man,' said someone.

'What else?'

'He was also a very lucky man, to have so many talents,' said Viraf.

'Yes, but what else?'

There was silence for a few moments. Then Jehangir said, timidly: 'He was a man searching for happiness, by trying all kinds of different things.'

'Exactly! And he never found it. He kept looking for new experiences, and though he was very successful at everything he attempted, it did not bring him happiness. Remember this, success alone does not bring happiness. Nor does failure have to bring unhappiness. Keep it in mind when you listen to today's story.'

A chant started somewhere in the back: 'We-want-a-story! We-want-a-story!'

'Riiiight,' said Nariman. 'Now, everyone remembers Vera and Dolly, daughters of Najamai from C Block.' There were whistles and hoots; Viraf nudged Kersi with his elbow, who was smiling wistfully. Nariman held up his hand: 'Now, now, boys, behave yourselves. Those two girls went abroad for studies many years ago, and never came back. They settled there happily.

'And like them, a fellow called Sarosh also went abroad, to Toronto, but did not find happiness there. This story is about him. You probably don't know him, he does not live in Firozsha Baag, though he is related to someone who does.'

'Who? Who?'

'Curiosity killed the cat,' said Nariman, running a finger over each branch of his moustache, 'and what's important is the tale. So let us continue. This Sarosh began calling himself Sid after living in Toronto for a few months, but in our story he will be Sarosh and nothing but Sarosh, for that is his proper Parsi name. Besides, that was his own stipulation when he entrusted me with the sad but instructive chronicle of his recent life.' Nariman polished his glasses with his handkerchief, put them on again, and began.

'At the point where our story commences, Sarosh had been living in Toronto for ten years. We find him depressed and miserable, perched on top of the toilet, crouching on his haunches, feet planted firmly for balance upon the white plastic oval of the toilet seat.

'Daily for a decade had Sarosh suffered this position. Morning after morning, he had no choice but to climb up and simulate the squat of our Indian latrines. If he sat down, no amount of exertion could produce success.

'At first, this inability was no more than mildly incommodious. As time went by, however, the frustrated attempts caused him grave anxiety. And when the failure stretched unbroken over ten years, it began to torment and haunt all his waking hours.'

Some of the boys struggled hard to keep straight faces. They suspected that Nariman was not telling just a funny story, because if he intended them to laugh there was always some unmistakable way to let them know. Only the thought of displeasing Nariman and prematurely terminating the story kept their paroxysms of mirth from bursting forth unchecked.

Nariman continued: 'You see, ten years was the time Sarosh had set himself to achieve complete adaptation to the new country. But how could he claim adaptation with any honesty if the acceptable catharsis continually failed to favour him? Obtaining his new citizenship had not helped either. He remained dependent on the old way, and this unalterable fact, strengthened afresh every morning of his life in the new country, suffocated him.

'The ten-year time limit was more an accident than anything else. But it hung over him with the awesome presence and sharpness of a guillotine. Careless words, boys, careless words in a moment of lighthheartedness, as is so often the case with us all, had led to it.

'Ten years before, Sarosh had returned triumphantly to Bombay after fulfilling the immigration requirements of the Canadian High Commission in New Delhi. News of his imminent departure spread amongst relatives and friends. A farewell party was organized. In fact, it was given by his relatives in Firozsha Baag. Most of you will be too young to remember it, but it was a very loud party, went on till late in the night. Very lengthy and heated arguments took place, which is not the thing to do at a party. It started like this: Sarosh was told by some what a smart decision he had made, that his whole life would change for the better; others said he was making a mistake, emigration was all wrong, but if he wanted to be unhappy that was his business, they wished him well.

'By and by, after substantial amounts of Scotch and soda and rum and Coke had disappeared, a fierce debate started between the two groups. To this day Sarosh does not know what made him raise his glass and announce: "My dear family, my dear friends, if I do not become completely Canadian in exactly ten years from the time I land there, then I will come back. I promise. So please, no more arguments. Enjoy the party." His words were greeted with cheers and shouts of hear! hear! They told him never to fear embarrassment; there was no shame if he decided to return to the country of his birth.

'But shortly, his poor worried mother pulled him aside. She led him to the back room and withdrew her worn and aged prayer book from her purse, saying, "I want you to place your hand upon the *Avesta* and swear that you will keep that promise."

'He told her not to be silly, that it was just a joke. But she insisted: "*Kassum khà*—on the *Avesta*. One last thing for your mother. Who knows when you will see me again?" and her voice grew tremulous as it always did when she turned deeply emotional. Sarosh complied, and the prayer book was returned to her purse.

'His mother continued: "It is better to live in want among your family and your friends, who love you and care for you, than to be unhappy surrounded by vacuum cleaners and dishwashers and big shiny motor cars." She hugged him. Then they joined the celebration in progress.

'And Sarosh's careless words spoken at the party gradually forged themselves into a commitment as much to himself as to his mother and the others. It stayed with him all his years in the new land, reminding him every morning of what must happen at the end of the tenth, as it reminded him now while he descended from his perch.'

Jehangir wished the titters and chortles around him would settle down, he found them annoying. When Nariman structured his sentences so carefully and chose his words with extreme care as he was doing now, Jehangir found it most pleasurable to listen. Sometimes, he remembered certain words Nariman had used, or combinations of words, and repeated them to himself, enjoying again the beauty of their sounds when he went for his walks to the Hanging Gardens or was sitting alone on the stone steps of C Block. Mumbling to himself did nothing to mitigate the isolation which the other boys in the Baag had dropped around him like a heavy cloak, but he had grown used to all that by now.

Nariman continued: 'In his own apartment Sarosh squatted barefoot. Elsewhere, if he had to go with his shoes on, he would carefully cover the seat with toilet paper before climbing up. He learnt to do this after the first time, when his shoes had left telltale footprints on the seat. He had had to clean it with a wet paper towel. Luckily, no one had seen him.

'But there was not much he could keep secret about his ways. The world of washrooms is private and at the same time very public. The absence of feet below the stall door, the smell of faeces, the rustle of paper, glimpses caught through the narrow crack between stall door and jamb—all these added up to only one thing: a foreign presence in the stall, not doing things in the conventional way. And if the one outside could receive the fetor of Sarosh's business wafting through the door, poor unhappy Sarosh too could detect something malodorous in the air: the presence of xenophobia and hostility.'

What a feast, thought Jehangir, what a feast of words! This would be the finest story Nariman had ever told, he just knew it.

'But Sarosh did not give up trying. Each morning he seated himself to push and grunt, grunt and push, squirming and writhing unavailingly on the white plastic oval. Exhausted, he then hopped up, expert at balancing now, and completed the movement quite effortlessly.

'The long morning hours in the washroom created new difficulties. He was late going to work on several occasions, and one such day, the supervisor called him in: "Here's your timesheet for this month. You've been late eleven times. What's the problem?" '

Here, Nariman stopped because his neighbour Rustomji's door creaked open. Rustomji peered out, scowling, and muttered: '*Saala* loafers, sitting all evening outside people's houses, making a nuisance, and being encouraged by grownups at that.'

He stood there a moment longer, fingering the greying chest hair that was easily accessible through his *sudra*, then went inside. The boys immediately took up a soft and low chant: 'Rustomji-the-curmudgeon! Rustomji-the-curmudgeon!'

Nariman help up his hand disapprovingly. But secretly, he was pleased that the name was still popular, the name he had given Rustomji when the latter had refused to pay his share for painting the building. 'Quiet, quiet!' said he. 'Do you want me to continue or not?'

'Yes, yes!' The chanting died away, and Nariman resumed the story.

'So Sarosh was told by his supervisor that he was coming late to work too often. What could poor Sarosh say?'

'What, Nariman Uncle?' rose the refrain.

'Nothing, of course. The supervisor, noting his silence, continued: "If it keeps up, the consequences could be serious as far as your career is concerned." '

'Sarosh decided to speak. He said embarrassedly, "It's a different kind of problem. I . . . I don't know how to explain . . . it's an immigration-related problem." '

'Now this supervisor must have had experience with other immigrants, because right away he told Sarosh, "No problem. Just contact your Immigration Aid Society. They should be able to help you. Every ethnic group has one: Vietnamese,

Chinese—I'm certain that one exists for Indians. If you need time off to go there, no problem. That can be arranged, no problem. As long as you do something about your lateness, there's no problem." That's the way they talk over there, nothing is ever a problem.

'So Sarosh thanked him and went to his desk. For the umpteenth time he bitterly rued his oversight. Could fate have plotted it, concealing the western toilet behind that shroud of anxieties which had appeared out of nowhere to beset him just before he left India? After all, he had readied himself meticulously for the new life. Even for the great, merciless Canadian cold he had heard so much about. How could he have overlooked preparation for the western toilet with its matutinal demands unless fate had conspired? In Bombay, you know that offices of foreign businesses offer both options in their bathrooms. So do all hotels with three stars or more. By practising in familiar surroundings, Sarosh was convinced he could have mastered a seated evacuation before departure.

'But perhaps there was something in what the supervisor said. Sarosh found a telephone number for the Indian Immigrant Aid Society and made an appointment. That afternoon, he met Mrs Maha-Lepate at the Society's office.'

Kersi and Viraf looked at each other and smiled. Nariman Uncle had a nerve, there was more *lepate* in his own stories than anywhere else.

'Mrs Maha-Lepate was very understanding, and made Sarosh feel at ease despite the very personal nature of his problem. She said, "Yes, we get many referrals. There was a man here last month who couldn't eat Wonder Bread—it made him throw up."

'By the way, boys, Wonder Bread is a Canadian bread which all happy families eat to be happy in the same way; the unhappy families are unhappy in their own fashion by eating other brands.' Jehangir was the only one who understood, and murmured: 'Tolstoy,' at Nariman's little joke. Nariman noticed it, pleased. He continued.

'Mrs Maha-Lepate told Sarosh about that case: "Our immigrant specialist, Dr No-Ilaaz, recommended that the patient eat cake instead. He explained that Wonder Bread caused vomiting because the digestive system was used to Indian bread only, made with Indian flour in the village he came from. However, since his system was unfamiliar with cake, Canadian or otherwise, it did not react but was digested as a newfound food. In this way he got used to Canadian flour first in cake form. Just yesterday we received a report from Dr No-Ilaaz. The patient successfully ate his first slice of whole-wheat Wonder Bread with no ill effects. The ultimate goal is pure white Wonder Bread."

'Like a polite Parsi boy, Sarosh said, "That's very interesting." The garrulous Mrs Maha-Lepate was about to continue, and he tried to interject: "But I—" but Mrs Maha-Lepate was too quick for him: "Oh, there are so many interesting cases I could tell you about. Like the woman from Sri Lanka—referred to us because they don't have their own Society—who could not drink the water here. Dr No-Ilaaz said it was due to the different mineral content. So he started her on Coca-Cola and then began diluting it with water, bit by bit. Six weeks later she took her first sip of unadulterated Canadian water and managed to keep it down."

'Sarosh could not halt Mrs Maha-Lepate as she launched from one case history into another: "Right now, Dr No-Ilaaz is working on a very unusual case. Involves a whole Pakistani family. Ever since immigrating to Canada, none of them can swallow. They choke on their own saliva, and have to spit constantly. But we are confident that Dr No-Ilaaz will find a remedy. He has never been stumped by any immigrant problem. Besides, we have an information network with other third-world Immigrant Aid Societies. We all seem to share a history of similar maladies, and regularly compare notes. Some of us thought these problems were linked to retention of original citizenship. But this was a false lead."

'Sarosh, out of his own experience, vigorously nodded agreement. By now he was truly fascinated by Mrs Maha-Lepate's wealth of information. Reluctantly, he interrupted: "But will Dr No-Ilaaz be able to solve my problem?"

' "I have every confidence that he will," replied Mrs Maha-Lepate in great earnest. "And if he has no remedy for you right away, he will be delighted to start working on one. He loves to take up new projects." '

Nariman halted to blow his nose, and a clear shrill voice travelled the night air of the Firozsha Baag compound from C Block to where the boys had collected around Nariman in A Block: 'Jehangoo! O Jehangoo! Eight o'clock! Upstairs now!'

Jehangir stared at his feet in embarrassment. Nariman looked at his watch and said, 'Yes, it's eight.' But Jehangir did not move, so he continued.

'Mrs Maha-Lepate was able to arrange an appointment while Sarosh waited, and he went directly to the doctor's office. What he had heard so far sounded quite promising. Then he cautioned himself not to get overly optimistic, that was the worst mistake he could make. But along the way to the doctor's, he could not help thinking what a lovely city Toronto was. It was the same way he had felt when he first saw it ten years ago, before all the joy had dissolved in the acid of his anxieties.'

Once again that shrill voice travelled through the clear night: '*Arré* Jehangoo! *Muà*, do I have to come down and drag you upstairs!'

Jehangir's mortification was now complete. Nariman made it easy for him, though: 'The first part of the story is over. Second part continues tomorrow. Same time, same place.' The boys were surprised, Nariman did not make such commitments. But never before had he told such a long story. They began drifting back to their homes.

As Jehangir strode hurriedly to C Block, falsettos and piercing shrieks followed him in the darkness: '*Arré* Jehangoo! *Muà* Jehangoo! Bulsara Bookworm! Eight o'clock Jehangoo!' Shaking his head, Nariman went indoors to Hirabai.

Next evening, the story punctually resumed when Nariman took his place on the topmost step of A Block: 'You remember that we left Sarosh on his way to see the Immigrant Aid Society's doctor. Well, Dr No-Ilaaz listened patiently to Sarosh's concerns, then said, "As a matter of fact, there is a remedy which is so new even the IAS does not know about it. Not even that Mrs Maha-Lepate who knows it all," he added drolly, twirling his stethoscope like a stunted lasso. He slipped it on around his neck before continuing: "It involves a minor operation which was developed with financial assistance from the Multicultural Department. A small device, *Crappus Non Interruptus*, or CNI as we call it, is implanted in the bowel. The device is controlled by an external handheld transmitter similar to the ones used for automatic garage door-openers—you may have seen them in hardware stores." '

Nariman noticed that most of the boys wore puzzled looks and realized he had to make some things clearer. 'The Multicultural Department is a Canadian invention.

It is supposed to ensure that ethnic cultures are able to flourish, so that Canadian society will consist of a mosaic of cultures—that's their favourite word, mosaic—instead of one uniform mix, like the American melting pot. If you ask me, mosaic and melting pot are both nonsense, and ethnic is a polite way of saying bloody foreigner. But anyway, you understand Multicultural Department? Good. So Sarosh nodded, and Dr No-Ilaaz went on: "You can encode the handheld transmitter with a personal ten-digit code. Then all you do is position yourself on the toilet seat and activate your transmitter. Just like a garage door, your bowel will open without pushing or grunting." '

There was some snickering in the audience, and Nariman raised his eyebrows, whereupon they covered up their mouths with their hands. 'The doctor asked Sarosh if he had any questions. Sarosh thought for a moment, then asked if it required any maintenance.

'Dr No-Ilaaz replied: "CNI is semi-permanent and operates on solar energy. Which means you would have to make it a point to get some sun periodically, or it would cease and lead to constipation. However, you don't have to strip for a tan. Exposing ten percent of your skin surface once a week during summer will let the device store sufficient energy for year-round operation."

'Sarosh's next question was: "Is there any hope that someday the bowels can work on their own, without operating the device?" at which Dr No-Ilaaz shook his head: "I'm afraid not. You must think very, very carefully before making a decision. Once CNI is implanted, you can never pass a motion in the natural way—neither sitting nor squatting."

'He stopped to allow Sarosh time to think it over, then continued: "And you must understand what that means. You will never be able to live a normal life again. You will be permanently different from your family and friends because of this basic internal modification. In fact, in this country or that, it will set you apart from your fellow countrymen. So you must consider the whole thing most carefully."

'Dr No-Ilaaz paused, toyed with his stethoscope, shuffled some papers on his desk, then resumed: "There are other dangers you should know about. Just as a garage door can be accidentally opened by a neighbour's transmitter on the same frequency, CNI can also be activated by someone with similar apparatus." To ease the tension he attempted a quick laugh and said, "Very embarrassing, eh, if it happened at the wrong place and time. Mind you, the risk is not so great at present, because the chances of finding yourself within a fifty-foot radius of another transmitter on the same frequency are infinitesimal. But what about the future? What if CNI becomes very popular? Sufficient permutations may not be available for transmitter frequencies and you could be sharing the code with others. Then the risk of accidents becomes greater." '

Something landed with a loud thud in the yard behind A Block, making Nariman startle. Immediately, a yowling and screeching and caterwauling went up from the stray cats there, and the *kuchrawalli*'s dog started barking. Some of the boys went around the side of A Block to peer over the fence into the backyard. But the commotion soon died down of its own accord. The boys returned and, once again, Nariman's voice was the only sound to be heard.

'By now, Sarosh was on the verge of deciding against the operation. Dr No-Ilaaz observed this and was pleased. He took pride in being able to dissuade his patients from following the very remedies which he first so painstakingly described. True to his name, Dr No-Ilaaz believed no remedy is the best remedy, rather than prescribing this-mycin and that-mycin for every little ailment. So he continued: "And what about our sons and daughters? And the quality of their lives? We still don't know the long-term effects of CNI. Some researchers speculate that it could generate a genetic deficiency, that the offspring of a CNI parent would also require CNI. On the other hand, they could be perfectly healthy toilet seat-users, without any congenital defects. We just don't know at this stage."

'Sarosh rose from his chair: "Thank you very much for your time, Dr No-Ilaaz. But I don't think I want to take such a drastic step. As you suggest, I will think it over very carefully."

' "Good, good," said Dr No-Ilaaz, "I was hoping you would say that. There is one more thing. The operation is extremely expensive, and is not covered by the province's Health Insurance Plan. Many immigrant groups are lobbying to obtain coverage for special immigration-related health problems. If they succeed, then good for you."

'Sarosh left Dr No-Ilaaz's office with his mind made up. Time was running out. There had been a time when it was perfectly natural to squat. Now it seemed a grotesquely aberrant thing to do. Wherever he went he was reminded of the ignominy of his way. If he could not be westernized in all respects, he was nothing but a failure in this land—a failure not just in the washrooms of the nation but everywhere. He knew what he must do if he was to be true to himself and to the decade-old commitment. So what do you think Sarosh did next?'

'What, Nariman Uncle?'

'He went to the travel agent specializing in tickets to India. He bought a fully refundable ticket to Bombay for the day when he would complete exactly ten immigrant years—if he succeeded even once before that day dawned, he would cancel the booking.

'The travel agent asked sympathetically, "Trouble at home?" His name was Mr Rawaana, and he was from Bombay too.

' "No," said Sarosh, "trouble in Toronto."

' "That's a shame," said Mr Rawaana. "I don't want to poke my nose into your business, but in my line of work I meet so many people who are going back to their homeland because of problems here. Sometimes I forget I'm a travel agent, that my interest is to convince them to travel. Instead, I tell them: don't give up, God is great, stay and try again. It's bad for my profits but gives me a different, a spiritual kind of satisfaction when I succeed. And I succeed about half the time. Which means," he added with a wry laugh, "I could double my profits if I minded my own business."

'After the lengthy sessions with Mrs Maha-Lepate and Dr No-Ilaaz, Sarosh felt he had listened to enough advice and kind words. Much as he disliked doing it, he had to hurt Mr Rawaana's feelings and leave his predicament undiscussed: "I'm sorry, but I'm in a hurry. Will you be able to look after the booking?"

' "Well, okay," said Mr Rawaana, a trifle crestfallen; he did not relish the travel business as much as he did counselling immigrants. "Hope you solve your problem. I will be happy to refund your fare, believe me."

'Sarosh hurried home. With only four weeks to departure, every spare minute, every possible method had to be concentrated on a final attempt at adaptation.

'He tried laxatives, crunching down the tablets with a prayer that these would assist the sitting position. Changing brands did not help, and neither did various types of suppositories. He spent long stretches on the toilet seat each morning. The supervisor continued to reprimand him for tardiness. To make matters worse, Sarosh left his desk every time he felt the slightest urge, hoping: maybe this time.

'The working hours expended in the washroom were noted with unflagging vigilance by the supervisor. More counselling sessions followed. Sarosh refused to extinguish his last hope, and the supervisor punctiliously recorded "No Improvement" in his daily log. Finally, Sarosh was fired. It would soon have been time to resign in any case, and he could not care less.

'Now whole days went by seated on the toilet, and he stubbornly refused to relieve himself the other way. The doorbell would ring only to be ignored. The telephone went unanswered. Sometimes, he would awake suddenly in the dark hours before dawn and rush to the washroom like a madman.'

Without warning, Rustomji flung open his door and stormed: 'Ridiculous nonsense this is becoming! Two days in a row, whole Firozsha Baag gathers here! This is not Chaupatty beach, this is not a squatters' colony, this is a building, people want to live here in peace and quiet!' Then just as suddenly, he stamped inside and slammed the door. Right on cue, Nariman continued, before the boys could say anything.

'Time for meals was the only time Sarosh allowed himself off the seat. Even in his desperation he remembered that if he did not eat well, he was doomed—the downward pressure on his gut was essential if there was to be any chance of success.

'But the ineluctable day of departure dawned, with grey skies and the scent of rain, while success remained out of sight. At the airport Sarosh checked in and went to the dreary lounge. Out of sheer habit he started towards the washroom. Then he realized the hopelessness of it and returned to the cold, clammy plastic of the lounge seats. Airport seats are the same almost anywhere in the world.

'The boarding announcement was made, and Sarosh was the first to step onto the plane. The skies were darker now. Out of the window he saw a flash of lightning fork through the clouds. For some reason, everything he'd learned years ago in St Xavier's about sheet lightning and forked lightning went through his mind. He wished it would change to sheet, there was something sinister and unpropitious about forked lightning.'

Kersi, absorbedly listening, began cracking his knuckles quite unconsciously. His childhood habit still persisted. Jehangir frowned at the disturbance, and Viraf nudged Kersi to stop it.

'Sarosh fastened his seat-belt and attempted to turn his thoughts towards the long journey home: to the questions he would be expected to answer, the sympathy and criticism that would be thrust upon him. But what remained uppermost in his mind was the present moment—him in the plane, dark skies lowering, lightning on the horizon—irrevocably spelling out: defeat.

'But wait. Something else was happening now. A tiny rumble. Inside him. Or was it his imagination? Was it really thunder outside which, in his present disoriented state, he was internalizing? No, there it was again. He had to go.

'He reached the washroom, and almost immediately the sign flashed to "Please return to seat and fasten seat-belts." Sarosh debated whether to squat and finish the business quickly, abandoning the perfunctory seated attempt. But the plane started to move and that decided him; it would be difficult now to balance while squatting.

'He pushed. The plane continued to move. He pushed again, trembling with the effort. The seat-belt sign flashed quicker and brighter now. The plane moved faster and faster. And Sarosh pushed hard, harder than he had ever pushed before, harder than in all his ten years of trying in the new land. And the memories of Bombay, the immigration interview in New Delhi, the farewell party, his mother's tattered prayer book, all these, of their own accord, emerged from beyond the region of the ten years to push with him and give him newfound strength.'

Nariman paused and cleared his throat. Dusk was falling, and the frequency of B.E.S.T. buses plying the main road outside Firozsha Baag had dropped. Bats began to fly madly from one end of the compound to the other, silent shadows engaged in endless laps over the buildings.

'With a thunderous clap the rain started to fall. Sarosh felt a splash under him. Could it really be? He glanced down to make certain. Yes, it was. He had succeeded!

'But was it already too late? The plane waited at its assigned position on the runway, jet engines at full thrust. Rain was falling in torrents and take off could be delayed. Perhaps even now they would allow him to cancel his flight, to disembark. He lurched out of the constricting cubicle.

'A stewardess hurried towards him: "Excuse me, sir, but you must return to your seat immediately and fasten your belt."

' "You don't understand!" Sarosh shouted excitedly. "I must get off the plane! Everything is all right, I don't have to go any more. . . ."

' "That's impossible, sir!" said the stewardess, aghast. "No one can leave now. Takeoff procedures are in progress!" The wild look in his sleepless eyes, and the dark rings around them scared her. She beckoned for help.

'Sarosh continued to argue, and a steward and the chief stewardess hurried over: "What seems to be the problem, sir? You *must* resume your seat. We are authorized, if necessary, to forcibly restrain you, sir."

'The plane began to move again, and suddenly Sarosh felt all the urgency leaving him. His feverish mind, the product of nightmarish days and torturous nights, was filled again with the calm which had fled a decade ago, and he spoke softly now: "That . . . that will not be necessary . . . it's okay, I understand." He readily returned to his seat.

'As the aircraft sped down the runway, Sarosh's first reaction was one of joy. The process of adaptation was complete. But later, he could not help wondering if success came before or after the ten-year limit had expired. And since he had already passed through the customs and security check, was he really an immigrant in every sense of the word at the moment of achievement?

'But such questions were merely academic. Or were they? He could not decide. If he returned, what would it be like? Ten years ago, the immigration officer who had stamped his passport had said, "Welcome to Canada." It was one of Sarosh's dearest memories, and thinking of it, he fell asleep.

'The plane was flying above the rainclouds. Sunshine streamed into the cabin. A few raindrops were still clinging miraculously to the windows, reminders of what was happening below. They sparkled as the sunlight caught them.'

Some of the boys made as if to leave, thinking the story was finally over. Clearly, they had not found this one as interesting as the others Nariman had told. What dolts, thought Jehangir, they cannot recognize a masterpiece when they hear one. Nariman motioned with his hand for silence.

'But our story does not end there. There was a welcome-home party for Sarosh a few days after he arrived in Bombay. It was not in Firozsha Baag this time because his relatives in the Baag had a serious sickness in the house. But I was invited to it anyway. Sarosh's family and friends were considerate enough to wait till the jet lag had worked its way out of his system. They wanted him to really enjoy this one.

'Drinks began to flow freely again in his honour: Scotch and soda, rum and Coke, brandy. Sarosh noticed that during his absence all the brand names had changed—the labels were different and unfamiliar. Even for the mixes. Instead of Coke there was Thums-Up, and he remembered reading in the papers about Coca-Cola being kicked out by the Indian Government for refusing to reveal their secret formula.

'People slapped him on the back and shook his hand vigorously, over and over, right through the evening. They said: "Telling the truth, you made the right decision, look how happy your mother is to live to see this day;" or they asked: "Well, bossy, what changed your mind?" Sarosh smiled and nodded his way through it all, passing around Canadian currency at the insistence of some of the curious ones who, egged on by his mother, also pestered him to display his Canadian passport and citizenship card. She had been badgering him since his arrival to tell her the real reason: "*Saachoo kahé*, what brought you back?" and was hoping that tonight, among his friends, he might raise his glass and reveal something. But she remained disappointed.

'Weeks went by and Sarosh found himself desperately searching for his old place in the pattern of life he had vacated ten years ago. Friends who had organized the welcome-home party gradually disappeared. He went walking in the evenings along Marine Drive, by the sea-wall, where the old crowd used to congregate. But the people who sat on the parapet while waves crashed behind their backs were strangers. The tetrapods were still there, staunchly protecting the reclaimed land from the fury of the sea. He had watched as a kid when cranes had lowered these cement and concrete hulks of respectable grey into the water. They were grimy black now, and from their angularities rose the distinct stench of human excrement. The old pattern was never found by Sarosh; he searched in vain. Patterns of life are selfish and unforgiving.

'Then one day, as I was driving past Marine Drive, I saw someone sitting alone. He looked familiar, so I stopped. For a moment I did not recognize Sarosh, so forlorn and woebegone was his countenance. I parked the apple of my eye and went to him, saying, "Hullo, Sid, what are you doing here on your lonesome?" And he said, "No, no! No more Sid, please, that name reminds me of all my troubles." Then, on the parapet at Marine Drive, he told me his unhappy and wretched tale, with the waves battering away at the tetrapods, and around us the hawkers screaming about coconut-water and sugar-cane juice and *paan*.

'When he finished, he said that he had related to me the whole sad saga because he knew how I told stories to boys in the Baag and he wanted me to tell this one, especially to those who were planning to go abroad. "Tell them," said Sarosh, "that the world can be a bewildering place, and dreams and ambitions are often paths to the most pernicious of traps." As he spoke, I could see that Sarosh was somewhere far away, perhaps in New Delhi at his immigration interview, seeing himself as he was then, with what he thought was a life of hope and promise stretching endlessly before him. Poor Sarosh. Then he was back beside me on the parapet.

' "I pray you, in your stories," said Sarosh, his old sense of humour returning as he deepened his voice for his favourite *Othello* lines'—and here, Nariman produced a basso profundo of his own—' "When you shall these unlucky deeds relate, speak of me as I am; nothing extenuate, nor set down aught in malice: tell them that in Toronto once there lived a Parsi boy as best as he could. Set you down this; and say, besides, that for some it was good and for some it was bad, but for me life in the land of milk and honey was just a pain the posterior." '

And now, Nariman allowed his low-pitched rumbles to turn into chuckles. The boys broke into cheers and loud applause and cries of 'Encore!' and 'More!' Finally, Nariman had to silence them by pointing warmly at Rustomji-the-curmudgeon's door.

While Kersi and Viraf were joking and wondering what to make of it all, Jehangir edged forward and told Nariman this was the best story he had ever told. Nariman patted his shoulder and smiled. Jehangir left, wondering if Nariman would have been as popular if Dr Mody was still alive. Probably, since the two were liked for different reasons: Dr Mody used to be constantly jovial, whereas Nariman had his periodic story-telling urges.

Now the group of boys who had really enjoyed the Savukshaw story during the previous week spoke up. Capitalizing on Nariman's extraordinarily good mood, they began clamouring for more Savukshaw: 'Nariman Uncle, tell the one about Savukshaw the hunter, the one you had started that day.'

'What hunter? I don't know which one you mean.' He refused to be reminded of it, and got up to leave. But there was loud protest, and the boys started chanting, 'We-want-Savukshaw! We-want-Savukshaw!'

Nariman looked fearfully towards Rustomji's door and held up his hands placatingly: 'All right, all right! Next time it will be Savukshaw again. Savukshaw the artist. The story of the Parsi Picasso.'

1987

Dionne Brand

b. 1953

Born in Trinidad, Dionne Brand came to Canada in 1970. After receiving a B.A. from the University of Toronto in 1975, she began graduate studies at the Ontario Institute of Studies in Education (M.A. 1988). In Toronto she worked as a writer and editor for *Spear Magazine*, Canada's Black Family Magazine (1971-3), and later as a researcher for the Library of Black Peoples' Literature (1973-4). Her concern with minority and women's rights led her to join the editorial collective for *Our Lives*, Canada's first black women's newpaper (1986), and to work as a director and writer of films, such as the National Film Board's *Older, Stronger, Wiser* (1989). She became writer-in-residence at the University of Toronto (1990-1).

Brand has published several books of poetry—*'Fore day Morning* (1979), *Primitive Offensive* (1983), *Winter Epigrams and Epigrams to Ernesto Cardenal in Defense of Claudia* (1983), and *Chronicles of the Hostile Sun* (1984), as well as a 1980 book for children, *Earth Magic*—and has co-authored (with Krisantha Sri Bhaggiyadatta) an 'anti-racism educational text' that contains inter-views with native, black, South Asian, and Chinese people, as well as a summary of recent anti-racist political activity in Toronto, *Rivers Have Sources Trees Have Roots—Speaking of Racism* (1986).

'At the Lisbon Plate' appears in the collection *Sans Souci and Other Stories* (1988). In these stories the female protagonist often finds herself 'in enemy territory', whether in the Caribbean (where hostility takes the form of domestic violence) or in Canada (where racial hostility can be silent or spoken but no less damaging). Temporary refuge takes many different forms, both literal (tree trunks for the child, liquor for the adult) and figurative (the security of a grandmother's love, self-denial such as her aunt's). But, as a black woman who finds that enemy territory is everywhere, Brand's protagonist ultimately realizes that she can find a safe-house by claiming the precious legacy left by her female elders (like the old hag in 'At the Lisbon Plate'): at the heart of her black, female self lies the power and magic of story.

At the Lisbon Plate

The sky in the autumn is full of telephone and telegraph wires; it is not like sitting in the Portuguese bar on Kensington in the summer, outside—the beer smell, the forgetful waiter. I wonder what happened to Rosa. She was about forty and wore a tight black dress, her face appliquéed with something I could barely identify as life. Her false mole, the one she wore beside her mouth, shifted everyday and faded by evening. She had a look that was familiar to me. Possibly she had lived in Angola or Mozambique and was accustomed to Black women, so she looked at me kindly, colonially.

'Do you have fish, Rosa?' I would ask.

'Oh yes, good Portuguese fish.'

'From the lake or from the sea.'

'Ah the sea, of course.'

This would be our conversation every time I would come to the bar, her 'of course' informing me of her status in our relationship.

My life was on the upswing, and whenever that happened I went to the bar on Kensington. That was usually in the summertime. After twenty years and half my life in this city I still have to wait for the summertime to get into a good mood. My body refuses to appreciate dull, grey days. Truthfully, let me not fool you, my life was neither up nor down, which for me is an upswing and I don't take chances, I celebrate what little there is. Which is why I come to this bar. This is my refuge, as it is. I believe in contradictions.

So Rosa ran from Angola and Mozambique.[1] Well, well! By the looks of it she'd come down a peg or two. At the Lisbon Plate, Rosa seems quite ordinary, quite different from the woman who entertained in the European drawing rooms in Luanda and Lorençes Marques.[2] Then, she gave orders to Black women, whom she called 'as pretinhas.'[3] Then, she minced over to the little consul from Lisbon and the general, whose family was from Oporto and whom she made promise to give her a little gun for her protection when the trouble started.

I figured anyone who left Angola was on the other side, on the run. Rosa did have a kind enough look, personally. The wholesale merchant she was married to or his general manager, whom she slept with from time to time, had to leave. So, Rosa left too. This does not absolve Rosa, however. I'm sure that she acquired her plumpness like a bed bug, sucking a little blood here, a little there.

As I've said, my life was on the upswing. Most other times it was a bitch. But I had spent two successive days with no major setbacks. Nobody called me about money, nobody hurt my feelings, and I didn't wake up feeling shaky in the stomach about how this world was going. And, I had twenty clear bucks to come to the bar. This is my refuge. It is where I can be invisible or, if not invisible, at least drunk. Drinking makes me introspective, if not suicidal. In these moments I have often looked at myself from the third floor window of the furniture store across from the bar. Rheumy-eyed, I have seen a woman sitting there, whom I recognize as myself. A Black woman, legs apart, chin resting in the palm of her hand, amusement and revulsion travelling across her face in uneasy companionship; the years have taken a bit of the tightness out of my skin but the expression has not changed, searching and uneasy, haunted like a plantation house. Surrounded by the likes of Rosa and her compadres. A woman in enemy territory.

It has struck me more than once that a little more than a century ago I may have been Rosa's slave and not more that twenty-five years ago, her maid, whom she maimed, playing with the little gun that she got from the general from Aporto. My present existence is mere chance, luck, syzygy.

Rosa's brother, Joao the priest, was now living in New Jersey. He used to live in Toronto, but before that he lived in Angola. One day, in a village there, during the liberation war, two whites were kidnapped and the others, including Rosa's brother, the priest, went into the village and gunned down a lot of people—women,

---

[1]Both Angola and Mozambique were Portuguese colonies and centres of a flourishing slave trade. During the 1960s independence movements in both countries gained enough strength to oppose foreign rule and, after intense fighting, the Portuguese withdrew in 1975.
[2]Luanda is the capital of Angola; Lorençes Marques was once the capital of Mozambique.
[3]Little black ones.

children—to death, everything. He told this story to Maria de Conseçao, my friend, and she told me. Women and children, everything. People think that saying women and children were killed makes the crime more disgusting. I was sorry that Maria de Conseçao told me, because whenever I think about it I see Joao the priest confiding this crime as if he relished it, rather than repented it. I think Maria de Conseçao told me the story just to get rid of it. It's the kind of story which occurs to you when you're doing something pleasant and it's kind of story you can't get rid of. I've kept it.

I am not a cynical woman under ordinary circumstances, but if you sit here long enough anyone can see how what appears to be ordinary, isn't.

For, on the other hand, I look like a woman I met many years ago. As old as dirt, she sat at a roadside waiting her time, an ivory pipe stuck in her withered lips and naked as she was born. That woman had stories, more lucid than mine and more frightening for that.

The day I met her, her bones were black powder and her fingers crept along my arm causing me to shiver. She was a dangerous woman. I knew it the moment I saw her and I should have left her sitting there, the old grave-digger. But no. Me, I had to go and look. I had to follow that sack of dust into places I had no right being. Me, I had to look where she pointed. She wanted to show me her condiments and her books. I thought nothing of it. Why not humour an old woman, I said in my mind. They were old as ashes. All tied up and knotted in a piece of cloth and, when she opened it up, you would not believe the rattling and the odour, all musty and sweet. A bone here and a fingernail there. They looked like they'd been sitting in mud for centuries, like her. When it came to the books, it was before they had pages and the writing was with stones, which the old thing threw on the ground and read to me. I never laughed so much as I laughed at her jokes, not to mention her stories, which made me cry so much I swore I'd turn to salt water myself. It was one of her stories which led me here, in search of something I will recognize, once I see it.

But back to things that we can understand, because I want to forget that harridan in the road and her unpleasantness.

Today I am waiting for Elaine, as usual. She likes to make entrances of the type that white girls make in movies. The truth is she's always getting away from something or someone. She is always promising too much and escaping. Which is why we get along. I never believe a promise and I, myself, am in constant flight.

Elaine is a mysterious one. Two days ago she told me to meet her here at one o'clock. I've been sitting here ever since. I know that she'll turn up a new woman. She'll say that she's moving to Tanzania to find her roots. She'll have her head tied in a wrap and she'll have gold bracelets running up her arms. She'll be learning Swahili, she'll show me new words like 'jambo' and she'll be annoyed if I don't agree to go with her. Elaine wants to be a queen in ancient Mali or Songhai. A rich woman with gold and land.

The bar has a limited view of Kensington market. Across the street from it there's a parkette, in the centre of which there is a statue of Cristobal Colon.[4] Columbus, the carpet-bagger. It's most appropriate that they should put his stoney arse right where I can see it. I know bitterness doesn't become me, but that son of a bitch will

---

[4]The Spanish form of Christopher Columbus.

get his soon enough too. The smell from the market doesn't bother me. I've been here before, me and the old lady. We know the price of things. Which is why I feel safe in telling stories here. They will be sure to find me. For fish you must have bait; for some people you must have blood. Spread the truth around enough, and you must dig up a few liars.

In the summertime, I come to the bar practically every day. After my first beer I'm willing to talk to anyone. I'm willing to reveal myself entirely. Which is a dirty habit, since it has made me quite a few enemies. Try not to acquire it. The knots in my head loosen up and I may start telling stories about my family.

I keep getting mixed up with old ladies; for instance, I have an old aunt, she used to be beautiful. Not in the real sense, but in that sense that you had to be, some years ago. Hair slicked back to bring out the Spanish and hide the African. You could not resemble your mother or your father. This would only prove your guilt. This aunt went mad in later years. I think that it must have been from so much self-denial or, given the way that it turned out. . . .

Anyway, when I was a child we used to go to their house. It was made of stone and there was a garden around it. A thick green black garden. A forest. My aunt worked in the garden every day, pruning and digging. There was deep red hibiscus to the far right wall. The soil was black and loose and damp and piled around the roots of roses and xoras and anthuriums and orchids. In the daylight, the garden was black and bright; in the night, it was shadowy and dark. Only my aunt was allowed to step into the garden. At the edges, shading the forest-garden were great calabash mango trees. Their massive trunks and roots gave refuge from my aunt when she climbed into a rage after merely looking at us all day. She would run after us screaming, 'beasts, worthless beasts!' Her rage having not subsided, she would grab us and scrub us, as if to take the black out of our skins. Her results would never please her. Out we would come five still bright-black little girls, blackness intent on our skins. She would punish us by having us stand utterly still, dressed in stiffly starched dresses.

Elaine never reveals herself and she is the most frustrating storyteller. She handles a story as if stories were scarce. 'Well,' she says, as she sits down at the table. Then she pauses, far too long a pause, through which I say, in my mind, 'I'm going to last out this pause.' Then quickly getting upset, I say, 'For god's sake, tell me.' Then I have to drag it out of her, in the middle of which I say, 'Forget it, I don't want to hear,' then she drops what she thinks is the sinker and I nonchalantly say, 'Is that it?' to which she swears that never again would she tell me a story. The truth is that Elaine picks up on great stories, but the way she tells them makes people suffer. I, on the other hand, am quite plain. Particularly when I'm in my waters. Drink, I mean. I've noticed that I'm prepared to risk anything. But truthfully, what makes a good story if not for the indiscretions we reveal, the admissions of being human. In this way, I will tell you some of my life; though I must admit that some of it is fiction, not much mind you, but what is lie, I do not live through with any less tragedy. Anyway, these are not state secrets, people live the way that they have to and handle what they can. But don't expect any of the old woman's tales. There are things that you know and things that you tell. Well, soon and very soon, as they say.

Listen, I can drink half a bottle of whisky and refuse to fall down. It's from looking at Rosa that I get drunk and it's from looking at Rosa that I refuse to fall down. I was a woman with a face like a baby before I met Rosa, a face waiting to hold impressions.

I saw the little minx toddle over to the statue of Columbus, the piss-face in the parkette, and kiss his feet. Everyone has their rituals, I see. And then, before her mirror, deciding which side to put the mole on. Her face as dry as a powder. Perfuming herself in her bedroom in Lorençes Marques, licking the oil off that greasy merchant of hers. Even though the weather must have been bad for her, she stuck it out until they were driven away. It's that face that Rosa used cursing those 'sons of bitches in the bush,' when the trouble started. 'When the trouble started,' indeed. These European sons of bitches always say 'when the trouble started' when *their* life in the colonies begins to get miserable.

I never think of murder. I find it too intimate and there's a smell in the autumn that I do not like. I can always tell. The first breath of the fall. It distracts me from everyone. I will turn down the most lucrative dinner invitation to go around like a bloodhound smelling the fall. Making sure and making excuses, suggesting and insinuating that the summer is not over. But of course, as soon as I get a whiff of that smell I know. It's the autumn. Then the winter comes in, as green and fresh as spring and I know that I have to wait another ten months for the old woman's prophecy to come true. That hag by the road doesn't know what she gave me and what an effort I must make to see it through. On top of that, I have to carry around her juju belt full of perfidious mixtures and insolent smells and her secrets. Her secrets. My god, you don't know what a soft pain in the chest they give me. I grow as withered as the old hag with their moaning. She's ground them up like seasoning and she's told me to wear them close to my skin, like a poultice. I thought nothing of it at first. A little perfume, I said, a little luxury. I now notice that I cannot take the juju off. I lift up my camisole and have a look. It's hardly me there anymore. There's a hole like a cave with an echo.

The old hag hates the winter too; says it dries her skin out. God know she's no more than dust, but vain as hell. She migrates like a soucouyant[5] in the winter, goes back to the tropics, says she must mine the Sargasso[6] for bones and suicides. I must say, I envy the old bagsnatcher. Though she's promised me her memories, her maps and her flight plans, when it's over. Until then, I wait and keep watch here, frozen like a lizard in Blue Mountain, while she suns her quaily self in some old slave port.

At this bar, as I have my first beer and wait for the African princess, Elaine, I discover substantive philosophical arguments concerning murder. The beauty is, I have a lot of time. I have watched myself here, waiting. A woman so old her skin turned to water, her eyes blazing like a dead candle. I'm starting to resemble that bag of dust, the longer I live.

Now they have a man waiting on tables at the bar. I suppose the pay must be better. Elaine says he resembles Rosa except for her beauty mole and her breasts. It doesn't matter how Rosa looks in her disguises, I am doomed to follow her like a bloodhound after a thief. He is quite forgetful. Twenty minutes ago I asked him for

[5]In Trinidadian mythology a 'soucouyant' sheds her skin at night to become a ball of fire. On her night roamings she is believed to take blood from her victims.
[6]A sluggish part of the Atlantic Ocean situated between the Azores and the islands of the West Indies, known for surface gulfweed or 'sargasso'; in old sailors' legends the Sargasso Sea was a place of lost ships.

another beer and up to now he hasn't brought it. Elaine's the one who got me into beer drinking anyway. In the old days—before the great mother old soul in the road and before I sussed out Rosa and her paramour, Elaine and I used to roam the streets together, looking. The old bone digger must have spotted my vacant look then. Elaine, on the other hand, had very definite ideas. Even then Elaine was looking for a rich African to help her make her triumphal return to the motherland.

Still, a rumour went around that Elaine and I were lovers. It wouldn't have bothered either of us if it were true at the time or if it wasn't said in such a malicious way. But it was because of how we acted. Simply, we didn't defer to the men around and we didn't sleep with them, or else when we did we weren't their slaves for ever or even for a while. So both factions, those we slept with and those we didn't, started the rumour that we were lovers. Actually, Elaine and I laughed at the rumours. We liked to think of ourselves as free spirits and realists. We never attempted to dispel the rumours; it would have taken far too much of a commitment to do that. It would be a full time job of subjecting yourself to any prick on two legs. And anyway if the nastiest thing that they could say about you is that you loved another woman, well. . . .

Elaine and I would take the last bus home, bags full of unopened beer, or pay a taxi, after I had persuaded her that the man she was looking at was too disgusting to sleep with, just for a ride home. Elaine takes the practical to the absurd sometimes.

We've been to other bars. Elaine looked for the bars, she scouted all the hangouts. She determined the ambience, the crowd, and then she asked me to meet her there. There's no accounting for her taste. I'd get to the appointed bar and it would be the grungiest, with the most oily food, the most vulgar horrible men and a juke box with music selected especially to insult women. This was during Elaine's nationalist phase. Everything was culture, rootsy. The truth is, I only followed Elaine to see if I could shake the old woman's stories or, alternately, if I could find the something for her and get her off my back. It's not that I don't like the old schemer. At first I didn't mind her, but then she started to invade me like a spirit. So I started to drink. You get drunk enough and you think you can forget, but you get even greater visions. At the beginning of any evening the old woman's stories are a blip on the horizon; thirteen ounces into a bottle of scotch or four pints of beer later the stories are as lurid as a butcher's block.

I had the fever for two days and dreamt that the stove had caught afire. My big sister was just standing there as I tried furiously to douse the fire which kept getting bigger and bigger. Finally, my sister dragged the stove from the wall and with a knowledgeable air, put the fire out. When I woke up, I heard that the stock exchange in Santiago had been blown up by a bomb in a suitcase and that some group called the communist fighting cell had declared war on NATO by destroying troop supply lines in Belgium. Just as I was thinking of Patrice Lumumba.[7] For you Patrice! From this I surmised that my dreams have effects. Though, they seem somewhat unruly. They escape me. They have fires in them and they destine at an unknown and precipitous pace.

I followed Elaine through her phases, though there were some that she hid from me. Now we come to this bar, where we cannot understand the language most of the

[7]Former Premier of the Republic of the Congo (Zaire Republic since 1971), deposed in 1960 and killed in 1961.

time. Here Elaine plans the possibilities of living grandly and, if not, famously. As for me, I tolerate her dreams because when Elaine found this bar I knew it was my greatest opportunity. All of the signs were there. The expatriates from the colonial wars, the money changers and the skin dealers, the whip handlers, the coffle makers and the boatswains. Their faces leathery from the African sun and the tropical winter. They were swilling beer like day had no end. Rosa was in her glory, being pawed and pinched. Of course, they didn't notice me in my new shape. Heavens, I didn't notice me. It scared the hell out of me when the juju[8] surged to my head and I was a thin smoke over the Lisbon Plate. What a night! They said things that shocked even me, things worse than Joao, the priest. The old-timers boasted about how many piezas de indias[9] they could pack into a ship for a bauble or a gun. The young soldiers talked about the joys of filling a black with bullets and stuffing a black cunt with dynamite. Then they gathered around Columbus, the whoremaster, and sang a few old songs. The old woman and I watched the night's revelry with sadness, the caves in our chest rattling the echo of unkindness, but I noticed the old woman smiling as she counted them, pointing and circling with her hand, over and over again, mumbling 'jingay, jingay where you dey, where you dey, where you dey, spirit nah go away.' Before you know it, I was mumbling along with her too, 'jingay, jingay, where you dey. . . .' We stayed with them all night, counting and mumbling. Now, all I have to do is choose the day and the spot and it's done. The old woman loves fanfare and flourish, so it will have to be spectacular. If Elaine knew what a find this bar was, she'd charge me money.

Elaine never cared for Rosa one way or the other, which is where Elaine and I are different. Some people would have no effect on her whatsoever. This way she remained friends with everyone. Me, I hate you or I love you. Always getting into fights, always adding enemies to my lists. Which is why I'll never get any place, as they say. But Elaine will. Elaine, sadly, is a drunk without vision. I, unfortunately, am a drunk with ideas. Which is probably why the old woman chose me to be her steed.

I pride myself with keeping my ear to the ground. I read the news and listen to the radio every day, even if it is the same news. I look for nuances, changes in the patter. It came to me the other night, when listening to the news. One Polish priest had been killed and the press was going wild. At the same time, I don't know how many African labourers got killed and, besides that, fell to their deaths from third floor police detention rooms in Johannesburg; and all that the scribes talked about was how moderate the Broderbond is. We should be grateful I suppose.

It occurred to me that death, its frequency, causes, sequence and application to written history, favours, even anticipates, certain latitudes. The number of mourners, their enthusiasms, their entertainments, their widows' weeds, all mapped by a cartographer well schooled in pre-Galileo geography. I'm waxing. Don't stop me. I couldn't tell you the things I know.

Meanwhile back at the bar, still waiting for Elaine to surface, there have been several interesting developments. Speaking of politics. First, I hear that the entire bourgeoisie of Bolivia is dead. It was on the radio not more than half an hour ago. The

---

[8]juju: marijuana.
[9]Since slaves were once referred to as 'pieces', this phrase (which literally means 'pieces of Indian') has a particularly distasteful connotation.

deaths are not significant in and of themselves. What is interesting is that only a few days ago, when I heard that president Suazo was kidnapped in La Paz and that there was possibly a coup, I said in my mind, that the entire bourgeoisie should perish. It was the Bolivian army who killed Ernesto Che Guevara, you see. They put his body in the newspapers with their smiles. Now, I hear the news that the entire bourgeoisie of Bolivia is dead. Of course, from this I learned that as I become more and more of a spirit, I have more and more possibilities. First Santiago and Belgium and now Bolivia.

Second, and most, most important, the big white boy has arrived here. He's ordered a beer from Rosa's brother. I would know those eyes anywhere. The last time I saw them, I was lying in the hold of a great ship leaving Conakry[1] for the new world. It was just a glimpse, but I remember as if it were yesterday. I am a woman with a lot of time and I have waited, like shrimp wait for tide. I have waited, like dirt waits for worms. That hell-hole stank of my own flesh before I left it, its walls mottled with my spittle and waste. For days I lived with my body rotting and the glare of those eyes keeping me alive, as I begged to die and follow my carcass. This is the story the old road woman told me. Days and days and night and nights, dreaming death like a loved one; but those hellish eyes kept me alive and dreadfully human until reaching a port in the new world. His pitiless hands placed me on a block of wood like a yoke, when my carcass could not stand any more for the worms had eaten my soul. Running, running a long journey over hot bush, I found a cliff one day at the top of an island and jumped—jumped into the jagged blue water of an ocean, swimming, swimming to Conakry.

Elaine has also arrived and disappeared again, she's always disappearing into the bar to make phone calls. I never get an explanation of these phone calls mainly because I simply continue with my story. But I have the feeling, as the afternoon progresses into evening, and as different moods cross Elaine's face after every phone call, that some crisis is being made, fought and resolved. I have a feeling that Elaine needs my stories as a curtain for her equally spyish dramas.

The big white boy was sitting with his dog. I did not see his face at first, but I recognized him as you would recognize your hands. His hair was cut with one patch down the middle. He was wearing black and moaning as he sat there smoking weed. Like Rosa, he had fallen on his luck. I heard him say this.

'I don't have nobody, no friends, I ain't got no love, no nothing, just my dog.'

He was blond. At least, that was the colour of his hair presently. I felt for him the compassion of a warship, the maudlin sentiment of a boot stepping on a face. He said this to Rosa, who gave him an unsympathetic look as she picked her teeth. I'm not fooled by their lack of affection for each other. They are like an alligator and a parasite. I felt like rushing to his throat, but something held me back. The old woman's burning hand. I've seen him and Rosa whispering behind my back. What would a punk ku klux klansman and a washed-up ex-colonial siren have in common. Except me and the old lady. I suppose they're wondering who I am. Wonder away you carrion! I wonder if they recognize me as quickly as I, them. I saw them do their ablutions on the foot of the statue in the parkette. How lovingly they fondled his bloody hands. They have their rituals, but I've lived longer than they.

[1]Seaport capital of Guinea, West Africa, known as an important port during the time of the slave trade.

Listen, I neglected to say that my old aunt of the forest has gone mad. She told my sister, and indeed the whole town of Monas Bay, that on Easter Sunday of 1979, this year, jesus christ had descended from the heavens and entered her bedroom and had been there ever since. She had had a vision. After days of fasting and kneeling on the mourning ground, she had entered a desert where nothing grew. No water and inedible shrubs. The sun's heat gave the air a glassiness upon looking into the distance. Then she saw christ. He was withered and young as a boy of twenty. Christ and my aunt conversed for many days and planned to marry three years from the time of their meeting. They would have a son who would grow to be the new christ. My aunt related this incident to any one who would listen and cursed into hell and damnation anyone who did not believe. Few, needless to say, didn't. Anyone with a vision was helpful in bad times and people said that at least she had the guts to have a vision, which was not like the politicians in those parts.

Even my aunt's garden had descended into sand and tough shrub. It had become like the desert of her vision. She no longer made any attempt to grow plants, she said that armageddon was at hand anyway. Her bedroom, she turned into a shrine on the very day of her meeting with christ. On the wall hung bits of cardboard with glossy photographs of her fiancé cut out of the *Plain Truth*,[2] and candles burnt endlessly in the four corners of the shrine. Sundry chaplets of jumbie beads, plastic and ivory manoeuvred themselves on the windows and bedposts. My aunt knows that some people think that she is mad; so, in the style of her affianced, she prays for their salvation. If she is mad. . . . Which is a debate that I will never personally enter, having seen far too much in my short life and knowing that if you live in places with temporary electricity and plenty of hard work, jesus christ (if not god) is extant. Not to mention that, the last time that I saw her, she stood at what was once the gate to the forest garden and was now dead wire, wearing a washed-out flowered dress and her last remaining tooth, even though she was only a woman of fifty, and told me that the land taxes for the forest and the stone house was paid up or would be as soon as she went to town. This, to me, attested to her sanity. Come hell or high water, as they say, though these might be the obvious causes of her madness, if she were mad, they were certainly legal. Anyway, if she is mad, her vision is clearly not the cause of it. Rather it has made her quite sane. At any rate she no longer uses face powder.

This trick that I learned in Bolivia and the dream in Santiago has set me to thinking. She, the old poui stick, is not the only one who can have plans. The dear old lady only gave me seven red hot peppers and told me to write their names seven times on seven scraps of paper. Then put the seven pieces of paper into the seven red hot peppers and throw them into seven latrines. This, she said, would do for them. This and sprinkling guinea pepper in front of their door every morning. Then, she said, I should wait for the rest. The old hag is smart, but she never anticipated the times or perhaps that's what she means.

Elaine thinks I'm taking things too far, of course. But, I cannot stand this endless waiting. I've practically turned into a spirit with all this dreadfulness around the Lisbon Plate. I want to get back to my life and forget this old woman and her glamorous ideas. So, what must be done, must be done. Elaine's on her way to Zaire, at any

---

[2] A publication of the Christian evangelical organization known as the World Wide Church of God.

moment anyway. I think she's landed Mobutu Sese Seku.[3]

For now I've taken to hiding things from her. She doesn't care about anything. Each time I mention it she says, 'Oh, for god's sake, forget them.' As if it's that easy. You tell me! When there's a quaily skinned battle-axe riding on your shoulder and whispering in your ear. Well fine, if Elaine can have her secret telephone calls, and I don't think that I mentioned her disappearances, I can have my secret fires too. She can't say that I didn't try to warn her.

Wait! Well, I'll be damned! They're coming in like flies, old one. I eavesdrop on conversations here. I listen for plots, hints. You never know what these people are up for. This way, I amuse myself and scout for my opportunity. Listen,

'Camus' *Outsider* can be interpreted as the ultimate alienation!'

Ha! Did you hear that? Now, literature! Jesus. That's the one who looks like a professor, all scruffy and sensitive. If the truth be known several hundred years ago he made up the phrase 'Dark Ages,' then he attached himself to an expedition around the Bight of Benin from which, as the cruder of his sea company packed human cargo into the hold of their ship, he rifled the gold statues and masks and he then created a 'museum of primitive art' to store them. Since his true love was phrase-making he made up 'museum of primitive art,' elaborating his former success 'Dark Ages.' Never trust white men who look sensitive. They're the worst kind of phonies. They want the best of both worlds. Compared to him, the big white boy looks like a saint.

Anyway, alienation, my ass! Camus! Camus wrote a novel about a European, un pied noir, killing an Arab on a beach outside Algiers. He works it so that the sun gets into the European's eyes (they have their rituals) and the heat and his emotionlessness to his mother's dying and all this. But killing an Arab, pumping successive bullets into an Arab is not and never has been an alienating experience for a European. It was not unusual. It need not symbolize any alienation from one's being or anything like that. It was customary in Algeria, so how come all this high shit about Camus. Didn't it ever strike you that Meursault was a European and the Arab on the beach was an Arab? And the Arab was an Arab, but this European was Meursault.

You want to hear a story? Let me tell you a real story. I have no art for phraseology, I'll warn you.

Ahmed. Ahmed. Ahmed. Ahmed came to the beach with Ousmane to get away. The town, stiffly hot, drove him from the bicycle factory, making an excuse to his boss. Headache, my little brother has a headache three days now. He needs the salt air. The grimy hands of the boss closed around a dry cigar in the tin can ashtray. 'Ahmed, if you leave I don't pay for the week. That's it. That's it you hear.' Ahmed retreating, feeling free already, sweat trickling and drying under his chin. He would go to the beach, Ousmane was waiting for him, the sand would be damp. Ousmane was at the corner, he held his flute anxiously looking up and down the narrow street. His face lit up as he saw Ahmed. 'You got away, good Ahmed,' running beside Ahmed's bicycle. Ousmane climbed onto the handle bars. Ahmed pedalled in the hot silence toward the beach. Nearing the sea, their legs and arms eased from the tension of the town. Ousmane's bare feet leapt from the makeshift seat at the same

---

[3]President of Zaire since 24 November 1965.

time that Ahmed braked. They headed for their favourite rock wheeling and lifting the bicycle through the sand, hot and stinging. Already he felt tranquil as the thin wind shaking the flowers. He dropped the bicycle, raced Ousmane to the water, crushing softly underfoot the vine and silky mangrove. Ahmed and Ousmane fell into the sea fully clothed, he washing away the sticky oil of the bicycle shop, Ousmane drowning his headache. Then they lay beside the rock, talking and falling asleep.

Ousmane awakening, felt hungry; his dungarees, still damp, felt steamy on his legs. Shading his eyes from the sun which had narrowed the shadow of the rock, his headache came back. He stood up, lifted his flute and played a tune he'd made over and over again as if to tame the ache in his head. After a while he wandered down the beach, looking for a foodseller.

Ahmed. Ahmed. Ahmed awoke, feeling Ousmane's absence at the same moment that he heard an explosion close to his ear. Ahmed felt his eyes taking an eternity to open into the glassy haze of the afternoon. A blurred white form wobbling in the heat's haze. Sound exploded on the other side of Ahmed. He barely raised his body, shielding his eyes as he made out the white form of a European. Far out in the ocean a steamer was passing. The sand around Ahmed pulsated with the heat and the loud ringing in his ears. Ousmane! Run!

Ahmed's vision pinpointed the white's face, the toothpick between the white's teeth and lip moving. The gun transfixed his arms. Beneath a veil of brine and tears, his eyes were blinded; they watched the steamer's latitude longingly. 'Born slackers!' Ahmed's chest sprang back, tendrilled. 'Born liars!' A pump of blood exploded in his left side. 'Born criminals!' Sheets of flame poured down his ribs. 'Born. . . !' Ahmed![4]

That is what happened! And as for Camus. Murderer.

This is it baby. The old woman has given the go-ahead. Now that they're all gathered—Rosa, the big white boy, the professor, the money-changers and the skin dealers, the whip handlers, the coffle makers and the boatswains, the old timers and the young soldiers. I'm going to kill them. I'll tell them I have something to sell. That'll get them going; it always has. Then we'll strangle them. It'll be a night for the old woman to remember. That'll make up for it. Then that'll be the end of it.

We chained them around the statue of Cristobal Colon, the prick head. The old woman and I slashed his face to ribbons then we chewed on the stones and spit them into the eyes of the gathering. When that was over and they were all jumping and screaming, the old woman drew out her most potent juju and sprayed them all with oceans of blood which, she said, she had carried for centuries.

'En't is blood all you like?!' she whispered in their ears maliciously.

Then we sang 'jingay. . .' and made them call out everything that they had done over and over again, as they choked on the oceans of blood from the old hag's juju. Then we marinated them in hot peppers, like the old woman wanted. What an everlasting sweet night we had. The old woman was so happy, she laughed until her belly burst.

---

[4] "Ahmed's death" is intended to echo and counterpoint the corresponding scene in *L'étranger* and therefore echoes the language of the Penguin edition, English language translation' [Brand's endnote in *Sans Souci and Other Stories*]. The novel *L'étranger* by Albert Camus was published in 1942. It is sometimes translated as *The Outsider*.

When Elaine returned from her continuous phone call, I convinced her to stuff the bodies in her trunk to Zaire. It wasn't easy, as she almost could not see me and kept saying how much my face had changed. I promised her the Queendom and riches of Songhai. She bought it. The old lady has promised me her big big juju, so this is where the African princess and I must part. I'm off to see my new love and companion, the old hag of a banyan tree.

1988

Erin Mouré

b. 1955

Erin Mouré was born and raised in Calgary. In 1974 she moved to Vancouver, where she worked for the passenger service of the Canadian National Railway. Since 1978 she has worked for VIA Rail. Wishing to integrate her work with her writing, Mouré became an active member of 'The Vancouver Industrial Writers' Union', a group formed in 1979 to support and promote creative writing about the workplace. In 1984 she moved to Montreal, where she now oversees the writing of manuals and other documents for VIA.

Mouré has described the artist as the 'focal point' where the thoughts, feelings, and concerns of ordinary people intersect (*Rubicon*, 1984). To speak to, and for, her community, is a task she undertakes in six books of poetry: *Empire, York Street* (1979), *The Whisky Vigil* (1981), *Wanted Alive* (1983), *Domestic Fuel* (1985), *Furious* (1988), and *WSW (West South West)* (1989).

Her recent poetry shows an interest in feminist and deconstructive literary theory that is derived to some extent from the influence of the literary critic Gail Scott, with whom she lives.

Mouré writes for a community of readers, and her poems are often about communities and the need for change and development. In 'Professional Amnesia' movement does not bring change; the women's running, like the absences at family gatherings, suggest family relationships that do not develop. The speaker's inability to remember growth and change parallels the family's inability to reach beyond its hollow rituals of domestic tranquillity. But the speaker in 'Miss Chatelaine' finds herself moving, along with her female friends in the baggage car, towards a clearer understanding of their changing relations, both with each other and with representations of women in the media.

It Is Only Me

For Aline Kouhi Klemencic

Say there is a woman
in the locked-up cornfield.
She is making a desert for herself, not me.
Like the poet[1] said: Fumbling the sky's queer wires,
asking for
mercy, abstract collusion, a kind of awe;
she hikes across the frozen furrows in mid-November
ready to observe nearly anything,
self-consciously, as if the turned dirt
would see her singing,   10
would answer with arguments on Kandinsky[2] & Klee.

At least she can't hear
the saxophone playing scales in the next room,
taking the colours out of the air;
they become discordant sounds & no longer answer.
The words stay silent on the page, their usual selves,
picking lice from under their collars,
not yet torn, or interested, or censored,
or even free.
There are never enough groceries, does the woman   20
know this in the strange field?
Probably she has thought of it before, a few minutes,
but now the long furrows
are turning her over & over, like a leaf
in the wind.

Never mind the sound,
the saxophonist is in another country, its mountains
stop him from reaching her.
It is only me, with my bad language, my long distance whisky:
I see her far away, it is very cold, I am   30
calling her out of her field.

1983

---

[1]Al Purdy; in lines 3 to 5 Mouré alludes to his poem 'Wilderness Gothic' (see pp. 388).
[2]Wassily Kandinsky (1866-1944), Russian painter and pioneer of abstract expressionism; Kandinsky
and the Swiss abstract painter Paul Klee (1899-1940) were members in Germany of the *Blue Rider*
group of artists and colleagues on the Bauhaus faculty.

Barrington

For Tony Klemencic

There was the hard day you told us of,
nineteen stories into the sky; with your grey
shirt-sleeves rolled, the metal box filled
with tools, hammers,
fixing some thing on the roof of the building.
You couldn't tell us what.
Or if it was sunny.
If it was the shingles, or something to do with the drains.

You told us you worked with an old man, that between
his hands & the tools there was   10
no withholding.
All day you tried to work as he did, moving slowly
across the roof like a cat
high up into the daylight.
For you this happened;
for us it is just an image like a film, you & this man
nineteen floors up the building on Barrington,
the light is hard, all your arms move together,
tacking the roof, feet spread over it,

you & the workman high above us in the sky.   20

Then you told us what you dreamed then,
that the roof was done, you both
had turned your arms back thru the sleeves of your jackets,
& locked the tools, when
the old man jumped off the side of the building.
Holding his box of tools, that evening.

& we see you as you tell it, awake with our glasses of beer
on the twelfth floor of the same building, where you live,
gazing with you
into the dark where the old man fell.   30
How he fell, you told us: like a lamp, like a skiff of paper,
easily, you dreamed him falling like a seed,
slowly, ready to land.
Waiting for you.
& you jumped after him, you too with your tools.

It was like jumping off a stair, you said, when you landed.
You had seen the whole city thru its haze, the sun
pushing the lake into the towers, the light
as it sparked
each window in your long floating,   40
nineteen stories to the street & the old man outside the door.

Then we take our beer again, the same grainy film
of your dream runs past us, its defiance of the layered city,
the people in their houses along Barrington
eating dinner,
& your jacket floating, sunset, the hard speck that was
the box of tools, & your wild trust of the man,
that carried you down to us

1983

Professional Amnesia

He remembers family reunions at Lake Somewhere; each summer
the women running toward the water
laughing,
holding eggs in spoons
In his memory they keep on running,
he can't remember when they reach the water,
their clothes streaked with sand & grass
Or is it
the target shoots he claims had happened,
shooting at old records, ribbons, plastic soldiers   10
thrown up by the other children,
his cousins, who never grew

In his memory the women are still running,
the water does not rise to meet them,
they run right out of his life
so their names are forgotten
Family names
Family memories, the accusations one parent made
against the other
while he sat outside, his head   20
pressed against the cold tree that shaded his room

He remembers who stayed away each Christmas but not who came,
who wouldn't cut the turkey,
who stood up in shirt & tie & armbands
& sharpened knives against the steel.
The eaters are forgotten, the celebrations spontaneous
combustions;
when he speaks of family
the women are running out of it, into a summer lake of air

1985

Miss Chatelaine

In the movie, the horse almost dies.
A classic for children, where the small girl pushes a thin
knife into the horse's side.
Later I am sitting in brightness with the women
I went to high school with in Calgary,
fifteen years later we are all feminist, talking of the girl
in the film.
The horse who has some parasite & is afraid of the storm,
& the girl who goes out to save him.
We are in a baggage car on VIA Rail around a huge table,   10
its varnish light & cold,
as if inside the board rooms of the corporation;
the baggage door is open
to the smell of dark prairie,
we are fifteen years older, serious
about women, these images:
the girl running at night between the house & the barn,
& the noise of the horse's fear mixed in with the rain.

Finally there are no men between us.
Finally none of us are passing or failing according to   20
Miss Chatelaine.
I wish I could tell you how much I love you,
my friends with your odd looks, our odd looks,
our nervousness with each other,
the girl crying out as she runs in the darkness,
our decoration we wore, so many years ago, high school
boys watching from another table.

Finally I can love you.
Wherever you have gone to, in your secret marriages.
When the knife goes so deeply into the horse's side, a   30
few seconds & the rush of air.
In the morning, the rain is over.
The space between the house & barn is just a space again.
Finally I can meet with you & talk this over.
Finally I can see us meeting, & our true tenderness, emerge.

1988

INDEX